ETHNIC ESCAPISM AND THE BLACK BURDEN
Vol. 1
—

Holistic 360 Publishing

3rd Floor
86—90 Paul Street
London EC2A 4NE

The Library of Congress has catalogued the paperback and hardcover editions as follows:
Names: Ifé, Diego
    Title: Ethnic Escapism and the Black Burden / Diego Ifé
Description: 1st Edition. | London: Holistic 360 Publishing, 2023.
Subject(s): LITERARY COLLECTIONS / Essays.
Classification: LCO01000

Paperback ISBN: 978-1-8381450-0-2
Hardcopy ISBN: 978-1-8381450-1-9

This book is available to be purchased in bulk for promotional, educational, or business use.
For orders, please email orders@diegoife.com

For further titles please visit author's website: www.diegoife.com.

In Blessed Memory of My Dad and Grandma,
May You Both Continue to Rest in Peace.

CONTENTS

FOREWORD

The inspiration for writing this book came from my university elective *The Politics of Race and Diaspora*. I became fascinated by the histories and politics that birthed the African diaspora. Beyond my studies, I felt a strong desire to contribute to existing writings on the African diaspora and black studies in general. As time has passed, the inspiration has waxed stronger—almost as if it's a divine assignment, and without doubt this has enabled me to stay the course.

Over the course of this journey, I have introspected and reflected on key events in my life—dating back to my formative years. In doing so, I wondered whether the sum total of my experiences had already—albeit subconsciously—set me on the path to writing this book. An overview of some of these thoughts and experiences are perhaps revealing.

Identity is a sensitive topic. In my case, my sense of 'blackness' took root as a young boy, consuming glimpses of prevailing popular culture: programs such as *The Fresh Prince of Bel-Air*, *Desmond's*, re-runs of the *Cosby Show*; films such as *Cool Runnings* and *The Best Man*; music by the likes of *Aaliyah*, *the Fugees*, and *Mobb Deep* and the music review show *The Lick with Trevor Nelson*—both on MTV; Radio shows such as *Choice FM's* Slow Down Zone hosted by the 'Lady Of Soul,' Jenny Francis—whose smooth and sultry voice evokes much nostalgia, and the pioneer Steve Jackson's slot on *Kiss FM*. I was so taken by the music of the day that I began writing rap lyrics and poems in earnest—one of which was titled *It's a Black Dream*. These recollections, among others, reflect the tendencies of many in the diaspora to navigate their identities through the gazes of popular culture.

Perhaps more significant were some of my experiences during my secondary school years. One which comes to mind was when I had a haircut in the third week of September in year 7. A few days prior, I had earned £35 delivering leaflets for a local salon and had chosen to treat myself to a rare haircut by a barber, having previously settled for 'home cuts,' and the attendant fear of existential damage to my hairline. What I considered a neat 'short back and sides,' level 1.5 fade with a high-top was deemed an inappropriate, rebellious haircut by myriad teachers scrutinizing my head as if it was an abomination—the punishment for which was a minimum of 2 weeks in library isolation until my hair grew back. Yet what was ostensibly a punishment, with hindsight, was serendipitous—even more so the refusal to give me the work assignments I would have otherwise undertaken had I attended class. The school library was unlike anything comparable to my local library—honestly the resources were truly immense. I was able to read *The Financial Times* broadsheet newspaper—which I had always been intrigued by due to the sight of City of London professionals engrossed in its contents during my morning commute. I was also able to indulge in reading books about football—ranging from tactics to sports science, history, and the soccer legend *Pele's 125 Greatest Footballers of all Time*. It is perhaps unsurprising that reading these books instilled in me an interest in history, global economics, finance, and politics—all of which are relevant to both volumes of this book. This tilted me towards employment in financial risk management, a short-lived professional football career and moonlighting as a football agent. The most memorable book I read was about the most significant black Civil Rights and pan-African activists of the 19th and 20th centuries. This featured summarized biographies on W. E. B Du Bois, Booker T Washington, Frederick Douglass, Malcolm X, Martin Luther King, and a certain Marcus Garvey. Eerily enough, during this same period I used to deliver newspapers and leaflets on the same Talgarth Road (No. 53 precisely) in West London that Garvey once resided. Remarkably, I passed by his address on a daily basis without realizing how significant he was in the era of Black liberation politics. Moreover, this may or may not—depending on perspective—be coincidental, but I later attended Birkbeck College, University of London, an institution of which Garvey is also an alumnus.

Having received elocution lessons between the ages of 6 and 7 to improve my speech patterns and address an intermittent speech impediment, I developed a somewhat distinct RP (received pronunciation)

English accent, complete with some cockney and urban inflections. Despite my speech-related inhibitions and self-consciousness owing to my quirkiness, I was accepted by my friends and elders in the West London Afro-Caribbean community. Contrarily, however, this acceptance wasn't forthcoming during my first year of university when I came into contact with more British African and particularly [international and British] Nigerian students. My increasing encounters with the latter group only occurred from age 18—19 onward; this perhaps reflected the increase in the non-Caribbean African segment of the total UK black population between 2001 and 2011—surpassing the Afro-Caribbean subcategory as the majority. Again, popular culture shifts were indicative of this change in the black demographic. Black social spaces in London during the 1990s and 2000s had a discernible Caribbean—particularly Jamaican—influence across music, nightclub events, the popular consumption of Caribbean cuisine, the annual Notting Hill Carnival, and the so-called Urban speech— which in this book I call the *London Creole English* (LCE) dialect to reflect the evident cockney and Jamaican patois contributions. However, from the latter 2000s and up to the 2020s the African cultural imprint began to predominate: Afrobeats—the musical emblem of African-Brits; increased availability of jollof rice in a variety of London restaurants / takeaways; and even 'African' inflections and the use of the odd Yoruba and Ga words which are now part of the evolving LCE dialect. While I assumed my own Nigerian background and awareness of the unfolding shift in popular culture would foster an even greater affinity with my fellow Nigerian students than what I shared with my Caribbean peers, ironically, I couldn't have been more wrong. I experienced much hostility, derision, aloofness, and our perceived mutual differences were weaponized against me—my mode of speech being the most derided. While this was a painful experience, there was a vital lesson therein: 'black' people in the UK are not a monolith, and the all-encompassing label *black* belies the significant diversity among diasporans.

Growing up I had been nominally exposed to my 'Nigerianness'. Despite hearing elders at cultural events speak Igbo, Yoruba, and pidgin; regularly reading BBC Africa news updates; watching Nollywood movies; reading Ovation magazine editions; and watching the Nigerian National Football teams perform at World Cups, African Cup of Nation tournaments, and Olympics, I still felt a void. This void intensified when my father passed away and I went back to our village to attend his funeral. What was initially a painful experience, later sparked this desire to establish deeper roots in my ancestral homeland. I learned more about the country, gradually became a stakeholder, and grew deeply interested in its problematic political history, and dysfunctional economy—the latter of which was the subject of my MSc Economics dissertation. To this end I embarked on many trips, especially to the capital city of Abuja, and the commercial center of Lagos. Both were intriguing, such was the degree of globalization that I observed. One instance is the degree of discernible western influence in the Lagosian city of Lekki [Phase I]. Upon entering the city from the tollgate separating it from Victoria Island, the U.S. flag is hoisted at full-mast on an American car dealership; there are several Western-style shopping malls—complete with outlets stocking western goods and selling Western-style fast foods; Western-style architecture houses and décor; the occasional Texan or Californian number plate; Western-style lounges and nightclubs, and much more. I and my friends jokingly refer to it as a 'satellite Babylon' and playfully ascribed its residents the demonym *Lekkonian*.

As much as I found the Westernization of Lagos and other parts of Nigeria amusing, I admittedly felt a sense of 'comforting' familiarity with the evident Black American cultural influences, which are also discernible in Black UK social spaces. This influenced my decision to buy a house in Lagos and invest in an ecommerce business as part of my transnational plans. While both projects proved to be abortive, they were a key part of what has been a remarkable journey of self-discovery. My journey also coincided with the writing of both volumes of this book, and the writing of another book *Pirates in Power: Nigeria, its Perils, Problems and Promise*. With respect to both, I necessarily read hundreds of sources—many of which shed light on

Nigeria's pre-colonial and historical connections with the Transatlantic Slave Trade. Curiously, the names of several of my ancestors' homelands in Eastern and Western Nigeria—Awka, Mgbakwu, Udi, Ihiala, Uli, Orumba (all Igbo), and Ibadan, Abeokuta, and Ondo (all Yoruba), recurrently appeared as places that were the subject of multiple slave raids. This influenced me to read about my ancestors ways of life, and others from African polities which were also affected by the Atlantic trade—including the events that foreshadowed their enslavement. Moreover, I embarked on genealogical research and DNA tests with the likes of MyHeritage, 23andMe and Ancestry. I discovered close to 5,000 distant cousins from first to eighth cousins, most of whom are based in the U.S., Jamaica, Trinidad, Haiti, Grenada, St. Lucia, Venezuela, Guyana, Suriname, and Montserrat, in addition to other New World countries. I also discovered that I have African ancestors from present-day Benin/Togo, Angola/DR Congo, and according to MyHeritage—North Africa (Algeria) and Kenya. It has been pleasant connecting with distant family members, and in many ways these encounters have enriched the writing of this book.

Moreover, my evolving interest in African history and its current affairs, has aided my writings on the [continent's] *Black Burden*—in short, the factors behind the Africa's seemingly perpetual problems, and litany of state failures.

The following themes are central to both volumes of this book: the politics of race in the diaspora, the Black Burden theory—both in terms of diasporic identities and continental issues; the relevance of the Western World to the Black experience, and the connective tissue of globalization among the different peoples of the English-speaking Black Atlantic. This is an unusually long foreword, so I do appreciate your patience up to this point. I sincerely hope you derive value from reading this book and I thank you in advance for your support.

ACKNOWLEDGMENTS

There are many people that have helped and inspired me along this journey who I would like to acknowledge: Dr. William Ackah of Birkbeck College— my former lecturer on *The Politics of Race and Diaspora* elective and who was influential in my decision to write this book; Adaobi for her enduring support and patience where I may have been unreliable when frenetically writing at odd hours; Ronique for her support, encouragement and thoughtfulness; Birkbeck College for its highly useful library resources; Eghosa for her encouragement and helping me access rare books; Louis, Tina, Fil, Tunde, Sam, Ola—all for their encouragement and support in the early stages of writing the book; and though they might not know it, books written by the likes of Akala, David Olusoga, Clare Alexander, Afua Hirsch and Reni Eddo-Lodge were useful and thought-provoking in the early stages of this journey. It is possible that I may have missed some names, however, those who know they have helped me, should be rest assured I appreciate you immensely.

INTRODUCTION

This first volume of *Ethnic Escapism and the Black Burden* consists of 3 sections.

The first section is about the origins of the African diaspora. It chronicles the events from the 17th century that triggered the dispersals of Africans from their homelands, their experiences in captivity, post-manumission life and black liberation politics up the first half of the 20th century. This is referred to as the *Old diaspora*.

The second section is about the diaspora's trajectory from the second half of the 20th century to the present. This is referred to as the *New Diaspora*.

The third section is the concluding part of the book. The diaspora's prospects are evaluated, as is the degree of collective consciousness in the present day, and the diaspora's possible fate in relation to changing demographics in recent decades.

Below are some important terms and definitions which will feature throughout the book:

i)   *Diaspora*: This is derived from the Greek word *diaspeirein* which means to 'disperse' in English; *dia* is 'across' + *speirein* 'scatter'. The term first appeared in the Septuagint—the Greek translation of the bible — Old Testament, Deuteronomy 28: 25:

         'Thou shalt be a dispersion in all kingdoms of the earth'.

ii)   *Ethnic*: This is derived from the Greek word *ethnos* which means 'nation'. *Ethnikos* is also derived from the same word and means 'heathen' in older forms of English which was used to denote 'a person not of the Christian or Jewish faith'.

iii)   *Escapism*: An activity, a form of entertainment, etc. that helps you avoid or forget unpleasant or boring things. The origin of the word is from the old French word *escapher* which is taken from the Medieval Latin words: 'ex' meaning *out*, and *cappa* meaning 'cloak'.

iv) *Creole/Creolization*: This term was first used between the late 17th—early 18th century. The term initially appeared in its Portuguese form *crioulo*—denoting a 'white' person born in the colonies; its French and Spanish forms are créole and criollo respectively, both of which denote persons of mixed black and Spanish/French white. It has also been used to refer to a pidgin which has evolved into a mode of speech / language over subsequent generations i.e., Haitian Creole, Jamaican Patois and so forth. In the context of these sections, it will be used to denote languages, cultures and other distinguishing characteristics that have evolved in the diaspora.

THE OLD
AFRICAN
DIASPORA

—

THE [OLD] AFRICAN DIASPORA

The idea of an *African Diaspora* is age-old but in recent times the term has grown popular in usage. Informally, it often appears on several social media platforms. More formally, the Declaration of the Global Diaspora Summit (2012) recognized the need to build sustainable partnerships between the African continent and the African diaspora through dialogue and effective collaboration with African governments. Moreover, the African Union designated the African Diaspora as the 6th Region of Africa. These developments underline the importance of covering the African Diaspora's evolution up to the present day.

There have been many seminal books written about diasporic communities. One of the flaws commonly identified by authors is how casual the term diaspora is used. The following quote from Gabriel Sheffer is instructive:

> "*The highly motivated Koreans and Vietnamese toiling hard to become prosperous in bustling Los Angeles, the haggard Palestinians living in dreary refugee camps near Beirut and Amman, the beleaguered Turks dwelling in cramped apartments in Berlin, and the frustrated Russians in Estonia all have much in common. All of them, along with Indians, Chinese, Japanese, Africans, African-Americans, Jews, Palestinians, Greeks, Gypsies, Romanians, Poles, Kurds, Armenians, and numerous other groups permanently residing outside of their countries of origin, but maintaining contacts with people back in their old homelands, are members of ethno-national diasporas*".

Many writers have tried to give the concept of a diaspora more coherence by using some of the following measures: i) ethnic and/or religious persecution; ii) civil wars; iii) enslavement; iv) economic crises, among others. To this end Robin Cohen produced his own influential framework *the Common Features of a diaspora*:

1. Dispersal from an original homeland, often traumatically, to 2 or more foreign regions.

2. Alternatively, or additionally, the expansion from homeland in search of work, in pursuit of trade, or to further colonial ambitions.

3. A collective memory and myth about homeland, including its location, history, suffering and achievements.

4. An idealization of the real or imagined ancestral home and a collective commitment to its maintenance, restoration, safety, and prosperity, even to its creation.

5. The frequent development of a return movement to the homeland that gains collective approbation even if many in the group are satisfied with only a vicarious relationship or intermittent visits to the homeland.

6. A strong ethnic consciousness sustained over a long time and based on a sense of distinctiveness, a common history, the transmission of a common cultural and religious heritage and belief in a common fate.

7. A troubled relationship with host societies, suggesting a lack of acceptance or the possibility that another calamity might befall the group.

8. A sense of empathy and co-responsibility with co-ethnic members in other countries of settlement even where home has become more vestigial; and

9. The possibility of a distinctive creative, enriching life in host countries with a tolerance for pluralism.

This author will use Cohen's framework in the concluding part of the book to evaluate the African Diaspora's degree of collective consciousness.

Life in The Old World & Subsequent Captivity

Prior to the onset of the Transatlantic slave trade, the conditions, culture, and circumstances in the captives' primordial homelands informed their search for identity in the New World.

Throughout the Americas, diasporic Africans and their immediate descendants created new worlds. The enslaved were forcibly displaced from their ancestral homes and then bound upon ships which transported them to far away destinations. These captives were transported alongside others with whom they shared cultural similarities. After their Atlantic crossing, these peoples drew on familiar practices and lifestyles to survive as slaves. Initially, distinct 'nations' of Africans—and perhaps distinctive 'African' notions of nationalism—emerged while in chattel slavery. The survivors (and their children) also drew on many cultural contributions from other Africans, influences from their masters and additionally from New World indigenes to fashion distinctive local and regional cultures.

The 'Igbo Peoples'

Ife Na-azo Na-egbu,

Ife na-Egbu Egbu na-dzo Azo

"What saves also kills,

and what kills also saves."

—Igbo Proverb

At its greatest, the Nri sphere of influence covered perhaps half of Yorubaland; nevertheless, it constituted its ritual heart, like Ife did among the Yoruba. Both are encrusted with legend, and in both, ancient sculptures and other treasures have been found. 'The street of the Nri family is the street of the gods, through which all who die in other parts of Igboland pass to the land of Spirits.'

The Eze Nri is a ritual figure rather than a king (he's alternatively referred to as a priest-king). Chosen, after an interregnum, through manifestations of supernatural powers, he was installed after a symbolic journey to Aguleri, on the Anambra River. Here, by magical means, he collects stones from under the water, undergoes a symbolic burial and exhumation, and is anointed with white clay—symbolizing purity. When he dies, he is buried seated in a wood-lined chamber. The Igbo myth of the creation of the world is located, not at Nri, but at Aguleri: 'All the first things happened at Aguleri. There the land was made dry, and food given to the world.'

Nri and Aguleri are part of the Umueri clan, a cluster of Igbo village groups which trace its origin to a sky being called Eri, and significantly, includes (from the viewpoint of its Igbo members) the neighboring kingdom of Igala. The land—originally a quagmire—was dried by the bellows of an Awka smith; the chameleon—a magical being—walks with great care because it was created in the world's morning. Nri tradition provides a mythical charter for the foundations of Igbo life: yam and cocoyam were

11

obtained at the cost of the death of Nri's son and daughter, an oil palm and a breadfruit tree by the sacrifice of slaves.

According to Douglas Chambers a great many African captives taken to New World plantations—such as those in Chesapeake, Virginia—were from the Bight of Biafra in West Africa. The specific region most severely affected by slaving throughout the hinterland was central and northern Igboland—in particular, communities within the cultural ambit of the ancient Nri civilization. Centered at the village known in the colonial era as Agukwu (Great Lion), the Nri civilization has been antedated to the 9—10th centuries. From his analysis of the *eze* or king lists, M. A. Onwuejeogwu infers that Nri was founded in 948, but this date may be too early as it is based on 15 'reigns', and it seems more likely that the *Odinani Nri* (Nri culture) founded at Agukwu dates from the 14th century.

Nri was both a place and a culture. Its union of several villages was located between 2 small lakes in the Anambra River Valley. The Eze Nri claimed a special relationship with the deified Earth force (*Ani*, var. *Ale*).

The Nri were the "first Igbo" for many reasons. They were said to be the descendants of the oldest ancestors (the *ndi ichie*), or the elder brothers of Igbo, whose *Eze Nri* owned the original ancestral staff of authority (*ofo*). They were connected directly with practices that defined institutional culture such as *nso* and the ideology of abominations; yam cultivation and *njokku*; the cult of achievement (*ikenga*); the multitiered *ozo* titles system, with its ennobling ichi facial scarification and other insignia of exalted rank; the drum, and, most importantly, a pacifist ideology that abhorred the shedding of human blood. Moreover, the people of Nri have had a strong commitment to peace, rooted in the belief that it is an abomination to pollute the sacred Earth. 'The white men that came started by killing those who did not agree with their rules. We Nri never did so' (in reference to colonial occupation through military means).

With respect to the foregoing cultural practices and mores, it can be said

That the Nri were the arbiters of Igbo custom (*omenani*), or what ancestors said was done.

Igbo people recognized that *omenani* was a function of local arrangements. As one proverb states, "The bush fowl of a village cries in the dialect of the village." Or put another way, "The hawk of Ezalo catches a fowl of Ezalo and goes to the cotton tree of Ezalo." Each village or village group might do things in its own fashion or produce its own footprints, which made local custom seem ever new. Often, however, the appearance of particularism merely colored a more fundamental unity of form and function. As another proverb collected early in the 20th century put it, "I am a drum; if there is no wedge, the drum has no head."

At Nri, as elsewhere in Africa, many of the most important archaeological discoveries were incidental. In 1938, a farmer was digging a cistern in his compound at Igbo-Ukwu, 9 miles from Nri, when he stumbled upon remarkable bronze sculptures. More than 20 years elapsed before the area was professionally excavated, and much longer before the excavations were published. When they were, they revealed the existence of a hitherto unsuspected Igbo Bronze Age in the 9th century CE. Following on from this, there were several archaeological sites excavated in the early 1960s. While the dating did not go unchallenged, it has never been disproved; moreover, these discoveries were immediately explicable in terms of later Nri culture.

Between the 1930s and 1960s, the following—among others—were discovered: large caches of intricately decorated pottery; ivory tusks; a treasure hoard; forged metal objects; several fine specimens of textiles; bead ornaments; regalia and burial practices that strikingly resemble royal Nri material culture, and a dignitary buried in a sitting position in a wood-lined chamber, with slaves and valuables. Furthermore, in terms of the above bronze discoveries, one was a human face sculpture from Igbo-Ukwu which was incised with facial scarification that mirrors the distinctive hachure of Nri men; another bronze depicts a woman with *ichi* facial scars, and only one woman had these scars—the eldest daughter of Eze Nri. The incised designs on the pottery were very similar to modern woodcarving patterns. One motif of surface decoration was a snake with an egg in its mouth, a praise name for the Onitsha king.

The Igbo-Ukwu excavations elucidate the institution of sacred kinship, which still flourishes at Nri and among the riverain and western Igbo, and was much older than could have been deduced from oral tradition alone. The finds also yielded evidence of a hitherto unsuspected involvement in international trade, hundreds of miles from the southern termini of the Saharan routes; there was a great treasury of beads, some of glass and some of carnelian, many of which seem to have originated in Venice and India. Much research has been devoted to the raw materials used in the sculptures: tin bronze and leaked tin bronze, which may have been obtained in ancient mines in Abakaliki in eastern Igboland. They depicted, among other things, a horse, and a seashell. Nri is far from the sea, and because of tsetse fly, horses cannot survive there. The dignitary was buried with slaves and ivory; the economic importance of both is mirrored in oral tradition, and Ogubenyi, Elephant Slayer, is a widespread personal title.

Bronze is only one of many sculptural media; it has attracted perhaps disproportionate scholarly attention because of its durability and its value in western eyes. Much sculpture, among the Igbo, as among other West Africans, was in wood or terracotta. Sculpture in unbaked clay is intrinsically ephemeral, but this medium was often chosen to honor *Ala*, the sacred Earth. The *mbari* houses of the Owerri Igbo are not dwellings but collections of clay sculpture, which is part of the Earth cult; once completed, they were allowed to crumble away.

With respect to spiritual matters in Nri, the *Eze Nri* delegated the power to render judgements to his representatives. These were often the most accomplished local men who had achieved high status in a complicated title society, the *ozo* society. Not only were these delegated powers confined to render judgements in disputes, they also included: the ritualistic performance of removing curses that breaking taboos wrought; the performance of rituals to ensure a bountiful harvest and restore harmony in local affairs; setting the agricultural calendar, the regulation of markets and controlling the elements; and addressing any other transgressions in a society governed by rules—and not rulers, thus ensuring peace and prosperity. Ideally, *ozo* title holders operated in areas influenced by *Odinani Nri*, and travelled from village to village to undertake their work.

The representatives of the *Eze Nri* received a special and distinctive facial scarification called *ichi*. The *mgburichi* (mbreechi)—those marked with the ennobling hachure—were singled out as men who were full citizens; above all, the hachure denoted (spiritual) royalty and qualified one to be a representative of the priest-king and eligible to receive the spiritual inspiration to become king. As the 18th century (1745—1797) Igbo-born Olaudah Equiano recalled, the "elders or chiefs" in his home district were "styled Emrenche; a term, I remember, importing the highest distinction, and signifying in our language a mark of grandeur. . . . Those Emrenche, or chief men, decided disputes and punished crimes; for which purpose they always assembled together." To be within the Nri cultural ambit meant to ascribe to the *nso* ideology, and its institutional apparatus: the *Eze Nri*, the yam spirit (*ifejioku*, var. *njokku*), the *ozo* title society, the *ikenga* cult, and the Agbala oracle of the blacksmiths at Awka, among other beliefs and practices. As one customary praise song performed during the multiday scarring ritual suggests, *ichi* marks were closely associated with royal status: "*Nwaichi nyem ma aguu/agbunem Ichi Eze, Nwadiokpal*a" (Ichi child give me food so I will not starve/Facial scar for kings, facial scar for first sons).

Pioneering Nigerian ethnoanthropologist, M. Angulu Onwuejeogwu neatly summarized the core religiopolitical concepts of the Nri civilization:

> The concept of peace, harmony and truth was ritually symbolized
> and enacted in the ceremonies of the ozo-titled men, who were also
> the political elite. Nri men who had taken the *Ichi* title always carried
> in their hands the spear of peace called *otonsi*. With the spear of peace
> in their hands and the *ichi* marks on their faces, they were identified as

15

the "sons" of Eze Nri, *Nwa nri*, who controlled the mystical force. They travelled generally unmolested from one Igbo settlement to another as agents of Eze Nri to perform political and ritual functions associated with the removing of abomination, the dissolving of the codes of abomination and the enacting of new codes, the ordaining of ritual and political officials, the crowning of chiefs, the making of peace and the creating of markets and shrines. In the performance of these activities Nri people spread into different parts of Igbo land and Eze Nri held some degree of control over the external and internal politics of the older Igbo settlements.

In short, these settlements saw themselves as under the spiritual protection of the *Eze Nri*. And the prestige and power of the *Nwa Nri* came from their ability to ensure peace and prosperity and to safeguard the people from the misfortunes that plague human existence. At its height, Nri influence extended across the densely populated region generally in a great arc from beyond the Niger in the west to Nsukka in the north, Bende in the east, and Owerri in the south. By the 20th century, however, the area where Nri lineages were still found had contracted to the plateau region at the headwaters of the Imo River and west of the great escarpment that divides northern Igboland longitudinally from Nsukka through Enugu and Awgu and above a line roughly westward through Okigwe, Orlu, and Oguta and across the Niger north of Aboh.

The history of the Nri civilization can be divided into 4 periods. The first is the formative period, comprising the reigns of the first 3 *Eze Nri* (Ifikuanim, Namoke, Buife), or roughly 1225—1425. This was the initial period of primary migration and of the introduction and institutionalization of divinely inspired priest-kingship in the original or core settlements. This period was marked by the articulation of many of the institutions of Nri social and political culture.

The second, or classical era, roughly 1425—1700, began with the distinguished reign of Jimofo I, a great leader who spread Nri influence throughout northern Igboland and established the *ikenga* cult of achievement. This era included a period of severe drought (ca. 1500—1530), which was followed by the magical reign of Fenenu (ca. 1530—1630), who acquired many wives as well as the ability to fly and lived so long that it is said he refused to die." But he was arrogant and eventually was cursed by the Council of Advisers (the *Nzemabuo*), which led to his death. During Fenenu's reign, the Nri first came into contact with the Delta Igbo and other coastal peoples. He was succeeded by Agu (r. ca. 1630). Even though his ascension marked the apogee of the Nri civilization, "when Nri was real Nri" (*oge Nri bu Nri*), Eze Agu was the first to abdicate his title because he refused the rigors of the office. The classical era closed with another innovation, the dual kingship of Alike and Apia (ca. 1635—1710). They are remembered for living a very long time and for profoundly valuing human life, banning the ancient practice of abandoning "deformed" babies and the ritual sacrifice of slaves because they defined all people as human with the universal right to life. During their reign, and likely toward the latter part, slavery and slave trading became an issue, and they defined the status of a slave for the first time. They formally declared that such a person was "an unfortunate human being held in captivity" and therefore that it was an abomination to kill or bleed a slave. Alike and Apia also authorized the selling of slaves. By doing so, the kings acknowledged for the first time that the organized slave trade had reached the Umu Nri. The formal recognition of slavery and slave trading marked the classical era of Nri.

The third period was an era of crisis from the early 18th to the early 20th century. It was marked by ritual anomalies and was inaugurated by the supreme abomination of the murder of a sitting *Eze Nri*, Ezimilo (r. ca. 1710—25). He had ascended to the title as the dark clouds of social violence and slave trading were gathering across central Igboland. His murder brought a severe drought and famine throughout the land, understood as collective punishments, which continued through the reign of his successor, Ewenetem (r. ca. 1725—27). At the close of the 18th century, an even more serious abomination occurred. The newly installed Eze Nri Enewelana (r. ca. 1790—1889), who had forcibly deposed his successor, Nwankpo, formally

17

authorized the use of force. He created an anti-Aro (anti-Ndelkelionwu) military alliance (the *Amakom*) and then launched a war against the Aro. Hence, a very long interregnum occurred after his death.

But the sense of things falling apart continued into the modern era. Shortly after the coronation in 1889 of Obalike, the British arrived in a series of punishing military expeditions, and in 1911, British forces disgraced the Eze Obalike in the supreme crisis of the Nri civilization. The British forced him to leave his shrine residence (the first *Eze Nri* ever to go outside the palace during his tenure) and travel to Awka. There, the British demanded at gunpoint that he formally renounce the powers of the *Nwa nri*, which he did. His death in 1926 marked the advent of the modern era and triggered a further crisis of succession with a contested coronation and the secret installation of a second *Eze Nri* (1935—36). Thus, an unreconciled divided kingship existed between about 1935 and 1947. The succession crisis has continued, though a new *Eze Nri*, Enwelani II, was officially coronated in 1988. The contemporary crisis pits the people of the 2 oldest villages of Nri (Diodo and Akampisi), who still contest other villages and lineages, the *Adama*, and secular political authorities.

Eboan Africans, as Equiano termed the people of village-level Igboland, relied to a great extent on yam agriculture. Although Igboland was just one part of the larger yam belt of West Africa, the cultivation of *Dioscorea* was of particular importance for the Igbo, for whom it indeed was "the king of crops." Yams were central to the social conception of being Igbo and signified the deepest sense of Igboness. For example, traditionally, whenever an Igbo man's life was in peril outside of his local community, he could shout for "Igbo who eat [domesticated] yams" (*Igbo neri ji*) and expect immediate assistance. In the early 20th century, many Igbo still made eating yams a key to understanding shared ethnicity.

Yam agriculture was time-consuming and required constant attention. The work included making clearings by burning the surrounding bush, making the mounds in which the seed yams were planted, tying up the runners with stakes, weeding, and harvesting and storage. A series of other crops, including cocoyams (but no cassava until the 20th century), guinea corn, plantains, black-eyed peas, watermelons, various fruits, and the oil palm tree and cotton, were intermixed with yams. By the mid-18th century, Eboan Africans also produced cotton and tobacco. Though Eboan agriculture centered on the production of yams, which all primary and secondary sources emphasize was characteristic or essential to Igboland, regional agriculture was actually a mixed-farming system with a continuous round of work. In fact, yam agriculture was largely inseparable from oil palm cultivation. This is one reason why constant human habitation of a particular area resulted in the reduction of the tropical rainforest to what became known as oil palm bush. Oil palms provided kernels and oil of course, but also the basic beverage of Igboland, palm wine (*mimbo*).

Foodways were an important way of defining *omenani*. Igbo did not just eat anything, and what was edible was often a consequence of what the ancestors approved. The proverb "if vultures were edible birds, our forebears would have eaten them all up" captures this perfectly. Another common proverb closely identified folkways with foodways: "The type of firewood that is native to a village is the one that cooks the food of the people who live there." In fact, the relationship between the common garden crop okra (from the Igbo word *okro*)—the pods of which were used to thicken soups and which Igbo thought had aphrodisiac properties—and the wisdom of the ancestors as distilled in proverbs was itself proverbial.

The food staple throughout Igboland was *fufu* (boiled and pounded yam). Variously described as yams "boiled and then beaten into a consistence like dough" or "pounded until they become like a stiff dough," *fufu* in Igboland was invariably made of yams, not cassava. Heavily peppered soups served in calabash bowls, greens "of the Calilue kind," and stews rounded out the Eboan diet.

The built world in Igboland—houses, juju structures, and living compounds—also reflected a local logic based on a rectangular model. There were no round structures or round buildings, as were preferred in the east and north. Captain Hugh Crow, who traded extensively at Bonny in the 1790s and 1800s, described the houses there as being "six or seven feet high," which means they must have been between twelve and thirteen feet wide (using standard assumptions about vernacular architecture), or twelve feet on a side. Present-day "traditional" Igbo houses tend to be square, and if historical Igbo built on a twelve-foot-square model, such an Igbo protoform was nearly half as large as the supposed "West and Central African norm" of ten feet square. All available evidence suggests that Igbo built on the template of rectangles, with compounds coming to resemble mini villages behind fences or walls that enclosed house yards. Most daily living took place in such yards, as people tended to live out-of-doors, and the women planted their garden plots of kitchen crops, including *okro*.

For most people in historical Igboland, the world was circumscribed by the limits of family compounds. As Equiano remembered, they typically were "a large square piece of ground, surrounded by a moat or fence, or enclosed with a wall made of red earth tempered." Neighborhoods or villages were composed of adjoining compounds together with the outlying fields, which often were "some hours walk from our dwellings." Adjacent villages, or the village group, comprised "one little state or district."

The extreme localism of most Igbo meant that personal loyalties rarely extended further than one's village or group of adjoining villages. This discouraged large-scale state formation but encouraged a culture of honor and the investment of political power in the village-level patrilineage. As Igbo in Owerri say, there was "a king in every lineage" (*Eze no na nchi*). In fact, every village had its leader (*eze*) or set of leaders (the holders of the Nri-based *ozo* title, of which the *eze* title was the highest), which Europeans later saw as so many little kings and chiefs, just as every compound had its headman and every lineage its Okpara. As Samuel A. Crowther noted, "A king is acknowledged in every district of the Ibo country," and there also was a "superior class of men, who have paid enormous sums to obtain this rank." He also observed that "every headman appears to be master in his own quarters."

20

Throughout Igboland, people attempted to gain mastery of their Eboan African world through the performance of ritual. The people prepared offerings, poured libations, and performed sacrifices to the spirits of their individual and collective ancestors (*ndi ichie*) as well as to "feed" and placate the many forces, gods, and "invisibles" (*ndi muo*) who inhabited the animistic Eboan African world. Equiano wrote, "Those spirits . . . such as our dear friends and relations, they believe always attend them, and guard them from the bad spirits or their foes." For this reason, he said, "they always before eating, as I have observed, put some small portion of the meat, and pour some of the drink, on the ground for them; and they often make oblations of the blood of beasts or fowls at their graves."

The core of historical Igbo ritual performance and thus of Eboan community culture, was sacrifice (*aja*). Throughout Igboland, as well as in heavily Igboized Elem Kalabari, Bonny, and Old Calabar, public ritual killings of consecrated victims—occasionally including even humans—was ubiquitous. Personal *aja* included pouring libations, apparently at every meal. Sacrifice was a fundamental religious act. As one modern scholar wrote, sacrifice was "the soul of Ibo cult," "the essence of their worship, and the heart of their religion." Sacrifice was performed most commonly by diviners (*obea* or *dibia*) as part of asking or demanding (*a-juju*) something from the multitude of invisible forces, powers, and spirits (*muo*) who inhabited the Igbo world. More importantly, though less commonly, people engaged specialists from Nri to make sacrifices to cleanse or remove "abominations" that had occurred as a result of breaking taboos. Sacrifice in historical Igboland reaffirmed the ideal existence of the invisibles largely because people thought of *aja* in terms of "feeding" the benevolent spirits (the *muo*) and of placating the bad or evil spirits (the *mo njo*).

Unlike other peoples in West Africa, however, Igbo generally did not eat the physical remains of sacrifices; thus, the religious act of aja was not a function of "eating the gods" but rather of petitioning and of "feeding" them. Indeed, sacrifice in Igboland tended to reaffirm the close connections between the gods and the people, between the invisibles and the visibles, rather than expressing the separation of the profane world from that of the sacred. As one recent scholar wrote, in Igboland, "the gods and men live a symbiotic life. . . . Men feed the gods and the gods provide health, fertility of soil and reproduction." As elsewhere though, sacrifice in Igboland also underscored the connections among the people, who struggled to live in a world inhabited by a host of invisible as well as visible beings. In this Eboan world, nothing happened by chance; therefore, leaving anything to chance was dangerous.

Sacrifice was the principal way that people in Eboan Africa attempted to create order out of the events of their individual and collective lives. Sacrifice, the ritual killing of consecrated victims to feed the spirits, to placate the powerful forces (visible as well as invisible) in Igboland, and to petition for answers, structured much of historical Igbo ritual life. Igbo people understood that they sacrificed living things because the deities demanded it. The more powerful deity or the more powerful the need for "asking" (*a-juju*), the more valuable the sacrifice must be. Conversely, some sacrifices, called *ichu aja* (joyless sacrifice), were of rotten or disfigured or ugly things, such as rotten eggs, sick chickens, abortive lambs, or lizards. These joyless sacrifices were done specifically to distract otherwise malevolent spirits, "much as a dangerous dog is given a bone to keep it busy."

Olaudah Equiano also gave his account of how common sacrifices were in Nri, and of which many marked special events, especially days of thanksgiving. Most sacrifices were performed by the lineage heads (*okpala*) and other leading men: "They have many offerings, particularly at full moons; generally, two at harvest before the fruits are taken out of the ground: and when any young animals are killed, sometimes they offer up part of them as a sacrifice. These offerings, when made by one of the heads of a family, serve for the whole. I remember we often had them at my father's and my uncle's, and their families have been present. Some of our offerings are eaten with bitter herbs. We had a saying among us to any one of a cross temper, 'That if they were to be eaten, they should be eaten with bitter herbs.' These sacrificial rites often included other forms of mass or collective performance, especially dancing and singing."

Performance, music, entertainment and so forth were a significant part of Nri culture. When Equiano attempted to capture the essential character of what he termed 'Eboan Africans' or 'natives of Eboe', he stressed the importance of group-based performances ('songs') as a metaphor for Igbo community culture. 'We are almost a nation of dancers, musicians, and poets,' he wrote in the 1780s. 'Every great event . . . or other cause of public rejoicing is celebrated in public dances, which are accompanied with songs and music suited to the occasion.' According to Equiano, these group dances always followed general rules of function and arrangement, with the assembly of people divided into 4 sections by age and sex. In particular forms or details, however, the actual performances often seemed to be newly constructed or *ad hoc*. Equiano wrote that because public dance was meant to convey a narrative, 'and as the subject is generally founded on some recent event, it is therefore ever new'. This topicality gave 'our dances a spirit and variety which I have scarcely seen elsewhere'.

The dances, music, and poetry that Equiano believed defined Igbo-speaking people as 'Eboan' demonstrate the existence of a group of people, culturally conversant with each other and bounded by time and space, who would understand the performances. As an Igbo proverb states: 'A new man does not sing' (*onye ofo edekwe*). In other words, 'Eboan' community culture was something that people at the time recognized guided their behavior in concrete ways. As Equiano understood, in historical Igboland every person belonged to a specific group, and every group had its rituals, its customs, its beliefs, its ways of life—in short, its community culture (*omenani/odinani*).

The Aro (Igbo) and Involvement in the
Transatlantic Trade — An Overview

The Aro origins derive from oral traditions that state the group formed the Arochukwu Confederacy—between the 1600s and 1720s—as part of an "Igbo-Akpa" alliance. The latter was said to have helped the Aros prevail in a civil war between themselves and the Ibibio 'ethnic' group; the Ibibios resultantly fled postwar, while others were assimilated into the Aro. Three confederates—Ezeagwu, Okennach, and Ibom Isii—were at the Apex of the confederacy and between them comprised a total of 9 inalienable lineages which were called the *Otusi*. The *Otusi* formed an umbrella for several of the 19 Arochukwu lineage groups/or sections, which the British referred to as "towns," and the Aros classified as "villages". The various Aro diaspora settlements were connected to these units, from which the founders of the respective diaspora settlements were drawn. The heads of the 9 *Otusi* (singular form: Eze Otusi) constituted *Okpankpo*, the highest ruling council headed by a troika—*Nna Ato* (Three Fathers)—chaired by Eze Aro (Aro king), who must be the senior *Otusi* of his lineage-group cluster or confederate. In effect, Eze Aro was not an absolute ruler but a committee man.

Using the traditions of the Niger Delta corporate kin groups, G. I. Jones concluded that the Aro oracle, *Ibiniukpabi*, played a crucial part in their formation. Developments relating to the Middle Belt state of Kwarafara [in particular] throw light on Aro origins and political structure, and on the Biafra trade. The demise of the long-troubled state of Kwarafara dovetailed with the formation of the Aro state. The firearm-bearing Akpa who intervened in the crisis that produced Arochukwu appears to have represented advance elements of Kwarafara migrants, in an exodus that had commenced in the 16th century.

The notion that Arochukwu was founded in the early 17th century is also concordant with recent evidence of the antiquity of the major slave market at Bende (present-day Abia State, southeastern Nigeria). The Bende market was organized around the Aro trading networks; its major and minor fairs, respectively, were named after the Aro families *Agbagwu* and *Bianko*, so that evidence of its existence implies Aro trading activity. Indeed, Bende was thriving by the 1670s. French mariner, John Barbot, who made at least 2 voyages to the Biafra coast between 1678 and 1682, wrote in 1682 that "There is . . . large market for slaves in Belli, a large town west of *Old Calabar inland*". In July 1699, James Barbot and John Grazilhier referred to a "Bendi" market where 247 bars were exchanged for 23 captives. The inland market was, according to them, 3 or 4 days away from the New Calabar port. The descriptions of both "Belli" and "Bendi" fit into the location of Bende, situated in Cross River Igboland. These observations were made a century before Mathew's projected date of Aro formation—the second half of the 18th century.

Firearms/guns and gunpowder were one of the main goods procured by the Aros and are known to have been imported in the second half of the 17th century: over £1,000 (£187,195 in 2022) worth of these goods were imported between 1662 and 1703, and importation may well have begun even earlier. Such arms are part of the supporting evidence that Arochukwu was formed during the early Atlantic slave trade era in the Bight of Biafra. This event fits into a general pattern of immigration into the region, aimed at taking advantage of the coastal trade in captives. The contemporaneous formation in the 17th century of the Niger riverine states—Abo, Oguta, Onitsha, and Osomari—has been linked to non-Igbo people interested in the slave trade. Indeed, these societies all came to be deeply involved in the slave trade.

The Aro formation appear to have resulted from 3 related developments:

1. Conflict between expanding "Igbo" and "Ibibio" over a frontier region.
2. Migration of Kwarafara elements away from their troubled homeland under the weight of conflicts with Sudanic and, later, with emergent Middle Belt states.

3. The fledging Atlantic trade in which the Kwarafara diaspora and, perhaps, local Igbo and Ibibio sought to partake.

The Atlantic trade provided the incentive for Aro expansion, just as Aro modes of organization made the expansion possible and enduring.

The Biafra trade was in its infancy up to the mid-17th century, a period for which there is insufficient evidence of Aro expansion. Between 1501 and 1650, captives leaving the region's ports accounted for only 4.7% of captives from all African regions combined. If the sample of enslaved Biafrans in the Americas that Alonso de Sandoval recorded in 1627 is anything to go by, the proportion of the Igbo in the Biafra trade was still small; there was only one captive who was of "Igbo" origin among 15 captives from the Bight of Biafra. This indicates that the slave trade still drew heavily on coastal populations.

The opening up of new plantation regions in the Americas generated significant increases in the volume of captives exported from Africa in the second half of the 17th century. Between 1651 and 1680, the Bight of Biafra supplied as much as 16% of all captives exported from Africa. Though absolute numbers remained strong for the remainder of the century, captives from the Bight of Biafra, as a percentage of all African captives exported to the America, entered a period of decline after 1680. Resultantly, while the volume of captives exported from all African regions combined increased by 68% during the 25-year period 1676—1700, the number of exports leaving the Bight of Biafra actually declined by 14.5%. And the Biafra share generally remained small from 1700—40, when overall captive exports continued to increase appreciably. The upsurge of captive departures that began in the 1651—75 period suggests that there was a concentration of Aro activities in neighboring Ibibioland at a time when the Aro had not yet expanded westward and northwestward, and when Calabar was still Biafra's principal port.

Two demand conditions also influenced the trend observed in export volumes in the Bight of Biafra before the 18th century. The first was that captives from the Calabars "were not in high favor with the English."

Discrimination against captives from the Old Calabar, in particular, was reported in Barbados as early as 1675—76. They were referred to as "supernumerary Negroes" in 1679. Reinforcing this negative attitude was what European sailors in the late 17th century described as the turbulence of Old Calabar waters and its "intemperate air". "Intemperate air" conspired with malaria and high mortality to discourage Europeans from establishing a permanent presence in the region, as they did elsewhere in Atlantic Africa.

Though a significant increase in the Biafra slave trade did not happen until after 1650, there was some increase during the first half of the 17th century. Out of the estimated 5,278 Africans who were enslaved in Peru between 1560 and 1650, entries for "Biafra" and "Caravali" totaled 682—or nearly 13%. Indeed, Biafrans "became quite numerous" in Peru between 1610 and 1640. The Spaniards at Jamaica and Barbados were buying captives from the Bight of Biafra as early as the 1660s. In circa 1668 and 1693, a total of 215 captives from "Callebar" were imported into the island of Bermuda. In 1672, a Royal African Company (RAC) document concerning New and Old Calabar read in part, "whither many ships are sent to trade [and where' slaves and teeth ... are to be had in plenty".] Up to 1705, the British were trailing the Dutch, who had "the greatest share" in the Old Calabar trade. In June 1669, James Barbot learned of an English ship commanded by one Captain Edwards, who "got his compliments" of 500 captives in 3 weeks' time in New Calabar. Barbot Jr., claimed to have seen 10 or more slave ships in New Calabar in October 1700. In October 1702, it was expected that there might be too many ships in New Calabar, but the situation was deemed considerably undesirable again in Old Calabar. Prices correspondingly increased, though Barbot Jr.'s comment in December 1705 that New Calabar suppliers "rais'd price of negroes from 40s.—50s. to £12 or £14" (£2,192—£2,557 in 2022) probably reflected short-term phenomena. Supply had fallen behind demand, and though the market was still not as tight as it was elsewhere in Atlantic Africa, this trend could indicate a hinterland situation in which protracted resistance on the part of central Igbo checked captive supplies before the Aro eventually gained influence in the region.

In spite of increasing prices—probably due in part to fluctuations in the value of the iron bar, which was in use then as currency—the British Board of Trade reported in 1709 that, along with the situation at the ports below the Equator, prices of captives were lowest in the Bight of Biafra, "from whence the greatest number of Negroes are exported". The Board of Trade was either behind the times in its appraisal of the volume of the Bight of Biafra trade or it based its report on a short-term fluctuation. Relatively smaller numbers of captives left the region during the first 4 decades of the 18th century. Shortfalls in supply and competition from independent traders compelled the RAC to send factors "to try if an allayance cannot be made with the princes of the Country of the Bight, and to learn what sort of Trade may be carryed on there," according to an internal report of February 1721 from the Royal Africa Company. Clearly, demand was increasing at a faster rate than supply because of the expansion of the American plantation complex. This condition provided an incentive for hinterland slave traders to expand the sources of captives.

Aro efforts had yielded results by the 1740s, when captive exports from the Bight of Biafra increased dramatically. During the 1740—45 period, the volume of captives leaving the ports of the Bight of Biafra increased 61% over the foregoing 5-year period, representing a 7% increase in the Biafra share of the African total. Whereas the region supplied 66,833 — 6.1% of a total of 1,088,909 captives exported from all African ports in the first quarter of the 18th century, it supplied 182,006, or 12.4% of an African total of 1,471,725 during the second quarter. This upward trend continued until the end of the second phase of Aro expansion in 1807. The slave trade was expanding across the board, but the Bight of Biafra branch was expanding at a higher rate.

The rise in the Biafra Atlantic trade during this period was accompanied by a drastic increase in the turnaround rates for ships buying captives at Bight of Biafra ports. This phenomenon was obvious to Alexander Falconbridge, who sailed frequently to the region as a slaver's surgeon in the third quarter of the 18th century.

> The time during which the slave ships are absent from England, varies according to the destination of the voyage, and the number of ships they happen to meet on the coast. To Bonny, or Old and New Calabar, a voyage is fully performed in about 10 months. Those to the Windward and Gold Coasts, are rather more uncertain, but in general from 15 to 18 months.

The dramatic rise of the Biafra Atlantic slave trade from the 1740s onward reflected not only the supply conditions that facilitated fast loading rates, but also trajectories in Euro-American demand. While captives from the region were generally not considered premium grade by the planters, there seemed always to be pockets of plantation Americas that desired them, reflecting ambivalent perceptions about the enslaved Igbo, sometimes in the same regions, and perhaps a rising profile of Biafra captives in the New World over time. Planters of the Carolinas and to an extent those of Saint-Domingue rejected Igbo captives, but not those of Jamaica; Virginian planters accepted them enthusiastically. While Michael Gomez is able to quote a report that described the Igbo in 16th century Mexico as "difficult to manage and disposed to committing suicide when subjected to the slightest punishment or ridicule," Colin Palmer reports that they "were considered tractable and hence were highly sought after by some of the slaveholders" in early 17th century Spanish America. Writing in 1793, Jamaica-based British planter Bryan Edwards dwelled on suicide as cause for "the great objection to the Eboes as slaves," and after heaping scorn on the Igbo and their ways, he still took care to add that he could not "draw any conclusion of natural inferiority in these people to the rest of the human race". Despite Edwards's somber characterization of the Igbo, the course of the 18th century reveals what seems to be an incremental willingness to accept Igbo captives. One Theodore Morris in Barbados bemoaned to Bristol merchant, Isaac

Hobhouse in January 1730/1731 that "there has not been a cargo of Ebbo Slaves here a long time, and many People are Enquiring for them".

Some slaveowners even had reasons to prefer the Igbo. Gwendolyn Hall has suggested that Chesapeake planters—and to a lesser extent, planters in Louisiana as well—sought Igbo females, probably because of the high reproductive powers that were ascribed to Igbo women. In his memoirs, published in 1789, Olaudah Equiano stated that "[t]he West India planters prefer the slaves of Benin or Eboe to those of any other part of Guinea, for their hardiness, intelligence, integrity, and zeal". Equiano's observation corroborates that of Captain Hugh Crow, who made regular trips to the Bight of Biafra in the last 20 years of the 18th century. Crow gives the impression that favorable comments on captives from the Bight of Biafra had become the norm in his day.

> The Eboes [are] a superior race, and the inhabitants, generally, are a fair dealing people, and much inclined to a friendly traffic with the Europeans, who humor their peculiarities.... The Eboes, tho' not generally robust, are a well-formed people, of the middle stature: many of their women are of remarkably symmetrical shape, and if white, would in Europe be deemed beautiful. This race is ... of a more mild and engaging disposition than the other tribes ... and though less suited for the severe manual labor of the field, they are preferred in the West India colonies for their fidelity and utility, as domestic servants, particularly if taken young, as they then become the most industrious of any of the tribes taken to the colonies.

Impressions were mixed, but captives from the Bight of Biafra had gained wide acceptance by the second half of the 18th century, and possibly, half a century earlier. Though he noted in 1788 that Biafra captives were "weakly, and more liable to disorders," Liverpool merchant James Jones considered "the Trade [in Biafra] most Advantageous ... both as to Our Manufacturiers [sic] and the Number had from thence." All this suggests a shift in Euro-American attitudes toward Biafra captives or, at the very least, that an ever-increasing need for labor left planters with no choice but to take captives from wherever they could be found. Some who expressed very negative views of the Igbo even offered advice on how to make them better slaves. In 1864, physician and poet, James Grainger, opined that they needed to be "bought young" and Edwards recommended "the gentlest and mildest treatment".

The entry of Liverpool merchants and their subsequent takeover of the trade from their Bristol counterparts in the Bight of Biafra is relevant to understanding the trade despite the negative reviews of the region's captives. Liverpool merchants preferred to buy lower priced captives and were willing to accept lower prices in New World ports. The conditions in the Bight of Biafra suited this strategy well. Whereas the Bristol ships alone carried 300,000 captives from 1680—1700, Liverpool became dominant toward the mid-18th century. At least two-thirds of the voyages in which the Liverpool tycoon of the second half of the 18th century, William Davenport, invested, were dedicated to the trade in Old Calabar and the Cameroons, both in the Bight of Biafra. Of 144 of these voyages that have been traced, out of a total of some 160, as many as 98 went to the Bight of Biafra—55 to Old Calabar and 43 to the Cameroons. In January 1736, two mariners wrote to their owner in Britain that "we buy Callabar and Angola Negroes ... on which account we take as many ... as we can, in order to render the Negroe Account proffitable [sic] to the Company". Thus, Liverpool operations emphasized turnover, illuminating why the increase in the size of slave ships from 1664—1807 was greatest in the Bight of Biafra, where it rose by 50% in comparison to the previous 200 years. Liverpool domination correlates with this development.

Certain demand factors, including a continuing New World demand for labor and the rising profile of Biafra captives, especially the "Eboes" from the port of Bonny, justified this strategy and contributed to the expansion of the Biafra trade. Prices were resultantly impacted, notwithstanding increased supply. The average prices of Biafra captives in the New World, especially the "Eboe," hovered at quite competitive rates during the peak years of trade. This phenomenon was particularly striking in late 18th century Spanish Louisiana, when the mean price of Igbo men was highest among the most numerous ethnicities". The trend reversed in the U.S. from 1804 onward, but the fact that enslaved Igbo men commanded high prices in different regions and over long spells complicates planters' apparent lukewarm attitude to them.

If increases in the volumes of captive exports from the Bight of Biafra reflected increasing demand for captives, they also manifested greater organization, on both side of the Atlantic to meet the labor needs of a rapidly expanding plantation complex in the Americas. On the Biafra coast, there was a "trust" system in which European buyers advanced goods to coastal traders who in turn advanced these goods to the Aro. The rise of the Biafra trade has been attributed to this peculiar practice, which was made possible by the operation of the indigenous Ekpe society. This institution was important, but like other important factors, it only partially explains the rise of the region's trade. Developments in the hinterland—anchored by Aro organization—facilitated the supply of captives to the coast and justified European credit investment in the region.

The pivotal relationship of Aro organization to developments on the coast manifested by the mid-18th century in Bonny's supersession of Old Calabar as Biafra's principal port as the Aro expanded westward. The shift occurred during the 1726—50 period, when the volume at Old Calabar rose to 66,800, nearly doubling the 34,400 in the previous quarter century, while Bonny's rose to 93,200—22 times the paltry 4,200 in the previous period. Thereafter, the numbers embarked at both Old Calabar, and Bonny continued to rise, but while exports from Old Calabar rose appreciably to 103,800 or 55.3% in the 1751—75 period, the rise at Bonny was exponential—193,000 or 107%. In the last quarter of the century, the volume from Old Calabar declined to 82,500, while the number who embarked from Bonny rose further to 207,900. Bonny not only became the busiest port in the Bight of Biafra; it also became the busiest in Atlantic Africa north of the Equator.

Concomitant with the expansion of trade was the exceptionally fast loading rate that occurred at the Bonny port. Captain Simmons of the *Vine*, from Liverpool, "apparently [broke] the record" in 1766 when he sailed with 400 captives from Bonny to Dominica. He "accomplished the round voyage in 7 months and 10 days. The development was considered remarkable.

Many historians have pondered how the foregoing expansion came about, and cited the declining demand at Old Calabar as a factor. They have paid considerable attention to the role of Euro-American buyers in bringing about the relative decline of Old Calabar. Relatively poor health conditions at Old Calabar, the disinterest of West Indian planters in Old Calabar captives, prohibitively high duties—or 'comey'—payable to secure trading rights, and the rivalry between the Liverpool and Bristol ships. European traders could make £60—62 per head from Bonny and New Calabar captives, "against only £28—30 for slaves from Old Calabar". Indeed, the Liverpool-Bristol rivalry seems to have been more intense at Old Calabar and may have been put off by some buyers by 1767, when one Liverpool sailor wrote in 1767 that he "never saw a worse prospect for making a voyage than at present". Conversely, Bonny's more convenient anchorage relative to Old Calabar also made it more attractive.

The one demand condition that has been adduced to have been significantly impactful has barely received attention. The poor reputation of Biafra captives in the Americas affected Old Calabar much more than Bonny. The captives from Old Calabar tended to revolt aboard slave ships which was viewed as stereotypical by 18th century British slavers. That they were prone to suicide was another stereotype of the Igbo held by planters in several regions of the Americas. James Jones, who sent ships regularly to Bonny in the 1780s, claimed that he "always declined sending" ships to Old Calabar (and the Cameroons) because the ports "are Sickly, and Slaves inferior to any other, very Weakly and liable to great mortality". Indeed, mortality rates among captives leaving the Bight of Biafra were 7.5% higher than among those departing from the rest of Atlantic Africa, and within Biafra, the mean mortality rate involving vessels from Old Calabar was a significant 5.7% higher than those departing Bonny. One Euro-American and coastal element that may have been instrumental to the shift and high turnaround rates in the region is the possibility that the Aro moved captives to the ports where they could obtain higher prices, in this case Bonny, and where they could sell their captives as "Eboe" rather than the opprobrious "Calabar". This phenomenon buttresses the importance of Euro-American preferences.

A combination of factors—external and domestic—accounts for the ascendancy of Bonny. Eltis, Lovejoy, and Richardson have identified several conditions that favored the major ports—their proximity to "large stocks of potential slaves," accessibility to slave vessels, greater information there about commercial conditions, personal and commercial ties between indigenous merchants of the ports and their European counterparts, and domestic political factors. This perspective offers a greater range of possibly explanatory factors but does not necessarily explain the trajectories of any one port. One example of this is that the idea of Old Calabar's intrinsic unhealthiness as attributable to European mortality rates does not hold water—pun unintended—as these rates were brought about by long wait periods, occasioned by a shortage of available captives at the port; thus, it cannot be concluded that Bonny was any healthier. Even Harry Johnston, the vice consul in the Bight of Biafra during the 1880s appraised Old Calabar to be "relatively healthy". Citing high comey rates was also tenuous because the rates were also high at Bonny. Furthermore, the ease of anchorage argument regarding Bonny does not stand up to scrutiny as Euro-American buyers were aware of this advantage by the start of the 1800s, yet it was not until 1726—50 that Bonny superseded Old Calabar.

To this end, it has been said that declining supplies at Old Calabar and increasing supplies at Bonny reflected the shifting focus of Aro operations, rather than Euro-American demand patterns. It has been said that this best explains Bonny's supersession of Old Calabar as Biafra's principal port.

Nwokeji attributed the relative attractiveness of the ports to overseas buyers based on their supply links with the hinterland—from which most captives were drawn. The location of Bende (eastern Igboland), which had been well established since the 1670s, suggests the existence of a trade-route network that crisscrossed Igbo and the Ibibio countries down to Calabar. These routes led southward to the ports of Bonny and New Calabar and northward into the Igala and Idoma lands in the Nigerian Middle Belt, probably from the early 18th century and toward the end of the second phase or beginning of the second phase of Aro expansion. This would partly have resulted from the policies of the Atta dynasty of the Igala kingdom of Idah, which came into existence from 1687—1717. The Atta dynasty "turned energetically to the development of slave trading and became a major supplier to the Niger River markets and the Aro overland system". Of particular interest are the changes that took place in the trade-routes network. Four north-to-south routes had emerged by 1750, according to Afigbo:

1. The Niger waterway in the westernmost extreme of the region.
2. An overland route from the Middle Belt towns of Ejure and Idah on the Benue River, through Nsukka, central Igboland, and Akwete in southern Igboland to Bonny.
3. An overland route from the Middle Belt town of Ibi on the Beune through Ejure to central Igboland and "to the coast".
4. The easternmost route from Ibi through Wukari and Ogoja in the Ejagam region, Ezza in northeastern Igboland, to Cross River Igbo towns of Ubutu and Bende, Arochukwu, and the Ibibio town of Itu. This route most likely terminated at Calabar.

The second and third of these routes passed through central Igboland and headed toward the central Niger delta, and the second route terminated at Bonny. The Niger route was probably the oldest. This picture squares with the trends in Biafra Atlantic exports. The pattern of exports from Old Calabar suggests that the easternmost route was also older than the central routes; New Calabar was the oldest port of significance and received most of its trade from the Niger route closest to it, as did Brass, the westernmost port in the region. As Biafra's easternmost port, Old Calabar, "dealt with the

Ibibio along the lower Cross River" and brought captives from the Aro. Whereas the captives sold at Brass included significant numbers of non-Igbo from farther north, Bonny received its trade principally from the Aro network. It was more practicable to reach the Niger through the Brass River than through the Bonny River; the Bonny River was not even a branch of the Niger. Thus, Bonny received its captive supplies almost exclusively from central Igboland. Its rise as the principal port had to await the development of the central route. Old Calabar, which superseded New Calabar, received its trade from the easternmost route via Arochukwu, so that a higher proportion of non-Igbo captives were exported from there than from Bonny. The 2 central routes leading to Bonny through the Igbo heartland were the new elements in the trade-route system during the 18th century. The Bonny port—which became preeminent by the mid-18th century—linked these 2 routes via the major Aro settlements in the greater upper Imo River area. Thus, both internal and external dynamics were linked. The Aro mobilized captives from the hinterland, and Euro-American traders bought and transported those captives overseas, underscoring the fact that both internal processes and external Euro-American circumstances shaped the region's trade.

The Aro trading complex had not only an Atlantic context but also a regional political and economic one. The most spectacular development of the 18th century was the establishment of Aro settlements virtually everywhere in the region. Aro settlements maintained cultural and political fidelity to the Arochukwu metropole.

To this end, the Aro had 5 key elements of trade diasporas: *first*, a "central place" which was Arochukwu and the seat of the major Aro institutions, such as the central council (Okpankpo), the Ibiniukpabi oracle, and Eze Aro (Aro king), and each diaspora settlement was institutionally tied to the Aro world only through its parent Arochukwu lineage-group. A *second* element is in the relationship of trade diaspora to their host communities, which range from dominated diasporas to dominant ones,

36

with most falling into the former category. The *third* similarity between the Aro and other trade diasporas is cultural aloofness from the host population. Whatever their size, structure, or specific history, Aro settlements stood out from the local population. *Fourth*, in spite of the tendency to emphasize cultural exclusiveness, trade diasporas were "cross-cultural carriers of culture" or "cultural brokers". For example, though the trade diasporas of Senegambian groups, such as the Maraka, the Juula and the Jahaanke, "adopted the language[s] and some aspects of the culture of the [host societies]," they continued to claim Soninke origin. The Aro diaspora settlements, too, shared much and mixed with the groups among whom they lived, notably the Igbo, but they steadfastly held on to a separate Aro identity. *Fifth*, trade diasporas historically made ideological and / or religious references to universalist monotheism, and often claimed a special place within it. This is in like form to the Jews and the use of Islam by the African trade diasporas of the Hausa and the Soninke-speaking groups of West Africa, and the Swahili of East Africa. The Aro used the monotheist *Chukwu* deity.

The period from the 18th century onward marked the onset of the era of private enterprise. It was accompanied by the introduction of violence into the process (there is no evidence that indicates the Aro resorted to violence before the 18th century). Warfare intensified as groups jostled to take advantage of the slave trade. Aro wars in the 18th century did not involve the entire Aro community; typically, merchant-warlords and their followers were involved. Aro diaspora settlements sprang up in response to opportunities created by the expanding Atlantic slave trade; it was trade, more than political ambition, that originally motivated the establishment of Aro settlements. The merchants did not create political formations initially, but "trading centers". Consequently, they lived in Arochukwu throughout their lifetime; it was their descendants and dependents who settled permanently in the diaspora. The merchants-warlords of the 18th century came from various backgrounds—from within Aro ruling groups recent immigrants, and recently acculturated ex-slaves. Many Aros built 'rest houses' rather than permanently settle away from Arochukwu and several were invited by non-Aro communities to establish themselves there so as to benefit from Aro trade and protection. One example of the esteem the Aros were held in comes from a saying by the Ngwa of southern Igboland: *Onye Aro Mbi la ke ya whe oma mmera ya* (Harboring the Aro is good fortune). Some of these non-Aro communities paid regular tribute to Aro in the form of slaves, labor, and food, and those that threatened others were sometimes Aro allies. In the desperate fight for survival, the Aro would have been "invited" by one side, or the other, or both.

Non-Aro communities also welcomed the Aro because of their ability to dispense "justice"—including the removal of categorized persons to Atlantic slavery. Where the Aro were required to pay rent, it was usually a token amount. The annual tenancy renewal required the presentation of kola nut in Ngwa communities in one of the areas with strong Aro presence. In one community, the "rent" consisted of only two gallons of palm wine, eight manillas, and one cock. In Ibibioland, the acquisition of land required a case of drinks, a piece of cloth, a gun, and some salt. The Aro contracted *igba ndu* (covenant) with their hosts as an instrument of protectionism. Igba ndu often involved mixing protagonists' blood for mutual consumption. This ritual was deemed to carry a spiritual force capable of killing a protagonist who defaulted from the terms of an agreement. Kinship ties were forged and exploited. Marriages figured prominently among these ties. This practice created "the obligation of in-laws," and as in-laws and sons of local women, the Aro widened their contacts and increased their trade. Kinship ties were reinforced by massive immigration. Immigrants into Aro settlements operated freely in their natal homes under the umbrella of Aro enterprise.

Despite the formation of ties, strategies and practices that facilitated the establishment of Aro settlements among non-Aro hosts, the Aro deemed force to be particularly effective in the Igbo heartland. Here, the Aro did not always wait for pre-existing groups to "invite" them. Their massive and consistent application of force in this region is widely recognized as atypical Aro methods. Wars were not ordinarily in the interests of Aro trade. This seems to have been the key deterrence for wars, not that the Aro made war on numerically inferior groups, but instead on such populous groups as Onitsha, Ogidi and Igbo-Ukwu. The view that the presence of populations of potential adversaries was the primary criterion for Aro to make war on any group gives the impression that the Aro were warmongers who would make war on any group—except those strong enough to give them a good fight. The Aro resorted to wars in central Igboland despite strong opposition from populous societies, including the Nri during the 19th century. There were other reasons the Aro did not make war on certain groups, whether large or small. In the first instance, the Aro would have seen little purpose in making war upon communities with whom they enjoyed peaceful relations. Besides, speculating on the size of the communities which the Aro did not make war against runs the risk of anachronism: present-day populations are not always an accurate measure of the historical strengths of societies. Wars had severe impact on many communities and subsequent demographic developments have been uneven. Some societies gained from immigration out of devastated areas, while others lost out in the same process. In one extreme case, Ora, in the vicinity of Arondizuogu, was completely destroyed during the establishment of the Aro settlement. Present-day population densities reflect, in part, the effect, rather than the cause of wars. Rather than being a deterrent, the presence of numerically strong groups could have been the very cause of conflicts in the region.

If the size of potential foes was not necessarily a determinant of Aro invasions, it still needs to be explained why warfare prevailed during the mid-18th century establishment of the principal Aro settlements in the great upper Imo / Nri-Awka region. The resort to warfare was more likely a consequence of the tighter land-tenure rules that were a corollary of population pressure in the area and that anthropologist, Thurstan Shaw, attributes to "the antiquity and effectiveness of yam cultivation and the exploitation of the oil palm." The quest for space would likely have increased the levels of intransigence in the pre-existing societies and led to the breakdown of diplomatic alternatives. The situation was probably helped by Aro's determination to establish themselves strongly in a region that had great potential for them; Aro incursions into the heartland were, in the first instance, a function of the search for captives, and as abovementioned, were met with some resistance. This point is important because in pursuing their interests, the Aro generally preferred peace to war. They made war part of their overall strategy in order to dominate trade.

In summary, the Aro created a spiritual aura and authoritative air about them through the Ibiniukpabi, the temple of their universalist Aro God, Chukwu, and this was highly effective when dealing with non-Aro communities, especially when siphoning off captives and maintaining their influence. They developed a reputation for clairvoyance and through their oracle became known us *Umu Chukwu*—"children of God". When captives were taken, they were said to have been "eaten," which was a euphemism for being sold into Atlantic slavery; groups were required to pay fees / fines in captives, and failure to do so would result in non-transgressors being sold into slavery. The Aros were sought by the non-Aro to dispense justice and mediate in communities where disputes arose; they were shrewd and learned about all the communities' customs to maintain their reputation. It is noteworthy that the Aros did not consult the oracle against their fellow Aro, and it was solely applied to outsiders.

The further expansion of Aro merchant warlord settlements beginning in the mid-18th century was reflected in the growing power of their client village groups in the Nri area. This shift resulted in the massive increase in the exportation of slaves from the coast of Calabar that continued through the rest of the century. By the 1790s, slaving was so destructive that even the Nri had to resort to violence to defend themselves. The added exigencies of sustained drought and even famine during at least the first half of the 18th century also probably helped pave the way for Aro influence. The consequent slave raiding and trading and the general increase in social violence directly undermined the core cultural premises of the Nri civilization, with tragic consequences even for those who escaped enslavement. By the 20th century, perhaps only half of the area that had once been part of this civilization still maintained its ancestral connections with the "first Igbo."

In the 18th and 19th centuries, the rise of a new meritocratic elite in the heavily populated interior regions of Nri-Awka and Isuama (north-central Igboland), whose wealth was fueled by the importation of commodity currencies such as iron bars and copper rods, brought by new traders such as the Aro, encouraged the export of people as slaves. The community culture of Eboan African society, with its volatile mix of gerontocracy and meritocracy, of fatalism and localism, of *obia* (doctoring) and *aja* (sacrifice) and respect for *ikenga* (cult of achievement), lent ideological support to a growing system of exchange that increasingly transferred large numbers of people as slaves to the coast. As elsewhere, slavers in Igboland manipulated the political fragmentation of the region and benefited from the legality of enslaving one's enemies as well as of groups defined as Others. The destructive reach of the transatlantic slave trade extended deep into the Biafran hinterland and ravaged communities over 150 miles away from the coast. Again, the key turning point was the first half of the 18th century, the same time that transatlantic shipments from Calabar were flooding far-off Virginia with Igbo slaves, many of whom would have been enslaved from communities within the ambit of the Nri civilization.

The transformations that were ultimately both cause and effect of the growing transatlantic slave trade "out of Calabar," included the rise of Bonny in the central littoral, the ascendance of the Aro throughout the Igbo hinterland, and the slow collapse of the ancient Nri civilization—all of which crystalized in the first half of the 18th century. This was precisely the period when slave exports from the Bight of Biafra were sent disproportionately to the Chesapeake region of North America and to Virginia in particular. Not only were the great majority of these enslaved people likely Igbo, but they came from villages and village groups in the central and northern regions, and many of these people shared historical and cultural experiences rooted in the way of life of the "first Igbo."

The Atlantic Igbo — A
Virginian Eboesque Case Study

From the perspective of Virginia, the Bight of Biafra was the most important source of slaves for planters in the colony. Of the 83,500 Africans taken to Virginia in the century after 1676, about 37,000 came from the Calabar coast, and of these, perhaps 30,000 were Igbo. Most Biafran Africans (and Igbo) were taken in the first half of the 18th century, when the transatlantic slave trade to Virginia was at its height. Even though the Virginia market generally was a minor one in the Anglophone Americas, the flow of slaves from the Bight of Biafra during these decades was a demonstrable wave of Africans to the colony, and the Virginia market was significant for the initial expansion of the slave trade along the Calabar coast. In the 40 years after 1716, 57% of Africans sent to Virginia originated in the Bight of Biafra and thus came "out of Calabar." This wave of Biafran Africans and thus of Igbo heritage, resulted in 30,000 Calabars (of whom a likely 25,000 were Igbo) landing in Virginia in one generation. This Biafra-Virginia connection was especially concentrated in 1716—1730 and 1741—1750, when Biafrans constituted 62% and 75% respectively of imports in these cohorts. The forced migration of largely Igbo peoples had important consequences for the historical development of Creole Afro-Virginian slave culture and society, especially in the district around Montpelier.

The Igbo peoples, especially those from within the cultural ambit of the ancient Nri civilization, were a distinct ethnohistorical group whose members shared distinctive ancestral traditions and drew on the same or very similar material, social and ideological resources to adapt to the conditions in which they found themselves as slaves in the diaspora. They were a people that modern scholars began to study as a separate "nation" in the African diaspora.

During the 18th century, as the flow of enslaved Igbo turned into a tidal wave, the American market shifted rather dramatically from the Chesapeake region to the West Indies, especially Jamaica. But in the first half of the 18th century, between a quarter and a third (29%) of the estimated 93,000 Biafran Africans sent into the diaspora wound up in Virginia. The apparent Biafra-Virginia nexus was even more concentrated in the quarter century after 1716, when more than 55% of shipments sent from Calabar with a known destination went to Virginia. Between 1716 and 1740, Virginia was the major market (destination) for Biafran Africans. Slaves taken from this region were at least 6 times more likely to wind up in Virginia than in the next 2 major markets for these Africans—Jamaica, and South Carolina.

In the Virginia Piedmont in the second quarter of the 18th century, Igbo forced migrants were the first arrivals. They set the basic patterns of material, social, and ideological culture of enslaved communities to which successive waves of saltwater (Central African especially) and Creole (Tidewater) slaves acculturated. In other British Atlantic areas, such as Jamaica and the Lesser Antilles, especially after 1750, Igbo arrived as latecomers who then Igboized pre-existing institutions and cultural patterns. In both cases, people made do with what they had to sustain themselves, to forge connections among and between each other, and to make sense of their new worlds. This process of *historical creolization* in the Chesapeake was one of bricolage, of mixing and matching, of adapting and adopting a combination of new and old ways of doing things and of being people, and it resulted in an *Igboesque* regional "common tradition."

Igbo cultural dominance in the Chesapeake was not a forgone conclusion, given the known presence of other Africans in the region. Central Africans seemed to have been the major secondary group, and because of the use of political terms such as Congo (possibly derived from *manikongo*) and Angola (*ngola*) as toponyms and personal names, they seem to stick out. Since most Central Africans were brought in a second wave of slave imports in the 1740s and 1750s, they may have had to acculturate to pre-existing Igboized slave communities. And not only were Igbos the first arrivals in much of what became the Black Belt, but the high proportion of Igbo women in the colony may have given them disproportionate influence in the socialization of Creole children.

It is probable that Igboized slave communities incorporated some material, social, and ideological artifacts of Central African peoples, especially when they paralleled those of the Igbo. On a large scale, since Congo and Angola were also important in the slave trade to the Carolina low country (1720s—30s and 1790s—1807) and in the Spanish trade to New Orleans (1789s—1808), it is expected that there will be "Bantuisms" in antebellum southern life. But in the Upper South, what is most noteworthy is the relative lack of such markers of a Central African presence—for example, Kongolese political marronage, use of the term *gombo* for okra, slave "king / queen" festivals, and the term *wanga* for charm. Instead, for the Upper South one sees creolized Igboisms like decentralized authority (rules not rulers), yams as a staple, the term okra for the vegetable, Jonkonnu, and the term *mojo* for charm.

The other 2 major groups, Mande/Fulbe and Akan, were also rapidly absorbed into the Igboesque Creole culture.

The Igbo, as well as other Africans in early Virginia had to adapt to a new physical landscape that differed from Igboland. Virginia was hotter in the peak summer months, with temperatures rising to over 100 degrees Fahrenheit, and it was of course much colder during the winter. The radical seasonality of the New World would have seemed strange to people from subtropical lands relatively close to the Equator where the temperature usually stayed in the 80s and where the 2 "seasons" were those of the dry Harmattan from November through February (of the Western calendar), when hot dusty air blows south from the Sahara, and the perhaps hotter wet rainy season that prevailed through much of the rest of the year. Furthermore, the Igbo in Virginia might have found odd the fact that creeks and rivers flowed from north to south, or across the sun's daily path. In Igboland, clayey soils tended to be found in low-lying areas, with sandy soils in the uplands, whereas the opposite was the case in Virginia. Finally, even though large parts of historical Igboland were "derived savanna," or dry woodland, rather than the lush rainforest of myth, the mostly pine or deciduous forests in the interior of the Chesapeake would have seemed quite new and different.

Given these differences, however, a number of physical realities of the Virginia landscape would have seemed quite familiar to the diasporic Igbo, especially those in the Piedmont region. Much of the interior of both Igboland and Virginia had, in the words of a Nigerian archaeologist describing the Anambra Valley of northern Igboland, "a gently rolling topography." Mosquitoes and malaria were common to both regions as well. In Virginia, for example, some captives considered yams to be a prophylaxis against malaria: Uncle John Spence (b. 1857) remembered that the slaves in King George County "used to cultivate a lot of sweet potatoes (as a yam substitute) because they kept off malaria."

In Virginia summer, as throughout much of the year in Igboland, the land was alive with cicadas, fireflies, and tree frogs. On the Calabar coast in the 1820s and 1830s, at least 2 Europeans commented on the chirping of "the land Crabs" and the swarms of fireflies. When walking through Bonny in 1825. R. M. Jackson stated, "my ears were absolutely stunned by the chirping of the land Crabs existing here in vast numbers, whilst myriads of fire flies flitting before us plainly showed the grass from which they sprang." On the Niger River at the town of Eboe (Aboh), R. A. K. Oldfield remarked that "at night, the atmosphere was loaded with millions of fire-flies, illuminating it as far as the eye cold reach." The author of a 1922 collection of African-American folk rhymes commented on 2 rhymes with idiosyncratic language that he termed "Guinea or Ebo rhymes," both of them about frogs (and one specifically about tree frogs).

Much of the flora and fauna would have been new to Igbo exiles. There were no hippopotamuses, crocodiles, parrots, monkeys, duikers (bush antelopes), among other familiar animals, nor were there the many varieties of ferns and broad-leafed ground plants of Igboland. The important towering *iroko* tree (*Chlorophora excelsa*), used to make dugout canoes in riverine Igboland and a sign of ritual permanence, did not appear in the

Chesapeake. But the towering tulip poplar tree (*Liriodendron tulipifera*) in Virginia was called the "Canoe tree" in the third quarter of the 18th century, and Native Americans used its roots as a medicine for malaria. As early as the 1730s, Anglo-Virginians generally used the wood of this tree for a number of things, as William Byrd noted around 1737: "beautiful troughs, sticks, as well as walls in houses, roof shingles, chests for all needs, likewise for millwork, since it is very tough and lasting." Apparently, its association with canoes came later, perhaps with Africans.

Other plants and animals would have been familiar. In Eboan Africa, the Igbos raised pigs, poultry, bush bullocks (*muturu*), dwarf sheep, and goats; in Virginia they had hogs, "Guinea keet," and in the 18th century often sheep (raised for wool and for mutton for masters' tables). In Igboland, people fished creeks and lagoons for crabs, prawns, crayfish, catfish (*Clarias*), and tilapia as well as sardines, oysters, and perch, and land tortoises were well known. In Virginia, slaves nearer the Chesapeake Bay gathered crabs and oysters while Afro-Virginians in general would find turtles (terrapins), crayfish, catfish, perch, herring, and other edible creatures in the many creeks and rivers. Deer would have substituted for duikers, and rats, hawks, and vultures (buzzards) lived in Virginia as well as in Igboland. Clearly then, and contrary to the assertion that Africans in the New World faced "an almost completely strange environment," the Igbos would have found many things in Virginia at least partly familiar.

Moreover, tobacco, cotton, and perhaps maize were grown in Igboland in the mid-18th and 19th centuries, as attested by Equiano as well as by early Niger River explorers. Equiano noted that "our vegetables are mostly plantains, eadas [cocoyams], yams, beans, and Indian corn"; perhaps exaggerating, he claimed that in Igboland, people had "plenty of Indian corn, and vast quantities of cotton and tobacco." In the 1830s, Oldfield noted that on the middle reaches of the Niger, "Indian corn . . . is much cultivated," and when traveling up the river, he commented on "several fields of corn" he saw growing. In Virginia, where slaves grew tobacco and corn using mostly iron hoes or other primary tools and cultivated yams (and other familiar

47

domestic cultigens) in their Quarters, the Igbos would have had to shift emphasis from their old staple to the buckra's new ones but would still have been operating within a familiar agricultural system.

The ubiquitous West African oil palm (*Elais guineensis*) and kola nut of Igboland, however, did not exist in Virginia. The lack of oil palms, and thus of palm wine (*mimbo*) and eating oil (for *fufu*) meant a major shift, but perhaps the abundance of berries in Virginia (including blackberries and what some people in the Piedmont called "wine berries") as well as persimmons (a favorite food of opossums that people processed into persimmon beer) and fermented fruits (apples, peaches), would have made up the difference for palm wine, at least for drinking purposes. Lard would have sufficed for frying foods, and gravy or melted butter would have worked for mashed potatoes instead of the pungent castor-like palm oil for pounded *fufu*.

The technology of slave work in the first half of 18th century Virginia, with its hoe-based agriculture and cultivation of corn and tobacco in hills rather than in drilled rows, would have made sense to Igbo exiles. In fact, because tobacco was such a troublesome crop, requiring great care in planting, weeding, worming, tending, cutting, stripping, curing, and pressing into large barrels for shipment, the skills of Igbo farmers—women included—may well have been as important to the tremendous expansion of tobacco and corn production in the 18th century Chesapeake as the skills of other Africans were to the development of rice agriculture in colonial South Carolina. The eventual shift to plow-based Piedmont agriculture and the diversification into wheat in the second half of the century followed the creolization of the slave population. Those successive generations, however, continued to draw on Igbo material, social, and ideological resources to adapt to enslavement in the region.

Igbo exiles and their Afro-Virginia descendants had to rely on ancestral material resources because their masters, the buckra, were so niggardly in their provisions. Slave owners stinted the slaves, throwing the people back onto their own resourcefulness for sustenance. In the 18th and 19th centuries, masters provided slaves with only the barest necessities. Weekly or monthly rations consisted of salt fish and / or pork, corn or cornmeal, salt and perhaps molasses. The largest plantation holders usually doled out salted herrings as well as smoked pork and corn, which the slaves pounded and mixed with beans and boiled into hominy.

The 18th-century inclusion of salted fish, usually herring, is interesting. Equiano, for example, wrote that in his Eboan community, "dried fish . . . we esteemed a great rarity, as our waters were only brooks and springs." The Igbos had also made vegetable salt out of "wood ashes" and may have expected salt from their masters in Virginia. By the 19th century, the common custom in Virginia was to give slaves cornmeal, bacon, salt, and molasses. In the 19th century moreover, a colloquial Virginia term for flour was *ingany*, a word that intriguingly resembles the 19th century Igbo word for millet, *inyari*.

Captives augmented their meager food rations by hunting wild game and growing their own staple vegetables while using the corn or meal supplied to make either bread or mush or both. As might be expected in a society where the night was "negur day-time," slaves primarily hunted nocturnal animals such as raccoons and opossums. The basic diet, and the use of one-pot stews, remained largely consistent over the course of a century and a half. Hugh Jones wrote in 1724 that in Virginia, corn (maize) was "of great Increase and most general Use; for with this is made good Bread, Cakes, Mush, and Hommony for the Negroes, which with good Pork and Potatoes (red and white, very nice and different from ours) with other Roots and Pulse, are their general Food." This basic outline of the Afro-Virginian diet, along with such slave specialties as "'possum and sweet potatoes, ham hock cooked with cabbage or turnip greens, hoe cake and watermelon," also remained the norm throughout much of the 19th century.

Most importantly, slaves in Virginia relied on a number of garden cultigens, nearly all of which were West African plants that people commonly grew in Igboland. Scholars have identified a number of these "southern" garden cultigens as indigenous to West Africa. In Virginia, however, where the Igbo were the first to arrive, many of these food crops were Igboisms.

The Igbo in Virginia substituted yams for their old primary staple (*Dioscorea*) but maintained nearly all the secondary subsistence crops of their ancestral village agriculture except for cocoyams and plantains (and tropical fruits such as pawpaw / papayas). The loss of plantains and bananas seems to have been made up with maize and meal. Okra, associated with fertility as well as with proverbial knowledge in some parts of Igboland, black-eye peas (which in Virginia and indeed the entire South still brings good luck if eaten on New Year's Day), squashes, watermelons, and gourds and "greens" and others quickly reappeared and continued as staples of Afro-Virginian slave foodways.

Many slaves in 18th century Virginia made their own low-fired ceramic cooking pots and eating bowls, now termed *colonoware*. These *colonowares* were previously assumed to be imports from local American Indian groups, but evidence now indicates that slaves applied African conceptions and techniques of potting to make the ceramics.

Except for the uses of specialized plants and leaves and local mineral "decoctions," some of which may have had juju as well as functional purposes and which might have been quite easily re-created or substituted in Virginia's physical environment, the description of precolonial Igbo potting technology fits quite well with what is known of 18th century Virginia *colonoware*, thereby further supporting the thesis that the enslaved made the pottery.

Other aspects of Afro-Virginian material culture signify an Igbo connection. Dugout canoes, ideally made out of the canoe tree, evoke the canoes of riverine and coastal Igboland, especially compared to the reputedly short canoes found in the Carolina low country. The use of tulip poplars in Afro-Virginia is especially interesting given that at about the same time in western Jamaica, the most Igboized part of that island, black people there chose a single tree, the towering Cotton tree (*Eriodendron*) for their large dugout canoes.

Other historical Igbo crafts, such as blacksmithing and woodworking, may have found expression in early Virginia. Though no carved doors or panels such as those for which Igbo woodcrafters were noted in the late 19th and 20th centuries have been found in Virginia, southern black craftsmen sometimes fashioned ornate wooden canes, often with serpent motifs. Other objects, such as an 18th century wrought iron sculpture recovered in Alexandria, Virginia, and presently held in a private collection (last exhibited in the 1960s), may evoke an Eboan aesthetic. Though John Michael Vlach views this sculpture as "a powerful work" whose execution appears "to suggest the primal essence of human form," to Chambers it evokes the kinds of figurines made from wood or clay that inhabited southern Igbo *mbari* (ritual-art) structures or even Igbo *ikenga*.

Throughout Igboland, patrilineal groupings of kindreds (*umunne*), for whom the descent was bilateral, and the kinship idiom predominated, also organized themselves in 2 socially defined halves—what ethnographers call "moieties." Dual division meant that any grouping, whether kindreds in a clan, clans in village, or villages in a village group, had a rival, but related grouping of people. The historical Igbo social-political world was one of concentric circles of relations at diminishing degrees of consanguinity. A kindred was part of a clan (*ebo*), at least 2 clans made up a town / village (*ogbe*), and at least 2 towns made up a place / district (*ala*). Such a nested sense of social relations could also have described the world in which the enslaved perceived themselves: first part of a Quarter, at least 2 of which made up a farm, 2 or more of which comprised a plantation, which was often part of a *buckra's* holdings. In the mid-18th century, Anglo-Virginian planters who could afford to do so, shifted slaves around among and between their plantations, farms, and Quarters. Such ruthless planter capitalism may have unintentionally encouraged rather than disrupted the development of slave community life in the Chesapeake.

Afro-Virginians also forged a number of plantation customs that facilitated the creation and reproduction of slave social relations. Exogamy, or marrying out of the group, was the rule in historical Igboland (as indeed throughout Atlantic Africa). In 18th century Virginia, slaves may have applied this concept to Quarters so that people married between settlements, and the localism suggests an Igboized version of the concept rather than, for example, the applying of exogamous rules to the whole plantation or to a particular master's entire slave population.

The ancestral Eboan tradition included cyclical and seasonal time concepts as well as age grades, in which the year (as Equiano explained) was dated from when "the sun crosses the line." More important, however, was the belief that each child born was the reincarnation of some previous period, usually a remembered ancestor. The many Igbo women in early Virginia would have had to reckon with reincarnation whenever they give birth. It makes sense to believe that individual birthdates were not important because conceptions of a totally unique individuality may not have made sense to the people then; therefore, birthdays were not celebrated as discrete events. The importance of the group of reincarnation in the ancestral Igbo tradition found expression in the common Afro-Virginian tradition of not marking children's birthdates.

Much of early Afro-Virginian dance and music was performed in a distinctively African way. Igbo instruments like box drums and a banjo-like stringed instrument were common in Virginia and North Carolina. The word *banjo* itself signifies Igbo, as in *ba-njo* (being bad), and it is curious that in Jamaican Creole *banja* means "to play the fool." The banjo, as Thomas Jefferson noted, was an instrument "brought hither from Africa," and many Central African peoples called their version of a stringent gourd by variations of *mbanza*. Equiano also remembered that slaves in his area had "many musical instruments, particularly drums of different kinds, a piece of music which resembles a guitar, and another much like a stickado." In the early 20th century, an anthropologist among the Igbo also noted, in racist idiom of the time, that "the most interesting of Ibo instruments is the 'ubaw-akwala,' a sort of primitive guitar—or is it the original of the nigger banjo."

The term *banjo/banjer*, however, apparently was first used in the Chesapeake. It became the common word for this instrument between 1754 and the 1780s, whereas in the West Indies the term *banza* predominated until a general shift to *banjo/banjo* after about 1810.

Slaves on the North Carolina plantation where Harriet Jacobs grew up also used a drum made of a "box, covered with sheepskin [and] called the gumbo box;" Igbo slaves on a Jamaican plantation at about the same time relied on a similar box drum that they called "Gambys (Eboe drums)." In 1774, Edward Long described such "goombah" drums in the West Indies as "a hollow block of wood, covered with sheepskin stripped of its hair."

One of the most distinctive forms of antebellum African-American slave dancing, juba, had become an important part of the slave common tradition by the 19th century. Juba was a type of rhythmic jump-step dance that only black folks did. Dancers often patter their legs, arms, and chest (perhaps what subsequently came to be called doing the hambone) or "patting juba," There are a number of references to juba and patting juba in the antebellum published primary literature, though none in 18th century sources. Though Winifred Vass has assigned a Kongo or "Bantu" origin to the word, it was also associated with another Upper South slave artifact, Jonkonnu, which was also likely a creolized Igboism. Juba and patting seem to have been products of the elimination of drums (such as the 18th century "qua qua" in Virginia) from the 19th century common tradition.

Jonkonnu, known by various names including *John Canoe* and *John Koonering*, was common in slave societies throughout the British Americas. A Christmastime slave masquerade with a distinctive cow-horned masker who demanded gifts from the powerful sometimes wielded a whip, Jonkonnu was like an African men's masking society transported to the New World. Not known or at least not mentioned before the third quarter of the 18th century, Jonkonnu became a highly visible aspect of Afro-Caribbean societies at roughly the same time as 500,000 to 750,000 Igbo peoples flooded onto Caribbean sugar islands—after 1750. The masquerade has also been identified in 1820s Suffolk Virginia as well as 18th century North Carolina and perhaps late-19th century Rappahannock County, Virginia.

Generally given a Gold Coast provenance, this slave social fact was most likely an artifact of Igbo people in the Diaspora. The association of Jonkonnu with "gambys" and with cow-horn and other animal masks as well as with distinctive peaked-hat masks identical to mid-20th century Kalabari masks, plus the temporal association of the Afro-Caribbean version with the period of greatest Igbo importation (1760s—1820s), point toward Igboland as the source of the African-American performances.

Njokku, the "yam-spirit," was an important institution in historical Igboland (cognate terms included *njoku*, *onjoku*, and *ifejioku*), and there was also the yam-associated *okonko*, or Igbo secret society equivalent of Efik *ekpe*. 19th century sources attest to animal and ragman maskers in Bonny and Elem Kalabari, and these read much like both "root Jonkonnu" and 20th century northern Igbo *omabe* and *odo* masquerades. Diasporic Igbos combined elements from both shared traditions into a Creole institution. In effect, moreover, the Jonkonnu troupe may have served as an all-male slave "secret society" much like a masking version *okonko*. Jonkonnu clearly was a male preserve, with a leader who wielded a whip or stick in association with fierce animal-masked others. What slaves got was an annual visitation by *njokku* in *mmuo* (fearsome masking); those who participated as maskers gained honor and prestige within the save community. African-American Jonkonnu was a creolism but not randomly so.

Though there are no known descriptions of Jonkonnu in the 18th century Chesapeake, slaves in colonial Virginia also had a holiday at Christmas, ranging from one day to a week, in which they engaged in some sort of reveling. If Jonkonnu was a creolized reinterpretation of the Igbo *njokku* or a diasporic expression of *okonko* clubs, which celebrated the new year as well as the yam-spirit (which seems much more plausible than the other attempts to explain the phenomenon in terms of a minor trade chief on the Gold Coast during the 1720s), the continuing reliance of Igbo in Virginia on yams would suggest that those Christmas revels may have been an early form of Jonkonnu. Also, the southern Igbo men's clubs, *okonko*, could have provided a secondary model for organizing such masking performances.

Another social resource was the use of buttons as gaming pieces and perhaps as a form of amulets. Archaeologists of slavery in the Chesapeake have been puzzled by large numbers of buttons routinely found in the root cellars of slave sites. At one plantation in Prince William County, 97 buttons (mostly metal and bone) were found; at Monticello, one building on Mulberry Row yielded 40 such buttons. William Kelso has suggested that these caches of button represent the by-product of slave quilt making. It is also possible that these buttons were counters or game pieces for a complicated betting game known as *okwe* (similar to mancala) that people all over Igboland (and throughout West Africa) played.

There is also a possibility that 18th century Afro-Virginian slaves used buttons as a form of money. In general, buttons in the colonial era were used by men, as most women's clothing used clasps and hooks, and were often made of metal or bone. It fell out of circulation by the early 19th century, when even captives gained access to small coinage. The buttons left in root cellars had not been discarded so much as stored, like any other devalued money. Exploring the Niger River north of Aboh during the 1830s, Oldfield "purchased several bunches of plantains for a button each: blue cut beads were also in great demand here."

Buttons in colonial Afro-Virginia therefore were most likely the creolized analog of cowries in large parts of historical Igboland. In general, the Atlantic African "cowrie zone" in the 18th century included interior Mande (Bambara) and central and northern Igboland (Nri-Awka, Ika / Anioma) as well as the Slave Coast in general and Angola but did not include Gold Coast and Windward Coast areas or coastal Senegambia. Equiano, however, observed that the system in one of the areas to which he was taken to on his initial passage resembled that in his home village; their money "consisted of little white shells, the size of the finger nail."

How African slaves used these cowrie in Virginia is not clear. They may have been used as amulets or as part of divination kits. For example, in one slave burial in Barbados, archaeologists found a necklace of "European-made glass beads, drilled dog teeth, fish vertebrae, and a carnelian bead," and seven cowries. It is likely that cowries had multiple uses, including serving as protective charms, personal adornments, status markers, part of divining kits, gaming pieces, and even tokens doled out by *buckra* to reward good behavior. They could have served as tiny *lieu de momoire*, or constant reminders of African background.

The Atlantic [Mostly Caribbean] Experiences of the Igbos

Igbo peoples constituted one of the largest 'nations' of the Transatlantic slave trade, and thus of the early modern history of the Americas. They were found in sizeable numbers throughout the Caribbean and North America, especially anglophone areas, from the late 17th through the mid-19th century. But just as the peoples of the hinterlands of the Bight of Biafra had earlier created a plethora of local societies and yet united in a way that justifies their being characterized as all sharing 'Igboness,' so their uprooted cousins creatively adapted themselves to their own particular historical circumstances in specific times and places, by mixing the familiar with the functional, and not in simply random ways.

When Olaudah Equiano (c. 1745—97) was taken aboard the slave ship that departed from the Bight of Biafra he feared for his life. He initially feared being eaten by the 'whites' (whom he suspected were evil spirits), however, other people of 'my own nation … in small degree gave ease of mind'. These people whom he recognized as fellow 'natives of Eboe', or 'Eboan Africans', or simply 'my countrymen', told the young boy what little they knew: that 'we were to be carried to these white people's country to work for them'; 'that thus country was a far distant one'. Upon arriving he saw several 'Africans of many languages'.

Years later, in 1772, when he was a grown man, Equiano went to

Kingston, Jamaica, where he was impressed by the numerous Africans he saw there, and especially how those people grouped themselves by their particular ethnicities during their free time. On Sundays, he noted, African slaves gathered in large numbers at a general meeting place outside the town. 'Here', wrote Equiano, 'each different nation of Africa meet and dance after the manner of their own country. They still retain most of their native customs; they bury their dead, and put victuals, pipes and tobacco, and other things, in the grave with the corpse, in the same manner as in Africa.'

Though Equiano did not mention seeing other Igbo among 'each different nation of Africa' in Jamaica, other near contemporaries did. In 1788 Captain Hugh Crow, who became a major trader at Bonny in 1791—1810, witnessed the public execution of an Igbo man in Jamaica. He reported that the man's 'Eboe friends continued to cheer him with the hope that he would return to his own country [after his death] until he was turned off the scaffold.' Over 25 years later, Matthew Lewis, who kept a journal of his time in Western Jamaica in 1815—17, observed how his slaves grouped themselves according to their ethnicity; he noted, for example, that one day he 'went down to the negro-houses to hear the whole body of Eboes lodge a complaint against one of the book-keepers'. Even recent arrivals such as Lewis quickly learned to identify individual slaves by their African ethnicities. In one passage Lewis described a conflict between 2 of his male adult slaves named Pickle and Edward, both of whom were said to be 'Eboes'. Pickle, Lewis reported, had accused Edward of breaking into his house and stealing some of his goods. Upon being asked by Pickle to use 'obeah' to find where the stolen goods were, Edward was said to have gone out at midnight and to have collected the requisite herb and prepared it the proper way, but then, according to Pickle, to have used obeah to poison him rather than using it to find the stolen property as promised. As proof being 'obeahed' by his fellow Igbo, Pickle claimed that 'he had a pain in his side, and, therefore, Edward must have given it to him'.

Of the 750,000 Igbos that reached the Americas from 1700—1809, most are said to have ended up in the Anglophone Caribbean. Since the Igbos were widely regarded as unsatisfactory slaves by their European masters, it is possible that disproportionate numbers of them were sold in the more marginal regions of plantation agriculture in the New World. This seems to have been the case in the French colonies, where according to David Geggus, 'Igbo slaves, in large measure females, show up disproportionately in Guadeloupe and the least-developed parts of Saint Domingue.' By contrast, slaves from the Slave Coast (Ewe, Fon and others), who were usually regarded with greater favor by planters, tended to be shipped to the prime areas of French Caribbean sugar-production. Whether this pattern was replicated in the British colonies is uncertain, but, if it was, then one might anticipate that, in the first half of the 18th century, relatively few Igbo went to Jamaica, Antigua, and St Kitts, where sugar production was expanding vigorously, and relatively large numbers went to Barbados, where sugar production was stagnating, the Bahamas, and the mainland North America, especially the Chesapeake. After 1760, when the tide of Igbo exiles was at its height, it is likely that the Igbo were shipped in relatively large numbers to the islands of the Lesser Antilles and to areas around Montego Bay and Savannah la Mar in western Jamaica.

Whereas the precise pattern of Igbo arrivals in the Americas has yet to be entirely determined, the majority went to Anglophone Americas, as well as the likes of St. Domingue (Haiti and Dominican Republic (DR)) and Cuba to a lesser extent. By the 18th century, the Chesapeake in Virginia, the Bahamas, Leeward Islands and Jamaica were the most common destinations of diasporic Igbo. Scholars have noted the striking similarities in Atlantic creole languages, especially in the Anglophone Americas, as well as the wide distribution of certain elements of slave culture, including obeah, Jonkonnu (especially the so-called root version with its associated cow-horn and ragman maskers, and 'gambys' or box-drums), and the term *buckra*. Given that in 1750—1807 British planters received probably twice as many Igbos as any other African ethno-historical group (and perhaps 4 times the number of people from Gold Coast), it is worth considering how the Igbo ethnicity of those arriving from the Bight of Biafra contributed to the 'bricolage' and historical development of the various Afro-Caribbean slave societies in the British Americas.

In some colonies, such as the Chesapeake piedmont in the second quarter of the 18th century, the Igbos were the 'first comers' of enslaved Africans. In such cases, they set the basic patterns of material, social and ideological culture of enslaved communities to which the succeeding waves of saltwater (for example, Western Bantu and Mande) and creole (or tidewater) slaves acculturated. In other colonies, such as post-1750 Jamaica, Igbo were 'second-comers' who 'Igboized' existing institutions and cultural patterns as people drew on ancestral material, social and ideological resources in order to adapt both to slavery and to the culture of slaves already there. In both cases, Igbos made use of what they had at hand to fashion what they needed in order to sustain themselves, to forge connections amongst and between each other, and to make sense of their new worlds—often manifesting in Igboesque regional 'common traditions'.

Masters generally provided their slaves with only the barest essentials needed to shelter, feed and clothe the people. Many slaves, therefore, had their own provisioning grounds, whether kitchen gardens, house-yards, or outlying plots, where they grew their own fruits and vegetables. One of the most common slave-grown vegetables was *Hibiscus esculentus*, whose podlike fruit was a staple of slaves' 'one pot' cooking practices. Slaves used okra to thicken stews and soups, and the mucilaginous vegetable practically represented slave [and, in the United States, southern] food ways.

As abovementioned, 'Okra' was an Igbo word (okro). People in other parts of western Africa knew and grew the vegetable, called 'nkru-ma' in Twi and variations of '-ngomo' in Western Bantu languages. But it was Igbo people who brought the most common name of 'okro' into English. The word appeared in English dictionaries in the 18th century, notably the Oxford English Dictionary (1707 and 1756 editions), though the plant remained largely unknown to whites until the 19th century. Thomas

Jefferson, for example, did not have okra grown in his garden until 1809. Okra was associated with fertility as well as with proverbial knowledge in some parts of pre-colonial Igboland.

There is also clear evidence of Igboization in slave power ways. Fischer has defined power ways as 'attitudes toward authority and power' and 'patterns of political participation'. Slaves in Anglophone America draw on similar social resources to order their individual and collective lives. Though the influence of Akan on the Maroons of 18th century Jamaica has attracted much attention from historians, there is evidence of a clear Igbo influence on those who stayed on the local plantations. The world of the plantation was divided into 2 largely separate spheres; that of the whites and that of the slaves. In the British Atlantic, whites learned to call blacks 'niggers' and slaves learned to call their masters (and other whites) 'buckra'. The widespread use of the latter term reflected the ubiquity of Igbo peoples in the diaspora or, for slaves of other ethnicities, the utility of Igboesque ways of defining whites. Though derived from the Ibibio *mbakara* (*mb*-plural); -kara, to encircle, rule, abuse, master, understand), slaves everywhere in Anglophone America used the term to denote 'white folk'. It was Igbo people who brought the term into English as *buckra*, and also supplied the social context of seeing the white man as 'he who surrounds or governs' or as a 'demon, powerful and superior being'. Or, as a slave saying from South Carolina in the 1770s put it 'Da buccary no be good fatru' ('That white man is not good, to be sure').

How did Igboized slaves perceive *buckra*? Monica Schuler has provocatively suggested that, in Jamaica at least, many slaves 'defined slaveowners as sorcerers' because of the slaves' common conviction that sorcery played a prominent role in their original enslavement. There is good evidence to support such a supposition, at least in terms of the initial interpretation that many West Africans had of Europeans as spirits and *jujus*. For example, John Jea, who had been born in 1773 in Old Calabar and then taken to New York as a slave, remembered that he and his parents 'were often led away with the idea that our masters were our gods; and at

60

other times we placed our ideas on the sun, mood, and stars, looking unto them, as if they could save us'. In general, however, one may suggest that many of the slaves saw the *buckra* in Igboesque terms, that is, as *eze* (masters) or as little kings. As a missionary resident in Onitsha in the 1850s explained. 'Eze literally means "Master" and is applied to kings and to those who are in an important office'. Just as *eze* were spiritually and materially powerful beings who could lord it over the people and yet were subject to the *omenani* or customs of the place, so slaves saw their masters as cruel and yet bound by customary law. Furthermore, slaves everywhere routinely addressed not just their owners but all *buckra* with the ritual salutation of some variation of 'master', whether 'massa', or 'mossa', 'marster', or 'marse'. It may well be that Igboized slaves appropriated familiar political terms to make sense of their masters' formal powers over them, even as they were coerced into signifying their own subordination.

One may also see how an Igboesque political consciousness contributed to the importance of resistance rather than rebellion in the slave worlds of the British Americas. It is perhaps not without significance that successful slave revolts—whether in 17th-century Palmares, among the Maroons of the 18th century Jamaica, in St. Domingue in the 1790s, or in Bahia in the 1830s—tended to occur in areas with relatively few Igbos. By contrast, in places such as the Chesapeake and western Jamaica, where there was a strong Igbo presence, slaves tended to resort to resistance within small-scale communities to force the *buckra* to abide by unwritten but well-known plantation customs. Such customs (Igbo *omenani*) varied from place-to-place but shared many core elements; these included 2 days off, abroad spouses, 'negro daytime', basic rations, and individual compounds. The growth of plantation customs also contributed to the shift from corporal punishment to systems of discipline and incentives. In the more marginal areas where planters routinely subdivided their slave holdings into plantations, farms and quarter, Igbo concepts of localism, dual division and segmentary social relations would have been adaptive for Igboesque communities, with the incidental consequence of discouraging large-scale revolutionary movements.

Igboized slaves drew on other Eboan African institutions to forge their own power ways and regulate their own lives. The best known (and perhaps understood) was the common Anglophone slave masquerade, *Jonkonnu*. Generally given a Gold Coast provenance, this slave social fact was more likely an artifact of Igbo people in the diaspora. This is suggested by the association of *Jonkonnu* (the 'root' version, that is) with 'gambys', or box-drums, instruments that Matthew Lewis in 1815—17 called 'Eboe drums'. *Jonkonnu* is also associated with cow-horn and other animal masks as well as distinctive peaked-hat masks, many of which are identical to mid-20th century Kalabari ones. Moreover, the development of *Jonkonnu* in its Afro-Caribbean form seems to have occurred between 1750 and 1830 when arrivals of Igbos were at their greatest. Such evidence points, therefore, towards Igboland as the primary source of *jonkonu* in Anglophone America.

As was the case in Virginia, there were traces of 2 important institutions in the Caribbean from historical Igboland: *njokku* (or ifejioku), the 'Yam spirit cult', and the yam-associated okonko (men's clubs). The latter was the southern Igbo secret society equivalent of the *Efik* ekpe society. 19th century sources attest to animal- and ragman-maskers in Bonny and Elem Kalabari, and these appear very similar to 'root *Jonkonnu*' and not unlike the 20th century northern Igbo *Omabe* and Odo masquerades. Masquerading was first recorded by Hans Sloane in Jamaica in the 1680s and was extended to Barbados, St Kitts and Nevis, Antigua and Monserrat by early Jamaican planters and captives that migrated to these places; this development saw the diasporic Igbo combine the foregoing shared traditions into a Afro-creole institution. Whites more widely came to call the Christmas-time masquerade 'John Konnu' because that is what the slaves chanted or yelled during the visitation of *njokku*; the rest of the year it may have served as a kind of men's club. So-called 'root' *jonkonu* was a male preserve whose leader wielded a whip or stick in association with fierce animal-masked others. From an Igboesque perspective, one can imagine that what slaves got was an annual visitation by *njokku* in *mmuo* (fearsome masking); those who participated as maskers against honor and prestige within the slave community. To those enslaved, therefore, *jonkonu* may have been an internal means of establishing status and hierarchy among the slave men independently of any of their relations, occupational or otherwise, with whites, or even with women. The slaves then masked its importance by turning it into a Christmastime buffoonery for the *buckra*'s viewing. During the rest of the year, though, it may have had a much more serious purpose.

Another important Afro-Caribbean slave artifact, the system of 'doctoring' called 'obeah', points finally towards an Igbo presence in the ideological domain of slave community-culture. Igbo slaves drew on ancestral ideological resources to make sense of their new world and in the process 'Igboized' slave religious traditions throughout British America.

Because of its association with Jamaican slave communities, Afro-Caribbean obeah, like *jonkonu*, has tended to be given an Akan provenance. This may, however, be misleading, for the functions of obeah men and obeah women in the third quarter of the 18th century were similar to those of the *ndi obea* (or *dibia*) of pre-colonial Igboland. In the West Indies, as Edward Long explained in 1774, obeah men were 'consulted upon all occasions in order to revenge injuries and insults, discover and punish thieves and adulterers; to predict the future, and for the conciliation of favor'. As in Igboland, therefore, obeah men (and sometimes women) in the Caribbean were diviners, doctors, and petitioners who specialized in finding out why things happened in daily life and in determining what needed to be done to placate the gods in given situations. In short, they were juju-men *par excellence*.

In historical Igboland, the *dibia* or *obea* was the person, usually a man, who could communicate directly with the spirits. Known across Igboland and the heavily Igboesque coastal settlements as powerful and dangerous, and thus both feared and respected everywhere, such 'doctors' provide the most common link between the visible and the invisible worlds. Privy to secret information, including a separate ritual language, and often idiosyncratic in their own lives (and thus thought to be gifted or 'touched'), *dibia* combined their sacred knowledge. The latter presumably required practical pharmacological knowledge and to spend time in the forest collecting herbs, to ascertain what troubled individuals, to determine the necessary remedies, and then to apply them. Not only were 'Obeah doctors, or Dibbeah' able to 'cure diseases by charms'; they could 'foretell things to come and discover secrets' as well.

The various magical and religious characteristics of *dibia* seem to have changed very little in Igboland between the 1750s and the 1920s. In southern Igboland, an 'Ibo chief' told P.A. Talbot in the 1920s that 'With our people a native doctor is called *Onye Dibia*. All know witchcraft, but some are good and only make medicine and yet others only busy themselves with bad ones; every *Onye Dibia* has great power, because everyone fears to offend him on account of his medicines.' 70 years earlier, at Onitsha, it was said that the 'doctor, or priest, called *Dibia*, is another person of consequence, and is very much feared by the people. He has a great sway over the people, from his pretension to be able to foretell things to come and discover secrets.' At Bonny in the early 1800s, *dibia* were said to combine the sacred and the profane and through their powers held 'the populace in the most absolute awe and subjection'. The author of such remarks, Hugh Crow, also emphasized the curative medical abilities of *dibia*, and wrote that though 'they apply certain remedies, chiefly decoctions of herbs and cupping, which they perform with a small calabash, after having made incisions, they depend upon charms, in a great measure, for relief'. In his vivid description of *dibia* medicine, Crow went on to reveal the role of sacrifice in their curing rites. Thus, he noted that, after killing a male fowl by slitting its throat, the *dibia* 'then threw himself into many strange postures, and while muttering some incantations over the sick men, he sprinkled the blood on their heads'. Presumably the *dibia* also applied some physical medicine, for Crow noted that in general, *dibia* 'make much use of pod pepper, palm oil and various kinds of herbs for the cure of diseases'.

Remembering his childhood in the 1750s near present-day Orlu in

Isuama and within the Nri/Awka cultural ambit, Olaudah Equiano in 1789 provided a description of *dibia* similar to Crow's, though Equiano seemed to conflate the work of *dibia* with that of another major group of ritual specialists, the *atama* or Nri-men. Equiano wrote:

> Though we had no places of public worship, we had priests and magicians, or wise men. I do not remember whether they had different offices, or whether they were united in the same persons, but they were held in great reverence by the people. They calculated our time, and foretold events . . . These magicians were also our doctors or physicians. They practiced bleeding by cupping, and were very successful in healing wounds and expelling poisons. They had likewise some extraordinary methods of discovering jealousy, theft, and poisoning ...[which] is still used by the negroes in the West Indies'.

In short, therefore, the *dibia* or *ndi obea* in historical Igboland and the 'obeahmen' of pre-modern Afro-Caribbean societies were responsible for ascertaining why things happened, remedying, or influencing them, and punishing transgressors. They also provided other things such as war-medicine to protect those who would shed him blood. The world of the invisibles was as real to diasporic Igbo as it had been in Eboan Africa because those hosts of invisibles had also survived the Atlantic crossing. Eboan peoples drew on this ancestral tradition of the *dibia* to make sense of their new world, calling it by the Igbo variant of *obea*, and in the process adding a major Igboesque artifact to the religious bricolage of slaves in British America.

Defining 'Igboness' in the Old and New Worlds

It has become widely known that the word 'Igbo' was known in Africa and used in ways that might be suggestive of 'ethnicity'. This has led many to question the point(s) in time when an Igbo ethnogenesis began to gain traction. To this end, is it possible or meaningful to talk of an African-derived collective identity in the Atlantic diaspora called 'Eboe'? To what extent can the construction of the 'Igbo' ethnicity be considered as a function of events in the New World?

Enslaved Igbo often reconstituted themselves as a diasporic 'nation,' perhaps based on the Igbo concept of the *Ebo* / Ehbo—a clan or set of kindreds, or on particular ideas associated with being Igbo / Iboe. At times, this collective identity was evident in communal performance such as foodways, 'powerways,' dances, orature, religious praxis and other aspects of slave-village habitus. As with other diasporic African nations, such as Coramantee (Akan), Nago or Lucumi (Yoruba), Congo or Angola (Western Bantu), Arada or Popo ('Gbe') and so forth, these initial African ethnic identities in the New World may have been newly constructed, the result of *diaspora ethnogenesis* (the formation or emergence of an ethnic group), as a first step in the process of creolization. Chambers, therefore, suggested that a historically operational 'Eboe' meta-ethnicity (a level of commonality that transcends an ethnic group, but does not necessarily transcend 'nationality') in the diaspora was derived from the cultures of the Biafran interior. An 'Eboan' collective identity developed, as captives, once thrown into the diaspora, discovered ways of doing and of being which Igbo-speaking and Igbo-acting slaves shared.

Social and cultural artifacts termed 'Ibo' or 'Eboe' in the New World are signs of a historical Igbo presence, varied in different times and places. It may be possible to construct a series of definitions or historical understandings of what it meant to be Eboe in Virginia, in Jamaica or in St. Domingue (or Carabali in Cuba), and so forth, but it would be anachronistic to read these social and cultural assemblages back into African history as core signs of continental Igbo ethnic identity. Instead, the challenge is to follow Eboan African (Igbo) ethnic peoples and history *from* the hinterland *into* the diaspora.

Central to the problem of defining 'Eboe' social signs and cultural referents is that, in the process of creolization, diasporic Igbo responded to the often-brutal conditions of slavery in ways that require more subtle analyses than searching for New Word 'carryovers' or 'retentions' of Eboan African 'traits'. Using a metaphor of formal linguistics to describe the cultural change which the term 'creolization' evokes, it seems that Igbo may have tended to 'calque,' that is, to copy-translate into another cultural code behaviors (including words, phrases and other social 'things) from the ancestral set. Therefore, even root things such as yam-growing and -eating, especially the D. rotunda, became identified as of 'Guinea' rather than from Igbo specifically (that is, in the anglophone Americas). Other aspects of slave culture may be termed *Igboesque creolisms*, while still others were clearly Igbo.

If people displaced from other ethnic groups tended towards being 'apports,' bringing 'words' and 'things,' in or nearly in their original form and function, to the New World situations, such as Coramantee (Akan/Ga) ancestral names, or the Nago/Lucumi (Yoruba) shango worship, Igbo may have tended to copy-translate ancestral cultural forms and functions into creole (or even Euro-American) forms, that acted as 'calques'. For example, in Carriacou in the Grenadines, so-called 'Ibo nation-dances' included not just 'Igbo' but also 'Jig-Ibo' and 'Scotch Ibo'. In Haiti, Igbo created independent *nanchons* (vodun nations) informed by their own *loa* (gods), and with their own drumbeats and songs and ceremonials, but these took hyphenated names such as Legba-Ibo or Ibo-Lazile, transparent calques like *Un Pied Un Main Un Je* (One Foot, One Hand, One Eye), apparently a translation of a common Igbo name, or other names that may have evoked directly ancestral Igbo deities—*alosi* (perhaps *Alusi*), *Barak, Akoupi, Takwa,* or *Ibo Hequoike*. These socio-religious forms were creolized—that is, most likely created in the diaspora context through an internal process of 'bricolage'. Igbo in Haiti, however, invested their hyphenated *loa* with 'the ancestral principle [which] is the point of cosmic departure' for members of the several Igbo-named *nanchons* there, so that even in the mid-20th century these Igbo *loa* were believed to be 'intimately authoritative for Ibo families'. In other areas, identifying Igboisms (as well as Eboe-isms) in slave and African-American folk lifeways, especially where the people did not use 'Ibo' to denote their ancestrally influenced forms, often requires a step or 2 of interpretation and, therefore, a qualified reliance on inference.

Diasporic Igbo used a variety of ethnonyms to group themselves, or were so grouped by others, in different times and places. In the early 17th century, as attested by Sandoval (1647), Igbo were seen as a subset of 'caravalies' (Kalabaris), as they also seemed to the Dutch in the second half of the century. Throughout the 18th century, however, British slave traders and planters usually equated Calabar and Eboe. In late-18th century Jamaica, and in the Lesser Antilles in the 19th century, another term for a subset of 'Calabars' was 'Moko,' whom European slave traders such as Hugh Crow learned were called 'Kwa' in Bonny and were 'mortal enemies to the Eboes'. Earlier, Sandoval (1647) had included 'moco' in his list of 'caravalies particulares', and Dapper (1668) thought they originated in the vicinity of Bonny to the north; in the late 18th century Captain Adams explicitly stated that 'Ibibbys' (Ibibio) were the same as 'Quaws' and were called 'Mocoes' in the West Indies. In the 1840s, however, Koelle learned in Sierra Leone that people called 'Moko' came from east of the Cross River and were sold through Old Calabar. In the 20th century, the Kalabari (New Calabar) word for Ibibio as a group was *Mboko*; likewise, Ngwa-Igbo call Ibibio *Nmogho*. It can therefore be surmised that in the 17th and 18th centuries most 'Moko' were Ibibio (and perhaps others from the lower Cross River), but that in the 19th century the term was extended to others enslaved farther to the north and east.

In 19th century Cuba the term Calabar ('carabalis') reappeared as a general ethnic marker used by slaves, freedmen, and masters to gloss various Biafran (including Igbo) connections when naming *cabildos* (mutual aid societies), which led Fernando Ortiz to note that 'many of the ibos entered Cuba as carabalis'. For example, in Havana circa 1900 one *cabildo* had the title of the 'carabali ibo'. Ortiz also noted in Havana 'there existed a rich cabildo of the carabalis *isuama isieque*'. Curiously, the term 'Moko' was not used in Cuba.

The shift in descriptive terms of 'nations' from the Bight of Biafra may have reflected shifting patterns in the slave trade from the hinterland to the coast. In the 17th century, 'Carabalis' referred to a mix of eastern Ijaw, southern Igbo, and western Ibibio; in the 18th century, Igbo predominated or, as Edwards (1793) put it 'All the Negroes imported from these vast and unexplored regions [in the Bight of Biafra hinterland], except a tribe which are distinguished by the name of Mocoes, are called in the West Indies *Eboes*'. In the 19th century the pattern shifted again, with a greater proportion of non-Igbo, sometimes called Moko and sometimes not, and perhaps representing more people taken from groups like the Ekoi and Ejagham in present-day western Cameroon, as well as Efik from Old Calabar itself, bound for places such as Cuba.

Over these centuries, Carabali (initially Ijaw, later perhaps southern and eastern Igbo), Eboe (Igbo) and Moko (Cross River) peoples influenced in various ways the creolization (Africanization) of various American slave societies. In the case of the Igbo, and because of the relatively high proportion of women in displaced Eboan populations, it may be that their influences were felt most directly in domestic spheres of life; that is, they were highly gendered. Or, possibly, the classical Igbo impetus to localism resulted in a constantly changing mosaic of folkways (cultures) as small groups of displaced people struggled to make sense of their new worlds, creating many constantly changing common traditions from loosely shared ancestral ones.

The many terms used by and for 'Calabars' contain historical, geographical and cultural clues about the people enslaved from the interior. This variability of what Chambers called 'primary creolization' reflects the diasporic ethnogenesis, shared experiences of upbringing, enslavement, displacement, and oppression. In the process of creating these communities, diasporic Igbo (in particular) fashioned new, African-derived identities in America (and Sierra Leone). Since the people who identified as 'Eboe' learned this term only after being taken out of Igboland, it may have signified a meta-ethnicity that seems fluid and essentially new and yet rooted in shared historical experiences. Thus, for enslaved Eboan Africans (Igbo), the term 'Eboe' was a diasporic sign (word), but one with important African meanings.

In the various dialects and subcultural areas of present-day southeastern Nigeria, the term *Igbo* contained a variety of meanings. There seem to be at least 3 categories of meanings associated with Igbo and close cognates: classificatory, geographical and mythic. The first set of meanings are the best-known historiographically; that is, *Igbo* used as a pejorative signifier for linguistically similar 'others' or 'slaves' or 'strangers', especially those associated with upland (forested) areas by riverine or lowland dwellers (*olu*). Other 'types' of people covered by *Igbo* included 'yam-easters' and generically, the 'community of people', as well as 'group of old ones' (*Ndigbo*). Thus, wrote Oriji, 'whenever an Igbo man's life was threatened outside his cultural environment, he simply shouted *Igbo neri ji na ede unu nokwa ebea?* (Igbo who eat yams and cocoyams), meaning "Who domesticated these crops, are you around?"'

Other words, phonetically close to 'ebo' (e.g., Ibo, Oyinbo), also had classificatory meanings. In 1832, R. A. K. Oldfield recorded that on the middle reaches of the Niger near 'Eboe' (Aboh), locals hid in the bushes and called out to them what he heard as 'Oh, Eboe! Oh Eboe!' (meaning 'White man, white man!'); in the 1850s, at Onitsha another such 'stranger' Revd J.C. Taylor, was called by the people *oibo*, to mean 'whiteman'. Isichei has noted that in southern Nigeria *Oyibo*, was a term used to denote 'Europeans'. In the early 20th century, *ebo* (without the labial-implosive gb phoneme) could also mean various things, including 'the man to whom a slave runs' (Asaba area), 'man who finds a thief', breaking down of wall by rain' (an interesting

70

metaphor that would be for 'slaves'!) and, in the case of *igbwo*, a long or English type of bead (obviously, a trade bead).

'Igbo' was also used as a geographical term, both by outsiders as well as by people in Eboan Africa, though not particularly frequently, given the meanings suggested above. By the mid-19th century, Europeans had learned to call the general country inhabited by various Igbo-speaking peoples 'Igbo' (Eboe). Some Eboan Africans also used the term, though more specifically. For example, in Isuama and Orlu (and indeed further south, in Owerri, Ikwerre and Ngwa) some people claim that their ancestors migrated from a place called 'Amigbo' (Igbo Homeland), perhaps mythic, perhaps real, but in any case, founded by a man named 'Igbo' (whose family was associated with the domestication of yams and cocoyams) and whose putative descendants were considered to be living in the 'homeland, cultural center' of southern Igbo. In fact, JaJa of Opobo, an Nkwerre-Igbo, was born in Orlu division circa 1821, in a village that was also called Amigbo.

In the 19th century there existed a town called 'Azigbo' in the Nri-Awka area (North-central), where the 'Igbos' owned a market called *Nkwo Igbo* (that is, the 'Igbo market on nkwo, one of the 4 days of the Igbo week). Farther to the north, near Nsukka, people called a main road running south *uzigbo* ('road [of the] Igbo').

As might be expected, individuals (usually men) named 'Igbo' (or variations thereon) show up in the charter myths of a number of the more important village-groups (*obodo*), as well as of quarters and villages (ogbe) that were part of them. The original inhabitants are often described as having been expelled from earlier settlements for some violation or conflict and then migrating to their current places (where, ideally at least, the direct patrilineal descendants retained the original staff of authority *ofo*). For example, in the Nnewi district, the founder is remembered as *Digbo* (*di*: husband; husband of Igbo); in 'Anioma' (west of the Niger), the mytho-historical founder was Odaigbo, who had accidentally committed murder at 'Nshi' (Nri) but was allowed to choose exile and was sent carrying a magic pot on his head to 'find' new place.

Significantly, Olaudah Equiano, like hundreds of thousands of others from the hinterland of the Bight of Biafra, first learned to call himself Igbo only after he had been taken out of Eboan Africa. Equiano recognized his countrymen in places as diverse as Barbados, Jamaica, and London. When Equiano published his memoirs in 1789, he included his Igbo name in the manuscript's title.

Maureen Warner Lewis, in her book *Archibald Monteith: Igbo, Jamaican, Moravian*, writes of Equiano's fellow Igbo and former slave [from present-day Anambra State, southeastern Nigeria] Aniaso (Anaso)—better known as Archibald Monteith. Monteith was born in Africa and evidence points to him having learned a form of the Igbo language, such that he knew the meaning of his name, and also knew the role of the adult male in Nri culture; moreover, his knowledge of Igbo customs was also supplemented by that known of his fellow Igbo Jamaicans.

In the 19th century, Koelle's discussions in Sierra Leone—an extension of the Atlantic African experience—with informants were revealing of the fact that the Igbo identity, as it came to be known from the 20th century onward, had not congealed, and thus, Igbo-speaking recaptives were explicit in stating that they had never heard the term until they were sent or taken away. Koelle, a German missionary, solicited information from Igbo-speaking recaptives who were sent by the British to Sierra Leone in the 1820s and the 1830s. Koelle noted that "speaking to some of them respecting this name (Igbo), I learned that they never had heard it till they came to Sierra Leone." Before being drawn into the slave trade such people knew "only the names of their respective districts or countries."

Though fiercely localistic in their home areas, once thrown into the diaspora they embraced a collective identity derived from being a member of "my own nation," as Igbo-born former slave Olaudah Equiano put it. As the early English explorer W. B. Baikie explained in the 1850s, "In I'gbo each person hails from the particular district where he was born, but when away from home all are I'gbos."

The Yoruba

The word 'Yoruba' originally referred to Oyo and was first used in its modern sense by a missionary in 1832. It reflects a common language, but one with marked dialectal differences, a body of shared religious concepts and sociocultural pattern, none of which are common to all Yoruba. Not all the Yoruba kingdoms shared the tradition of a founder prince from Ife—but Benin did.

'Yoruba' Oyo looked on 'Yoruba' Ilesha or Ijebu as alien. The Ijebu 'were, before the [British] conquest the most exclusive and inhospitable of tribes.' Foreigners absorbed and reflected these stereotypes. 'I was now among a strange people, [the Ijesha] of bad repute among the [Oyo] Yoruba, with a language somewhat difficult and liable to suspicion.' The primary unit of identification, here as elsewhere, was the kingdom—*ilu* in Yoruba, *oman* in Twi. These varied greatly in size, from the vast Oyo empire of the late 18th century to small principalities such as the 16 Kingdoms of Ekiti.

Ife, like Nri, is famous both for its ritual pre-eminence and for its ancient sculpture. Here, tradition claims, the world was created, by separating the water from the dry land: 'from thence the sun and the moon rise, where they are buried in the ground, and all the people of this country, and even white men, have come from that town.

The enormously rich world of Yoruba myth and ritual has fascinated many scholars. Few peoples in black Africa have been so intensively studied. Unsurprisingly, their legends do not fit together to make a tidy whole, and historians differ radically in the way they interpret them. The gods of Yorubaland are sometimes understood as kings who were divinized in cults after their death—sometimes as divinities who have in tradition been given an unhistorical human face. Sango is alternatively the god of lightning or an early Alaafin of Oyo who entered the pantheon after his death. Obatala is the creator god or an early ruler of Ife. Oduduwa is a different creator god or an immigrant to Ife who overthrew Obatala and created his own kingdom. In a further variant, Oduduwa is Obatala's wife. The cult of Obatala is of great

73

importance in Ife religion as is the royal cult of Sango in Oyo. The worship of Ogun, god of iron, is centered at Ire in Ekiti.

Ife tradition tells of early settlers called *Igbo* (the word has a differential tonal structure from the name of the ethnic group, to which it is totally unrelated). Some scholars regard this as a historical indigenous population, but the word *Igbo* in the Yoruba language means 'bush,' and the legend may describe the conquest of nature by human culture. A heroic woman, Moremi, is said to have destroyed the Igbo by discovering the secret of their raffia masking costumes. This is one of a number of African legends which praise a woman who betrays her husband in the interests of their kin.

The Yoruba kings, who claim the jealously guarded right to wear a beaded crown, all claim an ancestor from Ife as 'the sons of Oduduwa.' In some versions, these number 16. This is a symbolic number: Ife is the center of Ifa divination, obtained by casting 16 palm nuts, and based on a corpus of sacred literature in 16 sections. Regional variants in myth are often politically determined: Oyo tradition states that the first Ooni (king) of Ife was a slave, and it seems likely that traditions of an Ife supremacy were elaborated as an ideology subversive of Oyo hegemony. An Ijebu man said in 1901, 'I deny that Oyo is the capital city of Yorubaland. Ife, the cradle home of the whole Yorubas and the land of the deified Oduduwa, has been recognized by every interior tribe (including Benin and Ketu) for all intents and purposes as the capital city.' The Oduduwa traditions can also be interpreted as a narrative of local chieftains and guild heads in the Ife area. (Ogun the blacksmith, Osanyin the physician).

Some have suggested that Ogboni, the secret male cult of the sacred Earth, is an institutional relic of an ancient past; 2 of its officials have the names of pre-Oduduwa kings, and its songs stress 'the rights of certain ancient local lineages *vis-à-vis* all "Interlopers"'. Ogboni was found in Oyo, Abeokuta and elsewhere—but not in Ilesha. In Ilesha, there are 3 ancient chieftaincy titles called *Ogboni*, which are linked with the Benin forest, and are the headships of local towns; like the Igala Mela in Igala, or the Uzama in Benin, they are an institutional fossil from a time before the dynastic kingdom. They have the same associations as the secret cult: elders, metal, and the earth. Do they share common historical roots, which evolved into different forms but retained the same name? There are some 'kings' at Ife who own beaded crowns they may not wear—a relic of otherwise vanished and forgotten polities.

Ife was a substantial town between the 9th and 12th centuries, with a splendid court, magnificent sculpture in terracotta and bronze, and elaborate potsherd pavements. Tradition associates the Ife pavements with a tyrannical women ruler, one of many apparently mythical woman royals who thread their way mysteriously through early West African history. The court may well have been sustained by the profits of Ife's glass industry; it died out before the 19th century, when glass was mined as if it were a mineral resource. While its origins in human technology have been forgotten, it was thought to be a gift from the gods. Yoruba royals wore abundant jewelry and crowns embroidered with beads in a symbolically significant pattern. They also symbolized the wounded herbalist god Osanyin: 'There was once born an amazing child. He came into this world with shining beads in many colors gleaming about his body.'

Ife is internationally famous for its terracotta and bronze sculptures. The latter are quite different in metal content from their counterparts in Benin and Igbo-Ukwu: some are leaded brass, and some of almost pure copper. Willett has calculated that the whole of the copper and copper alloy work from Igbo-Ukwu weighs 70 kg, and that from Ife 170kg. A single caravan across the Sahara carried 4 times as much. They are cast, like the Igbo-Ukwu sculptures, by the lost-wax technique; the metal is very thin, reflecting both its scarcity and the artist's superb virtuosity. But in style and subject matter, they are entirely different from the sculpture of Igbo-Ukwu. Most of the Ife bronzes are busts, idealized portraits, and one is a mask in the same style. They are thought to date from c.1100 to c.1400. Only 30 Ife bronzes are known to exist, and it is possible that they came from a single hand. There is a much larger corpus of terracotta sculpture, some, but not all in the same style. Several bronzes depict a victim awaiting sacrifice, gagged so that he cannot curse his executioner. Like the multiple interment at Igbo-Ukwu, they are a mute reminder of the underside of African history.

One of the mysteries of the Yoruba past is the contrast between Ife's importance in myth and the wealth reflected in its sculpture on the one hand, and its lack of political power in recent centuries on the other. Was an era of political strength succeeded by one of political decline, when ritualism became all-important? Ilesha, only 21 miles away, was probably founded in the early 16th century, and it may have taken over much of Ife's political role. A legend states that the ancestor of its first king, Obokon, was Oduduwa's youngest son, and that it was he who performed his father's burial rites, leaving behind a mere custodian at Ife.

Oyo, destined to be the largest of the Yoruba kingdoms, grew up on the northern edge of Yorubaland, hundreds of miles to the north of modern Oyo, which was founded in the 19th century. The lightning god, Sango, is said to have been an early Alaafin, an overambitious magician who brought disaster on his court, he was abandoned by his people, and committed suicide. In some versions he enters the ground by passing an iron chain into the earth; the same story is told of Nupe culture hero, Tsoede. The Yoruba say of Sango, *Oba koso* (the king does not die). But *koso* is not a Yoruba word and Oyo history is interwoven with that of its neighbors, Nupe and Borgu.

The original Oyo capital was founded in the 11th century; it became a larger city in the 14th century. Tradition suggests that it began as a small state—its putative founder, the Ife prince Oranmiyan (who is also the 'founder' of Benin), lacked a beaded crown and seized one from a neighboring king. Significantly, he is remembered as a youngest son. Nupe forces drove the Alaafin and his court into exile for about a hundred years, from the early 16th century to the early 17th. Nupe successes may well have been due to their cavalry.

Tradition claims that Oyo was ruled by a woman, Iyayun, during a long regency in the late 15th century. 'She wore the crown and put on the royal robes . . .and ruled the kingdom as a man.' It is a sad irony that later the Alaafin could not have a living mother. The Ondo state looks back to a mythical woman founder, sometimes described as the exiled mother of twins. Ilesha has traditions of no less than 6 early women Owa (rulers). Peel suggests that they were men, described as women to exclude their heirs from the succession, but it is likely that these and similar stories are really examples of a pattern—the use of inversion, to define and affirm the status quo.

The Yoruba in the New World

The collapse of the Oyo Empire in the early 19th century, and prolonged Yoruba wars, led to the enslavement of a great many Yoruba people.

Well before the 19th century the Oyo Empire exported significant numbers of slaves who passed through the ports of the Slave Coast on their way to the Americas. These included criminals, of whom a majority are likely to have been Yoruba speakers from Oyo and from other Yoruba-speaking peoples. Yoruba speakers were also captured in slave raids by Dahomey and then exported. But criminals very probably constituted only a small proportion of the total number of slaves exported from Oyo's non-Yoruba-speaking western and northern neighbors. Many Mahi and Bariba were captured in war, and many slaves were obtained by trade from Nupe, Borgu, and elsewhere. Even the greatly increased exports of slaves from Oyo in the late 18th century may have been fed in large part through trade from the north. Thus, Yoruba speakers are likely to have been a minority among the slaves who were exported from the Slave Coast in the pre-19th-century period.

From the early 19th century, however, Yoruba speakers came to dominate the exodus of slaves from the Slave Coast, including the rising port of Lagos and elsewhere, although Hausa slaves brought from further north in the Nigerian hinterland were also important in the Atlantic trade. Thousands of Yoruba and other slaves were also absorbed into slavery internally, within various Yoruba and other states, a process that continued well after the demise of the external trade.

The most common methods of enslavement of Yoruba speakers in the

19th century included warfare, raids, kidnapping expeditions, and brigandage. The 19th century was a period of almost continuous warfare and lawlessness in Yorubaland. Warfare was associated with the fall of Oyo and the rise of Ilorin. The city of Ilorin, which was situated in the northeast part of the Oyo Empire, was largely Yoruba in population. It became the center of an emirate of Sokoto/Gwandu Caliphate and made determined (and strongly resisted) efforts to carry the jihad (which had led to the setting up of the caliphate in the early 19th century) further south. The Nupe-Fulani emirate of Bida, also part of the caliphate, raided the small-scale northeastern Yoruba polities south of the Niger. Oyo provincial rulers and other chiefs seized the opportunity to carve out independent territories for themselves and to raid and control their neighbors. Warfare spread to the south and east in the Owu wars. The kingdom of Owu and the old Egba settlements were destroyed; the Egba founded a new settlement at Abeokuta and fought to obtain a safe trade route to the coast. The successor states to Old Oyo struggled among themselves. The rising city-state of Ibadan, which became the most successful of the successor states, eventually succeeded in destroying Kurunmi's city-state of Ijaye. Ibadan also embarked on wars of territorial expansion—affecting the Ekiti and Akoko Confederacies and the Ijesha Kingdoms; aided by Ilorin, these polities sought to regain their independence from Ibadan in the Ekitiparapo wars. All these wars, raids, expeditions, and attendant forms of lawlessness resulted in the "production" of large numbers of Yoruba slaves.

The city-state of Ilorin took over some of Oyo's role as a slave supplier by capture and by trade. Ilorin's pre-emirate ruler and rebellious Oyo general, Afonja, captured and enslaved people in the area immediately around the city of Ilorin and in the Igbomina, Igbolo, and Epo areas of the Oyo Empire, resettling them around Ilorin, absorbing male slaves into his army, and selling women and children to obtain arms. Afonja's Muslim allies moved west and carried out raids in the Ibarapa Province of the empire from a base at Iseyin. Among the slaves captured in these raids was a boy from the town of Osogun, who was sold into the Atlantic trade, freed by the

British antislavery squadron, and landed in Freetown. This was Samuel Ajayi Crowther, who became famous as an Anglican bishop and a scholar. Afonja's Muslim successors in Ilorin raided the Igbomina and Ekiti to the east, thus continuing Ilorin's role as slave supplier.

As the century wore on, Ilorin found itself competing with Ibadan and the Nupe-Fulani emirate of Bida in raiding the small-scale Yoruba polities stretching to the area of Niger-Benue confluence, but also raiding in cooperation with its competitor states. The Akoko area suffered from the competition between three raiding states, being, in the words of Hogben and Kirk-Greene "one of those unhappy districts alternatively raided by Nupe, Ibadan, and Ilorin." In an example of cooperative raiding, in 1875—76 Ilorin and Ibadan joined forces in the Wokuti campaign, which Samuel Johnson, the eminent Yoruba historian, described as an "expedition for slave-hunting" in the Ekiti, Yagba, and Akoko country.

In later years, Ilorin, in alliance with the Ekitiparapo, who were fighting for the independence of Ekiti, engaged in a prolonged conflict with Ibadan that also provided opportunities for Ilorin forces to seize slaves. In the course of Ilorin's long siege of its rebellious vassal town of Offa, for example, a certain Nathaniel Popoola Olawoyin was seized and sold to an Abeokuta man. He became a Christian, returned to Offa in 1907, and helped to found the Church Missionary Society (CMS) church there. Though Ilorin's activities had been to an extent circumscribed by competition with its powerful neighbors, it was still reported to have "started on a kidnapping expedition" as late as 1894, far to the east in "the Akoko country, distant about twenty days travel from Ilorin".

Nupe raids south of the Niger on the northeastern Yoruba may have begun even before the founding of Bida Emirate. According to a British official the raids had already started before the Fulani took over the Nupe kingdom: "It is largely owing to ... Majid's raids that the tribes in the Kabba Division are so mixed. The Yagba, Bunu, [and] Aworo [Oworo] ... seem to have paid the Nupe tribute unless left sufficiently long without a visit." Raids and demands for tribute continued through the 19th century and slave

seizures intensified for the last time in the final years before the defeat of
Bida Emirate by the Royal Niger Company in 1897. For example, according
to the account given by British official C. K. Meek in 1918:

> Towards the end of Maliki's and the beginning of Abubakr's reign
> the Bida Fulanis, fully appreciating the Niger Company's prepara-
> tions for war, made a final raid on Aworo [Oworo] and it is safe to
> say that in the Aworo district today there isn't a single male or
> female over the age of 30 who has not been a slave at Bida.

Another non-Yoruba state responsible for slaving Yoruba was Dahomey
to the west, which attacked the Egba regularly. During the siege of Ijaye by
Ibadan, for example, an invading Dahomean army attacked an Egba town
near Abeokuta and captured all the slaves they could.

Of all successor states to Old Oyo, Ibadan became the most powerful and
the most successful in obtaining and profiting from slaves. Soon after the
founding of the new Egba town of Abeokuta (dated by Saburi Biobaku to
1830), for example, Ibadan and Ijebu bands were overrunning its farms and
kidnapping "in broad daylight anyone who ventured beyond the town hall."
Ibadan's most successful slave-raiding period, however, appears to have
come in the 1850s and 1860s, during the decline of the Atlantic slave trade
and after its demise, while Ibadan was fighting for control over the Ekiti and
Ijesha countries. CMS missionary David Hinderer, for example, reported in
1855 on the captives the Ibadan soldiers had brought from Ekiti towns:

> The Ibadan war has at last terminated, and the warriors have
> come home with great riches, alas! I say, with hosts of slaves.
> Though not many are sold down to the coast except to Porto
> Novo by way of Abeokuta, yet is the price high . . . many of the
> rich warriors make new farms with them.

Consul Campbell at Lagos estimated that about 10,000 captives were
brought to Ibadan as a result of the 1855 Ekiti campaigns. In 1877 CMS
missionary James Johnson asserted that the Ijesha predominated among
slaves in Ibadan. In 1882 the Ijesha ruler, Owa Agunloye, reported that,

> I myself was taking [sic] captive . . . but I managed to escape;
> there is scarcely any man or woman in all the one thousand
> four hundred and sixty towns and villages that I rule over
> that were not three or four times slaves to the Ibadans.

Other Yoruba states also participated in slave-taking, including states which at other times were themselves the victims of slave raids. At the beginning of the 1830s the Egba of Abeokuta were victims of slave raiding. A few years later their war chiefs were bringing back "Oyo, Ife, or Ijebu captives whom they absorbed into their households, when not sold abroad, as domestic slaves." In 1862 Governor Freeman of Lagos asserted that the Egba had sold a larger number of Ijaye people, of whom they were supposed to be protecting, into slavery than Ibadan, Ijaye's enemy, had done. The Ijesha, preyed on by Ibadan, in turn raided weaker eastern Yoruba groups. Ijesha warriors, including the famed Ogedemgbe, conducted private military campaigns from which they returned with many slaves. The olupo (king) of Ajasse, in Igbomina, joined the Nupe in raiding Oworo to the east. The Ekiti warriors Aduloju of Ado and Eshu (Esugbayi) of Aiyede also raised the northeastern Yoruba for slaves.

Ambitious warriors, competing for power as the Oyo Empire collapsed, captured slaves to serve as members of their armies, to feed their households, and to be sold in order to buy weaponry. Afonja of Ilorin was one such warrior. Others included the Timi of Ede, who asserted his independence of Oyo and proceeded to attack his neighbors; Ojo Amepo, who left Ilorin, set himself up at Amese in the Epo Province, and raided widely from there; and Atiba, a son of Alaafin (King) Abiodun of Oyo, who joined Oja, a raider operating from Ago Oja. Later Abiodun himself became *Alaafin*, successor to the rulers of the old empire, and set up his court at Ago Oja, which became known as New Oyo. Another warrior, Kurunmi, migrated to Ijaye with many slaves and then continued to expand his following:

> [As] a young man, he was a notorious freebooter and slave-hunter.
> With a number of followers, who had attached themselves to his,
> fortunes, he would go out from [Ijaye] into some distant province

on predatory excursions. By kidnapping in the farms and plundering caravans he became rich and powerful and the leader of a party
which favored his ambition to become the ruler of the city.

Similarly, the warrior Oluyole used his many slaves to establish his base
at Ibadan. Ogedemgbe, other Ijesha warriors, and Ekiti warriors in later
years imitated their Ibadan mentors.

Less prominent warriors and even slave soldiers also joined in the
process of enslavement. In Ilorin an informant asserts that a slave who
caught slaves for his master though "still a slave ... was given different
treatment." Elsewhere in Yorubaland a slave who caught slaves might retain
some of them, to use for his own purposes, or be given a monetary reward.
A war chief might also reward a soldier slave by freeing him.

In addition to acquiring slaves by warfare, powerful states might obtain
slaves as tributary payments from vassal groups. Among the northeastern
Yoruba, for example, who became tributary to Bida, tribute payment in the
form of slaves rather than cowries (currency) seems to have increased from
the reign of Masaba (d. 1873) on, as cowries became increasingly devalued.
Those who were given as tribute may already have been slaves before they
were handed over, but this was not always the case. The reverend C. E.
Wating, who traveled in the northeastern Yoruba country with Bishops
Tugwell and Phillips in 1894, reported on Ayeri, a town near Kabba, where

> the king came to call on us ... and told us the English king was the
> ruler of the world, and he besought us white men to come and help
> him. He said that four years ago, on his coming to the throne, the
> Nupes came and took away 300 of his people. He told us that oppress-
> sion has been the rule here for forty years; that at first the Nupes only
> demanded couriers [cowries?], then farm produce, and that now they
> will have slaves as well. As all their own slaves are gone as tribute,
> they have to give their own children, and many, after giving their
> wives and children for tribute, have left the town and not come
> back—among others his own brother and cousin; that there are
> hardly any young people in the country, and that their nation is

becoming extinct.

Slaves given as tribute to overlord states might include those who had been enslaved as punishment for a crime. As punishment for murder in Ibadan, Hinderer reported, "the headmen . . . are not satisfied to take life for life only, but in addition catch and sell all the family of the offender." And in most of Yorubaland, it was said, "a thief or burglar or anyone who was unable to pay his debt or fines inflicted on him was sold together with his wife and children". In addition, according to Samuel Johnson, there were "well attested cases where a member of a family would be condemned to slavery by a unanimous vote of all the relatives when he has brought disgrace on the family."

Though individuals might be sold into slavery as punishment for crimes, however, the majority of slaves entered the slave trade, whether external or internal, after they had been acquired as tribute, and, even more especially, as a result of warfare and raids carried out by states vying for importance as successors to the Oyo Empire, by non-Yoruba states, and by ambitious warriors.

Members of many Yoruba groups were enslaved at various times in the 19th century, along a moving and fluctuating enslavement frontier. David Eltis points out, large areas of what is now called Yorubaland were "unaffected at first," and there were "few hints of disruption in the western Yoruba societies through which Clapperton and the Landers passed in the 1820s." In the 1850s and 1860s, the Ekiti and Ijesha were heavily preyed on. But in the end it seems likely that the groups that lost the greatest number of people were the small polities of the northeastern Yoruba, including the Yagba, Ijumu, Bunu, Oworo, Akoko, and Owe, who were attacked by Ibadan, Ilorin, Nupe and even their own Ekiti and Ijesha neighbors.

At the time these small northeastern Yoruba polities were not considered to be "Yoruba". In the 19th and 20th centuries a distinction was made, both by Western-educated Nigerians and by colonial officers, between the more central Yoruba and the peripheral groups to the northeast who spoke dialects of the Yoruba language. At the same time, it is highly unlikely that the northeastern Yoruba had any idea of a "pan-Yoruba" identity that would embrace them. Even the Bunu ex-slave James Thomas, who returned to the confluence as a CMS missionary in the mid-19th century, differentiated between his people and the "Yoruba," though he allowed that their languages were "almost alike." It is possible that such a differentiation made it more acceptable for groups called "Yoruba" to enslave the peoples of the northeast, though their powerlessness to resist the city-states and their war leaders must have been a deciding factor. And in the fluid and perilous conditions of the 19th century even close cultural and linguistic ties did not necessarily prevent mutual enslavement.

There does seem, however, to have been general disapproval among Yoruba of those who attempted to enslave people from their own towns (other than criminals or those who had caused disgrace), especially, Oroge argues, after Oluyole and Kurunmi led an expedition against the town of Abemo, following a civil war in which members of the losing side were captured by the winners. A report from mid-century Abeokuta testifies to the severe punishment meted out to those found guilty of enslaving their own townspeople, though it also confirms that this practice still continued:

> Strict watch is kept over those suspected of stealing men.... the house of one individual who was executed for this crime in Abeokuta, was razed to the ground. It... was found to contain rooms within rooms, doors opposite doors, to facilitate the capture and concealme -nt of the victims. The practice is to decoy some unwary person and there confine him until some opportunity offers for shipping him.

Reports from Ondo and Ibadan also attest to the seriousness with which the crime of enslaving one's own townspeople was regarded. At the very end of the 19th century enslavement of people from one's own area may well have briefly increased, in a last desperate attempt to obtain slaves before the British took control.

Some accounts are available of individuals' experiences of enslavement.

One such individual was Samuel Ajayi Crowther, who was captured when Osogun was attacked by a force of "Oyo Mahommedans" (another version of Crowther's narrative has "Yorriba Mahommedans"), accompanied by Fulani, in 1821. He was about 15 years old at the time. Initially he was taken to Iseyin, the headquarters of his attackers. After being sold several times, he eventually reached Lagos, where he was sold to the Portuguese:

> Being a veteran in slavery ... and having no more hope of
> ever going to my country again, I patiently took whatever
> came; although it was not without a great fear and trembling
> that I received, for the first time, the touch of a White Man,
> who examined me whether I was sound or not. Men and boys
> were at first chained together, with a chain of about six fathoms
> in length, thrust through an iron fetter on the neck of every ind-
> ividual, and fastened at both ends with padlocks. In this situat-
> ion the boys suffered the most ... At last we boys [were] separ-
> ated from the men ... we were corded together, by ourselves.
> Thus we were going in and out, bathing together, and so on.
> The female sex fared not much better. Thus we were for nearly
> the space of four months.

Finally, Crowther and the other slaves were embarked on a Portuguese ship bound for Brazil. The ship was intercepted, and Crowther was landed in Freetown, Sierra Leone, in 1822.

Another Yoruba slave who has left a record of his experiences was Osifekunde, an Ijebu trader. He was a young man when he was captured in 1820 in the lagoons along the Nigerian coast on his way east by boat from Lagos where he had bought European goods, to a town that has been identified as Mahin. He was ambushed by Ijo pirates who took him to the Niger Delta port of Warri where he was sold and sent to Brazil. In the 1830s his owner brought him to Paris, where he was sold and where he described his early life, his enslavement, and his homeland to a French scholar, D'Avezac-Macaya.

Somewhat later, but before Abeokuta was founded in 1830, an Egba boy who later took the name of Joseph Wright was enslaved when his town was captured in the course of the attacks on the Egba after the fall of Owu. Years later he still vividly remembered his experience, and the fate of those who were even less fortunate than he:

> The enemies satisfied themselves with little children, little girls, young men, and young women; and so they did not care about the aged and old people. They killed them without mercy.

> I was brought [to their camp] the same day the city was taken ... When I came to that place, the man who took me in the city took me and made a present to the chief man of war who commanded the band which he belonged to; for the custom was when any of their company went with bands of war, if he catch slaves, half of the slave he would give to his Captain.

> While I was with these enemies in the camp ... I saw a child of about eighteen month old cast out of the camp because the child was so young that nobody would buy him. That poor orphan because the child was so young that nobody would buy him. That poor orphan was there crying at the point of death for about two days, and none [took] pity to pick him up.

Wright's account illustrates the types that were valued, and the brutal treatment that might be meted out to captives who were not considered salable, capable of transporting themselves, or able to work. While the enslavers were said to prefer young people, including "little children," this obviously did not extend to children so young that they could not walk or carry loads. And though older slaves might have their uses in a more settled economy, they were a hindrance in the mobile world of the raiders.

Like Crowther, Wright was eventually sent south and sold to the Portuguese in Lagos. The slave ship on which he was conveyed was intercepted by the British, and Wright was landed in Sierra Leone, received an education, and became a clergymen. But unlike Crowther and a number of other "recaptives" (slaves freed by the antislavery squadron) who eventually returned to Nigeria, Wright remained in Sierra Leone and engaged in Christian missionary work there.

Though the above events were indivisible from the upsurge in Atlantic slave exports from the region, it is noteworthy that Yoruba-speaking slaves were sent to the Americas long before the 19th century. Moreover, the Yoruba were present in the Americas from at least the early 17th century, known under the designations of "Lucumi" and "Nago." The number of Yoruba increased during the 18th century, becoming particularly significant in the last several decades of that century, and especially in the 19th century, when they represented the single most important ethnolinguistic grouping in the trade from the Bight of Benin. In the 18th century many Yoruba were taken to the French Caribbean, as well as to Bahia, whereas in the 19th century they went mainly to Bahia and then to Cuba, and in accordance with British anti-slave trade measures, to Sierra Leone and Trinidad.

The question of who are to be identified as Yoruba raises the complicated issue of defining ethnicity and the relative importance of a recognizable nomenclature for such an identification. Robin Law has demonstrated that the various terms ("Lucumi," "Nago," "Aku," "Yoruba") have their own history, and the use of the terms "Yoruba" was more than a convenience. Yoruba Christians consciously adopted the term in the mid-19th century to describe the pan-ethnic and linguistic grouping that had become cohesive in the Americas and Sierra Leone, and where, it was hoped, a similar consciousness would be developed in "Yorubaland" itself. As Adediran has demonstrated, the various terms for the sub-ethnicities of Yoruba are complex and closely tied to historical developments and specific localities. The choice of the term "Yoruba" is perhaps curious, specifically because it has Muslim origins and was adopted by Christians. The emergent intellectuals among the repatriates were committed to a national agenda that required a specific pan-Yoruba identity, as Matory demonstrated in his discussion of the influence of "Yoruba intellectuals" in the development of ethnic consciousness in Bahia in the latter 19th century, though it is unclear why they needed a Muslim term to describe themselves as community. Neither Law nor Matory addresses this question; yet Lovejoy suggests that, both symbolically and figuratively, the term is significant. Its use emphasizes the importance of Islam in helping to shape ethnic cohesion among those who came to see themselves as "Yoruba." Indeed, the use of a Muslim term serves to correct the underrepresentation of Islam in the discussion of the genesis of the Yoruba as an ethnic group, and thereby reinforces the analysis of John Peel in his discussion of the role of the religion in "the making of the Yoruba." In examining Yoruba ethnicity, it is necessary to understand the role of the umbrella of language, the similarity in culture as expressed through divination and worldview, and the interrelated historical tradition of common origins from Ife. The role of Christianity and Islam in shaping ethnicity was profound, as Peel has argued in addressing its meaning and how this changed over time.

"Yoruba" has been a descriptive category for people speaking a common language in the interior of the Bight of Benin since at least the 16th century, and likely earlier still. The first reference to the term is in the writings of Ahmed Baba in 1613 but by implication Baba was describing an ethnicity that had existed for some time. Moreover, the reference almost certainly was not restricted to a particular section of the Yoruba, such as Oyo, which at the time was only a minor polity. *Yarabawa*, in Hausa, refers to people, not a place, meaning the people of Yoruba, which suggests a country, not necessarily a political state. Again, the use of the term among the Hausa seems to predate the rise of Oyo, and hence appears to have had a wider connotation than any particular state. Similarly, the earliest term used in the Americas ("Lucumi") appears to have had a generic connotation and did not specifically refer to a particular state or section of the Yoruba, though, like "Yoruba," the term "Lucumi" is sometimes thought to refer to Oyo, Ife, or perhaps Ijebu. However, the term appears in the Americas at the time when Oyo entered its imperial phase. The term, as used by Alonso de Sandoval in the early 17th century, clearly referred to a broad category of people or a region that may have included others than those who spoke Yoruba, perhaps reflecting areas where Yoruba was nonetheless understood as a language. Lucumi were therefore a significant factor in the early trade of the Bight of Benin. The association of the term with other identifications, such as Lucumi Kakanda and Lucumi Arara, suggests that the term has a meaning that was inclusive of other designations not Yoruba in origin.

The term "Nago" as used in Brazil and French colonies does not appear before the early 18th century. The term is derived from "Anago," a subsection of the Yoruba who lived east of Weme River, but in the Americas it was a generic concept that was derived from Fon and Allada terminology for all Yoruba. The equation of Anago with a general term for Yoruba probably reflects the historical situation that squeezed the Anago homeland between the expansive activities of first Allada and then Dahomey, on the one hand, and Oyo, on the other. The Anago country was vulnerable to invasion from Allada and Dahomey to the west, and hence, among the Gbe languages, "Nago" became the term for all Yoruba. The adoption of the terms in Brazil may well reflect the fact that many of the earliest Yoruba to arrive there were indeed Anago, who seem to have been decimated in the struggle for power among Allada, Dahomey, and Oyo. Neither Lucumi nor Nago were used in Sierra Leone, where large numbers of Yoruba recaptives were settled in the 19th century, which is understandable because these recaptives did not come through the filter of Gbe terminology and were not identified according to Spanish usage in Cuba or Brazilian nomenclature. Instead, the term "Aku" was used as an ethnic designation, apparently reflecting a common Yoruba greeting.

The issue of Yoruba ethnicity is further complicated because many slaves are associated directly or indirectly with Oyo, which was not only a source of enslaved Yoruba but also was involved in a transit trade in slaves, some of whom became acculturated as Yoruba. These Yoruba-speaking slaves entered the trade in the 18th century through Oyo, especially during the time of Alaafin Abiodun and the development of the route through Egbado to Porto Novo as a means of bypassing Dahomey. Even though the origins of many of these slaves are unknown, they were nonetheless designated as being "Oyo." Other Yoruba may have been included in the general name used by the Portuguese for this section of the coast, "Mina," though the term was more generally used for Gbe language groups. It can be assumed that many people who were designated "Nago," "Lucumi," "Aku," or "Yoruba" probably did not speak Yoruba as their first language, and certainly some individuals had multiple ethnic identities and spoke more than one language. However, with the disintegration of Oyo in the early 19th century, slaves who were actually to be identified as people of Oyo became numerous. Moreover, as religion also became an indicator of ethnic origins in the 19th century, those identified as Yoruba included Muslims and Christians, as well as those who consulted the *orisha*.

The number of enslaved Africans leaving from the ports of the Bight of Benin from 1650 to 1865 has been variously estimated at just over 2 million people. According to Eltis, Yoruba constituted the largest proportion of the deported population, perhaps numbering as many as 968,200 of the total number of deportees. Historical evidence indicates a Yoruba presence in the Americas for the 17th century, though the numbers were nominal at the time. The number of Yoruba increased over time, especially after 1715, as Law has noted, and reached a peak only in the 19th century. As Manning first demonstrated, the early trade of the Bight of Benin was heavily concentrated along the western lagoon, with the various Gbe groups (Ewe / Fon / Allada) suffering the most in terms of population loss. These people were known in the Americas variously as "Gege," "Allada," "Fon," "Mahi," and sometimes only as "Mina." Yoruba came largely in the century after 1750, when the total number of slaves exported from the Bight of Benin was over 1 million individuals, divided almost equally between 1751 and 1800 and between 1801 and 1865. The number of slaves being deported decreased substantially during the European wars from the 1790s through 1815. Though British abolition in 1807 was a complicating factor, the elimination of Dutch and French ships from the high seas was the major reason for the collapse of trade after 1793. The British had been heavily involved in purchasing slaves in the Bight of Benin only in the 1770s and 1780s, and hence their withdrawal after 1807 had little direct effect on the Bight of Benin. Export volume rebounded after 1815, and especially from the late 1820s to the 1840s, with trade directed primarily toward Cuba and Bahia.

The demographic data reveal that the origins of the deported population changed over time. Initially the trade flowed from Oyo to the coast, via Allada or Dahomey and Ouidah. By the last third of the 18th century, the principal ports of the trade had shifted eastward, first to Epe and Porto Novo, then to Badagry, and finally to Lagos. This eastward shift was mirrored by a shift in the relative numbers of Yoruba among the enslaved population that was deported, and also coincided with the great migration of Yoruba to Bahia, Cuba, and Sierra Leone. Before the 1760s the overwhelming majority of slaves left from Ouidah, and the ports of Allada on Lake Nokue (Offra and Jaquin). The ports to the east of Ouidah became important in the 1760s, as a result of the development of alternate ports to Dahomey-controlled Ouidah. Despite this competition, the records of slave departures reveal the continued importance of Ouidah, with its competitors only gaining a significant portion of the market in the late 1780s. A large number of ships that traded to the Bight of Benin are only identified as leaving from "Costa da Mina", but it seems that in many cases this referred to Ouidah. As Eltis demonstrates, half the salves whose port of departure from the Bight of Benin is known left from Ouidah. Between 1662 and 1863, 272,500 slaves are known to have left Ouidah, whereas 189,100 are known to have departed from Epe and Porto Novo, another 85,500 from Badagry, and 317,300 from Lagos, which became the principal port in the 19th century. These eastern ports together accounted for 591,000 slaves, in comparison with the million who left from Ouidah. In the 1790s and the first decade of the 19th century, Ouidah's trade virtually collapsed when only 21 ships were reported to have departed. Undoubtedly other ships stopped at Ouidah, but the decline was still dramatic. Slave exports from Ouidah rebounded in the second decade of the 19th century, but the number of slaves being shipped never attained the levels of the previous century.

The eastward shift responded to the sources of supply for slave shipments—the Yoruba interior. Whereas Ouidah connected to Yoruba markets via routes along the west of the Weme River and then to the northeast, Porto Novo, Badagry and Lagos were directly south of the Yoruba heartland and hence the closest outlets for most of the Yoruba country. Before 1762 only 5,700 slaves are known to have come from this area, in sharp contrast to the extensive trade at Ouidah. Slave exports grew in the quarter century from 1762 to 1786 to levels where the majority of those deported were either Yoruba or people from the Central Sudan, many of whom were Muslims. The relative proportion of these 2 categories can be roughly determined, thereby isolating the Yoruba factor for analysis.

Eltis has conservatively and with acknowledged reservations estimated that almost 1 million Yoruba were deported between 1650 and 1865. In the last quarter of the 17th century, an estimated 22,000 appear to have been among those deported. The number of Yoruba doubled in the first quarter of the 18th century, rising to 41,700, before doubling again in the second quarter to 89,500, and continued to increase at a rapid rate (140,100 in the third quarter of the 18th century and 172,900 in the fourth quarter), increasing even more in the 19th century (211,400 in the first quarter and 257,400 in the second). These are, of course, rough estimates that minimize the blurring of ethnicity and multiple identities. The early 19th century was also the period in which exports from the Central Sudan became a noticeable feature of the trade; Central Sudan slaves were probably sometimes represented as Yoruba, especially if they had been retained in Yoruba country before being exported.

Ethnic categories for people from the Bight of Benin can be distinguished between the various Gbe groups, who have been in at least parts of the diaspora as "Mina" and sometimes "Gege," though the use of these terms has varied, and Yoruba have been variously known as Nago and Lucumi. There is also a distinction between the southern "Mina," Yoruba, or Nago and people from the savanna to the north, including those identified as Hausa, Nupe, Borno, Borgu, and "Chamba" or more generally Gurma. Those often referred to as "Mina" and representing Allada, Hueda, Fon, Ewe and Mahi were particularly numerous in the early period, through at least the conquest of Allada and Hueda in which Ouidah was located, in the 1720s. The estimates of slave exports based on shipping data do not distinguish these different identity categories, but the correlation of export figures with political history can provide a gauge of when Yoruba were taken into the trade, and hence implicitly where they went in the Americas; however, much of the information on ethnicity has to be inferred, as do the destinations of people in the Americas. The voyage database, for example, only identifies the destination of a portion of those leaving the Bight of Benin. Instead, Eltis's estimate can be used as a rough figure for the possible number of people who in some way can be identified as "Yoruba." This calculation can be compared to research on the ethnicity of slaves in the Americas, particularly in St. Domingue and Bahia, colonies that received disproportionate numbers of slaves from the Bight of Benin in the 18th century, in the first case, and in the 18th and 19th centuries, in the second. As might be expected, an assessment of the ethnic patterns of the trade from the Bight of Benin reveals a heavy concentration of Yoruba. Plantation records for St. Domingue reveal that Yoruba constituted an identifiable component of the slave population. The study of Geggus covers 4,552 slaves, including each decade from the 1720s through the 1790s, but is heavily weighted toward the end of the 18th century. Moreover, Yoruba were found throughout the francophone Caribbean, including Louisiana and Trinidad, where French planters moved after the uprising in St. Domingue in the 1790s. Yoruba also arrived in considerable numbers in Trinidad after 1807 because of the settlement of recaptives in Sierra Leone.

The concentration of Yoruba in Bahia can be traced to the second half of the 18th century. Cortes de Oliveira provides data on the ethnicity of 537 slaves in Bahia between 1775 and 1815 as recorded in inventories, emancipation documents, and census data. The data indicate the proportions of different ethnic groups from the interior of the Bight of Benin; of 267 slaves from the Bight, 104 were Jeje (38.9%), 100 were Nago (37.4%), and the remaining 63 were Hausa (50), Tapa (12), and Barba (1), who together constituted 23.6% of slaves whose ethnic identity was indicated in the records. The great influx of Yoruba is reflected in the inventories and other documents, as recorded by Cortes de Oliveria, which show the following identification of slaves: previously a substantial population came from Angola and other parts of West-Central Africa; the population now contained a preponderance of Yoruba. In the documents dating from 1815 to 1859, Yoruba constituted 69.1% of all slaves whose ethnic or regional identity is known (sample: 2,593 slaves). Those identifying with West-Central Africa declined from 50.2% to only 14.7%, whereas Yoruba increased from 18.6% to 69.1%. Within the Bight of Benin, the proportion of Yoruba increased from 37.4% to 82.3%. The sample used here is based on probate records and covers 1,612 free urban blacks and manumitted slaves at Bahia in 1819—35 studied by Brazilian historian Joao Reis. Reis also provides evidence for the ethnicity of the slaves and free blacks charged after the Muslim revolt in Bahia in 1835. Of the 250 descendants, 196 (78.4%) were Nago (Yoruba); 32, Hausa (12.4%); 10, Jeje (Ewe-Fon) (4%) 7, Borno (2.8%); 6, Tapa (Nupe) (2.4%). Similarly, Mieko Nishida has demonstrated that Yoruba were numerous in the Bahian slave population of the 19th century. According to Nishida, the proportion of Yoruba in the population of Bahia increased in the 19th century, reflecting what is known about the trade. The registries of freed persons for 1808—42 include records on 662 individuals, 318 men and 344 women. Of these, 31.3% were Yoruba, 24.5% "Gege" or Gbe-speakers, and 17.2% "Mina," which may be identified with Mahi and others in the Bight of Benin interior. Between 1851 and 1884 the registries record 410 individuals, of whom Yoruba were the overwhelming majority (73.9%). Nishida also analyzes the records of individuals who were listed as "Nago" in emancipation papers between 1838 and 1888. Of those listed as "Nago" between 1838 and 1848,

Yoruba constituted 53.6% of those freed, while from 1852 to 1888 Yoruba constituted 79.3%. Of these, 58.5% were women.

The gender and age composition of the enslaved Yoruba population that was exported changed from the 18th to 19th century. The most striking feature arises from distance from the coast—which seems to have a correlation with gender, age, religion, and, of course, ethnicity. There appears to have been conscious attempts to discriminate among the enslaved population being deported. Specifically Muslim Yoruba may have been subjected to expulsion from places, though Muslims also ended up as slaves in Ibadan, Lagos, Abeokuta, Ijebu, and other Yoruba cities. There were many enslaved Muslims, often from the Central Sudan, whose presence was considered a threat, but the extent to which Islam was a factor in the selection of those to be deported is still be determined. The proportion of males in the deported population increased, especially after 1810, when the numbers of political prisoners of the jihad that revolutionized the Nigerian hinterland were sold to European merchants. Especially after 1817, Muslims, including Muslim Yoruba, were prominent among these prisoners. The revolt of the Oyo army in 1817 produced a wave of exports, most of whom appear to have gone to Bahia. The Owu war in 1822—23 and the collapse of Oyo in the early 1830s accounted for additional waves of deportation, though many of these were not Muslims. The consolidation of Ilorin and the Nupe emirates was directly related to the enslavement of Yoruba, including the Yagba, Igbomina, and other northeast "Okun" Yoruba, and retaliation by Ibadan and other non-Muslim states resulted in the enslavement of many others, whether Muslim or not. Distinguishing among Yoruba who were Muslims and Muslims from further north who became recognized as Yoruba is often impossible, but men tended to come from the interior and were more likely to be Muslim of whatever background, whereas women and children tended to come from near the coast and were not Muslim.

The age and sex rations of the deported population suggest that women and children were initially an important part of the deported population from the Bight of Benin, but the proportion of men increased over time, as Eltis and Engerman have demonstrated. There was considerable variation over time and among the different regions for which ratios have been calculated. Based on a sample of 41,121 slaves shipped by the French from the Bight of Benin in 1715—92, Geggus has calculated that 48% of the deported population were men, 30% women, 13.8% were boys, and 8.6% were girls—that 61.8% of the enslaved were males and 22.4% were children. According to Eltis and Engerman, 61.1% were adults, while children comprised 16.9% of the deported population.

The ratios of males and females and adults and children shifted between the end of the 18th century and the height of the trade in the 19th century; generally, the trade involved more males and especially more boys, while the number of women declined. This shift in the gender and age composition of the exported phenomenon of the whole slave trade, not just that from the Bight of Benin, but the reasons in the Bight of Benin were unique to the region. In 1811—67 the proportion of males had increased to 68% of the total number of people deported. According to Eltis and Engerman, 46% were men, 21% were women, with an additional 22% boys and 12% girls. In effect, the proportion of adult females declined from 30% in the last part of the 18th century to 21% after British abolition, while the proportion of adult males remained largely the same. This pattern can be explained by developments in the interior, changes in transport costs, and the reduction of risks associated with moving slaves great distances. The ratios of adult males seem to have been sustained through deportation of men, mostly Muslims, from the interior. The figures for those ports through which slaves were deported from Yoruba country and the Central Sudan suggest that the decline in females, especially women, meant that fewer Yoruba were leaving. According to Eltis, males comprised 63.4% of the slaves leaving the ports of Porto Novo, Badagry, and Lagos before British abolition, but the proportion rose to 67.4% thereafter. The population, moreover, was increasingly younger. Adult males comprised 57.5% of

cargoes before abolition, with women making up most of the remainder—
33.8%. After British abolition, adult males declined to 44% of the departing
population, while women declined to 20.2%. Children, especially boys,
became more common. There were more boys than adult women on most
ships after 1810, with boys comprising 23.3% of cargoes. It is not clear why
this should be the case, except the intention to remove the younger
generation that might have lived to fight another day. It is also possible that
as the male slave trade reached further into the interior, male children near
the coast became more prized because of the increased cost of moving
slaves from the interior.

Many of the males came from the far interior, including those classified
as Hausa, Nupe and Borno males, as well as Yoruba. The women and
children from the coastal zone were entirely Yoruba. It has been estimated
that 95% of slaves who were identified as Hausa, Nupe, or Borno were adult
males. Though the interior trade was much smaller than Yoruba exports, the
numbers were still large enough to influence the overall pattern. In the
period after British abolition, the total has been estimated at between
43,000 and 108,000 slaves from Central Sudan. The other deportees appear
to have been Yoruba, comprised of about 120,000 women, 77,000 girls,
144,000 boys, and 168,000—230,000 from northern Yoruba areas were
also largely adult males, and most likely political prisoners of the jihad and
related wars and raids. The profile that emerges after estimates are adjusted
for the Central Sudan factor and enslavement of Yoruba in the interior
suggests a demographic picture that highlights the rising importance of
children who were taken from near the coast. It seems that the majority of
the deported population from areas immediately adjacent to the coast were
not only children but also included those women who were deported. This
pattern is reflected in the biographical materials that have survived.

The Yoruba, Hausa and other people who clearly came from the interior
included relatively few females, either girls or women, and very few boys. In
this respect, this analysis supports those who have claimed that the ratio of
males among exports to the Americas tended to increase with distance from

the coast. The identification of Muslim slaves among the deported population from the Bight of Benin during the century after 1750 should also be noted. Not only was there a correlation between gender and distance from the coast, but males from the interior of the Bight of Benin tended to be Muslims, some of who were Yoruba. Lovejoy, estimated the relative proportions of males and females, suggesting the significance of these ratios in calculating the relative number of males and females shipped from the Bight of Benin, and therefore the proportion of males and females in the Yoruba population. He ultimately concludes that that 95% of slaves from the Central Sudan were males, and since the gender ratio for the deported population has been calculated, it is possible to demonstrate that the enslaved population from the Yoruba areas near the coast had a higher proportion of females than the export figures indicate. Though the period was one of adjustment to the Napoleonic Wars and British Abolition, Yoruba nonetheless still formed an important proportion of the total trade, perhaps as many as half of all exports from the 1790s through the mid-1820s and more thereafter.

Two patterns of the trade existed: one was overwhelmingly adult males from distances of 100—200 kilometers from the coastal ports, and the other was extensively a trade in women and children from the zone near the coast. Far fewer adult men were purchased in local slave markets than from the interior. The paradox of differential prices between the interior and the coast has to be explained; in the interior women cost more than men, often by a third, and yet European factors were willing to pay more for men at the coast. This paradox seems to overlook the importance of ransoming in determining slave prices; freeborn men often commanded ransoms that were double the market price for slaves. There appears to have been 3 categories of slaves for sale to Europeans—girls and women obtained from markets near the coast; high-priced men, often political prisoners, from the interior; and males, especially boys, from near the coast.

Significant proportions of Muslims were part of the deported population by the early 19th century. In a sample of slaves from the far interior whose religious identity seems certain, about 56% can be identified as Muslims through their names. The prevalence of such identification does reflect that Muslims dominated the commercial system of the interior. Evidence from Bahia suggest there were significant of numbers of Muslims among enslaved Yoruba in the early 19th century. It is possible that northern Yoruba included large proportions of males and sizeable numbers of Muslims, thereby extending the argument about the importance of Muslim males in the enslaved population from the Central Sudan. By contrast, the deported population from southern Yoruba country had much higher proportions of children and women. In this sense, there appears to have been 2 patterns in the deportation of Yoruba in the 19th century that were correlated with age, sex, and religion, one for the interior extending into the Central Sudan and the other in the Yoruba areas near the coast that were subjected to periodic wars and population displacement.

It may seem surprising that women and children were most likely to come from near the coast and were not otherwise retained within West Africa, where it appears that the market price for female slaves were generally higher—often a third higher—than that of their male counterparts of the same age, whether they were children or in their prime. The prices for males and females became relatively equal only at an advanced age when neither had many productive laboring years remaining. It seems clear that there were internal, structural reasons why women and children ended up in the trade near the coast but were not brought south from the far interior. These reasons are related to the interconnection between the local market for slaves in Yorubaland and the articulation of local debt enforcement mechanisms with the slave trade. Some females and children, at least, became slaves because of default on debts for which they were being held as pawns. Females tended to be held as pawns more often than males, and hence defaults on pawning arrangements tended to be on females, whose value could most profitably be realized through a sale to slave buyers, which increased the possibility of a sale to European merchants. Prime male slaves, by contrast, were more likely to be political prisoners and "criminals" being deported from the far interior; because of the price differential that held females at a premium, women were less likely to be sold to the Bight of Benin coast.

The demographic data on the export of enslaved Africans from the Bight of Benin demonstrates a relatively clear picture of the importance of the Yoruba migration under the conditions of Transatlantic slavery. In order to identify the "Yoruba" population further, it is necessary to examine the specific sub-ethnic identities of the Yoruba, and the specific wars and military campaigns that account for the majority of slaves leaving the Bight of Benin in the 18th and 19th centuries. The registers of liberated Africans in Havana between 1826 and 1839 provide a window in the determination of Yoruba ethnicity for this period, which can be correlated with the aftermath of the Owu wars and overlapping the period of disintegration for Oyo. The distinctions among the "Lucumi" population include Oyo, Egba, Ijebu, Ota, Ijesha, Sabe, and other designations. The term encompassed people who also passed through Yoruba country to reach the coast, such as Hausa, Nupe and Bariba. In this sample of 3,663 individuals, 68% (2,497) were classified as Yoruba, 26% (946) were classified as one of the Gbe groups, and only 1% (32) are clearly identified with the Central Sudan. It may well be that those classified as Lucumi without further identification may have included individuals from the Central Sudan; otherwise, the sample seems to underrepresent the far interior.

The Yoruba Cultural, Religious and Arts Atlantic Contribution

There is a discernible Yoruba cultural imprint in many parts of the Americas, especially in places such as Cuba, Trinidad, Haiti, Costa Rica, and the U.S. among others.

In Cuba, the most popular *Orisha*, Chango (for Shango, originally the principal deity of Oyo in Yorubaland), became a macho womanizer in Cuba, and Ochun is a *mulata*, syncretizing the Yoruba deity Oshun with the Virgin of the Caridad del Cobre, the patron saint of Cuba and symbol of the mestizo nation. Yemaya, the Yoruba goddess Jemoja, became a *'linda negra'*, a pretty, black woman with fine features and long, flowing hair, whose transformation is explained in a myth that says she was originally white but fell into the Black Sea.

Myths of the *orisha*, or *patakin*, whose function, like that of the Yoruba Ifa divination corpus, has been to explain and validate ritual practices and relationship and relationships between the deities in the Yoruba pantheon, reflect the influence of other cultures encountered in Cuba. An extreme example of this diverse ethnic mix is the *camino* (avatar) of Chango, called Sanfancion or San Fan Kung, which was invented by Marcos Portillo Dominguez, a *santero* of Cantonese and African descent, and is supposedly based on a Taoist myth. A Pataki recounts how other orisha fail to recognize Chango in this *camino* because of his Chinese appearance.

Adapted forms of the Yoruba religion developed into the Cuban *regla de ocha* despite the cultural losses suffered by slaves in the Middle Passage and the adjustments they had to make to a new social context. Since the Cuban Revolution, the commitment to the atheist [now secular] state and the desire to recognize the African roots of Cuban culture have further tested the adaptability of the contradictory world in which the *regla de ocha* emerged.

African-derived religions in Cuba are called *reglas*, from the *reglamentos*, or rules, of the *cabilos de nacion*, mutual aid societies organized along ethnic lines and encouraged by the Spanish colonial government to keep Africans from uniting against the slave system. The ethnic designation of these cabilos de nacion were derived from those of the slave trade (e.g., *congo*, *mandinga*, *carabali*, *lucumi*), though Africans themselves had some power to determine their cultural and religious boundaries, and in practice the *regla de ocha* tended to counteract the colonial policy of ethnic division. Initially, the *regla de ocha* was the religion of the *lucumi* slaves, but by the end of the 19th century, the *regla de ocha* became increasingly open to Africans of other ethnic origins and to Cuban-born blacks and whites. Indeed, many famous *santeros*, *santeras* and babalawos have been white. The term *lucumi* (included all Yoruba speakers as well as some neighboring groups such as Ewe-Fon and Nupe and was subdivided accordingly: *lucumi eyo* (Oyo), *lucumi ife/fee* (Ife), and so forth.

The *regla de Ifa* is the Cuban version of the Ifa divination cult, whose male diviners are called *babalawos*. These *babalawos* provide the ritual and spiritual leadership of *santeria* (from santo, i.e., saint), the term that is commonly used to designate both the *regla de ocha* and the *regla de Ifa*. *Santeria* also includes the *arara* practices of Ewe-Fon (Gbe) origin. In contrast, the *reglas congas*, also called *palo monte*, are of Bantu origin.

The terminology reflects changing attitudes: *santeria* was originally called *brujeria*, or witchcraft, by those external to the practice. Spanish clerics used the term to refer to the unorthodox rites whereby African gods were worshipped under the guise of Catholic saints. The Yoruba religious term is used by some *babalawos* to emphasize its African origin. Those who wish to emphasize its Cuban-ness tend to call it *la santeria cubana*.

There is little concrete information on the process of transforming the orisha cults into santeria. Oral tradition refers to meetings and convenios (agreements) between *santeros* to reconstruct and regulate religious practices in the 19th century. However, according to Lydia Cabrera, a Matanzas *babalocha* (a *santero* who has initiated others) called Lorenzo Sama and a Yoruba woman called Latuan (a daughter of Chango), who arrived in Cuba in 1887, conceived the idea of unifying the different Yoruba *orisha* cults in Cuba into a single liturgical body which was called the *regla*

102

de ocha. The *casas de santo* or *ile ocha* (literally, 'houses of the *oricha*/saint,' usually the private houses of *santeros* and *santeria* where ceremonies are held, now also called *casa templos*) replaced the *cabildos*.

Practitioners of the *regla de ocha* worship a number of deities. For members of the relatively independent local and regional *orisha* cults of Yorubaland, the pantheon is more the concern of *babalawos*. In Cuba, a devotee 'makes' or becomes initiated into the cult of a specific orisha, or *santo de cabecera* (saint of the head), but other orisha, *santos de fundamento* (usually Chango, Ochun, Yemaya and Obatala), are received at the same time. The *santos de addimu* are orisha received before or after full initiation to resolve specific problems, or when deemed necessary. Divination becomes more central in Cuba determining which orisha (and which *camino* of the *orisha*) is to be the *santo de cabecera*. Outside the *iyesa*, *egguado* and *arara* (Ijesha, Egbado and Ewe-Fon) houses in Matanzas, whose practices differ from that of the Oyo-dominated *santeria*, orisha have not been inherited within families.

Santeria practice, like Yoruba *orisha* worship, is flexible. 'Cada practicantetiene su verdad'. (Each practitioner has his/her own truth). Membership of other religions also affects practices within houses, as in the use of spiritism for dealing with *egun* (lineal ancestors). Great power and efficacy are attributed to initiation into several different packages, and the divination systems and mythology reflect this multi-religiosity. For example, divination verses refer to, and sometimes recommend, elements from other religions.

Cuban traditions evolved out of the need to adapt to different social conditions and to compensate for gaps in the transmission of religious knowledge, both from Africa to Cuba and from older to younger generations of Cuban-born practitioners. Not all *orisha* were transferred to Cuba, and some that were became less relevant; their cults died out, and their rituals were forgotten. As in Nigeria, an *orisha's* power depends on having numerous and attentive devotees, but some orisha were linked with activities no longer important in a slave society, while others had their functions modified. *Ochosi*, the hunter, who in Africa represents order in society, became in Cuba the patron of jails and acquired the contrary function offering protection against the police.

Sometimes orisha from different regions in Yorubaland were fused, as in the case of *Olokun*, an independent deity in Africa, who in Cuba is sometimes a *camino* of Yemaya. *Orisha* also became fragmented into multiple *caminos*, who reflected regional variants or multiple conceptions of an *orisha*, as expressed in Yoruba oriki poetry. *Orisha* cults in West Africa also display the merging and fragmentation of orisha, as well as a tendency to incorporate new material from other cultures.

Social and economic factors also affected practice, for example when its external expressions were not socially acceptable. For example, new initiates (*iyawo*) normally have to shave their heads and wear white for a year, but those who did not want outsiders to know that they were devotees could arrange a dispensation from these requirements. After the Revolution, when rationing restricted the availability of animals for sacrifice, birds were substituted for four-legged animals. Because fabric and colored beads needed to represent the different *caminos* of the *orisha* were scarce, only one *camino* was represented in ritual objects. When the required items were again available in the dollar economy, some traditions could be restored.

The descendants of Yoruba settlers who arrived in 19th century Trinidad are an example of a group using songs, phraseology, and vocabulary to reinforce their cultural connection to the homeland.

The first Yoruba-speakers to arrive in Trinidad appear to have come as slaves before the British abolition of the Transatlantic slave trade in 1808, but Yoruba immigration was heavily concentrated in the period after the 1838 in Sierra Leone and at Caribbean ports, having been freed from captured slave ships. Some of them were settled in villages in Freetown, Sierra Leone, and on the outskirts, while other were hired almost immediately as laborers and re-shipped to the West Indies under indentureship arrangements which lasted for varying periods, between 3 and 7 years. Yet others were recruited into the British-led West India regiments to prosecute colonial battles in Africa itself as well as in the Caribbean. Thus, while most Yoruba came to Trinidad as free immigrants, their migration still took place within the period of Transatlantic slavery and under conditions that might well replicate some of the conditions of slavery.

The Yoruba in the Caribbean, as was the case in Brazil, succeeded in establishing a New World identity that was palpably based on their native culture; they underestimated the degree of Yoruba cultural influence due to the presence of other cultures in the Americas. In both regions Catholicism provided the Yoruba with an institutional structure that they used to appropriate physical and cultural space, both of which led to the vibrant, Yoruba-based identities of "Nago" and "Lucumi".

Another example of the Yoruba cultural presence in the America's came in the form of the African American intellectual, W.E.B. Du Bois (1868—1963) involving the Orisha in a theatrical performance. A member of the Board of Governors of the National Emancipation of New York, Du Bois wrote an opera in 1913 entitled *The Star of Ethiopia*. It commemorated the 50th anniversary of the Emancipation Proclamation of 1863. Aimed at inspiring fellow blacks to rediscover themselves, to reclaim their cultural heritage, and then to fight for total freedom, the opera synthesized characters and artistic elements from different parts of Africa and the black world. As Freda Scott notes:

> Du Bois started the first of several drafts of The Star
> of European in 1911. At first he called the work *The
> Jewel of Ethiopia: A Masque in Episodes* (there were
> six in the first draft). Since the masque is more alleg-
> orical than commemorative, he began with a scene
> in which Shango, the God of Thunder, gives the Jewel
> of Freedom to Ethiopia in return for her soul. The Jewel
> finally reaches the United States after being lost and
> found several times. There the foundation stones of

> Labor, Wealth, Justice, Beauty, Education, and Truth
> are laid and the jewel is finally ensconced on a Pillar
> of Light and placed on this foundation . . . The thirteen
> leading characters included Queen of Sheba, Nat Turner,
> Toussaint L'Ouverture and Mohammed Askia.

The Yoruba deity Sango is associated not only with the thunderstorm but also with retributive and social justice. That Du Bois included the deity among the 13 leading characters in *The Star of Ethiopia* reveals his awareness of Sango's potential as an instrument for empowering the African-American struggle for social justice and cultural emancipation. He probably encountered Sango in the course of his avid collection of materials on African history and culture or as a result of his interactions with African-Americans who had migrated to the U.S. from the Caribbean where many of the Yoruba Orisha had survived in various forms. However, the *Orisha* did not attract public attention in the United States until the 1940s when more immigrants arrived from the Caribbean (especially from Cuba and Puerto Rico), bringing with them the African-inspired religion called Santeria, that is, the worship caught the attention of Katherine Durnham, the famous African-American choreographer. She employed some of the new arrivals in her dance company, and also organized monthly concerts featuring Cuban orchestras that played Yoruba-influenced music. In 1947 the jazz trumpeter and behop maestro, Dizzy Gillespie, collaborated with the Cuban Yoruba songs in honor of *Yemoja*, the Yoruba personification of motherhood. In Dizzy Gillespie's words:

> Chano taught us all the multi-rhythm; we learned from
> the master . . . . He'd teach us some of those Cuban chants
> and things like that . . . You have different ones, the Nanigo,
> the Arara, the Santo (music of the Yoruba orisha) and seve-
> ral others, and they each have their own rhythm . . . . They
> are all of African derivation.

Such collaborations between African-Americans and Afro-Cubans generated a lot of interest in musical circles, culminating in Cubop Jazz, which sometimes included bata rhythm, Sango's sacred music. The jazz drummer Mongo Santamaria is credited with staging the first public concert of *Orisha* music in 1956 at the Palladium Night Club in New York. The concert was dedicated to Sango whose name was already familiar to American theater audiences through Katherine Durnham's dance-drama Carib Song staged in New York in 1945. One of the first African-American converts to Santaria was Walter Eugene King (b. 1928), a graphic artist and member of the Katherine Durnham Dance Company, who was at that time searching for African alternatives to Christianity and Islam. King traveled to Matanzas, Cuba in 1959, where he was initiated and became a priest of Obatala, the Yoruba creative deity.

The early 1960s marked a turning point in the African-American experience. A combination of events such as the emergence of independent African states, the intensification of black nationalism in the U.S., as well as the struggle there for desegregation, equal opportunity, and cultural emancipation, encouraged many blacks to identify more closely with their motherland. The creation of the Peace Corps and Operation Crossroads programs, coupled with the availability of travel grants, enabled many African-Americans to visit Africa. Some did so as a kind of homecoming. Others traveled and lived in Africa for some time either to conduct research or simply to have a firsthand experience of their cultural heritage which they had only learned about till then in the ethnographic literature. The creation of African and black studies programs in American universities offered a unique opportunity for blacks who could not leave the U.S. to deepen their knowledge of Africa and its cultural traditions. One consequence of the new development is that some African-Americans abandoned the Christian faith and converted to Islam or indigenous African religions.

In 1960 Walter Eugene King established a Yoruba temple in Harlem, New York and began converting fellow blacks to *Orisha* religion. He broke with the Cuban tradition of worshiping the *Orisha* in the guise of Christian

107

saints, restoring to the deities their original Yoruba identity and calling the reformed religion *Orisa-Vodou*, instead of Santeria. He did away with the Christian images of Catholic saints used by Afro-Cubans to represent the *Orisha* on alters, replacing them with sculptures in the Yoruba style. Being an artist himself, he carved some of the altar sculptures dedicated to the *Orisha* in the Yoruba temple. He also introduced the performance of Egungun masks which the Yoruba use to signify the souls of deceased ancestors returning to the physical world to interact with living descendants. He opened a fashion store in Harlem that popularized among blacks the wearing of African dresses, especially the Yoruba "agbada," "daniski," "fila," "buba," "ira," and "gele," which soon became symbols of black nationalism and the black quest for cultural redemption. Some blacks adopted Yoruba names. King himself changed his name to Efuntola Oseijiman Adefunmi. In 1970 he founded the Oyotunji Village in South Carolina, which has since become a Mecca for Yoruba religion, art, and culture in the U.S. The village, influenced by Yoruba architectural design, is headed by Adefunmi who wears a beaded crown like a Yoruba king. By 1972 he had visited Yorubaland several times, and he spoke the Yoruba language. Admittedly, as Mikelle Smith Omari aptly observes, the revival of Yoruba traditions at Oyotunji Village cannot be traced directly to "survivals of slave cultures" as in Brazil, Cuba, Haiti, and other parts of the Caribbean. This point is also reflected in the eclectic nature of the revival which incorporates ancient Egyptian, Fon, Edo, and Asante elements. Yet, according to a resident of the village, the experiment constitutes an act of reclamation and reintegration of a lost and found heritage that has been of tremendous therapeutic value to thousands of African-Americans at critical periods in their struggle for survival in North America.

Many American cities now have a growing population of *Orisha* devotees or individuals who identify with the Yoruba tradition and use its tenets to enrich their lives. The number of botanicas (shops selling herbs and *Orisha*-related goods) has increased over the years. Some of the goods are imported from Yorubaland, Brazil, and the Caribbean; others, including Yoruba-looking images and beadwork, are made in the U.S. There is a general belief, however, that materials and images from Yorubaland are more effective ritually. This partly explains why members of the *Yemoja* Descendants Society of New York (*Egbe Yemoja*), founded in 1988, traveled to Ibadan (Nigeria) in 1990 to commission a special image of the goddess for use in its rituals. In short, shrines for the *Orisha* combine Yoruba- and American-made images and ritual furniture.

The Africans of the Gold Coast

The Ewe of Ghana and Togo, the Fon or Aja of ancient Dahomey and the Gun of Porto Novo (both in the modern Republic of Benin) all speak much the same language. Barbot referred to 'the *Fidafians* [of Whydah] using the same language as those of *Andra'* and to 'their uniformity of manners and practices.' The Ewe / Aja / Gun are now divided by the boundaries of no less than 4 modern nations, 2 of which are anglophone and 2 francophone. This, and the diversity of their ethnonyms, means that their essential unity is often not realized, even by other West Africans. The Ewe call the Gun and Fon—but not themselves—Aja, and western Yoruba, such as the people of Ketu, do likewise. Because of this a new name, Gbe, has been suggested for their common language but it has not yet won general acceptance. Aja-speaking communities trace their origins to the inland town of Tado, which has much the same ritual supremacy as Ife among the Yoruba. Some traditions say that Tado was founded by a migrant from Yorubaland, either from Ketu or from Oyo. From Tado, tradition claims, one section moved west to Nuatje, also in Togo, the center from which the Ewe trace their origin. Both Tado and Nuatje have substantial earthworks.

It seems likely that the Tado tradition does not reflect real historical movements but is essentially a charter of social relations. Some traditions speak of a leopard ancestor and others of an escape from royal tyranny, in myths which are strikingly similar to others told in far distant parts of Africa (the king who placed thorns in the mud to be trodden for a building). But in the last 300 years or so, there have been well attested cases of the formation of states after a migration, usually of a small body of royals and their entourage rather than whole populations. Refugee royals from Accra founded Little Popo in the late 17th century, and dynasts from Allada did the same at Porto Novo in the early 18th. If these movements were not fully documented, many might well believe traditions about them to be charters of social relations.

Different Aja-speaking groups made different political choices: the Ewe remained in the decentralized villages which probably originally characterized all Aja speakers. There are hints that kinship sometimes evolved out of clan headship—the Aja word for 'king' was *Ahosu*, which originally meant 'clan head.'

The hundred Anlo villages were on the coast in a zone of lagoons, sandbanks, and barren clay soils, where cultivable terrain was very limited. All Anlo are members of one of 15 clans, obeying the same ritual prohibitions, respecting the same totem, and tracing descent from a common ancestor. As with the Asante, or the Igala—but unlike the Igbo— clan members do not live in a single area but are scattered through many different settlements.

The conventional view is that clans are very ancient (a founder whose descendants are ever more numerous). But in the case of the Anlo, it has been suggested that the clans were developed in the late 17th and 18th centuries to protect their limited areas of agricultural land, when refugees reached the area from the west.

The study of language relationships sheds a great deal of light on the history of the Akan-speaking peoples and their neighbors. Volta Comoe languages fall into 3 main branches—western, central and Guang. The western branch consists of 2 languages spoken by small ethnic groups in Ivory Coast. The central branch has 2 sections, Bia and Akan. Bia included Agni and Baoule, also spoken in Ivory Coast, and Aowin and Sefi, found in western Ghana. Akan divides into 3 dialect clusters: the northern dialect of Brong, and Asante and Fante. The last 2 languages are known as Twi. Linguistic evidence suggests that the original home of Volta-Comoe was western Brong-Ahafo, near the present Ghana-Ivory Coast frontier, and that western Brong was the original point of dispersal for Akan. It is noteworthy that the type site for the Late Stone Age Kintampo culture is in this area.

The Fante lived on or near the coast; further east, Ga and Dangme were spoken, and there were some Guan-speaking enclaves. The relationship between language and population is complex; a lineage in Accra speaks Ga and regards itself as Ga, but its ancient heritage of oral literature is in Akan. Some Akwapim towns, such as Mamfe, changed from Guang to Akan, and Kpone changed from Dangme to Ga.

The use of the word Akan has changed over time and is chronically ambiguous. Its most appropriate modern use is linguistic, referring to speakers of Akan languages. In Twi, the prestigious term *akan-fo* meant 'us,' 'the true people,' as opposed to *apoto-fo*, 'them,' 'foreigners.' In modern academic discourse 'Akan' is inclusive and fixed rather than exclusive and situational,' a usage apparently derived from 19th century Basle missionaries.

Early European visitors wrote of 'Heccanys,' 'Hacanys' and 'Quiforo' (Twifo, the Twi people). Forms of 'Akan' thread their way through 16th- and 17th-century records and disappear in the 18th century. It is likely that the earlier references are to specific states, and though there is no general agreement on the identification, Akan and Adansi were clearly located in the Pra-Ofin basin. Guang is now spoken by scattered communities along the Black Volta and Volta, as well as near the coast in south-eastern Ghana. The linguistic evidence suggests a move from north to south. It is likely that Guang was once much more widely spoken, and that in some areas it has been supplanted by Akan.

The earliest Akan states developed north of the forest, in Bono and Bighu (Bitu), a commercial center on the Dyula trade route to Jenne. The area has yielded ironworking dates from the second century CE, though settlement would have begun long before involvement in far-flung trade routes. There were Brong and Dyula quarters; this hole was an ancient water cistern, surrounded by grinding hollows and traces of the Kintampo culture.

In 1895, the Gold Coast historian Reindorf wrote: 'Adance [the Pra-Ofin basin] was the first seat of the Akan nation, as they say by tradition: there God first commenced with the creation of the World.' Neolithic tools have been found near Kumasi, which was sparsely settled and cultivated from that time. In the 15th and 16th centuries, there was a major transformation; the forest was more densely settled, and there was extensive clearance. Oral tradition remembers this in terms of woman 'ancestors,' descending from heaven or emerging from the ground. They were not properly ancestors at all—they imposed a social order on existing populations. The Brong do not have the great totemic matriclans of the forest Akan. What these myths describe is the growth of a new socio-economic order.

The capital of the Asante kingdom, founded in the late 17th century, was at Kumasi, about 50 miles within the rainforest zone. There was an earlier settlement 20 miles further south which the Asante regarded as a sacred shrine: 'The *Asante Hene* . . . sent a yearly offering as "Santemanso," whence he came.'

In the 16th and early 17th centuries, the forest Akan exported gold and imported labor; they purchased slaves from both the Dyula to the north (these apparently came from the small-scale societies of the Volta basin) and the Europeans in the south; these captives were rapidly absorbed in Akan society. Small states were founded by entrepreneurs; these 'Big Men' used slave labor to mine gold and clear the forest.

Gold was extracted, sometimes by slaves, and sometimes by family units; as in Bambuk, men hacked out the ore from shafts which were sometimes as much as 30 meters deep. Women extracted the gold from the ore and also panned for alluvial gold on riverbanks. The labor involved was enormous—the maximum amount which a woman could wash in a day was 50 pounds of soil; in the 1880s, this earned a profit of between 2s 6d and 10 shillings.

The number of the matriclans has changed over time; Bowditch referred to 12 in 1819; 8 were listed by the Asantehene in 1907. They have almost ceased to exist. 'For a quite surprising number of Asantes today, clan affiliation is a matter no longer within, or but vaguely within, the level of consciousness.' Wilks suggests that the matriclans evolved as a way of organizing labor in the era of forest clearance; when this had been done, they declined, and the size of the unit of production shrank to the lineage. The Anlo developed clans as a way of protecting access to land and the Asante as a way of controlling labor.

Coromantee in the Atlantic World

The history of the Coromantee's homeland is important to understanding their cultural contribution in the New World. Historically the Coromantee's homeland lacked a common place name among its inhabitants; the Gold Coast moniker—which preceded its present-day name *Ghana*—was originally derived by16th century European traders from the Portuguese term Costa da Mina (the Coast of Mines) where they were based due to the lucrative coastal trade in gold. The former Gold Coast region included over 300 miles of coastline in Atlantic West Africa situated between the Comoe River in the west and the Volta River in the east—encompassing parts of modern-day Ghana, Cote d'Ivoire, and Togo. Depending on the century, or decade in some instance, the Gold Coast extended inland to the Volta basin in the north and—at least in terms of potential slave procurement or catchment areas—as far north as modern Burkina Faso. Much of the northern reach of the Gold Coast depended on the expansion and wide-ranging political influences of the Asante kingdom, particularly during the course of the mid- to-late-18th century.

Despite its small size relative to other coastal regions in Atlantic Africa, the Gold Coast was a land of stark contrasts. Within its diverse and shifting boundaries, the Gold Coast included 3 vastly different ecological zones— coastal grasslands, forests, and savannas. From south to north, flat coastal lands, salt marshes, and lagoons give way to hills, mountains, and dense forestation—representing a seemingly impenetrable "bush" in the early-modern European imaginary. In the view of Ludewig Romer, a trader stationed at Christiansborg Castle in the 1740s, "Africa (the seacoasts excepted) is still wholly unknown," a fact he blamed on "Nature herself," which created thick stands of forest and bushes that even the inhabitants had difficulty managing. The land was not as foreboding and impenetrable as outsiders believed, though its tropical disease ecology—complete with such lethal afflictions as malaria and yellow fever—made the Gold Coast, and much of Atlantic Africa by extension, truly a "white man's grave."

Despite its lethality to Europeans, the fertile coastal lands and inland savannahs sustained life to the degree that high population and settlement densities led to the wide proliferation of settled agricultural communities and large towns in the Gold Coast prior to 1600. On this note, Gerard Chouin and Christopher Decorse contend that as early as 800 CE. Akan-speaking peoples in the southern Gold Coast created a "pre-Atlantic" agrarian order in which they carved out—with iron tools and no less—agricultural spaces and dwellings from the dense inland forests. Within these habitations, people cultivated palm oil and yam and used iron digging tools to create the entrenched earthwork settlements they lived in from 800—1500 CE. The pre-Atlantic agrarian order, however, collapsed abruptly as the possible result of epidemic disease that caused a demographic catastrophe and served a devastating blow to the rise and growth of polities in the Gold Coast when it struck. In the wake of rapid population collapse, a new "Atlantic agrarian order" emerged that coincided with the arrival of the Portuguese in the 15th century. In this case, the Gold Coast was still recovering from the demographic and sociopolitical legacies of epidemic disease, and the previous earthwork settlements and agrarian spaces of the pre-Atlantic agrarian order were largely reforested by the 1400s.

By the 1600s, both populations and agrarian settlements had rebounded. Indeed, the Gold Coast witnessed a veritable demographic explosion, perhaps and not, as argued by Wilks, a new shift to crop cultivation. Wilhem Muller, a Lutheran pastor residing at a Danish fort near Cape Coast from 1662—69, described various "large and populous" towns in the region, including Efutu, Wimba (Winneba), Enkinne-Fu, and Ando-Crum. Reporting historical narratives passed on to him by the Ga-speaking residents of 18th century Accra. Romer noted, "The old Blacks tell us about millions of people once living on the Accra coast alone . . . It was not only the coast that was densely populated . . . where the mountains begin, [the district] was full of towns and people everywhere." In sum, the Gold Coast was "full of people" in Romer's view owing to a number of causes. "Blessed" and fertile land as well as efficient modes of agricultural production and labor mobilization combined to help sustain high population and settlement densities that later represented deep "recruitment" pools from which Europeans extracted enslaved Atlantic African labor.

The peoples of the Gold Coast were just as diverse as the physical geographies they inhabited. As abovementioned the 4 largest ethnolinguistic clusters in the region, both numerically and in terms of geographic expanse, include Akan or Volta-Comoe (Fante, Twi, Guang), Ga-Adanme, and Ewe. These language groups were joined by a range of others—including Gur in the north and Estii, Efutu, Eguafo, and Asebu in the south. Particularly in the coastal south, some of these smaller ethnolinguistic groupings became amalgamated by larger language clusters through complex processes of ethnogenesis, often as the result of military conquest or the political exigencies arising from the threat of northern invasion.

Questions have arisen as to why there has been a bias towards Akan-speakers as they feature disproportionately in historical accounts of the Gold Coast. This is understandable when one considers that even if they formed the majority of people in the southern Gold Coast, they lived among and interacted with speakers of Ga, Adanme, and Ewe. It is possible then that research of the region focused more on centralized, expansionist kingdoms of Atlantic Africa, of which the Akan [Asante] featured in addition to Benin, Dahomey, and Kongo. Those who lived in decentralized societies and small polities constituted a majority of the people in the Gold Coast and throughout Atlantic Africa and, by the fact of their relative powerlessness vis-à-vis centralized kingdoms, they were overrepresented among the enslaved the [dis]embarked, and the dispersed. It is for this very reason that their collective stories form an important aspect of the Gold Coast diaspora.

Before 1700, Akan was the most widely spoken language throughout the Gold Coast. It also had, by far, the largest geographic scope and spread. By the 17th century, the range for Akan speaking peoples encompassed much of the coastal portion of the Gold Coast, reaching northward beyond the region between the Afram and Volta rivers. From west to east, Akan speakers inhabited the area between the southeastern portion of what is now Cote d'Ivoire and parts of the coastal region east of the Volta River's outlet into the Gulf of Guinea—in the western portion of modern-day Togo. Certainly, given the long history of human migrations and the rise and fall of powerful states throughout the Gold Coast, the region in which Akan speakers lived experienced constant expansions and contractions, rendering it difficult if not impossible to convey a sense of stable ethnolinguistic geography. They, like others, were a people in continuous motion. Even the mapping of Akan-speaking habitation patterns in the 17th and 18th centuries becomes more complicated, considering the 'Akanization' of people from a variety of language communities conquered by Akan polities or through the more benign adoption of Akan as a political or commercial lingua franca. Due to many intersecting political and sociocultural processes, many peoples throughout the littoral and near-inland regions of the Gold Coast were familiar with Akan or a mutually intelligible dialect and could likely speak it as a secondary or tertiary language by the early 18th century.

Though many Akan traditions of origin speak of ancestors who descended from the sky or from under bodies of water, the corpus of "terrestrial" genesis traditions—in which the first people originated from underground—point in useful historical and archaeological directions. Due to the precision of the geographic locales at which Akan ancestors sprang from the ground, Wilks hypothesized that they represent "exact sites where farming began" in the 13th or 14th century. Some of the earliest Akan materials—including ceramics and samples of charcoal, were also discovered and were carbon dated to 800—930 C.E. In the "long memory" represented by Akan oral traditions, the sites where their ancestors emerged from the ground may have actually represented the point of settlement after lengthy migrations from elsewhere.

Though several writers have theorized the Akan people originated from the ancient kingdom of Ghana, these claims have been largely unsubstantiated. While origin stories and histories linking Akan-speaking peoples to migrations from Ghana and Egypt require imaginative leaps, a handful of oral traditions make more reasonable claims that Akan speakers originated somewhere in the north from either the "Great White Desert" or the Sahelian and savannah regions of Atlantic Africa.

Another set of traditions centers on the town or state of Adanse. Originating from the north to inhabit the forest fringe, Akan speakers arrived at what became Adanse and created a permanent settlement. Other traditions tell of Adanse as the very site of Akan-speaking origin and the place where their sky god, *Jamcompon*, began the project of creating the world and humanity. This is situated south of Kumasi, east of Denkyira and west of Akyem. Adanse's central locale in what became the Akan heartland perhaps explains its central place in oral traditions as the home of most Akan clans. Adense appears in several oral histories, and now in written accounts by professional historians, as one of the 5 great towns of pre-Atlantic Akan-speaking states. 17th and 18th century map makers frequently located "Acanji" or "Akanni"—the alleged home of the Akani or Akanist community of gold merchants—at or near Adanse. Whether Adanse was previously the capital of a centralized Akan kingdom or a pseudonym for an "Akanni" state may not be as important as the place in the collective Akan consciousness of this region as birth home to most, if not all, icons of Akan political culture—including court linguists (*akyeame*) and swords of state. Even now, many Akan-speaking clans trace their origins to Adanse, which is often said to be the "first Akan state" or the place where Akan speakers built the first houses in oral traditions. Recent archaeological findings support some of these claims. According to Brian Vivian, archaeological analyses conducted in the 1990s "from the site of Adansemanso indicate that a significant level of cultural complexity was attained within the central forest region of Ghana 2—3 centuries earlier than previously thought." This places the origins of Adanse in the 12th or 13th century, which greatly conflicts with the former view held by a range of historians that Akan polities first developed near the forest fringe as late as the 15th century. In sum, the archaeological record and the various oral traditions about the primacy and centrality of Adanse mostly concur.

Ga speakers inhabited a much more circumscribed and less fluid ethnolinguistic geography. According to Carl Reindorf, a Ga-speaking Basel missionary who collected several Ga oral traditions in the early- to mid-19th century, Ga refers specifically to "the people and country bounded on the east by the lagoon Tshemu near Tema, west by the [Lesser Sakumo River], south by the sea, and north by the Akwapem mountains." Representing about 30 miles of coastline and radiating out from its political and geographic center at Accra, the region inhabited by Ga speakers—the Accra Plains—was tiny in comparison to the lands of their far more numerous and geographically spread Akan-speaking neighbors. Their close physical proximity to, and long historical domination by, their Akan neighbors shaped fundamental aspects of Ga-speaking littoral communities. One example, among many, appears in the very naming of the Ga capital at Accra. The Ga name for the polity Accra is "Ga;" among Akan speakers, both the town and people were called "Nkran" (Accra)—a reference to a particular species of swarming ant and an Akan translation of the word "Ga". As a "powerful wandering tribe" that invaded other lands and subdued their inhabitants, Ga speakers named themselves after a species of invasive dark-brown ants that "wander about in great swarms and invade houses, killing and devouring every living thing they meet," according to Reindorf. While Ga speakers used the reference to swarming ants to connote military prowess and their ancient conquest of Guang speakers residing in the Accra Plains, the Akan-speaking appropriation and translation of this metaphor had a less than generous meaning. Instead of viewing Ga speakers as a formidable military force, the Akan-speaking term "Nkran" cast Ga peoples as pests or nuisances to be controlled or exterminated.

Both linguistic evidence and Ga oral traditions concur that Ga speakers migrated from what is now northern Nigeria, presumably to escape military and religious incursions by a Fulani sovereign. Another set of oral traditions claim that Ga and Adanme speakers migrated together or separately from either Tetetutu or Sameh in the east—both provinces of the kingdom of Benin. According to Parker, the fact that no archaeological findings support the linguistic evidence and oral traditions may mean that the migration trope should be interpreted as a metaphor for "their gradual rise to demographic, linguistic, and political ascendancy over neighboring Guang-speaking peoples." Though Ga is now lumped in with Akan, Adanme, and Ewe as part of the Western Kwa family of languages due to vast similarities in vocabulary, phonology, and grammar, this modern classification muddles a historical process in which Ga-speaking peoples and polities suffered military defeat at the hands of, and political domination by, a sequence of expansionist Akan-speaking polities. Over the course of 3 centuries, Ga speakers absorbed aspects of the cultures of their conquerors and neighbors. The significant amounts of cross-fertilization and linguistic intrusion between Ga and Akan obfuscates modern-day language classification systems, that don't take into the past. A plausible case then can be made that strong linguistic links between Ga, Adanme, and Ewe—for example—point to an earlier common proto-language that originated to the east of the Gold Coast. In this scenario, Ga, Adanme and Ewe may have more ancient, historical connections between each other that were not shared with Akan before the 14th or 15th century.

The Onset of the Gold Coast Diaspora

Perhaps the first real evil of the Transatlantic traffic in flesh was the social death suffered by its many victims. Nothing captures this truth better than the story of a Fante youth who went on to become one of the most strident abolitionist voices of the 18th century. When Quobna Ottobah Cugoano, "born in the city of Agimaque (Ajumako) on the coast of Fantyn" in 1757, remembered his life before his forced Atlantic sojourn and the months of toil in a Grenada slave gang, his focus centered on forever severed familial and social relations. Indeed, his recollections of his Gold Coast home moved immediately to his father, who served as a close companion and confidant to the Ajumakohene, perhaps in the capacity of caboceer or other court official. When the king died, his successor—Ajumakohene Ambro Accasa—sent for the young Cugoano to live with him at the royal court among his own children. After about 2 years in Accasa's court, Cugoano departed for an extended visit with his uncle, who had a residence 3 day's journey to the west of Ajumako near Assini. Three months with his uncle led Cugoano to consider returning back to his family and friends in Ajumako, but he notes, "By this time I had got well acquainted with some of the children of my uncle's hundreds of relations." In extending his stay with his uncle and other kin, Cugoano became caught up in the machinations of Atlantic commerce.

Captured in 1770 at the age of 13 with some 20 other children, Cugoano was sold to a European trader for a gun, a bolt of cloth, and some lead shot. His transformation from subject to object, from person to thing, and from social life to death continued after being warehoused and then later at Cape Coast Castle. His vain hopes that Ajumakohene Accasa would learn about his plight and redeem him led to heartbreaking despair when the realization of his fate finally dawned upon the young Cugoano:

> Let it suffice to say, that I was thus lost to my dear indulgent
> parents and relations, and they to me. All my help was cries
> and tears, and these could not avail; nor suffered long, till one
> succeeding woe, and dread, swelled up another. Brought from
> a state of innocence and freedom, and, in a barbarous and cruel

121

manner, conveyed to a state of horror and slavery: This abandoned situation may be easier conceived than described. From the
time that I was kidnapped and conducted to a factory, and from
thence in the brutish, base, but fashionable way of traffic, consigned to Grenada, the grievous thoughts which I then felt, still pant
in my heart.

However, the anguish of social death was not a totalizing experience for
enslaved captives. This notion, present in so much of the historiography,
limits the possibilities and range of human agency. For Cugoano, though he
deemed it a personal shame that some among his own "countrymen" had
captured and sold him to Europeans, his new life in Grenada was perhaps
made slightly more bearable by the many new companions with whom he
could speak Akan and form new connections and even a new sense of
community citizenship. No longer did Fante, Ajumako, or Assini have
currency or serve as viable identities or identifiers in Cugoano's mind. By
the time this "Son of Africa" penned his autobiographical account in 1787,
he could proclaim a new identity as "A Native of the Gold Coast, Africa." This
shift from natal alienation and physical separation from Ajumako to a
diasporic citizenship in the Black Atlantic, based on a broad Gold Coast
geography, found resonance with many untold thousands who experienced
similar Atlantic journeys.

There were many mechanisms that brought about the Gold Coast
diaspora in the 1760s. Indeed, there were very traceable patterns of the
many flows and fluctuations of Gold Coast and Atlantic commerce that
produced concentrations of people familiar with Akan languages and
cultures in specific locales throughout the Western Hemisphere. The very
mechanisms of slave procurement employed in the region before
approximately 1765 determined the fact that a significant proportion of
enslaved Gold Coast Africans were largely concentrated in British, Dutch,
and Danish colonies in the Americas during the 18th century—a fact
corroborated by the Du Bois Institute slave trade dataset. In the century

1665—1765, for example, 78% of all Gold Coast Africans that embarked on slave ships were destined for British, Dutch, and Danish possessions in the Western Hemisphere. The common bond they shared in the Americas was Akan, and this would mean that the existence of broad language communities they encountered on slave plantations would facilitate the ethnogenesis of Coromantee and (A)mina.

Rucker has produced comprehensive work which illustrates the common and linked geographies of slave trading in the Gold Coast and the Americas. His work details the Akanization of Ga-, Adanme-, and Ewe-speaking peoples and polities and the spread of Akan as a political and commercial lingua franca. Thus, the contention Rucker forwarded is that most Gold Coast Africans transported to the Americas knew Akan as a primary, secondary, or even tertiary language. This common thread and the heavy concentrations of Gold Coast Africans in specific circum-Caribbean and mainland colonies served as catalysts to ethnogenesis. Moreover, the dominance of Akan cultures in the Gold Coast meant that the influence of Akan-speaking peoples and polities went well beyond their languages. Aspects of their naming practices, religions, folkloric traditions, and political cultures became overlays in addition to—but not replacing or obliterating—the cultures of Ga, Adanme, and Ewe speakers. These levels of cultural interplay and exchange prefigured the kinds of collaborative enterprises Akan, Ga, Adanme and Ewe speakers engaged in after their New World sojourns.

Connected directly to language and linguistic Akanization, the spread and adoption of the Akan day-naming system throughout the Gold Coast represents another cultural tie linking what should be vastly diverse peoples and polities. Romer stated that the typical greeting given to Europeans living in and near Accra was based on the assumption that all Christians were born on a Sunday. Whether or not day-naming began as a uniquely Akan-speaking concept before spreading to others in the Gold Coast and beyond may be impossible to discover, especially given how intimately tangled cultures and peoples in the region became over time and through sustained contact. With this stated, it is likely that the Ga and later Ewe adoptions of day-names had their genesis among Akan-speaking neighbors and conquerors. Clues to this are embedded in Ga oral traditions claiming that the Ga-speaking settlers at Accra originally developed a calendrical system based on an 8-day week. By the 18th century, Ga-speakers not only adopted a 7-day week, but also used the 7 days of the week as the basis for part of the naming process for newborns. From his time in Ga-speaking Accra, Romer notes specifically that "each week every Negro has his own sacred day, the day on which he was born." Paul Erdmann Isert, a much later authority than Romer on naming practices in Ga-speaking Accra, wrote in 1788, "When a child is 14 days old a feast is held in order to give him a name. . . . Normally they have 2 names: the one taken from the day on which they were born, and the other given by the family."

Thus, day-names, or names assigned based on the day of the week on which a child was born, become not only a unique mark of Akan cultures in the Gold Coast, but also a cultural vector that helps trace the extent of Akanization. Perhaps the most insightful example of the use and embrace of Akan day-names among non-Akan speakers is the story of Cudjo (Kojo), a chief broker and caboceer of the Royal African Company based at James Fort in English Accra and the first *Alata Akutso Mantse* (or Alata division head). Cudjo, originally a Yoruba speaker from Allada named Ojo, was imported to Accra to serve as an enslaved worker at James Fort. Mastering English, Ga, and Akan, Cudjo quickly rose through the social ranks from enslaved laborer to wage-earning linguist and, ultimately, Royal African Company caboceer. By 1748, he ascended to a royal stool in Accra, becoming the head of the Alata quarter in James Town—a position his descendants continue to hold to this day. Not only did Cudjo adopt the Akan day-name for a child born on Monday, but also, he embraced the annual Akan Odwira festival procession. In many ways, the story of Cudjo epitomizes the degree and type of cultural transmutations characteristic of coastal and border cultures throughout Atlantic Africa.

In the intersecting realms of religion and folklore, Akan concepts dominated the Gold Coast regions in which Akan-speaking peoples and polities spread by the 18th century. This aspect of culture assumes elevated importance, as one 18th century observer noted, because "a people's nature and customs usually flow from their religion." In the case of Akan religions in the Gold Coast, the lack of uniform understanding of the otherworldly among their varied adherents—partly due to the absence of a unifying set of sacred texts—did not prevent several European observers from making extensive and sometimes insightful commentary.

Observing the religious values of the mostly Ga-speaking inhabitants of Accra, Romer demonstrates the penetration of Akan spiritual concerns and beliefs among non-Akan speakers as well as the multiple intersections between folklore and religion. In his discussion of the "universal spirit" and creator of the world among "All the negroes" in the Gold Coast, Romer states that this being's name was known as "Niumboo." Rask, another resident of Accra, noted that "The Akras call god Jungo, and the Aqvambues call god Jankumpung." In other 17th- and 18th-century records, the various renderings of the name of the sky god of creation in the Gold Coast include "Jan Commae," "Jan Comme," "Jancompon," "Iuan goemain," "Iancome," and "Yancumpong." In the modern Ga and Akan orthography, the sky god is rendered as *Nyonmo* (Ga), *Nyankon* (Akan), or simply *Nyame* (Akan).

In addition to the appearance of the Akan god of creation in the religious worldviews of Ga and Adanme speakers, one of Jancompon's subordinates—Ananse or Nanni—provided a vital bridge between religion and folkloric traditions. First mentioned in European accounts by Bosman as "Spider Ananse," this mysterious entity often appears associated by Akan speakers and others with the creation of humanity and with a set of didactic tales. While Bosman and other supposedly "better informed" Europeans sought to instruct Akan speakers they encountered about the impossibility

125

of a spider creating the first humans, he bemoaned the fact that "a great Number . . . remain of that Opinion, out of which Folly they are not to be reason'd." In his words, their faith in the powers of Spider Ananse was the "greatest Piece of Ignorance and Stupidty," especially considering that the Christian logic of Edenic gardens, forbidden fruits, and talking serpents should have been much more convincing to any reasonable listener. In sharp contrast, Romer offers a more extensive and nuanced commentary about the figure he refers to as "Nanni," explaining in full the religious and folkloric dimensions of the trickster spider.

Romer's version of Nanni came to him by way of Ga speakers in Accra, though the story has clear ties to Akan religious concepts and cultures. In this rendition, Nanni creates humanity out of woven cloth at the behest of the Akan sky god Jancompon. Instead of humanity appreciating Nanni, they ran in fear upon seeing her. With the extra cloth remaining, Nanni created another being—a male spider in her own image—and even named the new entity Nanni. It was this anthropomorphic spider, the male Nanni, who would become the subject of a corpus of didactic folktales in Akan-, Ga-, and Adanme-speaking regions of the Gold Coast. Compared by Romer to Ulenspeyl, a prankster character in German literature, Nanni ultimately becomes a trickster; his stories were acted out "in moonlight, sitting out of doors, 50 in a circle, while the old people tell the young about this Nanni." In the sample of a Nanni story given by Romer, Nanni does not resemble his more heroic diasporic counterpart in the 18th- and 19th-century British Caribbean. Instead of being depicted as a clever and witty hero, champion, and rebel against those who would abuse their power over the weak, Nanni in the story presented by Romer is wealthy, with many wives and children, yet lazy and greedy. In the end, Nanni has his hands amputated after a particularly petty and selfish act of theft. When his wives threaten to leave due to his weakened state, Nanni impersonates the voice of an oracle to convince them to return. In sum, Nanni and his associated tales serve as both a measure of the Akanization of populations in and near Accra and as a

126

backdrop against which diasporic folktales about Ananse the Spider—imbued, as they were, with the commoner consciousness—can be compared.

With some certainty, it is possible to trace the presence of Jancompon and Nanni among Akan peoples and polities and regions touched by Akanization throughout the early-modern Gold Coast. 17th and 18th century Akan religions and spiritual worldviews lacked any sort of uniformity, making a comprehensive description using contemporary sources close to impossible. In very broad outlines, Akan religions as practiced during the height of the Atlantic slave trade may have incorporated a handful of common features. The world of the Akan speakers was filled with spiritual forces to the degree that a sense of spiritual causality could explain most abnormal events. As Bosman observed, many coastal peoples believed in "nothing uncommon ever happening which is not attributed to some Miracle or another." He concluded that even "Death is never without a Cause." Mysterious deaths, illnesses, and bad or good fortune could be attributable to the activation of spiritual forces or the ancestors by an aggrieved party. Accidents or luck, therefore, would always have spiritual explanations. In these worldviews, there was no sharp line of distinction between the material and spiritual planes of existence. Few boundaries existed between the realms, allowing spiritual forces to permeate every area of life for Akan-speaking peoples and others in the Gold Coast. In this regard, while Jancompon was the omnipotent sky god, this entity remained distant and removed from its creation. Few if any priest- or priestess-hoods, shrines, and sacred groves honored the sky god directly. As one 17th century observer noted, because Jancompon was "righteous and good" and could do "no-one any harm," adherents of Akan religions deemed it unnecessary to worship or pray to him. Instead, a constellation of personal, local, and lesser deities, ancestral spirits, and oracles—collectively known as *bossum* (or *obosum* in the modern orthography)—became the recipients of prayers, sacrifices, libations, and

127

requests of various sorts by supplicants. Bossum or "fetisso," could represent an entire polity (as in the cases of Nananom Mpow or Lakpa), a lineage, or a household; they provided protection or could be activated as weapons to be used against enemies. Bossum played important roles in a hierarchically arranged spiritual universe among Akan speakers and others in the 17th and 18th century Gold Coast.

Another spiritual force that had personal uses and applications was a category known as suman. While bossum and suman seemed to overlap, at least in the mind of Muller, the latter refers to a more general type of protective spirit used as a "special domestic idol." Whereas bossum were attended to by a host of priests and priestesses—known variably in the 17th century Gold Coast *o-bossum-fu*, *comfu*, or *sophu*—and had shrines or sacred groves constructed in their honor, suman can be understood as personal ritual objects imbued with varying levels of spiritual power. This belief system was decentralized and mostly unregulated by polities; any supplicant could inherit, purchase, steal, or otherwise acquire a suman. Once activated, these objects had the potential of allowing anyone—from peasants to nobles—to tap into empowering and powerful forces. According to Muller, suman was the domain of a unique priesthood known as the *summan-fu*, who were "highly honored, but not as highly as *o-bossum-fu*," probably because they lacked state sanction and approval. Given the personal, quotidian, and even democratic nature of beliefs associated with suman, this complex of spiritual concepts survived Atlantic passages to the Americas and became a vital base for the worldviews of Gold Coast Africans in the New World. Suman and the Western Hemisphere system known as obeah became dimensions and extensions of the commoner consciousness as articulated throughout the 18th century Caribbean and mainland.

Beyond religion and folklore, another aspect of Akanization and the spreading influence of Akan-speaking politics becomes readily apparent in the political cultures throughout the Gold Coast. As far east as the Volta region, Akan concepts of matrilineal descent, stools, military formations

128

(e.g., the three-wing formation innovated by Akwamu), and asafo companies became hallmarks of Anlo-Ewe political and military culture by the early 19th century. Certainly, the Akwamu conquest and absorption of Ewe speaking states to the west of the Volta—Anlo, Little Pop, and Krepi—and its later and long-standing alliance with Anlo played a significant role in the adoption of Akan political and military cultures among Ewe-speaking polities extensively borrowed aspects from the military and political cultures of their Akan neighbors and conquerors. Indeed, given the longer history of Akan suzerainty in and around the Accra Plains, the interpenetration of Akan cultures was deeper among Ga- and Adanme-speaking people and polities. These people and polities, for example, adopted asafo companies and other forms of Akan military organization, matrilineal descent systems, and the Akan "paraphernalia of power"—stools, state swords, umbrellas, and palanquins.

As in the Ewe case, the adoption of Akan matrilineal descent was a sharp break from the cultural patterns established by both Guang and Ga speakers in Accra. Reindorf notes, for example, that "originally the inheritance in both the Guan and Ga races was by male line; but this was converted into the Twi [Akan] system during the time of the temporal reigns of Ofori and a few of the Akan kings." Such a fundamental change in sociopolitical culture among Ga speakers and other residents of Accra signals how deeply Akan and Ga concepts became intertwined with each other. Indeed, Reindorf—a Ga speaking resident of Accra who collected a number of Ga oral traditions in composing his *History of the Gold Coast and Asante*—credits a range of Asantehene with the creation of Accra asafo "bands" organized in every Ga-speaking town in the Accra Plains. Not only was the very organization of asafo militia companies in Ga towns an Akan cultural intervention, but the company names, their "symbolical mottoes," and their sigils or various "designs displayed by the bands . . . in the flags, swords, and state umbrellas" all bore the stamp of coastal Akan cultures.

Beyond all other markers of Akan political cultures in the Gold Coast, state and personal oaths and oathing ceremonies became central features, serving, ideally, as inviolable contracts for states, state and commercial actors, or armies. In most cases, taking an oath was a sacred act that involved eating or drinking substances believed by adherents to contain sufficient spiritual potency to kill anyone taking the oath on false pretense or breaking the terms of a sworn agreement. The ubiquitous practice of eating or imbibing during an oathing ritual led to the European description of an Akan oath as "eating fetish." In some descriptions, someone wishing to prove their innocence when accused of a criminal offense would be subjected to an oathing test or ordeal in which they would eat salt or bread on top of a ritual object—probably a personal suman of the accuser or the "fetisso" or bossum of a town or larger polity.

In a tangible sense, the related processes of capture and enslavement can be best symbolized as a sort of death for those suffering this fate. Following the logic of Orlando Patterson and others, the levels of violence and disruption involved in being torn from kin and kith only to be redefined as commodities to be traded and bartered—a sharp and abrupt discontinuity of a former existence—can only be described with the finality implied by death. As soul-rending as the processes of capture and enslavement had to be for their many victims, one should avoid overestimating the effects of social death as part of the continuity of experiences for Gold Coast commoners throughout the Black Atlantic. Cugoano, for instance, found some semblance of community among his Akan-speaking countrymen in Grenada and a sense of a transnational community citizenship in his life in freedom in the wider Black Atlantic. His example was representative of larger realities for many in the Gold Coast diaspora.

Outside of nobles enslaved after the defeat or collapse of their polity, the vast majority of those who suffered social death in the Gold Coast came from the lower orders of what were rigidly hierarchical societies. The 5 degrees or classes of Gold Coast peoples, as discussed by Bosman, did not suffer enslavement, humiliation, and social death evenly. Indeed, the first, second, and third degrees—kings, caboceers, and nobles, or *obirempong*—instigated expansionist wars, controlled political offices, collected tribute payments, and bartered with European factors and merchant companies to the disadvantage of the commoners and slaves who inhabited the fourth and fifth degrees. In reaping the benefits of those who were "imployed [sic] in the Tillage of Wines, Agriculture and Fishing" while forcing others into slavery through foreign acquisition and purchase, war, and debt, the various classes of Gold Coast elites presided over systems of exploitation that generated expanding pools of dependent and forced labor. Peasants living in rural hamlets undergirded expansionist city-states and kingdoms as the product of their collective labor fueled and fed wars that were often initiated by the wealthy and high-born but fought by the poor and dependent.

As Kea notes, there were "two categories of people that determined the continued social-economic existence of the *abirempon* [hereditary nobles] and the *afahane* [wealthy elite] as an upper class: retainers and free commoners." Within the hierarchical and corporatist structure of 17th and 18th-century Gold Coast states, kings, caboceers, and nobles conceived of their polities as "families" in which 'social lessers'—servants, retainers, and slaves—became part of a metaphorical kin simply as a means of providing the labor and social wealth necessary for elites to maintain their status and power. They were, in this sense, the hands that tilled and the feet that transported goods to market sustaining a body politic headed by ennobled economic and political elites. Though not comprising a class of dependent labor, even free commoners could be considered as essential elements in the ability of elites to define and retain power. In many ways, commoners became "pawns" to be acquired by nobility and other elites through the control of political offices. As a "class of political dependents or subjects," commoners—including petty farmers, fishermen, craftsmen, soldiers, market sellers, and low-ranking priests and priestess—generated revenues for political elites in the form of levies, tribute payments (in specie and in kind), and through a variety of specialized labor services. In the course of the slave trade, it would be among the poor, the downtrodden, the political or economic dependents, and the non-elite that new worlds across the Atlantic would be built. What would link them together would not just be a common range of dialects, languages, and broadly defined cultural practices. They became connected through a common consciousness that could be defined by a set of cultural and political performances that articulated distinctively subaltern worldviews.

Ultimately, the Gold Coast slave trade was made through commercial interests and networks on both sides of the Atlantic. In the castles and forts, the holds of slavers, and the slave pens and plantations, enslaved Gold Coast commoners became keenly aware of their new circumstances. In the process of Atlantic commerce, they proved the possibility of a social life after social death—forming connections with ever-widening circles of captives that went far beyond the shipmate bonds discussed by Mintz and Price. Slave ships were, in this sense, means of conveyance from one continent to others. They can even be understood as preindustrial "factories" that produced labor for plantation societies in the Americas. However, imaginings of slave ships literally giving birth to African-American peoples and cultures go a bit too far. The reality for Gold Coast Africans was that they were warehoused, shipped, and disembarked with others from the same speech communities and, in some cases, villages, and even kinship groups. Their cultures would not be forged in the belly of Atlantic seafaring beasts, or the liminal space represented by the middle passage, but within the context of both the Gold Coast past and the New World present.

In the continuum of realities that existed during the course of the Atlantic slave trade, there seem to be 2 radically different, yet characteristic historical poles. On one end of the spectrum, the specific and patterned trade link between one Atlantic African port of call and another in the Americas allowed for heavy concentrations of particular language cohorts in distinct Western Hemisphere regions. This appears to be the case in the much-studied link between Bunce Island off the coast of Sierra Leone and the coastal and Sea Island regions of South Carolina in the period between 1740 and 1800. The influx of rice producers from Greater Senegambia in general and Sierra Leone specifically meant that the resulting cultural matrix—Gullah and Geechee—was not due to the purposeful randomization of Atlantic African language or ethnic groups by European slavers and planters. While Gullah and Geechee borrowed a substantial amount of cultural material from West-Central African charter generations who predominated before the 1739 Stono revolt, the number of Mande loan words, the reliance on the knowledge of rice cultivation and livestock herding, and other markers of these unique cultures point to a Greater Senegambian provenance for the more recent threads woven into these rich cultural tapestries in the South Carolina Lowcountry. Ironically, Greater Senegambia may have been one of the most linguistically and culturally diverse Atlantic African slave trading regions. The diversity, however, was outweighed—at least in the case of coastal and Sea Island South Carolina— by the very focused and narrow Atlantic connections formed in the 18th century.

Sharply contrasting with the trade networks linking Greater Senegambia to South Carolina would be the much more chaotic trading experiences associated with various West-Central African ports of call and the destinations they "fed" with black flesh throughout the Western Hemisphere. In this case, over a number of decades the slave trading networks reached far into hinterland regions in West-Central Africa, bringing dozens of peoples and polities into the pull of Transatlantic commerce. The combined coastal and inland regions of West-Central Africa totaled more than 2.5 million square kilometers, and it was from this massive region that enslaved captives were drawn. Even if many of the language cohorts in this vast region spoke Bantu dialects, these were not always mutually intelligible and the amount of cultural homogeneity in the region has been greatly exaggerated by a range of scholars. Over time, the slave trade in West-Central Africans experienced much more scattered dispersal patterns in the Western Hemisphere, owing in part to their overrepresentation in the import and disembarkation statistics for the entire slave trade. As they accounted for more than 40% of all Western Hemisphere imports throughout the course of the slave trade, it would be difficult to show how they could be principally concentrated in any region outside of Brazil.

The Gold Coast trade, in the continuum of slave trading experiences, can be situated between the 2 poles represented by Greater Senegambia and West-Central Africa. If Greater Senegambia represents a culturally diverse yet focused Atlantic stream—especially into South Carolina, Georgia, and Louisiana—and West Central Africa a less culturally diverse and more scattered import pattern, the 18th century Gold Coast trade was both less diverse (owing to Akanization and the smaller scale of its coastal and inland trade networks) and meticulously patterned with heavy disembarkation concentrations in 18th century British, Dutch, and Danish circum-Caribbean colonies. With this said, 3 identifiable phases of the Gold Coast trade characterized the involvement of the region with Atlantic commerce from the time of the early Portuguese and other European goods and later enslaved peoples from the Slave Coast and West-Central Africa in exchange for gold mined in the Gold Coast Forest belt. As abovementioned, it would be during this phase that a number of near inland and coastal polities sought to gain control over trade roads—the vital commercial arteries in the region— to the coast and mines in the forest interior as a means of maximizing their economic, political, and military dominance over others.

Expansionist Akan-speaking polities in the Gold Coast—through their very actions—helped to inaugurate a shift in trade patters with European interests along the Coast and the rise of a new phase (1700—1760) in their involvement in Atlantic commerce. Polities that fought over control of trade roads, attempting to monopolize the commercial networks connecting interior gold mines to European factors and merchant companies at the coast, shifted to procuring and selling captives. During this second phase, the Gold Coast became a net exporter of slaves for the first time. In addition, the principal Gold Coast slave catchment shifted from the Slave Coast to the coastal and near-inland regions of the Gold Coast. This limited geographic zone for slave procurement meant that most of the enslaved peoples exported to the Western Hemisphere during this period knew Akan, facilitating their ability to connect with others from the Gold Coast shortly after disembarkation and to create viable language communities in the Americas. It was during this phase of the Gold Coast slave trade that the heavy concentrations of Akan-speaking peoples in particular locales in the Americas would spawn the creation of Coromantee and (A)mina identities and cultures.

The second phase of the slave trade shifted to a third and final phase (1760—1807) due to the actions of the Asante kingdom and expansionist Asantehene beginning with Opoku Ware. As the kingdom widened its sphere of influence, 2 related processes shifted the slave catchment regions from the coast and near inland to the northern reaches of the Gold Coast. First, the Asante kingdom expanded north, conquering a number of polities, and establishing a new "recruitment" pool for slave labor. In this case, hinterland slave markets, like Salaga in Burkina Faso, grew rapidly as the Gold Coast north and the Asante kingdom's capital at Kumasi became important hubs of Transatlantic commerce in black flesh. Along the coast, the multistate Fante coalition—which formed earlier in the 18th century— stood as the only force that could effectively repulse military incursion and political domination by Asante. With the spread of community and state militias or asafo companies, many towns, and smaller polities along the coast and near inland developed defense mechanisms against slave raiding and "panyarring" (kidnapping) that had plagued them between 1700 and 1760. The northern shift that characterized this final phase of the Gold Coast slave trade meant that a growing number of enslaved peoples embarking on European slavers came from non-Akan speaking groups—including

Tchamba speakers and others—in the northern regions. As a result, part of the lasting discourse of the slave trade in the imaginary of modern Ghanaians is that all or most slaves—during the long chronology of the slave trade—were northerners not directly related to coastal and mostly Akan-speaking populations. They were deemed collectively to be *donkor*, a term that implies northern Gold Coast origins and other more unfortunate attributes, including barbarians, stupid and uncouth. As Saidiya Hartman notes, 19th century Asante law held that by definition the term *donkor* was "applied to any man or woman, other than an Asante, who had been purchased with the express purpose of making him or her a slave." They became the quintessential "other"—a group that could be alienated and enslaved without generating sympathy or remorse in the more contemporary discourse about the slave trade and its many legacies in the former Gold Coast.

The Du Bois dataset corroborates the claim that export streams from the Gold Coast were much narrower and more focused than previously assumed. As Douglas Chambers shows, 76% of all Gold Coast Africans embarked on European slavers destined for the Americas at just 2 ports—Anomabu and Cape Coast Castle. In this circumstance, the trade activities of both Fante and British traders become central to commercial patterns emanating from the 18th century Gold Coast. While many scholars have emphasized the role of the Asante kingdom in the Gold Coast trade, Asante did not ascend to military and political dominance in the region until the reign of Asantehene Opoku Ware. In addition, it was not until 1744 that Asante controlled the major trade roads from the Gold Coast interior to the coastal trade centers. In sum, because Asante did not monopolize the supply end of the slave trade until after the 1750s, an unspecifiable but sizeable majority of Gold Coast Africans involved in the slave trade between 1680 and 1760 were Akan-speaking or from regions along the coast and the near inland that had experienced a significant amount of Akanization.

Though the Gold Coast was a net importer of slaves through the 1690s, this reality quickly changed during the first decade of the 18th century. This picture becomes acutely obvious when assessing the outflow of enslaved peoples embarking on ships at particular Gold Coast ports of call. In the 50-year period after 1700, the number of slaves embarked on European ships at Cape Coast, Elmina, Accra/Christiansborg, and Anomabu grew exponentially—ranging from two- to ten-fold increases. This massive expansion in slave trading operations did not result in more scattered patterns of import clustering in colonies linked to the merchant companies housed at the many castles, forts, and lodges built along the Gold Coast. In addition, enslaved Gold Coast Africans—a factor that influenced import concentrations and the active reshaping of import populations through the transshipment trade.

On both sides of the Atlantic, the Gold Coast slave trade—both exports and imports—can be characterized as regular and patterned, particularly during the second phase (1700—1760) of this commercial network. While the slave trade can be characterized as patterned, allowing for clusters of coastal and near inland peoples in the Gold Coast on European slave ships, this patterned flow of people across the Atlantic was mirrored in the ports of disembarkation in the Western Hemisphere. Enslaved Akan, Ga, Adanme, and Ewe speakers from the Gold Coast became concentrated in British, Dutch, and Danish colonies in the Americas during the 18th century; strong evidence for this can be found in the Du Bois slave trade dataset. In the century between 1665 and 1765, more than 78% (286,755 of 369,165) of all enslaved Gold Coast Africans boarded ships destined for British, Dutch, and Danish colonies in the Americas. More specifically, between 1700 and 1765, Gold Coast Africans represented significant percentages of Atlantic Africans disembarked in Curacao (14.8%), the Dutch Guianas (25%), Antigua (19%), Barbados (22.4%), Jamaica (26.9%), British Guiana (31.7%), and the Danish West Indies (46.6%).

These import figures reflect the dominating positions British, Dutch and

Danish trade companies had ever the many castles, forts, lodges, and other trading posts along the Gold Coast during the 18th century as well as the coastal ship trade near Fante-controlled Anomabu. In addition, these import figures include free traders, not connected to specific trade companies, from a range of Europe nations. However, disembarkation figures from the slave trade dataset only offer a partial window into a much more complex demographic terrain in the Gold Coast diaspora. For a range of reasons, Gold Coast import estimates are skewed downward, and heavier concentrations of enslaved peoples with some knowledge of Akan language were more likely to be the historical reality in the British, Dutch and Danish Caribbean and mainland.

Alone, the disembarkation percentages of enslaved Gold Coast Africans do not tell a complete story. If these estimates are solely to be relied upon, the enslaved Gold Coast contingent in disembarkation regions like Jamaica, Antigua, Curacao, and Suriname would seem inconsequential in comparison to the numbers of Atlantic Africans from other regions. Even in 18th century, British, Dutch and Danish Caribbean and mainland colonies, disembarkations from the Gold Coast could be dwarfed by imports from the Bight of Biafra and West-Central Africa.

As abovementioned, the enslaved speakers of Akan, Ga, Adanme, and Ewe did not meet for the first time during the processes in which they became Atlantic commodities and dehumanized "pieces," units, or heads. Therefore, the ethnogenesis of Coromantee and (A)mina peoples in the Americas, then, was not a product of embarkation or disembarkation, but their identity can be seen as a Western Hemisphere extension of an ongoing cultural process that was rooted deeply in the *longue durée* of Gold Coast history. The invention of Coromantee specifically, in the mind of Europeans, began in the associations that English and Dutch merchants drew between the coastal Fante towns of Kormantse and the captured men and women exported to their New World possessions. By the 1660s, the 'Coromantee' ethnic referent came into usage in the English colonies of Barbados and Suriname.

138

Coromantee diasporic characteristics include obeah, Ananse the Spider, loyalty oaths, Akan day-names, among others.

In the late-17th century British Caribbean and South American mainland, Coromantee could evoke an almost instantaneous set of mental images and assumptions of behavioral characteristics. The details of the 1675 Barbados plot led by "Coromantee or Gold Coast Negro's"—when combined with Behn's colorful description of the Coromantee of Suriname—further reinforced the idea of them as a group of noble and brave savages. Indeed, the governor of Barbados at the time of the conspiracy, Jonathan Atkins, noted that the plot was hatched "especially amongst the Cormantin negroes, who are much the greater number from any country, and are a warlike and robust people." On 12th June 1675, the Barbados Coromantees crowned a king named Cuffee, "an Ancient Gold [Coast] Negroe," precipitating a plan to set fire to sugar cane fields and kill as many whites as possible. This "Design amongst them the Cormantee Negro's to kill all the Baccararoes or White People in the Island within a fortnight" was betrayed when a young Coromantee woman named Fortuna overheard one of her countrymen attempting to recruit other Gold Coast Africans into the rebellious designs. After a series of trials, a number of the ringleaders were found guilty, and the courts sentenced 35 to a variety of torturous executions. When one conspirator, chained to a stake and awaiting death by fire, attempted to divulge the details of the plot, he was chided by a fellow countryman named Tony, who gave a grisly reminder of the fate of those already found to be connected to the plot: "Thou Fool, are there not enough of our Country-men killed already? Art thou minded to kill them all?" To this, the betrayer fell silent and the crowd of spectators— incensed by the effect of Tony's words—taunted, "We shall see you fry bravely by and by." Tony's response reveals the source of Coromantee bravery and tolerance for pain and torture; he replied, "If you Roast me to day, you cannot Roast me tomorrow." The person recording this exchange between Tony and the white onlookers opined that Coromantees believe "that after their death they go into their own Country." Transmigration, played a critical role in helping constitute one of the key behavioral traits associated with Coromantees and (A)minas in the Americas—their famed physical fortitude and pain tolerance.

The Kongolese of West Central Africa

The population of West Central Africa has always been low; it has been described as underpopulated, though the frequency with which famines occurred suggests otherwise. When the first Portuguese visitors reached the coast of West Central Africa, the Kongo kingdom was a substantial state, extending from the Zaire to Luanda Island. Its capital, Mbanza Kongo, later called Sao Salvador, was 200 kilometers inland. It had a population of approximately 500,000.

When the population of a given area expanded, it often led to a crisis—this happened in the Chokwe heartland in the mid-19th century, due to a buildup of the population by the acquisition of captive women. In good years, peopled tended to expand into marginal areas, but when the rains failed, they were forced back into the river valleys, often in a servile or client relationship. The coast was barren, and rainfall diminished steadily as one went south—hunger and drought are recurrent themes in the poetry of the Ovambo people of the northern Kalahari, on the southern margins of Angola.

One of the most striking facts to have emerged from the various statistical studies of the slave trade is the dominance of West Central Africa. It exported more slaves than any other region; while other areas, such as the Slave Coast or the Niger Delta, peaked at particular periods, it was of importance throughout the whole period of the slave trade. Possibly 40% of all slaves exported in the Atlantic trade came from Angola or the Congo River basin. This probably did not lead to absolute depopulation in the region as a whole, because the great majority of those exported were men, creating a gender imbalance which impacted both on marriage patterns and the distribution of work.

The introduction of New World crops, especially cassava and maize, helped sustain a denser population, but the dangers of the slave trade era encouraged settlement on mountain tops or in forests, chosen for their safety rather than for their suitability for cultivation. The Chokwe illustrate

141

the paradoxes which resulted; they opted for a forest home and their staple was cassava. Their name means, 'those who fled' (from the wars of the Ovimbundu), but in the late 19th century, they conquered much of the Lunda empire.

The history of West Central Africa societies in this period is shaped by a number of dominant themes: the impact of Atlantic trade, the varying exigencies of specific environments, and the profound cultural preferences which led some to opt for the vertical structures of the kingdom and others to prefer the horizontal linkages of ritual association. Some states were strengthened, at least in the short run, by external trade, and others were undermined by it.

The commerce between the coast and the interior was dominated by three trade routes. One great complex of trade canoe routes followed the Zaire and its many tributes, above Lake Malebo. Further south, land routes ran eastward from the ports of Luanda and Benguela, which were long dominated by the inland broker states of Kasanje and Matamba. The peoples of the small kingdoms of the Loango coast came to combine a broker role on the coast with caravan trade to Mpumbu, overlooking Lake Malebo; they developed a new identity as the *Vili*. The Bobangi, canoefarers on the Zaire above Mpumbu, developed an ethnic identity in the same way. The way in which the *Vili*, a coastal people, traveled inland was exceptional. It was more common for slaves or commodities to pass from one middleman to the next; since each exacted a profit, prices were inflated in the process. In the region which later became Gabon, goods were exchanged in a potlatch, a sequence of competitive exchanges of gifts.

Atlantic trade affected peoples who had never seen either a European or the sea. For centuries, the strangers were confined to the coast; even in Angola, they did not penetrate far inland. The first European to see the Zaire River above Lake Malebo was Stanley in 1877. But for centuries, inland peoples had heard rumors of strangers from the spirit world who purchased Africans in order to feed on their life force, who dyed cloth with their blood and processed their bones into gunpowder. Their king was Mwene Puto, Lord of the Dead. The Europeans had their own strange images of the African interior. 'No Christian has ever been there . . . The air is so unhealthy, that if a stranger travels by night by the light of the moon, his head will swell up and become as large as two.'

The slaving frontier and associated trade routes moved steadily to the east, until, in the 13th century, they reached what is now Zambia. Goods traveled vast distances from hand to hand—in the late 19th century it took as long as 5 years for a barrel of gunpowder from the coast to reach people living on the Zaire above the equator. And yet the lives of these distant villagers were profoundly affected by these changes.

The Foreign Factor and Kongo Slave Trade Origins

Slavery as an institution existed from the time that Kongo emerged as the dominant power in West Central Africa in the 14th century. By the time the Europeans had encountered the Kongo people, the region had grown over the preceding centuries to be highly developed and very complex. In this region a number of small principalities had coalesced into 3 states near the lower Zaire—the Loango, Kongo and Tio Kingdoms. The Kongo state was by far the largest. The Tio state was a confederacy of lords under a sacred king, north of the Zaire near Lake Maleo. Loango was the largest of 3 small kingdoms on what became known as the Loango coast; its people spoke a dialect of kiKongo. It is noteworthy that the 'Kongo' label does not refer to the Kongo Kingdom or the Bakongo people of the region; rather it is used as a generic term to refer to the linguistic and cultural area of the Kongo language zone, which includes peoples and languages of the Loango Coast south to Luanda in [present-day] Angola, and east of the Kwango River to the Yaka and Suku of modern Bandundu Province.

These states had shared equatorial traditions—matrilineal institutions and much shared political symbolism and vocabulary. There is some evidence that the culture of the Tio area was ancestral to the others: 'All the blacks who live along this [Loango] coast derive their laws and customs from those of Pombo [Mpumbu]'. These linkages were expressed in the idiom of kinship, the story of a woman with 4 sons—muTeke, muKongo, muWoyo and muVili.

While the Kingdom of Kongo was highly centralized, the Kingdom of Loango's power relied on economic, rather than political, power to control surrounding regions. The Loango Coast held a privileged geographic position in West Central Africa because it occupied the territory from the Cape Lopez in the north to the Congo River in the south and straddled the resource rich edge of the Central African equatorial rainforest, the southern fringe of which extended to the coast as far south as the port of Mayumba. French missionaries who arrived in Mayumba in June of 1773 described the natural splendor of Mayumba: "This plain is of a great beauty, well planted with greenery and surrounded by the most beautiful forests. [...] Nothing is more beautiful than the alwaysgreen forests" which are very abundant, "nothing is more agreeable than the plains that intersect them [.]" South of the rainforest fringe, the coastal area is made up of sandstone cliffs, such as those surrounding the Loango Bay. From Loango south to the Congo River, the coastline consisted of coastal plains varying in width between 6 to 35 miles. The Atlantic coast was an important site for fishing and salt collection. Savannas and light forests covered the coastal plains before giving way to heavier vegetation towards the mouth of the Congo River estuary. There, the Congo River stretched between 9 to 10 kilometers wide. Mangrove swamps dominated the north bank. To the interior of the coastal plains was a vast area of thick forest called Mayombe. In the eastern Mayombe forest lay a mountainous region containing deposits of iron, copper, and lead—minerals used and traded throughout the region for cultivation, hunting, and warfare. The Mayombe forest also marked the limits of European knowledge of the region in the early modern period; no European crossed into the Mayombe forest until the 19th century. East of the Mayombe rainforest the mountains gave way to the Teke plateau north of the Malebo Pool.

Before the arrival of Europeans, the Kingdom of Loango was the central political unit in the region. It was ideally positioned between the resource-rich equatorial forest to the north, the iron and copper mining regions of Mayombe to the east, and the Congo River estuary to the south. Loango's inhabitants travelled in groups to places such as the mining areas in the dry season in order to take advantage of these resources. This regional trade formed "an incipient caravan system" that would expand once Europeans arrived on the Atlantic coast. Loango's privileged position contributed to the importance of her coastal market where squares of raffia cloth called *mbongo* were used as currency. The kingdom itself boasted enviable natural resources: fertile land, savannas, and forests rich in wildlife, rivers, and coastlines apt for fishing and salt-making. At its height, the Kingdom of Loango's privileged geographic and commercial position allowed it to extend commercial influence throughout the entire region.

Each state had a sacred priest/ruler. Witchcraft was an important factor which mediated the competing traditions of big man centralization and equality. By vilifying those who accumulated too much, witchcraft promoted an "ideology of equality and cooperation." At the same time, political leaders—big men and later chiefs or kings—were believed to derive their power from the supernatural. Leaders were themselves perceived as a type of witch, using supernatural power for the benefit of their people. The role of leaders was both political and ritual, as was their power. The social order also reflected the cosmological understanding of the universe. The political and religious spheres were themselves inextricably intertwined, as seen in the ritual role of chiefs, belying the modern Western understanding of the separation between church and state. This equatorial African tradition expressed itself in every aspect of life—political, economic, and social domains—that were themselves interconnected aspects of a cosmological whole. The relationship between tradition and cosmology was a reciprocal one: both reflected fundamental meanings of the world. Equatorial Africans, therefore, not only shared a common political tradition, but also a common worldview.

The ruler—otherwise known as the *Mane Kongo*—was selected from the male members of a group of aristocratic clans, Mwissikongo, and his power rested essentially on his astute manipulation of the products of the ecological zones into which the area naturally divides—*nzimbu* (shell money from Luanda Island), salt from various coastal locations, and palm cloth from the interior. The Mane Kongo welcomed the Portuguese and was baptized as Joao; white was the color of the spirit world, and the strangers' supernatural standing was confirmed by their foreign tongue, exotic appearance, and associated with the sea.

Where it applies to the non-centralized states, the push and pull of the traditional esteem of big men as well as equality and decentralization are imprinted on the institutional history of the region. As late as 500 C. E., socio-political organization was highly decentralized—a reflection of both relatively low population density and the cultural value on local autonomy. Social organization centered on the House and the village. Big men (*mfúmú*, *mpfó*) led the House and the village. The village was characterized by relations of economic dependency rather than by blood or kinship relations. They included family members, clients, and local hunter-gatherers. Big men used wealth to attract followers. One of their central roles as leaders was to resolve conflicts through the institutions of the palaver. Subjects understood the power of big men as both political and religious, connected with charms (*nkisi*) or nature spirits (nkira). These political and religious powers were in turn tied to the land. This relationship can be seen in the title accorded to chiefs throughout the region: "master of the land." Among the Kongo the title was *ngáánsi*. The Tio similarly used *ngántsi*. *Nsi* and *ntsi* refer to the land. Both titles linguistically highlight the role of chiefs as political founders and their link with nature spirits or charms (Tio *nkira*, Kongo "Charms of the land" *nkisi ntsi*). Centers of ritual prestige laid the foundations for future

146

regions of political importance. The epicenter of spiritual life in the Kongo zone lay in the Mayombe rainforest and along the adjacent coast of the Congo River, the same region that would later develop into the kingdoms of Loango and Kongo.

West Central Africa was always of minor importance in Portugal's global perspectives, in comparison with Asia and Brazil, or even with the auriferous regions of Africa itself. Even when they enjoyed a virtual monopoly, they did not constitute a single monolithic presence, and the nature of their impact varied with time and place. Sao Tome was originally on uninhabited islands; the Portuguese began to settle there in the 1490s, founding sugar plantations worked with slave labor—a prototype of those which later developed in the New World. After the Oba of Benin prohibited the export of male slaves in 1516, the planters of Sao Tome obtained their slaves in West Central Africa, both for local use and for sale further afield. But the sugar of Sao Tome could not compete with that produced in the New World and the viability of its plantations was undermined by recurrent slave revolts, with the result that the settlers came to gain a living from slave trading, and from acting as carriers in coastal trade. Their interests were often at variance with those of the Portuguese crown and its agents. Those who came to West Central Africa were, on the whole, men who were marginal and relatively impoverished in their own society, and this was the cause of much of their rapacity and violence. Those who braved the diseased environment of sub-Saharan Africa were lesser nobles, struggling merchants, or younger sons. Their ranks included debtors, criminal degradados, Gypsies and Jews, then as later the victims of supposedly Christian Europe. Most died within a few months or years of their arrival. They turned to slave trading, in many cases, because of the failure of other initiatives such as agriculture or the quest for minerals. Like the slaves, but to a much lesser degree, they were the 'casualties of merchant capital.' Those who survived ended up impoverishing and depopulating the regions they had hoped would enrich them.

The immigrants married local women and an Afro-Portuguese community developed. Its members retained Portuguese names, European dress, and varying amounts of the Portuguese language, and of degrees of attachment to Christianity. These things were cherished because they helped to define what was perhaps an elusive sense of identity. By the 18th century, this Creole community was competing for trade with metropolitan Portuguese; these struggles were often the dynamic behind the expansion of the slaving frontier in the interior.

Giovanni Antonio Cavazzi, a Capuchin missionary who collected the earliest oral traditions on slavery from Kongo informants in the mid-17th century, noted that the first slaves in the kingdom appeared at its founding by Kongo's first conqueror king, Lukeni lua Nimi. The traditions that Cavazzi collected recalled that the lands that Lukeni conquered were 'ruled by a certain Mabambolo Manipangalla, whose descendants have been driven out by this insolent conqueror, [and] become slaves'.

The first Portuguese vessel anchored in the Zaire estuary in 1483. At first, the main commodity the new arrivals bought was copper from Mindouli, north of the Zaire, supplemented by ivory, raffia, cloth, pelts, and honey. The first reference to slaves comes from a legend found on the Cantino Atlas of 1502. The legend noted that by the 1520s, Kongo had commenced the sale of captives for 'things of insignificant value'. These captives were destined, first for the sugar fields of Sao Tome, and later for the insatiable markets of the New World; soon, the trade in slaves eclipsed all other exports. The Portuguese began to trade on the Loango coast in the 1570s, and Luanda, the original nucleus of Angola, was originally settled by clandestine traders evading the authority of the crown. In 1615, trade was developed at Benguela, for the same reasons. Angola, founded by a charter of 1571, was Africa's first colony, which African forces confined themselves to for decades due to the unhealthy coastal lowlands around Luanda.

Mane King Joao seemingly regretted his decision to welcome the Portuguese; when he died in 1506, there was a civil war, won by the pro-Portuguese and pro-Christian contender, Nzinga Mvemba, whom history knows as King Afonso, and who reigned until his death in 1543. The Portuguese assumed he was the heir, as the oldest son of the king's principal wife. Since his mother was not a member of the Mwissikongo, he had, in a matrilineal society, no right to succeed at all. An older historiography saw him as a Christian idealist, struggling unsuccessfully against the slave trade, but he sometimes opposed and sometimes supported it, depending on whether it strengthened or weakened his regime. Like the kings who came before and after him, he cemented political alliances by means of multiple marriages. He may well have seen in Christianity a new ideology appropriate for a non-traditional king. This does not mean that he was insincere, and there was much evidence, in the centuries which followed, of the depth of Kongo attachment to the new religion. Henceforth, the throne was monopolized by his descendants.

In the short run, the Portuguese presence strengthened the Kongo monarchy, and foreign goods augmented the resources available to the Mane Kongo to reward his followers. Successive kings imported firearms and employed Portuguese mercenary musketeers. At first, the Portuguese bought products such as copper and local cloth. Pereira noted at the beginning of the 16th century: 'In this land of Maniconguo there is no gold . . . but there is much fine copper and many elephants . . . we barter the copper and ivory for linen . . . In this Kingdom of Kongo, they make cloths of palm-leaf as soft as velvet satin, as beautiful as any made in Italy.'

But soon external commerce was overwhelmingly dominated by the sale of slaves, who were mostly obtained at markets outside the kingdom, and especially at Mpumbu, the strategic nature of whose site is reflected in the fact that it was roughly the future location of Kinshasa and Brazzaville. This became a great entrepot for both local and exotic commodities.

No slaves had been sold there previously; they were called people

149

acquired with *nzimbu* (Kongo shell money). A new route from Mpumbu to the sea ran through Mbanza Kongo, and a new class of Afro-Portuguese long-distance traders developed, called pombeiros, those who travel to Mpumbu.

While the Atlantic trade was under way in earnest, Kongo's King Afonso I (1509—43) wrote many letters to Portuguese kings which contoured his kingdom's different social categories and its indivisibility from slave status. In such letters, Afonso referred to freeborn Kongo people as *gente*. To stress that these people could be sold outside the country, he frequently used the term *peca* (piece), a Portuguese financial term referring to exported slaves, to describe them, including even those not immediately available for export.

In many references to slaves, Afonso noted that he had brought slaves back from his wars and had sent some to Portugal to cover various expenses. Afonso was using these slaves as commodity exports because they had monetary value in Portugal. In one case he referred to 50 slaves he sent to Lisbon 'to buy us succor[sic] that we need'. He also made note of another 500 slaves (with an additional 30 in case some of the originals died) that he sent to Lisbon in two large ships whose sale was meant to cover the upkeep of 'two of our nephews.' Moreover, the letter also contains several other references to the Portuguese purchasing slaves, and these references leave no doubt that Kongo already supported markets where slaves were bought and sold.

In 1568, the Kongo kingdom was almost overthrown by a people called the *Jaga*, who seized the capital, sacked villages and burnt churches. The King was forced to take refuge on an island in the Zaire River and returned to power only with the help of Portuguese forces from Sao Tome. Nearly 300 years later, a visitor was shown a swamp near the capital, formed by the tears of a local divinity, grieving over this invasion. Much has been written on the identity of the Jaga; they were an inland people—perhaps the forebears of the modern Yaka—and their rising may well have been a response to the pressures of the slave trade. Alternatively (and the 2 models are not necessarily incompatible), they may have been seeking to make a greater profit from it by cutting out the middlemen. The root of their name, *aka*, means stranger or brigand. Not all those sold by the Kongo elite were acquired outside the kingdom's borders, and rapacious nobles often preyed on the peasantry. As early as the reign of Afonso, there is evidence of kidnapping, and in the 17th century fathers branded their sons to protect them from enslavement—the implication being that they were already someone's property.

The profits of enslavement progressively distorted the patterns of social life. If someone broke a borrowed calabash, no repayment was acceptable but a slave, and it was said in the mid-17th century that 'they are made often to move to war to acquire a quantity of slaves ... than for political needs and matters of state.' The then-King Alvaro II (1587—1614) had a large army, and some thought, by then, that slaves outnumbered the free. Male slaves carried out the traditional agricultural tasks of women as well as those of men; their labors, combined with the impact of new crops, sustained an enlarged court. Literacy in Portuguese, perpetuated in local schools, enabled successive kings to keep records, and correspond both with the provinces and with European powers. By the 17th century, Kongo subjects paid a poll tax, which was collected in cash, and other dues were payable as well. Thornton suggests that these were not a heavy burden—the poll tax in Soyo was 2 mabongo; it cost between 80 and 120 mabongo to marry. But villages were built away from the main roads, out of the way of traveling notables and their retinues.

> To collect the tribute they almost always need to use violence,
> and this requires a lot of time and work ... The collectors, if they
> are not well accompanied, risk losing their lives because of the
> evils they inflict on the ... country-inhabitants to get them to pay.
> These, oppressed and vexed, frequently rebel, and if they cannot
> avenge themselves in any other manner, expel them from the country.

Sometimes peasants restricted production, to reduce the amount which could be appropriated—they 'refuse to sow abundantly and to raise cattle, [because they] would rather suffer penury than to work for someone else.' It was said that when nobles fought nobles or peasants fought peasants, the casualties were low; there were more deaths when they fought each other.

The king expelled by the Jaga went on to rule for 19 years; his successor, Alvaro II, also had an exceptionally long reign between 1587 to 1614—clear evidence of the kingdom's recovery. Alvaro II attempted to break free from the control the Portuguese merchants of Sao Tome exercised over his state's external relations by sending an ambassador to the Pope. He was held in Lisbon for 3 years—a symbol of Kongo's difficulties in joining the commonwealth of Christian nations on equal terms. Like Afonso I before him, Alvaro asked in vain for technical aid. The foundation of the Portuguese colony of Angola in 1571 did not immediately weaken the Kongo state—the main thrust of Angola's expansion was eastward into Ndongo and, by importing large quantities of Kongo cloth, for sale locally, it may have strengthened its economy. In the course of the 17th century, the Kongo state became weaker and more fragmented. Soyo, a Kongo province to the south of the Zaire estuary, successfully asserted its independence from the 1640s on. 'Towards the sea-coast are many lords who, though of inferior rank, usurp the title king.' In 1665, the king and many of his courtiers were killed by—largely African—Angolan forces at the battle of Mbwila. The kingdom never recovered, and for a long period the capital was deserted.

In this situation of crisis, a woman prophet emerged—Vita Kimpa, baptized as Beatrice, who claimed to be a medium of St. Antony. Her teachings were a fusion of traditional religion and Catholicism, and she proclaimed that Jesus and His Mother were black and locally born. Both nobles and poor responded to her teaching, and Mbanza Kongo was reoccupied. She was burnt at the stake for heresy in 1706, her baby son narrowly escaping the same fate.

A little later, Pedro IV (d. 1718), refusing to make war on a rebel, said:

> in no way would he make war, as it was the continual warfare which

had already destroyed the kingdom, and also the Faith. Nor did the
Congolese want any more troubles. They were already tired of being
Like beasts in the fields and wastelands: outraged, murdered, robbed
and sold, and their relatives, wives and children killed on all sides.

The unified Kongo kingdom had gone forever, and the patrimony of its
kings shrank to the area round their much-diminished capital. Atlantic trade
tended to go north to the Loango coast and an independent Soyo, or south to
Angola and Benguela. Christianity did not die out but mutated into
profoundly indigenized forms. Literacy survived and the Kongo elite
corresponded on banana leaves because of the high cost of paper. The
memories of a dramatic and remarkable history survived, and a certain
intangible mystique continued to surround the king.

It is important to note that the Portuguese did not enjoy a monopoly of
external trade for long, and before the end of the 16th century Dutch,
English and French vessels had begun to raid their settlements. The Dutch
began to trade in Loango in the late 16th century, and it became the center
of their commercial interests in West Central Africa (they briefly seized
Angola in the 1640s). They were not, at first, purchases of captives, for
which they had no use until they obtained their first possessions in South
America.

The British and French played a significant role in the 18th century slave
trade from the area. The demand for African slaves in Saint Domingue was
insatiable, and French slave traders had trouble keeping up with demand,
which was driven by the high mortality rate as much as by the growth of
agricultural production. "One commonly needed for the colony of Saint
Domingue alone a recruitment each year of 20—25,000 nègres, as much to
replace the mortalities as to increase the cultivation." The Loango Coast
became the focus of the French slave trade following the end of the Seven
Years war in 1763. In the last half of the 18th century, the French were
responsible for the majority of the slave trade on the Loango Coast and the

majority of Loango Coast captives went to the French colony of Saint Domingue.

Like the Dutch, the British and French had a commercial advantage over the Portuguese, both in the better quality and range of their imports and in their readiness to sell firearms and ammunition (prohibited by the Portuguese crown). The British were in a particularly strong position, as the manufacturers both of the most acceptable textiles and of the flintlock, which was a *sine qua non* for African trade.

For most of the 16th century, Kongo expanded militarily, foreign captives supplied Kongo's needs for slaves, and many of the people born in Kongo enjoyed the protection of the king and were not exported. The large-scale importation of firearms, often via Loango, began in the 18th century, and often those with access to guns fought their way to power, then and later—a pattern which, as in West Africa, contrasts oddly with the evidence of their poor quality. In 1759, only 200 of 4,000 trade guns examined were in good order. The fragmentation of Kongo's politics meant that kings could no longer protect their people from enslavement, resulting in many being enslaved as part of the Atlantic trade.

In the last third of the 17th century, the pattern of Atlantic trade on the Loango coast changed dramatically; almost a million captives were exported between 1660 and 1793, more than a quarter of a million more by 1835. Here too there is evidence of an increasing degree of social oppression, and people were enslaved for trifling offences.

In the third quarter of 18th century there was a protracted dispute between king and aristocracy, and the sovereign, who died in 1787, had no successor for over a century, partly because no one had the wealth needed for the ceremonies, and partly because the ritual prohibitions surrounding the office were incompatible with participation in foreign trade.

Kongo Captives in the New World

In September 1785, a concerned colonist of the French colony of Saint Domingue wrote to the Attorney General (*procureur général*) in the capital of Cap Français to "denounce" the activities of a "Monster." In the previous 6 months, the "Monster" had become so powerful that the author dared sign their letter only as "M." This "monster" was a "*négresse* [...] named *Kingué of Guinée*" said to have the ability "to kill and to bring back to life, to fight all sorts of illnesses" and to divine who was guilty of sorcery, witchcraft, and poisoning. She was "regarded by les nègres in general as a god." Worst of all, even the white colonists in the region had been turning to her for help. Marie Kingué's owner, Belhumeur of Port Margot, employed her to discover "criminals" in his slave workshops (*ateliers*) and allowed her to move and practice freely in the area. Indeed, Kingué's skill as a diviner was such that even the local Commandant, Sieur Chailleau, called on her to "examine his workshop." When Kingué was threatened with arrest, Chailleau went so far as to offer her protection in his own home.

"She has acquired a renown that extends across the entire North Province," one anonymous complaint claimed, where "she knows all the secrets of all the plantations." Demand for her services "to discover the Macandals [poisoners or sorcerers] in workshops" was so high that she and her assistant Polidor began initiating students, a fact all the more remarkable given that in principle '*le Vaudoux*' and African religious practices were illegal in the colony at the time. All of Plaisance was said to wear the *garde-corps* or talismans she sold, of which there were never enough, "as one wears a Saint-Suaire [a Catholic saint's medal]." The Royal Prosecutor of Cap Français, Jean-Baptiste Suarez d'Almeida, received similar complaints about Marie Kingué, which he summarized in this way: "This Négresse, or more accurately this Monster, attributes to herself a supernatural power, to divine the crimes of the *Nègres* & unfortunately, a superstition just as absurd has found believers among the whites, and made victims among the *Noirs*."

155

Who was this woman whose skill as a diviner was such that both the black and white population of the North Province turned to her, and who ultimately required a brigade from the capital to arrest her? According to court documents, her name was Marie Kingué, or Marie Catherine, she was aged between 35—40 years, and she was from the Kongo. Marie Kingué represents only one example of the Kongolese spiritual practitioners and cultural practices that flourished in the French colony of Saint Domingue in the last half of the 18th century despite colonists' attempts to stop them. West Central African spiritual practices in Saint Domingue included the packets called *"gris"* or *"macandal"* sold by Makandal in the 1750s, the "convulsive" dance of "Dom Pèdre" popular in the 1760s, the practice of "bila or pretend Magnetism" in Marmelade in the 1780s, and the song to the deity "Bomba" collected before the revolution. Taken together, it is clear there were many common elements to the ceremonies and practices cited above: the use of divination to identify *macandals*, poisoners or sorcerers; the use of alcohol to induce trance or possession; public healing rituals to address disease; and the production, sale, and use of power objects such as packets, weapons, and other *garde-corps* (talismans) for healing, poisoning, and personal protection. The most striking element they had in common, however, is that they all drew on elements of Kongolese cultural practices.

The powerful presence of Kongolese people—or known more generally as "Congos"—and practices in Saint Domingue was such that by the 1791 when the Haitian Revolution was underway, they comprised nearly 50% of the estimated 500,000 total of African captives. Many lived in majority Kongolese communities: West Central Africans represented the largest group of Africans in the colony, comprising the majority of the population of the North and South Provinces of Saint Domingue. West Central Africans also had dominated slave imports to Saint Domingue since the 1750s. By the mid-1780s, they comprised between one-half to two-thirds of the French slave trade to the colony, reaching a peak of 63% in 1784. In the decade preceding the Revolution, nearly half of the captives purchased by French slave traders came from West Central Africa. These numbers may have been higher. For some years, French records cite thousands more captives than the Trans-Atlantic Slave Trade Database (TSTD). For example, French slave trade documents cite a thousand more captives than the TSTD for the year 1785. A government summary of the slave trade for that year lists 34,045 captives on 90 ships, 46 from the "Angolan Coast" versus 29,835 captives on 83 ships, 36 from West Central Africa listed in the database. Using French documents, the percentage of French slave trade in West Central Africa in 1785 rises to 51.6%. Furthermore, the TSTD cannot account for French slave traders who underreported or failed to report their voyages to avoid paying customs duties or escape penalties for illegal trading activities. Slave traders had a new incentive to do so after the 1784 repeal of the highly lucrative (but corrupt) acquits de Guinée and again after 1789 when the French government passed a law requiring ships from the Indian Ocean to return to France with their goods and then re-embark for Africa. French legal cases at the time make it clear that French merchants attempted to skirt the new restrictions and tax laws by either underreporting the number of slaves they had purchased, not reporting Indian Ocean trade, or not reporting their voyage at all. Whatever the true numbers, it is clear that "Congos" were the largest group of Africans in the colony.

The population of Saint Domingue was therefore not only overwhelmingly African, but also largely Kongolese. Once in Saint Domingue, many Kongolese chose to create communities away from the plantation in maroon settlements and later on, the lakou. Those who succeeded created a life largely apart from the one imagined for them.

The Kongolese dominance was most pronounced on coffee plantations, where they were 50% more numerous than on sugar plantations. Colonists responded to the demographic dominance of West Central Africans on plantations through complaint, resignation, and academic study. French scholars in the colony such as Louis Narcisse Baudry de Lozières, Mederic Elie Moreau de Saint Méry, and Etienne Descourtilz cataloged the geographic origins, physical and moral characteristics of "Congos." The latter were so numerous on Baudry's plantations that he spent the 1780s studying the language of his "Congo" slaves, writing a *Dictionnaire ou Vocabulaire Congo* so that other "planters" would be able to communicate with the newly arrived "bossals." Baudry (who incidentally was Moreau's brother-in-law and escaped from France with him in 1793) believed that many of the newly arrived captives perished "often a short time after their arrival, because they cannot make themselves understood." Unfortunately for Baudry, the Haitian Revolution prevented him from publishing his *Encyclopodie Coloniale*, and so he was unable to establish whether linguistic knowledge would address the high mortality rate among the colony's enslaved Kongolese. However, it is an incredibly useful document that bears testimony to the important influence this demographic group had in the colony.

The Kongolese slaves became central to Saint Domingue's economy, which was, in turn, central to the economy of France. By the end of the 18th century, Saint Domingue had long been the wealthiest colony in the Caribbean, "the centerpiece of the Atlantic slave system." Despite being small in size—Saint Domingue covered only 10,600 square miles or roughly the size of Maryland or Massachusetts—in 1789 Saint Domingue boasted around 8,000 plantations and the colony was still growing. At the time of the Haitian Revolution, Saint Domingue produced nearly one-half of both the sugar and coffee consumed by Europeans and Americas, as well as significant quantities of cotton and indigo. Saint Domingue was the world's largest producer of sugar and coffee, exporting more sugar than Jamaica, Cuba, and Brazil combined. The exports produced by the colony "generated some two-fifths of France's overseas trade, a proportion rarely equaled in any colonial empire."

> "The livelihood of as many as a million of the 25 million inhabitants of France depended directly on the colonial trade [...] In 1789, 15 percent of the 1,000 members of

the National Assembly owned colonial property, and

many others were probably tied to colonial commerce."

It is noteworthy that though these Kongolese captives—taking their name from the collective term of the *Bakongo* people of the Kongo Kingdom—came from the Loango Coast and Mayombe rainforest, north of the Congo River, they had many cultural and linguistic variations. These would cross the Atlantic to Saint-Domingue, especially those concerning *nkisi*, *simbi*, and *nkita*. The significance of these captives' north Loango Coast origin is that its inhabitants had little or no contact with European religious beliefs and those from the inland forest had none at all. Mobley asserts, therefore, that these captives were not "Atlantic creoles" with prior knowledge of European culture and religion. Enslaved West Central African men and women such as the abovementioned Marie Kingué, used identifiable Kongolese cultural practices across the Atlantic in Saint Domingue and later Haiti. They drew on specific instrumental knowledge and spiritual technologies such as divination, possession, trance, and power objects to address the material problems of plantation life. This demonstrates the remarkable durability of Kongolese ontology on both sides of the Kongolese Atlantic world.

Within the Kongo zone there are important regional variations regarding religious concepts, especially concerning *nkisi*, *simbi*, and *nkita*. South of the Congo River, different regions define *simbi* as protective, local nature spirits who inhabit rivers or 2 types of nature spirits who inhabit rivers (*bisimbi bi masa*) or land (*bisimbi bi nseke*), who are seen in opposition to terrestrial spirits, *nkita*, who are themselves variously considered to be either the spirits of people who died a violent death or the spirits of founding ancestors.

Many aspects of religious beliefs and practices, even regarding these 3 concepts, differ greatly north of the Congo River. According to recent research by Dunja Hersak, neither the *Vili* nor the *Yombe*, for example, refer to themselves as Kongo, nor do they venerate their ancestors. Instead, they focus on ancient nature spirits, *nkisi si*, such as *Mbumba*. *Mbumba*, the central mythic figure of the *Yombe*, is now unimportant south of the Congo River. And though the *Yombe* recognize the words *nkisi*, *simbi* and *nkita*, they mean radically different things to them. For example, south of the river, *nkisi* (*pl minkisi*) are power objects. North of the river, they are powerful nature forces that occupy the central position in the spiritual hierarchy. North of the river, it is these terrestrial gods, the *bakisi ba nsi* (*nsi* among the *Yombe*, *tsi* among the *Vili*, meaning 'terre', earth, land), who are the principal focus of religion. In Ngoyo, the *simbi* are merely emissaries of local, terrestrial *bakisi ba si*. Both the *simbi* and the *nkita* disappear completely among the *Vili* of Loango. Only the *Yombe*, occupants of the rainforest inland of the coastal kingdoms of the Loango coast, recognize the *bakisi ba nsi* of the Loango coast and the *simbi* and *nkita* seen south of the river. Among the African spiritual leaders who practiced in Saint Domingue, none attained either the renown or the infamy of François Makandal. In the words of one colonist, "Of all the leaders of the maroons none had a reputation more grand or more merited than Français Macandal executed in 1758." Indeed, Makandal is a figure of legendary proportions. His life and especially his death loom large in the myth and history of slavery in Saint Domingue. Accused of attempting to poison the white population of Saint Domingue, 18th century French colonists reviled and feared him. For the white population, Makandal symbolized and embodied fears of poison, slave uprising, and the danger of African knowledge about plants, medicine, and religion. For the free and enslaved population and their Haitian descendants, Makandal has been lauded as a hero, his actions seen as a precursor to and inspiration for the Haitian Revolution.

Makandal was, in fact, a Kongolese spiritual practitioner—known as a Kongolese *nganga nkisi* or Kongolese priest—who created powerful packets for his followers. It is noteworthy that Makandal's name is derived from the Yombe word *makanda*, used to refer to packets of animal, vegetable, or mineral material wrapped in a leaf. Though both the white and black population of the colony associated these packets with poison, there is no evidence that Makandal was guilty of a conspiracy to poison the white population of the colony. Furthermore, no evidence supports the claim that Makandal was a revolutionary leader in the region or the colony. Rather, his followers appear to have been local. Makandal's was a spiritual rather than a military or political leader. Indeed, at least one of his "accomplices" was an *nganga tesa* or diviner. Each makanda was ritually empowered by an nkisi spirit, invoked by an nganga nkisi priest, and was named after the spirit or the power of the packet. Some packets were created for luck or protection. Others were aggressive: merely placing one in or near someone's house could cause them to fall ill. Makandal's name therefore indicates, first, that he was an nganga or Kongolese priest.

According to sources, the enslaved population turned to the spiritual technologies provided by Makandal and his "accomplices" such as power packets and divination for reasons including luck, protection, aggression, and to identify guilty parties. According to numerous sources, François Makandal was born in Africa. Captured and brought to Saint Domingue, he was a slave on the le Normand de Mézy plantation in Limbé, in the North Province of Haiti. On the plantation, Makandal worked in the dangerous sugar mill, where he lost one of his arms, after which he was made guard of the plantation's animals. At the time of his arrest, he was said to have been a maroon, or runaway, for variously 10 or 18 years. By that time, Makandal was already well known in the area. During his time as a maroon, Makandal was said to have amassed a huge number of followers and carried out the murder, by poison, of an "innumerable" number of people. According to a letter written by the colonial intendant and governor dated 27th February 1758, the poison had been used against blacks more often than whites and was responsible for the deaths of more than "6,000 nègres" in and around Cap Français in the preceding 3 years. Decades later, Moreau wrote, "During his desertion he [Makandal] made himself famous by his poisonings which spread terror among the nègres, and who all submitted to him. He openly maintained a school in this execrable art, it had agents in all parts of the Colony, and death flew at the least signal that he made." Moreau's description is an example of the mythic and monstrous character ascribed to Makandal by French colonists. For many, Makandal was not only guilty of 'maroonage' and poisoning, but also of planning to eradicate the entire white population of the colony. For example, Moreau asserted, "In the end in his vast plan, he had conceived the infernal project to make disappear from the surface of Saint Domingue all the men who were not black [.]"

The nganga held a central position in early modern Kongolese society. Documents written by visitors to the Kongo zone in the early modern period indicate that the nganga were "the most frequent and most influential experts in the population." The variety of social and ritual functions performed by *nganga* is reflected in the sources. Proyart wrote: The doctors [médicins] are revered as invaluable men, & even [as] necessary for the society: their art belongs to the religion. They bear the name of Ganga [...] one consults them to know the future and discover the most secret things: one asks them, as the King, rain and good weather; one believes that by the virtue of their enchantments, they can make themselves invisible, and pass through doors, be they made of the hardest wood, or even of iron. "There is among them," Proyart added, those "who exercise Medicine, and made a trade in curing, by blowing [soufflés] and enchantments." Grandpré defined the *nganga* as a "conjuror;" "One consults the great Gods on important occasions, in imminent danger, before a great voyage and for the trials of a culprit." Often translated as "priest," the term *nganga* referred to a wide variety of Kongolese spiritual experts.

According to Kongolese scholar Kimpianga Mahaniah, the *nganga nkisi* played 3 roles, all of which he was able to perform thanks to an *nkisi*. First, he neutralized the power of forces of the invisible or occult world to do harm—witches, ghosts, displeased ancestors. Second, he acted as a medical expert using magico-medical remedies to heal illnesses. Last, he used the *nkisi* to act as a prophet or seer to see events happening far away and learn the causes of diseases, deaths, and disasters. Early modern sources connected the *nganga nkisi* with medicine as well as the creation and use of power objects and knowledge of medicine and healing. For example, Grandpré defined the *nganga nkisi* as the "conjuror" of "little idols": "These little idols [*Kissy* or *nkisi*] influence health [la santé]; their conjuror is named Ganga'm Kissy; among them he is what doctors [médicins] are among us."

Both the name and associations with *nganga nkisi* existed in Saint Domingue. For example, in the Congo Vocabulary Baudry created in Saint Domingue he defined "*gangan kizi*" or *nganga nkisi* as "surgeon" ["*chirurgien*"]. One of the principal roles of the *nganga nkisi* was the composition and use of powerful objects. It is therefore not surprising that it is precisely with this crime that colonial officials charged Makandal. Despite Makandal's association, among colonists, with a widespread poison conspiracy, at the time of his arrest, he was in fact known for the powerful packets for which he was named. Court documents generated by his arrest show Makandal was in fact convicted of creating "allegedly magic packets." For example, according to the Arrêt du Conseil to Cap published against Makandal, he was charged and convicted with: "making himself formidable among the Negres, and to have corrupted and seduced them by prestiges (Illusion produced by magic or a magic spell; diabolic artifice), and made [them] devote themselves to impieties and profanations [...] by mixing holy things in the composition and use of allegedly magic packets [paquets prétendus magiques], and tending to evil spells, that he made and sold to the Negres; to have moreover composed, sold, and distributed poisons of all type [.]"

In other words, Makandal's crime was making powerful packets using holy items that he sold to others and in so doing not only corrupted them but also made himself into a powerful leader. Makandal's crime was therefore not plotting to kill the entire white population of the colony.

163

Indeed, contrary to the claims of colonists in later decades, colonial authorities failed to find any evidence of a colony-wide conspiracy to poison white colonists. Their failure to do so was not for lack of trying. According to a letter written from Cap Français 24th June 1758, colonists had burned alive 4 or 5 slaves a month since Makandal's execution; one source stated "there has already been 24 slave Nègres or Nègresses, and three free Nègres, who have suffered the same thing."

Despite the widespread arrests, tortures, and executions that were carried out in the wake of Makandal's execution, no evidence of a conspiracy emerged. Indeed, the colonial intendant at the time concluded that there was no colony-wide conspiracy to poison white colonists. Instead, Makandal and his accomplices were executed for the packets that were considered to be "a sacrilegious desecration, by the abuse of the Holy things that they use and that use alone is criminal."

As in Saint Domingue, the fear of both poison and sorcery appears to have been widespread throughout the Kongo zone in the late-18th century. This fear can be seen among Europeans as well as among the Kongolese of the Loango Coast and the Kingdom of Kongo. The Kongolese attributed sudden illnesses or deaths to poison and sorcery. Part of the reason was that the Kongolese believed that illnesses that were too short or too long—with sudden onset or chronic duration —did not occur naturally and therefore were caused by an unnatural cause such as sorcery or witchcraft. According to Kongolese scholar Kimpianga Mahaniah:

> Among the Kongo, illness is always the manifestation of a cause.
> Thus, the patient is not regarded as a biological machine put out
> of order, [or] a simple malfunctioning organ, but as an individual
> with all the various influences that implies: past, personality, familial
> context, social role, cultural environment, cosmological and religious
> beliefs which, as well as the physiological state, are the interdependent
> aspects of health. In other words, illness is not simply the result of the
> malfunctioning of an organ, provoked by a material cause, but could be

also due to an 'intangible force': Gods, local spirits and ancestors. Thus, the treatment must utilize not only material substances but equally resources borrowed from the cosmic or immaterial world.

In the case of a natural illness such as a headache, stomachache, or cold, an *nganga* treated the patient with medicines made mostly from plants. However, illnesses that did not respond to medical treatment, that were chronic or had a sudden onset, or that appeared following other misfortunes were considered abnormal and unnatural—*kimbevo kia nza*. Unnatural illnesses were seen as the result of social conflicts or of disequilibrium between the visible world of the living and the invisible world of the dead and spirits. The possible causes included "God, the ancestors, a ghost, a witch, the clan or an active *nkisi*." To identify the cause of the disease and cure it, the Kongo performed both socio-medical and magical religious rites. These were both individual and collective. In collective rites, the entire community was mobilized to perform a public healing ceremony to purify the community, pacify the causal agents, and neutralize the *nkisi-* empowered object causing harm. Unlike collective rites, in which the entire community assumed responsibility for the illness, in individual rites the goal was to identify the specific person who had caused the sickness. In order to do so, the Kongolese used divination as well as trials by poison and fire.

It is noteworthy, that the Atlantic slave trade was instrumental in disrupting the stability of the West Central African region. Atlantic trade initially exploited pre-existing trade routes and markets dominated by the Kingdom of Loango. In the 18th century, however, the dramatic increase in the slave trade on the Loango Coast would challenge rather than reinforce the Kingdom's influence. By the mid-18th century, the Atlantic slave trade had become the central organizing principle of political and economic institutions in the region. The influx of wealth from the Atlantic slave trade challenged the Kingdom of Loango's economic dominance over the north coast region and undermined central authority in the kingdoms. In so doing, the Atlantic slave trade would initiate a period of internal and external warfare and instability that resulted in the enslavement of increasingly large numbers of coastal inhabitants.

A Summary and Statistics of the Affected Africans in the Transatlantic Trade

While the above accounts of the Igbo, Yoruba, Gold Coast and Kongo kingdom histories and the Atlantic experiences of the captives drawn from these areas center on the peak years of the trade—which was the 17th century, the onset of the Old Diaspora has actually been antedated to 1444 when the Portuguese pioneered the slave trade, forcefully capturing the first group of Africans at the mouth of the Senegal River. Thereafter, Africa became intrinsically linked to the large development of the plantation systems in the Americas. The ability to navigate the sea was linked to the European desire and search for commodities, and the extensive production of sugar and the labor to produce it. In this respect, slavery and the slave trade connected Africa to the world economy and to global history. Consequently, the grand narratives of world history cannot be accurately written without including the slave trade, and an understanding of the global economy and politics since the 15th century cannot omit the role played by Africans. Africa was an integral part of the Atlantic World and played a crucial role in the history of early modernity, the industrialization of Europe, and the plantation economies in the Americas.

The nascent stages of what would become the Transatlantic slave trade saw captive Africans drawn from several sources across the African continent: West Africa supplied the majority, and others were drawn from southwest and Central Africa (areas of Cameroon, Congo, Angola, Gabon, and the modern-day Democratic Republic of Congo). Estimates on the total number of Africans forcibly removed range widely. Some of the figures quoted have been as high as 23 million, which include those that were earmarked for exportation, but died en route from the hinterland to the coast; alternatively, a relatively more conservative figure, taking into account fatalities en route to the coast, has been put at 15 million. Most scholars agree between 11.5 and 12 million left Africa, with between 9.6 million and 10 million actually reaching the Americas. Whatever the figure for those shipped, some 2 million is a conservative estimate for those who died while making the voyage, whether from illness, violence, starvation, suicide and so forth. It is important to realize that a census of slaves documented in written records will always be lower than the actual number exported. Not all records survive, and aspects of the trade—such as the activities of smugglers, interlopers and slaving captains packed more slaves on board than the law allowed—meant that many participants had a positive interest in concealment. It has been suggested that these areas of uncertainty invalidate all statistics or at best, are an underestimate. Both statements may well be true, but the general scholarly consensus is that the figures are remarkably accurate.

It is clear that the total demographic impact of the slave trade was much greater than the number of slaves exported. Many lost their lives in wars or raids partly or wholly motivated by the hope of gaining slaves. Many more died en route to the coast—as abovementioned—while awaiting purchase in slave barracoons, or during the Middle Passage. Estimates of all of this vary. Lovejoy suggests that these losses amounted to '6—10% at the port of departure and 10—14% or more en route to the coast' when the slave trade was at its height. This may well be conservative; an 18th century Loanda merchant claimed that slavers lost 40% of their captives between the original point of purchase and embarkment.

The Intercolonial Slave Trade of British America

A key part of the transatlantic slave trade era was *The Intercolonial slave Trade of British America, 1619—1807.*

In November 1755, over 300 Angolan men, woman, and children sailed into the Caribbean Sea, crowded aboard the French ship *l'Aimable.* They were bound for the French sugar colony of Saint-Domingue but never arrived. As *l'Aimable* traversed the Lesser Antilles, she ran across "his [British] majesty's ship" *Fowler*, armed to the teeth and cruising for prizes. Though official declaration had yet to arrive, the *Fowler* signaled war's descent on the Caribbean. At its helm, Admiral Thomas Frankland led a naval squadron that was getting a head start on privateering. *l'Aimable* was among the first victims. The African captives on board likely heard a warning shot from the *Fowler's* cannon but were probably spared the terror of a significant battle, as a slave ship was no match for a naval fleet. What capture by British privateers meant for the enslaved cargo of *l'Aimable* was a change of ownership and itinerary. Instead of heading to Saint Domingue, *l'Aimable* set a new course for Barbados, where the Middle Passage ended for these 327 survivors of the Atlantic crossing. For some, all that remained of their voyage to American slavery was a short, overland trip within the island. For others, however, much of the journey was still to come.

Under British naval custom, Admiral Frankland was entitled to one-eight of his fleet's prizes, so he claimed 146 of *l'Aimable's* captives—his share from not only that ship but also 2 other French slavers captured and sent to Antigua around the same time. Frankland did not sell his prizes locally. Instead, he partnered with a Bridgetown merchant, Gedney Clarke, in transshipping the Angolan people to South Carolina. Clarke maintained steady correspondence with traders in other colonies, and Charleston merchant Henry Laurens had informed Clarke of exceptionally high demand for enslaved Africans in South Carolina in recent months. Furthermore, Laurens had reported that the only expected slave shipments to South Carolina that year were from the Gambia River region, and the first ships to arrive from Gambia had reported that such vessels "are not likely to get half their Compliment of Slaves . . . [because] the small Pox is very rife in every part of that River." From this intelligence Laurens deduced that South Carolina would be undersupplied with African laborers, driving up prices relative to other American markets. Since ventures to Africa took months to plan and even longer to execute, Laurens recognized that traders from across the Atlantic would be slow to react to the rising prices. Sensing opportunity, he had proposed to numerous West Indian merchants that "there is a chance of making Money on a parcell [sic] of Slaves purchas'd with you to come down here in the Fall." Gedney Clarke and Thomas Frankland responded readily to Lauren's intelligence.

Thus, the convergence of smallpox in the Gambia River, the Seven Years' War between Britain and France, relative demand in South Carolina and Barbados, and the mercantile ambitions of Frankland, Clarke and Laurens forced 146 weary Angolan travelers back to sea after just 3 or 4 weeks of recovery from the Middle Passage in Barbados. For this next journey, they boarded a brig named—in bitter irony—*Relief*. Conditions were grim. Once at sea, the *Relief* proved "much out of kilter, [with] her Decks and all her upper works in want of Caulking." It was late December, so the temperature would have dropped considerably during the northbound voyage, but with "the Water that came down through the Deck," the Angolans were shivering before they even left the Caribbean. "Capt. Moses," who was not actually the ship's captain but rather the mate overseeing the captives, "was oblig'd to put their Cloaths on a few days after he left Barbadoes to preserve them." Moses likely delegated this task to the "three Negroes . . . put on board to take care of the rest." Unfortunately, the rough cotton garb typically given to captives simply soaked up the dripping water, offering little comfort. To fix the ship's problems, the *Relief's* captain, William Lightbourn, sailed the ship only as far as Anguilla before halting for 9 days of stopgap repairs. The *Relief* then pushed on to South Carolina and colder weather. Not surprisingly, "the Slaves . . . suffer'd very greatly." Six of the Angolans died at sea, and when the *Relief* finally reached Charleston's harbor on 12 January 1756, "6 or 7 more [were] very low and weak." A month had passed since their departure from Bridgetown.

Still, the suffering captives did not land in Charleston immediately. South Carolina law required the Relief to spend 10 days quarantined on Sullivan's Island in the harbor, where Laurens sent "a Doctor on board to visit and a carefull Woman as to nurse" the ailing captives. Laurens insisted that "Our Pest House where the Slaves are to be placed during their Quarantine is in good order and they have a plenty of Wood at hand," but surely for the Angolans, encountering their first winter outside the tropics, the fire was inadequate to chase away the chill. Even Laurens lacked confidence, adding, "We hope the Cloathing they have will be sufficient." At least on land they could stay dry. It was cold, but the unwilling immigrants "found the most favourable Weather that could be wish'd for at that Season of the Year or their mortality must have been much more considerable."

Laurens did not wait for his captives to survive quarantine before publicizing their availability. In the first issue of the South-Carolina Gazette after their arrival, Austin and Laurens announced the sale of "a Cargo of prime ANGOLA Men and Women SLAVES, Chiefly young People and healthy," scheduled for 22nd January, their first day out of quarantine. Charleston slave merchants advertised arriving Africans as soon as possible, a week or more in advance of a sale, hoping to attract distant buyers, and Laurens distorted the truth, however, when marketing the Angolan captives as "healthy." Despite "plenty of wood" and the visits of doctors and nurses, survivors of the *Relief's* leaky intercolonial voyage (not to mention the Middle Passage before that) struggled to recover. "The Flux"—probably dysentery—was rampant among them. Even "Capt. Moses was in a low poor state of health." By the time 22nd January came around, 13 survivors of the seaborne passage had perished in South Carolina, and there were "several more in great danger." Of the 127 surviving Angolans, Austin and Laurens "could only bring into the Yard 105" to be viewed by potential buyers.

"[T]he rest that remain'd alive were in a bad condition with the Flux," with 11 of them "sick in the Hospital." The additional voyage after surviving the Middle Passage had been too much.

From the merchants' perspective, the problems went beyond the dead and ailing human commodities. The event did not attract as many buyers as Laurens had hoped because "it unluckily happen'd that a Pereparamina [pneumonia] prevail'd . . . in many parts of the Province" at the time. Buyers still snatched up most of the enslaved people "that were able to appear in the Yard," but Laurens felt that the poor turnout had dampened prices. The sale was probably a "scramble," in which merchants allowed buyers to enter their "yard," or board a ship, only at a designated time, with the Africans arranged according to predetermined prices. Buyers could then rush in and literally grab individuals on a first-come, first-served basis. Traders hoped that in the frenzy, buyers would overlook blemishes and maladies that would otherwise drive down prices. But if few buyers turned out and the captives lacked the appearance of strength and health, the strategy could fall flat. Laurens reported that most prospective buyers deemed the Angolan people from the *Relief* "a very different parcel, that they were much too small a People for the business of this Country and in this Account many went away empty handed that would otherways have purchas'd." Laurens eventually "put off all [but] about 10" of those healthy enough to appear for the sale, but not before reducing prices. Another problem for the traders was that other speculators in the American slave market had noticed the high prices in Charleston. With Frankland's fleet delivering numerous French prize vessels to Barbados and Antigua, many intercolonial traders had bought up the twice-captured Africans and shipped them to Charleston. Intercolonial trade had glutted the market. "The monstrous prices given for a few Slaves in the month of October has produced all this Evil," Laurens explained. Traders "brought down parcel after parcel from the West Indias incessantly all this Winter."

Of course, such market conditions only mattered to the Angolan captives in terms of their personal situations and forced migrations. Those who were sold departed the yard of the Austin and Laurens mercantile house quickly, perhaps bidding a hasty farewell to fellow captives with whom they shared ties of kinship or bonds forged in the crucible of the slave ships. They faced yet another journey—this time overland to the home or plantation of their buyer. For some, this trip was mercifully short, just across town, but if Laurens was correct in predicting that the sale would draw planters "from the remote parts of the Country," some of the Angolans faced marches of more than 100 miles over several days. Meanwhile, others from the *Relief* remained unsold; a final plantation journey had to wait. Laurens found buyers for some of them over the following weeks, so they filed out of the merchants' yard one and two at a time. After a month, just 10 of the sickest remained. With the Charleston market glutted, Laurens figured that these stragglers "could not sell . . . in Town at any tolerable price being much reduced and ordinary." He decided to transship them once more. These last unsold survivors returned to sea. Only one woman was spared this move, "being very much swell'd and having Impostume on her Knee."

Thankfully, this last passage was just "round to George Town, a Port to the Northward" of Charleston by 60 miles but still within the colony. During the first month in George Town, 6 of the Angolans found themselves sold by Lauren's agents, fetching, in Lauren's words, "more than the whole 9 would have brought" in Charleston. Meanwhile, back in the entrepot, Laurens sold the woman he described as "the Wench that remain'd with us in Town." Sometime in April or May, one of the 3 Angolans who remained unsold in George Town finally succumbed to the hardships of the journey. The other 2 survived, however. They were finally sold more than 6 months after (and more than 200 miles away from) their first arrival in the Americas.

The Angolan men and women from *l'Aimable* who rode the Relief to South Carolina before dispersing across the colony endured a particularly convoluted journey to American slavery, but they were just a few among hundreds of thousands of enslaved people who faced final passages after

173

surviving an Atlantic crossing to British America. Time and again, African captives climbed off vessels that carried them from Africa to Jamaica or Dominica or South Carolina, only to be forced aboard a schooner that whisked them away again to North Carolina or Martinique or Cartagena. Studies of the Atlantic slave trade highlight the infamous Middle Passage, the forced crossing of the Atlantic, concluding the story with a sale of captives in the American port where the ocean crossing ended. Implicit in that choice of endpoint is an assumption that plantation owners—and others eager to exploit enslaved labor—were the buyers of enslaved people after the Atlantic crossing. But another type of buyer prowled the sales of recently arrived Africans in early America: one seeking captives to exploit, not as laborers, but as commodities. Trading between American colonies, these speculators monitored the prices for people in various ports and forged commercial connections across imperial borders. When opportunities arose, they pounced, buying newly arrived captives in one port, forcing them back aboard ships to another colony, and selling them all over again. For the traders, such dealings opened myriad economic possibilities because enslaved workers were among the most coveted assets in the colonial Americas. For the captives, such speculative endeavors meant that their forced migrations often continued after the transatlantic voyage. This intercolonial trafficking—its scale and reasons for existence, the strategies of the traders, its importance to imperial rivalries, its connections to broader commerce, and the final passages it entailed for African captives, are at the heart of this chapter in the history of the transatlantic slave trade.

For the African captives trafficked from the major ports of coastal Africa, their ports of disembarkation in British America—from where their migration continued to numerous plantations—were: Bridgetown, Barbados; Kingston, Jamaica; Charleston, South Carolina; and Roseau, Dominica. These ports were entrepots on the way to myriad colonies of the British, Spanish and French Empires (occasionally others). According to one source estimating the total number of captives at 12.5 million, Britain was responsible for over 3.5 million captives, or a quarter of the total taken to numerous new ports; only the Portuguese, including Brazilian traders, conveyed more Africans across the Atlantic, though they were outstripped by British deliveries during the peak years of the trade in the 18th century. Furthermore, British intercolonial traders engaged in a diverse range of slave transshipment activities. The outposts of British America—spread across the Caribbean, North America, and occasionally South America—adopted varied economic regimes and labor systems. In some regions, slave plantations anchored economies; in others, enslaved people toiled in more marginal tasks and professions. Not only did the labor demands of British colonies differ considerably over time and space, but so did the relationships of various colonies to Atlantic trading patterns. This diversity fostered a range of slave-trading activities within the empire. Transimperial commerce further bolstered the trade. British transatlantic traders delivered Africans to entrepots in British America, and then British colonists or foreign settlers navigated the transshipment of the human commodities across imperial lines—legally or otherwise.

To this end, Gregory E. O'Malley in his book *Final Passages* outlined five interrelated arguments in relation to the Intercolonial Atlantic slave trade. First, and most simply, the intercolonial slave trade was robust in scale. Of the roughly 2.7 million Africans forced across the Atlantic to British American ports from the mid-17th to the 18th century, approximately 15%—well over 300,000 people—promptly boarded new ships bound for other parts of the Americas. More than 200,000 of them departed the British Empire, bound primarily for French and Spanish settlements. Over 70,000 African people endured transshipment from the Caribbean to North America. Another 50,000 captives faced final passages from one British Caribbean territory to another. Many more were purchased by speculators who moved people within their colony of arrival for resale. This extensive intercolonial slave trading occurred for a variety of reasons. Colonists in many American regions wanted enslaved Africans but rarely saw vessels arrive directly from Africa, owing to both economics and geopolitics. In the broadest sense, demand exceeded supply. Europeans struggled to obtain as many captives on the African coast as they desired, and not all colonies could prevail in drawing shipments. Those settlements that lacked large numbers of potential buyers, sufficient capital, or well-connected merchants often failed to attract shippers directly from Africa who typically carried two or three hundred Africans per voyage. The need to sell all these captives quickly, without deflating prices or offering extensive credit, steered transatlantic slave ships away from small, underdeveloped British colonies—such as the Bahamas or North Carolina—and also from larger, more prosperous ones where the exploitation of African labor nonetheless remained marginal such as Pennsylvania or Massachusetts. Slave trading to these colonies could only be profitable on a smaller scale, a niche intercolonial slavers were keen to fill.

Trafficking between colonies was also robust because geopolitical and mercantile factors left many colonists outside British territory struggling to acquire enslaved laborers from merchants of their own empire. Most notably, the colonies of Spanish America relied on foreigners for slave shipments owing to treaties dating back to the 15th century, which barred Spanish merchants from Africa. In the 16th and 17th centuries, the Spanish turned chiefly to Portuguese and Dutch suppliers, but from 1660 onward, British slavers became increasingly important for providing Spanish America's African captives. Likewise, from the late 17th through the 18th century, French colonists looked to British traders to supplement insufficient deliveries from their own traders. The resulting British trade to foreign colonies often involved intercolonial shipments because relations between Britain and both France and Spain were tense. At times, commerce between the colonies of these powers was illegal in the eyes of one government or another, and even when condoned, it was complicated and perilous. Large vessels carrying hundreds of ailing African captives and out-of-date diplomatic information across the ocean typically avoided the risk of entering foreign harbors. Merchants trading people across imperial borders had to proceed with caution, so more nimble intercolonial traders possessed a great advantage due to their proximity to foreign markets. They could forge personal connections in foreign colonies and keep abreast of changes in policy or policing.

The second of O'Malley's arguments is that the extensive scale of intercolonial slave trading powerfully shaped enslaved people's experiences. The Middle Passage across the Atlantic was, for all its horrors, but one part of a long and multifaceted journey to American slavery. For many 21st century readers of books covering the slave trade, "Middle Passage" conjures thoughts of the plight of African people in their Atlantic crossings, but the voyage was actually termed "middle" to reflect the European, not African, experience. For many European traders, the transatlantic voyage formed the second leg of a three-part journey: a first passage, from Europe to Africa with trade goods; a "middle" passage, from Africa to America with slaves; and a third voyage, from America back to Europe with colonial staples. There were certainly deviations from this "triangle" trade, but it was such three-legged journeys that gave the Middle Passage its name. The irony is that, despite these Eurocentric origins, the term "Middle Passage" fits the experiences of many African migrants in ways that historians often fail to recognize. Their journeys did not usually begin at ports of embarkation for the ocean crossing, nor did they necessarily end when transatlantic vessels first reached the Americas. Instead, people fell into slavery both in African coastal regions and deep in the interior, with extended journeys to port cities increasingly common (especially for men) as the slave trade expanded in the 18th century. Stops to toil for African owners along the way, for a harvest season or even a few years, sometimes punctuated these trips. Only upon reaching the Atlantic coast were such people sold to Europeans for a further voyage to the New World.

Just as enslaved peopled funneled into the Atlantic slave trade from wide regions in West Africa, many spread outward from their ports of arrival in the New World. It is useful to think of the Atlantic slave trade as analogous to a major river system, such as the Nile. Like the tributaries of a river, slave traders within Africa channeled people from wide catchment areas to ports of embarkation, and from these ports, transatlantic vessels flowed into a metaphorical torrent, propelled across the Atlantic by the actual watercourse forged by the trade winds and equatorial currents. From the major American entrepots, forced migrants then branched out again, like the bifurcating streams of a river's delta—some great and some small. The routes of the intra-American phase of the slave trade meandered through time, with some channels flowing heavily for a few years, only to dry up in the next. Cumulatively, however, such intercolonial channels comprised an ongoing forced migration of hundreds of thousands of people.

The third argument is that intercolonial trade was not just incidental to the British transatlantic slave trade but vital to its growth and to the growth of American slavery more generally. Traders venturing from Africa to America in the 17th and 18th centuries tended to specialize in slave trading, so they usually transported hundreds of captives per shipment. As such, they concentrated deliveries on the largest, most established American markets for enslaved labor where demand was consistently strong. Intercolonial traders, by contrast, could operate on a smaller scale because they incorporated slave trading into a mixed commerce. As a result, they targeted a wider range of colonial markets. Many British colonies, in their early decades of experimenting with forced African labor, relied on intercolonial sources of enslaved workers. Likewise, some small British colonies—or larger ones where slavery remained marginal to the economy—continued to rely on intercolonial supplies through most of their histories with slavery. The intra-American trade was instrumental to the institution's spread from Barbados (England's first sugar-producing island), initially to the Chesapeake and Jamaica, and eventually to all the British colonies of North America and the Caribbean. Furthermore, the trade abetted slavery's growth outside the British Empire by connecting British transatlantic traders to French and Spanish colonial markets, where demand exceeded the supply of exploitable African laborers. Meanwhile, all of this intercolonial trafficking—foreign and domestic—spurred the African trade. As British American ports such as Bridgetown and Kingston became hubs of transshipment, British traders contemplating ventures to Africa came to rely on these entrepots as stable markets where hundreds of enslaved captives would sell quickly at almost any time. Robust intercolonial trade made the transatlantic slave trade a more reliable—and more expansive—business.

The fourth related argument is that the economic significance of this intercolonial commerce in human beings extended well beyond the profits from buying African people at one price and selling them at a higher one. For many merchants in the Americas, the intercolonial slave trade facilitated other branches of commerce, entangling the profits of many traditional trades with the buying and selling of people. As colonies on the North American mainland carved out an economic niche as provisioners to the sugar colonies of the Caribbean—exporting wheat, fish, pork, and timber to the tropical heart of Britain's colonial enterprise—traders sometimes struggled to find lucrative commodities for the return voyage from the Caribbean. North American markets often saw gluts of sugar and rum, but the British Caribbean produced little else. Enslaved people arriving from Africa, however, offered another commodity in which to take returns for North American produce, helping to complete a trade circuit that made North America the breadbasket of the Caribbean. Traders looking to export North American staples to Europe also found intercolonial slave trading useful. Chesapeake and Lowcountry planters often preferred to sell their rice, indigo, or tobacco to traders who offered enslaved workers in exchange. As a result, some merchants acquired enslaved people in the Caribbean with the principal aim of securing trader partners in North America.

In a similar fashion, British traders and imperial policymakers used the intercolonial slave trade to open other branches of commerce with French and especially Spanish America. Until the late 18th century, both France and Spain officially barred foreign traders from their American colonies, but high demand for enslaved Africans in both empires led to exceptions— sometimes official, sometimes ad hoc—for foreign merchants selling African people. From the 1660s and throughout the 18th century, Britain pursued this transimperial slave trade relentlessly, gradually asserting themselves as the primary slave suppliers to Spanish America and as important traders (rivaling the French themselves) to French colonies. To be sure, the British hoped to profit from the sale of enslaved people in foreign colonies, but such hopes were always entangled with dreams of opening foreign territories to the export of British manufactured goods. Because intercolonial slave trading enmeshed with other mercantile activities and geopolitical objectives, the profits derived from enslaved Africans in the Americas were not solely from their labor but arose out of this nexus of functions. Compared to other commodities, enslaved Africans were unique not only in their humanity but also for their ability to bring myriad trade partners to the table. The exploitation of enslaved Africans as laborers produced massive amounts of affordable staples from American soils; the exploitation of Africans as goods facilitated a bustling trade that aided Britain's rise to commercial supremacy in the Atlantic world.

Given this strategic and economic importance, O'Malley's fifth and last argument is that the intercolonial slave trade influenced imperial policy, gradually pushing Britain, France, and Spain away from mercantilism and toward policies of freer trade. By the late 16th century, Spain was exempting the slave trade from the empire's prohibition on foreign trade in the colonies to secure a labor supply. Spain's *asiento de negros* opened Spanish America exclusively to a series of merchants who contracted to supply enslaved Africans. By the mid-17th and 18th centuries, much of the asiento commerce became intercolonial as the Dutch and then the British used their own Caribbean Islands as trade barriers in times of acute labor shortage, allowing Spanish colonists to secure captives by venturing elsewhere. Likewise, starting in the 1660s, England granted exceptions to its own prohibitions against foreign trade with its colonies, allowing the export of enslaved people from the English Caribbean to rival colonies. Over the course of the 18th century, Britain pursued such commerce with increasing intensity, culminating in the 1760s with the creation of Caribbean "free ports" that welcomed foreign subjects to British territory to buy enslaved people and British manufactured goods. France's shift to freer trade came later and more suddenly. The French disapproved of any exceptions to trade barriers throughout the 17th and most of the 18th centuries, even to overcome labor shortages. But by the late 18th century, France, too, dropped prohibitions to secure supplies of enslaved Africans from the British. For all these powers, some of their first experiments with free trade were designed to facilitate intercolonial commerce in unfree people.

With respect to this topic of the intercolonial transatlantic slave trade, there is a paucity of firsthand accounts from captives in the slave trade, which has raised questions as to how to best label the persons involved. Slave traders and government officials seldom recorded much about the backgrounds of groups of captives, let alone individuals' names, stories, or personalities. Records usually label people simply as "Negroes" or "Slaves," offering the historian little to work with in the quest for more humanizing descriptors. To avoid endless repetition of the commodified term *slave*, writers such as O'Malley and this writer, often refer to those conveyed in the slave trade as *Africans*, or simply as *people*. Holding (and moving) people in bondage was a willful practice rooted in violence and coercion. In recognition of this, traded people are referred to variously as captives, forced migrants, or enslaved people. Where surviving evidence reveals that a group or individual is from a particular African region, they are referred to by the ethnicity, linguistic group, or region they came from, such as Angolan, Aja, Igbo, Gambian, or Akan, but with trepidation. Knowing that a group of captives departed Africa from a particular port or region does not equate to knowing their ethnicity, sense of identity, or language with precision.

Whatever their personal experiences, one thing the vast majority of captives in the British intercolonial trade shared was that they were Africans who had recently arrived in the Americas. Of the 26,830 people whose background is noted in the intercolonial database, 24,713 of them (more than 92%) were described as "New Negroes," "Africans," or a more specific African ethnicity. Fewer than 8% of people were described as "seasoned" or as otherwise having spent substantial time in the Americas. Furthermore, these statistics actually overstate the significance of American-born, or creolized, slaves to the traffic. Many port records labeled most captives simply as "negroes," only adding occasional qualifiers for particular groups as "seasoned," implying that the typical group of "negroes" was not acculturated to the American slave regime. But without more definitive proof of their background, such groups labeled only as "negroes" are not counted either way in calculating the statistics above. Additionally, port records documenting voyages that exported enslaved people from British colonies to foreign territories—the branch of the trade carrying the greatest numbers of people—rarely specified the origins of the "negroes" departing, yet anecdotal descriptions of such ventures in merchant and government accounts virtually never mention movements of seasoned people. Traders consistently describe the traffic as a transshipment within a matter of days or weeks of Africans' disembarking from the Middle Passage.

Two principal factors account for the predominance of recently arrived Africans in the intercolonial trade. First, Caribbean planters had little reason to sell acclimatized slaves. The biggest risk in slave investment was mortality, and this danger was greatest in an African's first year in the new disease environment of the Americas, while recovering from the slave trade. Enslaved workers also became more valuable to an owner after adapting to the plantation regime. The exceptions to this rule of increasing value after seasoning were the presence of acclimatized or American-born people in the intercolonial trade: most buyers preferred recently arrived Africans. Plantation owners and other prospective buyers questioned the motives of anyone offering acclimatized people for sale, wary that prior owners were seeking to unload problems. This fear of importing strong-willed or rebellious people pushed many colonies to enact prohibitive import duties on enslaved people who had resided in another colony for any considerable amount of time.

When traders did transship seasoned people, planters avoided them, a lesson James Burnett of Jamaica learned the hard way. In 1772, he sent a group of enslaved Jamaicans to South Carolina for sale, where his agent John Hopton "tried to barter [them] away for Produce and at private Sale but could not succeed." Hopton eventually resorted to an auction that netted low prices. When Burnett criticized Hopton for the cut-rate sales, the agent fired back that he had tried to warn Burnett. "Were they my own property I could not have done more in the disposal of them," Hopton argued, "for the people here as I mentioned to you before seem prejudiced against West India Negroes, that, with the heavy Duty laid on all season'd Slaves imported into this Province, have been a means of lessening the Value of them prodigiously." Indeed, the previous year, Hopton had cautioned Burnett that "People here in general object to the West India negroes as there are a great many of them sent here for their Roguery." Virginia trader Charles Steuart agreed, when he explained to Anthony Fahie why 2 enslaved men whom Fahie sent from Saint Kitts fetched low prices in 1751. As Steuart put it, "New Negroe Boys of 3 ft high will sell considerably better than the best West India Negroes, for it is generally supposed that they are ship'd off for great Crimes." Despite the linguistic and cultural barriers, most slaveholders preferred to buy recent African immigrants, taking solace in the knowledge that no prior European master has sold them owing to a rebellious streak or some unseen malady. When Charleston merchant Levinius Clarkson courted transshipments of Africans in 1773, during a moment of high demand in his province, the instructions he offered to would-be partners were standard:

"Should you meet with any new Negroes who have not been Six Months in any of his Majesty's Colonies . . . you may purchase ten or twelve on our joint Account."

The possible exception to this widespread preference for newly arrived Africans occurred in some northern colonies, especially during the 17th and early 18th centuries and in towns where Africans were employed as domestic servants. For instance, in 1715 Philadelphia merchant Jonathan Dickinson cautioned a correspondent in Jamaica against transshipping captives to his port, saying that Philadelphia did not want slaves, "save those that Live in other P'vinces." But Dickinson himself was not requesting seasoned slaves from Jamaica; he preferred that none be sent to him at all. And the prohibitive duties on seasoned slaves in Rhode Island and New York suggest that preferences for American-born or acculturated people were usual, even in the North, at least by the mid-18th century. Responding to both trade laws and market demand, intercolonial traders ensured that African captives fresh out of transatlantic vessels predominated in the slave trade between American colonies.

The Rigors of Plantation Life

Barbados

For Britain and Europe, the West Indian takeoff of plantation sugar, initially centered in Barbados in the mid-17th century, was a matter of strongly fortuitous timing. Spain's boom in New World silver had already begun to flag by around 1620. Confident with this was a downturn in the Baltic grain trade, in the woolens that were the mainstay of northern European commerce, and in the French wine trade. As a result, in the British historian of slavery, Robin Blackburn's words, as slave plantations gathered economic momentum, they "not only swam against the stream of the 17th century crisis; they became a dynamic pole of the Atlantic economy in the period 1700—1815.

Sugar thereafter quickly became that rare kind of product whose supply could rarely match its demand, and yet for which prices nonetheless declined dramatically over time. This came about mostly as a result of the ever-larger acreages of planted cane as the plantation-complex took over bigger and bigger islands. England seized Jamaica in 1644 and eventually re-created the Barbados experience on that much larger island, importing about 1.2 million kidnapped Africans there over time—more than it would elsewhere in the Caribbean. But after an initial lag, France—as abovementioned, determined not to be left out of this boom, began to catch up with British production on the islands it controlled. Between 1651 and 1725, slave departures from Africa bound for the French Caribbean increased from around 5,500 to roughly 77,000 per annum. And in the quarter century that followed, with the rapid emergence of Saint Domingue as the largest sugar producer of all, the volume of French slave shipments doubled again.

During the 40 years after James Drax founded his plantation, consumption of sugar increased fourfold in England, overwhelmingly on the back of Barbados's production. By the 1620s, Brazil's combined trade in sugar and slaves had eclipsed Portugal's Asia trade in overall value and had equaled the value of Spain's haul of American silver. In 1600 Brazil had supplied nearly all the sugar consumed in Western Europe. But in a striking measure of just how the sugar revolution progressed in the West Indies, by 1700, Barbados alone was producing more of the commodity than the Bahia region of Brazil, supplying nearly half of Europe's consumption—despite its later start and vastly smaller size. By 1660 it is estimated that tiny Barbados's sugar production alone was worth more than combined exports of all of Spain's New World colonies. And this was just for starters. From 1650 to 1800, as major new sugar islands emerged in the Caribbean, sugar consumption in Britain would increase 2,500%, and over this time, the market value of sugar would consistently exceed the value of all other commodities combined.

It stands to reason that a boom so large and so sustained would have been enormously stimulative, in ways both direct and indirect. In London the number of refineries shot up from 5 in 1615, to 30 in 1670, and perhaps to 75 by 1700; many other sugar refineries set up operations in smaller port cities and provincial centers. And these were not, by a long measure, the only commercial and growth-inducing effects of the sugar and slave complex. In fact, the sugar boom created a long succession of strong, systemic economic waves that were felt throughout the Atlantic world.

Barbados and the other Caribbean sugar colonies that followed in its wake not only provided a direct boost to the European economy in the 17th century, but perhaps even more critically, they threw a lifeline to the struggling colonies of British America, which were restricted from selling many types of manufactures into the protected English market. To the Americans' good fortune, they found avid buyers on Barbados for products both rough and finished. These included furniture, livestock (both for its meat and manure, which was highly prized as fertilizer), and lumber. Barbados imported such things and many more because once sugar monoculture had taken over on that booming island, productive land was deemed simply too valuable to farm for food or put to any other use and so, like a modern petrostate, pretty much everything required for local consumption was imported. In time, this even came to include New England rum. As Eric Williams wrote in *Capitalism and Slavery* of a time just a few decades later:

> In 1770 the continental colonies sent to the West Indies nearly one-third of their exports of dried fish and almost all their pick -led fish, seven-eighths of their oats, seven-tenths of their corn, almost all their peas and beans, half of their flour, all their butter and cheese, over-one-quarter of their rice, almost all their onions; five-sixths of their pine, oak and cedar boards, over half of their staves, nearly all their hoops; all their horses, sheep, hogs and poultry; almost all their soup and candles. As [an earlier historian] has told us, "It was the wealth accumulated from West Indian trade which more than anything else underlay the prosperity and civili-zation of New England and the Middle Colonies."

To better understand North America's dependence on trade with the sugar islands, it helps to put a figure on the kind of wealth disparities that existed within the British Empire. Taking Jamaica as an example, one historian has estimated that annual per capita income among whites on that island in the decade that Williams wrote of was more than 25 times higher than in Britain's mainland colonies, £2,201, compared with £60.2.

The plantation experiences of African captives in Barbados were hellish and miserable. The case of the Drax family was instructive, as revealed in the detailed memo of family patriarch, James Drax's grandson, Henry. The latter's memo was a 24-page instruction book to his overseer, which was duplicated and studied by other aspirational sugar barons on the island for more than a century. The picture it paints of the Draxes is one of "book farmers," or pioneers of capitalism, whose rigorous accounting practices and focus on labor organization sought to leverage very careful bookkeeping and the harnessing of data to steadily improve productivity.

Given the island's small size, once the early waves of land grabbing and fevered investment in sugar had passed, there was little left for newcomers to acquire, least of all the penniless indentured whites who had been the island's main source of labor in the early years of the colony. For ex-servants, this made Barbados "the worst poor man's country" in British America, a place that almost every white person who didn't quickly prosper desperately wanted to escape, which usually meant onward migration to other English colonies in the Caribbean or on the North American mainland. To sustain a supply of whites into indentured servitude on the island, as many as 50,000 prisoners had been shipped to the island by 1655, along with Scottish and Irish soldiers captured during Cromwell's campaigns and many other victims were inveigled in cities like London and Bristol and shipped off involuntarily to the Caribbean. The slang for this has been largely lost to the English language, but back then people spoke of being "Barbadosed," a term that was used in much the same way the word "shanghaied," came to be employed in the late 19th century. These and other factors, starting with the substantially lower cost of African labor, but also including crude racial notions that fancied Blacks as being better suited physically and temperamentally for unremittingly grueling work in the tropics, helped incline planters toward a preference for African labor, and within less than a generation this is what turned Barbados into an archetypal slave society.

Between 1630 and the 1680s, Barbados went from being an island with a tiny Black presence to one where people brought in chains from Africa constituted 75% of the population, and 95% of the workforce. In the West, new slave societies like these were largely confined to the Caribbean, where Barbados became both avatar and model. Even though Brazil received the largest number of slaves of any single country by far, at no point did it ever have a demographic majority composed of slaves, or even of slaves and mixed-race Creoles combined. In America, meanwhile, a racial composition so thoroughly dominated by Blacks was witnessed only in the Carolina Low

Country, where rice was farmed. There, by the way, the earliest recorded instance of African slaves being put to work on plantations was that of the third governor of the colony, Sir John Yeamans, founder of Charleston, who brought slaves from Barbados to clear his land and commence planting. To a significant degree, the populations of Carolina, Virginia, Maryland, and even Rhode Island and Massachusetts would be seeded by white people from Barbados as well.

Sugar planters in Barbados, and then later in much bigger production centers like Jamaica and Saint Domingue, were relentless tinkerers, searching through constant innovation to increase yields and profits, not just through farming techniques, per se, but through strict and exacting management of labor, as well, making them some of the most "accomplished capitalists of their time." It is hard to reconcile this with the fact that their wealth, as well as the very prosperity of the age, was built on the cruel foundation of bondage, but therein lie the roots of common modernity.

New notions about the ethical basis of labor and social values that might today be called *Humanist*, were just then beginning to arise in England, but Black slaves benefited little from this, if at all. It was permissible for Europeans to exploit African labor in maximalist ways, much "like a horse or a cow," that would not be socially acceptable in the case of whites. This extreme racial exploitation began with unremitting fieldwork, with workdays commencing before sunup and continuing until dusk and often beyond. The Royal African Company originally aspired to a ratio of 2 males for every female on its slave shipments but was never able to approach this target, possibly due in part to African resistance, and to the premium some African societies themselves placed on males. To make up for the shortage in men, the plantation regime as it emerged in Barbados and other islands began to assign women to some of the harshest tasks, such as the heaviest roles in the field. By the early modern era, these practices were already inconceivable among whites, even for indentured laborers, whose harsh treatment has sometimes been likened to that of African slaves. And as they planted, weeded, and harvested, Black women, even while pregnant, were almost equally subject to the lash.

More than tactics aimed merely at boosting productivity, the subjection of Blacks to such brutal and degrading regimes very early on became a key psychosocial factor in elevating white identity in the new mixed societies of the Americas; they became proof for whites, in a tautological sense, that people of European stock were a fundamentally different type of human being, people of an inherently superior nature to Blacks. As the historian Peter Thompson wrote, "The nature of labor on a sugar plantation was without parallel in the European experience, and even writers who prized its end product characterized the work itself, and hence the workers who carried it out, in animalistic terms." By being exempted from the most flagrant indignities inflicted on enslaved Blacks, even the lowest of whites gradually began to identify with "the strong sense of honor the experience of mastership generated," in the phrase of sociologist Orlando Patterson.

One of the most dehumanizing tasks was the seasonal handling of manure, an unavoidable requirement for successful sugar cultivation. Intensive dunging was another one of Drax's innovations. "Theire is No producing good Canes without dunging Every holle," he wrote. Roughly a ton per acre was applied on his lands each year. This involved the conveyance of large, sloshing 80-pound vats of feces, both animal and human, into the fields atop the heads of slaves, inevitably washing over the faces of people who bore them and drenching them, followed by the pouring of feces into the individual holes in which cane seedlings were planted. As one would expect, this produced soaring disease rates in the manure porters. In 17th- and 18th-century Barbados, female slaves from Africa generally dominated the ranks of those who performed this task, and indeed field labor in general.

During the grueling harvest season many slaves were obliged to work nearly all-night shifts, feeding cane into the boilers and keeping their fires stoked. "The only break in the work week was from Saturday night till

Monday morning. Otherwise, the 25 men and women in the factory worked continuously in shifts lasting all day and part of the night, or the whole of every second or third night." Slaves were sometimes kept going with cane juice, due to its high sugar content, and sometimes with cane spirits as well. And the dead-on-your-feet effect this produced led to many deaths of slaves by extensive burns or by crushing after being pulled into the rollers by their fingers. This latter type of incident occurred so frequently that it was common to keep a hatchet on a chain within reach so that an unfortunate slave's arm could be chopped off before the machinery consumed his whole body.

Though overseers were sometimes warned against excessively harsh treatment of slaves, the world of sugar plantations accepted the high mortality rates for Blacks driven in fields or put to work at the boiler in unabashed fashion; this was considered an ordinary part of the business, an ordinary fact of life. If Henry Drax's Black workforce included 327 slaves, for example, his writings assume a death rate of 3—5% per year. Other Barbados planters of that era spoke of 6% as being common. A common estimate for the average life expectancy of slaves ensnared in sugar production was 7 years or less.

Mortality rates on Brazilian sugar plantations were undoubtedly also high, but the approach of Drax and other members of the founding generation of big planters on Barbados marked a sharp break with practices in Pernambuco and Bahia, one that reflected the industry's important but unheralded role in the early stages of a shift from feudalism toward capitalism. As the historian Richard Dunn observes, "In Brazil the senhor de engenho, or lord of the mill was, as his name implies, a grandiose manner lord. He owned a huge tract, maintained a large force of salaried artisans, tenant farmers, and slaves, lived nobly in his Big House, and presided over a self-sufficient, paternalistic community complete with church, court, police force, and social-welfare agencies." In contrast to this *seigneurialism*, the big, early success stories among Barbados growers were men who, like Drax,

191

followed a much narrower, more hardnosed pursuit of profit and specialization, quite close, in fact, to the ethos of modern business. Significantly, many of them had commercial roots back in England, and hailed from families with experience investing in Atlantic trading and privateering. Dunn continues, "The English planter combined the roles of mill owner and cane grower. He did not attempt to produce food, clothing, and equipment for his workforce on his own estate, but depended on outside suppliers. He offered a minimum of social services."

As Britain came to see the abundant and regular provisioning of slaves to its sugar colonies as essential to its Atlantic empire and stepped up its involvement in the trafficking of Africans to the West Indies, what inexorably followed was a further de-emphasis on slave longevity or indeed even on their reproduction. Beginning no later than the 1660s, short life expectancies and low reproduction rates became a universal failure of plantation economy regimes as sugar spread throughout the Caribbean. In a region where the Barbados model became the leading template, including for the French, it was widely considered "cheaper to work slaves to the utmost, and by hard fare and hard usage, to wear them out before they became useless, and unable to do service; and then to buy new ones to fill up their places," as one Antiguan farmer put it in 1751. Robert Robinson, a clergyman-planter on the colony of Nevis, considered that in light of the low survival rate of infants, the loss of work to pregnancy by females, and the expense of feeding and clothing children before they could contribute much to the plantation, the gain from reproduction "cannot be great," so there was little point in encouraging it.

Brazil and Elsewhere in the Caribbean

The production of sugar in Brazil and the Caribbean consumed the majority of African slave labor, and another 5% worked in the Old South of the United States on cotton, rice, and tobacco plantations. In the case of Britain, it found its Empire in the Caribbean primarily for the purposes of sugar production plantations—the first of which was in Barbados, whereby captive Africans were part of the so-called "Triangular Trade". This involved the purchase of captured Africans who were then shipped to the Caribbean to produce sugar for export to Britain. Jamaica would—by the 18th century—emerge as the cornerstone of this system as the 4,874 tons of sugar exported in 1700, would rise to 17,399—and even more astonishingly to 73,849 annually by 1815.

In the case of Brazil, slave labor was the most characteristic aspect of both the rural and urban scene. Though a steady decline in productivity from the mid-17th century would see Britain—along with the French— eventually overtake Brazil as the leading producer of sugar, it was actually the Portuguese—colonizers of Brazil—that pioneered large-scale plantation agriculture in the New World. Nevertheless, sugar remained the colony's main cash crop, followed by cotton—accounting for 20% of exports by the beginning of the 19th century, cereal production, tobacco and cocoa cultivation, and diamond and gold mining. Captives worked on plantations and mines across the fertile coastal areas of Bahia, the fertile coastal strip of present-day Rio de Janeiro, Rio Grande do Sul, Santa Catarina, and Minas Gerais.

As the trade approached its peak between the 18th and 19th century, captives were subjected to some of the most unimaginable of dehumanizing conditions. Brazil, like any other colony or country, needed to regularly replenish its slave population—for the most part owing to very high mortality rates. Most individuals never survived their initial acclimatization and training, whilst others died due to a poor diet, insanitary living conditions and disease (cholera and smallpox epidemics). As it was deemed more economic to literally work field-based captives to death (brought on by ill-health and exhaustion), the demand for new arrivals remained constant to necessarily maintain productivity and mitigate the low fertility rate and high infant mortality rate.

The slave conditions in the British Caribbean colonies were no less brutal than was the case in Brazil. This was succinctly expressed by Elsa Goveia as "excessive intermittent labour" which was absolutely dependent on the "drawing" of blood. By the end of the 18th century, the [typical] working day in the Antiguan fields began at dawn, where groups of 20—60 (sometimes more) would work continually until 9am to have their breakfast. Thereafter, work would continue until noon before having their lunch, and shortly after resume until half an hour (c. 5pm) before sunset; other non-field jobs would be worked well into the night. The field workers as quoted by John Luffman were:

> under the inspection of white overseers... subordinate to these overseers are drivers, commonly called dog-drivers, who are mostly black or mulatto fellows of the worst dispositions; and these men are furnished with whips, which, while on duty, they are obliged, on pain of severe punishment, to have with them, and are authorised to flog wherever they see the least relaxation from labour; nor is it a consideration with them, whether it proceeds from idleness or inability, paying at the same time little or no regard to age or sex.

The diabolical nature of the above conditions has been the subject of attempts to "sanitize" the slave trade by treating it as just another business—something which has increased as capitalist ideology gained traction in the west. Unsurprisingly, historian, Herbert Klein, remarked as a corrective that while "violence and death were a significant factor... the overwhelming majority of slaves did reach America". Moreover "despite the *atmosphere* of violence, the experience may not have been as psychologically damaging as some have claimed" [author's emphasis]. Notwithstanding, he arguably attempted to counterbalance this by acknowledging that it is "undesirable and a basic fact of the slave trade" that millions of Africans were shipped to America against their will", and ultimately this was not done to "better their lives".

Perhaps more crucially, there were individuals within the supply chain of the slave trade who were well aware—by their own admission—of their activities offending contemporary standards. An example of this was an account given by William Bosman, the chief agent of the Dutch West India Company, who was based at its main trading location in modern-day Ghana (Cape Coast):

> When these slaves come to Fida [present-day Whydah, Benin Republic], they are put in Prison altogether... they are thoroughly examined, even to the smallest Member, and that naked too both Men and Women, without the least Distinction of Modesty. Those which approved as good are set on one side; and the lame and faulty are set by as Invalides... the remainder are numbered [sic], and it is entered [sic] who delivered them. In the mean while a burning iron, with the Arms or Name of the Companies, yes [sic] in the Fire; with ours are marked on the Breast ... *I doubt not but this Trade seems very barbarous to you, but since it is followed by mere [sic] necessity it must go on*; but we yet take all possible care that they are not burned too hard, especially the Women, who are more tender than the Men (emphasis added).

To ensure the submissiveness of the captive Africans—especially when they were conveyed in large numbers to numerous New World plantations—the cruelty was profligate. Some captives were branded several times over to prove ownership, to demonstrate that export duty had been paid, to show their vassalage to the king of the country concerned or, in a supreme act of double standards—to indicate that they had been baptized. In 1813, branding was replaced by a metal collar or bracelet, but it was restored 5 years later, this time with a silver branding iron and still with the evident intention of making clear that the captive was now an enslaved commodity, not a person.

In Brazil, save for minority voices advocating for the end of the trade and for this to be gradually substituted with free labor, most white Portuguese—planters, merchants, officials, and even priests—were deeply prejudiced on the subject of slavery and the slave trade. It was believed that Africans were born to serve and, that through the slave trade they were rescued from Barbarism in Africa and introduced to the benefits of Christianity in Brazil.

Oral Traditions and Folklore: Fostering Group Consciousness and Connection to the Homeland

In the cases of the Nri-Igbos, Gold Coast Africans (including the Akan and Ashantis), Yorubas, Kongoes, and myriad other African captives, several oral traditions, music, dance, folklore, myths, group economic strategies, principles, religious faiths, and philosophies were transported from Africa, and were contributory to the formation of New World identities. This led to a process of creolization through drawing on their respective cultures. One example of this was the creation of secular songs across the West Indies. In Haiti, it was documented that the inspiration and themes of the lyrics of these songs were derived from playful gossip, ridicule, lovemaking, scandal, reproach, misfortune, mistreatment, deprivation, hunger, sickness, and death.

There were also work songs to simultaneously maximize their productivity and provide a form of entertainment. This was present among the agricultural groups known as the *coumbites* and *societies* in Haiti. The men, and in some cases women, gather to the beating of drums, wooden cylinders, or the blowing of conch shell horns to till the earth together as their hoes rise and fall in a long rhythmic line across the field. In Jamaica, these work songs are called *iammas*, and were sung in much the same way as in Haiti.

Reaping a bountiful harvest was celebrated among the Africans in the Caribbean, as can be in this chorus sung by these Jamaican village traders:

> *Dis a day is working-day,*
> *Dis a day is feasting-day,*
> *Dig away, dig away, dig away.*
> *Mouth an' hand mus' go togedder,*
> *Lak a sistah and a breddah,*
> *Dig away, dig away, dig away.*

The above cooperative system was very important in the workers

196

regulating their agricultural output—a feature common across the rural Caribbean. This custom is discernibly related to comparable groupings in West Africa of which a distinctive form is the *dokpure* of Benin: the workgroup, as an instrument of cooperative labor and mutual self-help, with its tradition of giving no pecuniary reward for work done, but of making the feast which comes at the end of the day's labor adequate return.

One writer covering the African Haitian experience noted that the institution of the market in the Caribbean is itself inherently African. In Africa as it is the Caribbean, most market traders and distributors are women; generally, the men are the producers of the goods. Women were empowered in this economic relationship as they controlled market prices and ultimately kept the proceeds from their trading activity. This sense of independence is a carryover from the African tradition, which was unique and sharply contrasted from the conventional European practice.

The Stone Feast and Big Drum of Carriacou

On the island of Carriacou—a dependency of Grenada, Lorna McDaniel observed similarities between the *Stone Feast of Carriacou* and "*the Igbo Second burial.*" Both events are final death rituals which incorporate music and dance, and which [ceremonially] "assures the deceased final rest" among the ancestors of "Old Parents."

The *Stone Feast of Carriacou* comprises the laying of the headstone, the celebratory feast, and the performance of the Big Drum ritual of nationhood.

> . . . at the home of the person setting up the tomb the beasts
> are sacrificed, while the tombstone is collected from the ma-
> son's shop in Hillsborough. Five libations of rum and water
> are made to the stone: first by his kinsman, normally the head
> of the deceased's descent-line, . . . next, on its arrival to the home
> of the feast, the household head will sprinkle it in the yard; then
> when it is removed from the hall to the bedroom, being "dressed"
> it will be sprinkled again by the deceased's family; and when it is
> removed from the bed to the tomb the next morning, the fourth

libation is made. Finally at the tomb the mason also sprinkles it. .
. . Throughout the rite the stone represents the deceased . . . *Thus
the Stone Feast is a second and final burial which brings peace to
the dead and living alike.* [author's emphasis]

In some instances, the family may gather around the white-sheeted bed
and may even address the robed stone in this manner: "Dear Mama, we
haven't forgotten you. Open a way for us. Help us to pray for strength, long
life and prosperity." The family may weep, for "this stone represents the
person. While the others are outside enjoying, it is likely the body is there".
In the festive procession to the gravesite the stone is borne like a coffin on 2
poles by up to 6 men. The sounds of bass drum and tambourine contribute
to the triumphal atmosphere, which differs from the solemnity
accompanying the burial of the deceased's body.

The installation of the tomb is the central focus of the Stone Feast and is
the final death observance in the possible series of programs for the dead:
the wake; the funeral; the 3rd-day, 9th-day, and the 40th-day prayer
meetings; and finally, the Stone Feast. It is usual practice on the night before
the installation to participate in the *Big Drum* nation dance. The *Big Drum*
rites are usually held under a tent (made of a ship sail or a tarpaulin) in the
yard of the deceased. The ensemble and guests will walk there and perform,
after which they return to the tent for a brief respite and food. The second
half of the ceremony commences with a particular genre of "mid-night
songs."

The dance ring is formed by members of the community, who surround
3 drummers, the dancers/chorus, and the ritual and music leader, called the
chantwell. Two drummers play with open palms on open-bottomed, *boula*
drums that are held between their legs and slightly tilted from the ground.
Between these drummers sits the master drummer at the *cutter* drum. He
also plays with open palms, but his drum rests on the ground. All 3 drums
are constructed from wooden kegs, the *cutter* differing from others because
of a thread (with pins attached) that is strung over the head to produce a

raspy tone for the bold improvised drum statements. The instrumental ensemble is completed by the *chac-chac*, a stick-held maraca played by the *chantwell*.

After a preliminary, "warm-up" piece, someone strikes a hoe blade with a spoon or iron, then the male sponsor consecrates or "wets" the ring with rum and his wife consecrates it with water, thus inviting the participation of the ancestors. The dance circle is "free" for the ancestors; no humans are allowed to dance. The traditional, African-gong pulse seems to awaken—despite it appearing to be a predominantly Igbo-inspired ritual ceremony—a sense of history and nationhood among the creolized Carriacou descendants of the Cromanti (Akan), Igbo, Manding, Congo, Temne, Moko, Chamba, Arada (Dahomean), and Banda peoples.

If one has lost the knowledge of his kinship, it is felt that he might find himself dancing, propelled by the rhythm of his nation for:

> The blood tells your nation. I wouldn't dance any other.
> I feel good for the drum tells you what to do. Move as
> the drum tells you. The drum is speaking, telling you
> how to get on, how to wheel, how to come back, work
> your shoulders. The drum is speaking; without it you
> could do nothing.

Musical inspiration, directed by the "blood," perpetuates, reinforces, and reestablishes the intense patrilineal structure that prevalent male migration (most of the captives transported to the island were males) could have dispersed. The Carriacou patrilineality was discovered by M. G. Smith in the 1950s, who found it to be unique in the then British West Indies.

Music, dance, and ritual behavior contribute a wealth of information towards the understanding of culture, concepts and patterns of kinship, oral genealogies, and historical accounts. The Big Drum songs are sung in a French-creole *patois*, and the elderly residents of the island's southern section—*L'Esterre*, can translate proper Cromanti songs, such as "Ananci-o, Sari Baba,"—inspired by the Anansi [Akan] trickster spider and Creator-

God. Moreover, the following Cromanti and Igbo songs are particularly popular:

Cromanti Cudjoe	The ancestor Spirit
C'est nation mwe sa	That is my nation
Wé be nu	(meaning now lost)

Iama Diama Igbo Lé-lé	I am an Igbo
I'm a polin Igbo	Nothing can harm me
Mwe polin Igbo	
I ent ba ka fé Igbo	

When people are asked how they came to know the songs, slave myths, and family history, they invariably respond with "My mother told me" or "My grandmother taught me." Norman Paul, the founder of the Spiritual Baptists of Grenada, illustrates in his autobiography one way in the Big Drum culture of Grenada developed:

> I was seven . . . my grandmother took me to live with her.
> She was my mother's mother, Mistress John Noel. I called
> her "tante" . . . at night she used to practice us for singing.
> All in the house were "grans" besides me in the house. She
> used to practice us to sing Big Drum and dance, she used to
> practice us Ibo, and I would pick that up quick. She used to
> make all of us dance till we dead! I remember the songs; one
> she taught us was:

E-e, Ibo, Lele-lele	Baya-mamma se fa ma
Ba ya mamma ka-ki-ti	Ibo Bayo

. . . it mean she is Ibo family and she won't live for the other nations. She will trample them—that's Ba-kakite Ibo.

A Profound Slave Song

Earlier in this part of the book, reference was made to the British intercolonial slave trade. The following creole song—which has been passed down by successive generations—is redolent of the pain felt by a New World family that was torn apart, and each individual made available for sale in Trinidad, Haiti and Antigua:

> Pleéwé mwe Lidé, Pléwé Maiwas, oh
> Héle mwe, Lidé, héle oh, Maiwas
> Héle pu nu alé
>
> Dimash pwoshi batma-la-vol-a Haishi
> Vadi ya batma-la-vol-a kite, oh, Maiwaz
>
> Sa ki kota mwe, kosolé yish mwe bam we
> Sa ki kota mwe, kosolé Zabette bam we
> Sa ki éme mwe, kosolé Walter bam we
>
> Weep for me, Lide, weep, Maiwaz
> Lament for me, Lide, lament, Maiwaz
> Lament for our going
>
> Sunday next, the schooner sails for Haiti
> Friday the schooner leaves Haiti
>
> Whoever loves me, console my children for me
> Whoever loves me, console Zabette for me
> Whoever loves me, console Walter for me.

New World Folklore and Myths

The Caribbean and United States are rich in folklore and myths. Haiti for example, provides a case of 2 contrasting myths. A 'macho' man might have beaten his chest and boasted that he was a *neg Ginin* (a black from Guinea). 'Guinea,' purportedly derived from the Portuguese *Guine* for Africans living South of the Senegalese river during the Columbus' age of 'discovery', had come to symbolize the 'mythical origin of valor and virtue'. It referred to a mythical place of origin that had become an ideal of resistance to slavery, its suffering, and its humiliation'. Contrastingly, Haitians would feel offended by being called *neg Congo* (a black from Congo) as this designation was deemed to apply to Westernized Haitians—especially those Christianized; even those in Africa. They were viewed as docile and house slaves, similarly to the much-maligned 'Uncle Tom' trope, and was in sharp contrast to the sturdy, solidarized field hands.

Guinean spiritual deities were also in binary form. One set of spirits—*Iwa Ginin*—were bold, strong, helpful, and efficient, whereas the *Iwa Congo* were uninterested in the destiny of people. However, through more positive lenses the latter were viewed as gentle, encouraged joyful dances, expressed good humor and the desire for a happy life; after living an exiled existence, their souls would transition to their ancestral sanctuary.

Afro-Bahamians combined their storytelling folklore with leisurely singing and African folk fire-dances. Participants were usually in 2 groups—one of which comprises a drummer close to the fire. The drum is held over the fiery blaze until it sufficiently tightens to produce the desired tone—culminating in a flourish of beats to signify readiness. A clapping chorus ensues, followed by the drummers cries "Gimbay!"—a creolized word taken from the Kikongo (Angola/ Congo) word translated by many Africans in Jamaica and Bermuda as 'rhythm'; alternatively, as aforementioned, Chambers attributes this to an Igboesque development among the creolizing Africans in Virginia. It was usually an interactive event whereby the drummer didn't always decide what was played, but takes requests from other dancers, before one of the dancers takes to the center and is chorally clapped by everyone else encircled. The dancer makes a preliminary flourish during the first and second lines of the song, before nominating another dancer on third line; this is performed on rotation until the drum goes cold or out of tune—at which point the drummer fires the drum up again and the participants repeat the process.

The abovementioned heroic Anansi folklore—familiar to many—is a retention of a West African tradition, attributed to the spider legend from the Ashanti-land / Ghana. He has grown popular among many young people because he is considered dexterous, able to outwit all other forest creatures, and essentially can adapt to any situation in life. They believed God gave Anansi the meaning of order: lessons in architecture, the structure of dwellings, and the structure of life and society—all of which were signified through Anansi's spider web. The web also represents the sun and its rays, while the sun personifies God.

Another import to the New World was the *Mami Wata* folklore from West and West Central Africa—commonly referred to as *Water Mama* in Suriname and Guyana; *Ruba Mama* in Jamaica and *Mere de l'eau in Haiti*. She is portrayed as a woman with the tail of a fish who surfaces on moonlit nights near canals and rivers; she is found combing her hair and singing to herself. She is usually blamed as the cause of sudden drowning—usually a person who is the object of her love. In addition to *Mami Wata* folklore, the Surinamese also have the *flying slaves* legend which predates their 1st July Emancipation date. Legend has it that word was disseminated among the enslaved that a salt-free diet would enable them to fly back to Africa, but this wasn't an option for their wives and children forced to eat food in the houses they worked. As a result, the men deduced they would be able to fly back to retrieve their families, but their attempt ended in death for all of them. Nevertheless, their spirits are venerated as having returned to Africa and travelled to Suriname to celebrate the Emancipation Day anniversary.

The Gullah Geechee Africans of the Sea Islands in Georgia, United States of America, also have their own *flying Africans* legend. The legend is also found among African-Americans on the mainland. The legend is often associated with 2 other folk motifs: the tale of the independent hoe—and other iron tools that work by themselves—and the tale of the magic dish dispensing unlimited quantities of food.

The general outline of events in the legend is that during the period of

American slavery, some of African captives were brought to the islands, but they were not suited to the role and used magic to escape. In one variant of the legend, these Africans had magic power and refused to work as slaves. They could neither speak nor understand English. They were put to the fields with hoes to chop cotton but could not do it well. The white overseer approached them to whip them, and they uttered a magic incantation, arose, and flew back to Africa. They left their hoes standing in the field, continuing to work by themselves. Some variants of the legend say that the Africans enacted as part of their escape, a ritual in which they joined hands and moved in a circle steadily more rapidly until they were aloft, all the while chanting in unison. Some tellers use the simile "like a bird," and some identify the bird as a buzzard. In other variants, they actually transform into birds. Some variants hold that the leaders were a man and his wife who had magical power, but they also had children who did not have such power and were not able to fly away to Africa. Because the children were left behind, their parents had to return to the islands from time-to-time to visit them. One variant explains that one of the children left behind was a daughter who wanted to learn to conjure but was told that she had to undergo a sort of formal apprenticeship to gain such ability.

One of the core motifs in the legend, which is sometimes found in other tales, is the magical tool that has special powers that are accessible to anyone who knows how to wield it. The tool may be an ax, a sword, a spear, a nail, a needle, or a knife, and this motif occurs commonly in some African tales. In an Ashanti narrative, for example, *Porcupine*, the hoe's owner, uses it daily and hides it when he stops work. But spider watches him, steals the hoe, and set it to work but cannot stop it because he does not know how to halt the command. Likewise, on Wilmington Island, the tale is that *Brer Rabbit* steals Brer Wolf's magic hoe, but though Wolf informs Rabbit of the magic word to start the hoe, he neglects to tell him the formula for stopping it, and it continues chopping until it ruins Rabbit's crop. In another variant in which *Brer Rabbit* is the owner and *Brer Fox* is the thief, the hoe works

Fox to death because he is too stupid to remember the halt command. Among the Bambara—an African group, the narrative juxtaposes Hare as the owner and Hyena as the character who borrows the hoe to work a field and earn a wife. Hare does not reveal the halt command and lets Hyena die from exhaustion so he can take the wife for himself. The iron in the hoe and other such objects is the source of magical power that enables transformation to occur. The flying Africans use the hoe that works by itself as a tool in their ritual of transformation and escape.

The legend has come to symbolize the ability of enslaved Africans to maintain cultural and psychological connections to Africa and an Afrocentric identity and value system. As such, it represents cultural resistance to enslavement. Allusions to the legend surface in various forms in African-American oral tradition, literature and visual art. For example, "I'll Fly Away" and "If I had Two Wings" are 2 common spirituals in which the motif is found. It also plays a central role in Toni Morrison's novel, *Song of Solomon*, and in filmmaker Julie Dash's *Daughter's of the Dust*.

Eshu Elegba Folklore

The Yoruba [of Nigeria] trickster deity *Eshu Elegba* was borrowed by the Fon of Dahomey (present-day Benin Republic) and transported by captive Africans to Haiti during the 17th and 18th centuries. Through the course of terrible migration and an extraordinary history, these mythic protagonists were re-rooted, grafted, pruned and reborn. The deity was known to his devotees by either of these names in like fashion to how Jesus and Christ are interchangeable, and connected to a pantheon of Orishas, which is grouped into approximately a dozen or so "hot" and "cool" subgroups. Worshippers of the hot / hard Orisha (Ogun of Iron, Shango of Lightning, Shapona of Smallpox and so forth) say Eshu represents vanity, handsomeness and being sexually prolific. Devotees of Oshun, mother of cool terrestrial waters, say she is married to Eshu and shares his same guile—a perfect match in many ways. In contrast, the foreign incongruent influences of Muslim and Christian Yoruba maintain he is simply Satan, the devil.

The Yoruba oral traditions flexibly allow for many cross interpretations, one of which was the *oriki* (praise poetry) venerate Eshu as:

"the biggest creature with a big wooden stick",
yet he is so tiny that he must
"stand on tiptoe to put salt in the soup".
He is both first and last born,
Old man and child, cunning and capricious.
Young or old, he disregards the normal code;
He enjoys the natural licence of the innocent
And the privileged licence of the aged.
As a child he is the experimenter who breaks the rules.
Thus ...
The Yoruba say he is the youngest of the orisha,
but the father of them all"

This flexibility is also evident through the Fon version of Legba. Legba is a randier and more overt form of the Yoruba Eshu Elegba, with greater, effective variety—inspiring fear and admiration among his devotees. Legba represents the divine linguist—as appointed by the androgynous high god Mawu Lisa—with daily reporting duties on all affairs of men and gods. Further myths reveal he has sexual intercourse with *Gbadu* the female personification of prophecy who sits atop a palm tree with all but 16 eyes closed. Legba does however manage to infuriate her and Mawu Lisa through his philandering ways... with her daughter! The punishment is a permanent erection and sexual insatiability which prompts him to revert to fondling Gbadu. Upon reproach from his god, he attributes his conduct to the eternal punishment handed down to him.

Nowadays *Eshu Elegba* is not so much remembered in extensive oral tradition but instead now features as a ritual performed in a vodoun service.

Whether its across self and externalized entertainments, the preservation of faith-based rituals, building strength of character, venerating resilience, encouraging adaptability—even in very adverse conditions, or maintaining and strengthening the collective memory of a primordial homeland, the similarity between West Indian and African folklore is based not only on the subject matter, but also on the method by which the stories are narrated. African storytelling is a highly dramatic art, interspersed with songs and dances and involving a great deal of audience participation. The same is true of West Indian storytelling. It is in these works that deal with Caribbean folk and their culture—their day-to-day existence, their customs, beliefs, legends, tales, songs, and dances—that African cultural retentions can be glimpsed.

The Ethnogenesis and Creolization
of New World Africans

While the ethnogenesis of Igbos, Yorubas, Akans, and Kongolese has featured above, what hasn't been covered thus far is the creolization process that led to these diverse Africans becoming amalgamated as Jamaicans, Barbadians, Grenadians, St. Lucians, African-Americans and so forth. In addition to the emergence of folklore, social activities, and creole institutions—such as the abovementioned Stone Feast ritual, their plantation experiences, the fostering of real and fictive kin-based networks, and resistance in the form of revolts, were all key to the evolution of new world identities.

Whites everywhere referred to unacculturated Outlandish Africans as *new Negroes*. In the Chesapeake Bay region, incoming Africans were also called "Outlandish," and Creoles were known as "country-born." In Jamaica, and for a while in South Carolina, whites occasionally used "nation" in place of country. Local-born slaves were called "Creoles" in the Caribbean and Carolina-born" in the Lowcountry.

As noted earlier, in some societies, incoming Africans were identified ethnically, as Igbo or Coromantee for instance, whereas in others, whites simply lumped them together as "Guiney Negroes". An example of the latter is in Andrea Stuart's *Sugar in the Blood* where she stated that as white laborers in Barbados started to realize the benefits of identifying as 'white men,' it resulted in the island's captives becoming amalgamated as 'blacks' whereas they would previously have been identified as Igbos, Coromantees or Kubas. In some instances a planter may have subjectively observed a female captive as 'looking more Igbo than Coromantee'.

The naming of Africans in some cases was careless, and in other cases it was deliberate—for example, depending on how menacing whites considered them to be. To this end, blacks in the Chesapeake Bay region were seen as mostly cooperative, their ethnic markers were not used, and rather they were grouped collectively as Africans.

However, whites in the Caribbean usually singled out Gold Coast Coromantees as threatening, while for a time South Carolinians thought similarly of Angolans. Moreover, during the 1760s when South Carolina and East Florida were being established as settlements, the Lowcountry became a 'cultural enclave' in which captives were identified by their tribal names, languages, and provenance. During this time, the royal governor of East Florida requested for more "young Gambians or Gold Coast [as] they are fit to work immediately & the next year will be as good hands as any & less inclined to wander."

When Carolina traders talked about Africans, 2 peoples drew more than a passing interest. Igbos were considered unsuitable for rice production, and Angolans were seen as inclined to run away to Spanish Florida. To the undercurrent of mildly ambivalent views everywhere that Igbos in some situations became suicidally despondent, Carolinians added the charge of physical frailty as well. "Our people are very delicate in what they buy," and although "mad" for Africans, wrote Henry Laurens, the mainland's biggest slave trader, "Callabars [Ibo] won't go down." Igbos came from the Bight of Biafra, a region that supplied 40% of all *new Negroes* imported to the Chesapeake—a much larger proportion than any other Africans imported. However, in South Carolina, Igbos only comprised 5%, whereas 40% were Congo-Angolans.

Jamaicans—who alone referred to slaves by their country of origin long after they were first unloaded and sold—sprinkled tribal designations throughout their plantation records. An estate attorney's report in 1771 that no more slavers were due from the Gold Coast, brought an absentee's rejoinder to "buy Eboes [then] from Calabar." "Gambia Slaves" he had sold previously had "gained good Reputation." In similar circumstances the representative of another buyer advised that those offered for sale "are what we call Windward Negroes, Chambas, Dunkerers &c, the worst kind of negroes imported here for labour except Angolas." To use Angolans "for Sugar Works," he continued, "is throwing away money." The same Jamaican proprietor was later informed in the 1790s that "Gold Coast Negroes," the males about 18, "& the females about 16 years of age [are] the best calculated for sugar Estates."

While much of this is opaque, more of it points to understandings that were common and assumed. While surveying the slaves of empire loyalists who came into his island at the end of the Revolutionary War, a Jamaican attorney initially identified them as "American" before he looked beyond that level of assimilation to their real origins, then he referred to them as "a set of soft Angola and Mundingo Negroes." Another group of new arrivals was dismissed abruptly by a manager as "many Mandingoes . . . I bought none." Earlier, the same buyer characterized Chamba by their distinctive ritual scars—"those with Cutt Faces"—and as a people who did not do well at his own plantation. Some understanding of the assumptions that supported remarks of this kind occasionally surface. An advocate general for Jamaica made the following stereotypical allusion to suicidal Igbos: Hope, who took his own life following a quarrel with friends, was "a very good Negroe generally, but an Eboe." When Igbo were not available to establish a settlement (a new plantation), a manager explained that they chose not to buy alternatives because Igbo constituted "the country that will answer best there." (Settlements were usually in upland wilderness areas and thus close to enticing villages of maroons. In this case, however, the choice of nationality made sense because Igbo in Jamaica were hardly ever reported as maroons).

These purchasing strategies should not be dismissed as peculiar. On 2 occasions, as revealed in separate plantation records, Igbo women were paired with Coromantee men, evidently as a way of domesticating a people who were notorious as warriors. Moreover, in a different kind of source (akin to a planter's how-to manual), William Beckford noted that often new Negro women, among whom he singled out Igbo, considered themselves as bound to "the spot" of their first born. In other words, in each instance, it

210

was assumed that as Igbo stuck and stayed, their new mates, the dangerous Coramantee, would be inclined to the same.

Thus a few patterns, do emerge once kinds or classes of sources are laid back-to-back. Plantation registers that list slaves by ethnicity, for instance, are usually Jamaican, kept by large estates, and chiefly from the western parishes of Cornwall County, the center of significant slave rebellion throughout the slavery era. A 1778 ledger for one such estate of 488 slaves (York in Trelawny Parish, belonging to the Tharp family, who with 10 plantations and more than 2,000 slaves were among the wealthiest planters in Anglo-America) listed men and women from the major supply sources of western and central Africa. The degree of refinement within an entity, as indicated in the ledger, was the same as that used by advertisers for slaver cargoes in the gazettes, for Gold Coast people (Coramantee, Fante, and Asante); for Biafran (Igbo and Moco); and for Congo-Angola (Congolese, Angolans, Mungola, and "Portuguese Congo"). Newspaper descriptions of fugitives from this vast region included a new Negro woman with a crucifix necklace, another as bearing a "Spanish" mark, presumably a cross shape (probably Chokwe); and a third as speaking "Portuguese." Mandingoes and Papaw-Nagoes are also prominent on the register. Jamaicans sometimes saw the latter as one, and sometimes separately; they were respectively, Manding of Senegambia, Yoruban and Fan of Dahomey from the Bight of Benin.

Ethnicity was also used to distinguish slaves of the same name in plantation registers. In an 1807 list from Westmoreland Parish, Jamaica, slaves numbered 44 and 45, both named Peter, were then distinguished as Banda and Igbo; 3 Fannys were Creole, Igbo, and Congo. Also from the western parishes, an official in the 1790s reported matter-of-factly that a driver had "harangued his countrymen and others—Cormantee and Mandingo—to join him [as maroons] in the woods."

If a people were singled out in evidence of this type, they were usually

Coramantee—the most conspicuous and important nationality in Anglo-America. Written on the border of a slave register was a special count of Africans imported from the Gold Coast, followed by a note that in 1765 and 1766 the number halved because of "the War between the Ashantees & Fantees." West Indians, officials particularly, kept close watch on Coramantee, who were singled out in a 1772 census for Tobago, where their importation had been prohibited. Like Jamaica, Tobago was volatile, and it, too contained large interior communities of maroons. Meanwhile, in stable and secure Barbados, where ethnic labels were uncommon, Coramantee were so popular that one planter accused unscrupulous slave traders of altering the ritual scars of "other Negros to make them pass for this country."

In many ways for white Jamaicans, Igbo and Coramantee were opposites. Igbos were despondent and suicidal; Coramantee were physically and mentally tough, enterprising, and uncommonly stoic when tortured and executed. Bryan Edwards, who spiced his ethnic stereotypes with more insightful anecdotes, mentions the branding of a group of *new Negroes*, young Coramantee and Igbo men (brands, according to John Steadman, were small, silver, bore the owner's initials, and were applied over a dab of olive or palm oil to the face or chest). Led forward at the branding, an Igbo boy who happened to be first in line "screamed dreadfully." His countrymen immediately took up his cries. Meanwhile the Coramantee youths, laughing aloud, came forward, thrust out their chests and took the brand without flinching "in the least," and then "snapt their fingers in exultation over the poor Iboes."

But the most careful and systematic use of ethnic distinctions are found in thousands of newspaper advertisements for runaways. The advertisements are also highly comparable in format and content from one region to another and make the debate about the importance of ethnicity more precise by providing the largest number of slaves whose distinctively African features—ritual scarring, languages, and dialects—were attributed to members of specific west and central African societies. They were also the best indication of the increasing objectification of black people in the South, rather than to their continual reputation as the carriers of African traditions into New World slavery in the Caribbean.

The gist of an effective advertisement, in a form like contemporary classifieds, was to save money and time by using a minimum of words to help readily identify and ultimately recapture 'valuable property.' From long experience, Jamaicans knew a great deal about shipmates, countrymen, and the *new Negroes'* first reactions. They said as much in notices that, being succinct and informative, were the most effective that appeared anywhere. Advertisers wrote for a public able to depict Africans by reference to norms or stereotypes of national characters: "Looks more like an Eboe than a Coramantee;" and "Chamba but may be taken as a Coramantee." Whites identified ethnicity in the plantation correspondence; designations such as "looks Ibo" defy ready explanation and serve as a reminder of a lore that has been lost. "Looks Coramantee" or "Congo" were common in Jamaica throughout the slavery era, especially before 1800, but figured only twice in the South in 1773 in South Carolina for an Ibo and in 1734 in Virginia in reference to Madagascars, a people whose physical features were conspicuous (neither very African nor white) to settlers who became increasingly obsessed with their slaves' physical rather than cultural characteristics. This was a basic sign of a society in which blacks were relatively assimilated and so assumed to be under control.

Scarring patterns, the second way of establishing ethnicity, vary considerably among a people, even from village to village. The purpose of ritual scarification ranges from the cosmetic to the cosmological, and its use declined sharply in the 20th century. 18th century West Indians used the patterns confidently—"Eboe with marks of Moco"—and expressed surprise when noting adults that did not have them: "no Country marks whatever."

These comments are by Jamaicans who distinguished slaves by ritual scars long after they were assimilated. An urban slave and a baker, for instance, who in other societies would have been depicted solely on the basis of his skill, was also characterized by ritual markings (of which there were a few instances but these markings were mostly absent among the second generation Creoles). Jamaicans were most adept at identifying Chamba by scars, which comprised 3 or 4 angled and paralleled slashes on each cheek or a temple: "Supposed to be a Chamba (4 or 5 cuts on each cheek)"; Mungola Country but "country marks somewhat like Chamba"; or simply, "some small cuts on her temples . . . or rather, as called, cambas."

While Southerners usually described marks literally and said little more, Caribbean whites sometimes pushed further. Unsure of a fugitive's nationality, one owner nonetheless wrote appreciatively: "countrymarks on his Face, chest & belly which have been finely carved in his Country." When at the end of the 18th century *new Negroes* were incorporated as soldiers in the new black West Indian regiments, they were identified more thoroughly than usual. A recruit's village or district, as well as nationality, was included in the regimental succession registers.

The third way of depicting ethnicity, and for Jamaicans the primary means, was by reference to a language or dialect. Two *new Negroes* said to be "marked like Chamba Negroes" were, nonetheless, identified as Nagoes (Yorubans); another, without scars, was said to "speak . . . Chamba"; or, more specifically, "Country can't be discovered as his language can't be understood by any Negro on said Property;" or, "none of [my] Negroes . . . can understand her [but] supposed to be Chamba, Nago or Papaw."

These depictions are important because they contradict the common assumption that for reasons of security, incoming Africans of the same language group were scattered so that those who were kept together could not readily understand one another. Instead, in certain times and places, speakers of the same language were grouped together. Some learned another African language while acquiring their captors' English. From Jamaica, an Igbo was identified as "speaks Moco may pass as Moco;" a

Chamba woman, who had only been in the country 12 months, already spoke Mungola "well" and English "very well." A Mandingo woman in 5 months already spoke sufficient Coramantee and English "to be understood." A man 14 years in the country spoke "French and other Negro languages besides his country language," which may have denoted simply a patois, but the word "language" suggests otherwise. In distinguishing Africans by their languages and dialects, Jamaicans were most discriminating about Coramantees, and some cases sought to precisely identify where they came from in the Gold Coast.

An African's self-definition began as soon as some were brought ashore. While aboard the slaver these *new Negroes*—as they came to be known—made a plan to escape at the first opportunity and to return to the point of disembarkation in order to find a way "back home" to Africa: 4 Fante (Coramantee), for instance, were described in an 1801 Jamaican newspaper advertisement as fugitives who "told some of their shipmates, whom they solicited to go with them, they would proceed to the sea-side by night, and remain in the bush through the night, and the first Canoe they found by the seaside they would Set sail for their Country, which they conceived was no great distance."

The Fante may have been tragically ignorant of the great distance they had been carried. However, their design to return to where they were first unloaded, among other choices they would make, and the whites' attempts to understand these decisions, provide a straightforward way of talking about the combinations of African carryovers and local circumstances that channeled the choices and learning that are labeled variously as acculturation, assimilation, or Creolization.

If incoming Africans were brought to such colonies as Jamaica, help was available from those who spoke their own language and had been enslaved for some time. This network, subsequently, forced whites to speak more precisely about the newcomers—not as commodities but as the people they were—in order to make their societies more secure. Whites began to refine

the generic *new Negro* and instead spoke of "countrymen" and "shipmate"—
respectively, Africans of the same language group and of the same slaver
cargo—in order to recapture fugitives readily.

As ways to reduce the expenses of slave maintenance, planters chose—
among other methods—to give land and time-off to enslaved persons to
grow their own food. This method became entrenched in both the
Caribbean—especially in such mountainous and volcanic islands as Jamaica
and the Ceded Islands (Tobago, Dominica and St. Lucia) where only a
portion of the land was suitable for sugarcane. The remainder—the slope,
the ridges of the interior spine—was given over to the slaves as their
"mountain," where they could grow their own food.

   Through hard work, luck and holding on grimly to the advantage of
providing for themselves (other than allowances of salt fish and imported
grain) the mass of West Indian blacks in time acculturated amounts and
kinds of property that are startling if one begins with a perspective of slave
maintenance that was southern and antebellum. The enslaved persons on
all islands owned flocks of fowl and such small stock as pigs and goats,
which, along with other marketable products such as fodder (Guinea and
Scotch grasses), firewood, fruit, vegetables, and fish, generated the
Caribbean's justly famous large and flourishing slave-dominated markets.
This enterprise, as Sidney Mintz and Douglas Hall argue in a seminal essay,
was important for the future as well. It provided the base for the modern
internal marketing system in the West Indian Islands. No equivalent
development occurred in the American South, where generally slaveholders,
not their slaves, controlled surpluses including livestock and did not allot
provision grounds anywhere close to the size and distance from the home
plantation that were the case in the Caribbean. The argument is not that
there was not a modicum of slave-controlled food in the South, or even
some scratch marketing, but rather that it was negligible when compared to
the cluster of social developments that stemmed from the internal
economies of Caribbean plantation societies. The argument here is that

planation authority was a function not so much of paternalism or plantations as prisons, but rather more directly of the slave's experience of the organization of maintenance. Through time, Southerners came to realize that the cultivation and distribution of food as "allowances" conveniently and effectively controlled slaves. West Indians agreed but were often unable to use food in this manner because slaves provisioned themselves.

Slaves who grew much of their own food and marketed surpluses constantly and readily traveled beyond plantation boundaries. Those who did not, namely the mass of Southern slaves, were susceptible to stifling organizational schemes (as described in the "Management of Negroes" articles) that made plantations "their only home." In the South, slaves were fed allowances, a practice that enhanced views of them as chattel, while enforcing a slave's sense of being confined and dependent. By contrast, where blacks fed themselves, as in the Caribbean, the process diluted white power, and slaves acted as if planters owned only their labor, not their lives or personalities.

To examine the problem of slave maintenance is to uncover the institutional origins of what appears to be variants of Creolization, one Southern, the other Caribbean. What began in some societies as a simple expedient of allowing slaves to grow and gather their own food and dispense with surpluses became a formidable strategy, advancing a family's interests through time by using property for inheritances and to venerate the dead. Africanists call this combination the "family estate," which when refashioned in the Caribbean shaped plantation authority, control, and resistance decisively. The family estate enforced cultural conservatism on the slaves' part that until the last years of slavery served as a brake on significant forms of resistance. It is important to note that separating the economic strategies of slaves from other modalities of their ways of life may facilitate discussion, but to do so is to obscure the slaves' view of property acquisition as part of domestic and religious outlooks and practices. Thus, when women, who dominated marketing in the islands, "divorced" they tore in half the *cotta* [headcloth] used to support the market basket.

Hence, it is the social dimensions of food production and distribution that make the regional contrast so important. The exclusively Caribbean features of slave maintenance deserve emphasis in 3 respects. The first was the mobility of the ordinary slave (of women particularly) from plantation to mountain to market, creating sizeable and usually expanding hinterlands that (by the time artisans moved to the fore) were to an extent beyond the routine control of whites. The second, the rise of the family estate, gave slaves a stake in the plantation, the promise of a future, and in time the means and determination to defend their future. Third, the Caribbean food system provided opportunities for slaves to accumulate the surpluses and property that sustained families and religions that were African in character. Consequently, an indispensable task that is long overdue in slavery studies is to uncover the linkage, if any, between the domestic economy and religion throughout plantation America. Of this difficult problem, a noted specialist on West Indian slavery, Barry Higman, perceives Africans brought to the New World as isolated individuals who had lost their social cohesion, including family norms. Nonetheless, Higman locates a central issue when he describes, as a source of the Africans' isolation, a process that "dislocated their linking of genealogy and locality, and the veneration of specific pieces of land." This veneration was achieved through the Africans rechanneling the pain and tragedy from being dislodged from their homes. *New Negroes* opted to retain their native languages and coordinate an escape "back home" with their countrymen and shipmates. As this wasn't physically possible, this was symbolically achieved in the blood oath and play which linked them to a particular part of the plantation.

Basic regional differences in systems of slave maintenance were set in motion the moment Africans arrived on the plantation and *seasoning* began. In both Southern and Caribbean usage *seasoning* comprised the familiar idea of acclimating incoming Africans to new and often dangerous weather and disease environments. However, in the Caribbean, an additional and paramount meaning was to establish a *new Negroe's* maintenance, which was principally a matter of housing, food and training. "When a new Negroe has been two or three years in the country," explained a plantation physician, "and acquainted with the language and manners of it, and has got his provision ground in such a state as to supply himself with food, we consider him then as a seasoned Negro." Another doctor, appointed to inspect new Negroes brought to Trinidad, also connected seasoning with provision grounds. This official observed shrewdly that generous allotments of grounds would alleviate high mortality rates by helping the new arrivals to overcome the "chagrin" of enslavement.

New Negroes in the Caribbean were introduced to plantation slavery not by whites, but by other Africans who were often the new arrivals' countrymen. These *seasoned* Africans either boarded slavers or went into the merchant yards, where they tried to quiet fears and tell *new Negroes* in their own language what to expect. Once on the plantation, the Africans were put as inmates for several months in the households of established slaves. For instance, Thistlewood once noted that when his employer sent up a *new Negro*, "our Negroes have Nam'd him Hector, I put him to live with London."

One of the best descriptions of *seasoning* in the islands is by William Young, a wealthy absentee and author of a late-18th century travel account. Young said inmates were "the practice" and a trade-off between white supervisors and slaves who took the Africans in. In turn, the *new Negroes* were shown how to survive and get by as they worked in their mentors' provision ground and were fed by the owner or supervisor until their own plots were bearing.

However, according to the rich and experienced Jamaican attorney, Simon Taylor, care was to be taken that established slaves did not make "slaves" of inmates. Complementing this view is Young's observation that "competition" for inmate's labor was "violent, and troublesome in the extreme" because "every negro in his garden, and at his leisure hours [is] earning much more than what is necessary to feed him." An inmate's labor would make larger "surplus for sale, market, and for feeding his stock." To these warnings, however, Thistlewood added another side—the bonds that the shadowy institution engendered could be deep and long lasting, "Old Phibbah, an Invalid, died, had her grave dug, and buried, gave old Sharper Some dram as She took him a New Negro, and he got her a Coffin made."

Seasoning also set in motion the practices now commonly known as the "internal economy" of slavery. Important regional differences in that feature of slave life may be examined more thoroughly in the case studies that further expose variations in the way *new Negroes* and their descendants obtained food, property, and the ability to market. Thistlewood's diary, for instance, provides rare glimpses of the reception of incoming Africans and their incorporation into an ongoing plantation economy.

The diary describes 3 types of slave economy activity—provisioning, marketing, and gift-giving. First, provisioning included the "hand-feeding" of Africans who had just arrived from the slaver, the gardens of older residents, and the extensive use of local markets during annual late-summer droughts when food was scarce. Second, Thistlewood wrote of 2 kinds of marketing, his and the slaves.' The former was carried out by itinerant slave peddlers, usually favored women who sold such household products as beeswax, candles, seeds, and vegetables from the manager's large garden. The latter was by slaves who bartered or sold their own commodities. Third, a continual circulation of goods by way of both gift exchanges and loot taken from slave poachers reinforced plantation communities that were mean, harassed, and fragile. Most important, Thistlewood's jottings provide contexts: the physical setting of an economic activity and its place in a sequence of events. These demonstrate a relationship between food and resistance (typical of plantation slaves) that was monotonously periodic. In dry summer months trouble increased precipitously, particularly in such drought years as 1760 (the eve of Tackey's Rebellion) and produced such evocative jottings as "many Negroes from the Country Estates, Armd'd with Knives, Bills, Cutlasses, Maschets, clubs, fought our Negroe Men and got away." Moreover, drought and hunger for locals, both black and white, set in play "you scratch my back I'll scratch yours." Conversely, unusually wet and bountiful years yielded very few entries regarding hunger, resistance, and whippings.

Family Affairs

In making new families Africans had to negotiate continually between their own traditions and the demands of slavery. The compromises inherent in this process are exposed in a remarkable will by a Jamaican slave whose bequests stemmed from his plantation existence (including the disposition of the kind of slave property that was customary and widespread in a provisioning system such as Jamaica's) while his funeral instructions, about chorusing and shipmates, point forcefully to the African past. In March 1758 Thistlewood wrote a "Memorandum, how mulatto Will's goods are to be disposed of at his Death: his Wives Shipmate Silvia to have his Cow, her daughter Hester, the heifer . . . and that no Negroe should Sing."

Slave family and religion blended African traditions and plantation routines. This was reflected in the mullato's will, which was said to be an economic, religious, and cultural statement. As such, it was argued that slave families were culturally conservative in the Caribbean, yet assimilative in the South because of the system of maintenance there. As either provision or allowance, these systems steered slaves toward domestic arrangements that in orientation were either African and polygynous or Christian and monogamous. Because black families in the Caribbean were based on provision grounds, they were imbued with African notions of property as corporate; that is, as owned by the dead, used by the living, and thus a focal point for ritual. In the South, however, slave families were landless, customarily monogamous, and rarely if ever focused by property strategies meant to perpetuate a family conceived as comprising both the living and dead. Within these parameters, gender relations in the 2 regions indicate that the stereotypical black family—mother-centered, with anomalous father-husband—was in a formative stage. However, these familiar institutional forms were rather different in meaning and function from one region to the other because the Caribbean family was more conspicuously African in character than its Southern equivalent.

Probably more than is often realized, attitudes about the beginnings of the black family have been shaped by our own cultural biases. These biases are fortified by an uncritical acceptance of a view of Africans as victims who barely scraped by, and of antebellum slavery as representative of slavery generally. Undeniably, by the early 1800s Africans, always hard-pressed in North America, were no longer culturally influential. In the South, most couples with children were, or wanted to be, part of two-parent, monogamous unions. A comparative view complicates this conventional picture while opening a different line of inquiry. Living in the midst of Africans, Caribbean whites talked about black families as organized around shipmates, the born ground, polygamy, and inheritances. As for the slaves, it is suggested that the sexual predation of white men and the commanding participation of black women in grounds and marketing unexpectedly provided women with a bit of freedom and leverage, which thereby may have further strained slave gender relations. In any case, it does seem that account should be taken of both the skewed sex ratios on many 18th century estates (far greater numbers of men than women) and of the possibility that having children was no longer as important as it had been in Africa.

The *new Negroes'* struggles in the Caribbean to create networks and instant kin based on countrymen, shipmates, and inmates constituted the beginnings of the African-American family. It was understood that as shipmates, men and women of the same slaver cargo regarded one another as brothers and sisters and would not mate, even though they were not related biologically. This effort by *new Negroes* to sort out and anchor ideas of who should have intercourse with whom was important. In effect, it established an incest sanction which, anthropologists argue, is the basis of family formation.

Once slave households were underway, they varied considerably from one parent to two, father or mother centered, with children belonging to either, or to neither head of household. Historians who make reconstitutions usually base them on plantation registers of slaves listed by household. This convenient method raises problems, however. How the registers were made is usually unclear. Was the census taken on the spot by a driver or clerk? Reported individually by the head of household? Or (more likely) was it drawn up in the manager's house in a reasonable and tidy fashion to show an absentee that all was in order despite the incessant movement of slaves on and off the plantation? The registers also make an impression that households were stable and static when in effect, they were remarkably fluid, porous, and extended and in other ways inaccessible to the whites' surveillance and recordkeeping. Plantations were confining, so slaves often courted and mated elsewhere if they could. As one owner, unhappy with this tendency, put it for so many:

> it is better that the ladies should see company at Rooms's [Estate], than that the Gentlemen of Rooms's should be Obliged to see the company of the Ladies elsewhere, the child becoming the property of the Proprietor of the female. With respect to the preference to be given between the purchase of raw Slaves and that of seasoned Negroes, it is to be consider'd, that, the former will be more likely to remain at home than the latter, as they will of course attach themselves to those with whom they get first acquainted or at least in the Neighbourhood; but, Negroes who have lived in any other parts of the Island, having formed attachments elsewhere, will ramble, let the distance be what it, may, to their old Quarters, and thereby become of little use to their owners from undergoing more fatigue than they

are able to bear.

Given the practice by Caribbean slaves of making hidden households on and off the plantation, Sidney Mintz's warning about what did and did not constitute a slave household is apt. One should not postulate that a household occupied by "what is called a 'family' necessarily includes a co-residing sociological 'father.'" Nor should households automatically equate to family or "marriage" with a sacramental or civil service. "We cannot suppose that serial unions are the equivalent of 'promiscuity', or that the *irrelevance* of societal norms means the *absence* of societal norms." In short, Mintz concludes, terms like *family* and *marriage* raise the same problem as do *monarchy* and *theocracy*, even though "for many purposes we are inclined to suppose that such terminology has a genuine cross-cultural validity."

Plantation registers as informal censuses will continue to mislead until they are correlated with other sources. A facet of family life highlighted in the fugitive slave advertisements, for example, is geographical mobility to the degree that was self-imposed; Caribbean slave families were extended to a remarkable extent. Members lived separately and perhaps often by choice, occasionally on different properties where women as well as men customarily kept their own households and grounds.

The fugitive slave advertisements expose ordinary usages of kin nomenclature. As in the case of ethnic designations, the identification of sisters, aunts, grandparents, and the like was minimal in the South and far richer in the Caribbean. This is odd. Given that the advertisements' purpose was to recover valuable property expeditiously and that the majority of plantation slaves everywhere ran off to visit kin, it made good sense to be as explicit as possible about a fugitive's "connections" and their whereabouts. One would expect, then, to find the most refined use of kinship terms in societies such as Virginia and Barbados, where the slave trade was no longer important. In such places slaves had the time—and thus the Creole, not African, survival rates—to establish extensive networks of 2 or 3 generations' duration and depth. However, in South Carolina and Jamaica, where the trade thrived throughout the 18th century and kept many plantation communities in flux, families presumably would develop more slowly. One would expect that the use of kin terms to specify a fugitive's whereabouts were Caribbean, the most rudimentary were from the Chesapeake Bay region, and South Carolinian usage ranged between the 2, that is, between an expansive or a minimal recognition of slave kin. Caribbean advertisers referred to aunts, uncles, grandparents, and a godmother while alluding to polygamous, monogamous, extended, or nuclear families. Southerners, however, acted typically as if slave families were always and exclusively nuclear.

Planters in the Chesapeake Bay region used only the unavoidable designations—fathers, mothers, and occasionally a brother or sister—to focus attention on where a fugitive might be found. In this region where absenteeism was rare, paternalism was something more than an ideological sleight of hand to blunt abolitionist attacks. A planter's reticence to see family as much more than women and children stemmed from a truly patriarchal and proprietary view of blacks as members of the master's family. By contrast, planters in the Carolina Lowcountry and in the Caribbean seldom implied that their own—itinerant—families included blacks as well.

Given the heavy spiritual burdens that West Indian slaves (and maroons) placed on family members living and dead, and their tenacious hold on particular "spots"—born grounds and gravesites—a case can be made that what the more established black families tried to do in the Caribbean was based on the way land was thought of and used in Africa. There, Africanists refer to the "family estate," a concept that calls attention to the sacred and corporate nature of a family's land, which is not seen as a marketable commodity but rather traditionally as tilled collectively and controlled by the eldest male, but corporate in the sense of belonging to the ancestors and being the focal point of commemorative ritual. Thus, the presence or absence of slave property and markets does not fully explain the diverging paths of acculturation and resistance in the Caribbean and the South. Rather, it is what slaves did domestically with their economic leverage that made for the significant differences, and the concept of "the family estate" may sharpen regional comparisons of slave domesticity.

Distinctive courtship and marriage practices flowed from and reinforced the slaves' diverse meanings and uses for property. In the Caribbean, slave domestic relations were polygynous, African in origin, and the most difficult to change. Alone among missionaries, who usually regarded the practice of "plural mates" (the common term) as "licentiousness," one cleric argued that slaves' domestic bonds were "by no means to be regarded in the light of promiscuous concubinage" but rather as "Polygamy." The anonymous author of the 1826 birthrate study noted that though slaves would accept baptism, to interfere in their domestic concerns led to "acts of poisoning & obeah." Among them "polygamy" was an "innate Custom" and African, whereas attachment to one woman was "entirely an adoption from the European [and] . . . daily increasing as Africans die off."

"Unconscious evidence" in plantation records and newspapers also indicates that polygamous households may have been more common than previously realized. On one of the runaway fugitive notices in the face-to-face society of Barbados, there was a certain 'Ned Boy,' who was one of 2 carpenters described in the same notice as having 3 wives. Moreover, 11 fugitives out of 283—roughly 4%—in Barbados were advertised as having 2 or 3 wives.

In Jamaica, only 6 runaways were listed as polygamous. One, Fanny, had a "Plurality of husbands," and a waitingman was described as having "several wives." As Jamaica was large, its plantations more open than those elsewhere, and because owners did not know their slaves as well, they lacked information about the mates of a fugitive that whites in compact Barbados had at their fingertips.

It is also noteworthy that in the advertisements of each of the 4 plantation societies women were listed as mates, that is, as "wives." From Maryland, a fugitive said to "keep . . . three wives" was also described as "pretends to be religious." Another man was characterized in part as "supported and concealed . . . by several Negro Women whom he calls his Wives." And Cambridge, a waterman was "so well known as to need no other description . . . [he] has a Wife at almost every landing on *Rappahannock*, *Mattapony*, and *Paumunkey* Rivers."

Among the 1,280 fugitive men in Virginia a negligible number, 2, were listed as polygamous—a fraction compared to Barbados. And in South Carolina, only a few among the 2,582 fugitive men were listed as having more than one mate. An impressionistic source suggests otherwise, however. An English traveler noted that on the great antebellum Heyward family rice estate, the master did not interfere in any way that did not concern his own interest. "[The slaves] may have two or three wives apiece so long as they do not quarrell." These examples notwithstanding, for the whole of the American South, where evangelical Christianity mounted a largely successful assault on plural mates, a more convincing overview of slave domesticity is that of *Time on the Cross* and the Gutman study. After initial sexual trysts young black people usually settled into monogamous unions.

When the alien Judeo-Christian ethic did begin to orient slave gender relations and strategies, the results contrasted sharply from one region to the other. Agricultural reformers pursued different objectives regionally, in part because Southern slaves comprised a naturally growing population and Caribbean slaves did not. Caribbean reforms centered, therefore, not on behavioral modification, but on "the causes of depopulation," about which planters and managers, by the 1790s, were surprisingly knowledgeable. They recognized the importance of sex ratios and the connections between infertility on the one hand, and venereal diseases on the other. They were also aware (without the germ theory or disease) that cutting the umbilical cord could lead to tetanus ("lockjaw") and that breast feeding inhibited conception.

Thistlewood's diary indicates that before the 1780s whites were not too concerned about slave "promiscuity" and its effects on rates of conception. This attitude changed, however, when monogamy came to be seen as indispensable to schemes of reform that would reverse population losses. If slaves made lifelong unions, reformers reasoned, they would no longer exhaust themselves by nighttime traveling and socializing in towns. Once encouraged to settle in at home, women would want to have children and take better care of those they had.

Such were the skewed sex ratios and circumstances, men understood that women were both shared and had considerably more say in the arrangement than in Africa, thus many of them became concerned about obtaining and keeping hold of wives. From the bottom of an early 18th century Virginia inventory, a note that Roger hung himself in the old tobacco shed ended with "not any reason, he being hindred from keeping other negroes men's wifes besides his owne." From the same is a note that George, who was sick in the stomach and eventually died, "Said his Country men had poysened him for his wife." The 18th century novelist Edward Kimber portrays a Coramantee revolt in Maryland that was motivated in part by the absence of available women. More than a century later in Jamaica during the trials following the 1831 rebellion, a slave testified that he had been married to Sarah Atkinson for 3 months but did not live with her. Asked why he married, he replied that "Mr Whitehouse [a missionary] told us if we marry nobody can take away our wives."

Slave Revolts and Rebellions —
In Search of Freedom and the Motherland

Africans in the New World demonstrated much resistance to their enslavement and fought to be liberated throughout the era of the Atlantic trade. These efforts transpired in the following ways: slave revolts in New York (1712); on the British Caribbean islands of Antigua, Barbados and Jamaica, the Demerara (Guyana) rising; the Male riots in Brazil; Nat Turner's Virginian rebellion; Samuel Sharpe's Jamaican Baptist War; and the widely renown Haitian revolution.

Further along the line was the founding of the Freetown Sierra Leone British crown colony at the beginning of the 19th century; the American Colonial Society's integral role in establishing Liberia to resettle its extraneous presence of free Africans; and the Brazilian, Cuban and Sierra Leonean (Saro) and creolized returnees' community of mostly Yoruba descent, of whom made an indelible contribution—culturally, religiously, artistically and economically—to Victorian and 20th century Lagos [later part of Nigeria].

In addition to the above, there was also the emergence of Pan-African political schools of thought spearheaded by Ed, Blyden, Casely-Hayford, W.E.B Du Bois, Frederick Douglass, Marcus Garvey—considered by many as the 'father' of the movement; his legacy grew to such a degree that it was the bedrock of Kwame Nkrumah's philosophy and in turn, an independent Ghana's nascent foreign policy.

The 1712 New York City Revolt

After midnight on 6th April 1712, a group of African captives and some "Spanish Indians" set fire to an outhouse on Maiden Lane owned by Peter Van Tilburgh—slave owner and resident of the East Ward. When unsuspecting whites arrived at the scene to stop the blaze from spreading, the group of above 30 armed with guns, knives, clubs, and hatchets, attacked them. Nine whites were killed, and 7 others injured before a militia unit stationed at the nearby garrison was notified. Governor Robert Hinter ordered a cannon to be fired from Fort George to warn others in the area about the revolt. The militia eventually dispersed the rebels, who escaped to the northern forest of Manhattan Island. Of the 28 individuals captured and facing charges ranging from murder to conspiracy, Governor Hunter writes, "twenty seven [were] condemned whereof twenty one were executed . . . some were burnt others hanged, one broke on the wheele, and one hung alive in chains in town, so that there has been the most exemplary punishment inflicted that could be possibly thought of." Six of the slaves killed themselves rather than be captured. On a practical level, suicide provided an escape from torture and public execution, though there were possibly spiritual reasons, tied to particular West African concepts, for this action. Seven slaves charged in this case were reprieved and never tried. The master of each slave executed received 50 ounces of "Pillar Plate" silver as compensation from the provincial treasury.

In his description of the uprising, Rev. Sharpe noted that an anonymous free African conjurer rubbed powder into the clothing of slaves "to make them invulnerable." Sharpe further claimed

> ... It was agreed to on New Years Day the conspirators tying themselves to Secrecy by Sucking y'blood of each Others hands, and to make them invulnerable as they believed a free negroe who pretends Sorcery gave them a powder to rub on their Cloths which made them so confident that on Sunday night Apr. 7 ab'2 a Clock about the going down of the Moon they Set fire to a house which alarming the town they stood in the Streets and Shot down and Stabbed as many as they could...

The Antiguan plot and Jamaican revolt

The nascent stages of an extensive conspiracy to achieve freedom was uncovered on the British Caribbean Island of Antigua in October 1736. The well-orchestrated plot was underpinned by a considerable number of the enslaved—comprising both Africans and Creoles (Antiguan-born). The initiators were 2 Africans, one named *Court* and a Creole named *Tomboy*. Their plan was to set off an explosion at the annual coronation ball on 11th October where the Governor and the planter of the elite would be in attendance. Gunpowder would be surreptitiously deployed in the cellar and upon ignition, the Whites would perish, and the Africans would establish their kingdom. However, the function was unfortunately postponed until the end of the month. Consequently, this interruption led to a difference of opinion on how to best adapt to the setback. On one hand, Tomboy was resolute in his insistence that the revolt should still be executed on the 11th as initially planned; on the other hand, Court—who ultimately won the argument—assertively argued the plan should be pushed back to coincide with the new date set for the ball. This would essentially prove to be the plot's undoing.

The Jamaican revolts, in addition to the Antiguan conspiracy can be seen as one of many episodes in what has been described as a "200 Years War" between slave and slave-owner in the British Caribbean. It isn't hard to see what inspired such revolts, given the cruelty that was meted out on the Africans. These included receiving excrement in the mouth—known as a "derby's dose"—for one who was caught eating sugar cane; a visitor to another Jamaican plantation in 1790 witnessed a master nailing a house slave to a post by her ear for breaking a plate, and though she freed herself she was later caught and "severely flogged" for her insubordination. Such pretexts for punishment were also useful for sadists and rapists to gratify their desires. However, one planter—Arthur Hodge was executed by hanging in 1811 due to murdering as many as 60 men, women, and children on Tortola in the Virgin Islands—another Caribbean Island; thus, demonstrating that there were some 'limits' to which such dehumanizing brutality was appropriate in the name of squeezing a 'respectable profit' out of the captives. Notwithstanding the white community's outcries to pardon Hodges, the declaration of martial law ensured the execution took place.

Jamaican captives angered by the above ill-treatment and racism of the most dehumanizing form—all in the name of pursuing profits—embarked on their first great revolt in 1760. This was consistent with being recognized as holding the most impressive record for slave revolts—averaging at least one large-scale revolt every decade over the course of 180 years the slave society existed. Not only was the rebellion leader a Ghanaian King, but additionally, what made the 1760 *Tacky's revolt* arguably the most serious of all that transpired was the fear it struck in the hearts and minds of the planters—given the involvement of 30,000 rebels. One witness Edward Long remarked rather bombastically that the rebels' purpose was "the entire extinction of the white inhabitants... and the partition of the island into small principalities in the African mode".

Haitian Revolution

Where many of the revolts and rebellions during this era ultimately failed, the Haitian Revolution succeeded and in the course of doing so, represents the most thorough case study of revolutionary change anywhere in the history of the modern world. Beginning on the August 22nd, 1791, a coalition of captives—the highest at 40% came from Kongo (currently Northern Angola and Western Congo), the Igbo and Yoruba from present-day Nigeria, and the Fon from Benin Republic set off the revolution. Though they were from different parts of Africa as well as representing diverse cultures, creole French (patois) aided communication amongst them, in addition to the mulattoes and white population. Additionally, the Africans' syncretized belief system of African voudou and Catholicism was a catalyst, such was its inherent rejection of their 'ethnic' status as slaves. This was evident by the voudou ceremony which was taking place just before the onset of a tropical storm involving thunder and lightning, thus proving ominous as later that night the enslaved killed their masters and plunged the colony into civil war.

The plantation owners had long pre-empted an attack from Africans given the latter's brutal experiences, and thus the revolution's crescendo was akin to the detonation of an explosive. Consequently, they ensured they were well armed and defensively prepared. Nevertheless, within the space of a few weeks the African rebels had reached the 10,000 mark, and the violence metastasized over the subsequent 2 months. This resulted in the deaths of 4,000 whites, the destruction of 180 sugar plantations, and several hundreds of indigo and coffee plantations—totaling 900 different plantation varieties and a value of 2 million francs. 1791 saw the French strike back and kill 15,000 Africans through organized militia groups. Below was the Haitian rebel's marching song:

> *To the attack grenadier*
> *Who gets killed, that's affair*
> *Forget your ma,*
> *Forget your pa,*
> *To the attack grenadier,*
> *Who gets killed that's his affair.*

Through sustained internal and international warfare between 1791 and 1804, a colony populated predominantly by plantation slaves overthrew both its colonial status and its economic system and established a new, more egalitarian political state of entirely free individuals—with some ex-slaves constituting the new political authority. As only the second state to declare its independence in the Americas, Haiti had no viable administrative models to follow.

The success of Haiti against all odds made social revolutions a sensitive issue among the leaders of political revolt elsewhere in the Americas during the final years of the 18th century and the first decades of the 19th century.

The Haitian model of state formation drove xenophobic fear into the hearts of all whites from Boston to Buenos Aires. Furthermore, the inhabitants of the erstwhile colony gave themselves—as part of an intellectual strategy—a new name *Haitians*, and defined all Haitians as "black," thereby giving a psychological blow to the emerging intellectual traditions of an increasingly racist Europe and North America that saw a hierarchical world eternally dominated by types representative of their own somatic images. In Haiti, all citizens were legally equal, regardless of color, race, or condition.

Bussa's Revolt—Barbados, 1816

The tinderbox that was Barbadian slave society exploded on 14th April 1816, when half the island went up in flames. Curiously, it had been a prosperous year. The Barbadian House of Assembly later commented that it 'was remarkable for having yielded the most abundant returns with which Providence had ever rewarded the laborers of the Inhabitants of this Island.' This was particularly true of the parish of St. Philip, which was the flashpoint of the revolt, where a plentiful harvest meant that bellies were full. The slaves therefore rebelled not because they were in material distress, but because they desired a different social order.

The rebellion that one army officer evocatively described as 'a hell-broth' was led by a slave known as Bussa. Today a statue widely believed to be a model of him is sited on one of the island's most prominent roundabouts. Positioned like a triumphant boxer, the figure stands cast in bronze, his face turned to the skies, clenched fist raised at right angles to his head, with broken shackles dangling from his wrists.

In 1816, Bussa was chief ranger on the Bayleys plantation in St. Philip. Later to be dubbed 'General' by his followers, he was probably somewhere between 30 and 40 years old and was an African-born slave. This was significant, since 'saltwater' slaves, with their memories of a free life, were traditionally regarded as the most refractory and prone to revolt. Some sources have documented Bussa as being of Igbo heritage. Alternatively, another source claims that it is likely that he was a member of the Bussa nation (hence his nickname), a faction of the powerful Mande people, who had spread over much of West Africa during the 14th—15th centuries as conquerors and traders in gold and kola nuts. Their commercial and political prominence emerged particularly in the context of their dealings with the Portuguese at Elmina, the infamous slave fort. If Bussa was by inclination rebellious, he also had more prosaic reasons to resist his enslavement. The plantation on which he labored had recently changed hands and its relaxed, liberal owner Joseph Bayley had been replaced by a new manager, Mr. Thomas, a hard man who had a reputation as a 'severe disciplinarian.'

Bussa had been plotting the uprising for over a year, along with a number of co-conspirators, who were also elite slaves. Among them was Jackey, a head driver at Simmons plantation; Johnny the Cooper, who also worked at Bayleys, and a free colored man called Joseph Franklyn. One of the most radical of the plotters was a woman called Nanny Grigg, who called for armed struggle long before her male counterparts were ready to take that extreme step. As skilled slaves, their privileged positions meant that while they had less material need to rebel, they were the kind of people who found the indignities of enslavement most difficult to bear. As John Vaughan, a manager of the Codrington plantation, acknowledged long before the rebellion: '[It] is those slaves who are our chiefest favorites and such that we put most confidence in that are generally the first and greatest conspirators.'

Their special status meant that this coterie of slaves was allowed to travel and thus, plot unnoticed, while their superior standing in the slave community gave their opinions great credence. In a sophisticated propaganda campaign that fed on the hopes that had been raised by the abolitionist movement in England, they spread the idea that the British government had actually granted slaves their freedom and that local planters were resisting this development. It was the slaves' patriotic duty, they argued, to rebel and implement the will of His Majesty's Parliament. As the island's House of Assembly concluded later, the 'insurrection was entirely owing to these hopes, so originating and so fostered, and that the slaves were led to attempt by force that which they mainly expected as an original gift from England.'

The conspirators' overall objective was to overthrow the planter class and free all black Barbadians from slavery. The plan was to unfold over successive days. The first evening would begin with a surprise attack when rebels would emerge from the thick vegetation and set fire to the canes and plantations. That night the whites, watching their investment burn, were to cry 'Water!' The next night armed combat would begin, and the planters were to cry 'Blood!' Each of the plantations involved had its own leader who had worked out battle plans with those above them. They used a series of messengers to communicate with the high command as and when they needed advice on how to proceed. The final evening of planning took place under the cover of a dance at River plantation on Good Friday, 12th April. It was decided that if victory were achieved, Joseph Franklyn would be appointed as governor of the island.

The timing of the rebellion was carefully chosen. The rebels hoped that the Easter celebrations would distract the white community and make them more vulnerable to assault. It was also the height of the harvest, so the mature sugar canes would provide good cover for both their ambushes and their flight, while the burning of the canes would mean that the planters would lose their most valuable asset. Finally, the choice of Easter had great symbolic value for the slaves: according to their understanding of Christianity, it was the start of a 'new life,' so it seemed an unusually auspicious time to launch their final emancipation. All-in-all, it was not a bad plan. But the slaves had an Achilles heel: their inability to get access to arms. It was to be their downfall.

The outbreak of arson that precipitated the rebellion began in St. Philip at around 8.30 pm on 14th April. From there it spread throughout the adjacent parishes, including Christ Church, where Burkes plantation was situated.

Rumors spread as swiftly as the flames. Was this just an accident, a 'burn' that had got out of hand, or a real rebellion, the first on the island for over a hundred years? At first the colonists were reluctant to believe anything was wrong: there were whispers of revolts all the time, but none in living memory had ever come to anything. And it seemed barely credible that the slaves could hope to resist the combination of local militia and the British troops stationed on the island. But the gravity of the situation became clear when a rider galloped up to the plantation to fetch Robert Cooper for militia duty: a revolt was indeed occurring. And in order to address the unfolding events, Cooper had to leave the plantation float (around $5,000) in the hands of one of his slaves, thus like many Caribbean planters at the time, their slaves may have often been their enemies, but they were simultaneously the only people they could rely on.

The Demarara Revolt

In 1823 another rebellion broke out in the British West Indies. This time it was in the British colony of Demerara, part of what is now called Guyana. The trouble began in the east of the territory, where slaves had been emboldened by rumors that the British Parliament had directed the colonial powers to improve their conditions. When the news reached the governor that they had downed tools, he set out to meet with the protestors accompanied by a regiment of militia. They were confronted by a crowd of slaves armed with pikes, machetes, and fowling hooks. When the governor asked them what they wanted they replied succinctly: 'Our rights.' After further discussion they explained that they wanted 3 days off and an opportunity to go to church on Sunday. The governor refused, and the plantations were soon ablaze.

The revolt peaked in the space of a few days. The rising consisted of a few small skirmishes, one large stand-off, and traces of the earlier artisanal plots. The rebels said they would kill every white in the capital of Georgetown, distribute ranks of emperor, king, and governor, and make the entire colony theirs.

Set in motion by the deacons of Bethel Chapel, the revolt was poorly organized; a sit-down for most, it was to be an insurrection for others. As one of a handful of massive statements that ranged between strikes and actual rebellions, the Demerara rising leaves one wondering what would have happened if, as in Haiti, momentum could have been sustained, and if leadership had been seen in an African-Catholic or bush Baptist way as sacred and concentrated in a few, rather than scattered among so many demystified, moralistic deacons and catechists. Acutely aware of the subversive nature of missions of any style, however, planters wished to see the revolt as the work of one person, a white man, the London Missionary Society's John Smith, "the Demerara Martyr." On the other hand, historians have argued that the rebellion was the slaves' from first to last. In light of the slaves' own testimony and the ambivalent character of their tactics, objectives, and leadership (including that of the enigmatic Smith), both viewpoints are arguable.

In the sources, the rebels' uncertainty about objectives makes an impression similar to that of the artisan's preoccupation with planning in the conspiratorial associations. But tentativeness in the case of the deacons seemed a matter of Christian ambivalence regarding violence and bloodshed. This manifested itself in loose talk of help from the most unlikely sources, city blacks and maroons, and in an unusual concern for legality and its corollary, writing. While swarming around plantation yards as they tried to roust reluctant field laborers from their huts, the rebels hit on a tactic that provided both a quick payoff and a resolution whether the revolt was to be a war or a protest. Turning the tables, they shoved supervisors into the hated stocks and kept them there until paper and pen were marshalled and the whites had symbolically signed over the estates.

Once in command of the stocks it was easy to put whites in, out, and then back in as mood dictated. Usually, only supervisors were locked up. An owner—an old woman "of good physick" who spent much time in the hothouse among sick slaves—was hidden away. A physician who tried to talk his way out of trouble—he had sick people to attend to that morning— was told "who wants you for a doctor again?" One slave offered to get a pillow for his manager; another, who dragged his out of the house by the heels and down a flight of steps, later apologized and said he would work Monday. In reply the manager gave him and several others a drink. He was also slapped by Kate who asked, "how do you like it?" Another—alluding to the ubiquitous Exodus story—called his manager "a second Pharoah".

The rebel's fixation on written documents as proof of freedom, or that the estate was theirs, let off steam in the midst of an explosive situation. One rebel who freed some managers was given 4 bottles of wine. But as the tactic of signing official-looking papers caught on, the slave just as readily helped shove whites into the stocks until they agreed to sign.

Nat Turner's Virginia Rebellion, 1831

During the mid-evening of the attack, Nat Turner met with a few men in deep woods around a smoldering fire. They moved out, and at about 2am on Sunday 19th August, struck the first blow. As momentum gathered, a few became 70, many of whom were well-armed and mounted. While killing around 60, the rebels followed a circuitous route that in a day and a half covered only about 20 miles, which at first view seems to complement later opinions that they were soon so drunk and disorderly as not to know what they were about. But Turner's tactics were sound, according to Henry Tragle, a former military officer who has studied the rebellion more closely than anyone while crisscrossing the terrain, searching out and photographing the remnants of the deadly march, and compiling the best documentary history of the event. According to Tragle, Turner had the instincts of a good battle commander. He stuck to the high ground and descended only to strike at relatively isolated farmsteads.

After hours of exhausting fighting and killing, however, the attack quickly unraveled. Some may have been drunk. More were certainly disillusioned, because at Parker's field, scene of the final ignominious skirmish, they faced armed slaves who fought to protect whites. For his part, Turner said that his men, expecting to be joined by kin at Parker's, persuaded him to pull up. This may have been a tactical mistake because the whites were initially stunned and probably closer to momentarily losing Jerusalem (the country seat) than is now realized. Still, once they rallied, their vastly superior weaponry, militia, and the posse organization were decisive.

Yet, this white victory could not conceal the galling fact that after nearly a century of no organized risings, Turner had marched, pillaged, and killed for nearly 2 days and then had simply disappeared. Worse yet, more than a week passed before the authorities were able to arrive at a reliable description of one who, after all, was the most notorious fugitive in Southern history. It is "remarkable," one reporter put it, "how little is known of Captain Nat. We could find no person who has seen him." The runaway notice that eventually pursued Turner read:

> Nat is between 30 and 35 years old, 5 feet 6 or 8 inches high, weighs between 150 and 160 lbs, rather bright complexion, but not a mulatto—broad shouldered, large flat nose, large eyes, broad flat feet, rather knock-kneed, walks brisk and active, hair on the top of the head very thin, no beard except on the upper lip, and the top of the chin, a scar on one of his temples, also one on the back of the neck, a large knob on one of the bones of his right arm near the wrist produced by a blow.

Turner was an intellectual, who near the end of the "Confession" confronts his formative years this way: "I must go back to the days of my infancy, and even before I was born." His parents, sending a special child, maintained a family tradition that one of the boy's dreams concerned events that had taken place before he was born. Coming to similar understandings later about his prowess, older slaves included Turner in forays on white people's property. But usually Turner was a loner, who in his teens preoccupied himself with experiments to make paper and gunpowder—convenient symbols of the Creole leadership's dilemma: strive peaceably for literacy and the knowledge it makes available or prepare for armed struggle.

Experiments of another kind were like those of other acutely religious seekers of his era. Religion—conventional and esoteric—pervades the "Confession," which on a first reading, recalls such famous contemporary prophets as Joseph Smith and the Millerites. Like them, Turner has visions and received messages from God, angels and "the Holy Ghost."

Initially, and for long periods during his quest, Turner fasted, and prayed, and otherwise pursued conventional routes to redemption and saintliness. He wanted to be baptized, for instance, and to baptize others.

The Baptist War: Jamaica, 1831—32

This rebellion was preceded by a classic combination of preconditions, a stubborn epidemic of smallpox, a bitter drought that wrecked provision grounds, and the whites' blatantly provocative decision to change ground rules and shorten the Christmas holiday. A precipitant (reminiscent of the spark for the 1795 Maroon War) was the whipping of a driver's wife by a white whom the slaves hated more than any other, Colonel Grignon ("Little Britches"), who as head of the western militia would be forced to retreat ignominiously following his defeat in the major battle of the rebellion. In England, which had "crea[ted] an unprecedented level of hope and excitement" among a people, Mary Turner argues, who were dangerously provoked on the eve of the Christmas holidays when the whites held a series of public meetings about how best to keep slaves down, defy the crown, and perhaps seek an arrangement with a slave power to the north, the Southern United States. As chapel attendance rose dramatically, slaves decided not to work after the first of the year unless they were paid wages, or freed and paid wages.

Armed conflict began in the Leeward parishes, the traditional center of major resistance in Jamaica. By 1831 assimilated leaders used Baptist prayer meetings to organize, but the oath—an old rite, was still a fulcrum. From his jail cell, a Baptist rebel warned in nearly the same words as those used by a Coramantee during Tacky's rising in 1760. "I tell you again, if the gentlemen do not keep a good look out, the negroes will begin this business in 3 or 4 years, for they think the Lord and the King have given from the gift [freedom], and because those who were joined in this business were all sworn."

Baptist chapels were sited in individual plantations, of which its leaders were slave drivers or chapel teachers. The chapels in turn were linked to the mother church, the large Baptist congregation in Montego Bay, whose "daddy" or chief of them all was the black elder, Samuel Sharpe.

In an extensive region where most estates were heavily damaged or completely burned to the ground, some were spared, or suffered damage only to their tempting and very combustible trash houses. Confronted by armed insurgents, who were often "strangers" (a potent term in the islands), slaves reacted variously by continuing to work, leaving to join the rebels, remaining near their houses and garden plots to see how matters progressed, or fleeing into the woods before militia and insurgents alike. Riding through several estates when the war first broke out, the Presbyterian minister, Hope Waddell's base, Barrett Hall, was "safe and quiet." Its people gathered around and said they were ready to return to work. At Crawle, the estate village was deserted: "door open, fires burning, and dogs barking;" at Spring Estate, the slabs were "bold and independent, and ready to debate the question of their right to freedom." And at Spot Valley Estate, the people, "unruly" and plundering, replied to a proclamation ordering them back to the field: "We have worked enough already, and will work no more. The life we live is too bad; it is the life of a dog. We won't be slaves no more; we won't lift hoe no more; we won't take flog no more. We free now, we free now; no more slaves again." They shouted, laughed, and clapped their hands, Waddell continued, and "I could not help laughing with them, and my doing so increased their good humour."

As revolution came, slaves riveted attention on their own plantation leaders, who played a primary role in determining which way their people turned. At Unity Hall, a driver, George Kerr, after a meeting of the chapel in the quarter ordered slaves "to make themselves easy and set down and eat their Christmas [meal], and not to meddle with no man, and they, must let no man meddle with them." Quietly preoccupied in their houses during the holiday, when ordered out afterward the slaves again gathered before the driver's house as the white leadership caved in. The overseer, threatening to call in the Round Hill guard, armed himself and the bookkeeper and left. Returning home at this point to arm themselves for a brief symbolic exercise, the people fetched their hoes, brought them up, and threw them into the overseer's yard as a boy, at the command of a driver, set fire to the overseer's house. In the following week this group also burned down the great house and killed one of the few whites to die in the rebellion, a man sent to collect the master's belongings.

Elsewhere, John Dunbar, a driver, head cook, and Baptist, "not a ruler but a Follower," was further described by his owner as "always attentive to . . . duty." That is, until suddenly, about 6 weeks before Christmas, when Dunbar became "insolent, disobedient and would do nothing." Demoted to the field before the revolt, Dunbar ordered the plantation set ablaze when conflict broke out. Another driver, Alexander McIntosh, also identified as a "Doctor-Man," was "put in charge," he said, by his owner, who had left before Christmas. McIntosh also ordered the burning of the estate.

At Kensington, the 30-year-old Creole driver, Blacque Lawrence put on his sash and rode on a horse to a neighboring plantation where he took a gun away from a Negro. "It's to shoot parrots eating my plantains," he said as he fired it around. He later said, "that as he was the Driver, he was the Captain of the place." Returning from a trip, which may have an alibi, and seeing that the great house had been torched, Lawrence ordered that nothing should be killed without his orders. He asked, "Why they burn it for?" and requested that the kitchen and stable not be fired, as he would live in them. To this, another witness added that Lawrence said that if he could get Mr. Morris, Joe Vernon, and Reid, "he would be satisfied." "The prisoner [Lawrence] said Mr. Ingram was the only person left whose head he wanted." A desire for personal revenge among other objectives thus mixed with the most unblemished principle. The man whose gun the driver took repeated Lawrence's remark that "free was sweet and he would fight hard for it."

At the climatic meeting in Montego Bay after Christmas worship, 2 artisans were the principal speakers, George Taylor, a Sadler, and the most prestigious teacher, Sam Sharpe. Sometime after his arrival in 1824, Burchell made Sharpe a deacon (or in slave talk "ruler" or "daddy") for the Montego Bay congregation. The largest in the island, the congregation had nearly 2,000 members and included in its circuit a station comprised of the congregation of Moses Baker, the "bush" Baptist who upon his retirement turned his large Convince society over to Burchell.

Sharpe, sometimes called "Schoolmaster," regularly received extra newspapers from a nephew who worked in a print shop. These included the *Watchman* edited by Edward Jordan, a free man of color, whose newspaper was a conduit of information on the antislavery campaign in England. Informed, literate, and an eloquent speaker, Sharpe was of medium build, "fine sinewy frame," and "jet" black, wrote Edward Bleby, a missionary who spent many hours among the condemned. Listening to Sharpe address his fellow prisoners "for a long time on various topics," Bleby was struck by the "power" and fluency of his delivery, which "kept all his hearers fascinated and spell-bound from the beginning to the end."

Referring to the many evils and injustices of slavery, Sharpe asserted the natural equality of man and used biblical authority to argue that whites had no right to enslave blacks. He also spoke a great deal about the newspapers he had read, "showing that both the King and the English people wished the Negroes to be emancipated and expressed his belief that the 'freepaper' had already been sent out." Of Sharpe's last speech, "He said the thing is now determined upon—no time is to be lost. The King of England & Parliament have given Jamaica freedom and as it is held back by the whites we must at once take it . . . [He] kept on talking this way which roused us and made us nearly mad."

There was a bluntness to the country people's articulation of motives that contrasts sharply with the bravado of the earlier conspirators. They would, one said, burn "the Blasted Estates and do away with all the sugar works, it was them that kept them from getting their freedom." Some of the strongest statements of this kind were made by women and town people, hitherto not a significant part of major plots or rebellions in any region. In sight of militia closing in, one put down her washing and with a torch ran to fire a trash house, crying out before she was killed "I know I shall die for it, but my children shall be free!" Ironically, though leaders and meetings centered in Montego Bay, country people by far did most of the fighting and dying.

Male Rebellion in Brazil

The term *Male* was a reference to enslaved African Muslims in Bahia. Though there is debate on the etymology of the name, it is clearly related to *Imale*, the Yoruba word for Muslims. The name was used on the coast of the Bight of Benin as early as the first decade of the 18th century in reference to Muslim merchants, and generically to all Muslims, and hence the term was not only a Yoruba word. Who these early "*Malais*" were is unclear, but by the late 18th century, as revealed in documents on the slave trade, most of these Muslims came from Central Sudan and either spoke Hausa or Nupe or came from Borno in present-day North-eastern Nigeria. The enslaved Muslims who were sent to Bahia in the first decade of the 19th century were almost entirely from the Central Sudan (an erstwhile reference to present-day Nigeria). Thereafter, increasing numbers of enslaved Yoruba, some of whom were Muslims upon arrival but many of whom were not, made up the slave cargoes to Bahia. By the 1820s, Muslim Yoruba were a significant factor in the Muslim community, though the Muslim leadership remained in the hands of Hausa, Nupe and Borno Muslims, and it is likely that some of those designated as Hausa were in fact Fulani, that is Fulfulde-speakers of the Central Sudan.

The Male riot of 1835 in Bahia was arguably one of the most remarkable— such was the extent of collaboration between the enslaved and formerly enslaved—to have occurred in the New World. The province (now state) of Bahia was one of the most sugar-producing regions in the New World, owing much to its fertile *Reconçavo* location, which was a well-drained wetlands area surrounding the Bay of All Saints. The view of the Bay itself was considered "... perhaps the most magnificent in the world", according to the British navy commander Sir Robert Wilson in 1805. Bahia had an estimated total population of 65,500 in 1835 of which 42% or 27,500 were enslaved. Though this was less than half the population the figure was closer to 72% once the 19,500 population of freed blacks and mulattos are considered. This is arguably significant because though the latter may have been theoretically 'free,' economic rigidity, legal, racial, and ethnic barriers were weighty impediments. In more contextualized terms, certain paradoxes were present such as the materially well-off slaves—or at least urbanized slaves—were higher up the Bahian social hierarchy than freed beggars or vagabonds; this paradox is all the more peculiar as one can't help but wonder which would be socially more edifying in that society: to be free and starving or enslaved and fat. The presence of homeless indigent freed persons was inevitable given the poorest 60% of the population laid claim to only 6.7% of the total wealth distribution. When it is also considered that the 'few fortunate' free blacks were mandated to *ethnically-escape* their African heritage by adopting a more 'White-Brazilian' way of life, the cost of this was deemed to be too high. This being so due to the loss of social alliances with other blacks, lost dignity, independence, and identity, thus this reluctance helped to foster a sense of togetherness through a shared struggle and collective hardship. Consequently, few attained economic prosperity.

Beyond any doubt, Islam played a central role in the 1835 rebellion. It had been planned to begin at dawn on Sunday, 25th January—the day of 'Our Lady of Guidance, then an important celebration in the Bonfim church's cycle of religious holidays. Bonfim—8 kilometers from downtown Salvador—was still a semi-rural settlement consisting mainly of planted fields and orchards. This specific celebratory Sunday was deemed a good day to rebel since the usual level of oversight would be relatively lower, and this also happened to coincide with the spiritual strength they had acquired during the holy month of Ramadan. Staging revolts on Sundays and holidays was part of the standard pattern for the enslaved in Bahia and throughout the new world. Contrary to modern rebels, who mainly protest and strike on workdays, slaves used to rebel more frequently on days of leisure. The reasons for this it can be argued, are owing to the advantages: rest days meant inevitable vulnerability for the upper echelons of society. However, in the present day, protests, and strikes—given the social chasm between rebels and the elite is narrower—furnish protestors with more leverage should they disrupt key economic activity.

The feast of Our Lady of Guidance had, in fact, commenced on Saturday, at which point the throng of worshippers and merrymakers gathered for prayers and celebrations. This holiday—like many other public holidays— bridged the division between the sacred and secular, as well as enabling the different social classes to freely mix. The world was thus symbolically turned upside down. However, in 1835 one group was conspicuously absent, and while the masters were celebrating their saint on one side of the city, on the other side was the enslaved also using their religious faith and celebration to prepare a real turning upside down of the world the masters had made.

Rumors and gossip of an uprising began to gather apace in Salvador's business district—Conceiçao da Praia. Early on Saturday evening, when Domingos Fortunato, a freed slave, reached home, he told his wife, Guilhermina Rosa de Souza, that some blacks had spent the day whispering back and forth about an intense, unprecedented movement of slaves coming in from the *Reconçavo*. Despite her attempts to sound the alarm out of obligation to Fortunato's [former] master, this wasn't taken seriously until Guilhermina's friend and fellow freed former slave, Sabina de Cruz, who was the wife of the rebellion leader Vittorio Sule, sounded the alarm for a second time. Prior to Sabina's revelation of the attempted rebellion, a row had ensued between her and an ostensible spokeswoman, Edum, who insisted she could only see her husband once the "Africans were the masters of the land," to which Sabina, leaving little imagination as to where her loyalties lay, replied "they'd be masters of the whiplash." Subsequently she informed her white neighbor, Andre de Silveira, who eventually transmitted the news to the Justice of the Peace, the President, and other key personnel, upon which general alerts of the coup plans were sounded, security tightened, African residences within the Guadalupe neighborhood raided, and the ports restricted thus limiting escape routes to the African rebels.

During one of the house raids, a mulatto landlord, Domingo, was housing some of the African rebels laying the final touches to their plans over ritual meal in observance of a key occasion in the Muslim calendar. Out of fear for his life he tried to throw off the officials pressing him for answers as to who he shared the residence with. His attempts to divert their attention elsewhere failed as 50—60 Africans burst the room door down, chanting "Death to Soldiers!" as well as shouting orders in an undisclosed (possibly Yoruba / Hausa) African language. Despite some Africans having split loyalties between the Africans and the European authorities, the rebellion gathered momentum as Africans without prior notice of the revolt supplemented the extant hoard. Several casualties were incurred on both sides—including policemen and rebels, as well as neutral and passive parties. Nevertheless, such developments were not enough to quell the growing group of rebels as they advanced to the city jail to free a Muslim leader—Pacifico Licutan—who was held in high esteem. This action was also possibly part of a military offensive to free all the Africans, thus swelling their numbers further and accessing more weapons from the prison guards.

The rebel group was reported to have unsuccessfully attempted to take over the National Guard barracks in the Sao Bento Convent, but were a dominant presence in the street. As further fatalities accrued on both sides of the conflict, the group advanced toward Itapagipe but only reached halfway, where they were stopped at the cavalry barracks in Agua de Meninos. It was here—where according to contemporary accounts—that the decisive battle of the 1835 rebellion took place. It was reported that as the Africans advanced through the streets beating a war drum, the Chief of Police Goncalves Martins ordered that guardsmen instruct people to seek refuge in the church. He reported seeing 50—60 Africans armed with lances, swords, clubs, and pistols, but did not attack anyone as their objective was to pass by. The police horses intercepted the first wave of rebels, sparking a direct confrontation in which they rushed into a fort so as to shoot at their adversaries from a position of safety—incurring a minimum of 70 fatalities in the course of eventually bringing the rebellion to a close.

Revolt and Rebellion Outcomes

Antigua and Jamaica

The African-led slavery revolts produced varying outcomes in terms of successes and failures. In the Antiguan case, the plot was betrayed before it could be executed. Consequently, a rippling effect of fear was struck in the hearts of the white population given they totaled less than 3,000—far outnumbered by the 24,000 Africans on the island. Moreover, the key ringleaders were among the most trusted slaves, artisans, and plantation drivers, which underscored the whites' fears. This resulted in 88 executions owing to what the judges described as that "unparalleled hellish plot". The instigators of the plot: Court and Tomboy were 'broken on the wheel' (death by broken bones and bludgeoning) along with 3 others, 77 were slowly burned to death and 6 gibbeted (hung up in cages to die of thirst and starvation). The only thing which limited the extent of the slaughter was the depletion of British government funds for compensating the owners of the butchered slaves.

In contrast to the Antiguan case, the Jamaican rebellion moved from plot to execution stage, albeit with a devastating impact. The British had long faced a "Maroon" problem which involved armed runaway communities beyond the scope of white control, and which were not only successful in resisting colonial military expeditions, but also provided sanctuary to further waves of escapees. After 70 years of what was described as a "slaves and masters cold war," the Jamaican Maroon communities of Windward and Leeward signed treaties with the British to perform the role of mercenaries in actively capturing runaway slaves and putting down slave revolts. It was this mercenary force which was used to quash the Jamaican rebellion and shoot the rebel leader *Tacky*, dead. Once the rebellion ended, 60 whites had been killed, over 400 rebels also lost their lives—2 of which had their feet burned to ashes whilst alive to make an example of them. Of the remaining survivors, 500 were deported to Honduras (now Belize) which didn't stop them from also contributing to further rebellious activity on the island.

The Akan Factor in Slave Rebellions in the Americas

Much like the Vodun spiritual component in the Haitian Revolution, *Tacky's* 1760 revolt was said to be "Kormantin" and was aided by several Obeah doctors. To this end, the abovementioned Jamaican planter and chronicler of Tacky's revolt, Edward Long, described one of Tacky's doctors, Peter, as

> "an old Coromantin, who, with others of his profession, had
> been a chief in counseling and instigating the credulous
> herd, to whom these priests administered a powder, which,
> being rubbed on their bodies, was to make them invulnerable;
> they persuaded them into a belief that Tacky . . . could not
> possibly be hurt by the white men, for that he caught all the
> bullets fired at him in his hand, and hurled them back with
> destruction to his foes. This old imposter was caught
> whilst he was tricked up with all his feathers, teeth, and other
> implements of magic . . . he was so easily put to death,
> notwithstanding all the boasted fears of his powder and
> incantations."

Like this Obeah man, the sorcerer in Sharpe's account rubbed powder onto the New York slaves to create the same desired effect. This connection suggests that Peter the Doctor was possibly an Akan-speaking Obeah doctor.

Obeah often served as an important impetus and influence for Akan slave revolts in the Americas. One example would be the 1685 Jamaica revolt. During the initial stages of the revolt, the Akan-speaking insurgents attacked the Widow Guy's estate but were forced to retreat, "having lost one of their conjurors, on whom they chiefly depended. The Leeward Maroons of Jamaica, a community established after 1690, were led by an Akan-speaker named Cudjoe who often relied on the advice of an Obeah man. A contemporary witness who visited the Leeward Maroons during the 1730s noted, "They were very superstitious having during their State of Actual Rebellion, a Person whom they called *Obea Man* who they greatly revered, his Words, Carried the Force of an Oracle with them, being Consulted on every Occasion."

In 1728, a figure named Queen Nanny emerged as the military and spiritual leader of the Windward Maroons in Jamaica. Her name was likely derived from a combination of 2 Akan words: *nana*, a term used to denote a respected chief or elder; and *ni*, which translates as "first mother." Her role was a very familiar one for Akan-speakers; Queen Nanny not only led the independent Akan polity in eastern Jamaica known as *Nanny Town*, but she was also described in contemporary accounts as an "Obea woman." Queen Nanny's involvement in the First Maroon War, 1724—39, was facilitated by her alleged abilities to catch bullets with her hands or between her thighs (or *Nantu-compong*), to heal injured warriors, and to produce magical charms that rendered her soldiers invulnerable.

In Antigua, at least three separate Obeah men—Caesar Matthew, John Obia, and Quawecoo Hunt—were instrumental in a 1736 conspiracy. Both John and Quawcoo administered Akan oaths of loyalty which involved drinking a concoction made from a mixture of blood, graveyard dirt, and rum. Quawcoo was known in contemporary documents to be "a Negroe Obiaman, or Wizard, who acted his Part before a great number of Slaves . . . and assured them of Success." He was so frightening a figure that Quamina—a slave who turned King's evidence and betrayed the plot— confessed to court officials: "By God if you had not Catched me I would not have you now. I am afraid of this Obey Man now, he is a Bloody fellow, I know him in Cormantee Country."

Obeah also played a role in Jamaica following the Second Maroon War, 1795—96. In 1798, a group of Akan-speakers led by a man named Cuffee conspired to kill their masters and establish their own independent community. In planning the revolt, Cuffee consulted on at least one occasion with Old Quaco—an Obeah doctor who reportedly used a magic anklet to determine the movements of the colonial militia.

Edward Long related the following account regarding the influence of Obeah doctors in 18th century Jamaica:

> The most sensible among them fear the supernatural
> powers of African obeah-men, or pretended conjurers;
> often ascribing those mortal effects to magic, which are
> only the natural operation of some poisonous juice, or
> preparation, dexterously administered by those villains
> ... Not long since, some of these execrable wretches in
> Jamaica introduced what they called the *myal dance*,
> and established a kind of society, into which they invi-
> ted all they could. The lure hung out was, that every
> Negroe, initiated into the myal society, would be invul-
> nerable by the white men; and although they might in
> appearance be slain, the obeah-man, could, at his pleas-
> ure, restore the body to life ... Not long ago, one of these
> myal men, being desirous of seducing a friend of his to be
> of their party, gave him a wonderful account of the pow-
> erful effects produced by the myal infusion, and particu-
> larly that it rendered the body impenetrable to bullets; so
> that the Whites would be perfectly unable to make the
> least impression upon them, although they were to shoot
> at them a thousand times.

Moreover, the Akan loyalty oaths were integral part of Akan rebellions—of which Edward Long wrote about in 1774:

> Their priests, or obeah-men, are their chief oracles in all
> weighty affairs, whether of peace, war, or the pursuit of
> revenge. When assembled for the purposes of conspiracy,
> the obeah-men, after various ceremonies, draws a little
> blood from every one present; this is mixed in a bowl with
> gunpowder and grave dirt; the fetische or oath administer-
> ed, by which they solemnly pledge themselves to inviolable

254

secrecy, fidelity to their chiefs, and to wage perpetual war against their enemies; as ratification of their sincerity, each person takes a cup of the mixture, and this finishes the solemn rite. Few or none of them have ever been known to violate this oath, or to desist from the full execution of it, even although several years may intervene.

So perturbed were Long and several other planters that they sought to prohibit the continued importation of Akan-speakers into Jamaica because of the power of this type of oath and the constant threat of resistance.

Haitian Revolution

The Haitian revolt stands out as one of the greatest revolutions of modern history. It was not only the first successful slave revolt, but it also survived massive assaults from both the British and French—striking a mortal blow in the heart of Caribbean slavery. Given it was only the second country in the New World to declare itself an independent sovereign nation, this rankled with many Europeans who considered Africans to be their inferiors; this would ultimately prove costly. In 1825 France used the threat of warships to coerce compensation from Haiti for loss of its colonies and slaves—totaling the 2015 equivalent value of $21 billion. In many ways this burden is emblematic of the many issues which have impeded Haiti's development since achieving its independence.

The Haitian revolution typified the recurrent themes of African solidarity fueled by common goals which were stronger than their ethnic differences, religious dogmas, and economic ideologies. Despite the failures documented, the spirit of solidarity, ambition, intelligence, bravery, and a will to 'risk it all' against very low odds—multiple betrayals and inferior resources—speak to the "fine line between having everything to lose, and ultimately having nothing to lose" mindset which informed their actions.

Bussa's Revolt—Barbados, 1816

Robert Cooper and his militia had their first battle with the rebels in the yard of Lowther's plantation. Several of the rebels were armed with muskets and were exhorting other slaves to join them; moreover, one provocateur was brandishing an eye-catching red flag that depicted a white woman and a black man making love—the ultimate taboo in plantation society.

The rebels undoing was ultimately due to being poorly equipped, armed only with machetes and billhooks, cudgels, and axes, that they had looted from a hardware store. Consequently, it was easy to quickly disperse them. According to Colonel John Rycroft Best: 'We pursued and killed some; their rapid flight however saved numbers. We had to march from estate to estate to quell the insurgents for they were all set to plunder and destroy the dwelling houses. We killed about 30 men!' There was only one militia casualty, who was slightly wounded by a pistol shot. 'The villain was shot down immediately.'

The victory at Lowthers was greatly facilitated, according to Best, by the 'intrepid courage' of the free colored men who belonged to the militia, who dashed 'singly into a house full of rebels without looking behind for support and dug out the fellows.' Their behavior must have dismayed the slaves, who might have hoped that they would make common cause with them as had happened in Haiti; but the free coloreds had other ideas. They had been struggling to ameliorate their situation for a long time through constitutional lobbying and saw this as an opportunity to prove their loyalty. They were rewarded the following year, when they were given the right to give testimony in court against whites, a much-longed-for objective in their fight for civil rights.

After the success at Lowthers, the militia engaged in a mopping-up expedition in which they killed another 10 blacks. In retaliation, the slaves resorted to widespread arson. Best reported:

Large quantities of canes were burnt and I think more

> on the second night than the first, which proved that
> although the rebels were subdued by arms, they were
> nevertheless determined to do all possible mischief.
> Houses were gutted and the very floors were taken up.
> The destruction is dreadful, the plundering beyond
> anything you can conceive could be effected in so short
> a time.

The early defeat was a terrible disappointment for the rebels, who had been counting on victory to pursue their full strategy. Their fortunes continued to decline when the British troops on the island tardily joined the conflict. Cannily, however, the commander of the garrison included among his force 150 black men from the West India Regiment, who were to fight alongside 250 other soldiers.

The black troops of the West India Regiment arrived outside Bayleys plantation on Monday evening at sunset. The battle started at dawn. On spotting the black soldiers, some of the slaves were disorientated. As one officer wrote: 'The insurgents did not think our men would fight against black men, but thank God they were deceived ... The conduct of our Bourbons Blacks, particularly the light Company under Captain Smith, has been the admiration of everybody and deservedly.' But these men had their own agenda, too. The army had given them special privileges, they had never been part of the general slave population and they had no allegiance to the rebels. Put on the back foot by the soldiers, the slaves hesitated, and 70 were taken as prisoners. A large group fled north and reassembled at Golden Grove plantation just under a mile away, where they took over the great house.

Despite their successes, the planters could not yet relax. Other groups of rebels were causing havoc in St. John and Bridgetown. Various contingents were dispatched to deal with these problems and by Tuesday night, according to Colonel Codd, 'conflagrations had ceased and the dismay and alarm which had seized the colonists in a great degree subsided.' By midday on Wednesday the 18th, the revolt was all but contained, the arson had stopped and so had the fighting. At least 150 blacks had been slaughtered and 400 had been arrested. Bussa had been killed in the battle at Bayleys and many of the other ringleaders were dead.

After 4 days of pandemonium, the most 'momentous crisis in the annals of the country was finally over.' Robert Cooper returned to Burkes in a cloud of heat and dust to discover that his family were safe, his plantation had survived virtually unscathed and the slave he had entrusted with his money had buried it safely under a tree. Whether this was out of loyalty or judicious forethought will never be known. But he was rewarded, and Robert Cooper claimed that his faith in his slaves was reaffirmed.

In the chaotic and violent aftermath of the rebellion, Burkes became a friendly outpost for militia contingents, whose horses thundered across the countryside, policing the island's still-smoking landscape to search for runaway rebels and sympathizers as well as to intimidate the general slave population. The atmosphere across the island was one of profound paranoia. The smoke from the fires lingered for weeks alongside the sickly smell of burnt cane and rotting livestock. Refugees were still in the capital, reluctant to return to their plantations, while armed parties of militiamen patrolled ceaselessly. The planters couldn't understand how the slaves had managed to keep this conspiracy a secret for so long or to plot so extensively. After all, Barbados was small and the rewards for informing on conspiracies, lucrative.

In their febrile state the colonists nervously rehashed tales of suspicious slave conversations, or secret slave ceremonies that were alleged to have taken place or recalled obeah tokens spotted around their plantations such as decapitated roosters, hatchets impaled in doors or marks painted in blood. Their fear made them implement even more brutal methods of domination to control their slaves, and discipline on the plantations became even more draconian. The slave quarters were searched and researched, while innocent slaves were roused from their daily routines, questioned, and frequently beaten. There were other, more terrible stories of female slaves being violated and children being tortured.

Unsurprisingly, retaliations by the military were speedy and cruel. Even before official judicial measures were put in place, some British troops were involved in the random executions of rebellious captives and other unlucky slaves. The rebels who were taken alive arguably suffered even more: the methods for extracting information in the sugar islands rivaled those of the Spanish Inquisition and few victims could withstand their torturers' efforts. Since a slave society functions on fear, trials were as public and as brutal as possible, and often took place at local plantations, where slaves were encouraged or even compelled to attend.

One of the primary 'contrivers' of the rebellion, Johnny, the cooper from Bayleys plantation, was transported to the parish of St. Peter and hanged on Trent's Hill 'for the sake of an example to the blacks in that part of the Island.' His swift and public execution would be followed by several others: some slaves were shot, others hanged, while unlucky ones were tied to wooden poles and burned by slow fire. These unfortunate souls sometimes took 3 days to burn with no opportunity to pass out or die quickly. 'By these means the planters hoped to imprint indelibly upon the consciousness of the blacks throughout the island, the full reality of the consequences of armed rebellion.'

Over the next couple of months hundreds of captives were tried for insurrection, others for inciting blacks to revolt; a few were acquitted, some were sentenced to transportation, some flogged or maimed. A large proportion, however, were executed. Soon the island's highways were festooned with the bodies of hanged slaves decomposing in the heat: a feast for the buzzards.

In June 1816 a white Barbadian described the post-rebellion feelings among the blacks and outlined the dangers it posed for colonial society:

> The disposition of the slaves in general is very bad. They
> are sullen and sulky and seem to cherish feelings of deep

> revenge. We hold the West Indies by a very precarious
> tenure — that of military strength only. I would not vie a
> year's purchase for any island we now have.

Long after martial law was lifted on 12th July, the planters were still not convinced that the rebels were fully rooted out. Inevitably some innocent slaves were convicted, and though a number of their masters interceded on their behalf, it was usually to no avail. In the fervid and pitiless atmosphere that prevailed immediately after the revolt, justice was a mere detail.

In September a small group of blacks were arrested for planning another insurrection. 'Murder was to have been the order of the day,' declared Colonel Best, who acted as judge in their trial. 'As on the former occasion, the drivers, rangers, carpenters, and watchmen were chiefly concerned and a few field labourers . . . I am under no apprehension as to the consequences . . . It is no longer delusion amongst the slaves . . .They convinced themselves to be sufficiently numerous to become the masters . . . of the island.' The desperate rebels had lost the battle, but they did not accept that the war was over. The struggle against slavery continued though at a less organized level.

In fact, though it failed in its immediate aim, the uprising was the beginning of the end of Barbados slave society. The Barbadian colonists realized that no one on the island, while white or black, was free from fear. But even though they could never truly feel secure while slavery existed, they couldn't imagine a world without it.

Bussa's Rebellion was a profound shock to both the Barbadians and the British. The oldest and apparently most settled of the sugar colonies had suffered a major revolt. If the Barbadian slaves, inhabitants of the cradle of the Empire's sugar production and prosperity, could erupt into violence, what hope was there for the rest of the region? And yet, for the enslaved population of the island, the aftermath of Bussa's Rebellion was a profoundly depressing time. Not only were they still slaves, but their hopes and dreams for a better life seemed further away than ever. Ironically, this was in part because of their rebellion. When sensationalized accounts of the uprising had crossed the Atlantic, the British oligarchy was so shaken that even the man whom the slaves believed was their 'champion,' William Wilberforce, was forced to back away from the abolitionist cause. The extent of his volte-face was made clear when he sponsored a Parliamentary Address which formally declared that 'there existed no plan for introducing emancipation into the West Indies.'

The Demarara Revolt

When the governor confronted the insurrectionists to ask what they wanted, he was told that they "were as good as white people . . . and they had no right to be slaves, nor would they be any longer, the king had sent out their freedom, and free they would be." Asking where they heard that "God made all men [free] . . . and that they were as good as whites," the governor later declared [that] the universal reply was 'At Chapel, at Chapel.'

In order to build a case that John Smith organized his chapel for purposes of subverting slavery, the military court left one of the best records of the workings of a mission. The prosecution focused on religious texts and their explication, slave leadership, and the collection and disbursement of fees. Sunday worship at Bethel Chapel began with prayer, songs, and a lesson from the Bible. Immediately before the revolt, a black teacher based his lesson on Luke 19:41—42. "When Jesus came near the city he wept over it." But excerpts from printed sermons make it difficult to imagine the excitement they undoubtedly generated in the charged atmosphere of imminent revolt. It was difficult to confidently infer intent from such ambiguous professions of faith, as the following in which (in court proceedings) an insurrectionist in the same breath went from "blessings for massa" to "fire for massa": "at our prayer-meetings we prayed to God to help us and to that we might be made good servants unto them, and they might be good masters unto us; and to give us health & strength to do what it might be our duty to do . . . we pray about our masters hearts, we pray to the Lord to bless, and change our hearts, and change our masters hearts likewise." But suddenly, "I have heard some of the boys who read the bible, speak about the Israelites and the Jews, about the fighting of the Israelites when they go to war; when the prisoner [Smith] read about the fighting of the Israelites, after[wards] they went home and read it again." The deacon testified that he tried to explain Exodus without controversy, "but the people applied the story . . . and put it on themselves . . . they began to discourse about it; they said that this thing in the bible applied to us . . .as well as to the people of Israel." To this another said emphatically that churchgoers "never" spoke of any other part of the Bible except Moses and the children of Israel.

Diligent and dedicated, Smith established a rapport with the slaves and delegated real responsibilities to the black deacons. The court record also includes a note that the slaves "always" chose their own teachers from among those who could read. When questioned about who Smith chose as catechists, Bristol, a deacon, replied, "I tell him."

What slave deacons did before they became rebels included looking after the conduct of new members who lived on the same plantation as they did and reporting the initiate's progress to Smith. They also kept track of fees collected, maintained quiet during chapel service, and distributed communion bread and wine. Black church leaders included Quamina, the head deacon and a carpenter, who held the position before Smith took over in 1808. Of this leader, his brother-in-law, Bristol, noted that the missionary considered Quamina "more than white men." A third deacon was an older freedman who lived with his slave granddaughter, and a fourth, Jack Gladstone, a cooper, was Quamina's popular son and an anomaly of sorts. Appointed by Jacob Wray, Smith's predecessor, and only occasionally in attendance, Gladstone was useful because he could read. One senses from the trial record that he enjoyed life too much to place himself resolutely under the mission's morally inhibited codes. In the bitter aftermath of this affair, Quamina became a maroon before he was killed by Indian trackers; his son complied with the state and so was spared and transported. At Smith's trial, both hostile and friendly witnesses agreed that the missionary never talked directly about slavery or slave treatment. However, in court, Smith admitted his "aversion" to the institution, while claiming that he had not read the Bible selectively but "right through." He then asked how it was possible to teach church history without an account of the Deliverance. Of this testimony, a military officer concluded aptly that Smith, who soon died from an illness, certainly did expound on those parts of the Bible that were "entirely relative to the Oppressed State in which he considered them [the slaves] to be." To this, a slave deacon added, "I always understood, as well as the rest of the Negroes, that although the parson preached in a way not directly telling us to take our freedom, yet [we] . . . understood he meant we could do so."

The Bethel mission gathered an even greater diversity of slaves, African and Creole, skilled and field, than the earlier associations, and it did so while providing them with an Old Testament ideology that the congregation readily turned to its own revolutionary objectives. Yet conversion in Demerara never attained the emotional sweep that occurred in Jamaica, where the blend of old and new ignited a large and prolonged rebellion.

As always, the retaliation meted out on the rebels was always worse than the actual rebellion itself. More than a hundred slaves were killed in the conflict and many more brutally flogged or executed immediately after. The Methodist minister whom the authorities believed had inspired the revolution, the Englishman and *Demerara Martyr*, John Smith, was sentenced to death, but he expired of consumption before the punishment could be carried out. And afterwards the bullet-ridden body of one of the ringleaders, the abovementioned slave, Quamina, was displayed in front of the plantation where the revolt first started. According to one witness, it was a ghastly sight: 'a colony of wasps had actually built a nest in the cavity of his stomach, and were flying in and out of the jaws which hung frightfully open.'

Nat Turner's Virginia Rebellion, 1831

By the morning of 23rd August, Turner and his rebel band's bloody swathe across Southampton, Virginia, left 57 white men, women, and children dead. Resultantly, militia units from Virginia and North Carolina, as well as federal troops, were called in to quell the insurrection and by the morning of 24th

August 1831, the whites of Southampton had largely survived the bloodiest slave rebellion in U.S. history.

After his capture on 30th October 1831, Nat was tried and sentenced to be executed on 11th November 1831. In total, 16 were executed and 12 were transported (deported) from Virginia. As many as 100 slaves reportedly died in the wake of the rebellion. The case against Nat Turner generated 2 important documents that unlock several mysteries regarding the causes of the revolt. The first document was the "confession" dictated to Thomas Gray from November 1st—3rd. Gray, a slaveholding attorney, was no doubt hostile to what Nat Turner' revolt represented. His editorial comments reveal both a deep-seated animosity and a begrudging admiration of Nat. Despite the fact that Gray's interpretation of the events may have colored certain aspects of the confession, Nat Turner's undeniable voice, as Black preacher in the tradition identified by Du Bois, is still present in this document. The "Confession" is rich with references to an ascetic regime, fasting, and watchings, to encounters with awesome spiritual powers and signs, and to such supernatural inclinations and feats as foresight and healing. Curious about the advice a particular spirit gave to Turner, Gray inserted in the "Confession" "I could not get him to explain in a manner at all satisfactory—nowithstanding [sic] I examined him closely upon this point, he always[s] seemed to mystify."

Nonetheless, Gray was either led to, or made shrewd guesses about, the real character of Turner's religious style. He says little about Turner as part of the familiar tradition of Black Baptist exhorters, nor does that denomination provide keys to understanding this rebellion. Rather, Turner's orientation was archaic. "He became a dreamer of dreams." "Like a Roman Sybil" and "the character of a prophet" are phrases Gray used as he tried to grasp the nature of Turner's cultic orientation. In the best newspaper account, he wrote:

> He traced his divination in characters of blood, on leaves alone in the woods, he would arrange them in some conspicuous place, have a

dream telling him of the circumstance; . . . I have in my possession, some papers given up by his wife, under the lash—they are filled with hieroglyphical characters, conveying no definite meaning. The characters, conveying no definite meaning. The characters on the oldest paper, apparently appear to have been traced with blood; and on each paper, a crucifix and a sun, is distinctly visible; with the figures 6,000, 30,000, 80,000 &c.

At one point, Turner witnessed black spirits and white fighting in the sky, and stated 'Then the Holy Ghost was with me,' and further said 'Behold me as I stand in the heavens." "More hallucinogenic visions, which Turner interpreted as signs that he was God's chosen instrument, followed a regime of fasting and prayer. When the spirit came, Turner was alone (once at his plow), as opposed to its customary entrance in the Caribbean—publicly and ritually. Following these experiences, the slave saw himself mistaken, Turner replied, "Was not Christ crucified?" In none of this, however, is there an indication that the insurrectionist's visions also inspired his men and thereby became a motor for rebellion.

Gray also got right Turner's simple and direct goal. From his time to ours, some have concocted elaborate objectives for the Southampton rebels: to break out of slavery completely and become maroons in the Dismal Swamp miles away from the only home base these insular people had known. Instead, as Gray put it, "His object was freedom and indiscriminate carnage his watchword. The seizure of Jerusalem, and the massacre of its inhabitants, was with him, a chief purpose, & seemed to be his ultimatum."

Gray is on the right track at this point. What Turner did after the revolt is probably the most important to its meaning then and now. By remaining both alive and in the neighborhood, he kept himself available. By finding shelter until the lynch-mob hysteria had spent itself, it may be suggested that he gradually set up a safe and uneventful capture that would assure the transmission of a final statement about slavery as he knew it in Virginia, and his role in it. This decision represented the most that a slave leader could expect to do given the police-state character of slavery in much of the antebellum South. A primary meaning of the revolt was that once Turner had focused attention, he had to keep himself alive and close at hand, and so able to deliver the "Confession" at the proper time and to the safekeeping of someone who would come his way.

That the revolt was a desperate act and doomed from its inception is a possibility Turner may have recognized. In this regard it is most comparable to the revolt in British southeast Africa of another Virginia-trained insurrectionist, George Chilembwe. Like Turner, Chilembwe, as he put it aptly for both, in a militarily hopeless situation desired to show the oppressed that Black people could organize resistance and that whites, most assuredly, were vulnerable. A revolutionary's objectives in circumstances of this kind were "to Strike a Blow and Die."

The other item that helps to create a more complete picture of Nat Turner, and further illustrates some of the African dimensions of the revolt, is the actual trial record. Additional details about Nat are revealed through the court proceedings, which very clearly demonstrate that he was heavily influenced by African cultural undercurrents.

However, due to the nature of this revolt, the trial record is not as useful as the records generated by the Gabriel Prosser and Denmark Vesey conspiracies. The relatively spontaneous nature of the planning and actual revolt, that there were no lengthy meetings or massive recruiting efforts, means that the collective voice of the slaves involved is relatively limited in the record of the proceedings. In addition, slave testimony was actively paraphrased, abbreviated, and edited by court officials. Since the revolt was formulated in the mind of one man, this increases exponentially the value of Nat's confession. What is not revealed in the court record can be found, in full detail, in this key historical document.

The Baptist War: Jamaica, 1831—32

Originally planned as a peaceful sit-in, the revolt soon took on a life of its own and became the greatest slave rebellion the British Caribbean had ever witnessed. The fighters were so disciplined that they had their own uniforms (blue jackets and black cross-belts). It began a couple of days after Christmas at the Kensington great house in St. James in the north of the island. The unrest soon spread to the neighboring parish, and as many as 40,000 of Jamaica's 300,000 slaves were swept up in the conflict. One onlooker noted that the rebels seemed to be animated with a rare passion. One female slave converted to the cause declared, just before she was shot: 'I know I shall die for it but my children shall be free!' Soon the sounds of the horns, shells and drums reverberated across the island and the great houses, boiling houses and warehouses were in flames.

It took more than a month to subdue the rebels, and at its end 200 slaves and 14 whites had died. At least another 400 slaves were killed in reprisals afterwards. In Montego Bay the Methodist missionary Henry Bleby described the executions.

> Generally four, seldom less than three, were hung at
> once. The bodies remained stiffening in the breeze . . .
> Other victims would then be brought out and strung up
> in their place, and cut down in their return to make room
> for more; the whole heap of bodies remaining just as they
> fell, until the workhouse negroes came in the evening and
> took them away to cast them into a pit dug for the purpose,
> a little distance out of the town.

The casualties included the rebellion's leader, Samuel Sharpe— described by one missionary as 'the most intelligent and remarkable slave I had ever met with.' Sharpe's composure as he was taken to the gallows, profoundly impressed the spectators, just as his oft-repeated last words were used to recruit more people to the abolitionists' cause: 'I would rather die upon yonder gallows than live in slavery.'

No slave rebellion in Anglo-America equaled the degree of preparation, duration, and spectacular destructiveness of the Jamaica rising from late December 1831 to early January 1832. Property losses to about 250 estates and smallholdings exceeded a million pounds, and all-in-all more than 500 were killed, nearly all Black. Unsurprisingly, Parliament ceased procrastination and accelerated preparations for emancipation, which by this point the momentum behind it had become unstoppable. The Baptist revolt was the worst in the history of the English sugar isles and had reinforced the abolitionist arguments that slavery was an institution Britain could not afford to maintain.

In 1833, a petition signed by 187,157 abolitionist women was presented to Parliament. They focused particularly on the plight of female slaves, reminding the nation's soon-to-be monarch, Queen Victoria, that women and fellow mothers were being raped, brutalized, and sometimes beaten to death. (Though the new queen said very little directly about slavery, she was assumed to be supportive of the abolitionists because of her willingness to entertain Blacks and anti-slavery personalities like Harriet Beecher Stowe. And certainly the belief that she was sympathetic to the abolitionist cause did nothing to diminish Victoria's well-nurtured image as matriarch of the nation.)

Male Brazilian revolt

The Male Brazilian revolt was outlawed by ways of Article 113, Chapter 4 of the 1830 Criminal Code. A violation of the law required that 20 or more slaves collectively attempted an escape to freedom—otherwise termed as a "crime of insurrection." Moreover, Articles 114—115 codified the sentencing of varying degrees of punishment to free persons supporting slave revolt efforts as either leaders or instigators. Consequently, 301 people—including many innocent parties—were either acquitted, sentenced to death, imprisoned, consigned to forced labor, flogged multiply, deported, or subjected to an undisclosed punishment. The key objective of the sentencing was to protect the institution of slavery—such was its importance to the economy. As a deterrent, sentences took place in public gaze, and there was a sustained institutional and media driven ethnic-persecution campaign to deport free Africans described as "barbarians" with "no place in the Political, civilized world". The deportees of whom many had worked hard to buy their freedom—were peaceful, well-integrated, socially-contributive and innocent—were deported to [namely] Lagos—proving particularly harsh due to major political changes over the course of the 20—30 years they had been away. The devastation of war meant few—if any—found family and acquaintances alive. Even the few rebels among the deportees had established positive, life-changing roots in Bahia in the event the rebellion had been successful, thus were not prepared for life on the other side of the Atlantic. For the Africans that remained in Bahia, an edict to eliminate slave conspiracies and rumors was signed by the police chief to subject them to a hostile environment, which included keeping families in a state of anxiety, imposing curfews on freemen (slaves moved around more freely in contrast) from 8pm and banning the gathering of African crowds coming together for entertainment and social activity.

The Evolution of Freedom in the New World

While many took up armed conflict to achieve liberation, there were not only several enslaved persons who were being concomitantly emancipated [or at least the next best thing] but even free persons of color. While free men of color were clearly present in the New World from the first years of the Atlantic slave trade, and there were significant numbers of free colored in every slave society, the patterns of emergence of these "communities" of free men varied considerably, as did the rates of growth and the relative sizes at particular times. At the 2 extremes were Curaçao, Brazil, and Martinique, on the one hand, and the British islands of Jamaica and Barbados, on the other hand. In several provinces of Brazil, the numbers of free colored rose above 50% of the total population a decade before general emancipation. Even in the late 18th century, the percentage of free colored in Minas Gerais surpassed 30. In the Dutch colony of Curaçao, the free colored made up more than 43% of the population in 1833. In Martinique, the percentage of free colored in the total population grew from 2.5 in 1696 to 32 in 1848, though the increase was not steady, dipping markedly in the 1730s and 1740s during the height of the sugar boom. At the other end of the spectrum, the percentage of free colored in the total population of Jamaica did not rise above one-tenth, even on the eve of emancipation, while in Barbados the comparable figure was less than 7%.

While a simple comparison of the proportions of the free colored population in several of the slave societies of the New World suggests outstanding divergences, a consideration of the internal rates of growth of the free colored indicates considerably less variation. Among the discernible groups in New World slave societies, the free colored seems to have been the only group capable of increasing through natural means. By contrast, slave and white groups tended to be incapable of maintaining their numbers, much less of sustaining a normal growth rate. Consequently, these 2 groups depended to a considerable degree on continual immigration and replacement. This contrast between the patterns of growth of the free colored and the white and slave groups is, of course, much less notable in the more temperate areas, and especially in North America, where white settlement was much more extensive, and rates of growth were much more vigorous.

But this is not to say that the patterns of growth of the free colored populations were similar throughout the New World—only that everywhere they shared the common achievement of apparent self-sustenance of population growth; moreover, with the notable exception of British North America, this achievement occurred well in advance of both the white and slave strata. Of course, the continuing accretion of new members to the free colored groups through the self-purchase of freedom and the emancipation of children born of mixed white and non-white unions remained a factor of importance in the growth of the free colored population. But in many of these societies there was a period when the pressures created by increased restrictions on manumissions slowed the rate of accretions to the group and made natural replacement and reproduction the primary generator of population growth.

The emergence and early growth of the free colored population in New World societies were developments of enormous complexity, and evaluating the many contributory elements is enormously difficult. However, much of the literature covering this field suggests that in the earlier phases of the development of the slave society, the manumission of black and mulatto females attached to whites in formal or informal unions and the inclusion of their offspring in the free group were the principal forms of accretion. Many of these relationships transpired even if the white [usually male] in the relationship had another marriage arrangement in Europe. The fact that these unions assumed such regularity during the early period may have ensured their survival in later years, even in the face of strong governmental pressure such as that which Martinique experienced following the Seven Years' War.

Almost certainly, such stable unions were exceptional, and it is highly probable that the character of interracial unions altered over time. At first, they were, for the whites, presumably unions of sexual convenience. But later, with the emergence of a free non-white group with some wealth and a considerable degree of assimilation to the European society, or at least to its colonial model, the interracial union in some societies also involved substantive economic, perhaps even social, considerations. An example of this was in Martinique where such unions brought substantial financial benefits to the whites; to this end, as free colored populations grew, more free colored people married whites, which supplanted earlier white-slave unions.

One may even suspect that, in the early phase of the emergence of the free colored (the first few generations), the complex, multi-tiered color-coding system (for example, *Negro, sambo, mulatto, quadroon, mustee, mustifino, quintroon, octoroon*) may have been operative in terms of marriage preference and social status. A. J. R. Russell-Wood notes that an intricate but less arithmetic system survived in Brazil right through the colonial period. But elsewhere these categories became increasingly vague and confused within a century of the beginnings of the slave societies. The persistence of marriages between free colored and slave—and the increasingly restrictive legislation limiting subsequent manumission—made the terms *free* and *mulatto* or *slave* and *Negro* less synonymous. Equally, the differential statuses achieved by free colored of various shadings obscured the fine correlations between shade and status which white observers and administrators had readily made at an early date. Lastly, new patterns of manumission—through self-purchase and heroic service to state or master—made white shade preference a much less operative factor and introduced numbers of "Negroes" into the free group. One can observe, however, a tendency for the shade preference or "somatic norm image" to refocus on the more general somatic referents of mulatto and black.

The importance of the interracial union and of the associated manumissions in the early phase of the growth of the free colored population initially created age and sex anomalies. In terms of sex, the free colored groups throughout the hemisphere included disproportionately large numbers of females, not only as a result of the manumission of female partners in mixed marriages or sexual unions, but also as a result of the general tendency to manumit female infants in greater numbers than males. This is shown quite clearly in the 19th century figures for Cuba and Brazil. The sexual composition of the free colored group is all the more striking when seen against the white and slave groups, both of which were marked by a preponderance of males.

Two "selective" factors affected the sex ratio within the free colored group. The first was the increasing appearance of self-purchase as a means to freedom. Self-purchase appears to have become comparatively common during periods of rapid economic growth, which opened up considerable opportunities for free labor, though the practice later came under sharp fire from unpropertied white immigrants and other anti-manumission groups in virtually every society. Where self-purchase of freedom was possible, however, males were likely to join the free colored group in greater numbers than females.

Certainly, the available evidence suggests that where the "pulling up" of wives and relatives by newly free men was a relatively common practice it was a reflection of the opening of the economy to colored traders and artisans. The second "selective" factor, which also moderated the tendency toward female predominance among the free colored, was the readiness of colonial authorities—notably, the French, British, and Dutch in the Caribbean, the Portuguese in Brazil, and both sides in the War of American Independence—to offer non-white combatants freedom in return for heroic service in the internecine and civil struggles of the 17th and 18th centuries.

The disproportionately young age ratio was also moderated by several factors. The first was the custom of delayed manumission, which prevailed nearly everywhere throughout the slavery era. This custom required a "manumitted" infant or child to perform involuntary service, usually to an age beyond 20—including that of legitimate and illegitimate offspring. A third practice which moderated tendency toward a very young free colored population was the not altogether humanitarian practice of manumitting aged and incapacitated slaves. Such manumissions seem to have been related to declines in planting productivity and were associated with the practice of selling slaves to escape financial ruin. This practice has been well noted for the Tidewater areas of the Southwest. It was at this time that state legislatures hurried to enact regulations requiring slaveholders who intended to manumit slaves to put up a bond or guarantee which would protect state and locality from having to provide for sustenance and burial of penniless and infirm freedmen.

While the campaign to limit manumission of the helpless may be considered morally ambivalent, if not relatively humanitarian, the general trend against manumission was unequivocally strident. Waves of legislation overtook every slave society during the late 18th and 19th centuries, though perhaps to a lesser extent in 19th century Brazil. The legislation had a number of proponents—the plantocracy, artisan and poor whites, and colonial and metropolitan administrators—and took a variety of forms, from taxes and notarial restrictions. In every one of the societies under consideration, the anti-manumission legislation was unassailing, if present at all, through at least the first half of the 18th century. In the American South and in Cuba, the hardening of manumission restrictions occurred during the sugar and cotton "revolutions" of the early 19th century. But such a direct relationship between agricultural transformations and the openness of manumission laws would appear to have been exceptional as well as closely associated with the fear that the slave trade would be restricted as a result of the increasing number of attacks mounted against it during the third and fourth decades of the 19th century. In this situation, even the free colored people found themselves in a precarious position, and many fell, or were dragged back into slavery.

Elsewhere, the relationship of periods of attack to periods of intensification of agricultural production or the potential drying up of sources of slaves tended to be limited. There are indications, in fact, that the agricultural revolutions actually opened up opportunities for free colored persons—in management, in the factories, and in all the peripheral trades that grew up around the centers of production. More important in stimulating the movement against manumission were the whites' increasing fears of economic competition from freedmen and revolt among the slaves. The importance of these fears is especially clear in the cases of Martinique, Curaçao, Barbados, and Jamaica, and would seem to have been operative elsewhere as well. The revolution in Saint Domingue was only the grandest of events that produced intense fears throughout the New World of revolts ignited by free colored and carried to the greatest possible excess by slaves. Administrators heard the pleadings and warnings of the increasingly important economic and military role of the free colored but were uncertain whether this development reinforced or threatened their authority. In almost every case, however, they tended ultimately to heed the advice of the worried and angry whites.

What is at least as significant is the fact that the statutory restrictions on manumission were often ignored, bypassed, unenforced, or at most received only delayed attention. As a consequence, the decrease in economic opportunities permitting self-purchase, and the increase in acceptance of "semi-freedom" without official papers, also must be seen to have played a role in slowing down the rates of formal manumission.

While it has been argued that the fear-alliance factor was a primary element in the anti- and pro-manumission surges, it is all the more notable that the anti-manumission campaigns seem to have been aimed much more at the slaves than at the "communities" of free colored. Those already fully free lost little beyond an increase in their numbers as a direct result of the legislation. Though in retrospect this loss might appear to have been crucial, little free colored anxiety over their relative numbers is evidenced in contemporary sources. The anti-manumission laws did, however, attack and affect the quasi-free—for example, the *emancipados* in Cuba and the *soidisant libres* in the French Antilles. This rough category of quasi-free included those who were bound through marriage to the slave stratum and for whom the restrictive legislation made the manumission of wives, husbands, children, parents, and siblings much more difficult and costly.

To the extent that they were enforced, the anti-manumission laws, like much of the racial legislation and many of the administrative practices in the colonies, drove a considerable wedge between the free colored and slave populations. In certain circumstances, whites conceived of the free colored and slaves as belonging to one inferior category, but, in cases in which it served their interests, the dominant whites were prepared to define much more rigorously, not only the interstice distinguishing white from colored, but also that distinguishing free colored from slave.

As the legal and terminological distinctions made between free colored and slave became functional, the slave society assumed the character of a three-tiered structure, which prevailed throughout the New World except in much of the American South. Though the dominant group did generally perceive and define the free colored as an intermediate group between white and slave, the question of whether this stratum might be defined as a "class" or "caste" seems to be a terminological cul-de-sac. Class or caste consciousness appears to have been a relatively late-blooming phenomenon and was first notable in the petitioning campaigns of the 18th century, which were generally directed against the class legislation aimed at the free colored as a group. Its appearance is more striking still in the reactions of the free colored to the stirrings of the slave population at the end of the 18th century and in the first decades of the 19th.

A variety of explanations may be offered for the apparently slow development of such a group consciousness among the free colored. First, most of the contributors note that the free colored tended to aspire to white plantocratic or managerial status, and that such a general tendency could hardly be seen as promoting a separate group identity or reinforcing a consciousness of class. Second, deep cultural divisions between assimilated and unassimilated free colored were not unusual. In Brazil, to cite a profound and perhaps exceptional instance, many free colored were first- or second-generation Africans, and many more preserved much of the tradition of their ancestors. Russell-Wood notes, as well, that a number of free colored made visits to Africa, some to the homes of their ancestors. A third explanation involves the persistence of racial distinctions within the free colored group. Though the very complex racial hierarchy was apparently short-lived, as abovementioned, the tendency to differentiate between free mulatto and free black survived and persisted among whites and non-whites in every slave society (except much of the American South) right up to general emancipation. The division of free non-white militiamen into mulatto and black companies has been noted in Martinique, Saint Domingue, Curaçao, and some Brazilian towns, as well as in prevailing marriage preferences and employment policies, and there are additional indications of distinctions in residence patterns. Still another explanation of the late and incomplete rise of class consciousness revolves around the fact that upward mobility was primarily effected through individual initiative or good fortune. For an individual free colored person to rise in status or wealth, therefore, he had to transcend the downward mobility or stasis that everywhere characterized the vast majority of the free colored group.

Another pattern of cleavage distinguished the established free colored, particularly of the second, third, and later generations, from the quasi-free and newly manumitted of the first generation. In some societies this pattern evidently reinforced—in fact replicated—the differentiation of mulattoes and blacks within the free group. The newly "freed" persons were typically enveloped in conditions of lingering servitude resulting from provisos in their manumission papers or from debts incurred in self-purchase. Many of them bound themselves or "free" members of their families into states of debt peonage in order to gain the funds to free a wife, a husband, children, parents, or other relatives. In many cases the consequent creditor-debtor relationship took on the same character as the former master-slave relationship. It is in this marginal zone between slave status and the position of free people of color that one squarely confronts the problems of defining the free colored as a "community" or as a "class" or "caste." Until the anti-manumission restrictions (together with other factors) began to severely limit the access of slaves to free status, numbers of slaves moved each year into the borderland of freedom. When set against the total population, their numbers were of course small, but, seen in relation to the total free colored population, their numbers were considerable.

The fact that there were slaves who could be considered in the same category as nominally free men make the problem of comprehending the role of the free colored no simpler. Much research demonstrates detectable linkages between free colored and slave (or, put another way, the very slender gap between the 2) made political alliance no more likely or feasible. All were in desperate circumstances—so desperate that many freedmen sought the protection of renewed servile relationships with former masters.

In every society there existed a considerable body of colonial legislation that defined the gap between white and free colored very clearly, there were links between the 2 groups which tended to strengthen the colonial hand of the whites at the same time to limit the coalition of non-white groups. Foremost was the development and use of free colored militia as the police arm of the slave society. Similarly, interracial marriage, miscegenation, the plantocratic aspirations of the free colored, and prevalent fears of slave revolts all cemented the tenuous but working relationship between the 2 minorities. More subtle and less measurable were the opportunities created for the free colored by the dependence of the plantocracies on them for skilled labor and for the provisioning of the plantations.

Of course, this service role was not the preserve of the free colored

279

alone. Crucial was the cheap competition offered in these fields by hired-out slaves, slaves purchasing their own freedom, and unpropertied white immigrants. An instructive case of this was the competition for labor in the American South. The important immigration of white workers and craftsmen into southern cities in the antebellum period may be seen as one of the principal factors effecting the reduction of the small middle tier that had been present in all the southern states in 1810, but that by 1860 was largely absent outside the Upper South and Louisiana.

Though it is difficult to determine the extent of problems that arose out of economic competition between the free colored and mobile slaves, there were sharp conflicts between unpropertied whites and free colored, not only in American cities, but also in Saint Domingue and the French Antilles on the eve of the French Revolution, in Brazil throughout the 18th century, and perhaps most clearly, in Cuba during the 19th century. The earliest indications of such conflict are found within the legislation drafted to limit the range of occupations open to free colored people—whether trading in Saint Domingue, shipping in the French Antilles, or diamond mining in Minas Gerais.

To say that free persons of color generally acquiesced in the slave system, identified with the whites and gave aid and comfort to the plantocratic regimes is not to say that their role in the political stirrings taking place in these societies in the late 18th century was inert. Consciously and unconsciously, free blacks and free mulattoes offered the seeds of revolt or threatened revolt to assist the unfree blacks. The free colored were usually among the first to raise the issues of personal liberty and class discrimination in their societies. Though a variety of conditions made direct alliance with slaves unlikely, the unfree blacks became conscious of world issues of which their status and condition were a part. The role the free colored played in inspiring rebellions did not go unnoticed by the white people. Even where revolt did not occur, new conditions emerged in the vortex of widespread white fear of slave insurrections, a fear enlarged by the articulated grievances and appeals of the free colored. Apart from the strident measures adopted to preserve and enhance distinctions between slave and free colored, considerations and exceptions were given by state and plantocracy to limited numbers of free colored in an attempt to quiet free colored resentment over exclusionist policies based on race. The fact that free people of color accepted privilege when it was offered says less about commitment and corruptibility than it does about the precarious circumstances in which most free colored people lived.

The British Caribbean in the Era of Abolition

The abolition of slavery came through a combination of events, and the pressure of popular opposition to the practice, whether from slaves themselves or from the abolitionist movement, was only part of it. One major factor was economic, for the financial significance of the colonies that relied upon slavery was beginning to wane. As the historian Robin Blackburn noted, the value of West Indian imports from the mother country was falling, while exports to Asia were rising; so, they were no longer such a vital market for English goods. And though the British colonies still produced most of the sugar consumed in the mother country, it was so heavily subsidized that many argued that the British public was propping up the West Indian proprietors. There was also greater competition from cheaper sugar from places like Cuba. Domestic politics played a role, too. In a Britain beset by internal unrest brought about by the challenging conditions of the industrial revolution, throwing the public a bone in the form of the abolition of slavery was a clever way of avoiding greater losses, at a point when the whole colonial system was in decline.

The road to emancipation was officially under way and in 1833, a new governor was dispatched to Barbados to sell emancipation to the Barbadians. This case study underlines the mood at the time as it had now dawned on these islanders that the battle to maintain slavery was lost and consequently, they had already shifted their attention to the matter of compensation. In July the Barbadian sent a strongly worded missive to Parliament. 'As England is avowedly the author and was for a long time the chief gainer [of slavery] . . . let her bear her share of the penalty of expiation . . . Let a fair and just indemnity be first secured to the owner of the property which is to be put at risk.' It ended with the warning that without 'the cooperation and instrumentality of the resident Colonists,' the hope for a peaceful emancipation process was doomed and could only be attained 'through rapine violence and bloodshed, destroying all the elements of civilization and ending in anarchy.'

The mood in Barbados was predictably gloomy. The slaves were impatient for change. Most of the West Indian planters felt paranoid and misunderstood. They resisted the spirit of the times and took whatever measures they could to maintain 'the distinctions they deemed necessary to their safety,' including the harassment of the missionaries, whom they felt were stirring up the black population. In the end, it was a relief when compensation was finally agreed on and Britain granted the West Indian proprietors the sum of £20 million [£17 billion 2020 value] in lieu of the 'loss of their lawful property.'

Critics of compensation who feared that it would be a drain on the Crown's reserves proved to be misguided: in fact it was a long-term money spinner since much of the sum went to the great sugar planters of the region, and then found its way back to England, invested in the city or real estate. A few years later an editorial in *The Barbadian* complained about this pernicious trend. 'We should like to know' enquired the editorialist,

> the number of proprietors of extensive landed interests
> and wealth who are living in England or luxuriating in
> the soft delicate climes of France and Italy spending their
> handsome income amongst strangers and leaving it to a
> few of inferior fortunes to carry out the business of their
> native country and to battle the watch on the numerous
> opponents of decency and order.

In August 1833, the Emancipation Bill that had been introduced in the House of Commons by the Secretary of State for the Colonies 3 months earlier was finally passed. The Act became effective on 1st August 1834. Despite the anxiety of the planters, the day passed peacefully, and the Bishop of Barbados was able to report favorably to the Society for the Propagation of the Gospel: '800,000 human beings lay down last night as slaves and rose in the morning as free as ourselves. It might have been expected that on such an occasion there would have been some outburst of public feeling. I was present but there was no gathering that affected the public space.' Indeed, the most raucous aspect of the slaves' festivities was the folk song 'Lick and Lock Up' with which they eventually celebrated her freedom. Between the period of the abolition of the Atlantic slave trade (1807) and emancipation (1834), the total slave population of the colonies fell from 775,000 to 665,000. This decline was matched by growth in other New World slave populations, so that the proportion of the total slave population of the Americas living in the British Caribbean dropped significantly during the period. The British Caribbean remained a very substantial component of the whole, however. The slave populations of the United States and Brazil, by far the largest in the Americas, barely exceeded 1,000,000 in 1807. In that year, then, the British Caribbean accounted for almost one-quarter of all slaves living the Americas. Within the Caribbean, the importance of the British colonies was even more significant. In 1807 there were 1,150,000 slaves in the Caribbean, two-thirds of them in British Colonies. The subsequent decline of the British colonies together with the rapid growth of Cuba meant that by 1834, when the total slave population of the Caribbean was 1,300,000, the proportion in the British colonies had fallen to little over 50% of the previous figure. But the British Caribbean remained of outstanding importance throughout the period.

The Slave Registration Requirement

Slave registration was meant to identify slaves brought to the West Indies in the illicit Atlantic trade that continued after the British abolition of 1807. The abolitionists believed that by taking a complete census of the slave population and recording all subsequent movements resulting from birth, death, sale, or manumission, the failure to account for any slave through the registration system could be taken as presumptive evidence of illegal importation. Thus, the origins of slave registration lie in abolitionist attempts to effectively close off the Atlantic trade by policing the movement of slaves within the West Indies. At the same time, the abolitionists worked to plug the African end of the trade by promoting the act that made slave trading a felony in 1811 and working for international abolition at the Congress of Vienna. The abolitionists' preoccupation with the slave trade, rather than the institution of slavery itself, lay in their belief that amelioration would occur only when the West Indian planter could see no hope of replacing his losses in his labor force by recourse to the Atlantic slave trade and would be forced to depend on natural increase in the population.

The abolitionists began to argue for the introduction into Parliament of a bill to require the registration of slaves in Trinidad as early as 1810, but the government avoided this by allowing James Stephen to draft an order in council in 1812. The first registration of slaves took place in Trinidad in 1813. A similar order in council was applied to St. Lucia in 1814, and the slaves were registered the following year. The campaign for a general registration was delayed until 1815, but the assemblies of the legislative colonies objected to parliamentary interference in what they regarded as their internal affairs and eventually accepted responsibility for passing slave registration acts of their own. Jamaica and Barbados passed acts in 1816, and the other colonies in 1817, except that the Bahamas delayed until 1821, Anguilla until 1827, and British Honduras (Belize) and the Cayman Islands until 1834.

The orders in council for Trinidad and St. Lucia, and the various colonial acts, contained provisions for the administration of the registration system, set fines for the omission of slaves, and specified the data to be included in the returns. In most of the colonies, the system was administered by a salaried Registrar of Slaves, appointed by the government, who received the returns and employed clerks to copy them into volumes, or "registrars." Duplicate copies of the latter were also made and sent to the central Slave Registry Office in London. Though many of the original registers no longer survive in West Indian archives, the duplicates exist as an intact series.

The order in council that applied to Trinidad required that the Registrar of Slaves must not be a slaveowner. Henry Murray, nominated by the Governor in 1812, sold his slaves and estates in order to qualify. The Privy Council at first refused to grant him the post, so Murray traveled to England to explain that it was impossible to find any person in Trinidad of sufficient "respectability" for the office who did not own slaves. In March 1813 Murray returned to Trinidad confirmed in his appointment, with a salary of £500 sterling and the right to fees. Two days after his return, a proclamation was issued requiring all persons owning slaves to deliver their registration returns personally, on oath, either at the Registrar's office, on Brunswick Square in Port of Spain, or to a deputy in the appropriate district. Returns were supposed to be made within one calendar month, but the difficulties of travel within Trinidad resulted in an extension of the period to 14th October 1813. Murray employed 2 clerks, alternatively relieved by 2 others, working 12 hours a day, transcribing the returns into ponderous volumes, one for "plantation" slaves and the other for "personal" slaves not attached to agricultural units. The masters were given a month to make good omissions resulting from accidental causes. Then duplicate copies were made for the Colonial Slave Registry Office in London. In February 1814 Murray's clerks were still busy making indexes, 8 of them working from 6am to 9pm daily.

This delay in the completion of the Trinidad registration created suspicion that the late returns comprised slaves imported illicitly, though the vast majority of the returns were in fact made in the first month. By January 1817 some 58 judicial cases had been heard concerning defaulters in the initial Trinidad registration, but 49 of these returns were admitted by the Registrar and another 3 on appeal to the Governor. Corrections were made to the original returns of some "absentees and incapacitated persons" by special commissioners who traveled around the island. This process was valuable, said the Governor, "for the original returns were generally defective and imperfect."

Subsequent registrations returns were designed to record all changes in the Trinidad slave population, whether resulting from birth, death, manumission, sale, purchase, marronage (desertion), or transportation. Slaveowners were also required to record changes in the stature of growing children, "by actual measurement," and changes in bodily marks. After a brief attempt to obtain annual returns, in 1815 and 1816, Trinidad adopted a triennial system of registration. The principal reason for this change was the difficulty involved in travel within Trinidad; no arrangements were made for the collection of returns in the countryside after 1813, and masters had to deliver their returns personally to the Registrar's office in Port of Spain. But the process of copying the masters' returns into volumes and then sending authenticated duplicates to London was continued. In 1821 Henry Murray resigned the post of Registrar and was succeeded by his son Edward. The final registration of slaves in Trinidad was carried out in 1834.

The registration procedures employed in Trinidad were followed quite closely in the other colonies, except that in Jamaica and the Bahamas no special registrar was appointed and the work was performed by the Secretaries of these colonies. In Barbados, the Registrar, Conrade Adams Howell (succeeded by his son Benjamin in 1824), also held the offices of Island Treasurer and Storekeeper, and was lieutenant colonel in the militia. Thus, in 1817, when he called for the usual poll tax returns on slaves, in his role of Treasurer, he warned that "as Registrar I shall have it in my power to detect all those persons who did not heretofore give in their slaves." The dates of registration period had elapsed. The masters were required to swear their returns, within 3 months, at the Registrar's office in Bridgetown, though the Registrar spent one day at each parish church and also announced that he would "feel pleasure in attending any number of ladies in Bridgetown, or within one mile of it, on being required to do so." Those who failed to make returns had a period of 2 months in which to petition the Governor, but thereafter were subject to prosecution.

The court of Policy in Demerara-Essequibo, taking the Barbados

Registration Act as its model, believed that the Registrar should be "an individual of weight and consideration in the colony and one to whom, if unavoidable the United Colony would safely commit the vindication of its integrity and humanity not only here, but at home." James Robertson, the colony's Registrar from 1817 to 1832, did in fact take his duties very seriously. In 1824 he submitted a report on the slave population, but only to be told "that the Court of Policy cannot recognise in the Registrar any power to publish any report connected with remarks relating to the state of the slave population." Robertson complained that since he had been provided with no office building for the Registry, he had to use his own house and had to employ 4 copying clerks at his own expense. He persistently petitioned the Court for an improved salary and began including detailed statistical analyses of the registration returns in his reports, some of them being printed in *British Parliamentary* Papers.

Similar administrative machinery was set up in the small colonies of the British Caribbean. In most cases the Registry was located in the capital town. But some registrars traveled from parish to parish to collect returns, as in Grenada, and in the St. Vincent Grenadines returns were collected by resident Justices of the Peace. Many of the Registrars held additional official posts, but some employed deputies who shared their salaries and fees. Some of them were substantial slaveowners.

Dates of registration varied from colony to colony. Most adopted a triennial interval, but in Grenada and Tobago returns were made annually. The month of registration also varied from colony to colony, occurring at different points in the seasonal cycle. In some cases, the month of registration for a particular colony varied from triennium to triennium (every three years). In Grenada and Tobago, masters were required to make their returns during January, providing data on events occurring in the preceding calendar year. Where the triennial pattern was followed, the masters were generally allowed 3 months in which to make their returns, resulting in some variability in the events included. In Berbice, for example, the return of 1822 was intended to cover the calendar years in 1819, 1820, and 1821, but some masters included events occurring early in 1822, in the month before they actually made their returns. In the case of Berbice these events were dated precisely in the returns and so can be allocated to the appropriate period. Few other colonies required such exact dating, resulting in some ambiguity regarding the true temporal attribution of events. But the vast majority of returns were made within a single month, thus reducing the potential for distortion. In St. Lucia, for example, 80% of 1,024 initial returns were made in December 1815; another 13% were returned in January 1816, and 3% in November 1815, while the remaining 4% were late returns, some of which did not come in until the end of 1817. Most of the latter related to small urban slaveholdings, however. In fact, 85% of St. Lucia's slaves were included in the returns made in December 1815, and only 2% in returns made later than January 1816. The legal extensions granted for making late returns at the initial registration were rarely applied to the subsequent triennial returns, so the problem was reduced.

Some of the information about the slaves recorded in the registration returns was obtained by questioning slaves, but all data were filtered by the owners, most of whom were white and male. Most of the errors made by the masters stemmed from ignorance or carelessness rather than deliberate falsification. Tax fines imposed on defaulters were substantial. In Barbados, for example, a fine of £100 sterling was levied for each slave not registered, and if the slave was African-born he would be freed, on the assumption he had been imported illicitly. These fines were in fact imposed.

Some of the colonial acts, however, made no provision for freeing slaves if their owners were convicted of importing them illicitly. The Demerara-Essequibo Act provided that owners so convicted be fined 6,000 guilders and imprisoned for up to 2 years, but no regulations were made to ensure the freedom of the slaves. In Antigua such slaves were merely surrendered "to the use of His Majesty." But Antigua, as well as Dominica, St. Vincent, and Grenada, offered rewards to informers. Dominica, for example, imposed a fine of £100 currency for each slave not registered, half this amount to go to the informer. The island also imposed a fine of £500 and prison for up 2 years for holding an African slave illegally imported; such slaves were to be freed and paid £6. 12.0 maintenance annually by the Treasurer. Fines were also levied for wrongful registration, but some duplication did occur when the hirer as well as the owner of slaves each made returns. The person making a return was required to swear an oath as to its accuracy, "to the best of my knowledge and belief," under heavy penalties. If this apparatus did not necessarily strike terror into the hearts of the slaveowners, it was sufficient to ensure that few actually omitted registering their slaves. But the owner's ability to provide accurate information about their slaves on each of the items required by the registration returns varied widely.

Slave names were used primarily as identifiers, especially in order to link demographic events through the initial and subsequent registration returns and in tracing kin relationships. For this purpose, the major problem is the duplication of names within a single slaveholding. Since the masters also used the names as identifiers, they generally attempted to avoid such duplication, but it could arise through sale or removal or through the recognition of slave preferences. Some labels (Mary old, Mary young), or relationship labels (Jemima's Mingo, Christian's Robert), or ethnic labels (Ebo Mary, Creole Mary), or occupation labels (Mary field, Mary cook).

One area where slave owners were incentivized to manipulate reported data was with respect to their compensation entitlements due to the emancipation Act. The compensation figure was calculated according to the value of the slaves. This value was derived based on the average prices paid for slaves sold between 1823 and 1830 (a total of 74,000 transfers). The £20 million compensation money was then divided between the masters at a rate ranging from 42 to 55% of the valuation. The slaves were classified after actual inspection by the Assistant Commissioners for Compensation, except that in the Bahamas the occupations listed in the registration returns of 31 July 1834 were used, to avoid the cost of visiting the scattered islands.

The Cayman Islands were excluded entirely. The system required that slaves be classified according to their usual occupations before August 1834, but the masters had a monetary incentive to try to have slaves placed in a higher class. There also seems to have been some inconsistency between colonies in the allocation of occupational groups.

Black Slaveowners

Barbados

There were several slave-owning freedmen who had no issues hiring or purchasing slaves when their financial circumstances allowed for it. Their attitude regarding this topic issue is revealed in an 1803 petition submitted to the legislature requesting it not to pass a bill that was aimed at, among other things, preventing them from acquiring slaves: "Although we have all our lives been accustomed to the assistance of slaves, we must immediately [by the proposed bill] deprive ourselves of them and perform every menial office with our hands . . . The greatest blessing attending upon freedom is the acquirement and enjoyment of property and without that, liberty is but an empty name." By 1814 it was observed that, among Bridgetown's freedmen, "many were slave owners;" indeed one source estimates 80.9% of these slave-owning freedman lived in Bridgetown. A further 5.5% were in rural St. Michael.

In spite of the relatively small size of the freedman population in Barbados, and the limited extent of landownership, some 650 slaveowners (a conservative estimate) were identified as freedmen in 1817. They owned 2,533 slaves, or only 3.3% of the total, but they comprised 12.1% of the total owners.

It was observed that though the sex ratio of the freedman population was somewhat evenly balanced, females held 74.2% of the slaves. Male slaveowners showed a somewhat greater rural concentration than females but did not approach the white pattern of overwhelming rural dominance. Within the freedman population, there was a strong contrast between the "free mulatto" and "free negro" groups. The mulatto group was only slightly larger, but it possessed greater wealth, much of it inherited from white ancestors, and owned almost 4 times as many slaves as the free blacks. Females dominated in each group, however, and there was relatively little difference in their spatial distribution. In Bridgetown there was little difference in the pattern of slave-ownership for white and mulatto women, thus the latter was a prominent figure among the town's slaveowners.

The pattern of freedmen slave-ownership was likely typical of the old sugar colonies, but in the windward Islands, Trinidad, and Jamaica it appears more certain that they owned a larger proportion of the slave population and more often employed their slaves in agricultural work. In St Lucia, for example, only half of the identified freedman slaveowners lived in the towns, but few owned more than 20 slaves and in similar fashion to Barbados, women of color owners featured prominently.

Barbados's slave-owning freedmen largely employed their slaves as house servants, shop assistants, occasionally agricultural laborers, or as hired-out tradesmen. In addition, some of the slaves owned by freedmen were their own children, whom, because they could not pay the fee, they were unable to manumit.

It is difficult to assess how freedmen treated their slaves and whether this treatment was any better or worse than the treatment of slaves by white. In the late 18th century, William Dickson, a critic of the Barbadian slave system and a defender of the freedmen, observed that "free Negroes are generally more severe, because less enlightened, owners, than white people," but, as the years progressed, and more freedmen became slaveholders, they may have come in for a disproportionate amount of criticism; an American resident of Bridgetown in 1814 observed that freedmen

had the reputation of being much more cruel to their slaves than

292

the white proprietors. I had no means of knowing how much of
this censure they deserved, but I suspect it must be received with
many grains of allowance, for it was a character given by whites
who seemed to entertain a hostile feeling against them.

J. Thome and J. Kimball, who visited the island in 1837, offered a more
general conclusion, for which no contradictory evidence has so far been
unearthed:

> We regret to add, that until lately, the colored people of Barbados
> have been far in the back ground in the cause of abolition, and even
> now, the majority of them are either indifferent, or actually hostile to
> emancipation. They have no fellow feeling with the slave. In fact, they
> have had prejudices against the Negroes no less bitter than those which
> the whites have exercised toward them. There are many honorable
> exceptions to this, as has already been shown; but such, we are assured,
> is the general fact.

It should be clear that the relationship between freedman and slave was
more involved than that between master and servant. In everyday life, and
in a variety of institutional contexts, the two groups were often and
inevitably in contact.

North America

The majority of black slaveowners in South Carolina were said to have been
members of the mulatto class, and in some cases were the sons and
daughters of white slave masters. Many of the mulatto slaveowners
separated themselves from the masses of black people and attempted to
establish a caste system based on color, wealth, and free status. According to
Martin Delany, the colored community of Charleston City clung to the
assumptions of the superiority of white blood and brown hues. By
extension, a great many married fellow mulattoes to 'retain the color' and
formed church congregations that excluded freedmen of dark complexion.

According to the first census of 1790, 36 out of 102—or 35%—of the free Black heads of family held slaves in Charleston City. In 1820, free black women represented 68% of slave-owning heads of households in the North and 70% of slaveholding heads of colored in the South. The high percentage of black women slaveowners was the result of manumission by their white fathers, or inheritance from their fathers / husbands. Black women accounted for most slave emancipations due to their sexual relations—as was the case in much of the Americas. 33% of all recorded manumissions in the U.S. were mulatto children, and 75% of all adult manumissions were females.

By 1830 there were approximately 319,599 free blacks in the United States. Of this, 13.7% of the total black population was free. A significant number of these free blacks were the owners of slaves. The census of 1830 lists 3,775 free Negroes who owned a total of 12,760 slaves. 10,000 of these slaves were owned by free blacks in Louisiana, Maryland, South Carolina, and Virginia. The majority of black slaveowners lived in Louisiana and planted sugar cane.

According to many scholars and writers who have covered this topic, black slaveowners mostly acted benevolently. Typically, this happened as a way of circumventing laws against manumission. In the late antebellum period one state after another passed laws that required manumitted slaves to leave the state, and, at that, made manumission as difficult as possible. As a result, a free Negro who wished to purchase the freedom of a wife, husband, child, parent, or friend normally had to acquire and maintain property rights in his or her person; if this was not done, the emancipated Negro faced expulsion from the state. The great majority of Negro slaveholders—the total number of which was never large, though it has yet to be tabulated properly—owned relatives or friends as a mere formality and entered their slaves into a relationship such as the one Judge Manly of North Carolina described as existing between free Negroes and particular whites—that of *"patron and client."* The frequency with which Negro slaveholders appeared as owners of their own children and grandchildren resulted from the particular difficulties attached to manumitting slaves under 30 years of age—even when manumission was still a legal possibility.

The efforts, successful and unsuccessful, of slaves and free Negroes to free themselves and their loved ones often reached heroic proportions. Slaves who bought their own freedom generally had been artisans or skilled workers whose masters had permitted them to "hire their own time." Slave hiring was extensive throughout the South, especially in the cities. Despite all laws to the contrary, countless thousands of slaves were permitted to hire themselves out under circumstances that allowed them to pay rent to their master, provide for their own sustenance, and still save something, if they chose to. Similarly, the economic position of a portion of the free Negro community made small savings possible. In some cases, free Negroes, themselves sometimes only recently freed, devoted their efforts to buying freedom for others and accomplished what can only be judged as extraordinary feats of industry and selflessness. To cite only one of many cases, Samuel Martin, who was called "the oldest resident of Port Gibson, Mississippi, "bought his freedom in 1829 with the greatest effort and difficulty and then worked to buy 6 others, all of whom he freed and took to Cincinnati in 1844.

Not all free Negroes who owned a few slaves were selfless owners. One reason arguably was that some Negroes had never been slaves in the first place, and thus held a different worldview—in certain instances—to those who had started out as slaves. Contrarily, they had been indentured servants for a fixed period, beyond which they were free men. One example of this involved a certain Anthony Johnson whose case in 1654 was one of the first known to legally sanction slavery. In this court suite, Johnson and his wife gained the services of their black servant, John Casor, for life. It was said ". . . slave owning by free Negroes was so common in the period of the Commonwealth as to pass unnoticed and without criticism by those who consciously recorded events at the time." John H. Russell in his *The Free Negroes in Virginia, 1619—1865* wrote "The most remarkable property right possessed by free Negroes was the right to acquire, own, and alienate slaves. Indeed, for more than 20 years from the time when free Negroes first appear in the courts there was no legal restriction upon their right to own indentured white servants [in Virginia]." There were black slaveholders in Boston as early as 1724; in Connecticut by 1783, and in Alabama by 1797. Among the earliest records in the "deed books" of St. Augustine, Florida, is a document recording the sale of a black slave to a free black—by a free black. By 1790, 48 Maryland black owners possessed 143 slaves. Nat Butler, a free black who lived near Aberdeen in Harford County, owned a small farm, and regularly purchased and sold Negroes for the Southern trade. Some considered black slaveowners "Hard taskmasters" and claimed "... free black owners were as a usual thing much more severe on their slaves than the white owners."

To this end, in several cases, black slaveowners were interested solely or largely in profitmaking. Thomas Bonneau of South Carolina, who founded a school for free Negroes, left 2 slave girls to his heir. His will stipulated that, if the girls did not behave, they were to be sold—"in that case," he added, "the money will be sure." In other cases, litigation arising from disputes over the condition of the merchandise indicates that even free Negro slaveholders sometimes were merely engaged in business.

Even when relatives were bought, their fate necessarily remained precarious as long as they were legally slaves. Carter Woodson found cases of husbands who bought their wives and deliberately kept them as slaves to ensure their fidelity and good behavior. In one such instance, a Negro shoemaker in Charleston, South Carolina, bought his wife for $700, found her impossible to please, and so sold her some months later for $750. In another case, there was a man in Cumberland County, Virginia, whose mother was purchased by his father, who had first bought himself. Being enamored of a man slave, she gave him her husband's manumission papers so they would be able to escape together to free soil. Upon detecting the plot, the officers of the law received the impression that her husband had turned over the papers to the slave and arrested the freedman for the supposed offense. He had such difficulty in extricating himself from this complication that his attorney's fees amounted to $500. To pay these he disposed of his unfaithful wife to meet the bill.

The sight of Negro slaveholders caused apprehension among the whites, but the most serious complaints were directed against those who were genuine slaveholders rather than against those who were merely protecting relatives. Although it is not possible to be certain, it would appear that the white community accepted the necessity of a few exceptions to the manumission laws and was prepared to look the other way, especially since the force of custom and local usage so often modified southern legal arrangements. As abovementioned, the right of Negroes to own slaves had been firmly upheld by the courts in Virginia as early as 1654; however, it was not until 1832 was this right effectively challenged, and then only to the extent of limiting further purchases by Negroes to their spouses or children. In North Carolina, the right of free Negroes to accumulate property was never seriously challenged except when that property consisted of slaves. Even so, the Supreme Court reaffirmed Negro slave-ownership in 1833. Not until the secessionist legislature of 1860—61 was this right withdrawn, and even then, it did not apply retroactively. Curiously, the decision of 1860—61 came when it was hardly needed. As John Hope Franklin points out, the decline transpired in the closing decades of the antebellum period. Only Arkansas and the virtually free state of Delaware specifically prohibited Negro slave-ownership, although other states increasingly created obstacles.

Black Settler Colonial Projects

Resettling Liberated Africans

As mentioned above, many political, moral, and economic developments transpired in Europe and its New World territories in the century 1750—1850. Moreover, and notably so, was a 'return movement' to Africa spearheaded by European and African-diasporic stakeholders. While there were waves of African returnees to [short-lived, British-occupied (1827—1834)] Clarence in Fernando Po, Bathurst in Gambia, Libreville in Gabon, and Senegal, the 2 most significant projects were the settling of present-day Sierra Leone and Liberia.

Freetown, Sierra Leone

Named *Serra de Leao* in 1462 by the Portuguese explorer Pedro da Cintra—meaning "Lion Mountain", Sierra Leone would become a key British colony beyond its erstwhile importance as a strategic location for the transatlantic slave trade prior to 1792. A British clergyman and prominent slavery abolitionist who was a member of the 'Clapham Sect' of abolitionists, Granville Sharp, used his charitable foundation *The Committee for the Relief of the Black poor*, to establish a settlement as an alternative to funding the poverty alleviation program in London. The black 'poor' comprised former seamen that had previously served on slave ships, persons imported from the West Indies to serve as domestic staff, *Black Loyalists* that had fought for Britain in the American War of Independence, and men who were free but destitute. While the immediate sufferings of the black poor were to some extent alleviated by the distribution of food, clothes and charity, there was no obvious long-term solution.

Britain in the 1780s was in the throes of a deep recession. Given the shockingly high unemployment and land enclosures, many of the poor in rural areas converged upon London. In their quest for survival, only a small handful—probably the most skilled amongst them—secured employment, and the presence of the rest in their indigent state was deemed an extraneous social problem. What followed was—despite a growing British public opposition to the slave trade—a desire to rid London of its black presence, a sentiment even held by many on the committee. Defenders of slavery embarked on a racist propagandizing campaign, spanning the period between the 1780s and 1830, during which they diffused the notion—which gained traction—that a growing presence of black men on the streets of London would result in abhorrent 'racial pollution'. Moreover, the presence of black men with their white wives and mixed-race children reinforced this sentiment.

Addressing this 'social problem' would not be a straightforward process, but it appeared a solution was in the offing. While a number of them favored a return to the West Indies or Nova Scotia (Canada) where there were other black 'loyalists', the scheme of resettling—or some would argue 'deporting'—them began to emerge, courtesy of a certain Henry Smeathman, who was an eccentric amateur botanist and elocutionist. Smeathman provided a virtuous pretext, even going as far as to embellish how pleasant, welcoming, and benign the later-Freetown environs were. It was portrayed as being habitable for settlers to be housed all year round in simple huts which provided ample shelter, favorable climates, and the prospect of eating well. Smeathman, however, and tragically for the *Black Poor*, was an amoral con artist scheming to advance his financial interests, which would be in the form of securing support from 2 London cotton merchants who would be enticed by the prospect to invest in large-scale cotton-growing. Significantly, he downplayed the prevalence of tropical illnesses, withheld his knowledge of storms during the rainy season—which potentially would strip away crops, and most malevolently had disclosed all these risks when addressing a previous committee. Nevertheless, the backdrop to his scheming was owing to his advancing years—44 years of age, his failing health culminating from long-term exposure to tropical diseases, and the pressing need to satisfy his creditor.

In February 1786, Smeathman pursued his agenda by outlining his *Plan of a Settlement to be made near Sierra Leone* in writing to the *Committee for the Black Poor*, during which he personally undertook to 'remove the burthen of the Blacks from public for ever, by transporting London's troublesome Blacks back to Africa.'

Come May 1786, the Treasury agreed to pay him £14 for each black emigrant who travelled to Sierra Leone, though due to their knowledge that the Sierra Leone coastline was a notorious slaving area, the *Black Poor* would need convincing to sign up to the scheme. Furthermore, it didn't help that they were refugees from one continent, poverty-stricken in another, and facing the prospect of uncertainty on a third continent, thus underlining the need for assurances. Jonas Hanway, Chairman of the Committee, appealed to them with all manner of persuasive rhetoric, but ultimately the Black Poor insisted on a formal agreement between themselves and Smeathman, which would guarantee their freedom upon arrival. Unfortunately, the agreement was such that neither the committee nor the government was bound by its the terms, but those who signed on were legally obliged to emigrate as it was enforceable through the courts. Furthermore, the Committee required black people to sign the agreement as a condition for receiving their daily handouts. Eight corporals—6 of which could read and 2 that could write well—were hired to act as recruiters for prospective settlers. Only 130 out of 437 gave an immediate promise to sign up to the scheme; however, a considerable number of the *Black Poors'* were reluctant to follow suit—including those who refused their allowances— due to Smeathman's unexpected death in early July due to a 'putrid fever', and the attendant uncertainty. The low confidence was further impacted by the attempts of the Committee to switch the place of resettlement from Sierra Leone to the Bahamas, where slavery was very much still a legitimate trade.

Smeathman may have passed, but his sweet-seeming portrayal of an

African utopia remained influential and earned the confidence of the abovementioned Granville Sharp.

Despite the Landmark ruling in the 1776 Somerset case, which rendered slavery unconstitutional, abolition in any meaningful form had not transpired and London's free blacks were still at risk of being recaptured and forcibly sold off in the West Indies. Sharp saw the Sierra Leone scheme as a unique opportunity upon which to build a new a society underpinned by English principles, Christian values, and an economic and morally superior alternative to the slave trade, and ultimately slavery.

For the few who signed up to the scheme, their circumstances worsened due to onerous delays brought on by both those who had remained indecisive on whether to sojourn to Sierra Leone, and the government and committee who continued to exert pressure on as many of the Black Poor into acquiescence. The resultant delays meant those residing on ships waiting to set sail contended with inadequate clothing, a lack of beds, insufficient wood for stoves, an acute shortage of drinking water and candles, poor rations of salted food and conditions that generally felt like floating prisons—fueling extant rumors they were bound for a convict station. Exacerbating such bleak conditions, was a debilitating 1786—87 winter during which November was one of the coldest months on record. Precipitous rates of sickness led to a conservative estimate of 50 deaths while the ships lay at anchor. These deplorable circumstances led to Olaudah Equiano—the former slave who was now the commissary in charge of the mission's supplies and stores—writing to another black Londoner Otobah Cugoano, detailing the misuse of funds and mistreatment of the prospective settlers. The letter made its way into the press, sparking an argument between Equiano and the Captain of the HMS *Nautilus* ship— Thomas Boulden Thompson—through which the former considered the latter to be incompetent. As in line with the spirit of the time, a black man was always going to lose an argument with a white one, and Equiano was consequently stood down from his role—the justification for which was his 'disruptive' influence; for his troubles he was awarded £50 (the 2019 equivalent of £7,911.81) compensation by the admiralty.

The small flotilla of the Belisarius, Atlantic, and Vernon led by the *HMS Nautilus* set sail in January 1787—a full 4 months behind schedule. A fever outbreak led to a further 14 casualties, whose bodies were slung overboard. Raging winter storms led to the travelers regrouping in Plymouth, before setting out again after recalibration, by which time 411 of the original 456 remained. The *HMS Nautilus* anchored at the patriotically renamed [by captain Thompson] St George's Bay, at the mouth of the Sierra Leone River, on 10th May 1787, with a reduced total of 380 black Britons. The following day Captain Thompson exchanged the usual pleasantries—including 130 gallons of rum, some clothes, and hats—in a meeting with the coastal-based King Tom. A King of limited autonomy, he agreed by Treaty without objection to Thompson's request to purchase 20 miles of coastal land. With the blessing of the eventual Tory Prime Minister, William Pitt the Younger, the new settlement was named the *Province of Freedom* by an enthusiastic Granville Sharp; the pioneers of the scheme also interchangeably referred to it as 'Granville Town'—named in honor of Sharp's role in the scheme.

Unfortunately for the settlers, Sharp's pious naivety and Smeathman's deadly propaganda would culminate to disastrous effect. The 4 months lost whilst stationary in the Thames resulted in the settlers arriving in Sierra Leone at the worst time of year, as the rainy season commenced within two weeks of their arrival. Washed away was much of the crops planted in designated cleared spaces—not helped by the clearing of natural vegetation. Vast swathes of the peninsula were waterlogged, and pests and mold rendered the remaining crops inedible. Forests for hunting local game were impenetrable, huts in which the settlers inhabited were washed away and tent supplies were also obliterated. The heat proved to be oppressive for those used to more temperate climes in the UK and North America. Preventable diseases, malaria, and fevered dehydration resulted in waves of further fatalities—only 130 of the initial settlers remained by September

1788; more indicting was that many of the casualties had survived the smallpox outbreaks that had decimated the Black regiments of the revolutionary war—in addition to other unpardonable adversities.

These setbacks influenced Sharp's white administrators to betray him by travelling to Bunce Island, ensuring their own survival and attaining employment, ironically, in the slave trade. This was as much of a blow to Sharp, as were the mounting casualties. What ultimately killed off the *Province of Freedom* social experiment was an accidental stray shot fired by a young marine from the crew of the visiting *HMS Pomona*, into a Thatched roof hut in a Temne village; the fire spread rapidly and razed the entire settlement. This proved the catalyst for violent conflict between British Forces and the Temne through which the latter burned down Granville Town in retaliation. By December 1788, the remaining settlers were given 3 days to vacate the area by King Tom. They were rescued by slave trader's canoes from the nearby Bunce Island—10 of whom ironically made their living working for them; the rest attempted to build a new settlement nearby Bunce Island.

The Freetown Project Revival

Given that Sharp had sunk £1,700 (the 2019 equivalent of £258,241.33) into the experiment, he was left with no choice but to discontinue his financial support. The *Clapham Sect* of clergymen and slavery abolitionists—William Wilberforce (most celebrated of all), Henry Thornton and Thomas Clarkson became involved in a revival of the initial settlement project. This was influenced by a settlement petition from the popular leader of the Nova Scotians—Thomas Peters—who also happened to be from a Yoruba-Egba wealthy background. After some resistance to the proposed revival given how the first attempt ended, the Sierra Leone Company was incorporated on the 30th May 1791—absorbing Granville Sharp's St George's Bay Company. Sharp took more of a backseat role such were his divergent ideals from the rest of his colleagues. For Sharp, the point of colonizing Sierra

Leone was to offer a new start to men and women whose lives had been debased by slavery, and the dignity, freedom, and justice of self-government was essential to this. For Thornton, Wilberforce, and Thomas Clarkson, the colony was a commercial enterprise for the defeat of the slave trade, to be governed by those who 'knew best' (themselves), and the settlers would work hard for them and submit to their rule out of gratitude.

The instrumental Thomas Peters' story was that he had escaped from his plantation in North Carolina, and thereafter, pledged allegiance to King George III of England to fight in American War of independence. Promises of 'freedom' had yet to materialize—much to his chagrin. Fertile land had been made available to White loyalists and settlers in Nova Scotia, leaving at best a scarcity of land for the black loyalists to subsist on. Through being made effectively landless and hungry, free blacks had been forced into indentures so punitive that 'they might as well be in chains;' what made this even more egregious was that some of the 'free' blacks had been sold off to the West Indies.

John Clarkson had struggled to find someone to oversee the revival of the settlement Project—now known as 'Freetown'. Thus, he was heartened to receive emphatically positive feedback from the previously skeptical Black Nova Scotians, who were traumatized by the way they had been exploited by white people, and remained concerned by the prospect of being hoodwinked back into slavery or made to indenture for a lengthy period. Whereas Clarkson had anticipated only needing 3 ships to convey 100 people, he had to make significant adjustments to convey 1,196 passengers on a fleet of 15 ships. Clarkson funded this by raising a £240,000 (£36,457,600 as of 2019) investment. Given the initial humanitarian and commercial objectives, a land tax levied on farmers was considered, and to humanize the prospective black settlers, Wilberforce proposed that they be addressed as 'Africans' rather than 'Blacks' or 'Negroes.' This was deemed more respectful given the loaded racial baggage attached to the latter designations. Furthermore, Peters and Clarkson promised that every man who emigrated would receive 20 acres of land, every woman 10, and 5 for each child, as well as assurances that they would be free of the racial prejudices that attenuated their life chances in British North America. The shipping conditions were to be of better quality than those which conveyed the Black Poor, and the Black loyalists were deemed to be more skilled than the former.

Facilitating the settling of the Black loyalist was not without its problems. The settlement had been deemed a debacle and the crossing—which was extremely rough—had taken 7 weeks. Rumors abounded, ranging from the prediction of imminent violence at best, and multiple murders at worst. Shipped supplies had not been used to erect habitable infrastructure, and food and beverages were consumed inefficiently. Clarkson was beset with a near-fatal illness though the extant problems had no more subsided upon his recovery. Racialized friction was also an ever-present issue either side of the Atlantic, as White loyalists seething with resent at seeing their best and ablest inexpensive field workers depart for Freetown, played on their fears of being exploited again by spreading 'malicious' rumors that the Sierra Leone Company would issue extortionate land taxes. Unfortunately for the black loyalists, the 'malicious' rumors turned out to be prophetic as despite Clarkson's promises to the contrary, the company did impose an annual tax of 1 shilling, rising to 4% after 3 years. Clarkson's colleague Henry Thornton justified this approach as the company's preferred method of recovering 'all our huge expenses,' rather than the alternative of a customs duty on their produce. Thornton went on to add, 'I trust the Blacks will not consider it a grievance'. Unsurprisingly, they did.

Whilst Clarkson was determined to do right by the guarantees given to Black loyalists, a conflict between him and Thomas Peters was brewing. This was due to feeling his authority was being challenged by Peters' forthright approach in complaining about a lack of land, provisions, and imperious white rule of the colony. Further intensifying the conflict was Clarkson uncovering what he thought was a conspiracy to sideline him. However, it emerged to the contrary that there was a proposal being discussed to establish a self-ruling Black Committee; one which would comprise a 12-man panel—which included Thomas Peters among them—tasked with solving internal disputes among the settlers. Despite Clarkson agreeing to Peters' Christmas beef allowance request for the settlers as a peace offering, and conciliatory admissions of mutual shortcomings, Clarkson sidelined Peters upon being promoted to the role of superintendent, despite the latter being the instigator of reviving the settlement project. Tensions between the 2 culminated in dramatic fashion as Clarkson melodramatically prophesied one of them would be left hanging from a tree, before matters were settled. Matters were arguably settled by Peters' passing away 3 months later; Peters passed having felt betrayed and mistreated in Sierra Leone, just as he had in Nova Scotia.

Though Freetown was a demonstrable example that it was possible to establish a lasting settlement, the settlers were still beset by similar problems which had afflicted the black poor of London, especially as there were 200 fatalities in the first few years. These problems were in the form of oppressive summer temperatures and heavy rains spanning a long cold season—conditions worse than the rainy season the 1787 group experienced. However, losses were partially mitigated by the fact that the Freetown settlers' group was higher than the initial settlers, as well as being supplemented with the remaining survivors from the latter.

The Liberia Resettlement Project

The makings of a serious race problem brewing became more apparent in America in the early 19th century, owing to polarizing views concerning the institution of slavery. Whilst a small number of liberal whites, mostly from the North, supported emancipation—contrary to the South who wanted to maintain the trade—they had little appetite to live 'equally' alongside them. In the face of the increasing visibility of free black people—108,000 out of a total population of 1 million at the start of the century. This further rose to 233,000 out of a 1.5 million total by 1820.

As a means of abating the issue, the American Colonization Society (ACS) was established in 1817. It was funded and controlled by whites attracted to 'benevolent causes,' with the immediate objective of removing all free blacks and eventually the entire population. One of the founders, Robert Finley remarked:

> Could not the rich and benevolent devise means to form a colony
> on some part of the Coast of Africa, similar to the one at Sierra Leone,
> which might gradually induce many free blacks to go there and settle,
> devising for them the means of getting there, and of protection and
> support till they were established?

Prior to formation of the ACS there were 2 endeavors to resettle Black Americans in Africa. The lesser known of the two was set up by Rhode Island freedmen in November 1794 who had formed the African Society of Providence. One of its officers, James Mackenzie was dispatched to negotiate arrangements for the settlement of American freedmen. He was answerable to the visionary of this project, Reverend Samuel Hopkins, who saw it as a big opportunity to propagate Christianity on the African continent, in addition to a colonization opportunity—particularly for raising agricultural produce. The failure of the province of freedom project, loss of key Africans in the revolutionary war, and challenges with raising transportation costs, were behind the forgone opportunity.

The better known of the 2 was set up by the Ashanti and Native Indian-descended Paul Cuffee, who was a successful Quaker ship builder, owner of a fleet of ships and an activist. He declared an interest in using his resources to facilitate free blacks' passage to Africa on compassionate grounds, especially as they were fellow Africans. Though he had no formal schooling, Cuffee had considerable involvement in the attainment of rights for free blacks in Massachusetts; one way in which this was evident was by teaching freedmen skills and employing them as seamen. Nevertheless, whilst he was reportedly a skilled man of 'very pious and moral character', his sincerity was questioned because he never expressed on record his motivations for being involved in a resettlement scheme; it wasn't clear if he planned to settle in Africa, and he was born a free man, thus it was argued he couldn't relate with the hardships of fellow Africans who had been enslaved. In 1816, a year before his passing, Cuffee did finance the passage of 38 Americans to Freetown Sierra Leone.

The ACS, which had previously been known as *The American Society For Colonizing The Free People Of Colour in the United States*, was an amalgamate of several state colonization societies—including the Maryland Society—which had the intention of colonizing the State of Maryland's free blacks. The ACS believed that the creation of a separate black Christian empire in Africa would ultimately parallel the white Christian empire in America—'twin beacons' of a sort.

The lack of financial support for the colonization project was due to polarized views, given that the South wanted free blacks out of view from enslaved blacks in case it encouraged the latter to agitate for freedom, whereas the northerners saw it—like Finley—as a colonization mission alongside abolishing the trade. African Americans whether bonded or free, were not uniformly enthusiastic—much like *the Black Poor of London*—about the Liberia project, yet a few were adamant it was their only option given their bleak prospects in America.

Eventually financial support was forthcoming through a complex system of traveling agents and prominent philanthropic associates. Further support also came from bequests, legacies, auxiliary societies, and church collections. There was a growing belief that the threat of insurrections was looming, and this spurred the ACS into receiving sanction declarations from Legislatures in 13 states, a drafted Constitution for the government of Liberia, and a Plan of Civil Government for the Colony—all by the 1830s. This supplemented the work achieved by 1827 of establishing 224 plantations of 5 to 10 acres each—all through irregular financial backing.

Between March 1820 and September 1843, between 4,472 and 4,751 Black people voyaged to Liberia, of which 2,198 passed away during the same period—many of the deaths attributable to tropical maladies. Another source estimates this figure to have been 2,409, along with the suggestion that internal conflicts also added to the total number of casualties. The mortality rate—between 49 and 57%, was one of the highest ever recorded in settler history. Furthermore, this comprised a considerable proportion of the estimated 15,000 Africans returned to the continent from America during the 19th century. As the settlements in Liberia developed and became more self-sufficient, the administrative costs continually increased, totaling $332,586.28 (the 2020 value of $9,334,112.54) to transport freed blacks to Liberia between 1817—1836. This understandably attracted criticism as despite the annual fatality rates—which indicated it was destined to fail, waves of emigrants were still transferred to Liberia. Many critics therefore, were led to believe that the ACS used a Christian pretext for their racist motivations to rid the U.S. of its black population; moreover, the society became heavily indebted, and thus attracted further criticism.

Successful settlements?

At face value both the Liberia and Sierra Leone schemes began with near identical objectives: the deportation of their extraneous black population; the creation of new homelands for Liberated Africans who would be Christianized and in turn Christianize other Africans through missionary work, whilst establishing foundationally western societies imbibed with British and American values respectively. Both projects also had colonial objectives—overlapping the abolitionary movements on either side of the Atlantic.

1807 saw not only the passing of the Slave Trade abolition Act, but also the transfer of the Sierra Leone Company from the Clapham Sect administrators to the British government as a crown colony to be administered by civil servants. Whilst the initial objectives had not entirely changed, there was an express intention to empower British entrepreneurs, enabling their acquisition of local knowledge and African languages in the course of making the company profitable. The multiple casualties of black people from the first 2 settlement attempts in Freetown meant that in 1811—4 years after the 1807 Act was passed—new arrivals of what were termed *Recaptives* outnumbered the extant Black Poor of London, Nova Scotian and Maroon populations which were now a minority. *Recaptives* were Africans that had been captured across West and West-Central Africa with the intention of transporting them to New World colonies such as Brazil, Cuba and the British Caribbean; however they were intercepted on occasion by the British Navy West African Squadron and diverted to Freetown—a refugee center of sorts—as it was not feasible to return every one of them back to their places of origin, and to also avert the prospect of being captured for a second time by slavers. The *Recaptives* were diverted to a designated area in the King's Yard where those that required medical treatment received it and were entered into a register which listed 84,307 names between 1808 and 1848. The register was populated initially with their distinctive African names, as opposed to the receiving new identities as would've been the case in the New World. Ironically, it became usual in Sierra Leone by this point for these Liberated Africans to adopt the European surnames—such as Weeks, Smart, and Wellesley-Cole—of benefactors sponsoring young children's education, and the missionaries working in the colony. Another way through which such names were adopted was through the provisions of the Abolition Act, which stated *Recaptives* were 'crown property' and their deliverers—almost exclusively the British Navy—were paid a bounty of between £10—£40 (2019 value of £926.26—£3,705.04) depending on whether they were children, women, or men. Thereafter, women were paired with off with male *Recaptives* for marriage, and the men and children were 'given' to Nova Scotian farmers and British colonists for $20 each and put under an 'apprenticeship scheme.' The locations at which these apprenticeship schemes took place were not solely in Sierra Leone, and many *Recaptives*—in excess of 15,000—were dispatched to Jamaica, Grenada, Barbados, Trinidad, and other islands to work indentures as replacements for the slave labor that was gradually being manumitted. They were assimilated into the broader black population at the end of their indentures and made cultural contributions that have endured up to the present day.

With respect to the work undertaken by the British Royal Navy, the vast majority of slave ships were not intercepted. When measured in raw statistical terms, the anti-slavery squadron was a failure. It has been estimated that around 20% of the approximately 7,750 slave ships that were illicitly engaged in the Atlantic trade between 1808 and 1867 were condemned by the courts established to punish illegal slave trading. 85% of these were down to Royal Navy interceptions. In all, 162,000 African captives were liberated (not all were taken to Sierra Leone and the British Caribbean Islands), which represented 6% of the 2.7 million Africans who were captured and put on slave ships bound for the Americas from 1836 to the mid-1860s.

The apprenticeship scheme in Freetown was deemed controversial as the scheme had a maximum term of 14 years under forced labor conditions, whereas the life expectancy on Caribbean plantations was 7 years, thus, the 2 schemes weren't considered much different. What elucidated this similarity was when the colonial Governor-General of Sierra Leone, Thomas Perronet Thompson, discovered a white 'master' had punished his 8-year-old 'apprentice' for unsatisfactory work by burning her back repeatedly with an iron. Once the matter was brought in front of Thompson to explain himself, he remarked "he paid money for the girl and therefore she is his," and "that he has a right to do as he pleases with his own." When told by the Governor that slavery was illegal, he answered "Lord sir I did not buy her, I redeemed her." Given such attitudes, it is hardly surprising that some of the most ill-minded masters illegally resold apprentices into slavery to maximize their 'return on investment.' Thompson was irate and vehemently opposed to apprenticeships which he declared null and void and criminalized such practices thereof. This led to angst among the Nova Scotians who complained, to which Thompson appealed to them that if slavery was made legal again, none of them could be guaranteed their freedom. Given the vested interests and unwillingness to cause upset, William Wilberforce—who had recommended the young Governor, told him "not to jeopardize a promising career by rashness;" it appeared that Wilberforce and the fellow abolitionists pre-emptively included a clause of apprenticeship to avoid the abolitionary act being rejected in parliament. The friction between maintaining a form of 'lesser' slavery and Thompson's opposition to the system proved to be irreconcilable as he was dismissed by Wilberforce and his director colleagues. The apprenticeship scheme was later stopped altogether in 1840.

The potential profitability of Sierra Leone and Liberia as colonies was reliant on field hands for irrigation, clearing of land for agriculture, and in both schemes, there was reluctance from the Blacks at the top of the social ladder to dirty their hands. In the case of Liberia, it was reported that the freedmen's abhorrence and avoidance of such work was due to its perceived association with manual labor under slavery, and the preference for imported American goods which produced a quick profit—though with arguably longer-term consequences. Where the Nova Scotians in Sierra Leone demonstrated a similar reticence to manual labor, at their expense Governor Thompson empowered the *Recaptives*, who were receptive to the pressing need for labor to clear land by paying them bi-weekly wages, allowing them to build their own houses and grow crops. Moreover, he established 2 new settlements for them—Kingston-In-Africa and Leicester, in addition to constructing roads. Thompson who was a champion of liberty, paradoxically replaced 'Freetown' with 'Georgetown'—albeit briefly—in frustration at the recalcitrant Nova Scotians he considered to have 'half-comprehended notions of American independence." Consequently, he abolished the local currency of dollars and cents which the Nova Scotians traded with, which was a similar system used by the Americo-Liberian settlers, who also accepted the US dollar as legal tender, in addition to adopting several traditions reminiscent of their American heritage.

Relations among the initial Nova Scotian settlers, and subsequent arrivals of Maroons—save for some conflicts over protecting British interests, and rewards thereof—were more peaceful than not. Whilst it was concluded by Governor Thompson in 1808 that 'Maroons were second class citizens compared with Nova Scotians' the 2 groups would later coalesce into the *Krio* ethnic group. This group was further supplemented by *Recaptive* Africans from a diverse range of backgrounds. In addition to African-American Loyalists to Britain and Black Canadian Nova Scotians, others were drawn from ruling elites from Imo State, southeastern Nigeria; Abeokuta (Ogun State) and Ogbomoso (Oyo State), Western Nigeria; Hausaland, Northern Nigeria via Trinidad; Timbuktu, Mali; Sokoto (formerly Gobir), the Fulani Emirate in Northern Nigeria; Jamaica—through which the Maroon's christened their settlement 'Maroon Town;' Cape Verde and Angola—many of whom settled in 'Portuguese Town;' and Congo—after which the district the 'Congo Cross' was named. Additionally, the Maroons adopted the Ashanti *Recaptives* due to tracing their own lineage back to the Ashanti, which was indicative that though they had crossed the Atlantic twice over several generations as slaves and then rebels respectively, they still identified with their African 'ethnocultural' groupings.

Similar to Sierra Leone, Liberia's Black westernized elite drew in not only African Americans, but were supplemented by Caribbean Blacks, as well as 5,000 *Recaptives* from the Congo, Dahomey—present-day Benin Republic and Igbos from southeastern Nigeria who were all rescued by the United States' West African Squadron, which were commissioned with the same mandate as Britain's equivalent to intercept illicit slave ships and divert them to Liberia. The *Recaptives* were the most successful farmers in the colony, thus deemed valuable for the wider interests of the colonists. These groups assimilated under the 'Americo-Liberian' umbrella identity and sought to expand their new state through further migration of their 'kinsmen,' as opposed to integrating with indigenous Africans—something which would prove costly in future generations. The latter group were forcibly designated to do domestic housework and manual labor. Even within the Americo-Liberian elite there were further polarities in the form of the literate vs. illiterates, and the apex of the socio-political structure being vied for 'between the blacks and mulattoes'.

Given both Sierra Leone and Liberia had diverse persons settled, it is no surprise several of them erected structures which were vestigial of their previous locations. The appearance of West Indian and North American architectural styles for Jamaican Maroons and Nova Scotian homes respectively—both erected upon stone foundations, with verandas—proved to be commonplace, and also influenced consumption choices among the wealthy *Recaptives*. Americo-Liberians in addition to bearing the vestiges of the Deep-South American culture—top hats, morning coats and masonic lodges, also built houses with pillared porches, gabled roofs and dormer windows resembling the 19th century architectural styles of Georgia, Maryland, and the Carolinas. It is therefore unsurprising the Liberia national flag is a near replica of the American Stripes and Stars, albeit with a single star in contrast to the 13 stars on the U.S flag.

Despite their American cultural allegiance, it was a source of frustration to the American Colonial Society that the Americo-Liberians were more preoccupied with their lifestyles, house building and the construction of American-influenced institutions and barely showed any interest in tending the fields and maximizing agricultural produce. Resultantly, this proved costly as the ACS had accrued substantial debts by 1833, such was the need to subsidize the administrative costs of the colony—ultimately leading to the organization encouraging a declaration of independence in 1847. In preparation of a post-independent Liberia, the *Liberia College*—an American-style institution—was inaugurated in January 1862, which coincided with the height of its agricultural and extraction economic output. However, this would prove short-lived as thereafter European shipping and declining world prices in the leading exports (coffee, camwood, palm kernels, and ivory) brought depression conditions with the resultant reduction in Liberian College enrolments.

By contrast, Sierra Leone's equivalent to the Liberia College was the *Fourah Bay College* set up by the English Church Missionary Society (CMS) in 1827. Whilst both colleges shared similar theological seminary and training objectives, the 2 differed in that the CMS evangelized not only the amalgamated Krio ethnic group, but also indigenous Africans in Sierra Leone, such as the Temne, whereas the Americo-Liberians only evangelized within their own circle, such was their unwillingness to engage with the 'uncivilized' indigenous Africans.

The creolized settlers of Sierra Leone helped to make Victorian Freetown a unique, cosmopolitan city. The unprecedented mass of residents brought about a real estate boom, courtesy of civic building constructions—namely hotels, goods and local agricultural produce freely exchanged hands between consumer and trader, a racecourse was built, and a society formed to promote the arts and sciences. Given the extent of urbanization, European artisans, drifters, and traders flocked to Freetown to set up micro enterprises; similarly, Liberia attracted European, Americans and Arab businesspeople as traders.

In many ways the greatest divergence between both colonies is the degree to which they produced enduring legacies. The Sierra Leone Colony was Britain's foothold into West Africa through which they were able to absorb the Gold Coast (Ghana) from 1821, and the Lagos Colony (Nigeria)—officially in March 1861—into its growing empire. Whereas political conflicts and power tug-of-wars in Liberia meant that their flagship College had a very mute impact, Freetown's *Fourah Bay College* grew to attract students from present-day Nigeria, Ghana, and Ivory Coast—producing a formidable alumni which includes Samuel Ajayi Crowther and James Pinson Labulo Davies. Crowther was a Yoruba *Recaptive* rescued at the age of 13 from Fulani and Portuguese slavers and through his education—which included time in Britain—specialized in languages. His polygot skills across English, Latin, Greek, Hausa, Igbo, Nupe, Temne, and Yoruba, earned him the distinction of being the first man to translate the Bible and Book of Common Prayer into the Yoruba language. In much the same way that Crowther saw his exposure to the Christian faith as focal to his redemption as a freedman, James Davies—a fellow Yoruba man—used his to leave a remarkable legacy. Born in Freetown of *Recaptives*, Captain Davies served in the Royal Navy West Africa Squadron intercepting and rescuing other Africans onboard illicit slave ships—a benign irony given his parents had previously been rescued by the same naval force. He went on to become a school teacher, independent ship-owner and business man—utilizing his naval experience for merchant trading; became a pioneer in cocoa cultivation near Lagos; successful real estate developer; Church renovator; a creator of jobs for Sierra Leoneans, Ghanaians and Nigerians across diverse professions in Lagos; and compassionately empowered a former slave trader—Madam

Tinubu—so she would abandon the trade altogether; he constructed the Church Missionary Society Grammar School in 1859 in Lagos; and funded several scholarships which also extended to accessing select foreign institutions. He derived joy from empowering those less privileged and demonstrated fortitude in the face of adversity when he was made bankrupt—due to an economic downturn—and lost his wife within a short space of time.

Nevertheless, he redeemed himself by being discharged from bankruptcy, cultivating cocoa and kola nut, and becoming a whisky merchant with a new business partner. Curiously, he identified with Victorian values, he was an outspoken critic of British colonial rule in Lagos and was one of the first Saro returnees to hint at a desire for Nigerian nationalism and self-rule.

Liberia's potential for an enduring, positive legacy was undermined by the thirst for power among the Americo-Liberian elite. The post-independence era was characterized by *colorism*; the system of white preference in the US was replaced with a 'near-white' preference by the Liberian settlers. The 'mulatto-class' were a favored group due to being the best educated, most prosperous traders, and dominating the political arena. The prominent Edward Wilmot Blyden was a notable rarity in being a pan-African man critical of the uppity mulattoes, and through his role as the Liberia College president, he attempted to 'Africanize' the institution through welcoming students from the marginalized indigenous population, introducing Liberian and Arabic languages—the latter for business purposes. However, concerns grew that the Christian influence would take a backseat to Islamic growth and thus undermine western interests, therefore Blyden's methods were consequently jettisoned. Though they were resettled on the African continent, the Americo-Liberians did not see themselves as Africans, and in some ways arguably maintained a 'diaspora within the continent'— indicated by the traditions they sought to uphold. Given most of them did not live the same lives in Liberia that they did whilst in the US, there was an air of haughtiness about their lifestyles and ideologies which put social distance between themselves and the indigenous Africans. Though distasteful in their approach, their orientation was American, the most literate among them believed as free blacks in America they should have had the same opportunities as fellow white Americans, they didn't for the most part share a strong desire to be resettled in Africa—though a small few saw it as the lesser of 2 evils vis-à-vis being an oppressed class in America, and crucially as the settlement began as a colony, it is foreseeable that many of the Americo-Liberian class saw themselves as being in an 'America away from America'. However, the relationship dynamic with the much-exploited indigenous population would culminate in an explosive, pressure-cooker style. Liberia didn't change much up until well into the 20th century—even as the decolonization era of the 1960s gathered momentum. From 1877 to 1980 power remained within the grip of 'The True Whig Party'—a one party system which rotated mostly between 3 families: the Barclays, the Kings, and the Tubmans, all of whom only absorbed a few indigenes such as small children, ambitious country folk and concubines into the elite. Corruption was a mainstay of the politico-economic environment as the US Firestone Rubber and Tyre company leased a million acres in 1926 for 99 years at 6 cents an acre, and iron ore deposits through the Liberian Iron Ore Company—both producing 50% of the government's annual revenue by 1970. Leasing their flag to 2,500 foreign vessels passing through international seas for 'suitable' fees also added to the ruling elite and their cronies' self-enrichment. Though the incumbent president—William Tolbert—implemented policies of increasing the price of rice by 50% to encourage local production, this significantly favored the president's cousin who was simultaneously the owner of the largest rice importing firm. Tolbert also permitted the creation of an opposition party for the first time; however, he undermined this action by jailing them on treason charges when they called for a strike in protest. Tolbert met his waterloo in gruesome circumstances on the 21st April 1980 when a group of 17 dissidents led by Samuel Doe—a 28-year-old master sergeant who scaled his house, fired 3 bullets into his head, disemboweled him, and threw his corpse into a mass grave, along with several of his security detail who also perished. Subsequently Doe declared himself the new leader of Liberia and was the youngest, lowest-ranking officer Head of State in Africa at the time. As this signaled the end of the order, his announcement was met with jubilant cheers, though these were to prove a false dawn as Doe proved to be not much different than the Americo-Liberian elite.

Notwithstanding the residual positive impacts of Sierra Leone, and Liberia's vain distinction of being one of two countries, along with Ethiopia, to remain 'independent' during the European scramble of Africa, the settlements have not been positive for Africans residing in either of the former colonies. Liberia's choice of name—taken from the word 'liberation' only extended as far as its Americo-Liberian class and meant something different [at least until 1980] to the settler colony's indigenous Africans. This was evident in the form of a 1931 indictment of senior government officials from an International Commission for their role in organized slavery.

The Liberia and Sierra Leone settler colonies were de facto extensions of their 'Mother' countries, and therefore the westernized African settlers' distinct cultural practices indicate to varying degrees that these people may have still seen themselves as part of a 'diaspora within the continent'—only changing upon independence in the case of Sierra Leone. Both countries experienced diamond-driven civil wars between 1989 and 2003—resulting in an estimated 250,000 deaths in Liberia, and 50,000 fatalities in Sierra Leone. Moreover, it is noteworthy that whereas 85,914 (or 90,000 according to another source) Africans were taken to Sierra Leone between 1787 and 1848, and 15,230 left to work in the West Indies between 1841-1863, due to varied reasons—namely the foregoing civil war, outward migration resulted in the growth of Sierra Leonean diasporic communities in the US and UK reaching a total of 51,209. Liberia's case is far more underwhelming given only 15,000 moved to the former colony from America, yet the current Liberian diaspora in the US is estimated to be 64,581.

Though America and Britain both made colonial gains through these settler projects, their objectives to remove the black presence from their respective countries ultimately failed.

Black American Freedmen
Against the Return to Africa Movement

It is important to note that the return movement back to Africa polarized much of the African-American population. The likes of Martin R. Delany declared in the 1840s that it was a "great principle of political economy that no people can be free who themselves do not constitute an essential part of the ruling element of the country in which they live." He saw no future for the black man in white America. Due to his belief that he and other Afro-Americans could enable Africa to advance toward civilization, he went to Nigeria and signed treaties with the Egba giving Afro-Americans the right to settle in western Nigeria.

The wholesale emancipation of Afro-Americans after the Civil War did not halt the black exodus to Africa. Indeed, the failure of the Reconstruction Era appeared to have encouraged the view that Afro-Americans could never achieve true equality in America. Bishop Henry McNeal Turner of the African Methodist Episcopal (AME) Church declared in December 1895:

> There is no manhood future in the United States for
> the Negro . . . I believe that two or three million of us
> should return to the land of our ancestors and establ-
> ish our own nations, civilization, laws, customs, styles
> of manufacture, and not only give to the world . . . the
> benefit of our individuality, but build up social condit-
> ions peculiarly our own, and cease to be grumblers,
> chronic complainers, and a menace to the white man's
> country, or the country he claims and is bound to dom-
> inate.

Emigrationism, far from dead among most Afro-Americans during the early 20th century, took the form of messianism. On the eve of World War I, Chief Alfred Sam was able to raise $100,000 to buy a steamship, and transport a number of Afro-Americans from the mid-western United States. Sam's movement failed, but a decade later, Marcus Garvey, a Jamaican living in New York, saw in the return to Africa movement a solution to the Afro-Americans' plight in America as well as an opportunity for the New World Africans to liberate their motherland. He was struck by the impotence of the black man and saw the problems of African peoples in global terms. Garvey declared:

> As far as the Negroes are concerned in America we have
> the problem of lynching, peonage, and dis-enfranchisem
> -ent. In the West Indies, South and Central America, we
> have the problem of peonage, serfdom, industrial and
> political governmental inequality. In Africa we have not
> only peonage and serfdom, but outright slavery, racial
> exploitation and alien political monopoly. We cannot
> allow a continuation of these crimes against our race. As
> four hundred million men, women and children worthy of
> the existence given us by the Divine Creator, we are deter-
> mined to solve our own problems, by redeeming our "Moth-
> erland" Africa from the hands of alien exploiters, and [to]
> found there a government, a nation of our own, strong en-
> ough to lend protection to the members of our race scatte-
> red all over the world and to compel the respect of the nat-
> ions and races of the earth.

While preparing to return to Africa, Garvey waged a vigorous campaign against Afro-American shame in being black and in being of African descent. He created Black nobility, Black Cross nurses, and black dolls for little girls; designed an African flag with the colors red, black, and green; and painted black almost all the symbols of Western Christendom.

The emigration strategy of Afro-Americans did not result in the creation of an African state powerful enough to challenge racism in America. Nevertheless, emigrationism had a profound effect on the psyche of Afro-Americans. Roi Ottley believed that this movement:

> set in motion what was to become the most competing

322

force in Negro life—race and color consciousness which is today that ephemeral thing that inspires "race loyalty"; the banner to which Negroes rally; the chain that
binds them together. It has propelled many a political
and social movement and stimulated racial inter-natio-
nalism. It is indeed a philosophy, an ethical standard by
which most things are measured and interpreted.

The vast majority of Africans never seriously considered returning to
Africa. Nevertheless, they made up a sizeable group of people of African
origin who considered themselves *African* and who identified themselves
with the entire continent rather than with specific regions, thereby
becoming Pan-Africanists. Moreover, they saw their future cultural,
economic, political, and social positions as being linked to that of Africa, and
they sought the freedom of Africa, and of African peoples wherever they
existed.

The critical problem for Africans in the North American diaspora was
the fate of their fellows still in bondage if the freedman and their leaders
departed. Richard Allen, James Forten, and others accused the American
Colonization Society of planning to ship away only the freedmen, leaving the
slaves at the mercy of their masters. Some, because they were so concerned
that any association with Africa would jeopardize their chances of
emancipation in America, advocated dropping the word *Africa* or *African*
from the titles of organizations and suggested that these words be chiseled
off the marble of their churches. Alarmed by Captain Paul Cuffe's project and
that of the American Colonization Society, members of the free Afro-
American community in Philadelphia stoutly refused to leave America and
issued the following declaration in January 1817:

We are NATIVES of this country, we ask only to be treated as well
As FOREIGNERS. Not a few of our fathers suffered and bled to purchase its independence; we ask only to be treated as well as those
who fought against it. We have toiled to cultivate it, and to raise it
to its present prosperous condition; we ask only to share equal

privileges with those who came from distant lands, to enjoy the
fruits of our labour. Let these moderate requests be granted, and
we [will] not go to Africa nor anywhere else to be improved and
happy. We cannot doubt the purity of the motives of those persons
who deny us these requests, and who would send us to Africa to
gain what they might deny us at home.

Underscoring their attachment to America, these free Afro-Americans
even denigrated the land from which their forefathers came. Their
spokesmen declared that "[w]ithout arts, without science, without a proper
knowledge of Government, to cast into the savage wilds of Africa the free
people of color seem to use the circuitous route through which they must
return to perpetual bondage."

When several decades later Martin Delany started to preach
emigrationism, Frederick Douglass denounced the back-to-Africa
movement. He declared:

> We have grown up with this Republic and I see nothing in the
> character of the American people as yet which compels the
> belief that we must leave the United States.

Douglass believed that the less said about the relationship of the Afro-
American to Africa the better off black persons would be:

> No one idea has given rise to more oppression and pers-
> ecution toward the colored people of this country than
> that which makes Africa, not America, their home. It is
> that wolfish idea that elbows us off the side walk and
> denies us the right of citizenship.

Frederick Douglass was later to concede that Africa was less the cause of
his undoing than the attitude of the white in America. He said:

> I have no love for America, as such; I have no patriotism.
> I have no country. What country have I? The institutions
> of this country do not know me, do not recognize me as a
> man. I am not thought of, spoken of, in any direction, out of

the anti-slavery ranks as a man. I am not thought of, or spoken of, except as a piece of property belonging to some
Christian slave-holder, and all the religious and political
Institutions of this country, alike pronounce me a slave and
a chattel.

Nevertheless, Frederick Douglass could not wholly embrace emigrationism. He did not believe that those Afro-Americans who were free should abandon those who were still captives. Nor did he believe that his contemporaries should return empty-handed to Africa or ignore the contributions that earlier generations of Afro-Americans had made in building America.

Another reason why many Africans in the diaspora did not wish to return physically to Africa was their growing prejudice toward that continent and its inhabitants. Despised in part because of their African descent, they remained ambivalent about Africa. In contrast to the Jewish situation, in which even anti-Semitic Christians sang of "Jerusalem my happy home/Name ever blessed to me," most Europeans and their descendants viewed Africa as a savage and "dark continent." Blacks felt compelled to rehabilitate Africa and African peoples in their own eyes and in the eyes of the world so that by extension both they and that continent would be saved. They would learn about Africa, help it become free, but not necessarily return there.

Pan-Africanism

'for my part, the deeper I enter into the culture
and the political circles, the surer I am that the
great danger that threatens Africa is the absence
of ideology'.

Frantz Fanon

One of the key building blocks between the African diaspora and mother continent is the Pan-African school of thought. Proponents of Garveyism ideology have long christened Marcus Garvey the 'Godfather' of the Pan-African movement. This is not surprising given the enduring weight of his adage: 'A people without the knowledge of their past history, origin and culture is like a tree without roots'. Considering his achievements, it's not hard to see why he's widely regarded as a pioneer of the movement; nevertheless, the movement arguably predates him.

Sons of Africa was a Pan-African political organization set up in the late 18th century by Olaudiah Equiano and Ottobah Cugoano—both free men and prominent members of London's Black Community at the time. Their work was holistically focused, as not only was it concerned with the abolition of the slave trade, but they—particularly Equiano—fought for working opportunities for both Africans in London, as well those that would be resettled in Sierra Leone.

It is noteworthy that the many New World slave revolts reflected pan-African collaboration. This was remarkable given they were drawn from a number of different nations across coastal and hinterland lying West, Central and South-West Africa, spoke different languages and practiced unique cultures with different traditions. Notwithstanding these differences, a common goal of self-determination compelled them to risk their lives and potentially venture into the unknown. Haiti, whilst holding the distinction of being only the second country in the Americas to declare independence, also provided a new homeland and the prospect of self-reinvention for the runaway Africans as free men and women in what was initially intended to be an egalitarian society.

Edward Wilmot Blyden was a key Americo-Liberian who sought to bridge the black settlers' ideological and cultural divergences with the indigenous Liberians—reflected in his attempts to modify the Liberian college from being an American-oriented, Christian-focused university to one which was more secular and would have a wider, resonating impact beyond the Americo-Liberians. The introduction of linguistic courses—such as [the Liberian] Kru and also Arabic—were with the express intention of economic empowerment and instilling an African-centeredness. Blyden however was not without his contradictions: despite being pro-African in his sentiments, he did not acknowledge the role of enslaved Africans in the persistent struggles to subvert the institution of slavery. On the contrary, though he did not justify the brutality of slavery, he believed goodness came out of slavery and that the wickedness of it was a 'necessary evil' which conferred advantages on Africans in America to modernize Africa and ultimately bring about the continent's enlightenment. He was an influential theorist, among many others, who called for the freedom of Africa 'for the purposes of African descendants' colonization of Africa'. Nevertheless, many of Blyden's benevolent ideas influenced 20th century pan-African thought leaders, including Marcus Garvey, George Padmore and Kwame Nkrumah.

The Physician, scientist, historian, writer, and Pan-Africanist, James Africanus Horton, is considered by many to be "the father of modern African political thought". Born in Sierra Leone in 1835 of Igbo parents, he was yet another attendee of the *Fourah Bay College*, which was followed by studying and graduating from the University of Edinburgh in 1859. Thereafter he joined the army medical service in what is now Ghana and went on to write many Pan-African literary books. In his book *West African Countries and Peoples* he stated his aim was to develop a "true political science", and "prove the capacity of the African for possessing a real political Government and national independence." He was very much a product of his time in viewing European civilization as the benchmark for the inferior indigenous African societies to aspire to—a sentiment no doubt unpopular with many present-day Africans. Nevertheless, his influence spread far and wide, impacting another attendee of the *Fourah Bay College*—the Ghanaian lawyer Joseph E. Casely-Hayford, who was another writer, Pan-Africanist, and politician from a prominent coastal family of partial European ancestry. He was the founder of *The National Congress of British West Africa* (NCBWA). He was also another advocate—much like Blyden and Africanus Horton—of developing a regional "West African nationality", which was rooted in 'modernizing' the region, albeit with the retention of its African character. That he also called Africa the "cradle of civilization", but sought to only reform, not end the British Empire colonial system and attain self-rule— such was the need for its values to progress Africa—was contradictory; moreover, his elitist stance failed to enlist the support of traditional African rulers, nor the masses across all four British West African colonies. Notwithstanding his 'nuanced' views, his creation of the NCBWA which he eventually presided over, brought together nationalists from Gambia, Nigeria, Sierra Leone, Ghana; furthermore, his ethos upon which West African nationalism was advanced, were foundational for Ladipo Solanke and Herbert Bankole Bright creating the West African Student's Union (WASU) in London in 1924.

WASU developed out of the activities of earlier student union organizations, such as the Union of Students of African Descent and the Nigeria Progress Union—also established with Solanke along with Amy Ashwood Garvey (Marcus Garvey's future wife). The organization campaigned not only against racism in Britain, but for independence in West Africa through producing a regular publication, establishing 4 hostels to provide lodgings and a 'home from home' for West African students and African visitors at a time when racism and the 'color bar' limited the availability of accommodation.

The union, which established branches in all of Britain's West African colonies, influenced many West African independence movements; one particular success story was Kwame Nkrumah's emergence as Ghana's president when it became independent in 1957.

Additionally, WASU's political ambitions from its base in Britain extended to establishing links with many organizations, including the *League of Coloured Peoples* (LCP) and the Communist Party. The union also had its own parliamentary committee of MPs through which it lobbied on African concerns in the House of Commons. It was one of the most important political organizations in Britain from the 1920s until the 1960s.

The Western world was replete with political activity for the advancement of the rights of African people globally. One way in which this was evident was through 5 *Pan African Congress* conferences before the post-World War II wave of decolonization: *Paris* in 1919, *London*—both in 1921 and 1923, *New York City* in 1927, and *Manchester* in 1945. Prominent attendees included Du Bois—organizer of the first 2 conferences, Nkrumah, Jomo Kenyatta of Kenya, Trinidadian Pan-African activist George Padmore, Malawi's Hastings Banda, prominent Jamaican barrister Dudley Thompson, as well as Nigeria's Obafemi Awolowo and Jaja Wachuku. WASU also sent delegates to the 1945 conference due to rapid transformations in West Africa coinciding with the outbreak of the second world war. Out of this milieu WASU pursued promises from the UK Labour Party for the attainment of self-rule and -determination.

Garveyism

Marcus Garvey and his fellow colleagues from the *International League For Darker People* sought to use the Paris 1919 conference as a lobbying opportunity to achieve improved rights for people of color, however this approach was undermined by an inability to obtain the necessary travel permits. Though they were eventually able to send a Haitian delegate in Eliezer Cadet, their wishes were largely ignored in favor of reasserting support for European colonialism. This was one of many self-sacrificial activities that Garvey was involved in, starting with his trade unionist activities in the Colony of Jamaica—culminating in the loss of his printer's job, and agitating with fellow Jamaican nationalists to remove the Jamaican colonial Governor Sydney Olivier, such were the economically challenging conditions he and Afro-Jamaicans experienced from Indian 'coolies', among other rival migrants.

Economic hardship led to Garvey leaving Jamaica. He travelled to Costa Rica and other Central American countries, taking up work as a casual itinerant worker, where his trade union political activities were resumed—which unsurprisingly landed him in trouble with their authorities.

Garvey's sojourns took him to London where he networked with a future Prime Minister David Lloyd George, taken up speaking slots at the renown Hyde Park's Speaker's Corner, and attended evening classes at Birkbeck College, University of London. On his voyage back to Jamaica he had a chance encounter with a fellow Afro-Caribbean who had undertaken missionary work in the Cape Colony (South Africa) and established a diaspora-continent link by marring an African lady; the encounter instilled in Garvey a desire and vision to politically unify Black people across the world.

Upon returning home to Jamaica in July 1914, Garvey made-ends-meet by selling imported greeting / condolence cards and then selling tombstones. Additionally, he launched the legacy-defining *Universal Negro Improvement Association And African Communities League* (UNIA by abbreviation), and though he received criticism from Jamaicans who deemed the choice of word 'Negro' offensive, an unmoved Garvey—who considered it empowering for persons of African descent—stuck with it. The UNIA adopted the motto *One Aim. One God. One Destiny*. The UNIA received many financial contributions—including from the likes of William Manning, the Governor of Jamaica; however, he experienced tension from middle class mulattos, quadroons, and octoroons which influenced him to seek funding directly from white elites. Amid dwindling financial support and unsubstantiated rumors of financial misappropriation, he moved to New York City in March 1916 to revive the UNIA. This arguably proved to be an inspired move as the UNIA's membership grew—surpassing 25 branches in the US, additional divisions in the West Indies, Central America, and West Africa, and reaching an estimated 2 million members by June 1919. This figure reportedly rose to 4 million by 1921. Furthermore, the organization established a restaurant and ice cream parlor, a Women's hat store in Harlem, and a weekly newspaper the *Negro World*—the latter of which was circulated not only in the US, but also in the Caribbean, Central and South America.

Given the lofty ambitions of the UNIA, Garvey attracted a deluge of adversaries for a host of different reasons. Among these were 400 rival newspaper publications who exposed his financial appeals to help keep the newspaper afloat—though he remained principled in the face of these challenges by a flat-out refusal to feature adverts for skin-lightening and hair-straightening products and exhorted black people to "take the kinks out of your mind, instead of out of your hair". A particularly prominent opponent was the Federal Bureau of Investigation's (FBI) J. Edgar Hoover who had sought to monitor him for using more 'militant language' in his many speeches than that which appeared in printed press; this was through the view he expressed "for every negro lynched by Whites in the South, Negroes should lynch a white in the North".

W.E.B Du Bois' more established National Association for the Advancement of Colored People (NAACP) initially saw its membership crossover with the UNIA. The 2 would eventually butt heads as the NAACP's 'Talented Tenth' modus operandi of appealing to potential members who were working as doctors, lawyers and teachers, was sharply at odds with the UNIA's recruitment of poor Black Americans and Afro-Caribbean migrants. Tensions further took a negative turn when Garvey's appeal to Du Bois for UNIA contributions was rebuffed. The acrimonious dynamic culminated in Du Bois branding him a 'demagogue' and ambivalently as "a little fat black man, ugly but with intelligent eyes and a big head;" Garvey arguably gave as good as he received: "Where did he (Du Bois) get his aristocracy from? He picked it up on the streets of Great Barrington, Mass," in a broadside at his bourgeoise sentiments. Furthermore, Garvey went on to say "... he has been trying to be everything but a negro. Sometimes we hear he's a Frenchman, another time he is Dutch, and when it is convenient he's a negro... anything that is black to him is ugly, is hideous, is monstrous, and this is why in 1917 he had but the lightest of colored people in his office, when one could hardly tell whether it was a white show or a colored vaudeville he was running at Fifth Avenue". Garvey was a race-purist and held reservations over the potential split loyalties some blacks may have had with their partial European heritage.

Garvey was ever the man with a plan and a steely determination—so much so, that he survived an assassination attempt, during which he was penetrated by 2 bullets to his leg, yet nevertheless was available to fulfil a speaking engagement just 5 days later. Arguably what surpassed this feat, and the others was bringing his Black Star Line shipping business project to life—in the face of negative slurs; accusations of poor accounting and misappropriation of funds levelled at him; and being banned from selling shares to fundraise the scheme due to not holding a license to do so—as required to conform with the Blue Sky Laws applicable in Chicago. Whilst he stopped short of raising the $2 million target, the scheme did generate $50,000 which was enough by 31st October 1919 to acquire the *SS Yarmouth* 30-year-old steam ship. Unfortunately, the ship ran into problems when attempting its first and second assignments to Jamaica and Cuba, which incurred a repair bill of $11,000. He attempted to float a second ship, putting a $10,000 down payment for it, but eventually sacked a couple of administrators for what he attributed to corruption, and sold the Yarmouth for scrap metal in 1922.

Garvey remained a target of rival African-American groups, attracted criticism from Jamaicans for his own critique of them, and was conspicuously charged by the FBI for 'mail fraud'—more specifically for fundraising to buy another ship, the *Orion*, in what appeared to be a politically-motivated move by J.Edgar Hoover. It nevertheless made mainstream press coverage which largely portrayed him as a swindling con artist. Eventually he would be sentenced to a a 5-year prison term. Notwithstanding this adversity, Garvey upon leaving prison, engaged in several political and social activities, putting on plays—one of which was the Coronation of an African King in August 1930; this foreshadowed the coronation of Haile Selassie of Ethiopia during the same year.

Pan-Africanism and Ethiopianism

The genesis of the Pan-African movement also transpired concomitantly with myriad political and religious movements such as *Ethiopianism*. This was a generic term for the black race or the continent of Africa. Later, the name Ethiopia came to refer to the specific geographical area of what was previously called Abyssinia.

The *Ethiopianism* synonym for black liberation emanated from the Old Testament which prophesied that "Ethiopia shall soon stretch out her hands unto God" (Psalm 68, verse 31). This messianic prophecy, *Ethiopianists* believe, is a covenant between the black race and God that he will deliver the black race from slavery and oppression and bring together all children of the African diaspora. In the 1920s a West African nationalist newspaper stated that, " ... when we speak of our prospects we speak of the prospect of the entire Ethiopian race. By the Ethiopian race we mean the sons and daughters of Africa scattered throughout the world." *Ethiopianism*, hence, became a kind of religion for some blacks through which they saw a ray of hope in the wilderness of history.

This messianic and quasi-religious movement gave hope to its followers, a hope in the rise of Africa and the coming together of her scattered children. *Ethiopianists* believe Africa will ascend, its children will come together, and God will punish those who caused them misery. The enemy is a reference to the colonizers of Africa, enslavement, and the adversities felt by the diaspora. Western civilization—followers of Ethiopianism believed— will be doomed by God for this action directed against Africa.

This messianic message of *Ethiopianism* as a movement, or Ethiopia as a generic reference for all black people, was indeed a psychological confidence-builder and a ray of hope to look forward to for all its followers. They believed that they were special people and superior to the other races. *Ethiopianism* glorified Africa and Africans of the past. Its vision was that Africa would be redeemed by God, its people would free themselves from the shackles of bondage and recapture their lost glory and civilization.

Ethiopianism, thus was a spiritual hope and an important ingredient in black messianic insurrection. Indeed, Ethiopianism stimulated the birth of the 20th century Pan-African movement. Pan-Africanists such as Du Bois, Garvey, George Padmore, and Casely-Hayford were thus influenced by Ethiopianism. As Wilson Jeremiah Moses wrote in his book *The Golden Age of Black Nationalism*, "... Ethiopianism had become not only a transatlantic political movement, but a literary movement well-known among all black people from the Congo basin to mountains of Jamaica to the sidewalks of New York". Even Booker T. Washington, who was ideologically different from DuBois, was aware of this African connection and attempted to capitalize on it for African progress. Washington was for African industrial education, self-improvement, and wanted to establish Tuskegee-style schools in Africa.

Ethiopianists also identified with the present-day country of Ethiopia. Ethiopia was an independent country more so than the other 2 independent countries of that time, Liberia, and Haiti, which were politically independent but were economic appendages of the U.S. At the time of the movement, Haiti was heavily indebted to U.S. companies and Liberia was more or less dominated by the Firestone Rubber Company. Ethiopia was the only independent black country that successfully resisted Euro-based cultural and political domination. Hence it became a symbol of independence and hope for blacks on the continent and those in the diaspora. Furthermore, it boosted the morale of many black people by successfully defeating an Italian force at the Battle of Adowa in 1896. Ethiopia, as one west African newspaper put it, "remained the only oasis in a desert of rank subjugation from the avaricious hands of foreign domination." This victory reinforced the messianic belief that the European power could be resisted by the independent African nation.

Ethiopianism significantly inspired several African independent movements. Moreover, it inspired African-American resistance efforts which predated the American civil war. Radical-minded African-Americans, including American socialists, formed the Ethiopian Peace Movement in Chicago during the 1930s, and South Africa also established its own equivalent.

In addition to the African-American and Africa-based Ethiopianists, west Indians were also swayed by the lure of redemption. One was the Barbadian Jew, Rabbi Arnold J. Ford, who heeded a call by the Ethiopian government to relocate to Ethiopia and serve their country under the promise of free land and high wages. Ford was also a noted musician and musical director of the Universal Negro Improvement Association (UNIA). The UNIA's national anthem was known as the *Universal Ethiopian Anthem*.

The Rastafarian movement, which started in the 1930s in Jamaica, was predicated on Ethiopia's ruler and *Ethiopianism*. It was named after Emperor Haile Selassie's title and name during his regency. The Rastafarian movement is another version of the Pan-Africanist movement which drew on the historical parallel with the adverse Jewish experience in Babylon.

Marcus Garvey was instrumental to the Rastafarian movement after he was deported from the U.S. to Jamaica in 1927. It was said that he told his followers to "Look to Africa, when a black king shall be crowned, for the day of deliverance is near." When Ras Tafari was crowned Emperor Haile Selassie in November 1930, as "King of Kings and the Conquering Lion of the Tribe of Judah", some Garveyite Jamaicans began looking to the Emperor as the Living God. The government of Jamaica sought to 'prick the balloon' of Selassie enthusiasm by inviting him on a state visit, but it had the inverse effect of intensifying his popularity. Many started preaching about Ras Tafari as the King of Kings and the descendant of King David. This growing group of Jamaican followers viewed Ethiopia as more symbolic of 'blackness' or 'Africanity' with a loose connection to the country itself. These followers assumed the name *Ras Tafari* or *Rastaman* and looked to Ethiopia as the promised land; as the 'heartland of African civilization'. Thus, Afro-Caribbeans in general played an important role in *Ethiopianism*, saw Ethiopia as a citadel of independence, and enhanced the Pan-African movement further.

The Selassie effect had gathered much momentum, and his exile due to the Italian invasion, galvanized Pan-African solidarity not only in Jamaica, but elsewhere, including in the US where African Americans in East Harlem assaulted their Italian neighbors due to perceiving them as an emblem of Mussolini's fascist Italy. Boxer Joe Lewis's win over Primo Carnera was also celebrated as a win against fascist Italians. Some 20,000 protestors waving Ethiopian flags marched in a rally through Madison Square New York. In capturing the zeitgeist of the time, a Cleveland doctor, Joe E. Thomas, exhorted: "every son and daughter of African descent should render assistance to their blood relatives in Ethiopia. We must not desert our Race in Africa. We must stand, "One for all. All for one."

The efforts of Selassie's supporters across the diaspora were not in vain as Britain reversed its initial support for the Italians in favor of restoring Selassie in 1935, which was motivated by avoiding mass revolt in its colonies. Additionally, this same fear also influenced the British government to adopt a more militant anti-fascist stance.

Emperor Haile Selassie tried to portray a positive image of Ethiopia throughout the black world. For example, he instructed an Ethiopian, Dr. Melaku Bayean, to establish the Ethiopian World Federation, Inc. (EWF) in New York in 1937, and Melaku Bayean, distantly related to Haile Selassie and married to an African-American, was a graduate of Howard University's Medical School. The purpose of the EWF was to enhance unity, liberty, solidarity, freedom, and the self-determination of black people across the world. The EWF also sought to maintain the integrity of Ethiopia. The EWF opened a branch in Jamaica and was active in the 1950s as the Rastafarian movement increased its political activities. In order to encourage black people of the diaspora to return to Ethiopia, the Emperor allotted 500 acres of fertile land in Shashemene (east of Addis Ababa) to black people of the

West through the EWF. The EWF had broader political, economic, and humanitarian objectives. It raised funds, and political and medical supplies during the Italo-Ethiopian war and facilitated immigration of African-Americans to Ethiopia. Leaders of various Jamaican nationalist groups who visited Ethiopia in 1961 to study large scale immigration to Ethiopia were told that Ethiopia " ... would always open its doors to people of African origin who wished to return."

Several scholars have argued that the relationship between Blacks of the diaspora and Ethiopia was not always smooth. One example of this when Selassie was forced into a UK exile by an invasion from Benito Mussolini's Italian fascist troops in 1935. Garvey, who had initially spoken in support of Selassie, later developed hostility towards him due to being blanked upon attempting to welcome him at the London Waterloo Railway Station.

Another example of discordance in this relationship was presented by Harold Isaacs and William Shack, who indicated that Ethiopians rejected association with diasporan Blacks. Ethiopians, because of their partial exclusion from the outside world, and insecurity because of foreign aggressions over the centuries, were always suspicious of the *ferenji* (foreigner), mainly whites. While they admired the white man's achievements in science, medicine, and technology, they nonetheless viewed him with contempt. As far as the word "Negro" is concerned, some Ethiopians equated it with slavery. Hence, they resented it. However, they did believe that they were Black (*Tikur*). This, Isaacs and Shack stated, was similar to the view(s) held by "Africans-American" pertaining to ethnic labels. Like other ethnic groups or nationalities, however, some Ethiopians were victims of ethnic or national chauvinism. These groups felt they were "superior" to others. Holding one's own as a superior group (be it racially, ethnically, religiously, or culturally) may be true in almost all societies at a certain stage of their social awareness and economic development. Hence, Ethiopians, in this regard, were not exceptional but were completely misunderstood.

Also noteworthy was that the Royal House of Ethiopia was rather slow in recognizing Ethiopia as an African country. For a long time, Ethiopian rulers preferred to see themselves as part of the Middle East rather than Africa. Seeing the widespread support of Africans and black people at large, not least a young and teary Kwame Nkrumah, following the Italian invasion of Ethiopia, marked an inflection point in Ethiopia's self-discovery from 1935 onwards as truly part of the African condition. These developments marked a new form of racial consciousness in the Royal House of Ethiopia—its self-discovery of which was as an African dynasty of an African people. Over time, Haile Selassie developed into one of the founding fathers, and in many ways *the* elder statesman, of post-colonial Pan-Africanism. This development was one of the reasons why Garvey's criticisms of Selassie made him unpopular with some Garveyites and those who believed—whether justified or not—that he was a symbol of Ethiopia's struggle against colonialism.

As the above has outlined, the New World experiences of African descendants, and the related pursuits of freedom and self-determination are an integral part of the Pan-Africanist movement. However, it can be argued that the role of slavery in Pan-Africanism is not widely recognized; moreover, many theorists and scholars believe the ultimate goal of the Pan-Africanist movement was to secure Africa's independence.

THE NEW
AFRICAN
DIASPORA

—

THE NEW AFRICAN DIASPORA

The *New African diaspora* is an extension of the old African diaspora which took shape several centuries prior.

Britain

In Britain, the 'Black African' / 'Black Afro-Caribbean' designations only first emerged as official ethnic categories in 1991. However, evidence of a Black African presence dates back to at least the Roman era when a 500-strong 'division of Moors' were recorded to have defended Hadrian's well over 1,800 years ago; some of whom held high-ranking positions. Thereafter, West Africans in the form of domestic servants, musicians, entertainers, and slaves became more common from 1555 and throughout the Tudor period, prompting Queen Elizabeth I's unsuccessful attempt to expel the *blackamores* from her kingdom in 1601.

While this section posits that the new British African diaspora was marked by the onset of the Windrush generation arrivals from the late 1940s, these arrivals were foreshadowed by 15,000 Caribbean settlers from the British West Indies Regiment who had come to work in munition and chemical factories during World War I (1914—1918). Significantly, this reflected the prevailing international division of labor, based essentially along color lines; a Black sailor signed on at a colonial port could be paid at a rate much lower than those applying at any British port. This provoked white hostility by undercutting the rate for the job, and, on the other hand, encouraged black sailors to settle in Britain. As one writer, Richmond, put it: "the Black sailor got the worst of both worlds: inferior pay if he signed on overseas; white retaliation if he tried to sign on in Britain". Unsurprisingly, this set the tone for tension with white seamen—culminating in the 1919 anti-Black riots. The main reasons behind this were rising unemployment due to the end of the war—occasioning more acute economic competition, and the hatred that society had for Black-White sexual relations. The fallout from the riots for the Black community was particularly harsh as the British authorities not only disproportionately arrested more of them than their white counterparts, but a *Times* report states that they were placed in an internment camp pending repatriation. Blacks were racially profiled by being issued with special registration cards and fingerprinted as a qualifier for receiving pay or signing onto a shipping job. Such was the 'success' of the scheme, it impacted local policing policy in another British port city—Cardiff, which also registered 'coloureds' as aliens, making them subject to arbitrary deportation despite being Black British Citizens. The registration scheme also served as a means of a color bar, thus restricting employment opportunities following on from the riots; the frustrations of one worker, a Nigerian by the name Elder Dempsey, captured the sentiment of many in the community when he lamented 'white men never finish', in response to being told 'No coloureds. When white men finish you get job'. Given these adverse circumstances, it is unsurprising that a 345-strong west Indian contingent of workers who had relocated to Liverpool in February 1941 experienced varying levels of tension with fellow Black workers from West Africa who were less skilled than them.

The Liverpool Race riots also took place in the same year as riots in the US cities of Chicago, Washington, and New York, leading to 30 fatalities and 500 wounded in Chicago alone. This was preceded by the 1917 East St. Louis massacres where the economic bone of contention mirrored that which also ignited the Liverpool riots—causing an estimated 250 African-American casualties, and leaving 6,000 homeless. Marcus Garvey was moved to brand the massacre as "one of the bloodiest outrages against mankind," "a wholesale massacre of our people," and asserted "this is no time for fine words, but a time to lift one's voice against the savagery of a people who claim to be dispensers of democracy". It was against this backdrop of statements in the face of unionized white-led violence that attracted the attention of the FBI's J.Edgar Hoover.

In the UK, the Labour Party's landslide victory in the 1945 general election was used as an opportunity for the Pan-Africanist George Padmore to petition the new Prime Minister (PM), Clement Atlee, to lift the 1919 color bar imposition. He was encouraged by the growing post-war aversion to racism, which was indivisible from the African and Caribbean independence movements; however, his open letter to Atlee condemning imperialism and appealing for the criminalization of racism was ignored. Of more pressing concern to the new PM was how to address Britain's acute labor shortage due to the debilitating cost of the war. In June 1946 research undertaken by the British Cabinet Manpower Working Party estimated that to reach its target, the economy would need 940,000 additional workers—raising this estimate to 1,346,000 by the end of the year.

Despite such pressing circumstances, Atlee and his cabinet were loath to welcome Black British subjects and launched the European Voluntary Workers' (EVW) scheme. EVW brought in 80,000 displaced Ukrainians, Latvians, and Poles; these figures were further swelled by the arrival of 100,000 Polish armed forces personnel fighting on the side of the Britain against the Nazis—along with their families; and an influx of Irish immigrants.

Contradictory messages were issued by both the thousands of UK job vacancies advertised in the South London Daily Press, and the Colonial Office official dispatches to the Caribbean to inform the people that no such jobs were available. In the end the former prevailed, much to the chagrin of the Ministry of Labour which went to the lengths in 1947 of conducting an evaluation reporting negative findings on the 'surplus of West Indian males'. Parochial claims to the effect the men were not fit to brave cold outdoor temperatures, or very warm ones in coalmines, were debunked by a previous group of 600 men from the tropical British Honduras working as foresters in frozen Scottish temperatures, and airmen successfully enduring sub-zero temps in unpressurized RAF bombers on missions over Germany.

The transition from a limited and fragile presence in the pre-war years to a significant and fundamentally 'unassimilable' presence, began with the unexpected 1947 arrival of 110 Jamaicans aboard the former troop ship, the *Ormonde*. This was followed by what has been commonly reported as the arrival of 492 migrants on the 22nd June 1948. However, the narrative of an uncomplicated route of the Windrush from Kingston to Jamaica, with its homogenized carriage of Jamaicans, is too simplistically documented. On the contrary the passage of 492 migrants only tells part of the story, as after omissions, inaccuracies and ambiguities, and the addition of stowaways are accounted for in the passenger log, the total actually adds up to 1027 which is over double the figure widely and consistently reported. Moreover, once women and children are factored into the total count the final count of Jamaicans increases to 531. Further challenging the Jamaican focus of the Windrush, is the presence of several passengers reporting their 'Country of last Permanent Residence' as British Guiana, St. Lucia, Uganda, Kenya, Barbados, Italy, and even Scotland.

Sojourning to what many West Indian migrants fondly called the 'Mother Country', indicated they considered themselves to be intimately linked with their destination; they felt a 'profound affiliation to the land that lay before them'. Unbeknown to them, however, the government didn't quite share the same enthusiasm and regarded them an embarrassment. During the same year, British governors in the West Indies warned London that thousands more West Indians were applying for passports which led to stealth activity—including attempts to intercept the Windrush and divert it to East African groundnut projects—to ensure that the Windrush didn't set a precedent for future arrivals; ironically the groundnut scheme proved to be a 'white elephant' project and was abandoned in 1951. In a similar vein, 11 Members of Parliament (MPs) wrote a letter to the Prime Minister on the day the Windrush docked at Tilbury sounding a "warning" that the British people who "enjoy a profound unity" would see such "harmony, strength and cohesion" impeded by "an influx of coloured people domiciled here". However, the Cabinet Economic Policy Committee acknowledged somewhat wistfully that as "private persons travelling at their own expense" they could not be stopped.

In contrast to the racialized hostility British West Indians were to experience, there was a warmer welcome given to both continental and Irish aliens whose entrance was perceived to be likely advantageous to the UK economy and because they passed an unwritten test of racial acceptability. Nevertheless, the number of white inward migration flows was a mere dent in fulfilling the government's labor quota, which the new Colonial Secretary, Arthur Creech Jones, informed his race-conscious colleagues that West Indians were well aware of the UK's labor shortage and of plans to remedy this with European Displaced Persons. In light of this, he further advised that West Indians "are British subjects and many of whom have had prior work experience in Britain, during the war years, to relieve the labor shortage in Britain."

Paradoxically the 1948 British Nationality Act was passed the same year the Windrush docked in Tilbury. It granted the rights of citizenship to all members of the British Empire which it had envisaged would mostly facilitate two-way migration flows of White Brits in the UK and Dominions of Canada, Australia, and New Zealand. It was also a public relations exercise to assert that the UK was the imperial center of the great Commonwealth of nations with the ability to compete with the US and USSR world powers, despite the irony of the post-war independence / decolonization movement taking shape simultaneously. West Indians, from Jamaica in particular, who had fought in the war faced the prospect of economic hardship upon returning home due to the evisceration caused by hurricanes to their homelands. Furthermore, the birth-rate—variously estimated at between 2—4%, and an unemployment rate between 20—35% were further adverse factors. These circumstances and the UK's pressing labor shortage culminated in a 'marriage of convenience,' though this was more of a push factor than the adverse conditions in the Caribbean. Given the prospect of bright new beginnings, the optimism these West Indians felt was memorably captured by the Trinidadian Calypso singer Lord Kitchener's new song "London is the place to be." Musically, this expressed the 'calm,' before a long, raging storm of racialized hostility. The initial arrivals were temporarily housed in South-West London at the Clapham South deep shelter. The British Rail and National Health Service (NHS) provided plenty of working opportunities for mostly those from Barbados and Jamaica, and though the government did not welcome their arrival, such was the labor needs required, they secured working opportunities for all but 12 of them. The rest were assigned work in essential industries nationally, such as in Gloucester and Scotland.

In the 10 years that followed the 1948 Windrush arrival, 125,000 Caribbean migrants voyaged to the UK. This was due to the devastation wreaked on Jamaica by the ferocious Hurricane Charlie on the 16th August 1951. 50,000 people were rendered homeless and 162 people died— electrocution through the falling of powerlines into floodwaters being one of the chief causes. Given subsistence was an issue prior to the raging storm, this event was a further imperative to leave the island.

Another contributory factor to the number of post-Windrush arrivals was the passing of the 1952 McCarran-Walter Act / Immigration Nationality Act which was the result of the US coming under domestic pressures to reduce its black population. The passing of the Act had the effect of imposing an annual limit of 800 West Indian arrivals—100 of which could be Jamaican. Prior to its passing it was reported that for every migrant who travelled to the UK, 9 migrated to the United States. This was facilitated by the generous British visa quota the US created—which included the Caribbean population—provided they could pass basic literacy and medical tests. The dramatic reduction in accessibility to US migration opportunities led to further waves of aspiring migrants looking towards the direction of the 'motherland.'

Though numbers of migrant workers to the UK dropped significantly in

1958 and 1959 to only 33,000 and 22,000 respectively, in 1960 the figures substantially increased to 58,000 and then more than doubled to 136,000 in 1961. From 1954 it appears there was a key turning point as the Home Secretary Gwylim Lloyd George, and some other Conservative ministers decided that the solution to their 'race problem' was to publicize the dangers of uncontrolled "coloured immigration". This incubation of a racialized 'hostile climate' was to attribute their immigration control policies to the attitudes of an illiberal public, though in reality this was more a case of projecting their own bigoted sentiments onto a public deemed to be too accommodating and liberal to initiate their own brand of racial hostility. This propagandistic move reflected prevailing sentiments. One sociologist at the time, Anthony Richmond, estimated in 1955 that one-third of the UK population could be said to be 'tolerant', one third mildly prejudiced, and one-third extremely prejudiced. Richmond, whilst not expecting much from the latter, believed that a "judicious educational campaign" on the part of the government could do much to give the lead against popular "bias and discrimination." Another academic, Michael Banton, recorded only 4 out of every 100 whites believed blacks to be "uncivilized," less than 10% believed mixing between people of different skin colors should be avoided. Though both academics acknowledged popular caution held by whites toward blacks, they believed initiatives would help broaden the understanding of the UK's colonial history and how such diverse peoples came to be in proximity with each other.

The potential for racial tolerance persisted into the 1960s. Though there were instances of racialized aloofness and confusion persisted, this was more to do with ignorance, and certain organizations sought to overcome this. One example of this was when 4 branch officers of the Trades Union Congress between 1954—1957 requested information to accommodate a more diverse labor force. Moreover, 8 out of 18 officers supported the rights of persons from the commonwealth countries; among these were officers from the Bournemouth and the Midland Regions. In a similar vein,

Shingfield and Bedford District Trades Councils condemned UK employers and Italian workers for operating a color bar against Jamaicans. Further support came in the shape of features in the *Daily Sketch* newspaper, which condemned a color bar in the midst of 300,000 unfilled vacancies, whilst the Economist branded the refusal of West Indians to access jobs as "an admission of both economic ineptitude and moral defeat". The publication described West Indians as an economic asset and ridiculed the notion that they were taking jobs and houses from natives of Britain as "a polite hypocrisy... a cover for some social problems." The Economist asserted that the real issue wasn't down to job limitations, but skin color. Both publications held that racial discrimination was due to social and economic practices after West Indians arrived, and not because of it; furthermore, they believed that a color bar in Britain would damage Commonwealth relations. This is understandable given the concomitant lobbying by Africans on the continent for independence, and the exposure of such actions in wider media would further play into Kwame Nkrumah's growing popularity, and thus strengthen Ghana's independence quest. In any case, the tidal wave of independence was acknowledged by UK Prime Minister Harold Macmillan, whose government moved to limit the potential political spillovers of violent confrontations in the Belgian [DR] Congo and Algeria. Macmillan gave his famous 'Wind of Change' Speech in 1960:

> The wind of Change is blowing through this continent
> and whether we like it or not, this growth of national
> consciousness is a political fact. We must all accept it as
> a fact, and our national policies must take account of it.

Macmillan's speech foreshadowed the independence of Ghana's West African neighbors Nigeria—which came later in the same year on October 1st, and Sierra Leone a year later in 1961. In East Africa, British Somaliland achieved independence in 1960, and Iain McLeod, the colonial secretary between 1959—1961, brought forward the original timetable of East

African independence for Tanganyika (Tanzania) in 1961, Uganda in 1962, and Kenya in 1963.

The Politics of Race and the Black British Diaspora

The UK Race Riots of the 1950s

The prolonged endeavors by the British government and policymakers to whip up racial tension inspired cleavages of civil unrest in 1958.

On Saturday 23rd August in St Ann's area of Nottingham, an innocuous discussion between a black man and white woman provoked a pub brawl which then escalated into a "major race riot." 90 minutes later once the riot had abated, over 1,000 whites had perpetrated violent attacks on West Indians—resulting in 8 of them being hospitalized. A week later in Notting Hill, a crowd of 400 whites armed with an array of homemade weapons, descended on black people—including their homes and businesses—for 2 successive nights. Blacks armed themselves and began to defend themselves on the third night, before the police drew the riots to an end and re-established order in the area. The response to this was of public hostility—reflected in the lead story in London's *Daily Express* on the 25th August 1958. The publication reported that bottles, knives, razors, and sticks had been drawn in a "pitched battle" on the streets of Nottingham, England, involving "Englishmen, West Indians, Pakistanis and African," going onto label it "one of the ugliest race riots ever known in Britain." *The Daily Gleaner's* 1st September publication and *The Times* 3rd September edition described the events of Notting Hill as "New Riot Terror", and "Renewed racial Disturbances in London" respectively. Whilst this event was privately considered a blow to ongoing efforts to stealthily limit 'colored' migration—which would be considered racist in light of the recent events, it was nevertheless an inflection point in the incubation of racial hostility. It was opportunistically presented as a breakdown in society and law and order, with the concern on racist treatment not so much a priority. What was particularly significant about the riots was the influence of American cultural colonialism, or alternatively—globalization, as it related to British white racist views held by many. This was evident when a local reporter covering the Notting Hill riots questioned one of the white rioters on the reasoning for attacking the "young West African student," Seymour Manning. The rioter's response was "just tell your readers that Little Rock learned us a lesson." The events of Little Rock, in the State of Arkansas, occurred in the Jim Crow segregation era. This saw the Arkansas governor reinforce segregation laws against young African-American children attending school—with the possibility of military force if necessary. This transpired on the 2nd September 1957—almost a year to the day of Seymour Manning being hunted down, and whilst media attention and the international community disapproved of the US's handling of racial segregation—given their global preeminent position, the way in which Black Americans were mistreated served to inspire bigotry across the Atlantic. PM Macmillan for the sake of public decorum officially condemned the "riots," denounced the violence, and upheld the right of British subjects of whatever skin color to walk the streets unmolested. However, he was more concerned with the inability to bring the riots within the control of the state, and rather opportunistically hoped that a coinciding increase in unemployment would provide justifiable grounds for suspending passport issuances to parts of the Commonwealth.

The Murder of Kelso Cochrane

The 1958 civil discordance also led to the racially-motivated murder of a former U.S. resident and Antiguan migrant, Kelso Cochrane, in the Notting Hill area. The murder shared parallels with the February 1991 and April 1993 racially-motivated murders of Rolan Adams and Stephen Lawrence respectively.

Cochrane's murder came at the hands of the Teddy Boys which was a movement influenced by Oswald Mosley's far-right Union Movement propaganda—very much pushing the narrative that West Indians were a problematic economic and socio-political presence. Cochrane had not long been released from hospital to treat a thumb fracture, when he met up with his girlfriend and younger brother before meeting his untimely end. When approached by the Daily Mail reporter, Arthur Cook, who was covering the story, a reluctant witness made his sentiments known *"If a coloured boy's been killed, that's one less of them, and it suits us. The whole 4,000 of them should be cleared out."* Unsurprisingly, the murder went unpunished despite several suspects being arrested.

24 hours after Cochrane's murder, the Committee of African Organizations held an emergency meeting in London which culminated in the writing of an open letter to PM Macmillan, which elucidated the influence of American racist popular culture. Referencing the Notting Hill Crime, it read that such developments "rival what we have seen at Little Rock or the recent lynching of Mr. M. C. Parker of Poplarville, Mississippi". Parker was a black man who had been conspicuously accused of raping a white woman. He had been abducted from his jail cell by white men in hoods, beaten severely and shot dead. A day later, a Labour MP, Barbara Castle, also made a connection with Cochrane's murder and the brutal deaths in British custody, 2 months prior, of Mau Mau rebels fighting colonial rule in Kenya by remarking: "If the British people are going to allow those responsible for the beating of 11 detainees to death in the Hola concentration camp in Kenya to go untraced and unpunished we shall have given the green light to every 'nigger-baiting' Teddy Boy in Notting Hill." MP Castle's contribution further supported the growing view on the role globalization played in harmonizing racist attitudes towards black people. Among the activists and campaigners applying political pressure was Amy Ashwood Garvey—the ex-wife of Marcus Garvey.

Whilst Cochrane's murder unfortunately went unpunished despite the murderer's identity reportedly being "an open secret" among locals, the racialized political climate within which it occurred was instrumental to the creation of the world renown Notting Hill Carnival (NHC). Originally established on 30th January 1959—following on from the 1958 Notting Hill race riots, it was utilized to address prevailing issues of structural violence by the Trinidadian radical activist and 'mother of the Caribbean Carnival in Britain' Claudia Jones. What initially took place as an indoor protest between 1959 and 1965 was taken to the streets of Notting Hill a year later in 1966 as a small street festival for local children who were attracted by Russell Henderson's steel bands.

As the annual event began to take shape, it symbolized a celebration of a shared Caribbean cultural identity within an affordable urban settlement, and its emblems included traditional masquerades, music and costumes. This was best encapsulated by another Carnival co-founder, Rhaune Laslett, who stated that the NHC's evolution to a street level event emerged through the motivation 'to prove that from our ghetto there was a wealth of culture waiting to express itself, that we weren't rubbish people.'

Against the celebratory cultural backdrop of the NHC were protests directed at poor housing conditions and the construction of the Westway flyover, which cut through the area. The NHC was a means through which these grievances could continue to be aired out, and though the Carnival in its nascent street-level form was inspired by the Black Trinidadian carnival, it increasingly became synonymous with Jamaicans. Though the UK enacted the 1962 Commonwealth Immigrants Act to restrict entry to persons from the Commonwealth and the 1972 Act, which applied further restrictions to holders of work permits, or people with UK-born parents or grandparents, and which also had the effect of stemming most Caribbean migration, the Jamaican presence nevertheless swelled to the extent it became the largest West Indian group in the UK by the 70s. Unabated hostility and antipathy directed at the West Indian community, however, particularly impacted the second-generation young people who were growingly feeling disaffected by their lived experiences in London and other parts of Britain. Recreationally and culturally, the predominance of Jamaicans during this period was expressed through the increased presence of big sound systems playing dancehall music, which was also emergent on the inner-city Kingston scene in Jamaica.

Much of the growing disaffection felt by the second-generation West Indian community coincided with Britain's economic turbulence during the 1970s and 1980s. Whereas the first set of West Indian migrants—many of whom came from regions with limited employment opportunities—were happy to take almost any work opportunities available, their children foreseeably compared their own prospects with their white counterparts with whom they schooled with. Industrial disputes involving unions foreshadowed a deep recession and rising unemployment which acutely impacted the African-Caribbean community. This was evident in the case of the second-generation school leavers who experienced unemployment 3—4 times greater than that of white school leaver counterparts. Finding themselves meeting resistance time and again in their attempts to assimilate into the mainstream society, they continued to face *contested citizenship*, and this was in no small part related to the criminalization of their image in the mainstream media following the 1958 Notting Hill riots.

Enoch Powell and 'The Rivers of Blood'

The spirit of hostility toward Britain's growing non-white presence—built up by British policymakers in the 1950s—transcended into the 1960s and beyond. Out of this milieu, opportunistic politicians, such as the Conservative MP, Peter Griffiths, were able to capitalize on it to further their own career ambitions. One way in which Griffiths achieved this was with his election campaign slogan 'If you want a nigger for a neighbour, vote Liberal or Labour.' It proved to be an effective strategy as it secured his 1964 electoral win in the Smethwick constituency. This not only provided the impetus for prior restrictions on colored migration, but also resentment from certain influential factions of society who saw their presence as synonymous with the decline in Empire. Another of Griffiths's political peers who left his own more prominent mark on British race relations history, was the Conservative MP and former Minister of Health, Enoch Powell. In his now-infamous 20th April 1968 'Rivers of Blood' speech—held at the

Birmingham Political Centre, Powell recounted a conversation with one of his middle-aged, working-class constituents during which the man remarked: "in this country in 15 or 20 years' time the black man will have the whip hand over the white man." Powell's sentiments, which weren't solely reflective of the first generation of migrants, but also their children, further went on to predict that African, Asian and mixed-race children in Britain were like 'the cloud no bigger than a man's hand that can so rapidly overcast the sky'. Powell's views reflected his position as a member of the Cabinet Commonwealth Migrants Committee which was instrumental in codifying the 1962 Commonwealth Immigrants Act. Though Powell was sacked from the shadow cabinet within 24 hours of his speech, its impact was far and widely resonant. Not only did he receive 110,000 letters—of which only 2,300 disapproved his speech, but a Gallup poll at the end of April reported that 74% agreed with him. Furthermore, within 4 days of Powell's dismissal, 2,000 London dock workers downed tools in protest at his sacking; a day later a 92-page petition of signatures—supportive of Powell—was submitted by Smithfield market meat porters.

Against the backdrop of Powell's sustained legislative debates over a second Race Relations Bill, a number of Powell supporters perpetuated a series of racist attacks—some of which were very serious—on black people in what has been described as one of the worst periods in UK history. The newspaper iconography of American racism and the KKK, and media coverage of Martin Luther King's murder by a white racist in Memphis, heavily influenced British racists who eerily erected and burned wooden crosses outside the homes of Black people.

The decision to sack Powell by his boss and future Prime Minister Edward Heath reflected the latter's aversion to the racist attitudes of several of his political contemporaries in the Conservative party that wanted to limit immigration. It is noteworthy that the Labour Party also shared similar sentiments to Conservatives with respect to immigration. To this end, it was Labour that also moved to further restrict migration in 1964 and 1968, not solely from the West Indies, but also East African Asians ironically fleeing from one hostile environment to another.

The Black British Civil Rights Movement

The spirit of disaffection impacted the second-generation such that many school leavers in the 1970s didn't take up vocational courses in the belief that their employment prospects would be bleak thereafter; others partook in resistance activity to improve their circumstances. To this end, the *British Black Panther Movement* (BBPM) was established by Black and South Asian activists in the summer of 1968. This development was inspired by certain British Broadcasting Channel (BBC) news coverage, Malcolm X's London 1964—65 visit and a 1967 Stokely Carmichael address given at the Dialectics of Liberation Congress at the Roundhouse venue in London. Recognizing the common ground shared by Black Britons and Americans, Obi Egbuna, a Biafran novelist, playwright, lawyer, and Imprisoned Black Power Leader, had previously traveled to the US where he "tramped the Black ghettos of the United States and delved into the soul of the grass roots." This groundwork inspired Egbuna to form the *Universal Coloured People's Association* (UCPA) in 1967 as a precursor to forming the BBPM.

Though it remains known by only small few, the BBPM were involved in 2 significant events during the early 1970s. One of these was on 2nd March 1970 when approximately 100 people protested outside the U.S. embassy in Grosvenor Square, London, in support of the U.S. Black Panther founder Bobby Seale, who was on trial for murder in New Haven, Connecticut. As the chant rang out—"Free Bobby!", protestors waved placards emblazoned with "Free Bobby Seale!" and "You Can Kill a Revolutionary but Not a Revolution," and Tony Thomas waved a Panther flag—prompting law enforcement to curtail their demonstrations. Claiming that "their joint actions amounted to a general threat to passers-by," the London Metropolitan Police arrested and charged a group of 16 protestors that day. The charges were issued on the grounds of threatening and assaulting police officers, distributing a flyer entitled "The Definition of Black Power," intending to incite a breach of the peace, and willful damage to a police raincoat. At trial, the judge dropped the raincoat charge and found 5 of the accused, named as "Black Panther Defendants," guilty of the remaining charges. The spirit of radicalism—instrumentally harnessed by Egbuna—attracted 778 new members who signed up to the UCPA in the first 7 weeks of the organization's existence. The UCPA's 14-page Panther credo included an objective to "explain to the British People what Black Power in [Britain] really [was] . . . [the] totality of the economic, cultural, political, and if necessary, military power which the black peoples of the world must acquire in order to get the white oppressor off their backs." It further read the Black Power advocates claimed to be "no initiators of violence. But if a white man lays his hand on one of us, we will regard it as an open declaration of war against all of us." Though a considerable degree of radicalism was evident in both the US Black Panther Party and the BBPM, the latter was arguably more radical than the former in at least one way: Egbuna was not welcoming of its US counterpart's relationships with the white Left and of the embrace of cultural nationalism, stating that "the 'White Marxists,' with their usual presumption that only they have read Marx, persist in deriding Black Power as narrow, nationalistic, and un-Marxian." He contended that the British Panthers should remain independent from sympathetic white liberals—claiming that they enjoyed a certain degree of security from the mainstream society. Whilst this position may have initially contrasted with the BBPM's US counterpart who viewed coalitions with whites as an essential component of their revolution, the BBPM eventually began to accept the support of some whites once they had also attained notoriety.

The Mangrove Nine

The other event of significance involving the BBPM was the *Mangrove Nine*. The Mangrove Restaurant, which was in Notting Hill, was the beating heart of the local West Indian community, as well as being a thriving nexus for activists and intellectuals from the surrounding area. Described by the late Darcus Howe—one of the *Nine*—as the "headquarters of radical chic," it was also concomitantly the target of considerable police attention from 1969 which seemingly sought its closure. The Mangrove was the subject of 12 drug raids in the space of 9 months, which led to protests a month later in August 1970 demanding "hands off the Mangrove". The subsequent outbreak of violence led to the arrests of 9 protestors including the restaurant owner, Frank Crichlow, Althea Jones Lecointe, and Howe. Though Howe unsuccessfully requested an all-black jury, all of the accused were acquitted on incitement charges, and 5 of the 9—including Crichlow and Howe, were acquitted on all charges at their 1971 trial. Howe, who had also been an attendee of the NHC for many years, and had in 1971 found the Renegades Steel band, eventually became the Chair of the Carnival Development Committee (CDC) in April 1977. Whilst the *Mangrove Nine* were widely considered to have "turned the fight against police racism into a *cause célèbre*," another event took place later in the 70s which arguably increased tensions with the authorities; this transpired at the NHC in 1976. A year previously, the carnival had been policed by 60 officers, but this rose to 1,200 Bobbies the following year, and scuffles with Black youth subsequently ensued. This was a 'watershed in the history of conflict between blacks and the police', and it provided the ammunition to further reinforce the myth of 'Black collective criminality'.

The War on Drugs and 'Sus Laws'—UK Edition

The largely slanderous and virulent media critiques which followed the events of the NHC in 1976 were seemingly timely. The Misuse of Drugs Act 1971 (MDA) had come into force due to one of the goals of American cultural imperialism to criminalize 'illicit' drug use—both domestically and globally. Whereas Britain's traditional approach to drug addiction had been to treat habitual users as patients first and control addictions through health consultation and legal prescriptions, the US's *War On Drugs* became codified in 1961 by way of the United Nations (UN) Single Convention on Narcotic Drugs. As the subsequent moral panic set in, the UK authorities—almost in copy and paste mode—drew inspiration from their US counterpart's copybook. A few decades previously, a certain Harry J Anslinger was appointed head of the US Federal Bureau of Narcotics (FBN) in 1930 during a time when alcohol prohibition was being repealed. Ainslinger enthusiastically embraced his mandate—embarking on a manipulative, comprehensive media and political campaign, and also set in motion an enduring influence which transcended his 32 years at the helm of the FBN.

Subsumed within Anslinger's campaign was race baiting. He whipped up hysteria by incessantly playing on racial fear and prejudice by linking cannabis to Hispanic people, cocaine to African-Americans and heroin to the Chinese. More vividly, he characterized Chinese men as having a 'liking for the charms of Caucasian girls' and using opium to force them into 'unspeakable sexual depravity.' He claimed an increase in drug addiction was 'practically 100 percent among Negro people' who apparently partied with white women, 'getting their sympathy with stories of racial persecution'—the result of which it was claimed was pregnancy. The British resented the heavy-handed US approach and did their best to undermine it and thus uphold their own traditions. This sentiment was captured in a lamentation by a British delegate at the UN Commission on Narcotic Drugs that had it not been 'for the white drug problem in the USA,' other nations would have been left to their own drug-administrative discretions.

To further underscore the level of force applied to the Drug War by the US, the 1961 convention has the distinction of being the only convention in the history of the UN to use the word 'evil'. 'Addiction to narcotic drugs constitutes a serious evil for the individual and is fraught with social and economic danger to mankind'. Significantly, torture, apartheid and nuclear war are not described in these terms. Genocide is referred to in UN documents as an 'odious scourge' or 'barbarous acts,' but never as actually 'evil'. That the UN, founded in the ashes of the world war and the Holocaust, finds drug addiction the only phenomenon worthy of this word, is testament to just how heavily American moralizing pressure was exerted on others.

It was against this global political backdrop and fractious community-police relations that the Brixton Police launched *Operation Swamp 81* in April 1981, flooding the area with police officers, making close to 1,000 stop and searches of predominantly young black men over a 6-day period. Brixton, which was initially an early 20th century South London suburb for the emergent middle-class, had become one of the most deprived areas by the 1970s, and the media had made it a synonym of poverty, violence, and criminality. It was home to Britain's largest Afro-Caribbean community—and in a similar vein to Notting Hill and other urban areas—had its fair share of struggles with integrating its second generation into the mainstream society. The war on drugs was weaponized by the local Police against mostly teenage and young black men who to varying degrees experienced police beatings as a 'rite of passage'. Spurious pretexts of robbery and drug dealing were deployed to make arbitrary arrests, and the Suspicious Persons Act, or 'SUS' laws from the 1824 Vagrancy Act, provided the 'legal' latitude with which to inconvenience young black men. The ease with which the police could also search black residents' houses—turning them upside down in the name of questionable drug searching, also instilled tension between the second generation and the typically, quiet, unassuming and church-attending first generation of African-Caribbean migrants.

Eventually the pressure-cooker-like tension exploded in the form of the 1981 Brixton riots, and this pattern was replicated across the British inner cities of Toxteth in Liverpool in the same year, as well as cleavages in Manchester and Birmingham. Rather curiously, despite the high volume of arrests for nominal cannabis possession, which was foundational in criminalizing the young black men of Brixton, the subsequent 255 page-long report by Lord Scarman assessing the wider reasons behind the riots, failed to mention cannabis usage once. The breakdown in trust between the

Brixton community and local police from the 1970s marked the onset of the [heavily politicized] British War on Drugs.

Further Political Events During the 1980s

Among the political events of the 1980s was the New Cross Fire / massacre of 1981 which was a suspected racist arson attack at 439 New Cross Road. It was at this address on Sunday 18th July 1981 that Yvonne Ruddock had been celebrating her 16th birthday. As the evening progressed a fire broke out which resulted in 13 of the partygoers being burned to death, which included Ruddock; one of the survivors committed suicide 2 years later.

The suspicions of foul play were not without validity given it came in the wake of a string of racist arson attacks in South-East London. Due to the deafening silence in the way of empathy, justice or satisfactory inquest, the largest demonstration by Black people in British history took place on a weekday as 20,000 marched on parliament chanting 'blood a go run, if justice na come'. As noted by Akala, it proved to be prophetic, not only in terms of the foregoing riots, but others including another in Brixton in 1985 due to the shooting and paralyzing of Cherry Groce; another riot also took place just a week later in Broadwater Farm Housing Estate in Tottenham, North London, due to the death of Cynthia Jarret which transpired during a police raid on her home. Handsworth in Birmingham—like Brixton, also had a second riot in the same year, and riots in Chapeltown in Leeds also took place in 1981 and 1987 respectively.

The riots were concomitant with the rise in unemployment by 1982 to over 3.5 million people—the first time it had reached this point since the 1930s. Furthermore, UK unemployment averaged 9.1% between 1979 and 1989, occasioning attendant racism, discrimination, homelessness, and oppressive policing which acutely affected the scapegoated Afro-Caribbean community. This was reflected by the estimated black youth unemployment rate of 55% during this era of recession. What further compounded the issue was the enduring, adverse educational experiences dating back to the 1960s and the consequences thereof. Their perceived 'educational sub-normality' led to demands from the parents of white children to have separate classes—thereby avoiding 'coloured' children and the possible retardation of their offspring's' progress. This led to the 'solution' by the Department of Education and Science (DES) to 'spread the children;' it was recommended that schools should not have more than one-third of its total number of pupils from immigrant backgrounds—though this recommendation was not universally mandated. Though there was an arguably useful recommendation from the DES in 1973 to establish school programs which identified the needs of black children in English schools, it did not widely take root, but contrarily, the caricature of the black 'immigrant scrounger' impeded any official understanding of institutionalized marginalization or xenophobia.

The Arts and Youth Identity Formation: 1970s—1990s

The Black British demographic has significantly contributed to the arts since the formation of the *New Diaspora*. For many of the first and early second generation West Indian community, the 1970s saw the broadcast of independent films, such as *Pressure*, which told the story of the first-generation willing to accept white rule and second-class status—in direct contrast to the second generation that sought more parity with their white peers. This film was insightful as to the polarizing views on survival held by 2 siblings; one sibling immerses himself in the black power movement, whereas another actively attempts to assimilate into the white mainstream society.

In what may retrospectively be considered a predictable pattern, many of the film and theatre productions either portrayed stories of West Indian settler experiences or covered historical events which were a source of pride throughout the African diaspora. One example of the latter was the production of the *Haitian Revolution, The Black Jacobins*—put on by the Jamaican-born Yvonne Brewster. Brewster drew on inspiration derived from the Trinidadian historian, CLR James's writing on the topic. The 1977 film, *Black Joy*—which featured the late *Desmonds* TV show's British-

364

Guyanese protagonist, Norman Beaton, was entered into the Cannes Film festival of the same year. The diasporic connections are evident through the fictional story of a young naive man from the Guyanese countryside, Ben Jones, who relocates to Brixton, South London, in the pursuit of a better life, only to find himself scammed by a 'good Samaritan', thwarting an attempted robbery of his belongings, and the ways of his fraudulent landlord. Nevertheless, Ben develops street wisdom, loses his virginity—signifying a rite of passage, and in addition, the film also features the topic of abortion, which was very much a taboo subject at the time. The influence of African-American popular culture is also evident in this Black British production, as the likes of Aretha Franklin and Gladys Knight & The Pips provided soundtrack music.

The 1970s music scene featured the reggae subgenre of *Lover's Rock*, which was popular among West Indian youth and an apolitical alternative to conscious Rastafarian music of that time. Drawing on the soothing sounds of Philadelphian and Chicagoan soul, music from the Jamaican rocksteady 1960s era, and reggae bassline rhythms, artists such as Carroll Thompson and Louisa Mark, birthed a distinctive female sound, proving popular among many of South London's young women. Hits such as *Loving Kind*, *Waiting*, and *Black Is Our Colour* were emblematic of the Black British youths' quest for self-love, recreational fun and a feel-good factor.

For many of the UK's black youth, music was at the core of identity construction during the 1970s and 80s. The Brixton record stores were a bubbling hive of music enthusiasts scanning the latest releases, or dance and social spots where the best sound systems were present. During an era in which many found themselves unwaged, deskilled—and in many cases—unemployable, black youth culture became a mediation between the experiences and lives of young people, yet also instilled in them a consciousness which emphasized their structural subordination in society. Neighborhoods with a densely populated West Indian community were safe havens for black youth cultural expression. The "rude boy" image was seen by some as symbolic of the hustler from the Jamaican ghettos. Emulating or embracing the stereotypes of living outside of the system, gambling, selling dope and / or pimping was a visible rejection of the white world of wage labor. For others, the Rastafarian movement, and its emblems appealed, such was its biblical metaphors, rejection of white supremacy, opposition to capitalism, resistance to injustices and survival.

Much like the economic adversities their UK counterparts faced, US Black communities were very adversely impacted by the implementation of President Reagan's *Reaganomics* supply-side policies from 1980 onward. These included cuts in 1982 of 20% to Summer Youth Employment Program, the removals in 1981 of Comprehensive Education Training Act (CETA) and Public Service appointment programs—all of which served the economically disadvantaged, and the unemployed by providing local government-subsidized jobs with a view to these being replaced by future private sector [unsubsidized] jobs. The significance of this was that the black unemployment rate, which was usually twice that of their white counterparts, had reached 15.2% relative to the whites' 6.2% by 1990; furthermore in some parts of the US, the unemployment rate was 50% for black young men between the ages of 16—19, which meant that the removal of such programs left these young men with skills and CV gaps which in turn, meant that Reagan's hopes of the private sector absorbing these men, did not materialize.

Hip hop groups arose out of these circumstances and attracted swathes of young people across the US and in the UK. One of the groups to emerge in this milieu was Public Enemy, which formed out of New York City (NYC) in the mid-1980s, and which meshed the hard-hitting style of another group, Run DMC, with lyrical material which reflected the adverse effect of politicking on the black youth. Indeed, the choice of name *Public Enemy*, was based on "underdog love and their developing politics," and cleavages of racially-motivated murder, police brutality and propaganda weaponized against black young men in NYC—giving rise to the idea that "the black man is definitely the public enemy." On the West Coast in Compton, California, *Niggaz With Attitude* (NWA) launched themselves on the hip-hop scene with 3 tracks which reflected the rising anger of the urban youth. The most memorable track from their debut album *Straight Outta Compton*, "Fuck tha Police," was a protest against police brutality, racial profiling, and another influential track—"Gangsta Gangsta" was prototypical in forming the consensus global view of the inner-City youth. NWA was a pioneer of the gangsta-rap subgenre and one of the most influential in hip-hop history. Their politically-charged material led to over 10 million records sales in the US alone, a conspicuous letter of disapproval from the FBI, censorship for a period in Australia, and a platform for the likes of the future *Death Row Records* producer, Andre "Dr Dre" Brown to advance his career in the industry. Furthermore, the reclamation of the term "nigger" in radical hip-hop culture by both Public Enemy and NWA was also invariably influential on UK black youth, who like their US counterparts, employed it as a term of affection and abuse among each other.

In addition to the foregoing music genres, black youth also watched Black family sitcoms. One of these was *The Cosby show* which was based around the memorable Huxtable family. Their New York upper middle-class status, polished image and uprightness appealed to Black Americans and Black Brits, both of whom admired the show's matriarch, Clair Huxtable, who was a high-flying attorney, and adopted the Doctor Cliff Huxtable's character as a father figure; indeed for Akala and many of his peers he was like a surrogate figure redolent of a West-Indian grandfather. Despite the comedic nature of the sitcom, the show addressed sensitive and serious issues such as Cliff's son, Theo's, associated challenges with dyslexia, and the teen pregnancy of his daughter, Denise's friend, Veronica.

Another popular sitcom centered on a black family was *Desmond's.* The show ran for 6 seasons from 1989—1994 and was the first time a show of its kind featured on British TV. Desmond Ambrose—the show's main character played by Norman Beaton, was the Ambrose family patriarch, and owner of an eponymous barbershop in the South London district of Peckham. The show's appeal was the aspirational nature of the characters, for example, Desmond's son Sean was a confident, intelligent young man who was concomitantly a skilled rapper and computer whizz who later went on to attend university; and his daughter passionately pursued her fashion design dreams. Another key feature of the show was the heart-warming lifelong friendship between Desmond and Augustus—more commonly referred to as *Porkpie*, and the role of Matthew, the eternal student from Gambia, who could be relied upon to reel off one African proverb after another. Light-hearted banter was ever-present among all 3 of them and especially memorable was the teasing of Matthew, the latter of whom had a penchant for the proverbial opening: "There's an Old African saying. . ."

As abovementioned, musical influences from America were very dominant and ever-present, however the tail-end of the 1980s saw the emergence of more Black British musical art with a global reach. Among the many popular musical acts were *Jazzie B* and *Soul II Soul*. Their song *Keep On Moving* was notable for its diasporic collaboration having been produced in the UK by the offspring of Caribbean settlers, then subsequently remixed in a Jamaican dub format in the United States by an African-American, Teddy Riley. This diasporic connection was also evident when both they and NWA—the latter promoting their *Straight Outta Compton* Album in the UK—shared the same performance space at the Brixton Nightclub *The Fridge*, which combined British Caribbean, African and African-American influences. The Lyrics from Soul II Soul's *Get A Life*:

> So there it is, work it out yourself,
> Yeah be Selective, be objective
> Be an asset to the collective,
> 'Cause you know you've got to Get A Life;

And *Feeling Free*:

Well take a look up, take a glance
At the Alternative
Of what you have to give
And put that in the way you want to live
Your life. . .

had universal appeal across Britain's black youth. This was reflected in *Sky Magazine's* September 1989 edition, in which one of their writers had observed: *"young black men were onto the dancefloor with a proprietorial air"*. Among the superlatives deployed were *"an explosion of new black pride,"* and perhaps more emphatically, *"'a cultural black explosion', an assertion of a culture and identity that had been hitherto largely ignored, or positively denied."*

Black UK and US Demographic Transformations And Identity Formation—From the 1990s to the 2020s

The Rationale for the British Census

The British Census is conducted with the authority of the Census Act 1920. Though the Act specifies that 'Nationality, birthplace, *race* and language' may be part of the census, the 1991 census was the first in which a question on ethnic group was included.

Britain has recorded the nationality of people living in the country, and their country of origin since 1841 as it has always received immigrants from elsewhere. When in the 1950s there began an influx of people from other continents—mainly from the West Indies, East Africa, and Asia—there was nothing historically unique about this event, except for the important fact that, unlike most of their predecessors, these later immigrants were clearly distinguishable from the indigenous population by the color of their skin(s).

Information collected from [pre-1991 and up to the present] sample surveys has shown that blacks and Asians in Britain tend to have higher levels of unemployment, less well-paid jobs, and poorer housing conditions than other groups and that their children have greater difficultly in realizing their full educational potential at school.

For these reasons and because of the need to measure the extent to which equal opportunity programs have been effective in reducing inequalities resulting from discriminatory practices, it has been deemed necessary by the British Government to obtain information about, Black, Asian, and other ethnic minorities at regular intervals.

The census is the most important statistical operation in Britain. It collects information about every person in the country and produces a wide range of essential information for government, commerce, and industry. This also influences the expenditure budgets set for local authorities to meet schooling, housing, roads / infrastructure, and other vital services.

Moreover, the resources allocated to health authorities are calculated based on figures provided by the census.

While in 1971 the Office of Population Censuses and Surveys (OPCS) relied on parents' birthplaces as indicator of ethnicity, it became evident that it was flawed, given that by this point many white people were born in India, and many East African births were of Asian descent. Moreover, the projected increases from that point onward in the UK black population would render birthplace as an indicator even less reliable of one's ethnic group. To this end, the local authorities in England and Wales were given access to funding of over £100 million annually (under section 11 of the Local Government Act, 1966) to support ethnic minorities.

Britain considered how other countries conducted their census, especially those which had culturally diverse populations. In some countries such as Canada, the emphasis is on the country from which a person's ancestors are thought to have originated. In other places (such as India) people are distinguished by religion and language, or caste/tribe. Elsewhere, such as in the U.S. and Caribbean, the population is classified by a variety of criteria, including skin color, national origin, language, and culture. Given the variation between these countries' methods, the United Nations (United Nations Economic and Social Council, 1977), though recommending the collection of data on ethnic group in national census, has concluded that there is no universally acceptable criteria for classifying a nation's population; therefore, discretion is to employed, thus Britain determined that race-related ethnic categories would furnish them with better a understanding of their increasingly diverse population. However, this has not been without its criticisms, as if the purported rationale for the census is to surmount conscious or unconscious bias, by employing this method, it is inevitable that opposite outcome(s) would be realized—at least in many instances.

Several experiments in the form of field trials were introduced from

1975 to determine how responsive Britain's population would be to disclosing their ethnic identities. Of the 4 tests conducted from 1975—77, West Indians felt it was inappropriate to describe British-born people as coming from their non-British-born ancestors' place(s) of origin. A 1979 field trial was carried out in the London Borough of Haringey in conjunction with a full-scale census test to rehearse arrangements for the 1981 census. About 75%—or 56,000 households were asked to fill the survey. This was impacted by local organizations' campaigns discouraging prospective respondents from disclosing *ethnicity*, *birthplace*, and *parents' countries of birth* categories. The rationale for discouraging cooperation was on the grounds that disclosing such data was linked with the ongoing proposals to change nationality laws in a manner that would jeopardize the status of all ethnic minority groups in Britain. The position was vindicated by the passing of the British Nationality Act of 1981—further restricting non-white immigration.

Resultantly, only 54% responded, whereas the usual response rates for such surveys were 70%. Only 14% of West Indian households contacted answered the race/ethnicity question correctly, and only 19% gave complete answers to questions on their parents' countries of birth. Additionally, the number of people who objected in principle to questions on ethnic group also rose to unprecedented levels—32% of Black and Asian survey respondents, and the rate for objections to the parents' birthplace question was 37%.

Ultimately, the government attempted to overcome objections to racial disclosures and accommodate the preferences of West Indian respondents by adding another category to the census classification specifically for Afro-Caribbeans [and later Africans] born in Britain: 'Black British___'. In this sense, Britain chose to emulate the use of the term 'black' in their census as the US and other countries in the Caribbean had done so. It was deemed that this would record persons of African descent more effectively and be compatible with the use of the word 'white' to describe people of European origin.

Black Britain

Though the black UK population is broadly referred to as *The Black Community*, governmental bodies—such as the *Office for National Statistics* (ONS), group its data into 3 subcategories: *Black African-Caribbean*, *Black African* and *Black Other*.

According to the 2021 Census, the Black population total for England and Wales is 2.4 million. This figure has broadly grown each decade from when the *black* category was introduced in the 1991 census. The 1991 black population total was 891,000, the 2001 census reported it had grown to 1.14 million and reached 1.9 million in 2011.

The *African-Caribbean* segment are mostly the descendants of the Windrush generation, whose trajectory has been chronicled earlier in this section from the 1940s up to the present. At the time of the 1991 census, their demographic stood at 500,000, at 564,000 in 2001, 595,000 in 2011 and 623,000 in 2021.

The African segment arrived in nominal numbers at the same time as the earliest arrivals of the Windrush generation, though their numbers began to increase considerably from the 1980s onward. In 1991, they totaled 212,000, in 2001 it was 480,000, in 2011 it was 990,000 and in 2021 it reached 1.5 million.

The *Black Other* segment totaled 178,000 in 1991, 96,000 in 2001, 280,000 in 2011, and 300,000 in 2021. It is important to note that the decline to 96,000 in 2001 from 178,000 in 1991 is the result of how data was collated for the 2001 census, and it is noteworthy that the 2001 census was the first time *Mixed White-African* and *Mixed White-Caribbean* ethnic options were made available. While in the 1991 Census respondents could identify with the black ethnic categories or declare themselves *other*, in 2001 they could identify as *Mixed*. 692,000 people (more than 1% of the population) identified collectively as *mixed white-black* and *other* in 2001, of which 46%—or 316,000 accounted for the mixed white and black demographic. It is also important to note concomitantly that persons identifying as [broadly] *other* in 1991 declined from 290,000 to 229,000 in 2001.

The British African sub-demographic garnered attention due to increasing by over 130% between 1991 and 2001, and while the growth rate between 2001 and 2011 was lower at 106%, the figure in absolute terms more than doubled and still had the highest growth rate out of all other ethnic groups. 38% of this growth occurred through natural increase (reproduction rate), and 62% was the result of net-migration for England and Wales. Between 2011 and 2021, it recorded its lowest growth rate of 50%, even though there was an increase from 990,000 to 1.5 million in overall figures.

The British Afro-Caribbean sub-demographic grew by 13% between 1991 and 2001, little over 5% between 2001 and 2011, and 5% between 2011 and 2021. These nominal growth rates over the course of 4 decades are due to a lower reproduction rate than their African counterparts. It is noteworthy that whereas the Caribbean population has grown from less than 30,000 in 1951, it has not moved far from half a million since the 1970s.

There are other contributory factors for the nominal growth. One is that Caribbean movement closely followed the demand for labor in Britain and came to an effective halt after the economic crisis caused by the 1973 Yom Kippur War / oil crisis. A second factor is that the Caribbean population represents a classic assimilation case. It is very anglicized in terms of mostly coming from English-speaking, Christian backgrounds, and being raised in a British educational system. The Caribbean population's trajectory has been a classic assimilatory one, albeit a segmented assimilatory pattern into the white working-class; nowadays it has low rates of residential segregation and has high rates of mixed marriage unions with the white population. Another assimilation proxy is that where the Black Caribbean population, as abovementioned, grew 5% between 2001 and 2011, the Mixed White-Black Caribbean population grew by 80%—from 237,000 to 427,000; and by 20%—or from 427,000 to 513,000 between 2011 and 2021.

Given that there is an inevitability that the number of British people with one sole Black Caribbean grandparent and the remaining 3 being white would have increased in recent years, this development—which is a further assimilative indicator for the Caribbean population—may at least partly have been recorded in the *mixed other* ethnicity category which grew by 86%—or from 156,000 to 290,000 between 2001 and 2011, and 61%—or from 290,000 to 467,000 between 2011 and 2021.

The 2021 Census also allowed for Black British Africans to disclose the specific country they have roots in: Nigerians—276,000, Somalis/Somalilanders—196,000, and Ghanaians—115,000 were the 3 largest subgroups on record. However, it is possible that the true figures are higher than officially recorded as under the *African Unspecified* category there are 614,000 people. It may well be that some within the latter figure may either identify with a more specific ethnic group or region in their forbearers' countries of origin; or they may view themselves as being on the path of assimilation but may not fully have identified as *Black British* at the time of submitting their responses.

Of the 2021 Black UK population total, approximately 1.37 million live in London, which is 18% of the city's population. The 10 boroughs with the highest number of black residents are: Croydon (88,000, 23% of the Borough's total), Lewisham (80,000, 27%), Southwark (77,000, 25%), Lambeth (76,000, 24%), Greenwich (61,000, 21%), Newham (61,000, 17%), Enfield (61,000, 18%), Brent (56,000, 16%) (Hackney (55,000, 24%), and Barking and Dagenham (47,000, 21%).

The largest populations outside of London are: Birmingham (126,000, 11%), Manchester (66,000, 12%), Leeds (45,000, 6%), Nottingham (32,000, 9%), Leicester (29,000, 8%), Bristol (28,000, 6%), Luton (22,000, 10%), and Wolverhampton (25,000, 9%).

Black US [Recent Immigrant] Population

The migration of Africans to the US substantially increased due to the lifting of quotas stipulated by the Immigration and Nationality Act 1965 / Hart-Celler Act—which amended The Immigration and Nationality Act 1952 (also known as the McCarran-Walter Act). Significantly, this passage of legislation also made accommodations for the intake of refugees, as well as allowances for the non-US citizen family members US of citizens' and residents' to be able to join them in the US.

According to a report by the Black Alliance for Just Immigration (BAJI), people from Jamaica, Haiti and the Dominican Republic began moving to the United States in greater numbers during the 1960s in response to national and geopolitical changes such as Jamaica's independence from the UK in 1962, the brutal Duvalier dictatorship in Haiti, or the civil war and subsequent invasion of the Dominican Republic. One out of three Black immigrants are from Jamaica or Haiti, and around 42% of Caribbean immigrants arrived in the U.S. before 1990.

On the other hand, though the Caribbean has historically been the largest source of Black immigrants to the US, African migration has increased by 246% since 1999—2000. Of the approximately 2 million Black African immigrants now estimated to be in the U.S., 69% of Black immigrants arrived prior to 2009, and 31% over the subsequent decade.

According to American Community Survey (ACS) data, there were 816,000 Black immigrants in the United States in 1980. These figures were further swelled by way of The Diversity Visa Program / green card lottery, which arose from the Immigration Act of 1990 which facilitated lawful migration. Africans as of 2013 submit the highest number of applications, and an estimated 19,000 African-born migrants are awarded visas annually which is 38% of the total 50,000 annual award.

By 2000, the number of Black immigrants stood at 2.4 million. As of 2019, Black immigrants now account for nearly 10% of the nation's black population at 4.6 million people. Within this group, the number of African immigrants has seen a significant increase: There were approximately 574,000 African immigrants in the US in 2000, and by 2019, that number had more than tripled to over 1.9 million. Furthermore, 9% of the total U.S. black population, or 4.1 million Black Americans were born in the US and have at least one foreign-born parent. The combined total is 8.3 million, or 18% of the entire Black American population as of 2019.

According to Pew Research Center the number of Black immigrants may increase to near 10 million by 2060.

Black immigrants tend to live in highly concentrated regions of the U.S. The top 7 states with the highest Black immigrant populations are: New York — 856,000, Florida — 713,000, Texas — 276,000, New Jersey — 223,000, Maryland — 225,000, Massachusetts — 188,000, and California — 179,000.

Nigerians, Ghanaians, Zimbabweans, Sierra Leoneans, Rwandan, Congolese, Somalis, Eritreans, Ethiopians, Kenyans, Ugandans, Sudanese, Cape Verdeans (the U.S. specifically) comprise most of the contemporary African migrations to both the US and the UK.

Migration flows have been attributed to a wide variety of reasons: from the more propitious factors such as filling key skill job positions, professional opportunities, teaching, academic roles professorships, and for business reasons. At the other end of the scale are civil wars; state failures; unfavorable economic circumstances; and refugee / asylum cases due to genocide / ethnic cleansings, political exile, and political volatility / insecurity.

The Evolution of a 'Black British' Identity

Since at least the 1990s, a broader *Black British* identity has emerged, which predominantly comprises the Afro-Caribbean, and African populations, along with, to a lesser extent, *Black others* from countries such as Brazil and Colombia. This identity is largely the result of being housed and schooled in proximity to each other—notably in the London Boroughs of Croydon,

Lewisham, Lambeth, Hackney, and Enfield; socializing in similar spaces, both online and offline; and the consumption of black popular culture—especially from the US. As of the recent 2021 census, there are 19,000 declared (though this figure may be higher than reported) British Africans and Afro-Caribbean that identify as *Mixed Black*. In other words, those who have parents with roots in more than one country—combinations of which may be: *half Nigerian-half Ghanaian, half Jamaican-half Nigerian, half Barbadian/Bajan-half Sierra Leonean, half Grenadian-half Trinidadian*, and so forth; moreover, some have roots in more than 2 countries / islands. When this figure of 19,000 is added to those who identify solely as Black British, there are 216,000 people that identify as a product of Black British coalescence.

Another evident marker of this black identity coalescence is the emergence of what this author calls *London Creole English* (*LCE*). *LCE*—which is variously known as *Multicultural London English* (*MLE*) and *Black British English* (*BBE*)—is a dialect spoken by both British African and African-Caribbean people in mostly informal settings. *LCE* is the product of English slang words, cockney inflections, words from [predominantly] Creole / Jamaican patois—which is attributable to the earlier waves of Jamaican arrivals, and the odd word from the West African pidgin / creole dialects; and Yoruba, Ga, and Arabic languages. *LCE's* popularity has been so wide-reaching that it is now also spoken by several non-black people. Furthermore, the informal speech patterns of many British Black people in Birmingham, swathes of the Midlands, Leeds, Bristol, Manchester, Luton, Cardiff and so forth also bear parallels with LCE, albeit predominantly Jamaican patois words and inflections.

In the US, both the African and Caribbean immigrants—especially the second generation, have invariably adopted the *African-American Vernacular English* (AAVE) spoken by many African-Americans. Variants of this dialect—including what has been commonly termed *Ebonics*—have been influenced by British English dialects spoken many centuries ago, in addition to grammatical structures, pronunciation methods, and tense usage drawn from the West and West-Central African Niger-Congo language tree. AAVE is spoken by both working-class and middle-class African-Americans.

Black Popular culture: 1990s—2020s

'Black' Popular culture has been instrumental to the development of UK and US black identities. In the UK, London-originated *garage, drum and bass, jungle,* and *dubstep* music genres have long been produced by artists and producers of Caribbean and African heritage. For example, *Grime* music emerged in the early 2000s and is the product of influences from *jungle, dancehall,* and *hip hop.* It has been pioneered by artists from both African and Afro-Caribbean backgrounds such as *Wiley* (Trinidadian & Antiguan); *Skepta* (Nigerian: Igbo / Yoruba); *Dizzee Rascal* (both Ghanaian and Nigerian); *Lethal* Bizzle (Ghanaian); *Chipmunk, Wretch 32,* and *Kano* (pronounced 'Kane-O' (all three are of Jamaican backgrounds)); *Ghetts* (Jamaican and Grenadian); and *Akala* (Jamaican, Scottish and Scots-Irish), among others. Due to globalization, the Black UK population is also a significant consumer of African-American genres such as Hip hop and R&B (Rhythm & Blues) as much as—if not more than—its own homegrown music.

Another influential music genre which emerged in late-2012 on the Brixton, South London scene is *Drill,* which was imported from the Chicagoan South Side. Such has been its popularity in the UK, the American roots of the genre haven't always been discernible to much of its UK fanbase. Among the newer generations—millennials and generation-Zs—of the diaspora there has been the emergence of transnational connections in the form of *Afrobeat, Afro-pop* and *Afro-fusion* music from artists such as *Burna Boy, Wizkid,* which have gained popularity among UK and US blacks, in addition to swathes of the African continent.

Whereas the US has its *BET* (Black Entertainment Television) and *Soul Train* Awards, the UK has the long-standing "Music of Black Origin" *MOBO* awards

Show which was launched in November 1996 and recognizes music from not just the UK, but across the African diaspora—the US, Brazil, and the Caribbean.

US Comedy from black comedians such as *Dave Chapelle* is just as popular with the Black populaces either side of the Atlantic—in the UK even more so than any of its domestic equivalents. *Netflix* has been a key medium for making US-produced art available to UK audiences, which has familiarized them with—in addition to cinematic platforms—the likes of *Denzel Washington*, *Samuel L. Jackson*, as much as it has its US audiences. And the chords of artistic familiarity have been deepened through Black British actors and actresses: *Idris Elba*, *John Boyega*, *Damson Idris*, *Daniel Kaluuya*, *Chiwetel Ejiofor*, *Joseph Patterson*, *Letitia Wright*, and *Naomie Harris* are some of many artists to prolifically feature in Hollywood productions.

Furthermore, the marvel film series *Black Panther* and *Black Panther: Wakanda Forever* has also proven popular on both sides of the Atlantic. The regal clothing / headpiece worn by Queen Ramonda (played by American actress, *Angela Bassett*) of the fictional African nation *Wakanda* is redolent of the Egyptian Queen headpiece worn by the Somali-American supermodel *Iman* in the music video for Michael Jackson's 1991 single *Remember the Time*. Moreover, *Eddie Murphy* also featured as an Egyptian King alongside *Iman*, and such portrayals of black royalty resonated with many African-Americans and black diasporans who appreciated it as a rare display of black royalty on TV. The other notable display of black royalty was in the 1988 film *Coming to America*, which also featured Eddie Murphy as crown prince of the fictional African kingdom of *Zamunda*. It is inevitable that these regal images were a welcome change from the more controversial Alex Haley's *Roots* which portrayed Black people as slaves on TV for the first time.

Religion

There are 34 million Black Christians (72% of the African-American population of 47 million) in the US. Of this figure, 16.5 million are Evangelical Protestants, 13.2 million are non-Evangelical Protestants, and 3.3 million are Catholics. The next highest demographic is listed as *unaffiliated* (atheism, agnostic, irreligious and so on) which totals 10 million. Jehovah's Witnesses total no more than 470,000; and there is approximately 700,000 in total that identify as either Latter-day Saints, Orthodox Christians, Jews, or Hindus. Furthermore, there is also nominal adherence to *Black Hebrew Israelite* dogma.

As the 2021 UK census left religion as a voluntary question, it has advised that previous data, such as that collected from the ONS—either from the 2011 census or ONS reports prior to the 2021 census—are reasonably accurate. Therefore, as of 2011, there are 691,000 Black Christians, 207,000 Black Muslims, 57,000 chose not to disclose their faith 28,000 declared irreligiosity, 1,800 are Hindu, 1,560 declared other religion, 933 are Buddhists, 618 are Jewish, and there are 554 Sikhs.

Both the US and UK black populaces also practice Pentecostalism, Charismatic Christianity, and prosperity dogmas, and regularly attend places of worship such as *Mountain of Fire and Miracle Ministries* (MFM), *Redeemed Christian Church of God* (RCCG), Cherubim and Seraphim, Christ Embassy, and the Seventh Day Adventists among others.

There are UK and US Nation of Islam chapters of which the latter has a membership in the range of 20—50,000.

Political Participation

In the political arena, the UK has elected many politicians as Members of Parliament (MPs) from both African and West Indian backgrounds. These include Bernie Grant (Guyanese), Diane Abbott (Jamaican) and Paul Boateng (Ghanaian father), all of whom were elected at the 1987 general elections.

Bernie Grant's legacy in-particular is arguably unmatched. He was not popular with the press due to his commentary in the aftermath of the Broadwater Farm 1985 riots—which he asserted was taken out of context. During this period, he explained how the disaffection among the youth in his constituency had built up and erupted like a pressure-cooker. He was a trailblazer in setting up the *Parliamentary Black Caucus* in 1988—inspired by US's Congressional Caucus—as a means of creating opportunities for Black and other ethnic minorities in the UK. Through its creation he brokered links between black people in Britain and people of African descent throughout the diaspora. These ties earned him the unofficial title of the 'Minister for Black people;' he also traveled across the Caribbean and Africa, through which he helped to foster pan-African consciousness among his Black British constituents and elsewhere globally. This extended to meeting Nelson Mandela on day of his prison release with Rev Jesse Jackson and establishing an eponymous information technology skills college in The Free State province of South Africa.

Grant also established the *UK Africa Reparations Movement (ARM)* in 1993 and used this opportunity to gather opinion from many in his North London Tottenham constituency as to whether they would be in favor of receiving government repatriation grants to resettle in the Caribbean and Africa. He was keenly aware of the importance of history and heritage for people of the African diaspora, commenting: "only if we understand our past can we as Black People move forward in the future. We must demand compensation for the biggest crime in history—the colonization and enslavement of our people." Another of Grant's actions was to publicize a petition for the repossession of the Benin Bronzes from the British Museum. This was on behalf of the Oba of Benin—based in southern Nigeria—and was submitted on 19th November 1996. He continued to campaign against racist policing methods, deaths in custody, apartheid, and as a member of the *Select Committee on International Development*, he continued to argue for the elimination of overseas debt for the recognition of the ongoing consequences of the past injustices of colonialism and slavery.

ETHNIC ESCAPISM AND THE BLACK BURDEN

The election of the above MPs set the tone for the elections of other black MPs such as the serving (as of 2021) *Shadow Secretary of State for Foreign, Commonwealth and Developments Affairs*, David Lammy (Guyanese), Kate Osamor (Nigerian), Dawn Butler (Jamaican), Florence Eshalomi (Nigeria), among many others. Other distinguished figures include the Labour Party politician and diplomat Baroness Valerie Amos who generously established the Amos Bursary and scholarship program for young black men.

African-Americans, as well as African and West Indian migrants to the US have also participated in the political arena. In addition to the US's 44th President Barack Obama (Kenyan father), Colin Powell (Jamaican and Scottish) served both as United States Secretary and National Security Advisor (NSA); Condoleeza Rice—like Powell—also served as NSA and Secretary of State; Eric Holder became the first Black US Attorney General (2009—2015) under Obama; Kamala Harris (Jamaican descent) simultaneously became the first Black (or multiracial/ethnic minority— depending on perspective) and first female Vice-President under the incumbent Joe Biden administration; and Joe Neguse was the first Eritrean-American politician to be elected to Congress as Colorado Congressman.

Black Diaspora Media

The UK's leading black publication and only weekly newspaper is *The Voice* which was founded in 1982 by the Jamaican accountant and media entrepreneur, Val McCalla. Initially it was established to cater to the British Afro-Caribbean Diaspora, and in more recent years, has also provided employment opportunities and media coverage for the British African diaspora. Other publications include the Black History Month magazine— covering Black History Arts and culture, and the Pride Magazine which has catered for Black women in the UK since 1991.

The US's most recognizable black media platform is *BET*, and others include the lifestyle and Entertainment channel *TV One*, and *The Africa Channel*—set up by the Zimbabwean James Makawa in 2005 and features African historical and cultural content; it is also aired throughout the Commonwealth Caribbean countries.

Elite Sports Participation

In the UK, as of 2022 black footballers (including those of mixed heritage) plying their trade in the premier league football (soccer) division represent 43% of the players registered. In the US, the number of African-American players in the National Football league (NFL) is 58% as of 2020. The figure is even higher in the National Basketball Association (NBA) at 72% as of 2022.

Black Cuisine in the Diaspora

Across both the US and the UK, the influence of the Caribbean and Africa is very evident in the cultural dishes consumed by its black populations. Yams, peanuts (peanut stew), rice, and okra are widely consumed on both sides of the Atlantic. The Senegambian-originated jollof rice is as accessible in the 'Little Lagos' South London district of Peckham, as it is in Brooklyn, New York. Moreover, globalization and black identity amalgamation also accounts for the more common appearance of Jamaican jerk chicken sold alongside Jollof rice in the diaspora.

Socio-Economic Position

A report into homeownership in England and Wales was undertaken by the government and the statistics recorded are valid as of September 2020. It revealed that British Black Africans had the lowest rates of homeownership across all the 18 ethnic groups surveyed at 20% (88,000 homeowners in total). Conversely, the rate of Black African-Caribbean homeownership rate is more than double at 45% (124,000 in total). Part of this is attributable to the Afro-Caribbean population being more assimilated than the African population, thus with a greater passage of time to have acquired property—in many cases at prices far lower than prevailing property prices. Furthermore, British Africans live in London in large numbers—749,000 as of the 2021 census, as compared to the Caribbean total of 340,000. Moreover, the average cost of purchasing an apartment in the 3 boroughs with the highest number of African residents are: Croydon—£266,000, Greenwich—£392,000, and Lewisham—£350,000. Given that the highest (based on industry) average weekly wage earned by Black people is £600, it is unsurprising that the group would find such prices prohibitively expensive and inaccessible in terms of income multiples and deposit requirements; moreover, even many of the highest earners in London—of all ethnicities—would struggle to meet the such requirements.

Additionally, as of 2018, 36% of Black Africans live in private rented Accommodation in England, whereas for the African-Caribbean people it is 20%. The rates of those in rented social housing are 44 and 40% respectively.

As of 2022, the combined black unemployment rate is 7%, which is only exceeded by the Chinese with 12% and is over double the white rate of 3%.

The percentage of self-employed UK Black African and Black African-Caribbean combined is 11%. The rates for the other British ethnic groups are: White British—15%, Indian—15%, Pakistani/ Bangladeshi—23%, and Chinese / Other Asian—15%.

In the US, as of 2019, 42% of Black-immigrant-headed households are homeowners, which also matches the rate of homeownership among US-born Black Americans. However, this rate is lower than the overall immigrant homeownership rate of 53%, and lower than the 64% rate for the entire country.

The rate of homeownership varies among Black immigrants from different parts of the world: African immigrants—33%, Caribbean immigrants—49%, Central America or Mexico—44%, and South America— 48%.

As of 2018, the gaps between Blacks' and whites' homeownership rates are: Killean in Texas has one of the smallest gaps in the South: out of just over 26,000 black households there is a 49% ownership rate, as compared with the white homeownership of 63%—a gap of 14%. Fayetteville, North Carolina (45 and 63% respectively, with a 17% gap) and Charleston, South Carolina (54 and 72% respectively, 18% gap)—both in the South, are the only other cities in the top 100 cities with ownership gaps below 20%.

   The gap is larger in North-eastern and midwestern cities. Atlanta, Chicago, New York City, Philadelphia, and Washington DC are 4 metropolitan areas with the highest number of black households. Minneapolis, Minnesota has the biggest gap at 50%; just 3.4% out of 2.7 million black households own their homes, of which there are more foreign black than US-born black homeowners. This was followed by Albany in New York which has a 49% gap. The Atlanta metropolitan area has a 45% ownership rate among black households, down from a 55% peak, before the impact of the 2008 housing crisis. DC has one of the smallest gaps in the country but the home values for black owners were around $102,000 on average than was the case for white owners.

With respect to black immigrant income levels, as of 2019, they have a lower median income—which is $57,200—than overall US immigrant levels—which is $63,000, but the figure is higher than the income levels of US born blacks—$42,000. The median income breakdown for the different Black immigrant groups is: Africa—$54,000, Caribbean—$58,200, Central America / Mexico—$50,000, and South America—$62,000.

Educational Attainment

In the UK, as of 8th October 2020, the House of Commons Library published a Briefing Paper in which it documented the educational outcomes for Black school pupils and progress into higher education and the workplace. At GCSE level, Black pupils have the lowest combined English and Math pass rates of any major ethnic group at 59%, as compared to the White and Other—both 64%, Mixed—65%, Asian—71% and Chinese—89%.

Black African pupils generally fare better than Black Caribbean pupils, and Black pupils eligible for Free School Meal (FSM) also rank higher on some key measures than White pupils eligible for FSM.

The percentage of black first year undergraduate entrants to universities increased from 8% / 48,000 in the 2015—16 academic year, to 9% / 51,000 students of the total enrolled in the academic year 2019—20. Of the latter figure, 40,000 were Black African, 8,600 Black Caribbean, and 2,400 from Other Black backgrounds.

According to UCAS (Universities Colleges and Admissions Service), 45% of Black 18-year-olds across England were accepted to higher education in 2019. While this was lower than the rates for their Chinese; and combined Indian, Pakistani, Bangladeshi, and Other Ethnic peers, it was well above the levels for White and Mixed ethnic groups and the overall 35% average. The entry rate of Black young people increased from 28% in 2010—representing the largest increase of any ethnic group.

It is noteworthy that UCAS breaks down entry rates by the 'tariff' level of different universities between high, medium, and low, which refer to average grades of students admitted. The Higher tariffs are generally considered more prestigious and while 45% of Black students entered higher education in 2019, only 8% were admitted to higher tariff institutions, and reflected the lowest rate of any ethnic group.

Moreover, it was noted in a 2016 study that in the case of Black Africans the offer rate of the top Russell Group of Universities (UK IVY league equivalent) was the lowest out of all other ethnic groups—drawing on a 10% random sample of 68,632 candidates of whom made 151,281 applications in total; academic performances at GCSE and A-level were also factored into the study, as well as university-administered tests and interviews. Another source indicates that pre-university qualifications are linked to teachers unfair treatment and low expectations of young people from African, Caribbean, and other minority backgrounds. However, since 2008 improvements have been more evident as the National Pupil Database reported 60%+ of students of the following heritage: Ghanaians, Mixed African/white, African, and Nigerian achieved 5+ GCSE passes at grades A* - C, but was markedly lower in the case of Somali—34%, and [DR] Congolese—28%. Furthermore, the London Mayor's 2011 report on education identified that children from Ghanaian and Nigerian backgrounds were 3 times as likely to reach the national benchmark of 5+ GCSE passes at grades A* -C (including English and Maths) as those from Congolese or Angolan backgrounds. It is worth noting that the countries of origin of young people from Somali, Congolese and Angolan backgrounds do not have English as a first language.

There were differences recorded between Black ethnic groups and genders entering higher education in 2018—19 from state-funded schools. Of the Black African group, this reflected 75% of females, 59% of males; of the Black Caribbean group, 55% female and 35% male respectively; and of Any Other Black Background, 60% female, and 44% were male respectively. The total gap between Black females (68%) and Males (51%) from state-funded schools entering higher education by 19 years of age was 17%, which was higher than the overall gap for females (48%) and males (37%) of 11%. Ultimately, more females than males enter into higher education.

In terms of degree classifications awarded to graduates in the 2020—21 academic year, 39% of white graduates received a first-class degree, in contrast to 20% of black graduates, which were the highest and lowest rates

389

respectively out of all ethnic groups. Graduates from the mixed (48%) and black (47%) ethnic groups were the most likely out of all ethnic groups to be awarded an upper second-class degree (2:1). Furthermore, the gap between white and black graduates attaining a first-class or 2:1 degree went down from 26% in 2014—15 to 19% in 2020—21.

Black students are also less likely to stay in higher education. As of 2016—17, Black students have the highest dropout rate of 15%, which is the highest of all other ethnic groups: Mixed—11%, White and Asian—both 9%.

Black students were also less likely than all other groups to attain High-Skilled employment or to progress to further (postgraduate for example) study, 6 months after the conclusion of their studies. The Black rate was 69%, whereas the other groups were: Mixed—71%, Asian—72% and White—74%.

In the US, the 2018—19 Public High School Graduation rate for Black students was 79%, which along with Hispanic students, was lower than the US national average of 85%. Only White students recorded graduation rates over the threshold, with 89%. The location with the lowest graduation rates for black students was in the District of Columbia (D.C) with 67%, and Alabama, Arkansas, had the highest black graduation rate at 88%. Only West Virginia—86% and Texas—87%, recorded Black graduation rates above the average.

26% of Black immigrants age 25+ have a bachelors' degree or higher, followed by Black Caribbean immigrants at 20% and the rate for US born blacks is 19%. All of these rates are lower than the 30% rate across the population. Moreover, the rate of Black immigrants—regardless of age—with advanced degrees such as a master's, Ph.D. or professional degree is 10%, which is similar to the overall 11% rate.

Labor Market Participation

As of November 2022, 67% of Black British between the ages of 16 and 64 were employed; only the Mixed and Pakistani/Bangladeshi groups—64 and 58% respectively were lower. The employment rates for the other groups were: Other—67%, Asian (non-Pakistani/Bangladeshi)—69%, Asian Other—69%, White and White British—both 76%, and Indian—82%.

The *Public Administration, Education and Health* sectors accounted for the highest percent of jobs worked by Black people in Britain. With a 47% rate—most of which is in the *health* sector—the Black cohort ranks number 1 of all other ethnic groups employed in the same sector, thus underscoring the considerable reliance the country has on Black labor in this sector. *Banking and Finance* was the second largest provider of employment—providing 16% of all jobs worked by Black people. The remaining sources and percentages are: *Distribution, Hotels and Restaurants*—12%; *Transport and Communication*—10%; *Manufacturing*—5%; *Other Services*—4%; *Construction*—4%; *Energy and Water*—2%; and *Agriculture, Forestry, and Fishing*—0.1%.

In the US, as of November 2022, the US Labor Department reported that the Age 20+ black unemployment rate was 5.7% overall, and the black male and female unemployment rates are 5.4 and 5.2% respectively. Given the recent economic shocks brought on by the global COVID-19 viral pandemic, and the Russo-Ukraine war's impact on energy and grain prices, this rate indicates that conditions have not been as adverse as one might have expected. It is only 0.2% higher than the overall record low unemployment rate of 5.5% reported in September 2019. The rate for black males also decreased by 0.5% from its 5.9 percent rate reported in July 2019, however, for women the most recent rate is an increase of 0.8% when compared to its record low rate during the same period. Moreover, the overall (for all ethnic groups) unemployment rate has increased by 0.5%—in September 2019 it was 3.2%.

For young black males and females between 16 and 19 years of age, 26% were employed, and 17 percent are unemployed. The Labor participation rate for persons aged 16—19 is 32% and for those above 20 it is 63%.

Out of the *Civilian Noninstitutional Population* (16 years+ resident in 50 states—D.C inclusive., and who are not inmates of prisons, mental institutions, or homes for the aged) of 34 million, there is a labor participation rate of 21 million, while the non-labor participating population is 13 million.

According to the White House, wage growth for Black Americans has been relatively strong. Drawing on the Current Population Survey (CPS) microdata for the 12-month horizon up to July 2022, median wage growth averaged 7.8% for non-Hispanic black workers, as compared with the overall rate of 6.3%.

While it would be easy to interpret this data as Black Americans gaining parity or surpassing other ethnic groups, this would be an erroneous conclusion to make. This is because Black Americans are over-represented in the healthcare while concomitantly being under-represented in many other sectors—notably in the private sector's most lucrative labor opportunities. Owing to the COVID-19 pandemic, it was of great importance to retain personnel and also add to extant headcount, and in accordance with the laws of supply and demand, demand outstripped the supply of healthcare personnel available. To further underscore this, there are 10 states facing severe nurse shortages in terms of the supply expected vis-à-vis what is needed to fulfill demand by 2030: 1. California faces the most acute shortage with an expected deficit of -44,000; followed by 2. Texas with -15,900; 3. New Jersey— -11,400; 4. South Carolina— -10,400; 5. Alaska— -5,400; 6. Georgia— -2,200; 7. South Dakota— -1,900; 8. Montana— marginal 200 surplus; and 9. North Dakota and 10. New Hampshire also expects 700 and 1,100 marginal surpluses respectively.

Management Consulting Firm, *McKinsey & Company*, undertook a particularly revealing report titled *Race in the Workplace: The Black*

Experience in the US Private Sector, which was published on 21 February 2021. The private sector report looked at 3 areas: 1. Their participation in the entire US private-sector economy; 2. Their representation, advancement, and experience in companies; and 3. A path forward that includes the key challenges to address, actions companies can take, and additional actions for a wider set of stakeholders to accelerate progress on diversity, equity, and Inclusion (DE&I). Their research drew on data from 24 participating companies ranging in size from 10,000 to 1.4 million US employees across all geographies, representing a total of about 3.7 million US employees—insights of which are below.

In the US, black workers account for 15 million—or 12%—of the 125 million US private-sector workers. The overall Black labor force, including the entire private sector, public sector, and unemployed seeking work is, as abovementioned, 21 million.

McKinsey's analysis discovered that Black workers are underrepresented in the highest-growth geographies and the highest-paying industries. Meanwhile, they are over-represented in low growth geographies and frontline jobs, which tend to pay less. To this end approximately 57%—or 11 million—of the Black labor force live in southern states, 9% in West and Pacific, Midwest—17%, and Northeast—18%. 3 in 5 Black workers work in the following frontline jobs: service workers, laborers, operatives, and office and clerical workers.

Overall, Black workers are not located in places where current job opportunities are and where job growth will likely rise the fastest through to 2030. For instance, 1 in 10 Black workers are located in the fastest-growing cities and counties (such as Provo, Utah). On the contrary, they overwhelmingly live in places where job growth will range from low-to-above average, with the bright spots being in megacities such as Chicago, and urban periphery, such as Clayton County, Georgia. For growth to be inclusive in these areas, workers need to be in closer proximity to more emerging in-demand jobs. Such job sectors with black under-representation are Information Technology, professional services and financial services.

45% of workers—6.7 million people—work in 3 industries with a large frontline service presence: healthcare, retail, accommodation, and food service. These industries also have the highest shares of workers making less than $30,000—in retail this accounts for 73% of Black workers and in accommodation and food service, this accounts for 84%. Transportation is the highest paying industry for black workers with the most states—21— paying its black employees $40—70,000 per annum.

Automation will prove to be disruptive in the labor force for years to come, but its impact will not be distributed evenly. For instance, 1 in 3 Black workers are in occupational groups such as production work, food service and office support—all of which are at heightened risk of conceding jobs to automation. The only encouraging trend which indicates increasing job demand through to 2030 is in the health sector—which is disproportionately filled by Black labor.

Black workers face higher hurdles to gainful employment than the rest of the labor force, creating stark disparities. For example, the employment rate for Black workers with a college or an associate degree is similar to the total population of workers who have a high-school diploma.

According to the report, companies which made successful Black hires into frontline and entry jobs, but there was a significant drop-off in representation at management levels and not enough is being done to connect Black employees with sufficient opportunities to advance. Black employees only account for 7% of managers with higher-than-expected attrition rates limiting representation—though the report noted that there were promising indicators that this could be reversed.

Entry-level jobs are a revolving door, and Black employee attrition is high. They compromise 12% of entry level jobs as software engineers, paralegals, and account associates. While the report states that hiring has been effective, what hasn't been addressed is why Black employees are more likely to leave their jobs than their white counterparts—at all levels, thus reducing Black representation when promotion opportunities arise.

Private sector companies have much work to do in addressing the trust deficit between themselves and their Black employees—23% of the latter believe that they are less likely to receive "a lot" or "quite a bit" of support to advance, 41% less likely to view promotions as fair, and 39% less likely to believe their company's DE&I programs are effective than white employees in the same company.

If the above issues are left to persist, it will take 95 years for Black employees to reach talent parity (12% representation) across all levels in the private sector. However, tackling the foregoing issues can cut the time horizon needed to achieve parity to 25 years.

Black Business Ownership Rates

US

At a 17th January 2022 event marking Martin Luther King Jr. Day, Treasury Secretary Janet Yellen said, "From Reconstruction, to Jim Crow, to the present day, our economy has never worked fairly for Black Americans—or, really, for any American of color." Yellen's remarks were an acknowledgement that US policymakers have established racially tilted rules for the economy, prohibiting generational wealth transfers among Black Americans—among many other harms.

According to the Federal Reserve, in 2019, the median household net worth of white families was $188,200—7.8 times that of their Black peers, at $24,100. That wealth gap translates to many other disparities, including business ownership rates, which are heavily influenced by individual and family wealth. In 2019, there was a total of 5,771,292 employer firms (businesses with more than one employee), of which only 2.3% (134,567) were black owned, even though Black people comprise 14.2% of the country's population.

To this end, *Path to 15/55* initiative has been established to grow the economy by expanding the number of Black businesses. Brookings published a report that used the Census Bureau's 2019 Annual Business Survey (ABS) to calculate the national proportion of both Black and non-Black Businesses in the prior year. The report also calculated the businesses, jobs, and revenue the US would gain if the percentage of Black-owned employer firms equaled the proportion of Black people in the country's population.

There are over 124,000 Black businesses, and to reach parity based on comprising 14% of the population, 806,000 more businesses would have to be established.

Currently, Black businesses bring in average annual revenues of $1.03 million, in contrast to $6.5 million by non-Black businesses. According to Brookings, if Black businesses increased their average revenue to the level of non-Black businesses, it would increase their total revenue by over $676 billion.

Black businesses create an average of 10 jobs per firm, compared to 23 for non-Black businesses. If the average employees per Black business increased to 23, it would create approximately 1.6 million jobs.

Black businesses pay their employees an average of $30,000, compared to non-Black businesses' average pay of $51,000. If Black businesses paid as much as non-Black businesses, then those employees would see an increase in pay by $26 billion.

If the number of Black businesses and its revenues matched the population size and revenue of its non-Black business equivalents, then the total revenue of Black businesses would increase by near $6 trillion—the equivalent of 26% of the US economy's GDP in 2021.

If the number of Black businesses matched the population size, and the employees per firm matched non-Black businesses, it would create 20 million jobs.

Among several obstacles that US Black businesses contend with, the Small Business Credit Survey (SBCS) revealed that Black businesses experienced financial challenges in 2020 owing to the COVID-19 pandemic at a rate higher than all other groups surveyed: 92% of Black businesses reported difficulties, followed by 89% of Asian-American-owned firms, 85% of Latino / Hispanic firms, and 79% of White firms.

Arguably the most critical issue that Black businesses contend with is access to credit. To this end, it is noteworthy that Black people with a positive net worth have assets that are primarily tied up in real estate—mainly homeownership. As of 2020, Black Americans had the lowest rate of homeownership at 46%, followed by Hispanic-Americans—51%, Asian-Americans—61%, and non-Hispanic White-Americans—76%.

Black families are not only less likely to own a home, but according to Brookings's *Hamilton Project*, "their homeownership yields lower levels." Among homeowners, Black families' median home value is $150,000, compared to $230,000 for white families. Black families are also under-indexed in businesses, stocks, bonds, and other assets that increase their net worth. In addition, assets held by Black people have a lesser value than white people, which in turn constrains their ability to start businesses.

46% of Black business owners contacted through the SBCS reported concerns about personal credit scores or loss of personal assets due to late payments. Moreover, Black people had the lowest average credit score at 677, followed by Hispanics—701, Other—732, White—734, and Asian—745.

A number of initiatives have been introduced, such as diversity hires to fill investment fund manager posts. One example of this is Texas University's *AssistHER grant program*, which provided $10,000 grants to 100 women-owned businesses; however, no such programs have been targeted at black male business owners similarly in need and without alternative sources of assistance. Brookings made the suggestion that *Urban Wealth Funds* should have at least 30% representation from women and people of color.

While the foregoing obstacles elucidate the challenges experienced by Black businesses—including the disproportionate hurt occasioned by the COVID-19 pandemic, there nevertheless was an uptick in the number of new Black businesses created during the pandemic. This was driven by a surge in new online microbusinesses—26% of which was by Black owners—up from 15% prior to the pandemic. There were also particularly high rates of business creation in Black neighborhoods.

It is noteworthy that commentators have correlated the increase in new Black-owned businesses with the loss of employment for Black workers. Of the 5 occupations that employ the largest number of Black and Hispanic workers, 4 experienced the highest job losses at the beginning of the pandemic: retail salespersons, cashiers, cooks, waiters, and waitresses.

UK

The data available for UK Black-owned businesses is not as extensive as it is in the US, however, some insights have been attainable. The Black Business Network, which has a research partnership with the Lloyds Banking Group, published a report in September 2021 entitled *Black British In Business and Proud*. 800 respondents took part in the study, of which 65% were female and 34% male, and another 1% chose not to disclose their gender identity.

In terms of ethnic breakdown: 37% identified as Black British, 37%—Black African, 16%—Black Caribbean, 4%—Mixed White-Black African, and 3%—Mixed White-Black Caribbean.

4 in 10 current entrepreneurs were aged 26—40 and 20% were younger. 88% of Businesses owned by Gen X—aged 41—55 and the older Boomer Generation had been in operation for over 10 years; 36% of Gen Z — aged 16—25 were the highest demographic in business for under 2 years;

Millennials had the highest rates of business ownership longevity for 2 years or less (with 44%), 2—5 years (57%) and 5—10 years (45%).

30% of start-up businesses were set up within the 12 months preceding 2020—21; 42% of businesses were established between 1—5 years and 27% over the 5 years prior to 2021 respectively.

More than half — 55% — of respondents set up their businesses alone, and more than 25% with a partner; only 15% of enterprises had more people involved.

Sector-wise, 31% of Black owned businesses operate in Leisure (Hospitality, arts, fashion, and beauty); 22% in Services (Auto business, energy, finance, IT, professions, PR); 16%—Public & Not-For-Profit (including health, transportation, education), 15%—Retail & wholesale (Retail & Wholesale); 4%—Blue Collar (Agri, construction, energy, manufacturing).

Of the Black businesses surveyed, only 43% trust banks to act in their best interests and only 27% trust the government. By contrast 80% believe their families have their best interests at heart. Moreover, 84% believe racism is a potential perceived barrier—of which 50% believe it to be a significant barrier; 53% stated they had experienced racism over the course of their entrepreneurial efforts.

Despite the challenges experienced by UK Black businesses, *The Centre for Research of Ethnic and Minority Entrepreneurship* reported that Black-owned enterprises contribute £25 billion annually to the UK economy—a figure which the Black Business Network called a powerful statistic. Though this figure is indicative of progress, the UK Black demographic represents 4% of the total population, and thus, based on the 2021 UK GDP of £2.2 trillion, Black parity would only be achieved if the annual contribution by Black businesses reached £88 billion annually. As far as growth prospects are concerned, the Black UK hair industry comprises part of the largest percentage of Black owned businesses and is worth £88 million annually. It is expected that the global black hair market will be worth £368 billion annually by 2024, thus underlining the potential that can be realized.

Regardless of the industry, increased financial savvy is essential to achieving business parity within the UK macroeconomy. As of 2021, 23% of Black businesses need financial skills and cashflow management support and 19% need help in understanding funding and eligibility criteria. While 57% of Black business owners were aware that bank financing was available, just 13% look to banks when seeking support—which ties in with the limited trust they have in banks. Furthermore, 52% are not confident in applying for finance, specifically in the form of business loans or grants.

Health and Medical Care

UK

A report commissioned by the *Black Equity Organisation*, a national civil rights organization launched in 2022 to tackle systemic racism in the UK, found that out of 2051 respondents, 65% of Black people surveyed said they had experienced prejudice from doctors and other staff in healthcare settings. This rose to 75% among black people aged 18—34.

The report cited particular issues around the experiences of black women in maternity care and the diagnosis of certain special educational needs. Survey participants felt as though they were not seen and that their concerns were not listened to or incorporated into their treatment decisions. "Specific to Black women, participants felt that due to the misguided stereotype of 'strong Black women,' practitioners were dismissive of their pain," the report said.

It noted that this finding had also been reported by the National Health Service (NHS) Race Health Observatory, which found evidence of negative interactions, stereotyping, disrespect, discrimination, and cultural insensitivity across maternity services. This made many women from ethnic minority groups feel "unwelcome, and poorly cared for." It also found that black patients in the UK were subject to more intrusive treatments, such as injectable antipsychotics, and were less likely to be offered talking therapy for severe mental illness.

Another report was published in February 2022 by the National Health Service (NHS) Race & Health Observatory entitled *Ethnic Inequalities in Healthcare: A Rapid Evidence Review*. The report identified maternal and neonatal health as an area of concern, and to underline the degree of ethnic inequalities in this area, it was revealed Black women were 4 times as likely to die in childbirth and 2.5 times as likely to birth babies deemed to be of low birthweight, compared with White mothers.

Workplace inequalities were also experienced by NHS Black and other ethnic minority employees. Such forms of discrimination were evident in training and recruitment processes which negatively impacts career progression and pay prospects. Among medics, ethnic minority doctors are 3 times less likely to secure a hospital job than White doctors—a situation that has changed little in 20 years. Inequalities also exist for clinical excellence awards (performance related bonuses for consultant staff) and career progression opportunities, with evidence of substantial under-representation of ethnic minority staff in senior leadership positions. Rates of discrimination, bullying, and harassment are higher among ethnic minority NHS staff than among White staff, and the behavior may be perpetrated by managers, team leaders, colleagues, or patients and relatives. In addition, employers are less aware of bullying and harassment problems experienced by minority staff than they are of incidents among White employees.

US

The Affordable Care Act (ACA) has helped to ensure health care coverage for millions of Americans, and its passage was followed by a decline in the uninsured rate among African-Americans: more than 20 million people gained cover, of which 2.8 million were African-Americans. Nevertheless, they were more likely to be uninsured than White Americans: as of 2018, the uninsured rate among African-Americans was 9.7%, while it was just 5.4% among Whites. Affordability is a major issue for Black Americans as the average annual cost for healthcare premiums is almost 20% of their average household income. Moreover, they make up 18%—or 16.7 million—of 87 million underinsured Americans; the coverage they have is usually inadequate, thus leading to unusually high out-of-pocket costs relative to income, which in turn places a strain on personal finances, and in many cases leads to the accrual of debt.

Beyond the financial disparities, a survey conducted by the Kaiser Family

Foundation (KFF) found that 18% of Black adults reported *Fair* or *Poor* health status in 2020 vis-à-vis 13% of Whites. For the Age-Adjusted Rate of Cancer Deaths per 100,000, as of 2018, Black Americans were reported to have 174 deaths, as against White Americans at 154. Black Americans accounted for 11 Infant Mortalities per 1,000 births, whereas it was less than half — 5 — in the case of White Americans.

KFF conducted another nationwide poll, which included interviews with almost 800 African-Americans and reported that 7 in 10 people believe they are treated unfairly on the grounds of ethnicity or race when seeking medical care. Moreover, other findings included:

1. 4 in 10 Black adults knew someone who had died from coronavirus—almost double the rate of White adults.
2. One-third of Black adults and [as of 2020] nearly half of Black parents are struggling to pay their bills as a result of the pandemic. 2 out of 3 Black parents have either lost jobs or had their incomes interrupted since the pandemic struck in February 2020.
3. A sizeable minority of all ethnic groups are distrustful of the medical system, but only Black Americans were in the majority with 55%.
4. Despite the considerable death toll from the COVID-19 pandemic, just half of Black Americans surveyed would be interested in taking the vaccine—even if it were determined to be safe and free of cost. By comparison, 2 in 3 white people said they would definitely or probably get vaccinated, as did 6 in 10 Hispanics. The vast majority of Black Americans who said they would not take a coronavirus vaccine did not think that it would be properly tested, distributed fairly or developed with the needs of Black people in mind.

Many commentators claimed Black American sentiments were an outgrowth of the broader discrimination they face in their daily lives. "We have a centuries-long legacy in this country of basically Black people, in particular, and other people of color as well, being treated poorly," said Dr.

Lisa A. Cooper, an internist who directs The Johns Hopkins Center for Health Equity. She further added "So why should Black people trust any institution? It has gone on for so long."

CONCLUSION &
PROSPECTS FOR
THE DIASPORA

—

There is a question mark over the future of the African diaspora, and the reasons for this are explored below. It is noteworthy that diasporic communities eventually—and inevitably—tilt towards assimilation into their host societies' dominant culture and mores, examples of which include: the many Italian diasporic communities which have now assimilated and creolized into their erstwhile host nations—Brazil, Argentina, the US and so forth. This is also the case for the Irish diasporic communities and thus it can be argued that any contemporary Italian or Irish expat communities are different and largely unconnected from the diasporic communities of the past. Consequently, these groups 'became white' and this was significant particularly in places like the US where racially they were once considered undesirable; their assimilation into the dominant ethnic group opened up a path to prosperity which was previously unattainable. Even the British imperial diasporic communities with roots in different regions and localities in Britain, Ireland, and parts of mainland Europe, in their various colonial outposts and settler colonies, coalesced into nations once they pursued self-rule. The Chinese, with their trading prowess, which makes them a valued presence globally, also assimilated into the dominant culture of several countries across the globe—Australia, the US, Thailand, and Malaysia among others.

However, the 'African diaspora' is a unique one—far different to any others studied across the globe—and gauging what its future holds is not entirely straightforward, not least due to varying rates of mobility—notably chasms in educational and socio-economic outcomes, and self-perception / identity.

The Black American population secured the Civil Rights bill in 1968, and thereafter several job and educational opportunities / initiatives were made available to Black women due to holding 'double-minority status' by way of their race and gender. The men on the other hand were almost immediately impacted by the era of deindustrialization; the 1980s drug epidemic; young men disadvantaged by the removal of training programs to gain a foothold in the labor market during the Reagan administration; and the increase in incarceration rates which quadrupled between 1980 and 2006—though by 2006 this had decreased by 34%.

But there has been a degree of mobility for Black American men, for whom 52% are single, never been married and childless; almost 57% have attained middle-class status; and 2.5 million (12% of the male total) hold upper-class status. This is a remarkable achievement in the face of discrimination and other vestigial limitations. To put this into context, a report from the U.S. Congress's Joint Economic Committee, states that from their 2019 study, 97% of the respondents vastly underestimated the huge gap between the median wealth held by Black families ($17,000) and White families ($171,000)—a ratio of 1:10. Respondents estimated the gap to be 80 percentage points smaller than the actual divide.

Despite some concerns from the U.S. public on how it may impact the taxpayer, momentum gathered in 2020 for a reparation package for Black American descendants of slavery worth a combined $10—12 trillion—or the equivalent of $800,000 to each eligible Black household. 143 members of Congress co-sponsored H.R. 40, the Commission to Study and Develop Reparation Proposals for the African-American Act, compared with only 2 in 2014. Even the incumbent President Joe Biden endorsed the study; his campaign manifesto for Black America pledged to address the disparity of being 13% of the population but of which only 4% are small business owners. This is understandable given African-American businesses often lack the capital they need to succeed and are rejected at a rate of 20% greater than their white counterparts when it comes to seeking business financing. Even worse, African-American businesses that do receive funding only receive 40% of the total requested, whereas it is 70% for white businesses. One of the potential measures to ensure accountability is the production of a weekly dashboard with specific data on small business beneficiaries. Moreover, it was stated that there will also be increased opportunities for African-American businesses to obtain or participate in the bidding process for federal contracts.

Given the impact of stimulus spending on Covid-19—which increased the national debt to $26—27 trillion, Michael Tanner—a senior fellow at the Cato Institute, believes that the timing isn't right, but can be addressed once government revenues increase. An alternative proposal put forward by Darrick Hamilton—a professor of public policy at Ohio State University—is to issue "baby bonds" trust funds to fund higher education, a home acquisition, or business startup capital. The rationale is that it is much cheaper than reparations as every year, about 4 million children are born. If every account was seeded by about $25,000, the program could cost the government about $100 billion. Hamilton further rationalized:

> "One hundred billion is about 2 percent of federal expenditures now. It is much less than we spend with our tax policy on subsidizing the assets of the wealthy... We spend about $500 billion on reductions in capital gains and mortgage interest reductions. So if one were to think about the cost of baby bonds, the scale of other asset expenditures, it pales in comparison."

At state level there have been more recent efforts to remedy the effects of the past, as evidenced by the state of North Carolina unanimously voting in 2020 to apologize for slavery—subsuming discrimination and the denial of basic liberties; making funding available to help Black Businesses and homeowners; as well as targeting the reduction of gaps in healthcare, education, employment and pay. The City of Evanston in Illinois also made a similar move in 2019, using tax proceeds from recreational cannabis sales to fund the program.

There are lingering concerns that if the reparation strategies aren't applied effectively, it may result in socio-economic chasms improving in the short-run, but not produce the desired impact in the longer-term. Furthermore, support for reparations among White Americans has increased from 4% in 2000 to 1 in 10 in 2020—a 150% increase in 2 decades.

The issue of reparations for the UK black population is much different to that in the U.S. The late British-Guyanese politician—Bernie Grant, launched a UK Reparations movement in 1993. Another development also took place in [April] 1993 at the First Pan-African Congress on Reparations held in the Nigerian capital of Abuja and which was sponsored by the wealthy Nigerian businessman Chief Moshood Abiola. Abiola was inspired to take up the cause by a chance discussion about the Holocaust with a Jewish businessman, and by his contacts with the Congressional Black Caucus in the United States. This followed on from 3 key developments: The first development involved the then-Nigerian President, Ibrahim Babangida, who promoted the idea of reparations and officially dedicated US$500,000 (almost $1.1million at the 2023 value) to it, though the group eventually received its funding from Abiola's private purse, and not the Government of Nigeria. Babangida had discussed the idea of reparations as early as in 1991 with the then Presidents of Senegal and Togo—the 3 agreeing that the African debt "should be written off as part of reparations due for '500 years' of slavery of Africans in Western Europe and America".

The second key development was the Organization of African Unity (OAU) (The OAU was dissolved in 2001, but later reincarnated as the African Union in 2002) forming a 12-person 'Eminent Persons Group on Reparations for Africa and Africans in the diaspora in June 1992—under the leadership of Chief Abiola and Dudley Thompson, the then-Jamaican High Commissioner to Nigeria and one of the principal Caribbean spokespersons for the international reparations movement. At the Abuja meeting the representatives from Africa, the Caribbean, and the Americas called upon the Western nations "to recognize that there is a unique and unprecedented moral debt owed to African peoples that has yet to be paid—the debt of compensation to the Africans as the most humiliated and exploited people in the last four hundred years".

The third was during a speech Abiola delivered in London in 1992 during which he said:

> "Our demand for reparations is based on the tripod of moral,
> historic, and legal arguments... Who knows what path Africa's
> social development would have taken if our great centres of
> civilization had not been razed in search of human cargo? Who
> knows how our economies would have developed ...?"

He went onto add:

> "It is international law which compels Nigeria to pay her debts to
> western banks and financial institutions; it is international law
> which must now demand that the western nations pay us what
> they owed us for six centuries"

Chief Abiola's support for the international reparations movement engendered the hostility of major Western nations, and though he won the Nigerian presidential election in June 1993, the election victory was annulled, and when he subsequently asserted his right to the presidential mandate he was imprisoned by the military in June 1994; he later died in prison in June 1998. Lord Anthony Gifford, a British jurist and a firm supporter of the reparations movement, believed the United States, Great Britain, and other nations accepted the military coup and formally recognized the ascent of Abacha to Head of State because of Chief Abiola's "dominant and determined role in the movement for reparations". Gifford believed that:

> "All Africans on the continent of Africa and in the Diaspora, who
> suffer the consequences of the crime of mass kidnap and enslav-
> ement, have an interest in this claim... All Africans around the
> world have been affected in some way by the crime of slavery.
> Even those who have succeeded in a business or a profession
> have had to face racial prejudice at the least."

Concomitant with the African / African-American reparation claim was a resurfacing of the discourse on Jewish reparations for holocaust survivors—during which Jewish groups demanded that unpaid life insurance policies on victims of the Holocaust be paid, and that monies deposited by Jews in Swiss banks before and during the Second World War be paid to Jewish survivors and surviving relatives of murdered Jews. Due to this, the belief that some groups were more / less racially favored when it came to the issue of reparations, gained traction among some Africans and African-Americans. In any case, Jewish communities in the U.S. provided consultation for the Black reparation claim, and another claim brought forward in 2004 against insurance market—Lloyd's of London, among other British and American corporations—stating that by insuring and financing the slaving ships they were complicit in genocide.

It is noteworthy that the former President of Senegal, Abdoulaye Wade said that if reparations were to be paid for slavery, then he might be liable to pay them, as his ancestors had owned thousands of slaves. He found the proposal for monetary compensation for slavery insulting: "It is absurd... that you could pay up a certain number of dollars and then slavery ceases to exist, is cancelled out and there is no receipt to prove it". At the preparatory African Conference, he angered participants by discursively arguing that there was far more racism and xenophobic violence within Africa than against Africans in Europe.

In more recent times, UK higher institution, Glasgow University, resolved to pay £20 million / $26 million reparations as an atonement for its historical links to the transatlantic slave trade. This was following on from the 2018 revelation that Glasgow University benefited financially from Scottish slave traders in the 18th and 19th centuries by up to the tune of £236 million once inflationary adjustments are made to reflect its 2023 value. The agreement was formalized on Friday 23rd August 2019 in a signed agreement with the University of the West Indies. Prior to this, All Souls College at Oxford University launched an annual scholarship in 2017 for Caribbean students and paid a £100,000 grant to a college in Barbados in recognition of a bequeathment of £10,000 (£2 million in 2023) from wealthy slave owner, Christopher Codrington.

Undeterred by then-British Prime Minister, David Cameron telling Jamaican politicians to "move on" from the topic of reparations during his 2015 visit, and on behalf of its Black and Creole populations, and diasporic communities in the UK, U.S. and elsewhere, the 15 countries which comprise the Caribbean Community (CARICOM) renewed its call for reparations on 6th July 2020—through which they emphasized its importance for the second stage of independence in the Caribbean. According to Barbados Prime Minister Mia Mottley, the Caribbean "were not given a development compact," and that despite the great post-independence strides made, "only reparations could help overcome the psychological, sociological, and economical inequalities that exist within Caribbean countries and between them and their former colonizers."

Since Mottley's statement, Barbados attained formal independence on 30th November 2021, which was followed by Jamaica announcing its plans to also attain independence by 2025, and Belize also, in 2022, announced plans to actualize Republic status.

It was reported in the media in November 2022 that the Barbados government plans to make the Conservative MP Richard Drax pay reparations for his ancestors' pivotal role in pioneering the sugar plantation system in the 17th century. The Drax family are worth at least £150 million. Barbados MP Trevor Prescod, chairman of Barbados National Task Force on Reparations—part of the CARICOM Reparations Commission, declared that it will pursue legal action in the international courts against the Drax family "for hundreds of years of slavery, so it's likely any damages would go well beyond the value of the land." Significantly this is the first case of a family being singled out for liability.

It was also reported in the media in February 2023 that BBC correspondent, Laura Trevelyan and members of her aristocratic family traveled to Grenada to apologize for the role their ancestors played in the slave trade, having owned 1,000 enslaved Africans. The apology followed Trevelyan investigating her family's link to the trade and with a subsequent promise to pay £100,000 in reparations to the University of the West Indies, which is to be drawn from her pending (as of 2023) pension.

While the Black UK population—similarly to its US counterparts—has greater visibility across Sports, Entertainment, media, professional/service sector in 2020 than at any time in the past, the structural issues—well documented in this book—still linger. Arguably the biggest injustice of all is the Windrush Scandal which broke in 2008.

Earlier in this book the story of the Windrush generation was chronicled, including the push-pull factors that brought them to the UK, and the incubation of a hostile environment to discourage further migration from the British Caribbean—culminating in several legislative measures in the 1960s, 70s and 80s to limit their passporting rights to visit or undertake working opportunities in the UK. The effect of the Commonwealth Immigrants Act of 1968 and Immigration Act 1971 was that anyone who had arrived in the UK from a Commonwealth country before 1973 was granted an automatic right to permanently remain unless they left the UK for more than 2 years. Since the right was automatic, many in this category were the children and grandchildren of Caribbean settlers and were never asked to provide documentary evidence of their right to remain at the time or over the next 4 years, during which time many continued to live and work in the UK, believing themselves to be British. Whilst the Immigration and Asylum Act 1999 specifically protected these long-standing residents from enforced removal, conspicuously, this provision was not transferred to the 2014 Immigration legislation as those under its ambit who had arrived before 1st January 1973 were considered to be adequately protected.

Unfortunately, many from the Windrush generation were caught in the crosshairs—or some may argue deliberately targeted—during an attempt to fulfil the 2010 Conservative Party manifesto. The 'hostile environment policy' purported to encourage those without permission in the UK to voluntarily leave, and made it a legal requirement for landlords, employers, the National Health Service (NHS), community interest companies and banks to carry out ID checks and refuse services if their legal UK residence couldn't be proven. Failure to comply had the consequence of fines being levied of up to £10,000.

Initial warnings were issued to the Home Office from 2013 onward to the effect that Windrush generation residents were being treated as illegal immigrants and that older Caribbean born people were being targeted. Indeed, a leaked memorandum stated the department had set a target of achieving 12,800 enforced returns by 2017—18. A professional services and outsourcing firm known as 'Capita' is a case in point: caseworkers from a Wolverhampton Refugee and Migrant Centre reported seeing hundreds of people receiving letters informing them they had no right to be in the UK and some were told to leave the UK at once. Roughly half of the letters issued were sent to people with extant permission to be in the UK ('leave to remain') or were in the process of formalizing their papers. Several people wrongly considered to have illegal status, lost jobs, or homes as a result of losing access to welfare benefits, and NHS medical care; some were confined to detention centers ahead of precipitous deportations and some were refused re-entry into the UK. Caribbean governments from 2013 expressed their concerns to the British government over wrongful deportations, first during a 2013 Commonwealth meeting, and attempted to do so again at another meeting in 2018, though their formal request on behalf of 12 Caribbean countries was rejected by Downing Street.

An independent review—*Windrush Lessons Learned Review*—by the Inspector of the Constabulary in March 2020 concluded that Theresa May's Home Office displayed "thoughtlessness," "ignorance" and that what had transpired was "avoidable" and "foreseeable. The report further documented that immigration controls were tightened "with complete disregard for the Windrush generation" and demands for legal documentation establishing rights were "irrational." A few months later in

June 2020, Britain's human rights watchdog—the Equality and Human Rights Commission (EHRC) launched a review into the 'Hostile Environment' immigration policy and to assess whether or not the Home Office had complied with its duties outlined in the Equality Act 2010, with subsequent recommendations to be issued by September 2020. In November 2020 the EHRC stated that the Home Office had broken the law by failing to obey public-sector equality duties by not considering how its policies affected black members of the Windrush generation".

Unsurprisingly the British government launched a 'Windrush Compensation' Scheme in April 2019, yet for a scheme expected to cost anywhere between £200 and £500 million, only £360,000 had been issued to a total of 60 victims or £4,400 on average per victim. This was out of a total of 1,275 applicants—barely 5% of the total. Bureaucracy and exhaustive documentary requirements were the reasons attributed to its limited distribution to date. Criticism was foreseeable given that the Home Office profited from its own error. The greater documentary burden placed on the victims to prove residency and pay for citizenship tests to avoid forced removal, brought in a profit of £800 million between 2011 and 2017.

In an effort to remedy the situation, the government announced on 14th December 2020 that the extant Compensation scheme had been overhauled and the Windrush victims will now receive a minimum of £10,000 which is 40 times the minimum figure for government compensation schemes. Furthermore, claimants can receive up to £100,000 in exceptional cases above this threshold—based on the severity of their individual cases. As of October 2022, the Home Office reported it had paid or offered over £60 million through the scheme, of which £51 million had been paid across 1,307 claims and the remaining £9 million sum was at the offer stage awaiting acceptance or pending review.

The Question of a 'Black Community'

In the U.S. the concept of a 'Black Community' has been called into question on many occasions. One such instance was in the build-up to the 2020 US General Election and how the question of which candidate to back caused a bifurcation among a subset of the community, comprising on one side a predominantly Black female pro-Biden camp, and on the other end, a sizeable Black male pro-Trump / open-minded camp. A myriad of social media platforms featured this bifurcation rather prominently, and while it is not uncommon for other ethnic communities to have polarized and even nuanced political views, there was evident tension on display during an episode of Fox Soul's *Cocktails with Queens*. Aired in October 2020, this particular episode featured a Black all-women panel and a sole black male in Ice Cube during which he put forward a $500 billion Platinum Plan for Black America—a reparation program of sorts for the Black community to then-President Trump and tried but failed to engage then-Presidential candidate Biden. In response to Ice Cube's proposal the women asked unanimously why his contract didn't make specific reference to Black women. Ice Cube responded that they were already part of black America and that they shouldn't count themselves as a separate demographic altogether. Nevertheless, the women disagreed and said they had needs specifically as Black American women not being met by the government—by implication seeking policies that solely favor a gendered subset of Black America.

Another instance of political tension was evident on the Joe Madison show during which Black Democratic congressional leader Rep. Maxine Walters stated she would "never ever forgive" Black men for casting Trump votes. It is noteworthy that such infantilizing rhetoric from Rep. Walters, and the political stance of the Black women on Fox Soul are not conclusively reflective of the current state of Black America. Given that 90% of Black female voters gave their votes to Biden, and 80% of Black male voters also backed Biden, political alignment was closer than contentious media reports suggested.

It may be argued that the roots of discordance within the community dates back at least 4 decades. As mentioned above, the 1980s was a very difficult decade for the US black population. One of the key reasons for this was the opioid epidemic (heroin consumption) which from between 1979 and the mid-80s, the opioid mortality rate was higher for the black population than the juxtaposed white population. Crucially, the study from which these percentages were derived stated that these rates were underreported nationally by 24%, and heroin mortality rates were particularly underreported in southern states such as Louisiana and Alabama, which have large black populations.

Another example of discordance—evident between both genders—transpired in 1985 when the film *A Color Purple* was released. *The Washington Post* in a December 23rd, 1985, edition printed a review of the film in which the reviewer, Dorothy Gilliam, noted that the film was "an amazing literary work". She further stated:

> "It's a great film. Spanning 40 years, it is the story of a black American family in the rural south beginning in the early 1900s. Starring Goldberg as the main character, Celie and Danny Glover as her bullying husband, Mr__, this troupe of actors unleashes a spate of emotions on the screen like a well-rehearsed repertoire company. Although its themes are often dismal—rape, incest, and brutal male violence against women—paradoxically, it is really a film about the purity and depth of love.
>
> The love between Celie and her sister, Nettie, stretches over years and continents like a band. It holds them together from the days they fought off their father/rapist and played among purple daisies in Georgia, over decades of absence when Celie thought her sister might even be dead.
>
> Although Celie reveals the depth of her self-hate when she advises her husband's son to beat his free-spirited wife, Sofia, in order to control her, Celie begins to discover the meaning of self-love with Shug, her husband's mistress, and ultimately, the meaning of freedom."

The above review sharply contrasts from this more concise review featured in the December 20th, 1985 edition of the Los Angeles Times paper:

"There is absolutely no balance in the movie"

This was said by Kwazi Geiggar of the Coalition Against Black Exploitation, a 20-member group of professionals and lay persons that monitor black-themed films and TV shows. He further went on to say:

"It portrays blacks in an extremely negative light. It degrades the black man, it degrades black children, it degrades the black family".

Geiggar, one of several coalition members who protested a special "Color Purple" screening the previous Tuesday for the Black Women's Forum, accused Spielberg of attempting to win awards at the expense of Blacks. In this vein, Geiggar remarked:

"There is not one single person with positive features in the movie. There is only one scene in which a black man kisses a black woman ... Men without exception are absolute savages and suffer no consequences for their actions".

Willis Edwards, president of the Hollywood/Beverley Hills branch of the National Association for the Advancement of Colored People (NAACP) said he found "Color Purple" "very powerful" and also "very stereotypical". Edwards also soberingly noted:

"We're happy that a lot of actors that happen to be black got to work and they did a fantastic job. They should all be nominated for awards. But for the Black male, the movie is degrading."

The feedback issued by Warner Bros when the LA Times tried to reach Steven Spielberg rankled with many:

"All I can say is that Alice Walker (author of the book upon which the film is based) loved it, and that every major black leader I have talked to loved it. I don't believe the people protesting the movie have seen it." [said Rob Friedman, Vice President of Worldwide Publicity at Warner Bros].

This was at odds with Geiggar's claim he had watched the film. It was also at odds with then-California State Assemblywoman Maxine Waters' view that:

"It was one of the most beautiful and most powerful films I have ever seen. I was overwhelmed with the central theme of how one gains strength and comes into being. I don't find 'Color Purple' degrading or dehumanizing. That movie could have been about any color."

Though Waters ostensibly claimed she didn't want to discourage the protestors from being diligent about the potential exploitation of black people, her role as a coordinator at the film's screening on behalf of the Black Women's Forum was conspicuous as her enthusiasm for the film was concomitant with the absence of express sympathy or empathy for black men / male concerns relating to the onscreen portrayal of their image. While her comments of any nature are of her own prerogative, she occupied an influential political position and her inability to sympathize with these concerns was at odds with the notion of a 'community' and gave an insight into the incipient gender bifurcation which was to deepen in the subsequent decades. To underscore the significance of this, Geiggar had for the preceding 9 months pushed the film studio to consult Black sociologists before going into production and was notified by letter to "trust them"— perhaps given the eventual outcome of the movie this added to the sense of incredulity. Additional feedback was provided by other women in a 5th January 1986 Chicago Tribune edition who enjoyed the production and couldn't relate with how black men were negatively impacted by the movie; remarkably, one of the interviewees claimed:

"Alice Walker's timid endorsement of the film confirms that the movie is a softened version of the book".

In light of the furor the film's release created, this statement is incongruent with community sentiment. Perhaps even more so when you consider the following statements—the first from Geiggar's colleague Legrand Clegg, the chairman of the Coalition Against Black Exploitation:

> "The black family is the foundation of the black race, and the fact that certain people would be out of work is little loss compared to the devastation this may visit on black youth . . . ."

And this passage from the above New York Times article:

> "These works confront the often uneasy relationship between black men and women. Eldridge Cleaver, in his book "Soul on Ice", described it as a war. Miss Wallace described it as a "profound distrust, if not hatred".

Though there are many possible factors attributable to tensions between the genders, the Color Purple film may have set the tone for what in recent times is called *Ethnomasochism*. The 'gender war' is now more egregious and toxic going by certain tweets, Instagram posts and YouTube channels diffusing ideas beyond the pale. One such example is the celebration of the intentional abortion of male children—solely due to their gender; sentiments which ought to be unthinkable. Moreover, gender tension is also evident in the forms of the 'divestor' / 'swirl' movements. Rather than organic and genuine relationship compatibility that incidentally happens to be along interracial lines, these movements disparage the other gender of the same ethnicity, while concomitantly bandying the idea that marriage / procreation along interracial lines is a panacea to a better life.

Then again, it may be argued that regardless of gender tensions, the last frontier of assimilation into a 'host nation' is racial assimilation. This is arguably inevitable due to the growth rates of the Black US population total. As of 2015, the U.S. Census bureau population projections for growth between 2014 and 2060 reported that the Black population as a percentage of the total country's population will remain unchanged from what it currently is at 14%. Since then, this forecast has reduced from 13.4% to 13.1% by 2045; another source estimates it will be 13.6% by 2060. In this time, the US multi-racial population will grow from 2.1 to 3.8% by 2050, and to 5% by 2060.

These demographic changes and the inevitability of greater social assimilation will change the prevailing 'black experience' and perceptions of identity. In the UK, the African-Caribbean population had peaked by the time of the 1991 census (it hasn't moved much past the 500,000 mark since the 1970s). Whereas the African subset choose another African partner 8 times out of 10, 50% of Caribbean men and nearly 40% of Caribbean women choose a non-Caribbean partner. Consequently, mixed-race children with one Caribbean parent under the age of 10 are twice as likely to be born as children with 2 Caribbean parents.

The above factors indicate that the idea of a monolithic, borderless black community is erroneous. While 'ethnicity' is used as a designation on census surveys and other government data, in the strictest sense of the word, ethnicity denotes belonging to a nation or a subnation. Given that there is no prevailing black nationalist movement, the *black* identity designation reflects the vestiges of structural racism and systemic inequalities that were particularly egregious in past generations.

Inevitable demographic changes naturally raise a question mark over the future of the African diaspora. Some of the above statistics may be profound for some readers—not least from the African diaspora—however, indications of these changes have been evident for some time. The U.S. government's racial de-segregation of public institutions, amenities and passing the civil rights bills—in addition to Love v. Virginia—all paved the way for licit interracial dating, marriage, and multi-racial offspring.

Furthermore, U.S. black art and popular culture draws on not just vestigial African influences, but many sources—all of which are a product of creolization. The term 'creole' has been used sociologically to refer to an identifiable fraction of colonial society and is commonly used in French territories and in the Anglophone Caribbean. Originally it was used for white Europeans to differentiate between those born in colonies who had lived there for so long that they picked up 'native' characteristics and had forgotten how to be 'proper' Englishmen and Frenchmen. Indeed, one sociologist, O. Nigel Bolland stated that with respect to the Caribbean, the people—slaves, peasants, freedmen, or laborers—fully participated in the fashioning of new cultures.

For many American and British people with Caribbean roots, this quote from West Indian novelist George Lamming may resonate: 'Africa invades us like an invisible force'. This was the impetus for defining the Caribbean on their own terms. The rediscovery of this African 'voice'—its return to the surface, in societies like Jamaica in the 1960s and 70s—constituted the basis of a cultural revolution, which made the place, self-consciously, for the first time, a 'black society.' Significantly, this cultural revolution simultaneously affected the diaspora not just in the U.S. but also in the UK—in the course of which it brought an enduring influence to the Leeds Carnival and world-renown Notting Hill Carnival; the sharp increase in the availability of West Indian restaurants, takeaways and foodstuffs; the significant contribution to the London Creole English (LCE) dialect spoken to varying degrees by Black Caribbean, African, Asian and White Brits in the UK; even the African-American Vernacular English (AAVE) dialect / language spoken in America is a product of creolization—though the latter is arguably less obvious as Black Americans have become more immersed in the broader U.S. mainstream culture.

For African-Caribbean diasporic communities, the creolization experienced in both the Caribbean and in the UK and U.S. could be called 'Twice Creolized.' Furthermore, African groups such as Nigerians-Brits, most of whom are from the Southern part of the country, have also had creole exposure, though perhaps this is less obvious. The following factors are attributable: embracing the influences of British-Caribbean popular culture—especially for many of the generation X and millennial generation cohorts; the creolization of Nigerians in terms of popular music consumption—its production infuses many different genres; the onset of

423

deeply-rooted western cultural influences; the *Wazobia*-effect of Nigerians absorbing words from the languages of myriad ethnic groups (mostly Igbo, Hausa, and Yoruba) into their everyday speech; and also the evolution of 'pidgin'—essentially a creole now successive generations speak it—which was a consequence of Lagos's absorption into the British Empire in the 1850s—60s. This was a continuum from the Krio dialect of Sierra Leone and was widely diffused in the nascent Southern Nigerian Protectorate by Sierra Leonean returnees of Yoruba, Igbo, and Ijaw heritage residing in cities such as Lagos, Port Harcourt, Onitsha, and Owerri. It was a useful communication tool to aid coastal trade and diffuse Christianity in the region(s), which was a priority of the British colonial administration, along with the diffusion of western influences, ideologies and so forth—all of which took root in nascent Nigerian society. The Krio foundation of Nigerian Pidgin was formed in Freetown, the British Sierra Leone Protectorate, and was contributed to by the indigenous groups like the Mende, Temne, as well as recaptives / returnees from Yorubaland, Igboland, Congo, Angola, the Ashanti Kingdom/present-day Ghana, Jamaica, Barbados, Fulani, Nova Scotia, and parts of present-day U.S.

Even Nigerian popular culture from the early post-independent era was influenced by creolization. One example was evident through the music produced by the popular musician and political activist, Fela Anikulapo Kuti, whose artistic style was cultivated in the diaspora while studying in Britain. Moreover, his choice of a Black American girlfriend, (later the mother of his son Femi) during the nascent years of his music career was an example of continental-diasporic connections.

The African diasporic experiences spanning both the old and new diaspora, bear many parallels, but also some distinct differences. The latter is particularly crucial as it speaks to the heterogeneity of the 'African' collective; this is often overlooked such is the emphasis placed on the biological marker of 'black' skin—both by Africans and non-Africans, rather than recognition accorded to their ethnocultural group of origin. As a case in point, many Black Africans in the UK contend that the Black African designation doesn't capture the complexities of their identities. Indeed, when given the chance, survey evidence has shown Black Africans identify more specifically with their 'national' origins such as "Nigerian" or "Ghanaian". Furthermore, it was found that Somalis in Camden, London, 'complained of not getting the same level of resources' as all other recognized ethnic groups because they were hidden within the 'Black African' amalgam, thus indicating a reluctance by some to be associated with the *Black British* designation.

In the case of the U.S., first and second-generation African and West Indian migrants who participated in a sociological study were polarized on the identity label(s) deemed most fitting. The "African American" designation was not one that the majority surveyed wished to be associated with. For some this was not a rejection of co-ethnic solidarity, but rather as respectful recognition of the differences in cultural backgrounds and the unique relationship generational blacks have with America, both historically and contemporarily. Others wished to not be known as African Americans due to perceived unfavorable stereotypes, synonyms, and other negative associations. And some respondents identified with African Americans as a 'black' amalgam which shared similar social experiences due to their hue.

With respect to the possible future of the African diaspora, below is Robin Cohen's *common features of a diaspora* framework [outlined earlier in this book], which is employed in this section to measure the degree of diasporic consciousness among the persons of the African diaspora:

1. *Dispersal from an original homeland, often traumatically, to two or more foreign regions.*

    The dispersal of Africans—whether it was during the Transatlantic slave era or during the more post-colonial migration waves, has always resulted in Africans settling in at least 2 regions, evidenced by the presence of millions of black people in North America, South

425

America, the Caribbean, the UK, and mainland Europe. This book has documented the vagaries of trauma experienced by displaced Africans—the dehumanization of captive Africans, pestilences, civil wars, and genocides.

2. *Alternatively, or additionally, the expansion from a homeland in search of work, in pursuit of trade or to further colonial ambitions.*

The more recent migrations of Africans and those of African descent includes persons taking up careers in the professions, undertaking undergraduate / postgraduate studies, and family members joining their relatives already settled in the diaspora.

3. *A Collective memory and myth about the homeland including its location, history, suffering and achievements.*

This book has detailed many instances of Africans communalizing among each other, such as in Haiti with their Guinea/Congo folklore; the 'transatlantic' flying ancestor folklore in Suriname venerated annually on the 1st July *Keti Koti* Emancipation Day; the Legba folklore among both the Yoruba and Fon; West and Central African *mamiwater* folklore kept alive in the New World; the singing, dancing, and drum-playing *Goombay* celebration in Jamaica, the Bahamas, and Bermuda; and the Bahian Africans in Brazil maintaining their religious and African traditions, which were integral to the 1835 Male rebellion.

4. *An idealization of the real or imagined ancestral home and a collective commitment to its maintenance, restoration, safety and prosperity, even its creation.*

The Haitian revolution was a collective commitment to both abolish the institution of slavery and establish an egalitarian and agrarian-driven economy which 'worked for all'. Given that Africans were

426

deemed at the bottom of the social hierarchy in these slave societies, their victory gave them a new lease of life. Though unsuccessful, the abortive Tomboy and Court 1736 Antiguan revolt, Tacky's 1766 rebellion in Jamaica, and the 1835 Male riots all had similar aims of establishing a free African society, and with it, the redemption of their African identities.

The Rastafarian movement's support for Haile Selassie during his exile and agitation for his restoration to the throne was a symbolic restoration of their imagined homeland. Whereas Ethiopia in more ancient times represented the cradle of black civilization, the contemporary Ethiopia was part of ancient Abyssinia. Nevertheless, the pursuit of an alternative identity and the rejection of a British, Georgian one, tilted the Rastafarians towards adopting Selassie's adversity as a wider part of their struggle.

5. *The frequent development of a return movement to the homeland that gains collective approbation even if many in the group are satisfied with only a vicarious relationship or intermittent visits to the homeland.*

There have been several 'return movements' across successive generations of the African diaspora.

The first return movement was the 1787 Province of Freedom Sierra Leonean experiment—followed by the 1791 revived Freetown project, and subsequently the creation of Liberia in 1822. However, though many African diasporans approved these return movements, the fundamental goal was to rid both the British and American host societies of their free black populations, and to aid British and American colonial interests. Ironically, the African descendants in Freetown were British-African hybrids based in what was effectively an extension of Britain. The same applied to Americo-Liberians who while physically now in Africa, retained their American mores— establishing 'an America away from America'.

Marcus Garvey's liberation politics included a *Return to Africa Movement* and he sought to purchase land in Liberia to actualize this plan.

Though not a return movement to Africa in the physical sense, Walter Eugene King, or Efuntola Oseijeman Adelabu Adefunmi—as he later came to be known—established the next best thing to this, which was the *Oyotunji* African Village (the subject of a Netflix documentary) founded in 1970 near Sheldon, Beaufort County, South Carolina. Adefunmi, raised as Baptist but left the faith in his youth, began to develop an interest in African culture and studies at the age of 16. At the age of 20, he traveled to Haiti to study vodou, and in 1959—just prior to the Cuban revolution—he became the first documented African-American initiate into the Obatala priesthood. The Oyotunji Village was named after the Oyo empire and means "Oyo returns" or "Oyo rises again." This was a reconstituted Yoruba society centered on Yoruba religious worship. The population of the village grew to as many as 250 people within a few years of its establishment.

Bernie Grant formed the UK reparations movement in 1993, which included a proposal for Black Britons to receive repatriation grants (up to £100,000 each when adjusted for inflation in 2022) to resettle in Africa.

Ghana's current President Nana Akufo-Addo personally launched The Year of Return (TYOR) in Washington D.C., in autumn 2018, which occasioned a Return Movement and has since become popular among African-Americans—evidence by rapper, Kendrick Lamar's 2022 documentary covering his journey to Ghana. The country's Immigrant Act of 2000 provides African diasporans with a *Right to Abode* status, thus granting them the indefinite right to live and work. Additionally, the 2000 Citizenship Act enables diasporans to apply for Ghanaian citizenship. A cohort of 34 people, mainly from the

Caribbean, were the first to receive citizenship certificates in 2016; notably the Ghana Caribbean Association (ghacarib) was founded in 1964 to foster links between Ghana and the Caribbean diaspora—helping the latter to integrate into Ghanaian society.

The UK's African-Caribbean newspaper *The Voice* produced an article in March 2022 entitled *BLAXIT: Black Brits Head For a New Life in Africa and the Caribbean*. It stated that there are increasing numbers of Black British people moving back to the Caribbean and Africa. One story in particular featured a Grenadian-British woman whose grandparents were part of the Windrush generation; she resettled in Grenada and created a YouTube lifestyle series called *The Exodus Collective*.

Between the late 2000s and mid-2010s, several Nigerian-Britons participated in the *MoveBackToNigeria* relocation trend. This was informed by an improvement in the economy—which at the time was on course to be one of the world's highest performing economies, the prospects of a better lifestyle, and the appeal of being closer to their families and ancestral roots. However, this trend has largely subsided due to the economic decline that has transpired under outgoing President Muhammadu Buhari from 2015 to the present day (April 2023); increasing insecurity in the forms of kidnapping, banditry, and terrorism; and a general decline in living standards, even for the wealthiest of Nigerians.

Many of the African diaspora have become contented with vicarious relationships, such as following showbiz pages online and popular culture trends from their homeland, listening to Afrobeats music, watching Nollywood / African TV productions, and occasionally reading about political developments in their home countries.

Several diasporans take intermittent trips to their homeland(s) such as those who participate in the annual 'detty December' Christmas trips to visit family, take in a warmer climate, and experience nightlife in a number of African cities: Accra, Abuja, Lagos, Freetown, Harare, and Kampala among several others.

6. *A strong ethnic group consciousness sustained over a long time and based on a sense of distinctiveness, a common history, the transmission of a common cultural and religious heritage, and the belief in a common fate.*

As mentioned above, group consciousness was at the core of [especially Caribbean] slave revolts.

Leading on from the post slavery-era, several Pan-African personalities and collaborators emerged in the diaspora: Marcus Garvey [from Jamaica but achieving his greatest reach in the U.S]; the Trinidadian, George Padmore; W.E.B du Bois from the U.S.; Ghana's Kwame Nkrumah and Nigeria's Nnamdi Azikiwe—while both were international students attending universities in the U.S. [and UK in the case of Nkrumah], to name some of many.

Malcolm X and both chapters of the British and U.S. Black Panther Movement established links with the mother continent as part of their Black liberation politics. Moreover, the founder of the Black British Panther Movement, the Biafran / Nigerian Obi Egbuna, was a student in the U.S.—during which time he stayed among black residents in the LA ghettoes to understand their lived experiences, and also participated in diaspora events organized by the Caribbean Artists Movement. His belief in the need for universal black collaboration also led him to form the Universal Coloured People's Association. These pioneering commitments denoted a shared ethnic group consciousness and belief in a common fate to actualize the liberation of Black people from their 'capitalist oppression.'

Music from the likes of Soul II Soul with Jazzie B, and NWA played a part in establishing popular culture diasporic ties on both sides of the Atlantic.

The lynchings of Black people in the US influenced racist attitudes towards Black people in Britain, thus helping to foster a sense of kinship across the Black Atlantic.

The riots of the 1950s in Notting Hill and Nottingham; and the riots of the 1980s in Brixton, Tottenham-Broadwater, and Chapeltown—involving first and second generation African-Caribbean youth—fostered a sense of shared consciousness.

Black UK solidarity was also evident in the face of police brutality meted out on African Americans —such as Rodney King, which occasioned UK-based protests and vocalizing their support on several mediums.

Black youth culture, alternately termed 'urban culture' in both the U.S. and UK arose out of socio-economic marginalization during a very challenging era. Young black people began to repudiate the image of [white] 'respectability' in the 1980s in favor of their own identity expressions. It was from this milieu that many talented artists from the African-Caribbean community achieved mainstream success in the entertainment industry(ies).

7. *A troubled relationship with host societies, suggesting a lack of acceptance or the possibility that another calamity might befall the group.*

The following apply: the miseducation of black—particularly male—youth in the diaspora; the rates of black youth unemployment in both the US and UK; studies which have shown that despite the significant contributory role of Black African nurses employed by the UK National Health Service (NHS), many commonly reported experiencing racism, bullying, discrimination, and lack of equal opportunities—notwithstanding the passing of the Equality Act 2010;

additionally, nurses were disproportionately [50%] more likely to be referred to the Nursing and Midwifery council (NMC), less likely to be accepted on to diploma courses—7.2% of the total number of applications were successful—far outweighed by their white counterparts who recorded a 79% success rate; the weaponization of the war on drugs on black males in the form of incessant stop and search treatment and / or over-policing under the 'sus laws'; imposter bias to varying degrees while participating in mainstream society— particularly in high-achieving environments; and daily microaggressions which can be disconcerting for many.

Furthermore, many Black Africans in the UK have been disadvantaged by only accessing insecure, poorly maintained privately-rented accommodation, and along with Pakistani and Bangladeshi groups, have the highest levels of overcrowding.

8. *A sense of empathy and co-responsibility with co-ethnic members in other countries of settlement, even where home has become vestigial.*

The commentary under point 6 above also applies here. The BLM movement, though it emanated from the murder of the African-American George Floyd, sparked protests in the UK after British African and Afro-Caribbean diasporans were influenced by their U.S. counterparts who were the first to hold protests.

The diaspora from across the U.S., UK, Canada, and the Caribbean demonstrated solidarity on several social media platforms with the Nigerian youths extrajudicially executed by the Nigerian Army— alternatively termed the *Lekki Massacre*. The massacred youth had been protesters involved in the decentralized End Sars social movement in October 2020 in Lagos Nigeria, which was inspired by human rights violations committed by the Special Anti-Robbery Squad (SARS) in the forms of illegal stop and searches, illegal arrests and detention, sexual harassment of women, and the brutalization of young men.

Moreover, there is also a popular culture example of this co-ethnic solidarity produced by the Nigerian-British rapper and actor *Dave*. Dave captured headlines for his February 2020 performance at *The BRIT Awards* (London) of his single *Black*. This is a breakdown of the lyrics and their meanings:

> *Look, black is beautiful, black is excellent*
> *Black is pain, black is joy, black is evident*
> *It's workin' twice as hard as the people you*
> *know you're better than 'Cause you need*
> *to do double what they do so you can level*
> *them,*
> *Black is so much deeper than just African*
> *-American,*
> *Our heritage been severed, you never got*
> *to experiment With family trees 'cause*
> *they teach you 'bout famine and greed*

What is revealing here is that despite Dave being a second-generation Nigerian-Briton, his considerable exposure to the Black American experience and its indelible imprint on Black popular culture has influenced him to meld the distinct history of African-Americans with his own. The severed heritage lyric is a reference to the dislodging caused by the transatlantic slave trade, and thus doesn't apply to him as he is acquainted with his Edo state roots in present day Southern Nigeria. That he included these lyrics is evidence of his empathy and racial solidarity with Black Americans.

Dave's global take on the black experience was evident in other lines such as:

Black is watchin' child soldiers gettin' killed by otherchildren
Feelin' sick like, "Oh shit, this could have happened to me"

Which by inference is redolent of the tragic, brutal, and genocidal events during the diamond-driven Liberian and Sierra Leonean civil wars.

Another extract:

Black is distant It's representin' countries that never existed while
your grandmother was livin'
Black is my Ghanaian brother readin' into scriptures
Doing research on his lineage, findin' out that he's Egyptian

This is profound as it differs from the narrative that Africans on the continent know 'their roots'. On the contrary, there are several Africans that have researched their myths of origin, family history and for reasons best known to them, have traced roots to location(s) other than the African country that they have recent roots in.

Another:

Black is people namin' your countries on what they
trade most
Coast of Ivory, Gold Coast, and the Grain Coast...

This line relates to the pre-colonial maps that nicknamed polities well known for producing 'commodities'—both human and non-animate—that could be procured in considerable volumes. Ivory Coast's name comes from its trade in elephant tusks which is in contrast to Ghana which replaced its former Gold Coast colonial designation with the name of an ancient West African empire when it gained independence.

And Dave's closing line:

...But black is all I know, there ain't a thing that
I would change in it.

Underlines Dave's diasporic consciousness and solidarity not only with the diaspora in the U.S., but also African people based on the continent.

9. *The possibility of a distinctive creative, enriching life in host countries with a tolerance for pluralism*

The Notting Hill Carnival (NHC) has been an integral part of the British African-Caribbean experience. This is due to both its political roots from the 1950s in Britain and its connection to the 19th century Trinidadian carnival marking freedom for the island's enslaved Africans. The steel band at the NHC for example, is a cultural carryover from Trinidad. Second generation British youth from Jamaican backgrounds—though carnival is not a Jamaican practice in the strictest sense—use the NHC occasion to celebrate their creole culture in the form of Jamaica corner (without Soca music) and the sale of Jamaican food. In more recent times the NHC has created an Afrobeats corner—reflecting the musical tastes of second-generation African-Britons.

Black history month (BHM) celebrations—February being the U.S.'s designated month, and the UK's in October—take place annually to commemorate the diaspora's most remarkable achievements and profound events. However, the UK version has been criticized for many years due to its predominant focus on Black American history with nominal coverage of the UK Black history, despite the latter's rich history. Other criticisms center on moves in recent years to make it a 'multicultural affair' in both the UK/US, thus sparking fears of the occasion losing its meaning.

It should be noted that in more recent times there has been an increase in the number of Black theater productions; art galleries featuring the lives of British African Krios in Freetown and other parts of West Africa; art and iconography redolent of key periods of resistance and achievement—all of which are tools to reinforce African diasporic consciousness.

The Assimilation Question and Future of the Diaspora

The 'African diaspora' is similarly diverse to the Italian, Chinese and Indian diasporas. It comprises persons with distant links to the African continent—from the myriad Caribbean islands and the U.S.—and the more recent arrivals from the African continent. Significantly, though slave-based and colonial propaganda produced a negative global image of 'Black' people, it belies the diversity of ideologies, worldviews, and future possibilities across the diaspora. It is important to note that cultural production in the diaspora has been largely reactionary to racism, discrimination, hostile environments, and [to varying degrees] limited participation in the mainstream society. While this has produced successive waves of talent and creativity, the adverse conditions from which such output arose are unprecedented in the Western World, and thus cannot be replicated verbatim. Given the rate of racial and cultural assimilation taking place, the lived experiences of the coming generations will be markedly different. To this end, what does it mean to be Black in the present-day?

The U.S. and UK black communities and Africans from the Caribbean islands are all the products of 'fictive kinship' ties to varying degrees. The ancestors of African-Americans and African-Caribbeans came from different polities and nations in Africa, thus their shared experiences in captivity fostered a sense of togetherness. Successive generations gradually creolized and congealed into a solitary African-American ethnic group in the case of the U.S., and as Jamaicans, Grenadians, Bajans and so forth in the Caribbean.

By contrast, the British African population is a diverse motley crew essentialized as black; despite shared tastes in popular culture and the increasing acceptance of an, albeit, ambiguous Black British identity, the group at best shares a weak form of fictive kinship.

Despite the politics of the BLM movement, the era of Black liberation politics that characterized the emergence of Malcolm X, Martin Luther King, and the Black Panther movements are long over. Whereas the older generations were vehemently against capitalism and in favor of socialism— and in some instances held Marxist leanings, the younger generations in the diaspora are markedly more consumerist and capitalist-leaning. So-called Black music genres in both the UK and U.S. are now effectively 'open source' in that many white artists performing these genres can realistically achieve greater popularity among Black audiences than even some Black artists can; examples of this include Eminem, Adele, Ed Sheeran, and more recently, the drill artist Central-Cee. The culmination of these realities is consistent with what this author calls the era of 'Decentralized Blackness'.

At the time of writing, Black people who exhibit behavior or dispositions that are not stereotypically 'black,' or 'urban' invariably attract slurs in the forms of 'coon,' 'Uncle Tom,' 'sell-out,' 'coconut' and so forth. Those who use such slurs effectively assume the role of 'arbitrary gatekeepers of blackness,' despite lacking the credibility to do so. Moreover, they almost certainly have no verifiable track record of making sacrifices or exhibiting altruism on behalf of the Black masses. For people with such sentiments, 'Blackness' ironically becomes a zero-sum game—despite its original use to foster community spirit—and a tool which is weaponized against those disliked by the self-styled gatekeeper.

Unfortunately, for many 'non-stereotypical' black people such derision may feel hurtful, yet to 'racially virtue-signal' is a fool's errand. The solution alternatively is to embrace the concept of *Decentralized Blackness*. Stopping short of *Ethnomasochism* and actively seeking to harm other Black people, no Black person should feel anxiety to 'perform Blackness' for the amusement of another. Not only is the age of black nationalism non-existent in the present-day, but most black people in the diaspora are assimilated into their host societies to varying degrees—many of whom have adopted white working class or middle-class values.

It is important to note that a cultural vacuum has emerged since the 1970s when the Black Panthers disbanded. In its place the following have emerged: the feminist movement, which has gained traction among many Black women who see it as more advantageous to identify with their fellow women than to lead with their racial identity; the cult of celebrity which has transformed Black popular culture; and a spirit of hyper-consumerism.

Consequently, there is now uncertainty over whether the term 'Black' is a noun, a verb, or an adjective. As race is a social construct in the Western World it is officially a noun; it is widely accepted that Black physical features can be described, thus it counts as an adjective, however, the point of contention is whether 'Black' is a verb—or in other words, performative. Performativity is imprecise and polarizing so 'Decentralized Blackness,' conceptually is the closest thing to 'Black or 'Blackness' being a verb.

Nowadays Black popular culture is widely accepted as the nexus of Black identities. Blackness is often affirmed or indexed by the consumption of celebrity culture, showbiz art, music, entertainment, awareness of social media trends and other emblems. The problem with this is that previously popular culture was more innocuous, wholesome, and community-centered—as noted in the case of the *Cosby Show* and *Desmonds*; whereas nowadays it is more consumerist and polarizing in spirit—gender wars, individualistic sentiment, select storylines on reality TV shows, and relentless exposure to materialistic lifestyles. Those deemed outside the framework of popular culture consumption will unfortunately have their Blackness called into question, thus triggering race-related anxiety and bruised sensibilities.

Blackness is indivisible from the title of this book *Ethnic Escapism and the Black Burden*. Part of the burden has been addressed above, thus the proposal of 'Decentralized Blackness' to alleviate the performative burden of blackness—especially in the diaspora (the other [African] Black Burden theory is covered at length in Volume 2).

When it comes to the concept of 'Ethnic Escapism' and its relevance to the diaspora, the term 'Ethnic,'—derived from the Greek word 'ethnos' meaning nation or subnation—is not entirely accurate. In the U.S., though the era of Black liberation politics is over, systematic discrimination and unique cultural practices—particularly from the South—means the vestiges of Black nationalism still abound. In the case of the Caribbean, nationalist spirit is evident in proudly identifying as Jamaicans, Grenadians, Haitian, St. Lucian, Antiguans, Trinidadian and so forth.

However, despite the evolution of the Black British identity, strictly speaking it does not constitute a nation thus terming it 'ethnicity' is a misnomer.

In terms of the word 'Escapism' the word 'escape' comes from the old French word of 'eschaper' which means to 'cloak or mask something'; the 'ism' from the Greek word 'ismos' which denotes distinctive action(s), practice(s), doctrine(d), a theory, or a system. The creolized cultures of the New World, such as those in the Caribbean and the U.S., cloak the individual African practices or mores traceable to specific African nations. Thus, though many proudly assert their nationalities as Jamaicans, Grenadians, Louisiana creoles, Gullah Geechee and so forth, they are often reminded of their African roots—which they can never entirely dissociate themselves from. Examples include the assertion of African roots by Caribbean politicians and scholars, the U.S. hyphenating the African-American designation, and the British Government similarly adopting the hyphenated African-Caribbean label. Analogously, several Brits, Americans, Australians, still celebrate their Irish heritage by participating in Riverdance and celebrating St. Patrick day; many Chinese with distant roots to their homeland celebrate the Chinese New Year; Argentines with Italian heritage celebrate their roots at the annual immigrants festival or *Fiesta Nacional del Inmigrante*, to name some of many examples.

Evaluating the prospects of the African diaspora is a rather composite exercise. Among African-Americans there are many different worldviews held and these are informed by whether they identify as Pan-Africanists, Foundational Black Americans (FBA), American Descendants of Slavery (ADOS) and so forth; however, one thing they do have in common is a desire to remain in the U.S. in perpetuity. This is entirely understandable and reflects the view held by the Freedmen of many generations ago who refused flat out to move to Liberia or resettle in Africa due to the contribution they had made to developing the U.S. and the belief that they had a stake in the country, much like the other settler groups. As such, this raises questions as to the level of diasporic consciousness among them. For example, how many are invested in the affairs of the African continent? Keep abreast of the latest news developments? Travel to at least one African country every so often? Practice distinctive residual African / Creole customs and traditions? Feel solidarity with African-Caribbeans, Black Brits and Africans? Remit money back to the continent for myriad reasons (business, family support and so forth)? The reality is that African-Americans are primarily concerned with their everyday lives in the U.S., and have largely assimilated into the mainstream—including the adoption of European-American values and mores. Moreover, any reparations received will primarily be re-circulated within the U.S. economy by the majority of recipients. However, African-Americans do reinforce their African diasporic consciousness by showing solidarity with Africans in other parts of the world; speaking AAVE; the consumption of 'Soul Food;' celebrating Black History Month in February; Juneteenth—the date of their ancestors' emancipation on 19th June 1865, and Kwanzaa between 26th December and 1st January to commemorate African-American culture and heritage.

Caribbean people of African heritage reinforce their African heritage in myriad ways: the consumption of callaloo, ackee and saltfish and other food ways; watching Nollywood movies; using kola nut for celebratory and medicinal reasons; partaking in Junkanoo festivals; music genres such as calypso and so forth. However, they distinctly and primarily identify with the islands they come from; are primarily concerned with Caribbean issues—and issues that affect their individual islands in-particular; they do not participate in intermittent travel to Africa on a widespread level, nor is there a popular return-to-Africa movement—at best, the followers of Rastafarianism may have such leanings. Ultimately the Caribbean is home and Africa as a homeland is vestigial at best.

The African diaspora in Britain is the most complex to evaluate in terms of their diasporic consciousness. Second, third, and fourth-generation British African-Caribbeans are largely assimilated into mainstream British society. They are 'twice-diasporans' in terms of being both a part of the African diaspora and their individual Caribbean island diasporas. Several reinforce their Caribbean diasporic consciousness by consuming Caribbean cuisine, being part of community hubs such as the Seventh Day Adventist (SDA) Church, intermittently speaking patois / creole, attending the Notting Hill Carnival, celebrating Black History Month, and identifying with the African-American experience largely through popular culture. They by and large do not partake in any return-to-Africa or return-to-the Caribbean movement, and Britain is now home. Any remittances are sent back to the Caribbean and not to the African continent. Caribbean-Americans have a similar diasporic consciousness to their British-Caribbean counterparts, moreover, several of the former have cousins based in Britain and vice-versa. Caribbean-Americans are more proximal to African-Americans and in many cases have intermarried with them, as well as having invariably adopted an American identity.

The British African component is arguably the most diverse, which is understandable as they do not have a shared experience beyond a generation—in marked contrast to the diasporic communities in the U.S., the Caribbean and the Windrush generation (including its descendants).

African and Bantu Brits are phenotypically similar to their Caribbean counterparts and share some relative cultural similarities, while British Somali and Eritreans have distinctly different phenotypes and cultures. Moreover, there is almost no uniform diasporic consciousness. For example, British Africans are more likely to identify with their individual countries—Nigeria, Ghana, DR Congo, Kenya, Zimbabwe, Sierra Leone, Uganda and so forth; more granularly, some will identify even more so with their individual ethnic groups—Asante / Akan, Bakongo, Yoruba, Igbo, Mende, Ndebele, Busoga and so forth. Therefore, their attendant loyalties will naturally be split and are arguably irreconcilable. Music and media consumption vary; intermittent trips are made to different homelands, remittances are sent to several countries, and there are many different Independence Day celebrations held; in essence, the heterogeneity is so great that one could make the argument that grouping them as one diaspora would be contentious. By definition it represents a Motley Crew, reflects weak fictive kinship at best, and any sense of togetherness is predicated on a shared appreciation of popular culture—such as Afrobeats, Amapiano, TV series, jollof rice, Pentecostal / Charismatic church attendances and so forth, and invariably emulating media portrayals of African-Americans.

While many British Africans are second-generation and still strongly identify with their parents' countries of origin, they are very much on the path to assimilation. Besides the blend of popular cultures consumed, their values, lifestyles and economic aspirations are largely indistinguishable from any other demographic. There is also no return movement among them, and though they do intermittent travel back to their homeland(s), their connection is foreseeably more distant than that of their parents. When it comes to annual remittances to Nigeria or Ghana for example, the $20 billion+ figure sent back to Nigeria is largely from the older first-generation migrants for the purposes of paying relatives' bills, small-scale business capital and / or building a home to return to in their retirement; by contrast the second and certainly third-generations are disinclined to emulate their parents' remittance commitments, and their earnings are more likely to be re-circulated in the diaspora / host nation's economy. In light of this, it is almost inevitable that remittance flows will precipitously decline in the coming years. The more recent African migrants to the U.S. are on a similar path of assimilation to their British counterparts.

But for the creation of diaspora airlines, hospitals / clinics, real estate, business investments, banks to maximize the value of remittances, educational institutes, and the like to foster transnational lifestyles in greater numbers—all of which can be established with a fraction of just the Nigerian diaspora's annual remittances alone, the sun will inevitably set on the African diaspora. The changing racial demographics in the diaspora merely reflect the inevitability of assimilation.

EPILOGUE

I am grateful for everyone that has invested in a copy of this book. I sincerely hope the long road, challenges and sacrifices were worthwhile, and all feedback will be humbly appreciated.

It is only foreseeable that there will be disagreements on some parts of this book that may be deemed contentious. While the compilation of research and the critical approach to writing this book is not intended to offend, the burden of performance is such that I had to risk the possibility of offence and the bruising of sensibilities. I contend that much of what has been written will resonate for some time to come, and any detractors may, with time, agree with varying aspects of the book. My intention from the outset was to produce a work as robust and as rigorous as possible and you the reader can be the judge of how effectively this was achieved. The field of Black studies and diasporic matters is ever-growing and I feel privileged to have made my own contribution; it would give me the utmost pride if writers are inspired to build on any theories I have advanced in this book. I very much welcome any enquiries or discussions to aid related research.

If you enjoyed reading this book, volume 2 will be definitely worth reading as it explores the notions of Ethnic Escapism and Black Burdens from a continental vantage point. Both volumes are essential reading.

INDEX

LIST OF SOURCES

[A pocketbook], "Barbados Memorandum, Prices &c" [1772—82], E23918, Fitzherbert-Perrin Papers

[A West Indian], *Notes in Defense of the Colonies*, pps. 29, 34

[anon.] ""La nommee Marie Katherine, dite Kingue'...","" [1785?], AN 27 AP 12, Archives Privees, Fonds Francois de Neufchateau, folder 2

[Kingston] *Daily Advertiser*, July 16, 1790, J. Stokes; *Jam. Royal Gaz.*, May 23, 1801-S., S. Waddington and Co

[Quoted in] Agiri, B.A., 'Early Oyo History Reconsidered,' *History in Africa*, 1975, pps.1, 9

[T. R. Gray], *Richmond Enquirer*, Nov. 8, 1831; "Nat Turner's Confession," pps. 307—9

"[Ac]count of the Number of Slaves exported from [Cape Coast Castle] Gold Coast of Africa to his Ma[jesty's] Plantations ... in America Since 1757," no. 41, bundle 471, Dickinson Papers, I. I, Somerset Record Office, Taunton. The Tobago census is in Lt. Gov. William Young to the Sec. of State, April 29, 1772, C.O. 101/16, f. 126ff; "State of the Island of Tobago from the 24th June 1771 to 1st of May 1773," in Gov. Leyborne to Dartmouth, Grenada, July 17, 1773, C.O. 101/17, f. 181

"1826 Barbados — Codrington College Remarks in Codrington Estate and Treatment of Slaves," series C/WI, box 8, Society for the Propagation of the Gospel Archives, London

"*ACS Demographic And Housing Estimates.*" U.S. Census Bureau. December, 2019. Retrieved 15th March 2020.

"Act of the General Assembly, July 15, 1715," in Donnan, ed., *Documents*, III, pp.114, 446—449, 456

"Antigua, December 9," *South Carolina Gazette*, Dec. 25 1755—Jan. 1, 1756. For more on *l'Aimable's* transatlantic voyage, see Voyages: *The Trans-Atlantic Slave Trade Database*, accessed August 2011, www.slavevoyages.org, Voyage ID no. 31523

"Antigua, November 4," *South-Carolina Gazette*, Dec. 4—11, 1755

"*Diversity Visa Program Statistics.*"Travel.state.gov. Retrieved 15th May 2020

"Does 'Purple' Hate Men?" January 5th, 1986. Chicago Tribune. Url: https://www.chicagotribune.com/news/ct-xpm-1986-01-05-8601020159-story.html [Accessed: 18th February 2021]

"Ecowas Defence Commission", West Africa, no. 3822, 11-17 February 1991, pp.197, cited in Daniel Tetteh OSABU-KLE (2000) pp.331

"Farrakhan Set To Give Final Address At Nation Of Islam's Birthplace." Fox News Channel. December 6th 2011. Retrieved May 15th 2020

"Governor Jonathan Atkins to Sir Joseph Williamson, 3 October 1675," *CSPC*, no. 690 (and CO 1/35)

"H.R. 40 – Commission to Study and Develop Reparation Proposals for African-Americans Act [116th Congress (2019-20)] Congress.Gov. Url: https://www.congress.gov/bill/116th-congress/house-bill/40/cosponsors?searchResultViewType=expanded [Accessed: 8th February 2021]

"Home Office 'was told about Windrush problems in 2016'". 25 April 2018. BBC News

"Johan Nieman's Letter from Gross-Friedrichsburg, 8 March 1684," in Jones, Brandenburg Sources, pp.88

"Letter from 'M' to Francois de Neufchateau, Attorney General, 16 September 1785," AN 27 AP 12, Archives Privees, Fonds Francois de Neufchateau, folder 2

"Letter from 'M' to Francois de Neufchateau, Attorney General, 3 September 1785," AN, 27 AP 12, Archives Privees, Fonds Francois de Neufchateau, folder 2

"Lift Every Voice: The Biden Plan for Black America". Battle for the Soul of the Nation. Url: https://joebiden.com/blackamerica/# [Accessed: 8[th] February 2021]

"List of Negroes on Kings Valley Estate taken 1 Jan[uar]y," no. 1455, Penrhyn Papers, Department of Manuscripts, University College of North Wales Library, Bangor, Depositions of William Stevenson, Esqr., C.O. 140/84, p. 39; attorney's report, letterbook fragment (1801—5) of Scarlett (no first name) minor and owner of Peru Estate, Langsdale MS, University of Hull Archives

"Lynch Him! Heard in London," Manchester Guardian Weekly, 4th September 1958, ibid Perry pp. 156
"Minutes of the Assembly of Barbadoes, 23—25 November 1675," *CSPC*, no.712

"N.C. city approves reparations for Black residents through community investment. NBC – A Gray Media Group, Inc station. July 15th 2020. Url: https://www.nbc12.com/2020/07/15/nc-city-approves-reparations-black-residents-through-community-investment/ [Accessed: 8th February 2021]

"Nat Turner's Confessions," pps. 306ff, 309, 313—34, 316—37

"New Race Riots in UK: Mostly Whites Held," Daily Gleaner, 1st September 1958; and "Renewed Racial Disturbances In London," The Times, 3rd September 1958; ibid Perry pp. 155

"Persons Charged Following The Black Panther Demonstration On The 2nd March 1970," London, Public Record Office, Director Of Public Prosecutions (DPP) 2/4827, 1970
"Race Riots Terrorise a City," Daily Express, 25th August 1958 cited by Kennetta Hammond Perry "Little Rock" in Britain: Jim Crow's Transatlantic Topographies. Journal Of British Studies, Vol. 51, No.1 (2012) pp. 155

"Reparations". City of Evanston. Url: https://www.cityofevanston.org/government/city-council/reparations [Accessed: 8th February 2021]

"Slave descendants file $1 billion lawsuit against companies with alleged ties to slave trade". April 26, 2004. Jet. 150 (17) pp.36-7

"Slave Papers," no. 9, Library of Congress, Washington, D.C.

"Some Undistinguished Negroes" (documents), Journal of Negro History, 3 (January, 1918), pp.91

"St John's in Antigua, November 4," *Maryland Gazette*, Dec. 26, 1755

"Table 10. Persons Obtaining Lawful Permanent Resident Status By Broad Class Of Admission And Region And Country Of Birth: Fiscal Year 2016." Department Of Homeland Security. 16th May 2017, Retrieved 15th May 2020

"Treaty between the Kingdom of Fetu, the Kingdom of Denmark and the Danish Africa Company, 20 December 1659," *German Sources*, 9, 9n26

"Wilhelm Johann Muller's Description of the Fetu Country, 1662—9," in Jones, *German Sources*, pps.118—19, 134, 137, 138—141, 158—63, 162—166, 170—173, 175, 178

"Windrush compensation scheme overhauled". 14 December 2020. GOV UK.

1959. "British Enterprise on the Niger 1830—1869." Ph.D. diss., University of London

1999. "Trust, Pawnship and Atlantic History: The Institutional Foundations of the old Calabar Slave Trade." *American Historical Review*, Vol. 102: pps. 333--55

2000. 'Identifying Enslaved Africans in the African Diaspora,'

A Professional Planter: Practical Rules for the Management and Medical Treatment of Negro Slaves, in the Sugar Colonies [London, 1811), pps.35—36

Abrahams, Roger D. & Szwed, John F. (eds.) After Africa: Extracts from British Travel Accounts and Journals of the Seventeenth, Eighteenth, and Nineteenth Centuries Concerning the Slaves, their Manners, and Customs in the British West Indies (New Haven, 1983), passim

Acemoglu, Daron; Johnson, Simon & Robinson, James "The Rise of Europe: Atlantic Trade, Institutional Change, and Economic Growth," *American Economic Review*, XCV (2005), pps.546—579

Adams, Richard. "Oxford college to launch scholarship in attempt to address legacy of slavery". Fri 10 Nov 2017. Fri 23 Aug 2019. The Guardian. Url: https://www.theguardian.com/education/2017/nov/10/oxford-all-souls-college-scholarship-slavery-legacy-caribbean-christopher-codrington [Accessed: 8th February 2021]

Addish, Sumaya. "African Immigration to the United States (1965—)." Blackpast.org. January 27, 2022. Url: https://www.blackpast.org/african-american-history/african-immigration-to-the-united-states-1965/ [Accessed: 12 April 2023]

Adediran, Biodun, "Yoruba Ethnic Groups or a Yoruba Ethnic Group? A Review of the Problem of Ethnic Identification," *Africa: Revista do Centro de Estudos Africanos da Universidade de Sao Paulo, Brazil* (1984), pps.57—70

AEBa Legislativa. *Abaxio-assinados*, 1835-1836, maco 979
Afigbo, A. E. 'Oral tradition and the history of segmentary societies,' History of Africa, 1985 pp.6

Afigbo, A. E. 'Traditions of Igbo origins: a comment,' *History in Africa*, 1983, pp. 9

Afigbo, A. E. 1987. *The Igbo and their Neighbours*, Ibadan, Nigeria: Ibadan University Press, pp.41

Afigbo, A. E. *Ropes of Sand: Studies in Igbo History and Culture.* (University Press: Nigeria, Ibadan, 1981) pp. 64

Agbedor, Paul & Johnson, Assiba, "Naming Practices," in Lawrance, Benjamin ed. *Handbook of Eweland: The Ewe of Togo and Benin* (Woeli Publishing Services: Accra, 2005), pps.162—65

Agiri, 'Early Oyo History,' cit., the Oba Alaye, Oba Loron and Ompetu

Agorsah, "Archaeology and Resistance History," pps.178—80

Agorsah, E. Kofi & Butler, Thomas "Archaeological Investigation of Historic Kormantse, Ghana: Cultural Identities." *African Diaspora Archaeology Newsletter* (September 2008) pps.2—6

Ajayi, J.F. Ade & Smith, Robert *Yoruba Warfare in the Nineteenth-Century*, 2nd ed. (Ibadan University Press: Ibadan, Nigeria, 1971), pp.108

Ajayi, J.F. Ade, "Samuel Ajayi Crowther of Oyo," in *Africa Remembered: Narratives by West Africans from the Era of the Slave Trade*, ed. Philip D. Curtin, chap. 9 (Prospect Heights, Ill.: Waveland, 1997 [1967]), incl' pps. 296, 302—4, 310—14, 326

Akala Natives: Race And Class In The Ruins Of Empire (Two Roads, 2018)

Akyeampong, Emmanuel *Between the Sea and the Lagoon: An Eco-Social History of the Anlo of Southeastern Ghana c. 1850 to Recent Times* (Ohio University Press: Athens, 2001), pps.1—7

Alagoa, E.J. 1986. "The Slave Trade in Niger Delta Oral Tradition and History." In *Africans in Bondage*, pp.127. See Lovejoy Paul E. (editor) 1986. *Africans in Bondage: Studies in Slavery and the Slave Trade.* Madison, WI: African Studies Program, University of Wisconsin, pps. 139—40, 153—7

Alagoa, Ebiegberi J. & Adadonye, Fombo, *A Chronicle of Grand Bonny* (Ibadan, Nigeria, 1972), pps.3—16

Alagoa, Ebiegberi, J. *A History of the Niger Delta: a Historical Interpretation of Ijo Oral Tradition* (Ibadan, Nigeria), pps.10—16, 123—71

Aldridge, Delores P. & Young, Carlene *Out Of The Revolution: The Development Of Africana Studies* (Lexington Books, 2003) pp. 350

Alexander, Claire *The Art Of Being Black* (Oxford University Press: New York, 1996) pps. 1, 6, cit Fryer (1984: 372), 57

Alexander, Monica J.; Kiang, Mathew V. & Barbieri, Magali *"Trends in Black and White Opioid Mortality in the United States, 1979-2015."* Social Epidemiology, Walters Kluwer Health Inc. Url: https://journals.lww.com/epidem/Fulltext/2018/09000/Trends_in_Black_and_White_Opioid_Mortality_in_the.16.aspx [Accessed: 16th February 2021]

Alleyne, Mervyn C. 'Continuity versus Creativity in Afro-American Language and Culture,' in Mufwene, Salikoko S. (ed.) *Africanisms in Afro-American Language Varieties* (Athens, GA, 1991) pps.167—81

Alleyne, Mervyn C., 'Continuity versus Creativity in Afro-American Language and Culture

Allison, Philip, *African Stone Sculptures* (New York, 1968), pp.11

Allison, Philip, *Cross River Monoliths* (Lagos, 1968)

Allsop, Richard (comp.) *Dictionary of Caribbean English Usage* (Oxford, 1996) pps. 302, 392, 400; see entries for 'Ibo (Nation) — dance' and 'nation dance'

Amelia Gentlemen. "Home Office told of Windrush error five years ago, experts say". 8 May 2018. The Guardian

American Colonization Society, *Fifteenth Annual Report* (1831) pp. 34. The annual report noted that New Hampshire, Vermont, Connecticut, New Jersey, Pennsylvania, Delaware, Maryland, Virginia, Georgia, Tennesse, Kentucky, Ohio, and Indiana had passed resolutions approving of the Society and recommending a system of foreign colonization.

American Colonization Society, Seventeenth Annual Report, Treasurer's Report (1833) pp. 26

Anderson, Richard *"The Diaspora of Sierra Leone's Liberated Africans: Enlistment, Forced Migration, and 'Liberation' at Freetown, 1808-1863".* African Economic History, vol. 41, 2013, pp. 103

Andrew, John *The Hanging of Arthur Hodge* (New York, 2000) pp.18

Angelo, Anne-Marie *The Black Panthers In London 1967-1972: A Diasporic Struggle Navigates The Black Atlantic.* Radical History Review (2009) No. 103 pp. 21

Aniakor, Chike, 'The Omabe Cult and Masking Tradition,' in *Nsukka Environment*, pps. 271—2, 286—306

Anquandah, James *Rediscovering Ghana's Past* (Longman Group: Harlow, UK, 1982), pps.126—127

Anstey, Roger, "The Volume and Profitability of the British Slave Trade, 1767—1807," in Stanley L. Engerman and Eugene D. Genovese, eds., *Race and Slavery in the Western Hemisphere: Quantitative Studies* (Princeton, N.J., 1975) pps.3—31

Antigua, May 12, 1790, D1610/C 19, Codrington Family Papers, Gloucestershire Record Office, Gloucester

Apetheker, *Herbert, American Negro Slave Revolts* (International Publishers: New York, 1993), pps. 7—9, 44, 299—300

Apter, A. 'The historiography of Yoruba Myth and Ritual,' *History in Africa*, 1987, pps.1—25,

Arinze, Francis, Sacrifice in Ibo Religion (Ibadan, Nigeria, 1970) pp.13—14, 37—8, 44, 57, 83

Asante, Molefi Kete, *Afrocentricity* (Africa World Press Inc: Trenton, N.J., 1989), pp.8

Asante, S. K. B., *Pan-African Protest: West Africa and Italo-Ethiopia Crisis 1931—1941* (Longman Group Ltd: New York, 1974), pps.14, 15 (quoted from the *Gold Coast Independent Accra*, 18 January 1936)

Askari, Eva K., "The Social Organization of the Owe," African Notes 2, no.3 (1964—65), pp.9

Aspinall, Peter J. & Chinouya, Martha J. *Migration, Diasporas, and Citizenship. The African Diaspora Population in Britain: Migrant Identities and Experiences* (Palgrave Macmillan, Spring Nature: London, 2016), pps.viii (intro), 1—9, 11—16, 62, 64, 105—07, 131—32, 135 cit., Office For National Statistics 2011 census data; 140—47, 153—55, 158—59, 160, 205—07, 227—8; cit. Anonymous respondent data on pp.228

Aspinall, Peter J. *The New 2001 Census Question Set On Cultural Characteristics: Is It Useful For The Monitoring Of The Health Status From Ethnic Groups In Britain*. Ethnicity & Health, (2000) 5(1), pp. 36

Axelson, S. *Culture Confrontation in the Lower Congo* (Uppsala, 1970) pps.136—41

Ayorinde, Christine, "Regla de Ocha-Ifa and the Construction of Cuban Identity" in *Identity in the Shadow of Slavery* ed. Paul E. Lovejoy (Continuum, London, 2000), pps.72—75

Ba, D.. "Senegal's Wade Calls Slave Reparations Absurd", Independent Online, 11th August 2001.

Babayemi, S.O., *The Fall and Rise of Oyo c. 1706—1905: A Study in the Traditional Culture of an African Polity* (Lichfield Nigeria: Lagos, 1990), chap.3

Baikie, William B. *Narrative of an Exploring Voyage up the Rivers Kwora and Binue* (1856; London, 1966), pp.307, 308—11, 314—15, 337

Baker, E. C., *A Guide to Records in the Windward Islands* (1968)

Balmer, W. T. *A History of the Akan Peoples of the Gold Coast* (Atlantic Press: London, 1926), pps.26—31

Bank of England Inflation Calculator. Url: https://www.bankofengland.co.uk/monetary-policy/inflation/inflation-calculator
Baraka, Amiri. *Black Music* (W. Morrow: New York, 1967), pps. 180—212

Barb. Merc. And B-T. Gaz., Dec. 2, 1786, George White's Ned Boy, enclosed in C.O. 7/1 (71); Aug. 3, 1805, J. Malloney, Sen., Oct. 6, 1807, Issac Agard; Oct. 8, 1788, E. G. Thomas; Nov. 2, 1805-S., Jacob Goodrige; Aug. 30, 1783, Richard Redwar; Jan. 11, 1806, J. C. Roach; and Aug. 16, 1788, Abel Hinds. A plantation record notes that slaves with two wives are "very common." Gill Slater to Lady Fitzherbert, June 3, 1793, E20565, Fitzherbert-Perrin Papers

Barbados Mercury (Bridgetown), 11 Jan., 20 May, 24 June 1817; 28 Aug. 1824 (obituary); *The Barbadian* (Bridgetown), 31 Aug. 1824, 8 and 22 Aug. 1828

Barber, 'Discursive Strategies in the Texts of Ifa and in the "Holy Book of Odu" of the African Church of Orunmila, in P.F. de Moraes Farias and K. Barber (eds.), *Self-Assertion and Brokerage* (Birmingham, 1990), pps.196—224

Barber, Karim, 'How Man Makes God in West Africa: Yoruba Attitudes Towards the Orisa,' *Africa*, 51, no.3 (1981), pps.724—45

Barber, Karim, 'Oriki, Women and the Proliferation and Merging of Orisa,' *Africa* 60, no.3 (1990), pps.313—37

Barbot, James Jr. & Grazilhier, J. 1699. "Abstract of a Voyage to New Kalabar, Bandi, Doni Rivers, in 1699." *Collection of Voyages and Travels*, Vol. 3. (London: Thomas Astley) pp. 109

Barbot, James Jr. "The Slave Trade at Calabar, 1700—1705." *In Documents Illustrative.* See Donnan 1931

Barbot, John 1682. "John Barbot's Description of Guinea." *In Documents Illustrative.* See Donnan 1930; pp.340

Barbot, John. 1732. *A Description of the Coasts of North and South-Guinea; and of Ethiopia Interior, Vulgarly Angola: Being a New and Accurate Account of the Western Maritime Countries of Africa*, in Six Books (London: Churchill) pp. 381, III: 244, IV: 418, 572

Barclay, James, *The Voyages and Travels of James Barclay, Containing Many Surprising Adventures and Interesting Narratives* (n.p., 1777) pp.26

Barczewski, Stephanie; Eglin, John; Heathorn, Stephen; Silvestri, Michael & Tusan, Michelle *Britain Since 1688: A Nation In The World* (Routledge 1st Ed., 2014) pp.30

Barken, E.. The Guilt of Nations: Restitution and Negotiating Historical Injustices (New York: W.W. Norton, 2000) pps.3-29, 88-111

Barnet, Miguel, 'La hora de Yemaja,' *Gaceta de Cuba*, 34, no.2 (1996), pp.48

Barratt, Leonard E. *The Rastafarian: A Study in Messianic Cultism in Jamaica* (Institute of Caribbean Studies: Mexico, 1969), pps.78, 90

Barrow, Steve & Dalton, Peter *"The Rough Guide to Reggae".* (Rough Guides, 2004) pps. 329-334

Barry, Boubacar. *Senegambia and the Atlantic Slave Trade* (Cambridge University Press: Cambridge, 1998)

Based on updated Guthrie Classifications Compiled by Jouni Filip Maho: Jouni Filip Maho, "The New Updated Guthrie Online," http://goto.glocalnet.net/mahopapers/nuglonline.pdf

Bastian, A. *San Salvador* (1859) cit, in Jan Vansina, *Kingdoms of the Savanna* (Madison, 1966) pp.68

Baucom, Ian *Specters of the Atlantic: Finance Capital, Slavery, and the Philosophy of History* (N.C.: Durham, 2005), pps.11, 28—32, 43—48

BBC News Africa *Liberia Country Profile* – Url: https://www.bbc.co.uk/news/world-africa-13729504 (January, 2018)

BDA: Book of Powers Index; 1832; Manumission of Sukey Ann and others RB 7/26

Beckford Jr., William, Remarks Upon the Situation of the Negroes in Jamaica (London, 1788), pps.23—24

Beckles, Hilary *Bussa: The 1816 Revolution in Barbados* (Cave Hill, Barbados: Department of History, University of the West Indies, and JBHMS, 1998), pps.17, 23, 28—29, 32—34, 38—40

Beckles, Hilary McD. & Downes, Andrew, "The Economics of Transition to the Black Labor System in Barbados, 1630—1680," *The Journal of Interdisciplinary History* 18, no.2 (1987), pps.227, 247

Beckles, Hilary *'The 200 Years' War: slave resistance in the British West Indies, an overview of the historiography'*, Jamaican Historical Review, 13 (1982), pp.13

Beckles, Hilary: *A History of Barbados: From Amerindian Settlement to Nation State* (Cambridge University Press: Cambridge, 1990), pp.27

Beckwith, Martha Warren, *Black Roadways: A Study of Jamaican Folk Life* (1929; reprint, New York: Negro Universities Press, 1969), pps.191—92

Behn, Aphra *Oroonoko* (Penguin Books: New York, 2003 [1844]), pps. xxi—xxiv

Bell, Howard H. *A Survey of the Negro Convention Movement, 1830—1862* (Arno Press: New York and the New York Times, 1969)

Benedict, Burton, "Slavery and Indenture in Mauritius and Seychelles," in Watson, *Asian and African Systems of Slavery*

Berlin, Ira & Morgan, Philip D., ed., "The Slaves' Economy: Independent Production by Slaves in the Americas," *Slavery and Abolition* 12 (May 1991)

Berlin, Ira *Many Thousands Gone: The First Two Centuries of Slavery in North America* [Cambridge, Mass., 1998], pps.17—63, 183, 48

Besson, Jean, "Land Tenure in the Free Villages of Trelawny, Jamaica: A Case Study in the Caribbean Peasant Response to Emancipation," *Slavery and Abolition* 5 (May 1984), pps.3—23

Bethel, Leslie *The Abolition of the Slave Trade: Britain, Brazil and the Slave Trade Question* (Cambridge University Press, 2010) pp. 2, 3, 4

Bettleheim, Judith, 'The Afro-Jamaica Jonkonnu Festival: Playing the Forces and Operating the Cloth' (unpublished Ph.D. thesis, Yale University, 1979) pps. 7—20 , 80—100

Biggers, John *Ananse the Web of Life in Africa* (Austin University of Texas Press, 1962) pp.1

Biobaku, Saburi O., The Egba and Their Neighbours, 1842—1872 (Ibadan University Press: Ibadan, Nigeria 1991 [1957]), pps.17—20, 22, 24—5

Bittle, William E. & Geis, Gilbert, *The Longest Way Home: Chief Alfred C. Sam's Back-to-Africa Movement* (Wayne State University Press: Detroit, 1964)

Black And Asian Studies Association. *'Liverpool's Black Population During World War II'*. Newsletter No. 20 (January, 1998) pps.6 & 9

Black Britons — The Next Generation. January 28th 2016. The Economist Newspaper.

Black Business Network. "Black, British, In Business & Proud Report." September 2021. Url: https://www.blackbusinessnetwork.online/_files/ugd/624676_832e0769c83d41f1ac7299101 7fc5aea.pdf [Accessed: 12 April 2023]

Black Men: Statistics — Population. Url: https://blackdemographics.com/population/black-male-statistics/ [Accessed: 8th February 2021]

Blackburn, Robin, *The Making of New World Slavery: From the Baroque to the Modern, 1492—1800* (London: Verso, 1997) pps.173, 339, 377

Blagrove, Ishmail & Busby, Margaret (eds) *Carnival: A Photographic And Testimonial History Of The Notting Hill Carnival* (London: Rice N Peas) pp. 345

Blassingame, John *The Slave Community: Plantation Life in Antebellum South* (1972, rev. ed., New York, 1979)

Bleby, Henry, *Death Struggles of Slavery: Being a Narrative of Facts and Incidences, which occurred in a British Colony, During the two years Immediately Preceding Negro Emancipation* (London, 1853), pps.111—12, 15; John Clarke, *Memorials of Baptist Missionaries in Jamaica* (London, 1869), 92ff; *Brit. Parl. Papers, Slave Trade* (1831—34), 80/222-25

Blindloss, Harold *In the Niger Country*. (William Blackwood and Sons: Edinburgh and London, 1898) pp.171

Boahen, Adu "Origins of the Akan." *Ghana Notes and Queries* 9 (1966) pp.9

Boahen, Adu, 'Arcany or Arcany or Arcania . . .,' *Transactions of the Historical Society of Ghana*, 1973, pp.105ff, 218

Board of Trade 1709. "Report on the Trade to Africa."

Boliver, Vikki *Exploring Ethnic Inequalities In Admission To Russell Group Universities*. Sociology Vol. 50 .2, (2016) pps. 252-3.
Bolland, O. Nigel *Colonialism and resistance in Belize: Essays in Historical Sociology* (University of West Indies Press; 2nd ed, 2003) pp. 29 (quoting Edward Despard)
Bosman, Willem A *New and Accurate Description of the Coast of Guinea: Divided into the Gold, the Slave, and the Ivory Coasts*. 2nd., London: Knapton, Midwinter, Lintot, Strahan, Round, and Bell. pps.123—24, 135, 149—151, 202, 217, 300

Bosman, Willem. A *New and Accurate Description of the Coast of Guinea: Divided into the Gold, the Slave, and the Ivory Coasts)* 2nd edition, London: Knapton, Midwinter, Lintot, Strahan, pps.26—41, 78, 112—13

Boundless Immigration Inc. "Black Immigrants in the United States: Status, Challenges, and Impacts." Url: https://www.boundless.com/research/black-immigrants-in-the-united-states-status-challenges-and-impacts/ [Accessed: 12 April 2023]

Bowcott, Owen *"Inquest Begins Into 14 Victims Of 1981 Fire"*. The Guardian, 3rd February 2004

Bowcott, Owen. "Jamaican PM and Labour PM call for Windrush Compensation". 18 April 2018. The Guardian

Gentlemen, Amelia. "Windrush cancer patient has UK residency status confirmed". 27 April 2018. The Guardian

Braidwood, Stephen J. *Black Poor and White Philanthropists: London's Blacks And The Foundation Of The Sierra Leone Settlement, 1786-91* (Liverpool University Press:1994) pp. 31

Braithwaite, Edward Kamau, "Caliban, Ariel, and Unprospero in the Conflict of Creolization: A Study of the Slave Revolt in Jamaica in 1831—32," in *Comparative Perspectives on Slavery in New World Plantations Societies*, ed. Vera Rubin and Arthur Tuden, Annals of the New York Academy of Sciences (June 1977), 292: 41—62

Brake, Mike & Shank, Gregory *Under Heavy Manners: A Consideration Of Racism, Black Youth Culture, And Crime In Britain*. Crime And Social Justice No. 20, Race, Crime And Culture (1983), pp. 10

Brandon, George, *Santeria From Africa to the New World: The Dead Sell Memories* (Indiana University Press: Bloomington, 1993), pp.106

Breen, T. H. & Innes, Stephen, *"Myne Owne Ground": Race and Freedom on Virginia's Eastern Shore, 1640—1676* (New York, 2005), pp.70

Breinburg, Petronella *Legends of Suriname* (London: New Beacon Books Ltd., 1971) pp.14-15

Brit. Parl. Papers, Slave Trade (1823—24), 10ff for Smith's Journal "containing Various Occurrences at Le Resouvenir ... March 18," London Missionary Society, *Quarterly Chronicle*, Dec. 9, 1816, London Missionary Society Papers [included in the Methodist Missionary Archives]

Brit. Parl. Papers, Slave Trade (1823—24), 66/166, 169, 177, 187, 200—201, 229, 232, 239, 277

Brit. Parl. Papers, Slave Trade (1823—24), 66/83ff, 66/166, 106; C.O. 111/42, f. 7 f. 436, f. 469

Brit. Parl. Papers, Slave Trade (1823—24), ff 7., 59, 81ff, 200, 66/166, 101—2 (cf. 232), 227, 239, C.O. 111/42, 457; J. Mortier to the Secretary, Georgetown, Sept. 8, 1823, 143/144, Methodist Missionary Society Archives

Brit. Parl. Papers, Slave Trade (1825), 59; cf. 61, 63, 65, 66, 67,109, and C.O. 111/42, f. 430, f. 450, cf. 463

Brit. Parl. Papers, Slave Trade (1831—34), 80/200, 222-23, 225, 226, 294—295

Brit. Parl. Papers, Slave Trade (1831—34), 80/217—18. Volume 80 is essentially the Jamaica House of Assembly's "Report of a Committee to enquire into recent Rebellion — Retn'd to England — 22 June 1832."

Britain's Black Power Movement Is At Risk Of Being Forgotten, Say Historians. The Guardian, Friday 27th December 2013

Broady, Kristen & Barr, Anthony. "The Avenue—December's Jobs Report Reveals a Growing Racial Employment Gap, Especially For Black Women." *The Brookings Institute.* Tuesday, January 11, 2022. Url: https://www.brookings.edu/blog/the-avenue/2022/01/11/decembers-jobs-report-reveals-a-growing-racial-employment-gap-especially-for-black-women/ [Accessed: 12 April 2023]

Brooks Jr., George E. *The Providence African Society's Sierra Leone Emigration Scheme: 1794-1795: Prologue to the African Colonization Movement.* The International Journal of African Historical Studies, Vol. 7, No. 2 (1974) pps. 183-191

Brown, George W. *The Economic History Of Liberia* (Washington D.C.: Associate Publishers, 1941) pp. 111

Brown, Scott Fighting For US: Maulana Karenga, The US Organization, And Black Cultural Nationalism (New York: New York University Press, 2003) pps. 113-120;

Brown, Vincent, *The Reaper's Garden: Death and Power in the World of Atlantic Slavery* (Cambridge, Mass., 2008), pps.32—38

Browne, B. *The Yarn of a Yankee Privateer*, ed. Nathaniel Hawthorne (New York, 1926), pp.103

Buah, F. K. A *History of Ghana* (Macmillan: Oxford, 1998 [1980]), pps.1—3

Bunce, Robin & Field, Paul *"Frank Critchlow: Community Leader Who Made The Mangrove Restaurant The Beating Hear Of Notting Hill."* The Independent, 23rd September 2010.
Bunce, Robin & Field, Paul. *"Mangrove Nine: The Court Challenge Against Police Racism In Notting Hill,"* The Guardian, 29th November 2010.

Burdo, Adolphe 1880. *Niger et Benue: Voyage dan l'Afrique Central*, Paris: E. Plon, pp.95

Burge, Ryan P. "Black Americans See the Biggest Shift Away From Faith: There Are More Unaffiliated African-Americans, But They're Also More Likely to Return." February 15, 2022. Url: https://www.christianitytoday.com/news/2022/february/black-american-nones-faith-unaffiliation-nothing.html [Accessed: 12 April 2023]

Burnard, Trevor G. & Garrigus, John *The Plantation Machine: Atlantic Capitalism in French Saint-Domingue and British Jamaica* (Philadelphia: University of Pennsylvania Press, 2016), pp.37

Bush, Barbara *Slave Women in Caribbean Society, 1650-1838* (ACLS Humanities E-Book, 2008) p.44

Byrd, Alexander X., *Captives and Voyagers: Black Migrants Across the Eighteenth-Century British Atlantic World* (Baton Rouge, 2008), pps.17—31, 32—56

Byrd, William L. "Nat Turner's Rebellion," *Magazine of Virginia Genealogy*. 36 (1998) pp.6

C.O. 137/182, f.286; Higman, Barry W. Slave Population and Economy in Jamaica, 1807—1834 (Cambridge, 1976), pp. 207. There is an official map of the extent of destruction, St. Elizabeth Situated in the County of Cornwall. . . . Constructed from Recent Survey by Orders From the Authorities in March 1832" (London, Sept. 1832). This map bears an "explanation," "The places underlined, in red were those Destroyed during the Rebellion in 1832." About 280 properties are underlined, and the very few on which trash houses only were burned, such as Roaring River and Deans Valley estates in Westmoreland, are so indicated, as are the locations of the killing of whites at Marchmont and Rock Pleasant. Tharp Papers, R63/20, Cambridge Record Office.

C.O. 137/185, 210v-11v, ff. 240, 246—46v, ff. 308v-13, 314ff, 357—58, 373-75v

C.O. 137/185, f. 553

C.O. 295/28, f. 148: Monro to Bathurst, 4 Sept. 1812; f. 154 Murray to Bathurst, 11 Sept. 1812; f. 365: Murray to Bathurst, 25 Oct. 1812; C.O. 295/29, f. 23: Monro to Bathurst, 5 Mar 1813

C.O. 295/28, f. 208; James Stephen to Robert Peel, 17 Jan. 1812; C.O. 295/28. f. 250: Order in Council, 26 Mar. 1812

C.O. 295/29, f. 26: Proclamation, 27 Feb. 1813; f. 41: Murray to Monro, 17 May 1814; C.O. 295/32: Woodford to Bathurst, 4 Jan 1814; f. 150: Woodford to Bathurst, 9 May 1814

C.O. 295/30, f. 157: Proclamation, 14 Oct. 1813; C.O. 295/32, f. 135: Murray to Woodford, 28 Feb. 1814

C.O. 295/33, f. 114: Woodford to Bathurst, 11 Apr. 1821

C.O. 295/33, f. 420: Order of Government, 6 Dec. 1814

C.O. 295/34, f. 13: James Stephen to Henry Goulburn, 4 Feb. 1814. Cf. C.O. 295/32, f. 150: Woodford to Bathurst, 9 May 1814

C.O. 295/42, no. 21: Registrar of Slaves, 25 Jan. 1817 (enclosed in Woodford to Bathurst, 9 Feb. 1817)

C.W. Michie, Political Situation Northern Provinces and History of Ilorin, Report on Local Government Reform in the Bala and Afon District of Ilorin Emirate, 1954, para. 11; NNAK SNP 10/4 304p/1916, District Assessment Report Osi by G.O. Whitely)

Cabrera, Lydia, *Yemaya y Ochun* (Madrid, 1974; Miami, 1980), pp.113

Calvocoressi, N & David, N, 'A Survey of Radiocarbon and Thermoluminescence Dates for West Africa,' *Journal of African History*, 1979, pps.19—20

Campbell, Mavis *The Maroons of Jamaica 1655-1796* (Africa World PR, 1988) | Prof Richard Price
Capo, H.C. 'Le Gbe es tune langue unique,' *Africa*, 1983, pp.321ff

Captain Adams, John, *Sketches Taken During Ten Voyages to Africa, Between the Years 1786 and 1800* (1823; New York, 1970 edition) pp.53

Captain Allen, William, *A Narrative of the Expedition Sent by Her Majesty's Government to the River Niger in 1841*, 2 vols, (London, 1848), I, pp.251

Captain Beecroft & King, J.B., 'Details of Explorations of the Old Calabar River in 1841 and 1842,' Journal of the Royal Geographical Society, 14 (1844), pp.261

Carney, Judith Ann. *Black Rice The African Origins of Rice Cultivation in the Americas* (Harvard University Press: Cambridge, MA, 2001)

Carrell, Severin. "Glasgow University to pay £20m in slave trade reparations". Fri 23 Aug 2019. The Guardian. Url: https://www.theguardian.com/uk-news/2019/aug/23/glasgow-university-slave-trade-reparations

Caryl Phillips, Wendy *'The Pioneers: Fifty Years Of The Caribbean Migration To Britain,' in A New World Order* (New York: Vintage, 2001), pp. 264

Cavazzi, Giovanni, quoted in J. Thornton, 'The State in African Historiography: A Reassessment,' *Ufahamu*, 173, pp.116

Censor, Jack R. & Hunt, Lynn *Liberty, Equality, Fraternity – Exploring the French Revolution* (Pennsylvania State University,2001)
Cf. Barbara Bush, *Slave Women in Caribbean Society, 1650—1838* (Bloomington, 1990), pps.84—91

Chambers, Douglas B. '"He Is an African but Speaks Plain": Historical Creolization in Eighteenth-Century Virginia,' in Joseph E. Harris et al, pps.100—33

Chambers, Douglas B. '"My Own Nation": Igbo Exiles in the Diaspora,' *Slavery and Abolition*, 18, no.1 (1997) pps.72—91; and '"My Own Nation": Igbo Exiles in the Diaspora,' in Eltis, David & Richardson, David *Routes to Slavery: Direction, Ethnicity and Mortality in the Atlantic Slave Trade* (Frank Crass: London, 1997)

Chambers, Douglas B. 2000, *Tracing Igbo into the African Diaspora In Lovejoy*, Paul E. (editor) *Identity in the Shadow of Slavery* (Continuum: London) pps. 55—66

Chambers, Douglas B. *Murder at Montpelier: Igbo Africans in Virginia* (University Press of Mississippi: Jackson, 2005) pps. 22—24, 30—33, 40

Chambers, Douglas B., '"He Gwine Sing He Country": Africans, Afro-Virginians and the Development of Slave Culture in Virginia, 1690 to 1819' (unpublished Ph.D dissertation, University of Virginia, 1996)

Chambers, Douglas B., 'Eboe, Kongo, Mandingo: African Ethnic Groups and the Development of Regional Slave Societies in Mainland North America, 1700—1820,' Working Paper no. 96—14. International Seminar on 'The History of the Atlantic World, 1500—1800,' Harvard University, 1996

Chambers, Douglas B., 'Source Material for Studying Igbo in the Diaspora: Problems and Possibilities,' in Robin Law (ed.) *Source Material for Studying the Slave Trade and the African Diaspora* (Stirling, UK, 1997) pp.90—118

Chambers, Douglas B., "Ethnicity in the diaspora: The Slave-Trade and the Creation of African 'Nations' in the Americas," *Slavery and Abolition* pps.25—26, 34n5

Chandler, M. J., *A Guide to Records in Barbados* (1965)

Chang, Jeff *Can't Stop Won't Stop: A History Of The Hip-Hop Generation* (New York: Picador, 2005) pp. 247

Charles Steuart to Anthony Fahie, July 13, 1751, in Charles Steuart Letter Book, 1751—1763, microfilm, M-32, John D. Rockefeller, Jr. Library, Williamsburg, Virginia. Clarkson: Levinius Clarkson to David van Horne, Charleston, Feb. 23, 1773, in Donnan, ed., Documents, IV, pps.456—47

Chikwendu, V. & Umeji, A [reported in] New Scientist, 10th June 1989, pp. 15

Chouin, Gerard & Decorse, Christopher "Prelude to the Atlantic Trade New Perspectives on Southern Ghana's Pre-Atlantic History," *Journal of African History* 51 (2010) pps. 123—25, 129, 138, 142—45

Chowdhury, Tanzil [Chapter title] *Policing The 'Black Party': Racialized Drugs Policing At Festivals In The UK*— [From the book by] Koram, Kojo *The War On Drugs And The Global Colour Line* (Pluto Press, 2019) pp. 50

Christian, Mark *An African-Centred Approach To The Black British Experience: With Special Reference to Liverpool*. Journal Of Black Studies Vol. 28, No. 3 (Jan., 1998) pp. 297

Church Missionary Society Archives, University of Birmingham, UK (CMS) CA2/049(a), Hinderer to Venn, 26 October 1855, quoted in E. Adeniyi Oroge, "The Institution of Slavery in Yorubaland with Particular Reference to the Nineteenth Century," (Ph.D. thesis, Centre of West African Studies, University of Birmingham, UK, 1971), pps.92, 161—2, 171, 176.

Clapperton, H., *Journal of a Second Expedition into the Interior of Africa* (Murray: London, 1829), pp.4

Clarke, *Memorials of Baptist Missionaries*, 103; cf. C.O. 137/185, f.220.f

Clarke, W.H., *Travels and Explorations in Yorubaland 1854—1856* (Ibadan, Nigeria, 1972) pp.125

CMS CA2/049(b), David Hinderer, *Journal for the Quarter* Ending 25 September 1851, quoted in Oroge, "Institution of Slavery," pp.132

CMS CA2/05, Johnson to Wright, 9 May 1879, cited in Oroge, "Institution of Slavery," pps.125, 133, 327—28

Cohen, David W. & Greene, Jack P. eds. *Neither Slave Nor Free: The Freedom of African Descent in the Slave Societies of the New World* (The John Hopkins University Press: Baltimore & London, 1972), pps. 3—5, 7—9, 11—13, 15—17

Cohen, Robin & Sheringham, Olivia *Encountering Difference — Diasporic Traces, Creolizing Spaces* (Polity Press, 2016)
Cohen, Robin *Global Diasporas: an introduction — second edition* (London: Routledge, Taylor & Francis Group, 2008) pp. 17, 22, 39, 43;pp. 28 cit., David J. Goldberg & John D. Raynor. *The Jewish people: Their History And Their Religion* (Harmondsworth: Penguin, 1989) pp. 92 & Philip K. Hitti, *History of The Arabs: From The Earliest Times To The Present* (London: Macmillan, 1974) pps. 533-4, 356-7

Colby, Sandra L & Ortman, Jennifer M. *"Projections of the Size and Composition of the U.S. Population: 2014 to 2016"*. United States Census Bureau. Url: https://www.census.gov/library/publications/2015/demo/p25-1143.html [Accessed: 16th February 2021]

Coleman De Graft-Johnson, John *African Glory: The Story of Vanished Negro Civilizations* (Black Classic Press, 1986) pp. 163

Collins, Lois M.. "Most black males reach the middle class or higher. Here's what drives her success. July 2, 2018. Deseret News. Url: https://www.deseret.com/2018/7/2/20648205/most-black-males-reach-the-middle-class-or-higher-here-s-what-drives-their-success [Accessed: 8th February 2021]

Committee Report, Henry Shirley, Nov. 12, 1788, *Votes of Assembly*, 80, 88, C.O. 140/73

Congressman Don Beyer, Vice Chair. "The Economic State of Black America in 2020". Joint Economic Committee. Url: https://www.jec.senate.gov/public/_cache/files/ccf4dbe2-810a-44f8-b3e7-14f7e5143ba6/economic-state-of-black-america-2020.pdf [Accessed: 8th February 2021]

Constitutional Whig, Richmond, Sept. 26, 1831, in *The Southampton Revolt*, ed. Tragle, pp.95

Cookey, S. J. S. "An Ethnohistorical Reconstruction of Traditional Igbo Society." In *West African Cultural Dynamics: Archaeological and Historical Perspectives*, e.d. B. K. Swartz and Raymond E. Dumett, pps. 327—47 (Longman, Hurst: London, 1980)

Cookey, Sylvanus 1974. *King Jaja of the Niger Delta: His Life and Times, 1821—1891*, New York: NOK Publishers Ltd, pp. 19

Coombs, John C., "Building 'the Machine': The Development of Slavery and Slave Society in Early Colonial Virginia" (Ph.D. diss., College of William and Mary, 2003), pp.103

Cornwall Chron., Nov. 10, 1781-S., Thomas Deane; *Jam. Royal Gaz.*, July 25, 1795-S., Mary Bees; Nov. 17, 1781-S., Richard Saunders; Jan. 3, 1801-P.S., Sam Wolinwood; Fanny an Ibo who "says she is Mundingo . . . and speaks Eboe, Mundingo and English very well": May, 11, 1782-S., James Watson

Cortes de Oliveira, Maria Ines, "Retrouver une identite: Jeux sociaux des Africains de Bahia (vers 1750—vers 1890_" (Ph.D. dissertation, Universite de Paris—Sorbonne, 1992), pp.98 cit., Testament et inventaires apres deces: Chartes de Libertie; Equete du Calundu de Cachoera; Liste des Africains resident dans la Paroisse da Panha

Cosentino, Donald *Who is that Fellow in the Many-Colored Cap? Transformations of Eshu in Old and New World Mythologies: The Journal of American Folklore*, vol. 100, No. 397, 1987, pp. 261-262

Courlander, Harold. *"Profane Songs of the Haitian People." The Journal of Negro History*, vol. 27, no. 3, 1942, pp. 320, 321. *JSTOR*, www.jstor.org/stable/2715328.

Coursey, D,G., Yams: An Account of the Nature Origins, Cultivation and Utilisation of the Useful Members of the Dioscoreaceae (London, 1967), pps.59—60, 64

Cowan, A.A. 1936. "Early Trading Conditions in the Bight of Biafra, Part II." *Journal of the Royal African Society*, Vol. 35, No. 138: pps. 53—44

Craton, Michael *Testing the Chains: Resistance to Slavery in the British West Indies* (Cornell Press University: Ithaca and London, 1982), pps.18, 108—9

Craton, Michael, 'Decoding Pitchy-patchy: the Roots, Branches and Essence of Junkanoo,' *Slavery and Abolition*, 16 (1995), pps.15—31

Craton, Michael, "Changing Patterns of Slave Families in the British West Indies," *Journal of Interdisciplinary History* 10 (Summer 1979), pps.1—35

Craton, Michael, "Hobbesian or Panglossian? The Two Extremes of Slave Conditions in the British Caribbean, 1783 to 1834," *William and Mary Quarterly*, 3d ser., 35 (April 1978), pps.324—356

Craton, Michael, "Jamaican Slave Mortality: Fresh Light from Worthy Park, Longville and the Tharp Estates," *Journal of Caribbean History* 3 (Nov. 1971), pps.1—27

Craton, Michael, *Searching for the Invisible Man: Slaves and Plantation Life in Jamaica* (Cambridge Mass., 1978)

Craton, Michael, *Sinews of Empire* (1974)

Crayon, Michael, "Hobbesian or Panglossian? The Two Extremes of Slave Conditions in the British Caribbean, 1783 to 1834," *William and Mary Quarterly* 35 (1978): pps.324—56

Creel, Margaret Washington. *A Peculiar People: Slave Religion and Community-Culture Among the Gullahs* (New York University Press: New York, 1988)

Crosbies and Trafford et al. 1762. "Capn. Ambrose Lace," see Williams, G 1897: 486—88

Crow, Hugh 1830. Memoirs of the Late Captain Hugh Crow (Longman, Rees, Orme, Brown, Green: London) pps. 26, 83, 146, 197—99, 212, 225, 252—3, 258

Crowder, Michael 1978. *The Story of Nigeria*, London: Faber and Faber, pp.65

Crowther, Samuel A. "Journal of the Rev. S. Crowther." 1859. In Samuel Crowther and John C. Taylor, *The Gospel on the Banks of the Niger — Journals and Notices of Native Missionaries Accompanying the Niger Expedition of 1857—1859* (Dawsons of Pall Mall, 1968) 19, 254, 264, 367—8, 430, 432, 434, 435

Crumpton, Taylor "Black women saved the Democrats. Don't make us do it again". Washington Post. November 7 2020

Cugoano, Quobna Ottobah *Thoughts and Sentiments on the Evil of Slavery* ed. Vincent Carretta (Penguin Books: New York, 1999), pps. x, 12—16, 27—28, 143, 153n19

Curtin, Philip D, "'The White Man's Grave,' Image and Reality, 1780—1865," *Journal of British Studies* 1 (1961) pp.95

Curtin, Philip D. 1975. *Economic Change in Precolonial Africa: Senegambia in the Era of the Slave Trade.* Madison, WI: University of Wisconsin Press, pp.64

Curtin, Philip D. 1984. *Cross-Cultural Trade in World History* (Cambridge: Cambridge University Press), pps. 2—3, 5, 25

Curtin, Philip D. *The Atlantic Slave Trade.* (University of Wisconsin Press: Madison, 1969), pps.34, 78, 85

da Roma, G., *Relation* (a mid-seventeenth-century Capuchin account) quoted in Thornton, *The Kingdom of the Kongo: Civil War and Transition,* pp.41

Daaku, K. Y., & Van Dantzig, Albert, trans. and eds. "Maps of the Regions of the Gold Coast of Guinea," *Ghana Notes and Queries* 9 (1966) pps. 70

Daaku, K. Y., Oral Traditions of Adanse (Legon, Ghana Institute of African Studies, 1969), pps. i—ii, 1, 3—4, 6

Daily Sketch, 3rd November 1954 and 8th December 1954; and The Economist, 6th June 1954, and 13th November 1954, ibid Paul pps. 140-141

Dakubu, M.E. Kropp, 'The Peopling of Southern Ghana: a Linguistic Viewpoint,' in C. Ehret and M. Posnansky, *The Archaeological and Linguistic Reconstruction of African History* (Berkeley and Los Angeles, 1982) pp.245ff, 248, 260

Dakubu, M.E. Kropp, *One Voice* (Leiden, 1981)

Dalby, David, "Ashanti Survivals in the Language and Traditions of the Windward Maroons of Jamaica," *African Language Studies* 12 (1971): pp.48; Karla Gottlieb, *"The Mother of Us All": A History of Queen Nanny Leader of the Windward Jamaican Maroons* (Trenton, NJ: Africa World Press, 2000), pps.10, 24—25, 44, 52, 58

Daniel Warner to Benjamin Spencer and Co., Antigua, March 14, 1756, no. 60549/246, Spencer-Stanhope Cannon Hall Muniments, Archives Department Central Library, Sheffield

Daniels, Roger *Guarding The Golden Door: American Immigration Policy And Immigrants since 1882* (Hill & Wang, 2005) pp. 120
Danquah, J.B. "Culture of Akan," *African Language Studies* 12 (1971) pps. 360, 363

David, Paul A. *Reckoning with Slavery: A Critical Study in the Quantitative History of American Negro Slavery* (Oxford University Press: New York, 1976)

Davis, David Brion *The Problem of Slavery in Western Culture* (Cornell University Press: Ithaca, 1966), pps.223—61

Davis, David Brion, *Inhuman Bondage: the rise and fall of Slavery in the New World* (Oxford University Press: New York, 2006), pp.81

Davis, David Brion, *The Problem of Slavery in the Age of Revolution 1770—1823* (Ithaca, 1975)

Davis, Lee Allyn *Natural Disasters* (Checkmark Books: New Ed., 2008) pp. 276

Davis, Nick. "Stuck in Jamaica: My pension, my house, my kids are in the UK". 21 April 2018. The Guardian;
de Carvalho Soares, *Mariza, Devotos da cor: Identidade etnica, religiosidade e escravidao no Rio de Janeiro, seculo XVIII* (Rio de Janeiro: Civilizacao Brasileira, 2000)

de Grandpre, Louis, *Voyage a la cote occidentale d'Afrique fait dans les annees 1786 et 1787* (Paris: Dentu, 1801), pps. I: xiv

De Marees, Pieter. *Description and Historical Account of the Gold Kingdom of Guinea*, pps. 20, 67—74

de Queiros Mattoso, Katia M. *Bahia: a Cidade de Salvador e seu Mercado no seculo 19* (Sao Paulo: HUCITEC, 1978) pp.161-69 and passim

De Sandoval, P. Alonso [1627] 1956. De Instauranda Aethiopum Salute: El Mundo de la Esclavitud Negra en America. Bogota: Empressa Nacional de Publicaciones, pp.94

Deakin, Nicholas "The Immigration Issue in British Politics" (Ph.D. thesis, University of Sussex, 1972), cited in Zig Layton-Henry, *The Politics Of Immigration* (Oxford: Blackwell, 1972) pp. 31

Debien, Gabriel, "Les origines des esclaves aux Antilles," Bulletin de l'Institut of Afrique Noire, ser. B, 23 (1961), pps. 363—87, 24 (1962); 1—41; 24 (1963); 1—38, 215—66, from French Shipping and Plantation Records," *Journal of African History*, 30, no.1 (1989), pp.32

Degler, Carl *Neither Black Not White* (Macmillan: New York, 1971)

Delzin, Gail, *The Folk Culture of Grenada and Carriacou through Story and Song* (St. Augustine, Trinidad: University of the West Indies, 1977)

Desch-Obi, T. J., *Fighting for Honor: The History of African Marital Art Traditions in the Atlantic World* (University South Carolina Press: Columbia, 2008), pps. 205—06

Desrochers, Jr., "Slave-for-Sale Advertisements and Slavery in Massachusetts, 1704—1781," *WMQ*, 3d. Ser, LIX (2002), pps.623—664

Dias, J. 'Famine and Disease in the History of Angola c. 1830—1892,' *Journal of African History*, 1981, pps.331, 352

Dickson, Kwamina B. *Historical Geography of Ghana* (Cambridge University Press: Cambridge, 1969), pp.24

Dickson, W., *Letters on Slavery* (London, 1789), pp.55

Dike, K.Onwuka 1956. Trade and Politics in the Niger Delta 1830—1885. (Clarendon Press: Oxford), pps.38—39

Dike, Kenneth O. & Ekejiuba, Felicia *The Aro of South-Eastern Nigeria, 1650—1980: A Study of Socio-Economic Formation and Transformation in Nigeria* (University Press: Ibadan, Nigeria, 1990), pps. 56—57, 132, 179

Directorate of Citizens and Diaspora Organizations African Union Commission *African Union Continental Symposium on the Implementation of the International Decade for People of African Descent* (African Union Commission, 2018)

Dirks, Robert *The Black Saturnalia* (University Press of Florida, 1989) pp. 161, 162

Dodwell, Aisha "Another blow for May's Hostile Environment for immigrants". 20 February 2018. Global Justice Now

Dominguez, Jorge I. *Insurrection or Loyalty: The Breakdown of the Spanish American Empire* (Cambridge, Mass., 1980), 55-56, 146-69

Donnan, ed., Documents, IV, 257 nn. 2, 4, 315 n. 2., 443—444

Donnan, Elizabeth 1930. *Documents Illustrative of the History of the Slave Trade to America, Vol. 1, The Eighteenth Century*. Washington, DC: Carnegie Institution of Washington, pps. 14—15, 282—301, 419—20, 431-33

Donnan, Elizabeth 1931. *Documents Illustrative of the History of the Slave Trade to to America, Vol. 2, The Eighteenth Century*. Washington, DC: Carnegie Institution of Washington, pps.49—81, 455, 589—92,

Donnan, Elizabeth 1935. Documents Illustrative of the History of the Slave Trade to America, Vol. 4, The Border Colonies and the Southern Colonies. Washington, DC: Carnegie Institution of Washington; Vol. IV pps.69—84

Drake, D. K. 1976. "The Liverpool-African Voyage c. 1790—1807: Commercial Problems." In *Liverpool*. see Anstey, R. *The Atlantic Slave Trade and British Abolition, 1760—1810* (Macmillan Press Ltd: London, 1975), pps.141, 149

Drapper, O. *Description de l'Afrique* (Amsterdam, 1686) pp.360

Dubois, Laurent *Avengers of the New World: the story of the Haitian Revolution* (Cambridge, Mass.: Belknap Press of Harvard University Press, 2004) pp.40—41

Dubois, Laurent The Avengers of the New World: The Story of the Haitian Revolution (Cambridge: Belknap Press, 2005) pps.40-44

Dubois, Laurent, "Complications," *The William and Mary Quarterly* 68 no. 2 (2011)

Dummett, R., 'Precolonial Gold Mining and the State in the Akan Region,' *Research in Economic Anthropology*, 1983, pp.95ff

Dunn, Richard S. *Sugar and Slaves: The Rise of the Planter Class in the English West Indies, 1624—1713* (University of North Carolina Press: Chapel Hill, 1972) pps.48, 64—65, 73, 257—58, Chap. 10

Dunn, Richard S., "A Tale of Two Plantations: Slave Life at Mesopotamia in Jamaica and Mount Airy in Virginia, 1799 to 1828," *William and Mary Quarterly*, 3d ser., 34 (Jan. 1977), pps.32—54

Dunn, Richard S., "A Tale of Two Plantations: Slave Life at Mesopotamia in Jamaica and Mount Airy in Virginia, 1799 to 1828," *William and Mary Quarterly* 34 (1977), pps.32—65

Dupigny, E.G.M, *Gazetteer of Nupe Province* (Waterlow: London, 1920), pp.20

Easton [Md.] Gazette, Aug. 27, 1831, Maryland Historical Society, Baltimore

Edwards, Bryan 1793. *The History, Civil, and Commercial, of the British Colonies in the West Indies; in Two Volumess* Vol. 2 (John Stockdale: London), pps. 74—75

Edwards, Bryan, *The History, Civil and Commercial, of the British Colonies in the West Indies*, 2 vols. (Dublin, 1793 [1794]), pps.2, 65, 73

Edwards, Walter. *"African-American Vernacular English: phonology."* In Bernd Kortmann (Ed.). A Handbook Of Varieties Of English. (Walter de Gruyter GmbH & Company KG, 2004) pp. 383

Edwin Betts (ed.), *Thomas Jefferson's Garden Book, 1766—1824*

Egbunga, Obi *Destroy This Temple: The Voice Of Black Power In England* (London: MacGibbon and Kee, 1971), pp. 17, 79, 145-146, 148;
Ekejiuba, Felicia I. 1991. "High Point of Igbo Civilization: The Arochukwu Period." *In Groundwork of Igbo History*. See Afigbo, A.E. 1991b. *Groundwork of Igbo History*. Lagos: Vista Books, pps.313—14

Elebute, Adeyemo *The Life Of James Pinson Labulo Davies: A Colossus Of Victorian Lagos 2nd Ed* (Kachifo Limited: Lagos, 2013) pp. xviii, 1, 7-14, 101, 105, 107

Elkins, Stanley M. "The Slavery Debate," Commentary 60 (Dec. 1975), 40-1, repr. in Elkins, *Slavery: A Problem in American Intellectual and Institutional Life*, 3d ed. (1959, Chicago, 1968)

Ellis, Alfred Burdon *Tshi-Speaking Peoples of the Gold Coast and West Africa* (1897; Palala Press, 2016), pps.1—3

Elnaiem, Mohammed. "Let's bring the Caribbean struggle for reparations to Britain" — Opinion. 19 July 2020. Url: https://www.aljazeera.com/opinions/2020/7/19/lets-bring-the-caribbean-struggle-for-reparations-to-britain [Accessed: 8th February 2021]

Elphick, Richard & Giliomee, Hermann, eds., *The Shaping of South African Society, 1652—1820* (Cape Town, 1979)

Elphinstone, K.V., Gazetteer of Ilorin Province (Waterlow: London, 1921), pps.30

Eltis, David & Engerman, Stanley, "Was the Slave Trade Dominated by Men?" *Journal of Interdisciplinary History*, 23 (1992), pps.237—57

Eltis, David & Richardson, David, "West Africa and the Transatlantic Slave Trade: New Evidence of Long-Term Trends," in Eltis, David & Richardson *Routes to Slavery: Direction, Ethnicity and Mortality in the Atlantic Slave Trade* (Frank Crass: London, 1997), pp.27

Eltis, David et al., *The Trans-Atlantic Slave Trade: A Database on CD-ROM* (Cambridge University Press: Cambridge, 1999)

Eltis, David, "Fluctuations in Sex and Age Ratios in the Nineteenth-Century Transatlantic Slave Traffic," *Slavery and Abolition*, 7, no.3 (1986), pps.259, 264

Eltis, David, "Fluctuations in Sex and Age Ratios in the Transatlantic Slave Trade, 1663—1864," *Economic History Review*, 46 (1993), pps.308—23

Eltis, David, "The Diaspora of Yoruba Speakers, 1650—1865: Dimensions and Implications," in Falola, Toyin & Childs, Matt D. *The Yoruba Diaspora in the Atlantic World* (Indiana University Press: Indiana, 2004), pps.17—35

Eltis, David, "The Slave Trade in Nineteenth-Century," in *Studies in the Nineteenth-Century Economic History*, ed. Toyin Falola and Ann O'Hear (Madison, African Studies Program, University of Wisconsin, 1998), pp.86, 88—9

Eltis, David, *Economic Growth and the Ending of the Transatlantic Slave Trade* (New York, 1987) pps.249, 250—2

Eltis, David. 1983. "Forced and Coerced Transatlantic Migrations: Some Comparisons." *American Historical Review*, Vol. 88, No. 2: pps. 260

Eltis, David. *The Rise of African Slavery in the Americas*. (Cambridge University Press: New York, 2000), chap. 7, pp.100

Eltis, David; Lovejoy, Paul and Richardson, David 1999. "Slave-Trading Ports: Towards an Atlantic-Wide Perspective." In Law and Strickrodt (editors), Ports of the Slave Trade, pps.20, 23—24

Eltis, David; Lovejoy, Paul E. & Richardson, David, "Ports of the Slave Trade: An Atlantic-Wide Perspective, 1676—1832," in *The Ports of the Slave Trade (Bights of Benin and Biafra)*, ed. Robin Law and Silke Strikrodt (Stirling, UK: Centre of Commonwealth Studies, University of Sterling, 1999)

Encyclopaedia Of Cross-Cultural School Psychology. Springer Science & Business Media. February 18th 2010, pp. 405. Retrieved 15th March 2020.

Engerman, Stanley L., "Economic Adjustments to Emancipation in the United States and the British West Indies," *Journal of Interdisciplinary History* 13 (Autumn 1982), pps.191—220

Engerman, Stanley, "The Slave Trade and British Capital Formation in the Eighteenth Century: A Comment on the Williams Thesis," *Business History Review*, XLVI (1972), pps.430—443

Enoch Powell's *'Rivers Of Blood'* Speech, Telegraph, 06.11.07, https://www.telegraph.co.uk/comment/3643823/Enoch-Powells-Rivers-of-Blood-speech.html

Enquirer editions of Oct. 21, 1831 and Nov. 8, 1831

Equiano, Olaudah. 1789. The Interesting Narrative of the Life of Olaudah Equiano, Written by Himself. Ed and intro. Robert J. Allison. Boston. Bedford Books of St. Martin's Press, 1995, pps. 5—16, 39, 45, 50, 54—5, 57, 145

Examinations taken by the St. Ann's milita (before J. J. and W. S. Sharker), Jan. 13, 16, 1832, James Johnson box, letters, 1770—1838/1877, folder: "Letters 1832," Powell Collection, Historical Society of Pennyslvania

Falconbridge, Alexander 1788. *An account of the Slave Trade on the Coast of Africa* (J. Phillips: London) pp.11, 51

Falola, Toyin & Oguntomisin, *Yoruba Warlords of the Nineteenth Century* (Africa World Press: Trenton, N.J., 2001) Chaps. 2—9, pps.3—8, 84—8

Falola, Toyin and Essien, Kwame *Pan-Africanism, And The Politics Of African Citizenship And Identity* (Routledge: New York, 2014) pp. 65-66

Falola, Toyin, "Slavery and Pawnship in the Yoruba Economy of the Nineteenth-Century," in Unfree Labour in the Development of the Atlantic World, ed. Paul E. Lovejoy and Nicholas Rogers (Frank Cass: London, 1994), pp.225, 230

Feldman, Susan (ed.) *African Myths and Tales* (New York: Dell Publishing Co., 1963) pp.12—13

Fields, Barbara J., "The Nineteenth-century American South: History and Theory," *Plantation Society in the Americas* 2 (April 1983): 9, 9n

Fields-Black, Edda L. *Deep Roots: Rice Farmers in West Africa and the African Diaspora* (Indiana University Press: Bloomington, 2008)

Finley, M. I., *Ancient Slavery and Modern Ideology* (London: Chatto and Windus, 1980), pp.66

Finney, Nissa & Harries, Bethan. Which Ethnic Groups Are Hardest Hit By The Housing Crisis? In Stephen Jivraj & Ludi Simpson (Eds.), Ethnic Identity And Inequalities In Britain: The Dynamics Of Diversity (Bristol, England: Policy Press, 2015) pp.
Fischer, David Hackett, *Albion's Seed: Four British Folkways in America* (New York, 1989) pps.7—11

Fladeland, Betty, "Abolitionist Pressures on the Concert of Europe, 1814—22," *Journal of Modern History* 38 (1966), pps.355—73

Fleary, Sinai. "BLAXIT: Black Brits Head For a New Life in Africa and the Caribbean". The Voice Newspaper. 31 March 2022. Url: https://www.voice-online.co.uk/news/features-news/2022/03/31/blaxit/ [Accessed: 13 April 2023]

Fletcher, Michael A. "Black Americans See a Health-care System Infected By Racism, New Poll Shows." October 16, 2020. Url: https://www.nationalgeographic.com/history/article/black-americans-see-health-care-system-infected-racism-new-poll-shows [Accessed: 12 April 2023]

Floyd, Barry, *Eastern Nigeria: a Geographical Review* (New York, 1969) pps.174—7

Fogel, Robert William & Engerman, Stanley L. *Time on the Cross: The Economics of American Negro Slavery.* 2 vols. (Little & Brown: Boston 1974), 1: 29

Foner, Laura & Genovese, Eugene D. *Slavery in the New World* (Englewood Cliffs: N.J., 1969)

Foner, Philip S., *The Life and Writings of Frederick Douglass* (International Publishers: New York, 1950), 2:441—47

Forde, D. (editor). *Efik Traders of Old Calabar* (Oxford University Press: London, 1956) pp.16

Forde, Daryll & Jones, G.I., The Ibo and Ibibio-speaking Peoples of South-eastern Nigeria (1950), passim; c.f. Baikie, who in the 1850s recognized 4 major groups and 6 or 7 other major subgroups, with a number of lesser districts or places;

Fox Soul: *Cocktails with Queens.* October 2020

Fox, Early Lee *The American Colonization Society 1817-1840* (Baltimore: The John Hopkins Press, 1919) pp. 57
Francis, Tam'Ra-Kay. "West Indian Immigration to the United States (1900—)." Blackpast.org. January 27, 2022. Url: https://www.blackpast.org/african-american-history/west-indian-immigration-to-the-united-states-1900/ [Accessed: 12 April 2023]

Franklin, "Free Negro in North Carolina," pps.224—5, 230

Franklin, John H. *From Slavery to Freedom* (New York: Alfred A. Knopf, 1967) pp. 184—5

Franklin, John Hope & Moss, Jr., Alfred A., *From Slavery to Freedom* (McGraw Hill Inc.: New York, 1994), pps.433—34

Franklin, John-Hope, *From Slavery to Freedom: A History of Negro Americans* (New York, 1974), pp.54

Franklin, V.P.. "Commentary—Reparations as a Development Strategy: The Caricom Reparations Commission. The Journal of African American History (2013), Vol. 98, No.3, pp.363

French, Howard W. Born In Blackness: Africa, Africans, and the Making of the Modern World 1471 to the Second World War (W. W. Norton & Company, Inc: New York, 2021), pps. 198—203, 208—212

Frey, William H. "The US will become 'minority white' in 2045, Census projects", The Avenue. Wednesday 14 March 2018. Url: https://www.brookings.edu/blog/the-avenue/2018/03/14/the-us-will-become-minority-white-in-2045-census-projects/ [Accessed: 9th February 2021]

Fryer, Peter Staying Power: The History of Black People in Britain (Pluto Press, 1984) pps. 195—197, 385

Fyfe, Christopher A History Of Sierra Leone 1st Ed (Oxford University Press, 1962) pp. 115—16

Fyfe, Christopher, A History of Sierra Leone (Oxford University Press: London, 1962), pp.170

Fynn, J.K., "Asante and Akyem Relations," pps. 60, 63—66

Fynn, J.K., Asante and Its Neighbours, 1700—1807 (Longman Group: London, 1971), pps.1—3, 27—29, 43, 45—51, 58, 60, 61—81

Gardner, W. J., The History of Jamaica from Its Discovery by Christopher Columbus to the Year 1872 (1873, repr. London, 1971), pp.182

Garigue, Philip The West Africans' Student Union – A Study In Cultural Contact. Africa: Journal Of The International African Institute, Vol. 23, No. 1 (Jan., 1953) pp. 62—63

Garnett, Henry Highland, The Past and Present Condition and Destiny of the Colored Race (Troy, N.Y.: J.C. Kneeland and Co., 1848), pps.6—12

Garvey, Amy Jacques, Garvey and Garveyism (A.J.: Kingston, 1963), pp.99

Garvey, Amy Jacques, Philosophy and Opinions of Marcus Garvey or Africa for the Africans (Frank Cass and Co.: London, 1967), pps.38—39

Gaspar, David Barry, Bondsmen and Rebels: A Study of Master-Slave Relations in Antigua (Durham: Duke University Press, 1985), pps.246—47; "The Antigua Slave Conspiracy of 1736: A Case Study of the Origins of Collective Resistance," William and Mary Quarterly, 3rd ser., 35 (April 1978), pp.322

Gberie, Lansana A Dirty War in West Africa: The RUF And The Destruction Of Sierra Leone (Bloomington, IN: Indiana UP, 2005) pp. 6

Geggus, David Patrick "The French Slave Trade: An Overview," The William and Mary Quarterly 58 no. 1 (2001), pp.128

Geggus, David Patrick Haitian Revolutionary Studies (Indiana University Press: Bloomington, 2002) pp.5

Geggus, David, "Haitian Voodoo in the Eighteenth Century: Language, Culture, Resistance," Jahrbuch fur Geschichte von Staat, Wirtschaft und Gesellschaft Lateinanerikas 28 (1991)

Geggus, David, "Sex Ratio, Age, and Ethnicity in the Atlantic Slave Trade: Data (1989), pps.23—44

Geggus, David, "Sugar and Coffee Cultivation in Saint Domingue and the Shaping of the Slave Labor Force," in Cultivation and Culture: Labor and the Shaping of Slave Life in the Americas, ed. Ira Berlin and Philip D. Morgan (Charlottesville: University of Virginia Press, 1993), pps.73—98, 314—18

Geggus, David, "Sugar and Coffee Cultivation in Saint Domingue."

Geggus, David, "The Demographic Composition of the French Caribbean Slave Trade," in *Proceedings of the Thirteenth and Fourteenth Meetings of the French Colonial History Society*, ed. P. Boucher (Lanham, Md.: University Press of America, 1990), pps.14—29

Genovese, Eugene D *In Red and Black* (Pantheon Books: New York, 1968), pp.159

Genovese, Eugene D, *Roll, Jordan, Roll* (Pantheon Books: New York, 1974)

Genovese, Eugene D., "The Slave States of North America" in *Neither Slave nor Free: The Freedmen of African Descent in the Slave Societies of the New World*, eds. Cohen, David W. & Greene, Jack P., pps.258—277

Genovese, Eugene D., *Roll Jordan Roll: the World the Slaves Made* (New York, 1974), passim

Gentlemen, Amelia "Caribbean nations globally demand solution to 'illegal immigrants' anomaly". 12 April 2018. The Guardian

Gentlemen, Amelia "Home Office broke inequalities law with hostile environment measures". 25 November 2020. The Guardian.

Gentlemen, Amelia "Londoner denied NHS cancer care: It's like I'm being left to die". Sat 10 March. The Guardian

Gentlemen, Amelia "Windrush scandal: only 60 victims given compensation so far". Thursday 28 May 2020

Gentlemen, Amelia. "Revealed: depth of Home Office failures on Windrush". 18 July 2018. The Guardian

Gerzina, Gretchen *Black England: Life Before Emancipation* (Allison & Busby: London, 1999) pp. 172

Gillespie, Dizzy (with Al Fraser), To Be, or Not to Bop (Doubleday: Garden City, NY, 1979, pp.319; quoted in Vega, "The Yoruba Orisha Tradition Comes to New York," pps.202—3

Gilliam, Dorothy. 'The Color Purple' Not as Simple as Black or White. December 23, 1985. *The Washington Post*. Url: https://www.washingtonpost.com/archive/local/1985/12/23/the-color-purple-not-as-simple-as-black-or-white/5f7bc0bc-ba59-4e5f-9f0b-221def1a8c66/ [Archive accessed: 16th February 2021]

Gilmore, Tony, ed., *Revisiting Blassingame's The Slave Community: The Scholars Respond* (Westport, Conn., 1978)

Gilroy, Paul *There Ain't No Black In The Union Jack* (London: Routledge, 2002) pps. 86, 116

Gocking, Roger. *The History of Ghana* (Greenwood Press: Westport, CT, 2005), pp.21

Gomez, Michael A. 1998. *Exchanging Our Country Marks: Transformation of African Identities in the Colonial and Antebellum South*. Chapel Hill, NC: University of North Carolina Press pps. 84—85, 90—105

Gomez, Michael A. 2003. "A Quality of Anguish: The Igbo Response to Enslavement in the Americas," in *Trans-Atlantic Dimensions of Ethnicity*. See Lovejoy, Paul E. and Trotman, David V. (editors) 2003. *Trans-Atlantic Dimensions of Ethnicity in the African Diaspora* (London: Continuum)

Gopert, David L. & Handler Jerome, ed. and trans. 1974. 'Captain de Corvette. Barbados in the Post-Apprenticeship Period: The Observations of a French Naval Officer,' JBHMS 35, no. 4

Gov.UK. "Employment by Sector," 27 July 2022. Url: https://www.ethnicity-facts-figures.service.gov.uk/work-pay-and-benefits/employment/employment-by-sector/latest [Accessed: 12 April 2023]

Gov.UK. "Employment." 3 November 2022. Url: https://www.ethnicity-facts-figures.service.gov.uk/work-pay-and-benefits/employment/employment/latest [Accessed: 12 April 2023]

Gov.UK. "Families and Households." Url: https://www.ethnicity-facts-figures.service.gov.uk/uk-population-by-ethnicity/demographics/families-and-households/latest [Accessed: 12 April 2023]

Gov.UK. "First Year Entrants Onto Undergraduate Study." 9 June 2022. Url: https://www.ethnicity-facts-figures.service.gov.uk/education-skills-and-training/higher-education/first-year-entrants-onto-undergraduate-degrees/latest [Accessed: 12 April 2023]

Gov.UK. "Homeownership." 15 September 2020. Url: https://www.ethnicity-facts-figures.service.gov.uk/housing/owning-and-renting/home-ownership/latest#:~:text=Mixed%20White%20and%20Asian%20households,lowest%20rates%20of%20home%20ownership. [Accessed: 12 April 2023]

Gov.UK. "Household Income." Url: https://www.ethnicity-facts-figures.service.gov.uk/work-pay-and-benefits/pay-and-income/household-income/latest [Accessed: 12 April 2023]

Gov.UK. "Renting Social Housing." Url: https://www.ethnicity-facts-figures.service.gov.uk/housing/social-housing/renting-from-a-local-authority-or-housing-association-social-housing/latest [Accessed: 12 April 2023]

Gov.UK. "Self-employment." Url: https://www.ethnicity-facts-figures.service.gov.uk/work-pay-and-benefits/employment/self-employment/latest#:~:text=Main%20facts%20and%20figures&text=15.3%25%20of%20workers%20in%20the,self%2Demployed%2C%20the%20lowest%20percentage [Accessed: 12 April 2023]

Gov.UK. "Undergraduate Degree Results." 25 November 2022. Url: https://www.ethnicity-facts-figures.service.gov.uk/education-skills-and-training/higher-education/undergraduate-degree-results/latest#title [Accessed: 12 April 2023]

Gramlich, John. "Black imprisonment rate in the U.S. has fallen by a third since 2006". Pew Research Center. May 6, 2020. Url: https://www.pewresearch.org/fact-tank/2020/05/06/share-of-black-white-hispanic-americans-in-prison-2018-vs-2006/

Grant, Colin *Negro With A Hat: The Rise And Fall Of Marcus Garvey* (London: Jonathan Cape) pps. xxii, 21, 53—54, 61, 104, 128, 135, 148, 155, 164 174, 212—214, 426, 441—442

Gray, Robert F., *The Family Estate in Africa: Studies in the Role of Property in Family Structure and Lineage Continuity*, ed. Robert F. Gray and P. H. Gulliver (Boston, 1964), 4ff

Great Newes from the Barbadoes, pps.9—12

Green, M.M. *Ibo Village Affairs* (1947; New York, 1964) pp.7

Green, M.M., 'Igbo Dialects in the Polyglotta Africana,' *African Language Review*, 6 (1967) pps.111—19

Green, William A. *British Slave Emancipation: The Sugar Colonies and the Great Experiment, 1830—1865* (Oxford University Press: London, 1976), pp.15

Greenberg, Kenneth, ed. *The Confessions of Nat Turner and Related Documents* (Bedford Books: Boston, 1996)

Greene, "Social Change in Eighteenth-Century Anlo: The Role of Technology, Markets and Military Conflict," *Africa: Journal of the International African Institute* 58 (1988) pps.70—72

Greene, Jack P. Evaluating Empire and Confronting Colonialism in Eighteenth-Century Britain (Cambridge: Cambridge University Press, 2013), pp.27

Greene, Jack P., Pursuits of Happiness: The Social Development of Early Modern British Colonies and the Formation of American Culture (N.C.: 1988) pps.51, 62, 67, 126, 144—45

Greene, Lorenzo Johnstone *The Negro in Colonial New England, 1620—1776*, 4th ed. (New York, 1942), pp.36

Greene, S., 'Land, Lineage and Clan in Early Anlo,' *Africa*, 1981, pp.451ff

Greene, Sandra "The Anlo-Ewe: Their Economy, Society and External Relations in the Eighteenth Century," Ph.D., diss., Northwestern University, 1981 pps.1—8

Greene, Sandra E. 'From Whence They Came: A Note on the Influence of West African Ethnic and Gender Relations on the Organizational Character of the 1733 St. John Slave Rebellion,' in George Tyson and Arnold Highfield (eds), *The Danish West Indian Slave Trade: Virgin Islands Perspectives* (Virgin Islands, 1994)

Greenwood, George "Home Office citizenship fees 'scandalous' ". 13 February 2018. BBC News

Grundy, Adam & Lee, Lynda. "Increase in Number of U.S. Black-Owned Businesses Between 2017 and 2019." United States Census Bureau. February 22, 2022. Url: https://www.census.gov/library/stories/2022/02/increase-in-number-of-united-states-black-owned-businesses-between-2017-and-2019.html [Accessed: 12 April 2023]

Gutman, Herbert G., *Slavery and the Numbers Game: A Critique of Time on the Cross* (University of Illinois Press: Urbana, 1975)

Haines, Julia. "The State of the Nation's Nursing Shortage." U.S. News & World Report L.P. Nov 1, 2022. Url: https://www.usnews.com/news/health-news/articles/2022-11-01/the-state-of-the-nations-nursing-shortage [Accessed: 12 April 2023]

Hair, P.E.H, 'An Ethnolinguistic Inventory of the Lower Guinea Coast Before 1700: part I', *African Language Review*, 7 (1968), pp.47—73 and Part II, *African Language Review*, 8 (1969), pps. 225—26

Hall, Douglas *In Miserable Slavery: Thomas Thistlewood in Jamaica, 1750-86* (London; [New York]: Macmillan, 1989) pp.72

Hall, Douglas, "The Flight from the Estates Reconsidered: The British West Indies, 1838—42," *Journal of Caribbean History*, 10—11 (1978), pps.643—66

Hall, G. M. *Slavery and African Ethnicities*, pps.56—57, 66, 80—100, 102—105, 144, 149—157, 159—164

Hall, Gwendolyn M. Africans in Colonial Louisiana: The Development of Afro-Creole Culture in the Eighteenth Century (Baton Rouge, LA. 1992)

Hall, Gwendolyn Midlo. *Slavery and African Ethnicities in the Americas*: Restoring the Links, (Chapel Hill, NC: University of North Carolina Press, 2005)

Hall, Rober L. 'Savoring Africa in the New World,' in Herman J. Viola and Carolyn Margolis (eds.), *Seed of Change: a Quincentennial Commemoration* (Washington, D.C., 1991) pps.79—80. 161—9

Hall, Stuart *Creolite And The Process of Colonization*, from Robin Cohen & Poala Toninato. *The Creolization Reader: Studies in Mixed Identities And Cultures* (Routledge: London & New York, 2010) pps.27-33; intro pps.6—17.

Halliburton Jr., R., "Free Black Owners of Slaves: A Reappraisal of the Wooden Thesis," *The South Carolina Historical Magazine*, July 1975, Vol. 76, No. 3, pps.129—142

Handler, Jerome S. & Sio, Arnold A. "Barbados" in *Neither Slave nor Free: The Freedmen of African Descent in the Slave Societies of the New World*, eds. Cohen, David W. & Greene, Jack P., cit., "Minutes of the Barbados Privy Council, November 1, 1803," BDA; pps.245— 6

Handler, Jerome S. "Slave Revolts and Conspiracies in Seventeenth-Century Barbados," *New West Indian Guide* 56 (1982) pps.13—19

Handler, Jerome S. *A Guide to Source Materials for the Study of Barbados History, 1627—1834* (1971)

Handler, Jerome S., & Bilby, Kenneth M. "On the Early Use and Origin of the Term 'Obeah,' in Barbados and the Anglophone Caribbean," *Slavery and Ambition* 22 (2001) pps.87—100

Handler, Jerome S., "Survivors of the Middle Passage: Life Histories of Enslaved Africans in British America," XXIII, no.1 (April 2002), pps.37—38

Handler, Jerome S., *The Unappropriated People: Freedmen in the Slave Society of Barbados* (John Hopkins University Press: Baltimore, 1974), pps.18—25, 150

Hargreaves, Susan M. 1997. "The Political Economy of Nineteenth Century Bonny: A Study of Power, Authority, Legitimacy and Ideology in a Delta Trading Community from 1700—1914." Ph.D. diss., Centre of West African Studies, University of Birmingham

Harms, R., *River of Wealth, River of Sorrow* (New Haven and London, 1981) pp.2

Harris, Joseph E. Global Dimensions of the African Diaspora (Howard University Press; 2nd ed, 1993) pps.160—164

Harris, Marvin, *Patterns of Race in the Americas* (New York, 1974), pps.71—74

Harris, Sheldon H. *Paul Cuffee, Black America, And The African Return* (New York, 1972) pp. 38—39

Hartman, *Lose Your Mother*, pps. 86—87, 151—161, 245

Heffer, Greg "Windrush: Human rights watchdog reviewing UK's 'hostile environment' policy". Friday 12 June 2020. Sky News.

Henderson-Quartey, David K. *The Ga of Ghana: History and Culture of a West African People* (Book-in-Hand: London, 2001), pps.19, 20, 39—43, 49

Hermon-Hodge, H.B., *Gazetteer of Ilorin Province* (London: Allen and Unwin, 1929) pp.272

Hersak, Dunja, "There Are Many Kongo Worlds: Particukarities of Magico-Religious Beliefs Among the Vili Yombe of Congo-Brazzaville," *Africa: Journal of the International African Institute* 71, no.4 (2001)

Herskovits, Melville J. *The Myth of the Negro Past* (Boston, 1958), pp.45

Herskovitz, Melville J. *Life in a Haitian Valley* (New York: A. Knopf, 1937), pp. 257

Heywood, Linda M. "Slavery and Its Transformation in the Kingdom of Kongo: 1481—1800," *The Journal of African History* 50, no. 1 (2009)

Higgins, W. Robert, "Charles Town Merchants and Factors Dealing in he External Negro Trade, 1735—1775," *South Carolina Historical Magazine*, LXV (1964), pps.205—217

Higgins, W. Robert, "The Geographical Origins of Negro Slaves in Colonial South Carolina," *South Atlantic Quarterly*, LXX (1971), pps.37—38

Higman *Slave Populations of the British Caribbean, 1807—1834* (1995), cit., M.C.P.D.E., 1817, pps.276, 361; *P.P.*, 1817, vol. 17 (338), pp.35; T.71/522, pps.180—81; index 10487, f. 93 (P.R.O.)

Higman, B.W., "African and Creole Slave Family Patterns in Trinidad," Journal of Family History, 3 (1978), pps.163—80, appendix, 178—80

Higman, Barry W., "African and Creole Slave Family Patterns in Trinidad," in *Africa and the Caribbean: Legacies of a Link*, ed. Margaret E. Crahan and Franklin W, Knight (Baltimore, 1979), pps.41—64

Higman, Barry W., "Household Structure and Fertility on Jamaican Slave Plantations: A Nineteenth-century Example," *Population Studies* 27 (1973), pps.527—50

Higman, Barry W., *Slave Population and Economy in Jamaica, 1807—1834* (Cambridge, 1976)

Higman, Barry W., *Slave Populations of the British Caribbean, 1807—1834* (Baltimore, 1983)

Higman, Barry W., *Slave Populations of the British Caribbean, 1807—1834* (UWI: Kingston, 1995), pps.1, 3, 6—10, 14—16, 46, 108—09

Higman, *Slave Populations in the British Caribbean 1807—1834* (1995) cit., M.C.P.D.E., 1817, pp.278: 12 Mar. 1817; M.C.P.D.E., 1824, pp.329, 20 Mar. 1824; M.C.P.D.E., 1826, vol. 2, pp.324: Petition, 9 Aug. 1826; 1827, vol. 1, pp.95: petition, 30 June 1827; 1828, vol. 2, pp.153: Petition, 28 July 1828; *P.P.*, 1833, vol. 26 (700), pp.427—49

Hill, Donald, "England I Want to Go": The Impact of Migration on a Caribbean Community" (Ph.D. dissertation, Indiana University, 1973), pp.1

Hill, Robert A. ed. *The Marcus Garvey And Universal Negro Improvement Association Papers, Vol. 1 1826-August 1919*. Berkeley And Los Angeles: University Of California Press (1983)

Hilton, A. 'The Jaga Reconsidered,' *Journal of African History*, 1981, pp.191—202

Hilton, A. *The Kingdom of Kongo* (Oxford, 1995), pps.6—7, 70, 69—72, 120, 122—3

Hiro, Dilip *Black British, White British: A History Of Race Relations In Britain* (London: Paladin, 1992) pps. 16 - cit Ceri Peach *West Indian Migration To Britain: A Social Geography* (London: Oxford University Press, 1969: pps. 2, 23-25)

Hobsbawm, E. J. & Ranger, T. O. eds. The Invention of Tradition (Cambridge University Press: Cambridge, UK, 1983)

Hochschild, Adam. *Bury the Chains: The British Struggle to Abolish Slavery* (Macmillan: London, 2005), pps.341—3

Hoetink, H. *Slavery and Race Relations in the Americas* (Harper and Row: New York, 1973)

Hogarth Blake *Flora Shaw gives the name Nigeria: Transcribed from an article 1st printed by The Times of London, January 8th, 1897* (Hogarth Blake, 2008)

Hogben, S.J. and Kirk Greene, A.H.M, *The Emirates of Northern Nigeria* (Oxford University Press: London, 1966) pp.300

Hogendorn, Jan, "Economic Modelling of Price Differences in the Slave Trade between the Central Sudan and the Coast," *Slavery and Abolition*, XVII, no.3 (December 1996), pps.209—222

Holsey, Routes of Remembrance, pps.40—41, 81—102

Home Office; Priti Patel. "Home Secretary's oral statement on the Windrush Lessons Learned Review by Wendy Williams". 19 March 2020

Hopkins, Nick & Stewart, Heather "Amber Rudd was told about migrant removal targets, leak reveals". 28 April 2018. The Guardian

Hopton to Burnett, Sept, 7, 1771, in Henry Laurens Paper, 1747—1860, South Carolina Historical Society, Charleston

House of Commons Seasonal Papers (1790), 29/218 also, 29/144, 189

Howard-Hassman, Rhoda E.. Reparations to Africa and the Group of Eminent Persons*. Discussion of claims for reparations to Africa made at the United Nations-sponsored World Conference against Racism held in Durban, South Africa in September 2001. Url: https://journals.openedition.org/etudesafricaines/4543?file=1 [Accessed: 8th February 2021] pp.85
Howe, Darcus "If I pleaded guilty, said the lawyer, I'd only get five years." New Statesmen, 4th December 1998.
http://www.slavevoyages.org

Hunt, Carl M., Oyotunji Village: The Yoruba Movement in America (University Press of America: Washington DC, 1979), pp.28

Hunwick, John & Harrak, Fatima, Mi'raj al-Su'ud: Ahmad Baba's Replies on Slavery (Institute of African Studies: Rabat, 2000)

Hurston, Zora Neale "Dance, Songs and Tales from the Bahamas", Journal of American Folk-lore, Vol 43 (1930) pp.294

Hutton, Frankie Economic Considerations in The American Colonization Society's Early Efforts to Emigrate Free Blacks to Liberia, 1816-36. The Journal of Negro History, vol. 68, No. 4 (Autumn 1983) pp. 376

Idowu, E.B., Oludumare God in Yoruba Belief (London, 1975), pp. 24

IES (Institute of Education Services)-NCES (National Center for Education Statistics). "Public High School Graduation Rates." May 2021. Url:
https://nces.ed.gov/programs/coe/indicator/coi [Accessed: 12 April 2023]

Ifemesia, Chieka C. 1978. Southeastern Nigeria in the Nineteenth /century: An Introductory Analysis. New York Publishers, pps.32—37

Igwe, G. E. Onye Turu Ikoro Waa Ya Eze (University Press: Ibadan, Nigeria, 1986)

Ijere, Martin O. W.E.B Du Bois And Marcus Garvey As Pan-Africanists: A Study In Contrast. Presence Africaine, Nouvelle serie, No. 89 (1er TRIMESTRE, 1974) pp. 197

Imoagene, Onoso Chapter Title: Forging a Diasporic Nigerian Ethnicity In The United States And Britain. Beyond Expectations — Second-Generation Nigerians In The United States And Britain. (University Of California Press, 2017)

Inikori, J.E., 'The Sources of Supply for the Atlantic Slave Exports From the Bight of Benin and the Bight of Bonny (Biafra),' in Serge Daget (ed.) De la Traite a l'Esclavage: Acts du Colloque International sur la Traite des Noirs, 3 vols. (Nantes, 1988), pp.31—2, 35

Isaacs, Harold R., The New World of Negro Americans (The Day John Co.: New York, 1963), pp.149

Isert, Paul Erdmann Journey to Guinea and the Caribbean Islands of Columbia (1788). Trans. and ed. Selena Axelrod Winsnes pps.129—130,175—76

Isichei, Elizabeth *A History of African Societies to 1870* (Cambridge University Press: New York, 1997) pp. 246—252, 389—

Isichei, Elizabeth *A History of Nigeria* (Longman, 1983) pp.28

Isichei, Elizabeth *A History of the Igbo People* (Macmillan: London, 1976) pps. 10—16, 19, 28, 64, 98

Isichei, Elizabeth ed. 1978. *Igbo Worlds*: An Anthology of Oral Histories and Historical Descriptions. Philadelphia Institute for the Study of Human Issues, pp. 21—67, 97

Jaafar, Ali *Screenonline: Desmond's (1988-94)*. Retrieved 12th May 2020

Jackson, Cit., Lewis M. Killian *School Busing In Britain: Policies And Perceptions*. Harvard Educational Review, (1979) 49(2), pps. 185-206; pps. 120-121

Jackson, Nicole M. *Questions of Empire And Belonging In Black British Educational Activism*, Cit., Ambalavaner Sivanandan *A Different Hunger: Writings On Black Resistance* (London: Pluto Press, 1982) in [Edited by] Kehinde Andrews & Lisa Amanda Palmer *Blackness In Britain* (Routledge, 2016) pp. 118

Jackson, Richard M., Journal of a Voyage to Bony River on the West Coast of Africa, ed. Roland Jackson (Letchworth, 1934) pp.68

Jalloh, Alusine and Maizlish, Stephen E. (eds), *The African Diaspora* (College Station, TX, 1996), pps.100—33

Jam. Royal Gaz., April 8, May 6, 1780-S., Daniel Singer; Simon Taylor to Chalonder Archdeckne, Mullet Hall, St. Thomas in the East, Sept 3, 1787, box 2, bundle 13, Vanneck MS, Manuscripts Room, Cambridge University Library

Jam. Royal Gaz., Aug. 26, 1797-P.S., David Owens

Jam. Royal Gaz., Feb. 22, 1794-P.S., W. Weir; Jan 3, 1801, Francis Ashir; July 3, 1801-S., Richard Brooks; Thistlewood's Journal, June 19, 1765

Jam. Royal Gaz., Jan. 18, 1794-P.S., I. Pearkins; Aug. 17, 1782-S., Dr. R. Davies; April 6, 1793-P.S.; Overseer at Dry Driver Course [Kingston] *Daily Advertiser*, Jan. 9, 1790, James Lawrence

Jam. Royal Gaz., Jan. 19, 1782—5, George McCormack; Aug. 26, 1780, Joseph Gaskarth; and Cornwall Chronicle and Jamaica General Gazette [Cornwall Chron.], Oct. 3, 1789-S., James Findlater

Jam. Royal Gaz., June 29, 1799-P.S., Elizabeth Burton; March 1, 1794-P.S., Richard Saunders; [Kingston] Daily Advertiser, Sept. 1, 1790, Jacob Pereira and Co.

Jam. Royal Gaz., June 29, 1799-P.S., Elizabeth Burton; Oct. 21, 1797-P.S., John Kelly

Jam. Royal Gaz., Nov. 28, 1801-S., Cleland and Bull; Oct. 20, 1781-S., John Cosens; "Socco Country, talks Coramantee," *Jam. Merc.*, Dec. 4, 1779-S., Mathew Hinegan

Jamaica Royal Gazette [*Jam. Royal Gaz.*], for uncle: Oct. 17, 1780, George Bannett, Aug. 16, 1794-P.S., Moses de Campos; May 30, 1795-S., Thomas Priddie, Oct. 17, 1795-S., R. Craighton; for aunt, Oct. 25, 1794-P.S., John Christopherz; May 23, 1801-S., James Wilson, grandfather: Oct. 14, 1797-P.S., Colin M'Larty. Barbados: kin terms in the *Barbados Mercury and Bridge-Town Gazette* [*Barb. Merc. And B-T. Gaz*], for-sale notice; for father-in-law; Oct 4, 1806, Jacob Blozada; Oct. 17, 1807, Gabriel B. Byer

James Crooks, Registrar for Tobago, owned Belmont Estate and 85 slaves: T.71/462, pp.228; Official Returns of Registrar of Slaves, Tobago, 1823 (T.A.)

James Wedderburn to Samuel Vassall, April 15, Sept. 13, 1774, William Vassall Letterbooks

James Wedderburn to William Vassall, Oct. 11, 1771; William Vassal Letterbooks, 1769—96, Archives Department, Central Library, Sheffield

James, Winston & Harris, Clive *Inside Babylon: The Caribbean Diaspora In Britain* (Verso, 1993) pp. 22

Jarmon, Laura C., "Flying Africans," in Anand Prahlad ed. African American Folklore: An Encyclopedia For Students (ABC-CLIO, LLC: California, 2016, pps.90—91, 103—04

Jeffries, M. D. W, 'The Umundri tradition of origin,' *African Studies*, 1956, pps.122—23

John Ferguson to Hugh Hamilton, Feb. 25, 1786, Hugh of Penmore Muniments, GD142/2/1, no. 32, Scottish Record Office, Edinburgh

John Jacques to Perrin, Feb. 8, 1794, E17141, Fitzherbert-Perrin Papers

Johnson, Katanga. "U.S. public more aware of racial inequality but still rejects reparations: Reuters/Ipsos polling". June 25, 2020. Reuters. Url: https://www.reuters.com/article/us-usa-economy-reparations-poll/u-s-public-more-aware-of-racial-inequality-but-still-rejects-reparations-reuters-ipsos-polling-idUSKBN23W1NG [Accessed: 8th February 2021]

Johnson, Leonard G. *General T. Perronet Thompson 1783-1869: His Military, Literary and Political Campaigns* (London: George Allen & Urwin, 1957) pp. 26 – Quoting the National Archives, Kew, CO 267/24 (*Sierra Leone Gazette*, 1 August 1808)

Johnson, Samuel *History of the Yorubas: From the Earliest Times to the Beginning of the British Protectorate* (1921; Cambridge University Press, 2010 reissue), pps.13, 19, 102, 156, 325—26, 403

Johnston, Harry H. 1888a. "A Journey up the Cross River, West Africa." *Proceedings of the Royal Geographical Society*, Vol. 10, No,7 (July): pp.753

Jonathan Dickinson to John Lewis, May 2, 1715, Jonathan Dickinson Letter Book, 1715—1721, Yi 2 / 1628, alcove 4, shelf 12, Library Company of Philadelphia

Jonathan R. Webb to Barham, St. Elizabeth, June 16, 1809, bundle 1, 1809—16, c. 358, Barham Family Papers; cf. Craton, "Changing Patterns of Slave Families," 12

Jones, G. I. 1939. "Who Are the Aros?" Nigerian Field, Vol. 8, No. 3: pps. 100—03. 1961. "Ecology and Social Structure among the North Eastern Ibo." *Africa*, Vol. 31: pps. 117—34

Jones, G. I. 1989. *From Slaves to Palm Oil: Slave Trade and Palm Oil Trade in the Bight of Biafra* (Cambridge: African Studies Centre) pps.34—36

Jones, G. I., *The Trading States of the Oil Rivers: a Study of Political Development in Easter Nigeria* (London, 1963), pp.9—48

Jones, G.I. 'Olaudah Equiano of the Niger Igbo,' in Philip D. Curtin (ed.), Africa *Remembered: Narratives of West Africans from the Era of the Slave Trade* (Madison, Wisconsin, 1967), pps. 60—9

Jones, James 1788. "James Jones to Lord Hawkesbury,"26 July. *Documents Illustrative* see Donnan 1931; pp.590

Journals of Thomas Thistlewood [Thistlewood's Journal], March 21, 1758, Monson 31, Lincolnshire Record Office, Lincoln

Journals of Thomas Thistlewood [Thistlewood's Journal], Monson 31, Lincolnshire Record Office, Lincoln, May 25, 1754, July 6, Dec. 10, 1761

July, *The Origins Of Modern African Thought*, 208-33; Wilson, Henry S. ed., *Origins Of West African Nationalism* (London: Macmillan, 1969), 227-62; Norbert C. Brockman, *An African*

Biographical Dictionary (Santa Barbara, CA: ABC-CLIO, 1994), 56; Hakim Adi And Marika Sherwood, *Pan-African History: Political Figures From Africa And The Diaspora Since 1787* (London: Routledge, 2003), 11-15
July, *The Origins Of Modern African Thought*, 433-57; Henry S. Wilson, ed., *Origins Of West African Nationalism*, 309-80; Brockman, *An African Biographical Dictionary* 75-76; Adi And Sherwood, *Pan-African History,* 82-85

Kaufmann, Elaine M., *Ibibio Dictionary* (California, 1972), pp.223

Kea, Ray A., *Settlements, Trade, and Polities in the Seventeenth-Century Gold Coast* (John Hopkins University Press: Baltimore, 1982), pps.1—7, 11—14, 23—32, 104—108, 159—160

KFF—The Independent Source For Health Policy Research, Polling, and News. "Disparities in Health and Health Care Among Black People." Feb 24, 2022. Url: https://www.kff.org/infographic/disparities-in-health-and-health-care-among-black-people/ [Accessed: 12 April 2023]

Killingray, David *Africans in Britain* (Frank Cass, 1994)

Kimber, Edward, The History of the Life and Adventures of Mr. Anderson, Containing His Strange Varieties of Fortune in Europe and America (Dublin, 1754), pp.129ff, 216

Kiyaga-Mulindwa, D, 'The "Akan" Problem,' *Current Anthropology*, 1980, pp.503ff

Klein, A. Norman, "Toward a New Understanding," *African: Journal of the International African Institute* 66 (1996) pps.248—253, 254, 260—263

Klein, Herbert 2001. "The Slave Trade and Decentralized Societies." Journal of African History, Vol. 42, No.1 pps.49—65

Klein, Herbert *Slavery in the Americas* (University of Chicago Press: Chicago, 1967)

Klein, Herbert, *The Middle Passage: Comparative Studies in the Atlantic Slave Trade* (Princeton University Press, Princeton 1978), pp.117

Knibb and Borthwick, P. *Defence of Baptist Missionaries from the Charge of Inciting the Late Rebellion in Jamaica* .... 2d ed. (London, 1833), 5ff. Thomas Burchell, Memoir of Thomas Burchell (London, 1845), pp.230

Knight, Franklin W. Slave Society in Cuba During the Nineteenth Century (Madison: University of Wisconsin Press, 1970), pps.193—94

Knight, Franklin W. *The Haitian Revolution*, The American Historical Review, Vol. 105, No.1, 2000, pp 103

Koelle, Rev'd Sigmund W. *Polyglotta Africana* (1854: Graz, Austria, 1963), pps.7—8, 28

Kolapo, Femi J., "The 1858—59 Gbebe CMS Journal of Missionary James Thomas," History in Africa 27 (2000), pp.190, entry for 17 July 1859

Kolapo, Femi J., "The Igbo and Their Neighbours During the Era of the Atlantic Slave-Trade," *Slavery and Abolition*, XXV (2004), pps.114—133

Kolapo, Femi James, "Military Turbulence, Population Displacement, and Commerce on a Slaving Frontier of the Sokoto: Nupe c. 1810—1857" (Ph.D. dissertation, York University, Canada, 1999)

Konadu, Kwasi *The Akan Diaspora in the Americas* (Oxford University Press: New York, 2010)

Kulikoff, Allan "A 'Prolifck' People," *Southern Studies*, XVI (1977), pp.392

Lacobucci, Gareth. "Most Black People in UK Face Discrimination From Healthcare Staff, Survey Finds." BMJ Publishing Group Ltd. 27 September 2022. Url: https://www.bmj.com/content/378/bmj.o2337. [Accessed: 12 April 2023]

Lagos Weekly Record, 29 September 1894

Laing to Perrin, Jan. 10, 1773, E16753—54, Fitzherbert-Perrin Papers

Lander, Richard & Lander, John, Journal of an Expedition to Explore the Course and Termination of the Niger, 2 vols. (New York, 1832), II, pps.174, 201

Langley, Lester D. *The Americas in the Age of Revolution, 1750-1850* (New Haven, Conn., 1996), 159-77.

Larkin, Colin. *The Virgin Encyclopaedia Of Reggae* (Virgin Books, 1998)

Latham, A.J.H *Old Calabar 1600—1891: The Impact of the International Economy upon a Traditional Society* (Clarendon Press: London, 1973) pps. 19—20, 27—28, 35—39

Laurens to Clarke, Jan. 12, 1756, Feb. 21, 1756, pps. 62—64, 100—101

Laurens to Clarke, Mar. 3, 1756, Apr. 5, 1756, pps. 123, 140—141

Laurens to Gidney [Gedney] Clarke, Jan. 12, 1756, in *Laurens Papers*, II, pps.62—65

Laurens to Law, Satterthwaite, and Jones, Jan. 12, 1756, Laurens to Clarke, Mar. 3, 1756, pps. 65, 123—124

Laurens to Law, Satterthwaite, and Jones, Jan. 31, 1756, Laurens to Clarke, Jan. 31, 1756, in both in *Laurens Papers*, II, pps.81—82, 82—84

Laurens to Thomas Frankland, June 4, 1756, pps.208—210

Law, Ian & Henfrey, June *A History Of Race And Racism In Liverpool, 1660-1950* (Liverpool, UK: Merseyside Community Relations Council, 1981) pp. 31

Law, R. *The Oyo Empire, 1600—1836: A West African Imperialism in the Era of the Atlantic Slave Trade* (Oxford, 1977), pp.308

Law, R. *The Slave Coast of West Africa 1500—1750: the Impact of the Atlantic Slave Trade on the African Society*, 7, (Clarendon Press: Oxford, 1991) pps.28, 70, 92, 187, 190—91

Law, R.C.C, 'Traditional History,' in S.O. Biobaku (ed.), Sources of Yoruba History (Oxford, 1973) pp.38

Law, Robin, 'Ethnicity and the Slave Trade: "Lucumi" and "Nago" as Ethnonyms in West Africa,' *History in Africa*, 24 (1997), pps.205—19

Law, Robin, "Ethnicity and the Slave Trade: 'Lucumi' and 'Nago' as Ethnonyms in West Africa," *History of West Africa*, 24 (1997), pps.205—19

Law, Robin, *Ouidah: The Social History of a West African Slaving "Port," 1727—1892* (James Currey: Oxford, 2004)

Law, Robin, The Oyo Empire c. 1600—c. 1836: A West African Imperialism in the Era of the Atlantic Slave Trade (Clarendon Press: Oxford, 1991), pps. 105, J225—7, 258, 274—76, 278, 280, 281—82,T 284—85, 295—96, 298, 306—8

Law, Robin, *The Slave Coast of West Africa, 1550—1750: The Impact of the Atlantic Slave Trade on an African Society* (Oxford, 1991) pps.182—191

Lawal, B. 'Dating problems at Igbo-Ukwu,' Journal of African History, 1973, pps.1—8

Lawal, Babatunde, 'Reclaiming the Past: Yoruba Elements in African American Arts' in The Yoruba Diaspora in the Atlantic World (eds.), Falola, Toyin & Childs, Matt D. (Indiana University Press: India, 2004), pps.304—08

Lawrence, Leota S. *The African Presence In Caribbean Folklore. New Directions*, vol 8, no. 3, 1981, pp. 21.
https://pdfs.semanticscholar.org/dc97/25b537ce6f1142b67c1df1f22e4c410aa8d8.pdf

Leonard, A. G. *The Lower Niger and Its Tribes* (London, 1906) pps. 36—7

Leonard, A. G., 'Notes of a Journey to Bende,' Journal of Manchester Geographical Society, 14 (1898), pp.191

Letwin, Olive *Biddy, Biddy Folk music of Jamaica Music Educators Journal* Vol. 63 No. 1 (1976) pp. 39

Lewis, Matthew G., Journal of a West India Proprietor (London, 1834), pp.129, 133—4

Liberia, Simon Greenleaf, and Pennsylvania Colonization Society. *The Independent Republic Of Liberia: its Constitution And Declaration of Independence: Address Of The Colonists To The Free People Of Color In The United States, With Other Documents: Issued Chiefly For The Use Of The Free People Of Color*. Philadelphia W.F. Geddes, Printer 1848

Likupe, Gloria *Experiences Of African Nurses And Perceptions Of Their Managers In The NHS*. Journal Of Nursing Management (2015), 23(2), 231—241

Lines, Rick *"Deliver us from evil?"—The Single Convention On Narcotic Drugs, 50 years on*, International Journal On Human Rights And Drug Policy, Vol. 1 (2010)

Lipking, Joanna, "Confusing Matters: Searching the Backgrounds of Oroonoko," in Todd, *Aphra Behn Studies*, pps.259—281

Livingstone, Thomas W. *The Exportation of American Higher Education to West Africa: Liberia College, 1850-1900*. The Journal of Negro Education, Vol. 45, No. 3 (Summer, 1976) pps. 249-250, 254, 260-61

Lloyd, P.C., "Political and Social Structure," in Sources of Yoruba History, ed: Biobaku, S.O. (Clarendon Press: Oxford, 1973), pp.209

Lloyds Banking Group. "Race Action Plan: Our Stand Against Racism." Url:
https://www.lloydsbankinggroup.com/who-we-are/responsible-business/inclusion-and-diversity/ethnicity/our-stand-for-racial-equality.html [Accessed: 12 April 2023]

Logan, Rayford W., "The Historical Aspects of Pan-Africanism," *African Forum*, I (Summer 1965), pp.90

Long, Edward, *The History of Jamaica*, 3 vols. (1774, repr. London, 1870), 2: 451—54, 413, 416—17, 473

Long, Richard A., *The Black Tradition in American Dance*, pps.72—3

Lopes and Pigafetta. *A Report of the Kingdom of Congo and of the Surrounding Countries; Drawn Out of the Writings and Discourses of the Portuguese, Duarte Lopez, by Fillippo Pigafetta, in Rome* 1591: pp.57

Lovejoy, Paul E. & Richardson, David, "Competing Markets for Male and Female Slaves: Prices in the Interior of West Africa, 1780—1850," *International Journal of African Historical Studies, XXVIII*, pps261—293

Lovejoy, Paul E. "Islam, Slavery, and Political Transformation in West Africa: Constraints on the Trans-Atlantic Slave Trade," *Revue francaise d'historie d'outre-mer* 89 (2002), pps.247—82

Lovejoy, Paul E. "Jihad e escravidao: As origens dos escravos Muculmanos de Bahia." *Topoi* (Rio Janiero) 1 (2000), pps.11—14, 22. 27

Lovejoy, Paul E. "The Yoruba Factor in the Transatlantic Slave Trade," in Falola, Toyin & Childs, Matt D. *The Yoruba Diaspora in the Atlantic World* (Indiana University Press: Indiana, 2004), pps.40—51

Lovejoy, Paul E. and Richardson, D. 1997. "Pawns Will Live when Slaves is Apt to Dye": Credit, Slaving and Pawnship at Old Calabar in the Era of the Slave Trade, London School of Economic History, No. 37/97, November

Lovejoy, Paul E. and Richardson, D., "'The Initial Crisis of Adaptation' The Impact of British Abolition on the Atlantic Slave Trade in West Africa, 1808—1820," in From Slave Trade to "Legitimate" Commerce, ed. Robin Law (Cambridge University Press: Cambridge, 1995), pp.40

Lovejoy, Paul E. and Rogers, Nicholas (eds), *Unfree Labour in the Development of the Atlantic World* (London, 1994), pps.151—80

Lovejoy, Paul E., 'The Volume of the Atlantic Slave Trade: A Synthesis,' *Journal of African History*, 23 (1982), pp.478, 480—1

Lovejoy, Paul E., "Biography as Source Material: Towards a Biographical Archive of Enslaved Africans," in *Source Material for Studying the Slave Trade and the African Diaspora*, ed. Robin Law (Centre of Commonwealth Studies, University of Sterling, UK, 1997)

Lovejoy, Paul E., "The Central Sudan and the Atlantic Slave Trade," in *Paths Toward the Past: African Historical Essays in Honor of Jan Vansina*, ed. Robert W. Harms et al. (African Studies Association Press: Atlanta, 1994), pp.354

Lovejoy, Paul E., Reviewed Work(s): Slave Rebellion in Brazil: The Muslim Uprising of 1835 in Bahia by Jose Reis, *The International Journal of African Historical Studies*, vol. 30, No.1, 1997, pp183.

Lovejoy, Paul E., *Transformations in Slavery: A History in Slavery: A History of Slavery Africa*, 2nd ed. (Cambridge University Press: Cambridge, 2000) [1983]), pp.51 (3rd edition, New York 2011—pps. 53—62, 73—83

Lowenthal, David, *West Indian Societies* (Oxford University Press: London, 1972), pp.40

Lynch, John *The Spanish-American Revolutions*, 1808-1826 (New York, 1973)

Lyndsey, Lydia "Halting The Tide: Responses To West Indian Immigration To Britain, 1946-52." Journal Of Caribbean History 26.1 (1992) pps.68, 70

Lyric Find. Songwriters: David Orobosa Omoregie & Fraser Lance Thorneycroft-Smith. *Black lyrics* © Warner Chappell Music, Inc, Kobalt Music Publishing Ltd.

Madden, Richard R. *A Twelvemonths Residence in the West Indies*, 2 vols. (London, 1835), 2: 168—69

Magubane, Bernard Makhosezwe *The Ties That Bind: African-American Consciousness of Africa* (Africa World Press Inc., 1987) pp.176 quoting Joe E. Thomas

Malcolm Laing to William Philip Perrin [Kingston, Jamaica], Jan. 10, 1773, E16753—54, Fitzherbert-Perrin Papers, Derbyshire Record Office, Matlock

Mann, Kristin, "Shifting Paradigms in the Study of the African Diaspora and of Atlantic History and Culture," *Slavery and Abolition* 22, no.1 (April 2001), pp.9

Mann, Kristin, "Slave Exports from Lagos, c. 1760—1851," *Canadian Association of African Studies*, Montreal, 1996

Manning, Patrick *Slavery, Colonialism, and Economic Growth in Dahomey, 1640—1960* (Cambridge University Press: Cambridge, 1982), pp.19

Manning, Patrick, "The Slave Trade in the Bight of Benin, 1640—1890," in *The Uncommon Market: Essays in the Economic History of the Atlantic Salve Trade*, ed. Henry A. Gemery and Jan S. Hogendorn (Academic Press: New York, 1979), pps.125—29

Manning, Patrick, *The African Diaspora: A History Through Culture* (New York, 2009), pps.101—113, 123

Manoukian, Madeline *Akan and Ga-Adangme Peoples of the Gold Coast* (Oxford University Press: London, 1950), pps.9, 66—69

Manzo, Ula C. & Manzo, Anthony V.. *Literary Disorders: Holistic Diagnosis and Remediation* (Holt, Rinehart and Winston, Inc, 1993) pp. 27

Mara Ostfeld & Michelle Garcia. "Black men shift slightly towards Trump in record numbers, polls show". NBC. Nov 4 2020.

Margin note to an inventory for the estate of Edmund Jenings, Esqr., Dec. 16, 1712 by John Hawkins, Francis Porteus Corbin Papers, Colonial Williamsburg Research Center, microfilm of the original at the Manuscript Division, Duke University Library

Maroon Societies: Rebel Slave Communities in the Americas (The Johns Hopkins University Press, 1996)

Marshall, B. et al., "The Establishment of a Peasantry in Barbados," in *Social Groups and Institutions in the History of the Caribbean* (San Juan, 1975), pps.85—104

Marshall, Rita *"Black Power Men Launch Credo,"* Times, September 11th 1967.

Marshall, Woodville K. ed., *The Colthurst Journal: Journal of a Special Magistrate in the Islands of Barbados and St. Vincent, July 1835—September 1838* (Millwood, N. Y.: KTO Press, 1977), pps.68—69

Martin, Guy *African Political Thought* (Palgrave Macmillan: New York, 2012) pp. 1 — quoting Frantz Fanon *Toward The African Revolution*: Political Essays, translated by Haakon Chavelier (New York: Grove Press, new ed. 1988)

Martin, K.K., "America's First African Dance Theatre," Odu: *A Journal of West African Studies*, n.s. 11 (January 1975), pps.123—24

Martin, P., The External Trade of the Loango Coast 1576—1870 (London, 1965) pp.46

Martin, Phyllis M. The External Trade of the Loango Coast, 1576—1870: The Effects of Changing Commercial Relations on the Vili Kingdom of Loango (Clarendon Press: Oxford, 1972)

Martin, Phyllis M., *The External Trade of the Loango Coast, 1576—1870: The Effects of Changing Commercial Relations on the Vili Kingdom of Loango* (Oxford, 1972), chap.4

Martin, Tony *Marcus Garvey: Hero* (Dover, Mass.: Majority Press, 1983) pps. 26-27

Mary [Turner] Record, "The Jamaican Slave Rebellion of 1821," *Past and Present* 40 (July 1968): 108—25; Edward Kamau Braithwaite, "The Slave Rebellion in the Great River Valley of St. James, 1821—1832," *Jamaica Historical Review* 13 (1982): 11—30; Craton, *Testing the Chains*, ch. 22; and, for an official overview, Gov. Belmore to Viscount Goderich, Jan. 6, 1832, C.O. 137/181, ff

Mason, John, "Yoruba Beadwork in the America," in *Beads, Body and Soul: Art and Light in the Yoruba Universe*, ed. Henry J. Drewal and John Mason (University of California Fowler Museum of Cultural History: Los Angeles, 1998), pps.87—177

Mason, John, Olokun: *Owners of Rivers and Seas* (New York: Yoruba Theological Archministry, 1996), pp.70

Mason, Michael, "The Jihad in the South: An Outline of the Nineteenth-Century Nupe Hegemony in North-Eastern Yorubaland and Afenmai," *Journal of the Historical Society of Nigeria*, 5, no.2 (1970): pp.201

Mason, Michael, *Foundations of the Bida Kingdom* (Ahmadu Bellow University Press: Zaria, Nigeria, 1981), pp.77; idem, "Jihad in the South," 205

Mateos, Pablo *Names, Ethnicity And Populations. Tracing Identity In Space* (Berlin, Germany: Springer, 2014).

Mathews, Jack *"Some Blacks Critical of Spielberg's Purple'"*. December 20th, 1985. Los Angeles Times. Url: https://www.latimes.com/archives/la-xpm-1985-12-20-ca-5050-story.html. [Accessed: 16th February 2021]

Mathieson, William Law, *British Slavery and Its Abolition* (1926)

Matory, J. Lorand, "'The English Professors of Brazil: On the Diasporic Roots of the Yoruba Nation," *Comparative Studies in Society and History*, 41, no.1 (January 1999), pps.72—103

May, Roy & Cohen, Robin *The Interaction Between Race And Colonialism: A Case Study Of The Liverpool Race Riots Of 1919* (University Of Birmingham Faculty of Commerce and Science, 1974) pp.118

Mayor Of London. (2015) *Chain Annual Report. Greater London. April 2014 – March 2015.* Greater London Authority.

Mazrui, Ali A., ed., *UNESCO General History of Africa: Vol. VIII Africa Since 1935—Unabridged Edition* (UNESCO: Paris, 1999), pps.8—9

McCargo, Alanna & Strochak, Sarah. "Mapping the Black Homeownership Gap." *Urban Institute.* February 26, 2018. Url: https://www.urban.org/urban-wire/mapping-black-homeownership-gap [Accessed: 12 April 2023]

McCusker, John J. & Menard, Russell R., The Economy of British America, 1607—1789 (N.C.: Chapel Hill, 1991), pps. 39—46 78—80, 92—110, 174, 198—203

McDaniel, Antonio *Extreme Mortality in Nineteenth-Century Africa: The Case of Liberian Immigrants*. Population Association of America Demography, Vol.29, No.4 (Nov 1992) pps.581, 583

McDaniel, Lorna, "The Igbo Second Burial," *The Black Perspective in Music*, Vol. 6, (Spring, 1978), pp.49

McDaniel, Lorna, "The Stone Feast and Big Drum of Carriacou," *The Black Perspective in Music*, Vol. 13, No. 2 (Autumn, 1985), pps.179—194

McGreal, C.. "Turning Racism on its head", Mail and Guardian (Johannesburg), January 30, 2001

McKinsey & Company. "Race in the Workplace: The Black Experience in the US Private Sector." February 21, 2021 [Report]. Url: https://www.mckinsey.com/featured-insights/diversity-and-inclusion/race-in-the-workplace-the-black-experience-in-the-us-private-sector [Accessed: 12 April 2023]

McKinsey & Company. "The Future of Work in America: People and Places, Today and Tomorrow." July 11, 2019 [Report]. Url: https://www.mckinsey.com/featured-insights/future-of-work/the-future-of-work-in-america-people-and-places-today-and-tomorrow [Accessed: 12 April 2023]

McLaughlin, James L and Owusu-Ansah, David *Britain And The Gold Coast: The Early Years* (1994)

McManus, Edgar J. *Black Bondage in the North* (Syracuse, N.Y., 1973), pp.20

Md. Gaz., Jan. 20, 1803; *Va. Gaz.* (Dixon and Hunter), Oct. 31, 1771, James French; *Va. Gaz.* (Purdie and Dixon), April 21, 1768, John Holladay

Mead, Matthew *Empire Windrush: Cultural Memory And Archival Disturbance. Moveable Type,* Vol.3, 'From Memory To Event' (2007) pps. 116-119

Meek, C. K. *Law Authority in a Nigerian Tribe: A Study in Indirect Rule* (Oxford University Press, 1937)

Meier, August & Rudwick, Elliot, *Black History and the Historical Profession, 1815—1980* (Urbana, 1986), pps.249ff, 267

Menard, Russell R., *Sweet Negotiations: Sugar, Slavery, and Plantation Agriculture in Early Barbados* (Charlottesville: University of Virginia Press, 2006) pp.18, 38, 45, 71, 84

Meredith, Henry *An Account of the Gold Coast of Africa: With A Brief History of the African Company* (Hurst, Rees, Orme, and Brown: London: Hurst, 1812), pp.144

Meredith, Martin *The State Of Africa — A History Of The Continent Since Independence* (Simon & Schuster: London, 2013) pps.545-48

Merewether, J. and Manning, E. 1736. "John Merewether and Edward Manning to Peter Burrell," January 6, 1736, see Donnan 1931

Metaferia, Getachew, "The Ethiopian Connection to the Pan-African Movement," *Journal of Third World Studies*, Fall 1995, Vol. 12, No. 2, Historical and Contemporary Third World Developments, pps.300—25

Meyerowitz, Eva *Akan Traditions of Origin* (Red Candle Press: London, 1952), pps.33—35, 63—64, 74, 95

Miller J. C., 'Requiem for the Jaga,' *Cahiers d'etudes africaines*, 1973, pps.121—49

Miller J. C., 'Thanatopsis' *Cahiers d'etudes africaines*, 1978, pps.229—31

Miller J., *Way of Death: Merchant Capitalism and the Angolan Slave Trade 1730—1830* (London, 1988) pps.4—5, 38, 77, 89—90, 395, [title of] Ch. 8

Miller, J.C., "The Numbers, Origins, and Destinations of Slaves in the Eighteenth Century Angolan Slave Trade," in Inikori and Engerman, *Atlantic Slave Trade*, pps.78—79, 104—110

Miller, J.C., *Way of Death: Merchant Capitalism and the Angolan Slave Trade, 1750—1830* (Madison, Wisconsin, 1988) pps. 71—104, 105—126, 141—153, 379—442

Miller, Joseph C. *Slavery: A Comparative Teaching Bibliography* (Waltham, Mass., 1977)

Mintz, Sidney & Price, Richard, *: An Anthropological Approach to the Afro-American Past. A Caribbean Perspective* (Philadelphia, 1976), pps.7, 9—11, 22—23

Mintz, Sidney & Price, Richard, *The Birth of African-American Culture: an Anthropological Perspective* (Boston, 1992), pps.43—44

Mintz, Sidney W. & Hall, Douglas, "The Origins of the Jamaican Internal Marketing System," in *Papers in Caribbean Anthropology*, ed. Mintz, Yale University Publications in Anthropology no. 57 (New Haven, 1960)

Mintz, Sidney W., "Slavery and the Rise of Peasantries," in Roots and Branches: Current Directions in Slave Studies, ed. Michael Craton (Toronto, 1979), pps.213—4; "From Plantations to Peasantries in the Caribbean," in Caribbean Contours, ed. Sidney W Mintz and Sally Price (Baltimore, 1985), pps.127—53

Mitton, Dr Lavinia & Aspinall, Peter J.. *Black Africans In The UK: Integration Or Segregation? Research Findings*. Understanding Population Trends And Processes [UPTAP]/ESRC. (2011, January).

Mobley, Christina Frances "The Kongolese Atlantic African Slavery & Culture from Mayombe to Haiti, Ph.D. Duke University, pps. iv, 1—9, 18—20—24,

Mohamed, Besheer & Diamant, Jeff. "Black Muslims Account For a Fifth of all U.S. Muslims, and About Half are Converts to Islam." *Pew Research Center*. January 17, 2019. Url: https://www.pewresearch.org/fact-tank/2019/01/17/black-muslims-account-for-a-fifth-of-all-u-s-muslims-and-about-half-are-converts-to-islam/ [Accessed: 12 April 2023]

Molesworth to Blathwayt, November 2, 1685, W. Sainsbury et al., eds., *Calendar of State Papers, Colonial Series, America and the West Indies* (London, 1862) quoted in Barbara Klamon Koptyoff, "The Early Political Development of Jamaican Maroon Societies." *William and Mary Quarterly*, 3rd ser., 35 April 1978): 298n, 300, 302

Moliner, Israel, Personal Communication, Matanzas, February 1997

Montessarchio Girolamode (seventeenth-century Capuchin), quoted in Thornton, The State in African Historiography,' pp.19

Moore, Stacy G., "Established and Well Cultivated": *Afro-American Foodways in Early Virginia,' Virginia Cavalcade*, 39 (1989), pps. 70—83

Morgan, Jennifer L., Laboring Women: Reproduction and Gender in the New World Slavery (Philadelphia: University of Pennsylvania Press, 2004)

Morgan, Kenneth, *Slavery, Atlantic Trade, and the British Economy, 1660—1800* (New York, 2000)

Morgan, Philip D. "The Cultural Implications of the Atlantic Slave Trade: African Regional Origins, American Destinations and New World Developments." *Slavery and Abolition* pps.122—145

Morgan, Philip D., 'The Cultural Implications of the Atlantic Slave Trade: African Regional Origins, American Destinations and New World Developments,' in Slavery and Abolition, 18, no.1, pps.122—45

Morris, Robert, '*The 1816 Uprising: A Hell Broth*,' JBHMS, 40: 1—15

Morton-Williams, Peter, "The Oyo Yoruba and the Atlantic Slave Trade, 1670—1830," *Journal of the Historical Society of Nigeria*, 3, no.1 (1964), pp.25—45

Moses, Wilson Jeremiah, *The Golden Age of Black Nationalism 1850—1925* (Archon Brooks: Hamden, CT, 1978), pp.24 as quoted from David Walker, *Walker's Appeal in Four Articles* (1829) and Henry Highland Garnet, *An Address to the Slaves of the United States of America* (Troy: N.Y., 1848)

Moslimani, Mohamad; Tamir, Christine; Budiman, Abby; Noe-Bustamante, Luis & Mora, Lauren. "Facts About the U.S. Black Population." *Pew Research Center*. March 2, 2033. Url: https://www.pewresearch.org/social-trends/fact-sheet/facts-about-the-us-black-population/ [Accessed: 12 April 2023]

Mulcahy, Matthew, Hubs of Empire: The Southeastern Lowcountry and British Caribbean (Baltimore: John Hopkins University Press, 2014) pp.81

Mullin, Michael *Africa in America: Slave Acculturation and Resistance in the American South and the British Caribbean 1736—1831* (Illini Books: Illinois, 1994), pps.13—15, 23—27, 59—60, 126—128, 130—131, 159—163, 167—168, 170, 249—257, 264—267

Murphy, Andrea *From The Empire To The Rialto: Racism And Reaction in Liverpool, 1918-1948* (UK: Liver Press) pp.
Murray, D. J. *The West Indies and the Development of Colonial Government, 1801—1834* (1965)

NAR (National Association of Realtors). "U.S. Homeownership Rate Experiences Largest Annual Increase on Record, Though Black Homeownership Remains Lower Than a Decade Ago, NAR Analysis Finds." February 23rd, 2022. Url: https://www.nar.realtor/newsroom/u-s-homeownership-rate-experiences-largest-annual-increase-on-record-though-black-homeownership-remains-lower-than-decade-ago [Accessed: 12 April 2023]

National Humanities Center. *'The Negro Silent Protest Parade Organized By The NAACP Fifth Avenue., New York City, July 28, 1917.'* The Making Of African American Identity Vol. 2, 1865-1917 (2014). Url: https://nationalhumanitiescenter.org/pds/maai2/forward/text4/silentprotest.pdf

Newman, Simon P. *A New World of Labor: The Development of Plantation Slavery in the British Atlantic* (Philadelphia, University of Pennsylvania Press, 2013), pps. 208—209

NHS (National Health Service) Race & Health Observatory. "Ethnic Inequalities in Healthcare: A Rapid Evidence Review." February 2022. Url: https://www.nhsrho.org/wp-content/uploads/2022/02/RHO-Rapid-Review-Final-Report_v.7.pdf [Accessed: 12 April 2023]

Nicholas, Tracy, *Rastafari: A Way of Life* (Anchor Press Doubleday, 1979), pps.21—25

Nigerian National Archives Kaduna [NNAK] SNP 7/13 4703/1912, Omu District—Offa Division—Assessment Report, June 1912 by C. S. Burnett] para 9; same file, Omu Islanu District Assessment Report by V. F. Biscoe, 1912, para. 6)

Nishida, "Manumission and Ethnicity in Salvador," pps.370, 378

Nishida, Mieko, "Manumission and Ethnicity in Urban Slavery: Salvador, Brazil, 1808—1888," *Hispanic American Historical Review*, 73, No. 3 (1993), pps.361—91

NNAK SNP 10 393p/1918, Assessment Report on Aworo District, by C. K. Meek, paras. 29—30

NNAK SNP 19 393p/1918, An Assessment Report on the Aworo (Oworraw) District of the Kabba Division, by Mr. C. K. Meek, Assistant District Officer, para. 45

Nokes, Caroline. "Immigration Minister: Immigration Status of the Windrush generation". 15th April, 2018. The Voice Newspaper
Norfolk and Portsmouth Herald, Nov. 4, 1831, Beinecke Rare Book and Manuscript Library, Yale University

Northrup, D., "Igbo and Myth Igbo: Culture and Ethnicity in the Atlantic World, 1600—1850," XXI, no.3

Northrup, D., *Trade Without Rulers: Pre-Colonial Economic Development in South-eastern Nigeria* (Oxford, 1978), pps.52—7, 60—2, 231, 35—9

Nwala, T. Uzodinma, *Igbo Philosophy* (Lagos, 1985) pp.19

Nwokeji, G. Ugo 1997a. "Biafra Markets and Slaves: The Aro and the Atlantic Slave Trade, c. 1750 to 1890." Presented at the Conference, "West Africa and the Americas: Repercussions of the Slave Trade," held at the University of West Indies, Mona-Kingston, Jamaica, February 20—22

Nwokeji, G. Ugo 2000a "The Atlantic Slave Trade and Population Density: A Historical Demography of the Biafra Hinterland." Canadian Journal of African Studies, Vol. 34, No.3: pp.621

Nwokeji, G. Ugo *The Slave Trade and Culture in the Bight of Biafra: An African Society in the Atlantic World* (Cambridge University Press: New York, 2010) pps. 26—27, 30, 32—35, 42—51, 53—55

Nwokeji, Ugo G., "African Conceptions of Gender and the Slave Traffic," William and Mary Quarterly, 3d, Ser., LVIII (2001), pps.47—48

Nwulia, Moses D. *The History of Slavery in Mauritius and the Seychelles, 1810—1875* (Fairleigh Dickinson University Press: East Brunswick, N.J., 1981)

O'Callaghan, *Documents*, 5: 138, 341

O'Carroll, Lisa "EU parents warned children need papers to stay in UK after Brexit". 28 March 2018. The Guardian

O'Hear, Ann, 'The Enslavement of Yoruba' in Toyin Falola & Matt D. Childs *The Yoruba Diaspora in the Atlantic World* (Indiana University Press: Indiana, 2004) pps.56

O'Hear, Ann, "Ilorin as a Slaving and Slave-Trading State," in *Slavery on the Frontiers of Islam*, ed. Paul E. Lovejoy (Princeton, N.J.: Markus Weiner, 2003)

O'Hear, Ann, "The Yoruba and the Peoples of the Niger-Benue Confluence," in Yoruba Frontiers, ed. Toyin Falola and Funso S. Afolayan

O'Hear, Ann, Power Relations in Nigeria: Ilorin Slaves and Their Successors (Rochester Press: Rochester, N.Y., 1997), pps. 26-27

O'Malley, Gregory M. Final Passages: The Intercolonial Slave Trade of British America, 1619—1807 (The University of North Carolina Press: Chapel Hill, 2014) pps.1—15

Obeyemi, Ade, "The Sokoto Jihad and the O-kun Yoruba: A Review," Journal of the Historical Society of Nigeria, 9, no.2 (1978), pps.61—87

Obichere, Boniface, 'Slavery and the Slave Trade in the Niger Delta Cross River Basin,' in Daget (ed.), *De la Traite*, II, pp.50

Odotei, Irene. "The History of Ga during the Gold Coast and Slave Trade Eras," Ph.D. diss., University of Ghana 1972, pp.259

Oettinger's Account of His Voyage to Guinea," in Jones, *Brandenburg Sources*, pps.193

Ogbar, Jeffrey O.G. Black Power: Radical Politics And African-American Identity (Baltimore: John Hopkins University Press, 2004) pps. 94-5, 195-96

Oguagha, Philip A., 'Historical and Traditional Evidence,' in Philip A. Oguagha and Alex I. Okpoko (eds), *History and Ethnoarchaeology in Eastern Nigeria* (Oxford, 1984) pp.271

Ohadike, Don C. *Anioma: A Social History of the Western Igbo People* (Athens, OH, 1994) pp.16

Okiy, G. E. O. "Indigenous Nigerian Food Plants." *Journal of the West Africa Science Association* 6, no. 2: 117—21

Olawoyin, J.S., My Political Reminiscences (John West: Ikeja, Nigeria, 1993), pp.10

Olden, Mark *Murder In Notting Hill* (Zero Books, 2011) pps.1-4, 6

Oldfield, R.A.K., 'Mr. Oldfield's Journal,' in Macgregor Laird and R.A.K. Oldfield, *Narrative of an Expedition Into the Interior of Africa, by the River Niger*, 2 vols, (London, 1837), I, pps.374, 386—7

Olusoga, David. *Black and British: A Forgotten History* (Pan Macmillan: UK, 2016), pp.498

Omari, Mikelle Smith, "Completing the Circle: Notes on African Art, Society, and Religion in Oyotunji, South Carolina," *African Arts* 24, no.3 (1991), pp.67

ONS (Office for National Statistics). "Businesses Ownership Broken Down by Ethnicity." 13 November 2020. Url: https://www.ons.gov.uk/aboutus/transparencyandgovernance/freedomofinformationfoi/businessesownershipbrokendownbyethnicity [Accessed: 12 April 2023]

ONS (Office for National Statistics). "Ethnic Group, England and Wales: Census 2021." Url: https://www.ons.gov.uk/peoplepopulationandcommunity/culturalidentity/ethnicity/bulletins/ethnicgroupenglandandwales/census2021#:~:text=%22Black%2C%20Black%20British%2C%20Caribbean,was%202.2%25%20(1.2%20million) [Accessed: 12 April 2023]

ONS (Office for National Statistics). "Ethnic Group, National Identity, Language, and Religion Quality Information for Census 2021." 29 November 2022. Url: https://www.ons.gov.uk/peoplepopulationandcommunity/culturalidentity/ethnicity/methodologies/ethnicgroupnationalidentitylanguageandreligionqualityinformationforcensus2021 [Accessed: 12 April 2023]

ONS (Office for National Statistics). "Population Estimates by Ethnic Group and Religion. England and Wales: 2019." 16 December 2021.

ONS (Office for National Statistics). "Religion in England and Wales 2011." Url: https://www.ons.gov.uk/peoplepopulationandcommunity/culturalidentity/religion/articles/religioninenglandandwales2011/2012-12-11 [AccesOlused: 12 April 2023]

Onwuejeogwu, M. Angulu *Igbo Civilization: Nri Kingdom and Hegemony* (Ethnographica: London, 1981), pps. 11, 14—16, 38—40, 79

Onyeneke, Augustine, *The dead Among the Living: Masquerades in Igbo Society* (Nimo, Nigeria, 1987)

Orenstein, Myrna. *Smart But Stuck: How Resilience Frees Imprisoned Intelligence From Learning Disabilities, 2nd Ed.* (Routledge, 2012) pp. 12
Organisation For Economic Co-operation and Development Country Of Birth *Database* (2008)

Oriji, J.N., 'The Slave Trade, Warfare and Aro Expansion in the Igbo Hinterland,' *Transafrican Journal of History* 16 (1987), pps.151—164

Oroge, E.A. 'The Institution of Slavery in Yorubaland, With Reference to the Nineteenth Century' (University of Birmingham, Ph.D. thesis, 1971) pp.6

Ortiz, Fernando Hampa Afro-Cubana: *Los negros esclavos* (Havana, 1916), pps.41, 50 (Chambers, D.B translation), reprinted as *Los negros esclavos* (Havana, 1975)

Ottenberg, Simon 1971. *Leadership and Authority in an African Society: The Afikpo Village-Group*, WA and London: University of Illinois Press, pps.24—27

Ottley, Roi, *New World A-Coming* (Houghton Miffin Co.: Boston, 1943), pps.68—74

Ottley, Roy *Black Odyssey: The Story Of The Negro In America* (New York: Charles Scribner & Sons, 1948) pp.235

Oyenuga, V.A., *Agriculture in Nigeria: an Introduction* (Rome, 1967) pps.134—9

P.P., 1817, vol. 17 (338), pp. 5; *Barbados Mercury*, 1 Mar. 1817

P.P., 1817, vol. 17 (338), pp.6; T.71/524, pp.519; T.71/525, pp.746

P.P., 1823 (16), "Papers, Presented Pursuant to Address, Relating to the Island of Trinidad," pp.76 Woodford to Bathurst, 9 Feb. 1817)

Packwood, Cyril Outerbridge, *Chained on the Rock: Slavery in Bermuda* (Eliseo Torres: New York, 1975)

Painter, Colin "Guang and West African Historical Reconstruction," *Ghana Notes and Queries* 9 (1966) pps.58—66

Palmer, C. 1981. *Human Cargoes: The British Slave Trade to Spanish America, 1700—1739.* Urbana, IL: University of Illinois Press, pp. 129

Palmer, Colin A. 'From Africa to the Americas: Ethnicity in the Early Black Communities of the Americas,' *Journal of World History*, 6, no.2 (1995) pps.223—36

Pares, Richard, *War and Trade in the West Indies, 1739—1763* (Oxford, 1936), pps.282—283

Pares, Richard, *Yankees and Creoles: The Trade Between North America and the west Indies Before the American Revolution* (Cambridge, Mass., 1956)

Parker, John *Making the Town: Ga State and Society in Early Colonial Accra* (NH. Heinemann: Portsmouth, 2000), pps. xxvi, 2, 6

Parliamentary Debates, 1st Ser., vol. 17, pps.659—89; 15 June 1810; vol 19, pps.223—40: 5 Mar 1811

Patterson, Orlando, "Slavery and Slave: A Socio-Historical Analysis of the First Maroon War, 1655—1740," *Social and Economic Studies* 18 (September 1970): pp.302

Patterson, Orlando, *Slavery and Social Death: A Comparative Study* (Cambridge, Mass: Harvard University Press, 2000) pp.11

Patterson, Orlando, *The Sociology of Slavery: an Analysis of the Origins, Development and Structure of Negro Slave Society in Jamaica* (1967; Rutherford, New Jersey, 1989, edition), pp.245

Pattison, Orlando *"Slavery and Slave Revolts: A Socio-Historical Analysis of the First Maroon War 1655-1740"*, *Social and Economic Studies*, 19 (1970), pp.289

Paul, Kathleen cit. DO35/3917 Ministry Of Labour Arrangements For The Transfer Of Workers From The Irish Republic To The United Kingdom, 3 August 1951; HO213/1322 Ministry Of Labour Circular, 141/30 Movement Of Work People Between Eire And Great Britain

Paul, Kathleen *Whitewashing Britain: Race And Citizenship In The Postwar Era* (Cornell University Press: Ithaca, 1997) pp. xiii, 141-142, 157

PBS News Hour. "3 ways that the U.S. population will change over the next decade". Jan 2, 2020. Url: https://www.pbs.org/newshour/nation/3-ways-that-the-u-s-population-will-change-over-the-next-decade [Accessed: 9th February 2021]

Peach, Ceri *West Indian Migration To Britain: A Social Geography* (London: Oxford University Press, 1969) pp. 16

Peel, J., *Ijeshas and Nigerians* (Cambridge, 1982), pps.21—2, 207—236, 275—6

Peel, J.D. Y, *Religious Encounter and the Making of the Yoruba* (Indiana University Press: Bloomington, 2000)

Peeren, Esther *Carnival Politics And The Territory Of The Street.* Constellations Of The Transnational: Modernity, Culture, Critique. Thamyris/Intersecting No.14 (2007) pp. 70

Pelton, Robert D. *The Trickster in West Africa: A Study of Mythic Irony and Sacred Delight* (Berkeley: University of California Press, 1980) pp.87

Perbi, Akosua Adoma. *A History of Indigenous Slavery in Ghana from the 15th to the 19th Century* (Legon-Accra, Ghana: Sub-Saharan Publishers, 2004) pps.25, 116—17

Pereira, Duarte Pacheco, Esmeraldo de situ orbis (trans. G. H. T. Kimble, Hakluyt, 2nd series, LXXIX), pp.14

Perry, Andre M & Romer, Carl. "To Expand the Economy, Invest in Black Businesses." *The Brookings Institute*. December 31, 2020. Url: https://www.brookings.edu/essay/to-expand-the-economy-invest-in-black-businesses/ [Accessed: 12 April 2023]

Perry, Andre M.; Seo, Regina, Barr, Anthony & Broady, Kristen. "Black-owned Businesses in U.S. Cities: The Challenges, Solutions, and Opportunities For Prosperity." *The Brookings Institute*. February 14, 2022. Url: https://www.brookings.edu/research/black-owned-businesses-in-u-s-cities-the-challenges-solutions-and-opportunities-for-prosperity/#:~:text=Nationally%2C%20as%20of%20the%20latest,supporting%203.56%20million%20U.S.%20jobs. [Accessed: 12 April 2023]

Perry, James *Arrogant Armies Great Military Disasters and the Generals behind them* (Wiley, 1st Ed., 1996)

Peyton, Nellie & Murray, Christine. "Calls for reparations gain steam as U.S. reckons with racial injustice". Everything News. Reuters. June 24, 2020. Url: https://www.reuters.com/article/us-usa-race-reparations-feature-trfn/calls-for-reparations-gain-steam-as-us-reckons-with-racial-injustice-idUSKBN23V2UO [Accessed: 8th February 2021

Phillips, Ulrich B., *Life and Labor In The Old South* (Boston, 1963), pp.172

Piersen, William D. *Black Yankees: The Development of an Afro-American Subculture in Eighteenth-Century New England* (Amherst, Mass., 1988), pps.6—7

Pigafetta, P. *A Report of the Kingdom of Congo* (based on information from Duarte Lopez) (1591, London, 1981 reprint) pp.32

Pilkington, Edward *Beyond The Mother Country* (I.B. Tauris, 1988), ibid Paul pps.155

Piot, Charles, "Of Slaves and the Gift: Kabre Sale of Kin During the Era of the Slave Trade," *Journal of African History* XXXVII (1996), pps.34,47

Postma, Johannes M., The Dutch in the Atlantic Slave Trade 1600—1815 (Cambridge, 1990) pps.1—25, 56—83, 106--25

Potter, Jess. "Is our personal data fair game in drive to create Theresa May's 'Hostile Environment'?" 25 January 2018

Powell, Enoch *Freedom And Reality* (Kingswood: Elliot Right Way Books, 1969) pp. 282 pps.46-49.

Price, Sally & Price, Richard *Maroon Societies: Rebel Slave Communities in the Americas* (John Hopkins University Press: Baltimore, 1996), pps.277—83, 308

Prince, Mary. *The History of Mary Prince, A West Indian Slave* (Penguin: London, 1831), pp.26

PRO CO 147/1, Freeman to Newcastle, 4 June 1882, quoted in Falola and Oguntomisin, *Yoruba Warlord*, pp.221

PRO CP 520/92, "The Laws and Customs of the Yoruba," in Egerton to Crewe, 11 April 1910 (section 8), cit., in Oroge, "Institution of Slavery," pps.131—32

PRO FO 84/976, Campbell to Clarendon, 7 December 1855, cit., in Oroge "Institution of Slavery," pp.162

PRRI (Public Religion Research Institute). "The 2020 Census of American Religion." 8th July 2021. Url: https://www.prri.org/research/2020-census-of-american-religion/ [Accessed: 12 April 2023]

Public Record Office, London (PRO) CO 147/48, Statements . . . made by His Majesty King Owa Agunloye-Oyibo . . . , 12 January 1882, enclosure 10 in Rowe to Kimberley, 14 March 1882, quoted in Oroge, "Institution of Slavery," pp.176

Public Record Office, War Office/25/644, pp.118, Feb. 18, 1820 entry

Q&A: The Scarman Report. BBC News, 27th April 2004, http://news.bbc.co.uk/1/hi/programmes/bbc_parliament/3631579.stm
Quarterly Chronicle of the Transactions of the London Missionary Society (London, 1825), box, West Indies, Odd 4; *Quarterly Chronicle*, Dec. 4, 1823; and Jane Smith, Affadavit, Nov. 13, 1812; all Methodist Missionary Society Archives

Quartey-Papafio, A. B. "Use of Names among the Gas or Accra People of the Gold Coast," *Journal of the Royal African Society* 13 (1914) pps.170—71, 178—81

Quoted material from Henry Laurens to Smith and Clifton, Jul. 17, 1755, in Philip M. Hamer et al., eds., *The Papers of Henry Laurens*, 16 vols, (Columbia, S.C., 1968—2022), I, pps.294—295, 316—318, 324—325, 331—332

R.L. Brooks. When Sorry Isn't Enough: The Controversy over Apologies and Reparations for Human Injustice (New York: New York University Press, 1999) pps.13-81

Ragatz, Lowell Joseph *A Guide for the Study of British Caribbean History, 1763—1834* (1932)

Randolph, Herbert *"Memoranda of S. Salvador or Bahia", in Life of General Sir Robert Wilson* (London: John Murray, 1862), I: pp. 342
Rask, *Brief and Truthful Description*, pp.77n53, 78, 180—183

Rattray, R.S., Ashanti Law and Constitution (1929; London, 1956 reprint), pp.132

Rediker, *Slave Ship*, pps.272 ,303—06, 324

Reindorf, Carl Christian, *History of the Gold Coast and Asante* (Ghana University, Accra, 2007 [1895]) pps.17, 21, 24—25, 48, 66, 85, 117, 124

Reis, Joao Jose Slave Rebellion in Brazil — The Muslim Uprising of 1835 in Bahia (John Hopkins University Press: Baltimore, 1993), pp.3, 6, 8-11, 73, 91, 221 & 225

Rev Waiting, C.E., quoted in Seymour Vandeleur, *Campaigning on the Upper Nile and Niger* (Methuen, 1898) pps.189—90

Reverend John Sharpe, "Journal of Reverend Sharpe," Pennsylvania Magazine of History and Biography 40 (January-October 1916): 421; James Grant Wilson, ed., *The Memory History of the City of New-York: From Its First Settlement to the Year 1892* (New York: New York History Company, 1892), 2: 139—40; Headley, Great Riots, 26—28; Riddell, "The Slave in New York," 72

Richardson, David 1976. "Profits in the Liverpool Slave Trade: The Accounts of William Davenport, 1757—1784," In *Liverpool*. see Anstey, R. and P .E. H. Hair (editors) 1976. *Liverpool, the African Slave Trade and Abolition: Essays to Illustrative Current Knowledge and Research*, Great Britain, Historical Society of Lancashire and Cheshire Occasional Series, Vol. 2

Richardson, David 2001. "Shipboard Revolts, African Authority, and the Atlantic Slave Trade." William and Mary Quarterly, Third Series, Vol. 58, No.1: pps. 69—92

Richardson, David, "The Slave Trade, Sugar, and British Economic Growth 1748—1776," in Barbara I. Solow and Stanley L. Engerman eds., *British Capitalism and Caribbean Slavery: The Legacy of Eric Williams* (Cambridge, 1987), pps.103—133

Richmond Enquirer, Sept. 30, 1831, *Richmond Whig*, Sept. 26, 1831, both in "Nat Turner's Confession," pps.92, 310. For reactions to allegations that Turner was a Baptist, see *Richmond Enquirer*, Aug. 29, 7, 1831

Richmond Whig, Sept. 7, 1831, Virginia Historical Society, Richmond; Gov. John Floyd to Brig. Gen. Richard Eppes, Executive Dept. [Richmond], Sept. 13, 1831 in *The Southampton Revolt*, ed. Tragle, pps. 274, 423

Riley, Rashawn. "Did the 1994 crime bill cause mass incarceration?". The Brookings Institutions. August 28, 2020. Url: https://www.brookings.edu/blog/fixgov/2020/08/28/did-the-1994-crime-bill-cause-mass-incarceration/

River, William James, A Sketch of the History of South Carolina: *To The Close of the Proprietary Government by the Revolution of 1719* (1856), pp.107—9

Roberts, G. W., "A Life Table for a West Indian Slave Population," *Population Studies* 5 (1952), pps.238—43

Roberts, Justin *Slavery and the Enlightenment in the British Atlantic, 1750—1807* (Cambridge: Cambridge University Press, 2018)

Roberts, Nery & Bolton, Paul. "Educational Outcomes of Black Pupils and Students," Briefing Paper No. 09023, *House of Commons Library*, pps.1—8. 8 October 2020 Url: https://researchbriefings.files.parliament.uk/documents/CBP-9023/CBP-9023.pdf [Accessed: 12 April 2023]

Rodney, W., *A History of the Upper Guinea Coast 1545—1800* (Oxford, 1980)

Rodrigues, Nina, *Os Africanos no Brasil* (Sao Paulo: Companhia Editoria Nacional, 1977 [1906]), pps.90—97, 178—79, 218—26, 334—65

Romer, Ludewig Ferdinand *A Reliable Account of the Coast of Guinea* (1760), Trans, ed. Selena Axelrod Wisnes (Oxford University Press: Oxford, 2000 [1760]) pps.16—19, 77—79, 80—83, 80n10, 95, 98—100, 101, 115—16, 136—37

Rotberg, Robert I., "Psychological Stress and the Question of Identity: Chilembwe's Revolt Reconsidered," in *Protest and Power in Black Africa*, ed. Robert I. Rotberg and Ali A. Muzrui (New York, 1970), pps. 337—73; cf. George Simeon Mwase, *Strike a Blow and Die; A Narrative of Race Relations in Colonial Africa*, ed. Robert I. Rotberg (Cambridge, Mass., 1967)

Rucker, *The River Flows On: Black Resistance, Culture, and Identity Formation in Early America* (Louisiana State University Press: Baton Rouge, 2006) pps.22, 27—28, 35, 37, 40—45, 191—2

Rucker, Walter C., *Gold Coast Diasporas: Identity, Culture, and Power* (Indiana University Press: Bloomington & Indianapolis, 2015), pps.23—31, 66—71, 83—91, 93—101, 125, 128

Russell, John H. "Colored Freemen As Slave Owners In Virginia," *Journal of Negro History*, I (July, 1916), pps.234—35, 241—42

Russell, John H., *The Free Negro in Virginia, 1619—1865* (Baltimore, 1963), pp.91

Samantrai, Ranu *AlterNatives: Black Feminism In The Postimperial Nation* (Stanford University Press, 2002) pp. 73

Sargent, Robert A. 1999. *Economics, Politics and Social Change in the Benue Basin c. 1300—1700.* (Enugu: Fourth Dimension), pps. 61, 218—19, 226, 236, 249

Sargent, Robert A. *A Regional Approach to Pre-colonial West African History* (Enugu, Nigeria, 1999), pps.190—195

Schaffer, William C., & Agorsah, Kofi E. "Bioarchaeological Analysis of Historic Kortmanse, Ghana." *African Diaspora Archaeology Newsletter* (March 2010) pps.2, 8—9

Schama, Simon *Rough Crossings: Britain The Slaves And The American Revolution* (Vintage, 2009) pps.235, 237, 259, 343, 398
Schildkrout, Enid & Gelber, Carol *The Golden Stool: Studies of the Asante Center and Periphery* (American Museum of Natural History: New York, 1987), pp.15

Schuler, Monica "Akan Rebellions in the British Caribbean," *Savacou* I (1970) pps.12, 15—16, 21

Schuler, Monica, 'The Life, History, and Unparalleled Sufferings of John Jea, the African Preacher [1815],' in Graham Hodges (ed.), *Black Itinerants of the Gospel* (Madison, Wisconsin, 1993), pp.90

Scott, Freda M., "'The Star of Ethiopia: A Contribution Toward the Development of Black Drama and Theatre in the Harlem Renaissance," in The Harlem Renaissance: Revaluations. Eds, Singh Amritjit, William S. Shiver, and Stanley Brodwin (Garland: New York, 1989), pp.259

Scott, William R., *A Study of Afro-American and Ethiopia, 1896—1941*. A Ph.D. diss., Princeton University 1971

Segal, Ronald *The Black Diaspora* (London: Faber & Faber, 1995) pps.28, 31

Sells, William *Remarks on the Condition of the Slaves in the Island of Jamaica* (London, 1823), pps.28—29

Shack, William A., "Ethiopia, and Afro-Americans: Some Historical Notes, 1920—1970," *Phylon*, Vol. XXXV, No. 2, 1974, pp.153

Sharpe, John, "The Negro Plot of 1712," *The New York Genealogical and Biographical Record* 21 (1890): pps.162—63

Shaw, T. 'Those Igbo-Ukwu radiocarbon dates: facts, fictions and probabilities,' Journal of African History, 1975, pp.15

Shaw, T. *Igbo-Ukwu: An Account of Archaeological Discoveries in Eastern Nigeria* (London, 1970, 2 vols

Shaw, Thurston, *Igbo-Ukwu: An Account of Archaeological Discoveries in Eastern Nigeria*, Vol.1 (Evanston, IL, 1970);

Sheffer, Gabriel *Diaspora Politics: At Home and Abroad* (Cambridge University Press, 2009), pp. introduction

Shelton, Austin J. *The Igbo-Igala Borderland: Religion and Social Control in Indigenous African Colonialism* (Albany, NY, 1971) pps.6—7

Shepperson, George, "Ethiopia and African Nationalism," *Phylon*, Vol. XIV, (1953), pps.9—18

Sherwood, H.N. *"The Formation of the American Colonization Society,"* The Journal of Negro History No. 2 (1917) pps.213—4

Shick, Tom W. *A Quantitative Analysis Of Liberian Colonization from 1820 to 1843 With Special Reference to Mortality*. The Journal of African History (1971) 12 Vol. 1 pp. 45—59

Shields, Francine, 'Pakm Oil and Power: Women in an Era of Economic and Social Transition in 19th-Century Yorubaland (South-Western Nigeria)' (PhD thesis, University of Stirling, UK 1997), pps.33—113

Shields, Francine, "Biographical Data on Enslaved Yoruba," Appendix 4, "All Incidents of Slavery and the Slave Trade for Area of Study, 1820—67," pps.297—317

Shirreff, David *Barefeet And Bandoliers: Wingate, Sandford, The Patriots And The Part they Played In The Liberation Of Ethiopia* (London: The Radcliffe Press, 1995)

Shumway, Rebecca. *The Fante and the Transatlantic Slave Trade* (University of Rochester Press: Rochester, 2011) 9, pps.3, 7—9, 13, 15, 23—24, 28, 37—40, 42—43, 47—51, 88—89, 93—101, 106, 132—53

Skinner, Elliott P., "Afro-Americans and Africa: The Continuing Dialectic" (The Urban Center, Columbia University: New York, 1973)

Skinner, Elliott P., "The Dialect Between Diasporas and Homelands" in *Global Dimensions of the African Diaspora* 2nd edition (Howard University Press: Washington D.C., 1993), Joseph E. Harris ed., pps.17—19, 21—22

Skocpol, Theda & Somers, Margaret, "The Uses of Comparative History in Macrosocial Inquiry," *Comparative Studies in Society and History* 22 (1980), pps.174—97

SlaveVoyages, "Trans-Atlantic Slave Trade—Estimates," https://slavevoyages.org/estimates/E1PNmWdH

SlaveVoyages, https://slavevoyages.org/estimates/pVr7i5

Smallwood, *Saltwater Slavery*, pps.5—6, 9—10, 16—20, 35—36, 166—176

Smith, Athelstone Carnota, John *Memoirs of the Marquis of Pombal: With Extracts From His Writings, and From Despatches in the State Papers Office, Never Before Published* (London: Longman, Brown, Green, Longmans, 1843), pp.125

Smith, D. S., Slavery, Family, and Gentry Capitalism in the British Atlantic: The World of the Lascelles, 1648—1834 (New York, 2006) pps.113—116

Smith, James E. *Slavery in Bermuda* (Vantage Press: New York, 1976)

Smith, M. G., *Kinship and Community in Carriacou* (New Haven: Yale University Press, 1953), pps.14, 162, 309

Smith, M. G.; Augier, Roy & Nettleford, Rex. *The Rastafari Movement in Kingston, Jamaica.* Kingston: Institute of Social and Economic Research, University College of West Indies, 1960

Smith, R. *Kingdoms of the Yoruba* (London, 1976)

Soares, "The Mahi-Mina in Rio de Janeiro in the 18th Century," Harriet Tubman Seminar, York University, Canada 2001 (unpublished); Gwendolyn Midlo Hall, "African Ethnicities and the Meanings of Mina," in Trans-Atlantic Dimensions of African Ethnicity, ed. Paul E. Lovejoy and David V. Trotman (Continuum: London, 2002)

Solow, Barbara I. & Engerman, Stanley L. eds., British Capitalism and Caribbean Slavery: The Legacy of Eric Williams (Cambridge, 1987), pps.103—133

Solow, Barbara I. "Caribbean Slavery and British Growth: The Eric Williams Hypothesis," *Journal of Developmental Economics*, XVII (1985), pps.99—115

Sommers, Jeffrey *Race, Reality, and Realpolitik: U.S. – Haiti Relations in the Lead Up to the 1915 Occupation* (Lexington Books, 2015) pp.124

Soul II Soul | Encyclopedia.com. Url: www.encyclopedia.com. Retrieved 12th May 2020

South Carolina Gazette [S. C. Gaz], Aug. 13, 1737, plantation of Isaac Porcher; *South Carolina Gazette and Country Journal [S. C. Gaz and Ct. J]*, workhouse inmate notices Oct. 11, Nov. 15, 1774, Jan. 31, 1775

South Carolina Gazette [S.C. Gaz.], Sept. 6, 1773, John Champneys; Virginia, *Virginia Gazette [Va. Gaz.]*, Nov. 5, 1726, Benjamin Neddler; March 1, 1737, Philip Lightfoot

South-Carolina Gazette, Jan. 15, 1756; Laurens to Law, Satterthwaite, and Jones, Barbados, Jan. 12, 1756, and Laurens to Clarke, Jan. 31, 1756, both in *Laurens Papers*, II, pps.64—66, 82—84

St. George's Chronicle (Grenada), 6 Dec. 1823 and 20 July 1833; *Grenada Free Press*, 2 Dec. 1829; *St. Vincent Gazette*, 27 Aug. 1825

St. Kitts Bluebook, 1832, pp.66 (S.K.G.A.)

St. Pierre, Maurice A. *Reganomics and Its Implications For African-American Family Life*. Journal Of Black Studies, Vol. 21, No. 3 (Mar., 1991) pp. 336

Stampp, *The Peculiar Institution*, pps.194—5

Starke, T. 1702. "Answer of Thomas Starke to James Westmore." See Donnan 1935

Statewatch News Online. "Hostile Environment" faces criticism from parliamentary committee as new migration checks on bank accounts come into force". Www.statewatch.org. January 2018

Staton, Bethan "Banks run immigration checks in Home Office crackdown". Friday 12 January 2018. Sky News

Stede, E. & Gascoigne, S. 1679. "Edwyn Stede and Stephen Gascoigne to the Royal African Company."

Stenhouse, Ann. "What is the Windrush Scandal – and how the Windrush generation got their name". 15th April, 2018. Daily Mirror Newspaper

Stephenson, R. F. 1968. *Population Growth and Political Systems in Tropical Africa*, New York and London: Columbia University Press, Chp. 9

Stewart, J. M., "Akan History: Some Linguistic Evidence." *Ghana Notes and Queries* 9 (1966) pps.54—58

Stone, R.H., In *Africa's Forest and Jungle; or, Six Years Among the Yorubans* (Anderson and Fernier, 1900), pps.53—4

Stuart, Andrea *Sugar in the Blood: A Family's Story of Slavery and Empire* (Portobello Books: London, 2012), pps. 102, 273—283, 293—94, 302—7

Stuckey, Sterling, *Slave Culture: Nationalist Theory and the Foundations of Black America* (Oxford, 1987), pps.68—73

Sweet, Leonard I. *Black Images of America, 1784-1870*. (New York: W.W. Norton and Company, 1976) pp. 37

Szwed, John F., "An American Anthropology Dilemma: The Politics of Afro-American Culture," in *Reinventing Anthropology ed. Dell Hynes* (1969, New York, 1972), pps.153—81

T. 71 (Public Record Office, London). Complete sets of the original registers survive in Jamaica, the Bahamas, and Belize, and Dominica, and St. Kitts

Talbot, David, *Contemporary Ethiopia* (New York, 1952), pp.252

Talbot, P. Amaury. 1926. *The Peoples of Southern Nigeria: A Sketch of Their History, Ethnology, and Languages with an Abstract of the 1921 Census* 4 vols. (Cass: London, 1969), pps.54

Tamir, Christine & Anderson, Monica. "[4] Most Black Immigrants Live in Northeast, South; New York City Has Largest Black Immigrant Population by Metro Area." *Pew Research Center.* January 20, 2022. Url: https://www.pewresearch.org/race-ethnicity/2022/01/20/most-black-immigrants-live-in-northeast-south-new-york-city-has-largest-black-immigrant-population-by-metro-area/ [Accessed: 12 April 2023]

Tamir, Christine & Anderson, Monica. "[5] Household Income, Poverty Status, and Home Ownership Among Black Immigrants." *Pew Research Center.* January 20, 2022. Url: https://www.pewresearch.org/race-ethnicity/2022/01/20/household-income-poverty-status-and-home-ownership-among-black-immigrants/#:~:text=Black%20immigrant%20households%20less%20likely,based%20on%20heads%20of%20households). [Accessed: 12 April 2023]

Tamir, Christine & Anderson, Monica. "One-in-Ten Black People Living in the U.S. Are Immigrants: Immigrants — particularly Those From African Nations — Are a Growing Share of the U.S. Black Population." *Pew Research Center.* January 20, 2022. Url: https://www.pewresearch.org/race-ethnicity/2022/01/20/one-in-ten-black-people-living-in-the-u-s-are-immigrants/ [Accessed: 12 April 2023]

Tamir, Christine. "Key Findings About Black Immigrants in the U.S." *Pew Research Center.* January 27, 2022. Url: https://www.pewresearch.org/fact-tank/2022/01/27/key-findings-about-black-immigrants-in-the-u-s/#:~:text=Between%202000%20and%202019%2C%20the,about%20600%2C000%20to%202.0%20million. [Accessed: 12 April 2023]

Tanna, Laura, "African Retentions: Yoruba and KiKongo Songs in Jamaica," Jamaica Journal 16 (Aug. 1983), pps.47—52

Tannenbaum, Frank *Slave and Citizen: The Negro in the Americas* (Vintage Books: New York, 1946)

Taylor to Archedeckne, Mullet Hall, St. Thomas in the East, Sept. 3, 1787, box 2, item 13, Vanneck MS; Journals of Thomas Thistlewood (Thistlewood's Journal], Oct. 13, 1763, March 17, 1761, Monson 31, Lincolnshire Record Office, Lincoln

Taylor, David Bewley *The United States And International Drug Control, 1909-1997* (London: Continnum, 2001) pp. 61
Taylor, Jamila. "Racism, Inequality, and Health Care for African Americans." The Century Foundation. December 19, 2019. Url: https://tcf.org/content/report/racism-inequality-health-care-african-americans/ [Accessed: 12 April 2023]

Terray, E. 'Gold Production, Slave Labor and State Intervention in Precolonial Akan Societies,' *Research in Economic Anthropology*, 1979, pp.44—6

The Amos Busary. Url: https://www.amosbursary.org.uk/about/ . Accessed on 16th March 2020
The Aristocratic Journey: Being the Outspoken Letters of Mrs. Basil Hall Written during a Fourteen Months' Sojourn in America, 1827—1828, ed. Una Pope-Hennesy (New York, 1931), pp.223

The Assembly estimated property damage at £1,154,589.2.1, C.O. 137/182, f.286

The Church Missionary Intelligencer, 1853, pp.58

The Condition Of Education. *Public High School Graduation Rates*. National Center For Educational Statistics. Last Updated: May 2020. Url: https://nces.ed.gov/programs/coe/indicator_coi.asp. Accessed: 21st May 2020

The Constitution and By-Laws of the Ethiopian World Federation, 1937, as quoted by M. G. Smith, Roy Augier, Rex Nettleford, *The Rastafari Movement in Kingston, Jamaica*, pps.10

The Cultural Implications of the Atlantic Slave Trade: African Regional Origins, American Destinations and New World Developments, in in Eltis, David & Richardson, David *Routes to Slavery: Direction, Ethnicity and Mortality in the Atlantic Slave Trade* (Frank Crass: London, 1997), pp.129

The favoring of "black" over "African-American" was based on *The Washington Post*-ABC Poll. See the Article "Men and Women of their World," *The Washington Post National Weekly Edition*, October 28-November 4, 1990. Also see the article "Poll Says Most Blacks Prefer 'Blacks' to 'African-American,'" *The New York Times*, January, 29, 1991

The National Archives. *Moving here – Migration Histories*. Url: https://webarchive.nationalarchives.gov.uk/+/http://www.movinghere.org.uk/galleries/histo ries/caribbean/working_lives/working_lives.htm#ffw (Archived on 5th Dec 2013)
The Southampton Revolt, ed. Tragle, pps. 67—70, 95—97

The WASU project *History of WASU* – Url: http://wasuproject.org.uk/history-of-wasu/
The White House. "Pandemic Shifts in Black Employment and Wages." August 24, 2022. Url: https://www.whitehouse.gov/cea/written-materials/2022/08/24/pandemic-shifts-in-black-employment-and-wages/ [Accessed: 12 April 2023]

Thistlewood's Journal, March 25, 1976

Thomas, Hugh, *The Slave Trade: The Story of the Atlantic Slave Trade, 1440—1870* (New York: Simon & Schuster, 1997), pp.203

Thomas, Northcote W. 1913. *Anthropological Report on the Ibo-speaking Peoples of Nigeria*. 6 vols. (Negro Universities Press: New York, 1969), 2: 27, 70, 104, 299, 157, 303, 382

Thomas, Northcote W. Law and Custom of the Ibo of the Awka Neighbourhood (London, 1913) pps. 49—50

Thome, J. A. and Kimball, J. H., *Emancipation in the West Indies* (New York, 1838), pp.76

Thompson, Eric T., "The 1991 Census of Population in England and Wales," *Journal of the Royal Statistical Society. Series A (Statistics in Society)*, 1995, Vol. 258, No. 2, pps.203—240

Thompson, Peter "Henry Drax's Instructions on the Management of a Seventeenth-Century Barbadian Sugar Plantation," *The William and Mary Quarterly* 66 no. 3 (2009), pps.569, 574

Thompson, Robert F., "' The Three Warriors: Atlantic Altars of Esu, Ogun, and Ososi," in *The Yoruba Artist: New Theoretical Perspectives on African Art*, ed. Rowland Abiodun, Henry Drewal, and John Pemberton (Washington, DC.: Smithsonian Institution Press, 1994) pp.227

Thompson, Robert F., *Flash of the Spirit: African and Afro-American Art and Philosophy* (New York, 1983)

Thompson, Robert Farris *Black Gods and Kings. Yoruba Art at U.C.L.A* (University of California 1st Ed., 1971)
Thornton, John K, "'I Am the Subject of the King of Congo": African Political Ideology and the Haitian Revolution,' *Journal of World History*, 4, no,2 (1993) pps.181—214

Thornton, John K, 'A Resurrection for the Jaga,' *Cahiers d'etudes africaines*, 1978, pps.229—31

Thornton, John K, 'African Dimension of the Stono Rebellion,' *American Historical Review*, 96, no.4 (1991) pps,1101-13;

Thornton, John K, "The African Experience of the '20. and Odd Negroes' Arriving in Virginia in 1619," WMQ, 3d Ser., LV (1998)

Thornton, John K, "The Coramantees: An African Cultural Group in Colonial North America and the Caribbean." *Journal of Caribbean History* 32 (1998) pp.167

Thornton, John K, "War, the State, and Religious Norms," in "Coromantee" Thought: The Ideology of an African American Nation pps.191—94

Thornton, John K, *Africa and Africans in the Making of the Atlantic World 1400—1680* (Cambridge, 1992), part 2; pps.98—125, 183—205

Thornton, John K, *The Kingdom of the Kongo: Civil War and Transition 1641—1718* (Madison, 1983), pp.19, 23—5, 41, 73, 78, 80, 82, 96, 106—13, 208—10

Tomkins, Stephen *The Clapham Sect: How Wilberforce's Circle Transformed Britain* (Lion Hudson plc, 2010) pp.93, 94-96, 103, 200-206

Truteneau, H. Max ed. *Christian Protten's 1764 Introduction to the Fante and Accra (Gafi) Languages* (Afro-Presse, 1971), pps.11—12

TUC Papers, MSS292/103.2/3 Bounemouth Trades Council to TUC, 12 August 1955, MSS292/103.2/4 Andover and District Trades Council to TUC, 28 October 1955. Shingfield District Council to TUC, no date TUC Advisory Committee Midland Region, 13 August 1958, Bedford and District Trades Council, 17 October 1959, cited in Kathleen Paul, *Whitewashing Britain: Race And Citizenship In The Postwar Era* (Cornel Univ. Press: Ithaca & London, 1997) pp.140

Turnbull, Gordon, An Apology for Negro Slavery, 2nd ed. (London, 1786), 21ff, 25; "Extracts from Minutes of Evidence taken by the Committee of Council for Inquiring into the Negro Character as Exhibited in this Colony [Trinidad]," *British Parliamentary Papers, Slave Trade* 73 (1826—27)

Turner, Henry McNeal in *Addresses and Proceedings of the Congress on Africa, Dec. 13—15. 1895*, ed. J. W. E. Bosen (Atlanta: Gammon Theological Seminary, 1896)

Turner, Lorenzo D. Africanisms in the Gullah Dialect (2001), pp.191

U.S. Bureau of Labor Statistics. "Employment Status of the Civilian Population by Race, Sex, and Age." Url: https://www.bls.gov/news.release/empsit.t02.htm [Accessed: 12 April 2023]

U.S. Bureau Of Statistics. *(1990 March). Monthly labor review.* Washington, DC: US. Department Of Labor.

Ullman, Victor, *Martin R. Delany: The Beginnings of Black Nationalism* (Beacon Press: Boston, 1971), pps.152, 273—74

Unearthing Igbo-Ukwu: Archaeological Discoveries in Eastern Nigeria (Ibadan, 1977)

United States Census Bureau *Place of Birth For The Foreign-Born Population In The United States, Universe: Foreign-born population excluding born at sea, 2007-2011 American Community Survey 5-Year Estimates* – Url: http://factfinder2.census.gov/faces/tableservices/jsf/pages/productview.xhtml?pid=ACS_11_5YR_B05006&prodType=table (2013)

United States Census Bureau *Total Ancestry Categories Tallied For People With One Or More Ancestry Categories Reported 2013 American Community Survey 1-Year Estimates* (September 2014)

United States Census Bureau. "2000 Shows America's Diversity," Monday, March 12, 2001. Url: https://www.census.gov/newsroom/releases/archives/census_2000/cb01cn61.html#:~:text=White%2075.1%20percent,Asian%203.6%20percent [Accessed: 12 April 2023]

United States Census Bureau. "2010 Census Shows America's Diversity." Thursday, March 24, 2011. Url: https://www.census.gov/newsroom/releases/archives/2010_census/cb11-cn125.html [Accessed: 12 April 2023]

United States Census Bureau. "2020 Census Statistics Highlight Local Population Changes and Nation's Racial and Ethnic Diversity." August 12, 2021. Url: https://www.census.gov/newsroom/press-releases/2021/population-changes-nations-diversity.html [Accessed: 12 April 2023]

United States Census Bureau. "Quick Facts." Url: https://www.census.gov/quickfacts/fact/table/US/RHI625221#RHI625221 [Accessed: 12 April 2023]

United States Census Bureau. "Race and Ethnicity in the United States: 2010 Census and 2020 Census. 12 August 2021. Url: https://www.census.gov/library/visualizations/interactive/race-and-ethnicity-in-the-united-state-2010-and-2020-census.html [Accessed: 12 April 2023]

United States Census Bureau. "The Vintage 2021 Population Estimates Available for the Nation, States and Puerto Rico". Tuesday, December 21, 2021: Url: https://www.census.gov/newsroom/press-releases/2021/2021-population-estimates.html#:~:text=21%2C%202021%20%E2%80%94%20According%20to%20the,rate%20since%20the%20nation's%20founding. [Accessed: 12 April 2023]

United States Census Bureau. Quick Facts – United States. Url: https://www.census.gov/quickfacts/fact/table/US/PST045219 [Accessed: 9th February 2021]

University of St. Augustine for Health Sciences. "The 2021 American Nursing Shortage: A Data Study." 25 May 2021. Url: https://www.usa.edu/blog/nursing-shortage/ [Accessed: 12 April 2023]

Urban Institute. *Mapping The Black Homeownership Gap*. Urban Wire: Housing And Housing Finance. February 26th 2018. Url: https://www.urban.org/urban-wire/mapping-black-homeownership-gap. [Accessed 19th May 2020]

Uzoie, L.C. 'Agricultural Land Use in the Nsukka Area,' in G.E.K Ofomata (ed.), The Nsukka Environment (Enugu, Nigeria, 1978), pps. 155, 170—1

Valdes, Rafael Lopes, 'Notas para el studio etnohistorico de los esclavos lucumi en Cuba,' in L. Menendez (ed.), Estudios afrocubanos (Havana, 1990), 2: pps.311—47

Valerie Lacarte. "Black Immigrants in the United States Face Hurdles, But Outcomes Vary by City." *MPI (Migration Policy Institute)*. February 10, 2022. Url: https://www.migrationpolicy.org/article/black-immigrants-united-states-hurdles-outcomes-top-cities [Accessed: 12 April 2023]

Van Stipriaan, Alex *"Between Diaspora TransNationalism and American Globalization – A History of AfroSurinamese Emancipation Day"* in Ruben S. Gowricharn (ed.) *Caribbean Transnationalism: Migration, Pluralization and Social Cohesion* (Lexington Books, 2006)
Vansina, Jan *Paths in the Rainforests: Towards a History of Political Tradition in Equatorial Africa* (London and Madison, WI, 1990), pps.71—100, 201, 249—63

Vansina, Jan. *Paths in the Rainforests: Toward a History of Political Tradition in Equatorial Africa* (University of Wisconsin Press, 1990), pps.95, 146—52, 258—260, 346n71

Vansina, Jan. *The Tio Kingdom of the Middle Congo, 1880—1892* (London: Oxford University Press for the International African Institute, 1973), pp.224

Vega, Marta Moreno, "The Yoruba Orisha Tradition Comes to New York," *African American Review*, 29, no.2 (1995), pps.210—12

Verger, Pierre, *Trade Relations between the Bight od Benin and Bahia, 17th to 19th Centuries* (Ibadan University Press: Ibadan, Nigeria, 1976)

Virdee, Satnam *Racism, Class And The Racialized Outsider* (Red Globe Press, 2014) pp.100

Vivian, Brian "Recent Excavations of Adansemanso," *Nyame Akuma* 46 (1996) pps.37—41

Votes of Assembly for 12 Nov. 1788, 94—95, C.O. 140/73; House of Commons Sessional Papers (1789), 29/112, pps.89, 157, 215, 260—62, 300, 207ff, 321ff, 30/351—52; E. Pool to Eliza Elletson, Sept. 10, 1778, Elletson Letterbooks, MS 29a, Institute of Jamaica

Voyages: The Trans-Atlantic Slave Trade Database, http://www.slavevoyages.org/tast/database/search.faces (accessed 31 March 2023)

Waddell, Hope Masterton, *Twenty-nine Years in the West Indies and Central Africa: A Review of Missionary Work and Adventure, 1829—1858* (London, 1863), 59, 63ff

Wagner, Mark, 'The Introduction and Early Use of African Plants in the New World,' *Tennessee Anthropologist*, 6 (1981), pps.112—23

Walsh, Conal. "Slave descendants sue Lloyd's for billions". 27 March 2004. The Guardian. Url: https://www.theguardian.com/money/2004/mar/28/insurance.usnews [Accessed: 8th February 2021]; Walsh, L.S. "Chesapeake Slave Trade," WMQ, 3d Ser., LVIII (2001), pps.139—170
Walsh, L.S., "The Differential Cultural Impact of Free and Coerced Migration to Colonial America," in David Eltis, ed., *Coerced and Free Migration: Global Perspectives* (Stanford, Calif., 2002), pps.117—151

Walvin, James *Black And White: The Negro in English Society, 1555-1945* (London, 1973), quoting The Times (19th June 1919) pp.208, 210
Warner, Maureen, "Africans in Nineteenth Century Trinidad," *African Studies Association of the West Indies Bulletin* 5 (Dec. 1972), pp.39

Warner-Lewis, Maureen, "Trinidad Yoruba: Notes on Survivals," *Caribbean Quarterly*, 17, no.2 (1971), pps.40—49

Warner-Lewis, Maureen, *Archibald Monteath: Imperial Pawn and Individual* Agent In Njoku, Raphael Chijioke & Falola, Toyin (eds) *Igbo in the Atlantic World: African Origins and Diasporic Traditions* (Indiana University Press, 2016), pps.218--227

Warner-Lewis, Maureen, Ethnic and Religious Plurality Among Yoruba Immigrants in Trinidad in the Nineteenth Century in Identity in the Shadow of Slavery, ed. Paul E. Lovejoy (Continuum: London, 2000), pps.113—14

Warner-Lewis, Maureen, *Guinea's Other Suns: The African Dynamic in Trinidad Culture* (Dover, MA, 1991), pps.9—15

Warner-Lewis, Maureen, Trinidad Yoruba: From Mother Tongue to Memory (Tuscaloosa, AL, 1996; Kingston, 1997), pps.28—31

Warner—Lewis, Trinidad Yoruba: From Mother Tongue to Memory (University of Alabama Press: Tuscaloosa, 1996)

Washington, Booker T., "Industrial Education in Africa," *Independent*, LX (March 15, 1906), pps.616—19, as quoted by W. Manning Marable, ", Booker T Washington and African Nationalism," *Phylon*, Vol. XXXV, No.4, 1974, pps.398—406

Washington, Booker T., *The Future of the American Negro* (Small, Maynard: Boston, 1899)

Wastell, R. E. P., *The History of Slave Compensation, 1833 to 1845* (Master's thesis, University of London, 1932), pps.29—47, 80; T.71/685—851; Lt. Governor's Correspondence, Tobago, 1835, "Report on the committee appointed to inspect the books of the Compensation Commissioners." (T.A.)

Watts, Carl Peter *"The 'Wind of Change': British Decolonisation in Africa"*, 1957-1965. History Review (2011) Vol.71, pps.12-17

Wax, "'New Negroes Are Always in Demand,'" *Georgia Historical Quarterly*, LXVIII [1984], pps.203—204

Wax, Darold D., "Preferences for Slaves in Colonial America," Journal of Negro History, LVIII (1973), pps.371—401

Webster, *Imagining Home: Gender, 'Race' And National Identity, 1945-64* (Routledge 1st ed., 1998) pp.26

Weeks Okrafo-Smart, Victor S. *Okrafo Over A Century In The Lives Of A Liberated African family, 1816-1930* (Palm Tree Publishers UK, 2006) pps.3, 14

Wellesley-Cole, Robert *Kossoh Town Boy* (Cambridge University Press, 1960) pp.21

West Africa (20 August 1921)

West Africa (9 August 1919)

Westbury, Susan Alice "Colonial Virginia and the Atlantic Slave Trade" (Ph.D. diss., University of Illinois at Urbana-Champaign, 1981), pp.94

Westbury, Susan Alice, "Slaves of Colonial Virginia: Where They Came From," *WMQ*, 3d Ser., XLII (1985), pps. 228—237

Westcott, Joan *The Sculpture of Eshu Elegba. Africa* (1962) Vol 32, no.4, pp.336-354

White, Gillian B.. *In D.C., White Families Are On Average 81 Times Richer Than Black Ones – Other Major Cities Aren't Much Better.* The Atlantic [Business section]. November 26th 2016. Accessed 19th May 2020

White, Miles. *From Jim Crow To Jay-Z: Race And The Performance Of Masculinity* (Urbana: University of Illinois Press, 2011) pps. 64, 74

Whitford, John [1877] 1967. *Trading Life in Western and Central Africa* (2nd edition) London: Frank Cass

Wikramanayake, Marina, "The Free Negro in Ante-Bellum South Carolina," (Ph.D. diss., University of Wisconsin, 1966) pp.97

Wilcox, W. Bradford. "2.5 Million Black Men Are in the Upper Class. July 23, 2018. Institute for Family Studies. Url: https://ifstudies.org/blog/2-5-million-black-men-are-in-the-upper-class [Accessed: 8th February 2021]

Wilder, Rachel. *Insight Guide to Barbados* (Houghton Muffin Co.: New York, 1994), pp.32, cit., William Hart Coleridge, Bishop of Barbados

Wilfred, Sidney Mintz, "History and Anthropology: A Brief Reprise," in *Race and Slavery in the Western Hemisphere Quantitative Studies*, ed. Stanley L. Engerman and Eugene D. Genovese (New York, 1975), pps.493—94

Wilfred, Sidney Mintz, *Sweetness and Power: The Place Sugar in Modern History* (New York: Viking, 1985), pps. 49, 73

Wilks, Ivor "Slavery and Akan Origins? A Reply." *Ethnohistory* 41 (1994) pp.661

Wilks, Ivor *Forests of Gold: Essays on the Akan and the Kingdom of Asante*, (Ghana University Press: Accra, 1996) pps.64—72, 92—97

Wilks, Ivor *One Nation, Many Histories: Ghana Past and Present.* (Ghana University Press: Accra,1966), pps.15—18

Wilks, Ivor, 'Land, Labour, Capital,' in Gareth Austin, *Slavery to Free Labour in Asante, 1807—1956*, pps.508—9, 522

Wilks, Ivor, 'The State of the Akan and the Akan states: a Discursion,' *Cahiers d'etudes africaines*, 1982, pp.231

Williams, Eric *Capitalism and Slavery* (N.C., Chapel Hill, N.C., 1944), pp.108

Williams, Gomer. *History of Liverpool Privateers and Letters of Marque with an Account of the Liverpool Slave Trade* (William Heinemann: London, 1897) pps.529, 535, 539—40

Williams, Joseph J. *Psychic Phenomena of Jamaica* (New York, 1934) pp.173

Williams, Wendy "Windrush Lessons Learned Review" An independent review. Ordered by the House of Commons to be printed on 19 March 2020

Wood, Peter H. "'More Like a Negro Country': Demographic Patterns in Colonial South Carolina, 1700—1740," in Engerman and Genovese, ed., *Race and Slavery in the Western Hemisphere*, pps.145—146

Woods, Neil & Rafaeli, JS *Drug Wars: The Real Inside Story Of Britain's Drug War* (Ebury Press, 2018) pps.23—24, 58—59, 62—64, 69—70

Woodson, Carter G., ed., *Negro Orators and Their Orations* (Associated Publishers: Washington, 1925), 23ff, pps.80—81

Woodson, Carter G., *Free Negro Owners of Slaves in the United States in 1830* (Washington, D.C., 1924), pp.vi

Woodson, Carter G., *The History of the Negro Church* (Washington D.C., 1921), pps.86—90

World Digital Library *Map of Liberia, West Africa* (2011) Url: https://www.wdl.org/en/item/446/

Wray's Letters are in box 1 "B. Guiana-Demerara, 1807—1814," Methodist Missionary Society Archives

Young OBE, Dr Lola & Bogues, Machel (editor). *Bernie Grant Trust: Guide To The Bernie Grant Archive. Inspiration | Innovation | Inclusion.* 16th March 2004, pps 6-10, 26. Retrieved 16th March 2020

Younge, Gary "Hounding Commonwealth Citizens is no accident. It's cruelty by design". 13 April 2018. The Guardian

Zoellner, Tom, *Island on Fire: The Revolt That Ended Slavery in the British Empire* (Cambridge, Mass.: Harvard University Press, 2020), pp.7

Zoopla. "House Prices in Croydon, London." Url: https://www.zoopla.co.uk/house-prices/london/croydon/ [Accessed: 12 April 2023]

Zoopla. "House Prices in Greenwich (The Royal Borough of), London." Url: https://www.zoopla.co.uk/house-prices/greenwich-royal-borough/ [Accessed: 12 April 2023]

Zoopla. "House Prices in Lewisham, London." Url: https://www.zoopla.co.uk/house-prices/lewisham/ [Accessed: 12 April 2023]